09/03
128.95

Automotive Engines

09/03
128.95

Prentice Hall Multimedia Series in Automotive Technology

Other books by James D. Halderman and Chase D. Mitchell, Jr., in the
Prentice Hall Multimedia Series in Automotive Technology include:

Automotive Technology: Principles, Diagnosis, and Service, 0-13-359969-8.

Advanced Engine Performance Diagnosis, 0-13-576570-6.

Automotive Brake Systems, Second Edition, 0-13-080041-4.

Automotive Chassis Systems, Second Edition, 0-13-079970-X.

Automotive Steering, Suspension, and Alignment, Second Edition, 0-13-799719-1.

Diagnosis and Troubleshooting of Electrical, Electronic, and Computer Systems, Third Edition, 0-13-520578-6.

Prentice Hall Multimedia Series in Automotive Technology

Automotive Engines
Theory and Servicing

Fourth Edition

James D. Halderman   Sinclair Community College

Chase D. Mitchell, Jr.   Utah Valley State College

Prentice
Hall

Upper Saddle River, New Jersey
Columbus, Ohio

Library of Congress Cataloging-in-Publication Data

Halderman, James D.
    Automotive engines : theory and servicing / James D. Halderman, Chase D. Mitchell,
Jr.—4th ed.
        p. cm.
    Includes index.
    ISBN 0-13-799701-9
    1. Automobiles—Motors.   2. Automobiles—Motors—Maintenance and repair.
I. Mitchell, Chase D.   II. Title.

TL210.H29 2001
629.25—dc21

00-044619

Vice President and Publisher: Dave Garza
Editor in Chief: Stephen Helba
Executive Editor: Ed Francis
Production Editor: Christine M. Buckendahl
Production Coordination: Kelli Jauron, Carlisle Publishers Services
Cover Designer: Rod Harris
Design Coordinator: Robin G. Chukes
Production Manager: Brian Fox
Marketing Manager: Jamie Van Voorhis

This book was set in ITC Century Book by Carlisle Communications Ltd., and was printed and bound by Victor Graphics. The cover was printed by Phoenix Color Corp.

10 9 8 7 6
ISBN: 0-13-799701-9

Contents

4

Starting and Charging System Operation and Diagnosis 56

5

Ignition System Operation and Diagnosis 81

6

Fuel and Emission System Operation and Diagnosis 109

7

Cooling System Operation and Diagnosis 144

8

Engine Condition Diagnosis   171

9

Engine Removal and Disassembly   202

10

Engine Cleaning, Crack Detection, and Repair   218

18

Crankshafts and Bearings   437

19

Engine Assembly   468

20

Engine Installation and In-Vehicle Service 498

APPENDIXES

Tech Tips, Frequently Asked Questions, Diagnostic Stories, and High-Performance Tips

Photo Sequences

Preface

The fourth edition of *Automotive Engines: Theory and Servicing* includes many new tech tips, diagnostic stories, and answers to frequently asked questions (FAQs), plus photo sequences that help illustrate many engine service procedures.

Diagnostic Approach

This textbook was written to satisfy the need for problem diagnosis as its primary focus. Time and time again, the author has heard that diagnostic procedures and skill development are needed most in the automotive field. Diagnostic stories are included throughout to help illustrate how real problems are solved. Each new topic covers the parts involved plus the purpose, function, and operation as well as how to test and diagnose each system.

ASE Content Approach

This comprehensive textbook covers the material necessary for the Engine Repair (A1) area of certification as specified by ASE and NATEF. The book also includes information on engine machining that will help the technician study for the Cylinder Head Specialist (M1), Cylinder Block Specialist (M2), and Engine Assembly Specialist (M3) tests.

Multimedia System Approach

Over 30 photo sequences are included in the text. Many of these photo sequences are included on a videotape for instructors upon adoption of the textbook. A multimedia CD-ROM that accompanies and supplements the textbook is informative and also makes learning more fun for the student. The CD includes sound, 3-D animation, color live-action video sequences with narration, a waveform library, a glossary of automotive terms, sample ASE test questions, sample worksheets, and the ASE (NATEF) task list for the Automotive Engine Repair and Engine Machinist series.

Internet (World Wide Web) Approach

Included with the book is a coupon that entitles the owner to free access to an ASE test preparation web site for an extended time period. Now you can practice and take the ASE certification tests with confidence. Included at this web site are ASE-type questions for Automobile Engine Repair (A1) and Engine Machinist series (M1, M2, and M3). The questions are presented 10 at a time, then graded (marked). The correct answer is then given as you scroll back through the questions. This feature allows the students to study at their own pace.

Worktext Approach

A worktext is also included with the book. The worksheets included in the worktext help instructors and students apply the material presented to everyday-type activities and typical service and testing procedures plus typical results and a listing of what could be defective if the test results are not within the acceptable range. These sheets help build diagnostic and testing skills.

Acknowledgments

The author gratefully acknowledges the following companies for technical information and the use of their illustrations:

Auto Parts Distributors

Automotion, Inc.

Automotive Engine Rebuilders Association

B-H-J Products, Inc.

Camwerks Corporation

Castrol Incorporated

Champion Spark Plug Company

Chrysler Corporation

Clayton Manufacturing Company

Curtiss Wright Corporation

Dana Corporation

Defiance Engine Rebuilders Incorporated

Dow Chemical Company

Fel-Pro Incorporated

Ford Motor Company

General Motors Corporation:
  AC Delco Division
  Buick Motor Division
  Cadillac Motor Car Division
  Central Foundry Division
  Chevrolet Motor Division
  Oldsmobile Division

George Olcott Company

Goodson Auto Machine Shop Tools and Supplies

Greenlee Brothers and Company

Jasper Engines and Transmissions

K-Line

Modine Manufacturing Company

Neway

Parsons and Meyers Racing Engines

Prestolite Company

Rottler Manufacturing

Sealed Power Corporation

Society of Automotive Engineers

Sunnen Products Company

TRW, Michigan Division

Technical and Content Reviewers

The following people reviewed the manuscript before production and checked it for technical accuracy and clarity of presentation. Their suggestions and recommendations were included in the final draft of the manuscript. Their input helped make this textbook clear and technically accurate while maintaining the easy-to-read style that has made other books from the same authors so popular.

Victor Bridges
Umpqua Community College

Dr. Roger Donovan
Illinois Central College

A. C. Durdin
Moraine Park Technical College

Herbert Ellinger
Western Michigan University

Al Engledahl
College of Dupage

Oldrick Hajzler
Red River Community College

Betsy Hoffman
Vermont Technical College

Carlton H. Mabe, Sr.
Virginia Western Community College

Roy Marks
Owens Community College

Kerry Meier
San Juan College

Fritz Peacock
Indiana Vocational Technical College

Dennis Peter
NAIT (Canada)

Kenneth Redick
Hudson Valley Comm. College

Mitchell Walker
St. Louis Community College at Forest Park

Photo Sequences

The authors wish to thank Rick Henry, who photographed all of the photo sequences. Most of the sequences were taken in automotive service facilities while live work was being performed. Special thanks to all who helped, including:

B P ProCare
Dayton, Ohio
        Tom Brummitt
        Jeff Stueve
        John Daily
        Bob Babal
        Brian Addock
        Jason Brown
        Don Patton
        Dan Kanapp

Rodney Cobb Chevrolet
Eaton, Ohio
        Clint Brubacker

Dare Automotive Specialists
Centerville, Ohio
        David Schneider
        Eric Archdeacon
        Jim Anderson

Foreign Car Service
Huber Heights, Ohio
        Mike McCarthy
        George Thielen
        Ellen Finke
        Greg Hawk
        Bob Massie

Genuine Auto Parts Machine Shop
Dayton, Ohio
        Freddy Cochran
        Tom Berger

Import Engine and Transmission
Dayton, Ohio
        Elias Daoud
        James Brown
        Robert Riddle
        Felipe Delemos
        Mike Pence

J and B Transmission Service
Dayton, Ohio
        Robert E. Smith
        Ray L. Smith
        Jerry Morgan
        Scott Smith
        Daryl Williams
        George Timitirou

Saturn of Orem
Orem, Utah

We also wish to thank Blaine Heeter (technician actor) and Bill Kirby (narrator) for their help with the production of the CD-ROM as well as the faculty and students at Sinclair Community College in Dayton, Ohio, and Utah Valley State College in Orem, Utah, for their ideas and suggestions. Most of all, we wish to thank Michelle Halderman for her assistance in all phases of manuscript preparation.

James D. Halderman
Chase D. Mitchell, Jr.

Tools, Fasteners, and Safety

Objectives: After studying Chapter 1, the reader should be able to:

1. Explain the strength ratings of threaded fasteners.
2. Identify hazardous materials.
3. Describe how to safely hoist a vehicle.
4. Discuss how to safely use hand tools.

■ THREADED FASTENERS

Most threaded fasteners used on engines are cap screws. They are called **cap screws** when they are threaded into a casting. Automotive service technicians usually refer to these fasteners as **bolts,** regardless of how they are used. In this chapter, they are called bolts. Sometimes, studs are used for threaded fasteners. A **stud** is a short rod with threads on both ends. Often, a stud will have coarse threads on one end and fine threads on the other end. The end of the stud with coarse threads is screwed into the casting. A nut is used on the opposite end to hold the parts together. See Figure 1–1.

The fastener threads *must* match the threads in the casting or nut. The threads may be measured either in fractions of an inch (called fractional) or in metric units. The size is measured across the outside of the threads, called the **crest** of the thread.

Fractional threads are either coarse or fine. The coarse threads are called Unified National Coarse (UNC) and the fine threads are called Unified National Fine (UNF). Standard combinations of sizes and number of threads per inch (called **pitch**) are used. Pitch

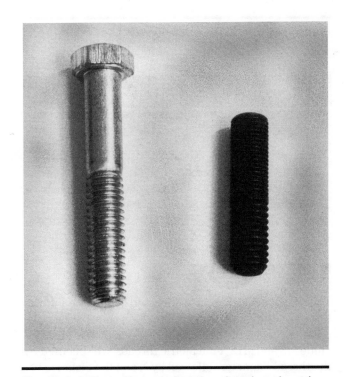

Figure 1–1 Typical bolt on the left and stud on the right. Note the different thread pitch on the top and bottom portions of the stud.

can be measured with a thread pitch gauge as shown in Figure 1–2. Bolts are identified by their diameter and length as measured from below the head as shown in Figure 1–3.

Fractional thread sizes are specified by the diameter in fractions of an inch and the number of threads per inch. Typical UNC thread sizes include 5/16-18 and 1/2-13. Similar UNF thread sizes are 5/16-24 and 1/2-20.

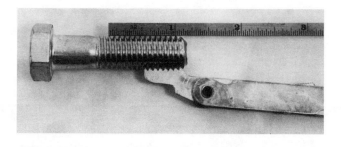

Figure 1–2 Thread pitch gauge used to measure the pitch of the thread. This bolt is 1/2 in. diameter with 13 threads to the inch (1/2-13).

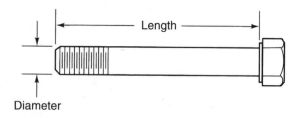

Figure 1–3 Bolt size identification.

Figure 1–4 Synthetic wintergreen oil can be used as a penetrating oil to loosen rusted bolts or nuts.

TECH TIP ✔

The Wintergreen Oil Trick

Synthetic wintergreen oil, available at most drugstores, makes an excellent penetrating oil. So the next time you cannot get that rusted bolt loose or find penetrating oil, head for the drugstore. See Figure 1–4.

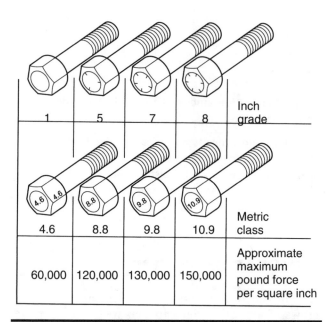

Figure 1–5 Typical bolt (cap screw) grade markings and approximate strength.

■ METRIC BOLTS

The size of a metric bolt is specified by the letter *M* followed by the diameter in millimeters (mm) across the outside (crest) of the threads. Typical metric sizes include M8 and M12. Fine metric threads are specified by the thread diameter followed by X and the distance between the threads measured in millimeters (M8 X 1.5).

■ GRADES OF BOLTS

Bolts are made from many different types of steel and for this reason some are stronger than others. The strength or classification of a bolt is called the **grade.** The bolt heads are marked to indicate their grade strength. Fractional bolts have lines on the head to indicate the grade, as shown in Figures 1–5 and 1–6.

The actual grade of bolts is two more than the number of lines on the bolt head. Metric bolts have a decimal number to indicate the grade. More lines or a higher grade number indicates a stronger bolt. In some cases, nuts and machine screws have similar grade markings.

CAUTION: *Never* use hardware store (nongraded) bolts, studs, or nuts on any vehicle steering, suspension, or brake component. Always use the exact size and grade of hardware as specified and used by the vehicle manufacturer.

Figure 1–6 Every shop should have an assortment of high-quality bolts and nuts to replace those damaged during vehicle service procedures.

■ NUTS

Most nuts used on cap screws have the same hex size as the cap screw head. Some inexpensive nuts use a hex size larger than the cap screw head. Metric nuts are often marked with dimples to show their strength. More dimples indicate stronger nuts. Some nuts and cap screws use interference fit threads to keep them from accidentally loosening. This means that the shape of the nut is slightly distorted or that a section of the threads is deformed. Nuts can also be kept from loosening with a nylon washer fastened in the nut or with a nylon patch or strip on the threads. See Figure 1–7.

Figure 1–7 Types of lock nuts. On the left, a nylon ring; in the center, a distorted shape; and on the right, a castle for use with a cotter key.

NOTE: Most of the "locking nuts" are grouped together and commonly referred to as **prevailing torque nuts.** This means that the nut will hold its tightness or torque and not loosen with movement or vibration. Most prevailing torque nuts should be replaced when they are removed to ensure that the nut will not loosen during service. Always follow manufacturer's recommendations. Anaerobic sealers, such as Loctite, are used on the threads where the nut or cap screw must be both locked and sealed.

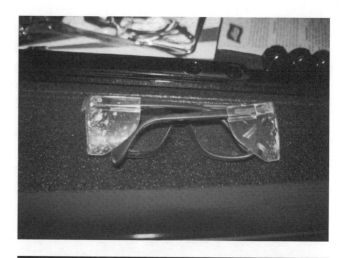

Figure 1–8 The most important tool in any toolbox is a pair of good-quality safety glasses.

 WASHERS

Washers are often used under cap screw heads and under nuts. Plain flat washers are used to provide an even clamping load around the fastener. Lock washers are added to prevent accidental loosening. In some accessories, the washers are locked onto the nut to provide easy assembly.

■ BASIC TOOL LIST

Hand tools are used to turn fasteners (bolts, nuts, and screws). The following is a list of hand tools that every automotive technician should possess. Specialty tools are not included. See Figures 1–8 through 1–37.

Figure 1–9 Combination wrench. The openings are the same size at both ends. Notice the angle of the open end to permit use in close spaces.

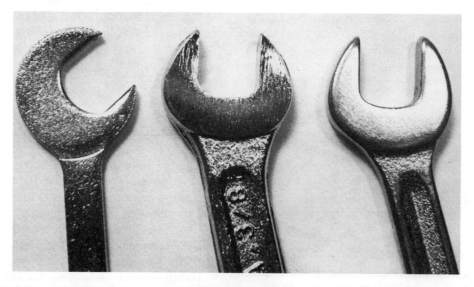

Figure 1–10 Three different qualities of open-end wrenches. The cheap wrench on the left is made from weaker steel and is thicker and less accurately machined than the standard in the center. The wrench on the right is of professional quality (and price).

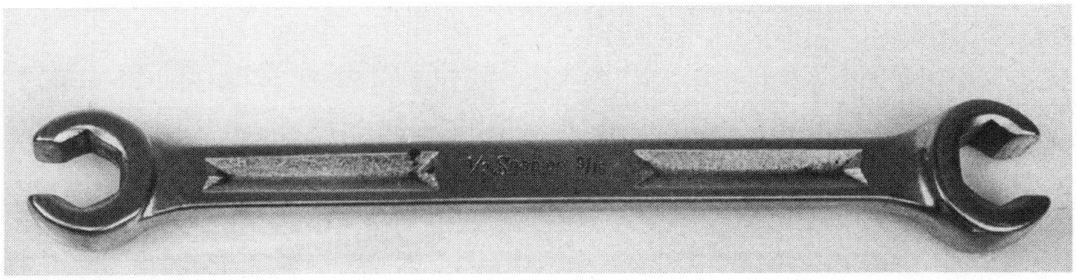

Figure 1–11 Flare-nut wrench. Also known as a *line wrench, fitting wrench,* or *tube-nut wrench.* This style of wrench is designed to grasp most flats of a six-sided (hex) tube fitting to provide the most grip without damage to the fitting.

Tool chest
Safety glasses
¼-inch drive socket set
¼-inch drive ratchet
¼-inch drive 2-inch extension
¼-inch drive 6-inch extension
¼-inch drive handle
⅜-inch drive socket set
⅜-inch drive Torx set
⅜-inch drive 13/16-inch plug socket
⅜-inch drive ⅝-inch plug socket
⅜-inch drive ratchet
⅜-inch drive 1 ½-inch extension
⅜-inch drive 3-inch extension
⅜-inch drive 6-inch extension
⅜-inch drive 18-inch extension
⅜-inch drive universal
½-inch drive socket set
½-inch drive ratchet
½-inch drive breaker bar
½-inch drive 5-inch extension
½-inch drive 10-inch extension
⅜-inch to ¼-inch adapter
½-inch to ⅜-inch adapter
⅜-inch to ½-inch adapter
⅜-inch through 1-inch combo wrench set
10-millimeter through 19-millimeter combo wrench set
1/16-inch through ¼-inch hex wrench set
2-millimeter through 12-millimeter hex wrench set
⅜-inch hex socket
13-millimeter/14-millimeter flare nut wrench
15-millimeter/17-millimeter flare nut wrench
5/16-inch/⅜-inch flare nut wrench
7/16-inch/½-inch flare nut wrench
½-inch/9/16-inch flare nut wrench
Diagonal pliers
Needle pliers
Adjustable-jaw pliers
Locking pliers
Snap-ring pliers
Stripping or crimping pliers
Ball-peen hammer
Rubber hammer
Dead-blow hammer
Five-piece straight slot screwdriver set
Four-piece Phillips screwdriver set
#15 Torx screwdriver
#20 Torx screwdriver
Crowfoot set (fractional inch)
Crowfoot set (metric)
Awl
Mill file
Center punch
Pin punches (assorted sizes)
Chisel
Utility knife
Valve core tool
Coolant tester
Filter wrench (large filters)
Filter wrench (smaller filters)
Circuit tester
Feeler gauge
Scraper
Pinch bar
Sticker knife
Magnet
Torque wrench
0–1″ micrometer
1″–2″ micrometer

Figure 1–12 Box-end wrench. Recommended to loosen or tighten a bolt or nut where a socket will not fit. A box-end wrench has a different size at each end and is better to use than an open-end wrench, because it touches the bolt or nut around the entire head instead of at just two places.

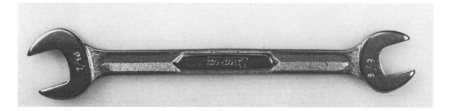

Figure 1–13 Open-end wrench. Each end has a different-size opening and is recommended for general usage. Do not attempt to loosen or tighten bolts or nuts either from or to full torque with an open-end wrench, because it could round the flats of the fastener.

Figure 1–14 A flat-blade (or straight-blade) screwdriver (*on the left*) is specified by the length of the screwdriver and width of the blade. The width of the blade should match the width of the screw slot of the fastener. A Phillips-head screwdriver (*on the right*) is specified by the length of the handle and the size of the point at the tip. A #1 is a sharp point, #2 is most common (as shown), and a #3 Phillips is blunt and is only used for larger sizes of Phillips-head fasteners.

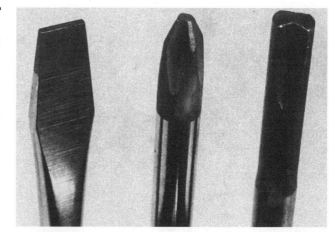

Figure 1–15 Assortment of pliers. Slip-joint pliers (*far left*) are often confused with water pump pliers (*second from left*).

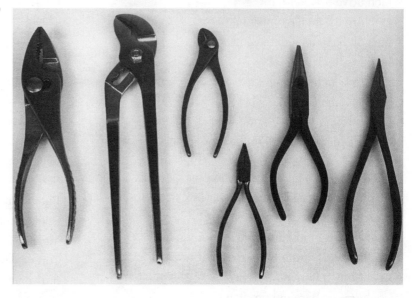

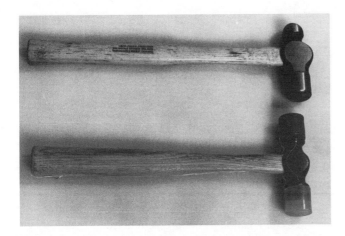

Figure 1–16 A ball-peen hammer (*top*) is purchased according to weight (usually in ounces) of the head of the hammer. At the bottom is a soft-faced (plastic) hammer. Always use a hammer that is softer than the material being driven. Use a block of wood or similar material between a steel hammer and steel or iron engine parts to prevent damage to the engine parts.

Figure 1–19 Twelve-point, six-point, and eight-point sockets. Six-point sockets are recommended because they contact all six sides of a typical bolt or nut and can exert more force without rounding the head.

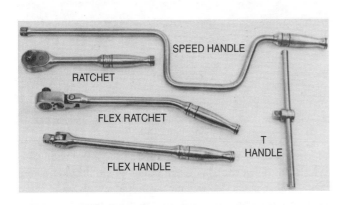

Figure 1–17 Typical drive handles for sockets.

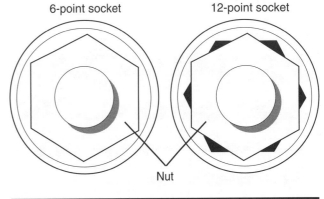

Figure 1–20 A six-point socket fits the head of the bolt or nut on all sides. A twelve-point socket can round off the head of a bolt or nut if a lot of force is applied.

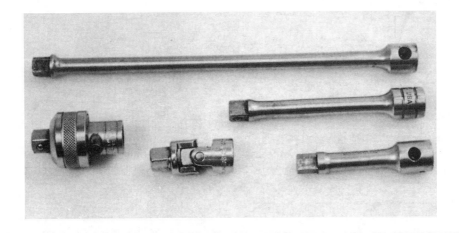

Figure 1–18 Various socket extensions. The universal joint (U-joint) in the center (*bottom*) is useful for gaining access in tight areas.

Figure 1–21 Standard twelve-point short socket (*left*), universal joint socket (*center*), and deep-well socket (*right*). Both the universal and deep well are six-point sockets.

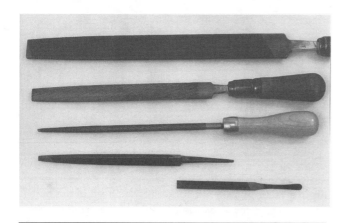

Figure 1–22 Typical files. Never use a file without a handle.

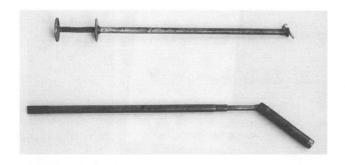

Figure 1–23 Mechanical pickup finger (*top*) and extendible magnet (*bottom*) are excellent tools to have when a nut drops into a small area where fingers can never reach.

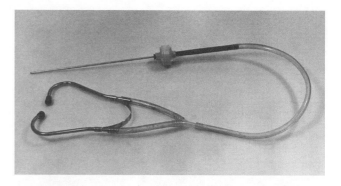

Figure 1–24 Stethoscope used by technicians to listen for the exact location of the problem noise.

Figure 1–25 A typical grinder. Notice the installation of eye shields. Even though an eye shield would provide some protection, the service technician should always wear safety glasses when using this or any other power equipment.

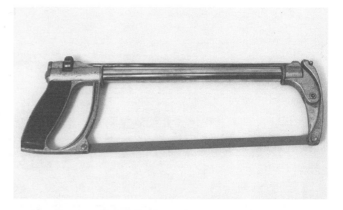

Figure 1–26 Hacksaw. The teeth of the blade should point away from the handle. The thinner the material being cut, the finer the blade teeth should be.

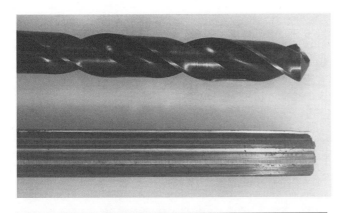

Figure 1–27 Drill bit (*top*) with twisted flutes (grooves), and a reamer (*bottom*) with straight flutes.

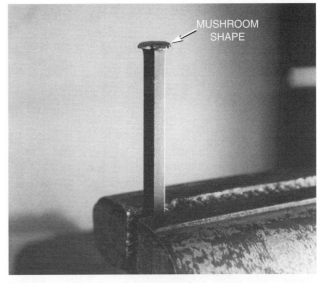

(a)

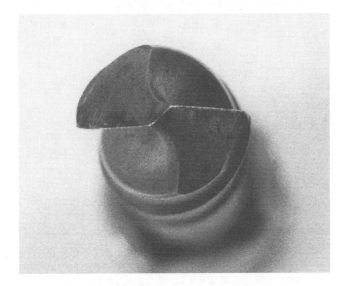

Figure 1–28 Cutting edge of a drill bit.

(b)

Figure 1–30 (a) The mushroom-shape top of this chisel can be dangerous. If a hammer blow strikes the top edge of the chisel, sharp chips could be forced off the top and cause personal injury. (b) When you discover a mushroomed tool, take a few minutes to grind the top to look like this to help prevent possible injury.

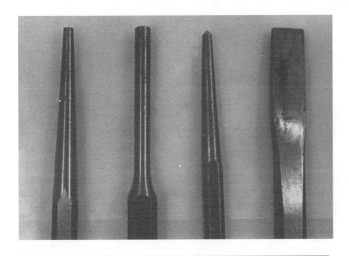

Figure 1–29 Various punches on the left and a chisel on the right.

Figure 1–31 Using a die to cut threads on a rod.

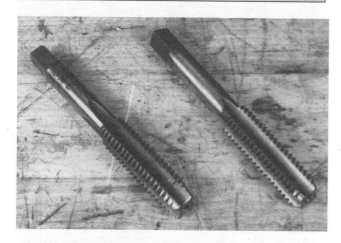

Figure 1–32 A standard and a bottoming tap. These taps are commonly used to "chase" or clean existing threads in blocks.

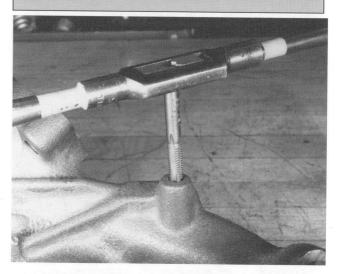

Figure 1–34 Starting a tap in a drilled hole. The hole diameter should match exactly to the tap size for proper thread clearance. The proper drill size to use is called the **tap drill** size.

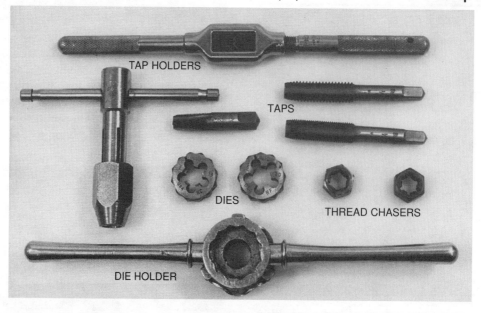

Figure 1–33 Dies are used to make threads on the outside of round stock. Taps are used to make threads on the inside of holes.

Figure 1–35 An inexpensive muffin tin can be used to keep small parts separated.

Figure 1–36 A good fluorescent trouble light is essential. A fluorescent light operates cooler than an incandescent light and does not pose a fire hazard if gasoline were accidentally dropped on an unprotected incandescent bulb used in some trouble lights.

(a)

(b)

Figure 1–37 (a) A beginning technician can start with some simple basic hand tools. (b) An experienced serious technician often spends several thousand dollars a year for tools such as found in this large (and expensive) toolbox.

■ BRAND NAME VERSUS PROPER TERM

Technicians often use slang or brand names of tools rather than the proper term. This practice results in some confusion for new technicians. Some examples are given in the following table.

TECH TIP ✔

The Valve Grinding Compound Trick

Apply a small amount of valve grinding compound to a Phillips or Torx screw or bolt head. The gritty valve grinding compound "grips" the screwdriver or tool bit and prevents the tool from slipping up and out of the screw head. Valve grinding compound is available in a tube from most automotive parts stores.

Brand Name	Proper Term	Slang Name
Crescent wrench	Adjustable wrench	Monkey wrench
Vise grips	Locking pliers	
Channel locks	Water pump pliers or multigroove adjustable pliers	Pump pliers
	Diagonal cutting pliers	Dikes or side cuts

■ SAFETY TIPS FOR USING HAND TOOLS

Consider the following safety tips when working with hand tools.

- Always *pull* a wrench toward you for best control and safety. Never push a wrench.
- Keep wrenches and all hand tools clean to help prevent rust and to provide a better, firmer grip.
- Always use a 6-point socket or a box-end wrench to break loose a tight bolt or nut.
- Use a box-end wrench for torque and the open-end wrench for speed.
- Never use a pipe extension or other type of "cheater bar" on a wrench or ratchet handle. If more force is required, use a larger tool or use penetrating oil and/or heat on the frozen fastener. (If heat is used on a bolt or nut to remove it, always replace it with a new part.)
- Always use the proper tool for the job. If a specialized tool is required, use the proper tool and do not try to use another tool improperly.

- Never expose any tool to excessive heat. High temperatures can reduce the strength ("draw the temper") of metal tools.
- Never use a hammer on any wrench or socket handle unless you are using a special "staking face" wrench designed to be used with a hammer.
- Replace any tools that are damaged or worn.

■ SAFETY TIPS FOR TECHNICIANS

Safety is not just a buzzword on a poster in the work area. Safe work habits can reduce accidents and injuries, ease the workload, and keep employees pain free. Suggested safety tips include the following:

- *Wear safety glasses at all times while servicing any vehicle.*
- Watch your toes—always keep them protected with steel-toed safety shoes. If safety shoes are not available, then leather-topped shoes offer more protection than canvas or cloth shoes.
- Wear gloves to protect your hands from rough or sharp surfaces. See Figure 1–38. Thin rubber gloves are recommended when working around automotive liquids such as engine oil, antifreeze, transmission fluid, or any other liquids that may be hazardous. See the Tech Tip, "Wearing Rubber Gloves Saves Your Hands."
- When working under a vehicle, wear a **bump cap** to protect your head against under-vehicle objects and the pads of the lift.
- Remove jewelry that may get caught on something or act as a conductor to an exposed electrical circuit.
- Avoid loose or dangling clothing.
- When lifting any object, get a secure grip with solid footing. Keep the load close to your body to minimize the strain. Lift with your legs and arms, not your back.
- Do not twist your body when carrying a load. Instead, pivot your feet to help prevent strain on the spine.
- Ask for help when moving or lifting heavy objects.
- Push a heavy object rather than pull it. (This method is opposite to the way you should work with tools—never push a wrench! If you push a wrench and a bolt or nut loosens, then your entire weight propels your hand(s) forward, and usually results in cuts, bruises, or other painful injury.)
- Always connect an exhaust hose to the tailpipe of any running vehicle to help prevent the buildup of carbon monoxide inside a closed garage space. See Figure 1–39.
- When standing, keep all ready objects, parts, and tools between chest height and waist height. If seated, work at tasks that are at elbow height.

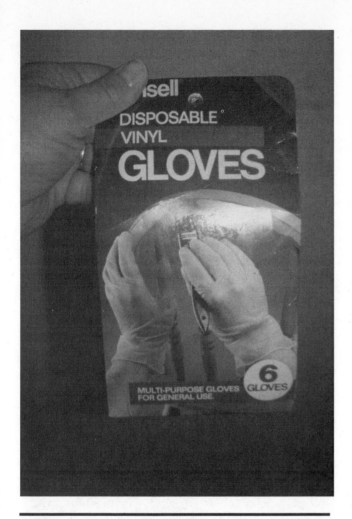

Figure 1–38 Protective gloves such as these vinyl gloves are available in several sizes. Select the size that allows the gloves to fit snugly. Vinyl gloves last a long time and often can be worn all day to help protect your hands from dirt and possible hazardous materials.

- Store all flammable liquids in an approved fire safety cabinet. See Figure 1–40.
- Always be sure the hood is securely held open. See Figure 1–41.

■ SAFETY IN LIFTING (HOISTING) A VEHICLE

Many chassis and underbody service procedures require that the vehicle be hoisted or lifted off the ground. The simplest methods involve the use of drive-on ramps or a floor jack and safety (jack) stands, whereas in-ground or surface-mounted lifts provide greater access.

Setting the pads is a critical part of this procedure. All automobile and light-truck service manuals include recommended locations to be used when hoisting (lifting) a vehicle. Newer vehicles have a triangle decal on the driver's door indicating the recommended lift points. The

Figure 1–39 Always connect an exhaust hose to the tailpipe of the vehicle's engine when run inside a building.

Figure 1–40 Typical fireproof flammable storage cabinet.

recommended standards for the lift points and lifting procedures are found in SAE Standard JRP-2184. These recommendations typically include the following points.

1. The vehicle should be centered on the lift or hoist so as not to overload one side or put too much force either forward or rearward. See Figure 1–42.

TECH TIP ✔

Wearing Rubber Gloves Saves Your Hands

Many technicians wear rubber gloves not only to help keep their hands clean, but also to help protect their skin from the effects of dirty engine oil and other possibly hazardous materials. Several types of gloves and their characteristics include:

- **Latex surgical gloves**—These gloves are relatively inexpensive, but tend to stretch, swell, and weaken when exposed to gas, oil, or solvents.
- **Vinyl gloves**—These gloves are also inexpensive and are not affected by gas, oil, or solvents.
- **Polyurethane gloves**—These gloves are more expensive, yet very strong. Even though these gloves are also not affected by gas, oil, or solvents, they do tend to be slippery.
- **Nitrile gloves**—These gloves are exactly like latex gloves, but are not affected by gas, oil, or solvents, yet they tend to be expensive.

Many service technicians prefer to use the vinyl-type gloves, but with an additional pair of nylon gloves worn under the vinyl. Nylon gloves look like white cotton gloves and when worn under the others help keep moisture under control. (Plastic gloves on a hot summer day can soon become wet with perspiration.) The nylon gloves provide additional protection and are washable.

2. The pads of the lift should be spread as far apart as possible to provide a stable platform.
3. Each pad should be placed under a portion of the vehicle that is strong and capable of supporting the weight of the vehicle.
   a. Pinch weld seams at the bottom edge of the body are generally considered to be strong.

CAUTION: Even though pinch weld seams are the recommended location for hoisting many vehicles with unitized bodies (unit body), care should be taken not to place the pad(s) too far forward or rearward. Incorrect placement of the vehicle on the lift could cause the vehicle to be imbalanced, and the vehicle could fall. This is exactly what happened to the vehicle in Figure 1–43.

   b. Boxed areas of the body are the best places to position the pads on a vehicle without a frame. Be careful to note whether the arms of the lift might come into contact with other parts of the vehicle before the pad touches the intended

(a)

HOOD STRUT CLAMP

(b)

Figure 1–41 (a) A crude but effective method is to use locking pliers on the chrome-plated shaft of a hood strut. Locking pliers should only be used on defective struts because the jaws of the pliers can damage the strut shaft. (b) A commercially available hood clamp. This tool uses a bright orange tag to help remind the technician to remove the clamp before attempting to close the hood. The hood could be bent if force is used to close the hood with the clamp in place.

(a)

(b)

Figure 1–42 (a) Tall safety stands can be used to provide additional support for a vehicle while on a hoist. (b) A block of wood should be used to avoid the possibility of doing damage to the components supported by the stand.

location. Commonly damaged areas include the following:
(1) Rocker panel moldings
(2) Exhaust system (including catalytic converter)

Figure 1–43 This vehicle fell from the hoist because the pads were not set correctly. No one was hurt, but the vehicle was a total loss.

SAFETY
ARM CLIP

Figure 1–44 The safety arm clip should be engaged to prevent the possibility that the hoist support arms can move.

    (3) Tires, especially if the edges of the pads or arms are sharp (See Figures 1–44 through 1–46.)
4. The vehicle should be raised about 1 foot [30 centimeters (cm)] off the floor, then stopped and shaken to check for stability. If the vehicle seems to be stable when checked at a short distance from the floor, then continue to raise and view the vehicle until it has reached the desired height.

CAUTION: Do not look away from the vehicle while it is being raised (or lowered) on a hoist. Often one side or one end of the hoist can stop or fail, resulting in the vehicle being slanted enough to slip or fall, and thus creating physical damage not only to the vehicle and/or hoist but also to the technician or others who may be nearby.

(a)

(b)

Figure 1–45 (a) An assortment of hoist pad adapters that are often necessary to use to safely hoist many pickup trucks, vans, and sport utility vehicles. (b) A view from underneath a Chevrolet pickup truck showing how the pad extensions are used to attach the hoist lifting pad to contact the frame.

(a)

(b)

Figure 1–46 (a) The pad arm is just contacting the rocker panel of the vehicle. (b) An example of what can occur if the technician places the pad too far inward underneath the vehicle. The arm of the hoist has dented in the rocker panel.

HINT: Most hoists can be safely placed at any desired height. For ease while working, the area in which you are working should be at chest level. When working on brakes or suspension components, it is not necessary to work on them near the floor or over your head. Raise the hoist so that the components are at chest level.

5. Before lowering the hoist, the safety latch(es) must be released and the direction of the controls reversed. The speed downward is often adjusted to be as slow as possible for additional safety.

TECH TIP

Do No Harm

As stated in the Hippocratic oath, a doctor agrees first to do no harm to the patient during treatment. Service technicians should also try to do no harm to the vehicle while they are servicing it.

Always ask, "Am I going to do any harm if I do this?" before you do it.

■ HAZARDOUS MATERIALS

The Environmental Protection Agency (EPA) regulates the handling of hazardous materials in the United States. A material is considered hazardous if it meets one or more of the following conditions.

- It contains over 1000 parts per million (PPM) of halogenated compounds. (Halogenated compounds are chemicals containing chlorine, fluorine, bromine, or iodine.) Common items that contain these solvents include the following:

  Carburetor cleaner

  Silicone spray

  Aerosols

  Adhesives

  Stoddard solvent

  Trichloromethane

  Gear oils

  Brake cleaner

  Air-conditioning (A/C) compressor oils

  Floor cleaners

  Anything else that contains a *chlor* or *fluor* in its ingredient name
- It has a flash point below 140°F (60°C).
- It is corrosive (has a pH level of 2 or lower or 12.5 or higher).
- It contains toxic metals or organic compounds. Volatile organic compounds (VOCs) also must be limited and controlled. This classification greatly affects the painting and finishing aspects of the automobile industry.

Always follow recommended procedures for the handling of any chemicals and dispose of all used engine oil and other waste products according to local, provincial, state, or federal laws.

To help safeguard workers and the environment, the following guidelines are recommended.

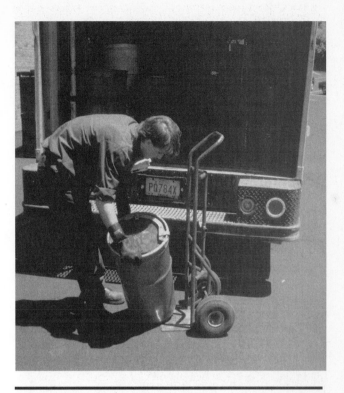

Figure 1–47 All solvents and other hazardous waste should be disposed of properly.

- A technician's hands should always be washed thoroughly after touching used engine oils, transmission fluids, and greases. Dispose of all waste oil according to established standards and laws in your area. See Figure 1–47.

NOTE: The EPA current standard permits used engine oil to be recycled only if it contains less than 1000 PPM of total halogens (chlorinated solvents). Oil containing greater amounts of halogens must be considered as **hazardous waste.**

- Asbestos and products that contain asbestos are known cancer-causing agents. Even though most brake linings and clutch facing materials are now manufactured without asbestos, millions of vehicles are being serviced every day that *may* contain asbestos. The general procedure for handling asbestos is to put the used parts into a sealed plastic bag and return them as cores for rebuilding or dispose of them according to current laws and regulations.
- Eyewash stations should be readily accessible near the work area or near where solvents or other contaminants could get into the eyes. See Figure 1–48.

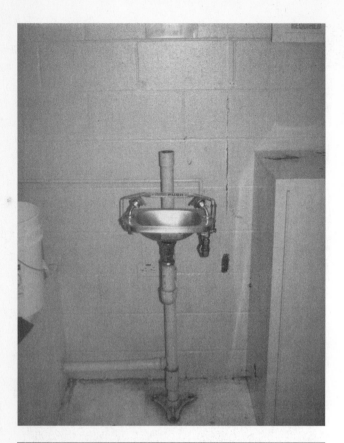

Figure 1–48 An eyewash station should be centrally located in the shop and near where solvent may be splashed.

TECH TIP ✔

Pound with Something Softer

If you must pound on something, be sure to use a tool that is softer than what you are about to pound on to avoid damage. Examples are given in the following table.

The material being pounded	What to pound with
Steel or cast iron	Brass or aluminum hammer or punch
Aluminum	Plastic or rawhide mallet or plastic-covered dead-blow hammer
Plastic	Rawhide mallet or plastic dead-blow hammer

Figure 1–50 A parts wash station.

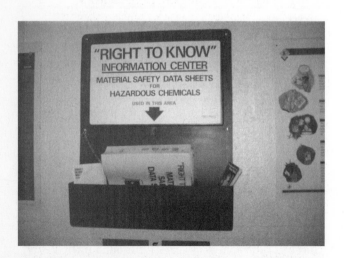

Figure 1–49 MSDS material must be displayed in plain view so that anyone can have easy access to information about possible hazardous materials.

■ MATERIAL SAFETY DATA SHEETS

Businesses and schools in the United States are required to provide a detailed data sheet on each of the chemicals or materials to which persons may be exposed within their buildings. These sheets of information on each of the materials that *may* be harmful are called **material safety data sheets (MSDS).** See Figure 1–49. Many of these potentially hazardous materials involve cleaning materials such as those used in a parts wash station as shown in Figure 1–50.

PHOTO SEQUENCE   Hoisting a Vehicle

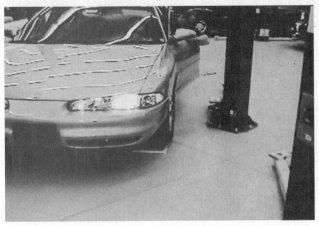

PS I–I The first step in hoisting a vehicle is to properly align the vehicle in the center of the stall.

TIRE PAD

PS I–2 Most vehicles will be correctly positioned when the left front tire is centered on the tire pad.

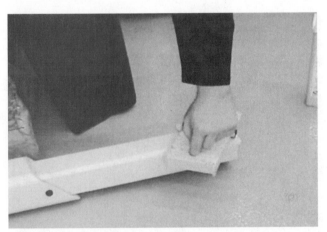

PS I–3 Most pads at the end of the hoist arms can be rotated to allow for many different types of vehicle construction.

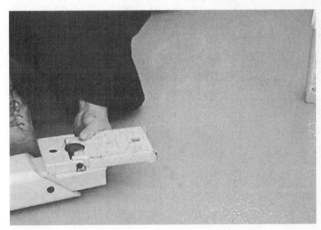

PS I–4 The arms of the lifts can be retracted or extended to accommodate vehicles of many different

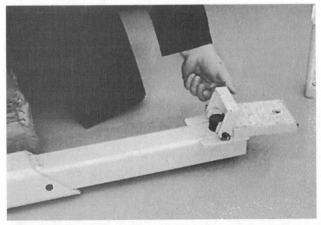

PS I–5 Most lifts are equipped with short pad extensions that are often necessary to use to allow the pad to contact the frame of a vehicle without causing the arm of the lift to hit and damage parts of the body.

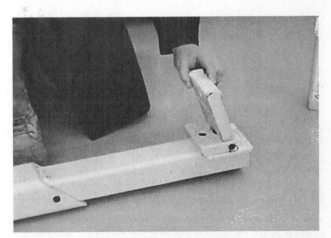

PS I–6 Tall pad extensions can also be used to gain access to the frame of a vehicle. This position is needed to safely hoist many pickup trucks, vans, and sport utility vehicles

Hoisting a Vehicle—continued

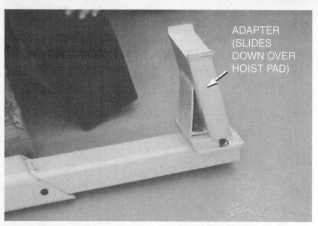

PS I–7 An additional extension may be necessary to hoist a truck or van equipped with running boards to give the necessary clearance.

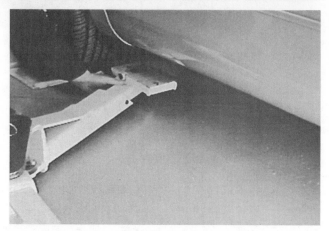

PS I–8 Position the front hoist pads under the recommended locations as specified in the owner's manual and/or service information for the vehicle being serviced.

PS I–9 Position the rear pads under the vehicle under the recommended locations.

PS I–10 This photo shows an asymmetrical lift where the front arms are shorter than the rear arms. This design is best used for passenger cars and allows the driver to exit the vehicle easier because the door can be opened wide without it hitting the vertical support column.

PS I–11 After being sure all pads are correctly positioned, use the electromechanical controls to raise the vehicle.

PS I–12 Raise the vehicle about one foot (30 cm) and stop to double check that all pads contact the body or frame in the correct positions.

PS 1–13 With the vehicle raised about one foot off the ground, push down on the vehicle to check to see if it is stable on the pads. If the vehicle rocks, lower the vehicle and reset the pads. If the vehicle is stable, the vehicle can be raised to any desired working level. Be sure the safety is engaged before working on or under the vehicle.

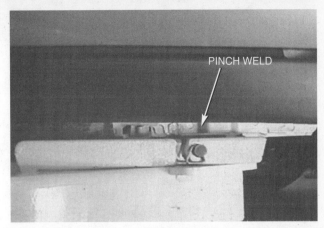

PS 1–14 This photo shows the pads set flat and contacting the pinch welds of the body. This method spreads the load over the entire length of the pad and is less likely to dent or damage the pinch weld area.

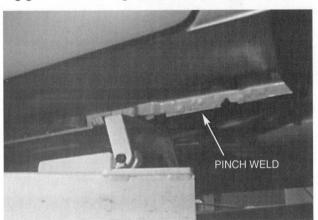

PS 1–15 Where additional clearance is necessary for the arms to clear the rest of the body, the pads can be raised and placed under the pinch weld area as shown.

PS 1–16 When the service work is completed, the hoist should be raised slightly and the safety released before using the hydraulic lever to lower the vehicle.

PS 1–17 After lowering the vehicle, be sure all arms of the lift are moved out of the way before driving the vehicle out of the work stall.

PS 1–18 Carefully back the vehicle out of the stall. Notice that all of the lift arms have been neatly moved out of the way to provide clearance so that the tires will not contact the arms when the vehicle is driven out of the stall.

PHOTO SEQUENCE Thread Repair

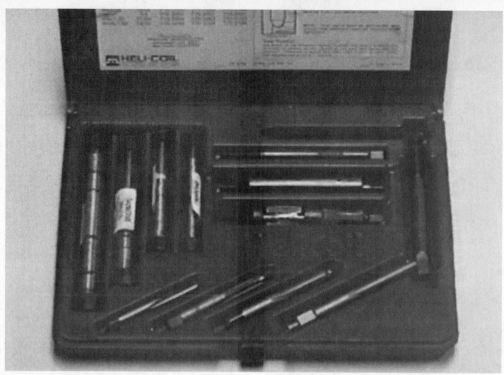

PS 2–1 To repair stripped out threads, a thread repair kit such as this is needed.

PS 2–2 The first step is to drill out the existing hole using the size drill bit specified in the thread repair kit. (The proper size drill bit may not be included with the thread repair kit.)

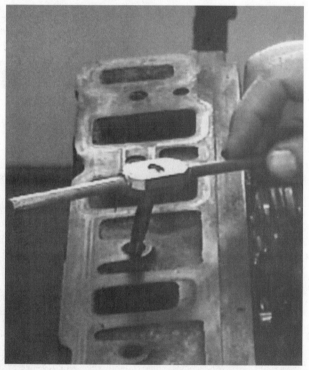

PS 2–3 The next step is to tap the hole using the specified tap that is in the thread repair kit. Cutting oil should be used on the tap to provide lubrication for the thread cutting process.

Thread Repair—continued

PS 2–4 After the hole has been tapped, use a cotton swab (such as Q-tip) to remove any cutting oil from the bottom of the tapped hole. This step is important to prevent the possibility of a hydrostatic lock occurring when the bolt is installed into the threaded hole.

PS 2–5 Install the thread repair insert onto the installation tool being sure that the tang is properly aligned on the tool as shown.

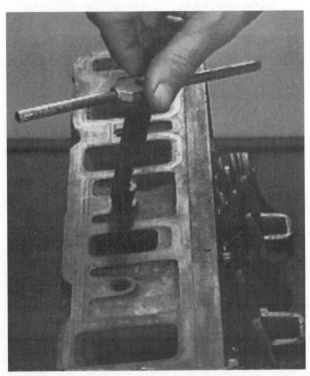

PS 2–6 The thread insert is then screwed into the tapped hole using the installation tool from the kit.

PS 2–7 Use a punch and a hammer to break off the tang of the insert after the installation tool is removed. Turn the cylinder head over to allow the broken tang to fall out of the hole. The threaded hole is now repaired with a new thread

■ SUMMARY

1. Bolts, studs, and nuts are commonly used as fasteners in the chassis. The sizes for fractional and metric threads are different and are not interchangeable. The grade is the strength rating of the fastener.

2. When a vehicle is raised above the ground, it must be supported at a substantial section of the body or frame.

3. Hazardous materials include common automotive chemicals, liquids, and lubricants, especially those whose ingredients contain *chlor* or *fluor* in their name. Asbestos fibers should be avoided and removed according to current laws and regulations.

■ REVIEW QUESTIONS

1. List three precautions that must be taken when hoisting (lifting) a vehicle.

2. List five common automotive chemicals or products that may be considered hazardous materials.

3. List five precautions to which every technician should adhere when working with automotive products and chemicals.

4. Describe how to determine the grade of a fastener, including how the markings differ between customary and metric bolts.

■ ASE CERTIFICATION-TYPE QUESTIONS

1. Two technicians are discussing the hoisting of a vehicle. Technician A says to put the pads of a lift under a notch at the pinch weld of a unit-body vehicle. Technician B says to place the pads on the four corners of the frame of a full-frame vehicle. Which technician is correct?
   a. Technician A only
   b. Technician B only
   c. Both Technician A and B
   d. Neither Technician A nor B

2. The correct location for the pads when hoisting or jacking the vehicle can often be found in the _____ .
   a. Service manual
   b. Shop manual
   c. Owner's manual
   d. All of the above

3. Hazardous materials include all of the following *except* _____ .
   a. Engine oil
   b. Asbestos
   c. Water
   d. Brake cleaner

4. To determine if a product or substance being used is hazardous, consult _____ .
   a. A dictionary
   b. A MSDS
   c. SAE standards
   d. EPA guidelines

5. For the best working position, the work should be _____ .
   a. At neck or head level
   b. At knee or ankle level
   c. Overhead by about 1 foot
   d. At chest or elbow level

6. When working with hand tools, always _____ .
   a. Push the wrench—do not pull toward you
   b. Pull a wrench—do not push a wrench

7. A high-strength bolt is identified by _____ .
   a. A UNC symbol
   b. Lines on the head
   c. Strength letter codes
   d. The coarse threads

8. A fastener that uses threads on both ends is called a _____ .
   a. Cap screw
   b. Stud
   c. Machine screw
   d. Crest fastener

9. The proper term for Channel Locks is _____ .
   a. Vise grips
   b. Crescent wrench
   c. Locking pliers
   d. Multigroove adjustable pliers

10. The proper term for Vise Grips is _____ .
    a. Locking pliers
    b. Slip-joint pliers
    c. Side cuts
    d. Multigroove adjustable pliers

Engine Operation and Identification

Objectives: After studying Chapter 2, the reader should be able to:

1. Explain how a four-stroke cycle gasoline engine operates.
2. List the various characteristics by which vehicle engines are classified.
3. Describe how engine power is measured and calculated.
4. Discuss how a compression ratio is calculated.
5. Explain how engine size is determined.

The engine converts part of the fuel energy to useful power. This power is used to move the vehicle.

■ ENERGY AND POWER

Energy is used to produce power. Chemical energy in fuel is converted to heat by the burning of the fuel at a controlled rate. This process is called **combustion.** If engine combustion occurs within the power chamber, then the engine is called an **internal combustion engine.**

NOTE: An **external combustion engine** burns fuel outside of the engine itself, such as a steam engine.

Engines used in automobiles are internal combustion heat engines. They convert the chemical energy of the gasoline into heat within a power chamber called a **combustion chamber.** Heat energy released in the combustion chamber raises the temperature of the combustion gases within the chamber. The increase in gas temperature causes the pressure of the gases to increase. The pressure developed within the combustion chamber is applied to the head of a piston or to a turbine wheel to produce a usable **mechanical force.** This force is converted into useful **mechanical power.**

■ FOUR-STROKE CYCLE OPERATION

Most automotive engines use the four-stroke cycle of events. The starter motor rotates the engine. The four-stroke cycle is repeated for each cylinder of the engine. See Figure 2–1.

- **Intake stroke**—The piston inside the cylinder travels downward, drawing the **intake valve** open and a mixture of air and fuel into the cylinder.
- **Compression stroke**—As the engine continues to rotate, the piston is forced upward in the cylinder, compressing the air-fuel mixture.
- **Power stroke**—When the piston gets near the top of the cylinder [called **top dead center (TDC)**], the spark at the spark plug ignites the air-fuel mixture. The piston is forced downward.
- **Exhaust stroke**—The engine continues to rotate, and the piston again moves upward in the cylinder. The exhaust valve opens, and the piston forces the residual burned gases out of the **exhaust valve** and into the exhaust manifold and exhaust system.

This sequence repeats as the engine rotates. To stop the engine, the electricity to the spark plugs is shut off by the ignition switch.

Figure 2–1 Typical four-stroke cycle of a spark-ignited gasoline engine.

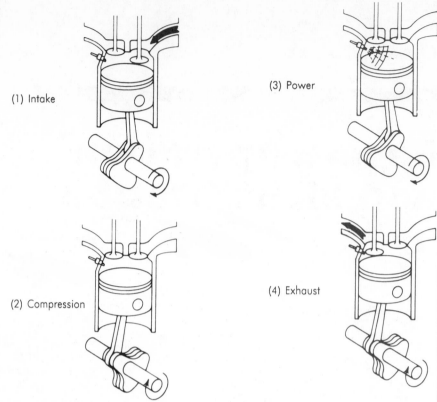

(1) Intake

(2) Compression

(3) Power

(4) Exhaust

VALVE LIFTER BORES

CYLINDER BORES

Figure 2–2 A V-8 engine block. The block is the foundation of any engine because it supports all moving parts necessary to make the engine operate.

Figure 2–2 shows an automotive V-8 engine block. A piston moves up and down, or reciprocates, in a **cylinder** seen as four large holes in the block. The piston is attached to a **crankshaft** with a **connecting rod.** This arrangement allows the piston to reciprocate in the cylinder as the crankshaft rotates. The combustion pressure developed in the combustion chamber at the correct time will push the piston downward to rotate the crankshaft.

■ THE 720-DEGREE CYCLE

Each cycle of events requires that the engine crankshaft make two complete revolutions, or 720 degrees ($360° \times 2 = 720°$). The greater the number of cylinders, the closer together the power strokes occur. To find the angle between cylinders of an engine, divide the number of cylinders into 720 degrees.

Angle with four cylinders = $720° \div 4 = 180°$
Angle with six cylinders = $720° \div 6 = 120°$
Angle with eight cylinders = $720° \div 8 = 90°$

This means that in a four-cylinder engine, a power stroke occurs at every 180 degrees of the crankshaft rotation (every 1/2 rotation). A V-8 is a much smoother operating engine, because a power stroke occurs twice as often (every 90 degrees of crankshaft rotation).

Engine cycles are identified by the number of piston strokes required to complete the cycle. A **piston stroke** is a one-way piston movement between the top and bottom of the cylinder. During one stroke, the crankshaft revolves 180 degrees (1/2 revolution). A **cycle** is a complete

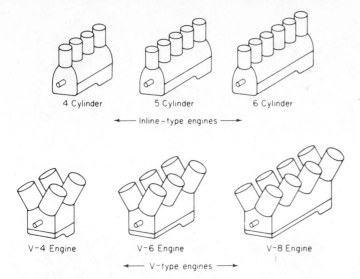

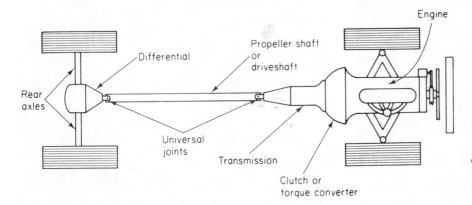

Figure 2–3 Automotive engine cylinder arrangements.

Figure 2–4 Typical front engine, rear-wheel drive.

series of events that continually repeat. Most automobile engines use a **four-stroke cycle.**

■ ENGINE CLASSIFICATION

Engines are classified by several characteristics including:

- *Number of strokes.* Most automotive engines use the four-stroke cycle.
- *Cylinder arrangement.* An engine with more cylinders is smoother operating because the power pulses produced by the power strokes are more closely spaced. An inline engine places all cylinders in a straight line. Four-, five-, and six-cylinder engines are commonly manufactured inline engines. A V-type engine, such as a V-6 or V-8, has the number of cylinders split and built into a V shape. See Figure 2–3.
- *Longitudinal or transverse mounting.* Engines may be mounted either parallel with the length of the vehicle (longitudinally) or crosswise (transversely). See Figures 2–4 through 2–6. The same engine may be mounted in various vehicles in either direction.

> **NOTE:** Although it might be possible to mount an engine in different vehicles, both longitudinally and transversely, the engine component parts may *not* be interchangeable. Differences can include different engine blocks and crankshafts, as well as different water pumps.

- *Valve and camshaft number and location.* The number of valves and the number and location of camshafts are a major factor in engine operation. A typical older-model engine uses one intake valve and one exhaust valve per cylinder. Many newer engines use two intake and two exhaust valves per cylinder. The valves are opened by a **camshaft.** For high-speed engine operation, the camshaft should be overhead (over the valves). Some engines use one camshaft for the intake valves and a separate camshaft for the exhaust valves. When the camshaft is located in the block, the valves are operated by lifters, pushrods, and rocker arms. See Figure 2–7. This type of engine is called a **pushrod engine.** An overhead camshaft engine has the camshaft above the valves in the

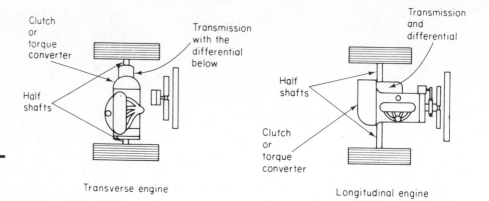

Figure 2–5 Two types of front engine, front-wheel drives.

Transverse engine

Longitudinal engine

Figure 2–6 A longitudinally mounted V-6 on a front-wheel-drive vehicle.

cylinder head. When one overhead camshaft is used, it is called a **single overhead camshaft (SOHC)** design. See Figure 2–8. When two overhead camshafts are used, it is called a **double overhead camshaft (DOHC)** design as shown in Figure 2–9.

NOTE: A V-type engine uses two banks or rows of cylinders. An SOHC design, therefore, uses two camshafts, but only one camshaft per bank (row) of cylinders. A DOHC V-6, therefore, has four camshafts, two for each bank.

- *Type of fuel.* Most engines operate on gasoline, whereas some engines are designed to operate on methanol, natural gas, propane, or diesel fuel.
- *Cooling method.* Most engines are liquid cooled, but some older models were air cooled.
- *Type of induction pressure.* If normal air pressure is used to force the air-fuel mixture into the cylinders, then the engine is called **normally aspirated.** Some engines use a **turbocharger** or **supercharger** to force the air-fuel mixture into the cylinder for even greater power.

Figure 2–7 Cutaway of an overhead valve engine showing the piston, valve, valve spring, rocker arm, and pushrod.

- *Engine VIN code.* Before service work begins, the vehicle must be properly identified to be sure that the proper replacement parts are ordered. A vehicle is first identified by make, model, and year. For example:

Make: Chevrolet

Model: Blazer

Year: 1998

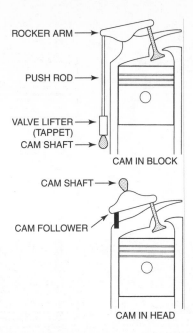

Figure 2–8 Camshaft locations.

Figure 2–9 A double overhead camshaft V-6 engine with the cam covers and timing belt removed.

The year of the vehicle is often difficult to determine exactly. A model may be introduced as the next year's model as soon as January of the previous year. Typically, a new model year starts in September or October of the year prior to the actual new year, but not always. This is why the **vehicle identification number (VIN)** is so important. See Figure 2–10. Since 1981, all vehicle manufacturers have used a 17-character VIN. Although every vehicle manufacturer assigns various letters or numbers within these 17 characters, there are some constants, including:

- The first number or letter designates the country of origin.

Figure 2–10 Typical vehicle identification number (VIN) as viewed through the windshield.

1 = United States	K = Korea
2 = Canada	L = Taiwan
3 = Mexico	S = England
4 = United States	V = France
6 = Australia	W = Germany
9 = Brazil	Y = Sweden
J = Japan	Z = Italy

- The model of the vehicle is commonly the fourth or fifth character.
- The eighth character is usually the engine code. (Some engines cannot be determined by the VIN number.)
- The tenth character represents the year on all vehicles. See the following chart.

■ VIN YEAR CHART

A = 1980	S = 1995
B = 1981	T = 1996
C = 1982	V = 1997
D = 1983	W = 1998
E = 1984	X = 1999
F = 1985	Y = 2000
G = 1986	1 = 2001
H = 1987	2 = 2002
J = 1988	3 = 2003
K = 1989	4 = 2004
L = 1990	5 = 2005
M = 1991	6 = 2006
N = 1992	7 = 2007
P = 1993	8 = 2008
R = 1994	9 = 2009

■ ENGINE DESIGN CLASSIFICATION

Internal combustion engines are described by reference number according to their different design features. Besides the four-stroke cycle gasoline engine, diesel-fueled engines and rotary combustion chamber engines also are used to power vehicles.

Diesel Engine

The diesel engine has been commonly used in heavy vehicles and on stationary machinery that generally operates at constant speeds. The diesel engine has high thermal efficiency, so it provides good fuel economy. The diesel engine produces exhaust emissions that are low in hydrocarbons and carbon monoxide. These characteristics make it a good alternative to the reciprocating gasoline engine used in automobiles. Mechanically, the two engines are very similar. The diesel engine is somewhat heavier and more expensive. The greatest difference is in their fuel and ignition systems. A diesel engine draws only air into the combustion. This air is compressed by the piston on the compression stroke. The compression is high enough to heat the air to about 1000°F (540°C). When the piston is near top dead center, fuel under pressure is squirted from a fuel-injection nozzle. The fuel is ignited by the hot air. The resultant burning fuel causes the piston to move downward on the power stroke. The crankshaft rotates and the piston is forced upward, thus forcing the exhaust out of the exhaust valve. Two factors limit the application of the diesel engine in passenger vehicles: the high price, and the fact that it is difficult for the diesel engine to meet the very low nitrogen oxide emission standards. See Figures 2–11 and 2–12.

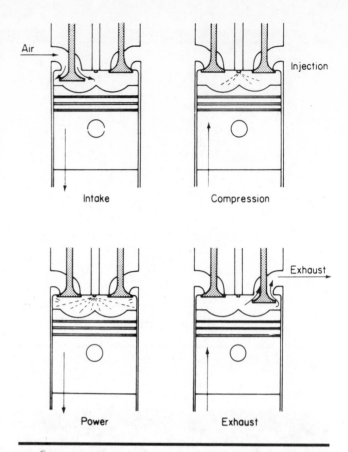

Figure 2–11 Four-stroke cycle diesel engine.

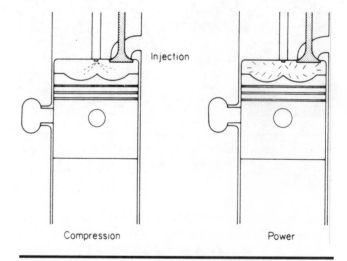

Figure 2–12 Two-stroke cycle diesel engine.

Rotating Combustion Chamber

A second successful alternative engine is the **rotary engine,** also called the **Wankel engine** after its inventor. The Mazda RX-7 represents the only long-term use of the rotary engine. It has some advantages over a piston engine. The rotating combustion chamber engine

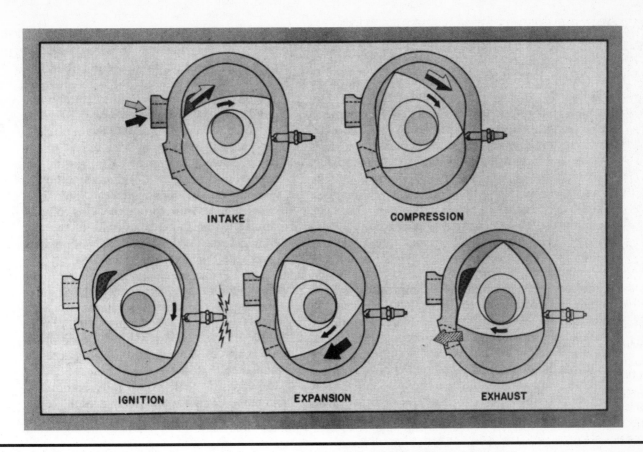

INTAKE

COMPRESSION

IGNITION

EXPANSION

EXHAUST

Figure 2–13 Rotating (rotary) combustion chamber engine. (*Courtesy of Curtiss-Wright Corporation*)

runs smoothly and produces high power for its size and weight. It operates on low-octane gasoline as a result of the large cooling surface around the combustion chamber.

The basic rotating combustion chamber engine has a triangular-shape rotor turning in a housing. The housing is in the shape of a geometric figure called a **two-lobed epitrochoid.** A seal on each corner, or apex, of the rotor is in constant contact with the housing, so the rotor must turn with an eccentric motion. This means that the center of the rotor moves around the center of the engine. The eccentric motion can be seen in Figure 2–13. This eccentric movement makes expanding and contracting chambers between the flat portions of the rotor and the housing. As a chamber expands, or increases in volume, an air-fuel intake charge is drawn in through an intake port. Figure 2–14 shows the port in the housing. When the chamber reaches its largest volume, the port is closed as the apex seal moves past it. Continued rotor rotation reduces the volume, compressing the charge. Spark plugs ignite the charge. The high-pressure gases developed during combustion force the volume to expand. This pulse of power provides the engine-rotating force. When the chamber again reaches its largest volume, one of the apex seals moves past an exhaust port, allowing the spent high-pressure gases to escape from the engine. Continued rotation reduces the combustion chamber volume to force the remaining exhaust gases

Figure 2–14 Disassembled Mazda rotary engine.

Figure 2–15 With the rotor removed, the housing shape (called epitrochoid) can be seen. The smoothness of the housing is a tribute to the manufacturing process.

from the engine. This completes a cycle similar to the four-stroke cycle of the reciprocating engine. Continued rotation of the rotor starts the next cycle with the next intake charge.

While the one chamber is going through its cycle, the other two chambers formed between the rotor and housing also go through similar cycles. This produces three power pulses each time the rotor makes one revolution.

Power produced by the rotor forces an eccentric shaft to turn. The action is similar to that of the connecting rod and crankshaft. The eccentric shaft makes three revolutions for each revolution of the rotor. This places the eccentric in the correct position to be pushed or rotated by each power pulse. An internal gear within the rotor meshes with an external tooth gear on one of the side housings. The purpose of the gear is to keep the rotor correctly indexed to the eccentric and housing. The gears do not carry any of the torque load.

Intake and exhaust ports are located in the rotor housing on some engines and in the side housings on others. A depression in the rotor forms the combustion chamber. Because the combustion chamber is relatively long, some engines use two spark plugs to ignite the charge for rapid, complete combustion. Two complete ignition systems are required when two spark plugs are used. See Figures 2–15 and 2–16.

■ ENGINE ROTATION DIRECTION

The SAE standard for automotive engine rotation is counterclockwise (CCW) as viewed from the flywheel end (clockwise as viewed from the front of the engine). The flywheel end of the engine is the end to which the power is taken to drive the vehicle, or the **principal end** of the engine. The **nonprincipal end** of the engine

Figure 2–16 Rotor with apex seal removed.

is opposite the principal end and is generally referred to as the front of the engine, where the accessory belts are used. See Figure 2–17.

Therefore, in most rear-wheel-drive vehicles, the engine is mounted longitudinally with the principal end at the rear of the engine. Most transversely mounted engines also adhere to the same standard for direction of rotation. Honda and some marine applications may differ from this standard.

■ BORE

The diameter of a cylinder is called the **bore.** The larger the bore, the greater the area on which the gases have to work. Pressure is measured in units, such as pounds per square inch (psi). The greater the area (in square inches), the higher the force exerted by the pistons to rotate the crankshaft. See Figure 2–18.

■ STROKE

The distance the piston travels down in the cylinder is called the **stroke.** The longer this distance, the greater the amount of air-fuel mixture that can be drawn into the cylinder. The more air-fuel mixture inside the cylinder, the more force will result when the mixture is ignited.

■ OVER SQUARE AND UNDER SQUARE

An engine with a bore larger in dimension than its stroke is called **over square.** An engine with a bore smaller in dimension than its stroke is called **under square.** An engine with equal-size bore and stroke is called **square.**

Engine operating characteristics differ as a result of many variables, including bore-stroke relationship; however, some general operating features include the following:

FLEX-PLATE
(DRIVE-PLATE)

PRINCIPLE
END

Figure 2–17 Inline four-cylinder engine showing principal and nonprincipal ends. Normal direction of rotation is clockwise (CW) as viewed from the front or accessory belt end (nonprincipal end).

Over Square Engine (bore larger than stroke)

- Usually is fast revving; reaches higher engine speeds (in revolutions per minute [RPM])
- Is responsive at higher engine speeds
- Tends to lack low speed torque (power)
- Is often used with a lower final drive ratio (higher number) to take advantage of faster engine speed characteristic

Under Square Engine (bore smaller than stroke)

- Usually slow to rev because of longer stroke
- Has good low-engine speed torque
- Is basically a low RPM engine
- Generally gives good fuel economy because of lower engine speed and usually is accompanied by a high final drive ratio (lower number)

Square (bore same as stroke)

- Is a good compromise between low RPM torque and high RPM power
- Provides good low-speed torque with good high-speed power

Bore = 4.000 in.

Stroke = 3.000 in.

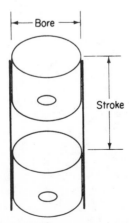

Figure 2–18 Dimensions used to determine the displacement of one cylinder.

- Allows use of higher final drive ratios (lower numbers) for fuel economy, yet still maintains drivability in slow city driving

■ ENGINE DISPLACEMENT

Engine size is described as displacement. **Displacement** is the cubic inch (cu in.) or cubic centimeter (cc) volume displaced or swept by all of the pistons.

A liter (L) is equal to 1000 cubic centimeters; therefore, most engines today are identified by their displacement in liters.

$$1 \text{ L} = 1000 \text{ cc}$$
$$1 \text{ L} = 61 \text{ cu in.}$$
$$1 \text{ cu in.} = 16.4 \text{ cc}$$

See Chapter 11 for explanations and formulas for calculating engine displacement.

■ ENGINE SIZE VERSUS HORSEPOWER

The larger the engine, the more easily the engine is capable of producing power. The following quotes are often heard about engine size:

There is no substitute for cubic inches.

There is no replacement for displacement.

Although a large engine generally uses more fuel, making an engine larger is often the easiest way to increase power.

■ COMPRESSION RATIO

The compression ratio of an engine is an important consideration when rebuilding or repairing an engine.

Compression ratio (CR) is the ratio of the volume in the cylinder above the piston when the piston is at the bottom of the stroke to the volume in the cylinder above the piston when the piston is at the top of the stroke. See Figure 2–19.

If compression is lower	If compression is higher
Lower power	Higher power possible
Poorer fuel economy	Better fuel economy
Easier engine cranking	Harder-to-crank engine, especially when hot
More advanced ignition timing possible without spark knock (detonation)	Less ignition timing required to prevent spark knock (detonation)

TECH TIP

All 3.8-Liter Engines Are Not the Same!

Most engine sizes are currently identified by displacement in liters. However, not all 3.8-liter engines are the same. For example, see the following table.

Engine	Displacement
Chevrolet-built 3.8-L V-6	229 cu in.
Buick-built 3.8-L V-6 (also called 3800-cc)	231 cu in.
Ford-built 3.8-L V-6	232 cu in.

The exact conversion from liters (or cubic centimeters) to cubic inches amounts to 231.9 cubic inches. However, due to rounding of exact cubic inch displacement and rounding of the exact cubic centimeter volume, several entirely different engines can be marketed with the exact same liter designation. To reduce confusion and reduce the possibility of ordering incorrect parts, the vehicle identification number (VIN) should be noted for the vehicle being serviced. The VIN should be visible through the windshield on all vehicles. Since 1980, the *engine* identification number or letter is usually the eighth digit or letter from the left.

A 5.0-liter V-8 also can be confusing to many owners and technicians. For example, some rear-wheel-drive General Motors vehicles may use a 5.0-liter V-8 (305-cubic-inch) engine made by Chevrolet. The same model of vehicle may also use a 5.0-liter V-8 (307-cubic-inch) engine made by Oldsmobile. The two GM 5.0-liter V-8s are not the same engine and no engine parts will interchange! Ford also sells a 5.0-liter V-8 of 302 cubic inches. Ford 5.0-liter V-8s also differ from year to year in such major characteristics as firing order.

Smaller, four-cylinder engines can also cause confusion because many vehicle manufacturers use both engines from overseas and domestically produced engines. Always refer to service manual information to be assured of correct engine identification.

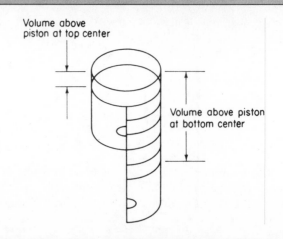

Figure 2–19 Dimensions used to determine the compression ratio of one cylinder.

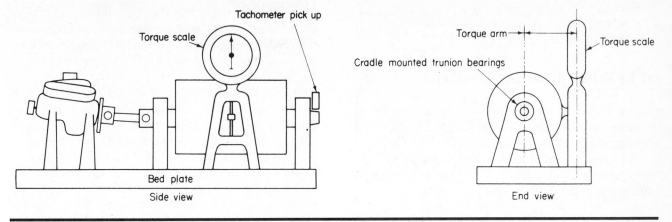

Figure 2–20 Line drawing of an engine dynamometer.

Frequently Asked Question ???

What Engine Part(s) Determines the Stroke of an Engine?

The stroke of an engine is the distance the piston travels from top dead center (TDC) to bottom dead center (BDC). This distance is determined by the throw of the crankshaft. The throw is the distance from the centerline of the crankshaft to the centerline of the crankshaft rod journal. The throw is one-half of the stroke.

If the crankshaft is replaced with one that has a greater stroke, then the pistons will be pushed up over the height of the top of the block (deck). The solution to this problem is to install replacement pistons with the piston pin relocated higher on the piston. Another alternative is to replace the connecting rod with a shorter one to prevent the piston from traveling too far up in the cylinder.

Changing the connecting rod length does *not* change the stroke of an engine. Changing the connecting rod only changes the position of the piston in the cylinder.

$$CR = \frac{\text{Volume in cylinder with piston at bottom center}}{\text{Volume in cylinder with piston at top center}}$$

For example: What is the compression ratio of an engine with 50.3-cubic-inch displacement in one cylinder having a combustion chamber volume of 6.7 cubic inches?

$$CR = \frac{50.3 + 6.7 \text{ cu in.}}{6.7 \text{ cu in.}} = \frac{57.0}{6.7}$$
$$= 8.5{:}1 \text{ (read as "8.5 to 1")}$$

■ HORSEPOWER

The power an engine produces is called **horsepower (hp).** One horsepower is the power required to move 550 pounds one foot in one second or 33,000 pounds one foot in one minute (550 lb × 60 sec = 33,000 lb per minute). This is expressed as 500 foot-pounds (ft-lb) per second or 33,000 foot-pounds per minute.

The actual horsepower produced by an engine is measured with a dynamometer. See Figure 2–20. A **dynamometer** (often abbreviated as **dyno** or **dyn**) places a load on the engine and measures the amount of twisting force the engine crankshaft places against the load. The load holds the engine speed, so it is called a **brake.** The horsepower derived from a dynamometer is called **brake horsepower (bhp).** The dynamometer actually measures the **torque** output of the engine. Torque is a rotating force that may or may not cause movement. The horsepower is calculated from the torque readings at various engine speeds (in revolutions per minute or RPM). **Horsepower is torque times RPM divided by 5252.**

$$\text{Horsepower} = \frac{\text{Torque} \times \text{RPM}}{5252}$$

See Figure 2–21.

Torque is what the driver "feels" as the vehicle is being accelerated. A small engine operating at a high RPM may have the same horsepower as a large engine operating at a low RPM.

NOTE: As can be seen by the formula for horsepower, the higher the engine speed for a given amount of torque, the greater the horsepower. Many engines are high revving. To help prevent catastrophic damage due to excessive engine speed, most manufacturers limit the maximum RPM by programming fuel injectors to shut off if the engine speed increases past a certain level. Sometimes this cutoff speed can be as low as 3000 RPM if the transmission is in neutral or park. Complaints of high-speed "miss" or "cutting out" may be normal if the engine is approaching the "rev limiter."

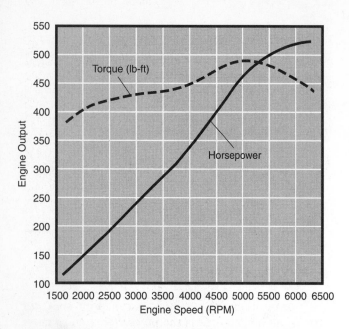

Figure 2–21 Typical torque and horsepower curves. Note that the torque and horsepower are the same (curves cross) at exactly 5252 RPM.

■ BRAKE-SPECIFIC FUEL CONSUMPTION

Brake-specific fuel consumption (BSFC) is another factor calculated by a dynamometer from engine test readings.

$$BSFC = \frac{\text{Pounds of fuel per hour}}{\text{Brake horsepower}} = \frac{lb}{bhp\text{-}hr}$$

The brake-specific fuel consumption is a measure of the amount of fuel an engine needs to create horsepower. The lower the number for BSFC, the more efficient the engine.

> **NOTE:** Most engines require about 0.5 pound of fuel per hour to produce 1 horsepower.

■ WHERE THE ENERGY GOES

In a spark-ignited gasoline engine, only 25% of the energy in the fuel is changed to useful work as engine power at the crankshaft. In a diesel engine, this percentage may be as high as 35%. The rest of the fuel energy is wasted as heat. About half of the wasted heat energy goes out of the engine with the exhaust gas. The other half leaves the engine through the cooling system. In this way, the friction heat is removed from the engine.

Unfortunately, all the power produced at the crankshaft, called **gross horsepower,** is not usable to drive the vehicle. A number of power-absorbing accessories are mounted on the engine. These include a water pump, cooling fan, electrical charging system, fuel pump, air-injection pump, air-conditioner compressor, power steering, and air cleaner. Some power is also required to pull the intake charge into the combustion chamber and to push the exhaust out through a catalytic converter and muffler. When all the power-absorbing accessories are being fully used, they will absorb about 25% of the power being produced by the crankshaft. The remaining 75% of the power at the crankshaft is usable power, and it is called **net horsepower.** This remaining useful power is further reduced as it goes through the driveline of the vehicle.

■ WATTS AND HORSEPOWER

James Watt (1736–1819) first determined the power of a typical horse while measuring the amount of coal being lifted out of a mine. For over 200 years, the power of a horse has been defined as 33,000 foot-pounds per minute. In Europe, power is commonly expressed in watts (W). It takes 746 watts to equal 1 horsepower. One kilowatt (kW=1000 watts) times 1.341 equals 1 horsepower.

■ TAXABLE HORSEPOWER

Taxable horsepower was developed as a means of taxation of motor vehicles based on engine size and number of cylinders.

Taxable hp = Bore × Bore × Number of cylinders × 0.4

For example, take a six-cylinder engine with a 4-in. bore:

Taxable hp = 4 × 4 × 6 × 0.4 = 38.4

Notice that the stroke dimension is not used. When taxable horsepower was first used, the bore and the number of cylinders generally determined the price range or value of the vehicle.

Taxable horsepower is still used by some state and local governments for tax or licensing purposes. The National Automotive Dealers Association (NADA) vehicle guides routinely list taxable horsepower in their listings of specifications.

■ SAE GROSS VERSUS NET HORSEPOWER

SAE standards for measuring horsepower include gross and net horsepower ratings. Gross horsepower is the maximum power an engine develops without some accessories in operation. SAE net horsepower is the power an engine develops as installed in the vehicle. A summary of the differences is given in the following table.

SAE Gross Horsepower	SAE Net Horsepower
No air cleaner or filter	Stock air cleaner or filter
No cooling fan	Stock cooling fan
No alternator	Stock alternator
No mufflers	Stock exhaust system
No emission controls	Full emission and noise control

Ratings are about 20% lower for the net rating method. Before 1971, most manufacturers used gross horsepower rating (the higher method) for advertising purposes. After 1971, the manufacturers started advertising only SAE net-rated horsepower.

■ METRIC VERSUS BRAKE HORSEPOWER

Engine power is usually expressed in watts or kilowatts (1000 watts equals 1 kilowatt). Metric horsepower differs slightly from brake horsepower because of slight differences in units and test procedures. The difference is minor, as the measurements are within 99% of each other. Metric horsepower may be labeled **pferoestarke (PS)** or **Cheval-Vapeur (CV)**. To convert metric horsepower (PS or CV) to brake horsepower, multiply by 0.986. For example:

$$150 \text{ metric hp} \times 0.986 = 147.9 \text{ bhp}$$

To convert from kilowatts to SAE net horsepower, multiply by 1.341. For example:

$$150 \text{ kW} \times 1.341 = 201.15 \text{ SAE net hp}$$

■ DEUTSCHE INDUSTRIE NORM HORSEPOWER VERSUS SAE HORSEPOWER

Deutsche Industrie Norm (DIN), or German Industrial Norm, is similar to SAE. The DIN testing standards for net horsepower vary slightly from the SAE testing parameters. All DIN horsepower ratings are net. To convert from DIN horsepower to SAE net horsepower, multiply by 0.963 to compensate for the slight differences in test conditions. For example:

$$150 \text{ DIN hp} \times 0.963 = 144.45 \text{ SAE net hp}$$

TECH TIP

Quick and Easy Efficiency Check

A good, efficient engine is able to produce much power from little displacement. A common rule of thumb is that an engine is efficient if it can produce *1 horsepower per cubic inch* of displacement. Many engines today are capable of this feat, such as the following:

Ford 4.6L V-8 (281 cu in.)—305 hp

Chevrolet 3.4L V-6 (207 cu in.)—210 hp

Chrysler 3.5L V-6 (214 cu in.)—214 hp

Acura 3.2L V-6 (195 cu in.)—230 hp

An engine is very powerful for its size if it can produce *100 hp per liter.* This efficiency goal is harder to accomplish. Factory stock engines that can achieve this feat are often supercharged or turbocharged. For example:

Toyota 2.0L 4-cylinder (turbocharged)—200 hp

Honda S2000 2.0L 4-cylinder—240 hp (@ 8300 RPM!)

■ JAPAN INDUSTRY STANDARD VERSUS SAE HORSEPOWER

Japan Industry Standard (JIS) is the standardization organization in Japan. After 1985, all JIS horsepower ratings are the same as SAE ratings, because JIS converted to SAE test conditions. For JIS net horsepower readings before 1985, multiply the reading by 0.984 to get SAE net horsepower. In other words, after April 1, 1985, JIS net hp = SAE net hp, whereas before April 1, 1985, JIS net hp × 0.984 = SAE net hp.

■ HORSEPOWER AND ALTITUDE

Because the density of the air is lower at high altitude, the power that a normal engine can develop is greatly reduced at high altitude. According to SAE conversion factors, a nonsupercharged or nonturbocharged engine loses about 3% of its power for every 1000 feet [300 meter (m)] of altitude. Therefore, an engine that develops 150 brake horsepower at sea level will only produce about 85 brake horsepower at the top of Pike's Peak in Colorado at 14,110 feet (4300 meters). Supercharged and turbocharged engines are not as greatly affected by altitude as normally aspirated engines, which breathe air at normal atmospheric pressure.

■ SUMMARY

1. The four strokes of the four-stroke cycle are intake, compression, power, and exhaust.

2. Engines are classified by number and arrangement of cylinders and by number and location of valves and camshafts, as well as by type of fuel used, cooling method, and induction pressure.

3. Most engines rotate clockwise as viewed from the front (accessory) end of the engine. The SAE standard is counterclockwise as viewed from the principal (flywheel) end of the engine.

4. Engine size is called displacement and represents the volume displaced or swept by all of the pistons.

5. Engine power is expressed in horsepower, which is a calculated value based on the amount of torque or twisting force the engine produces.

■ REVIEW QUESTIONS

1. Name the strokes of a four-stroke cycle.
2. Describe the operation of the rotary engine.
3. What does a dynamometer actually measure?
4. Define volumetric efficiency.
5. What is the difference between SAE net and SAE gross horsepower?
6. If an engine at sea level produces 100 horsepower, how many horsepower would it develop at 6000 feet of altitude?

■ ASE CERTIFICATION-TYPE QUESTIONS

1. All overhead valve engines _____ .
   a. Use an overhead camshaft
   b. Have the overhead valves in the head
   c. Operate by the two-stroke cycle
   d. Use the camshaft to close the valves

2. An SOHC V-8 engine has how many camshafts?
   a. One
   b. Two
   c. Three
   d. Four

3. Brake horsepower is calculated by which of the following?
   a. Torque × RPM
   b. 2 pi × stroke
   c. Torque × RPM ÷ 5252
   d. Stroke × bore × 3300

4. Torque is expressed in units of _____ .
   a. Pound-feet
   b. Foot-pounds
   c. Foot-pounds per minute
   d. Pound-feet per second

5. Horsepower is expressed in units of _____ .
   a. Pound-feet
   b. Foot-pounds
   c. Foot-pounds per minute
   d. Pound-feet per second

6. A normally aspirated automobile engine loses about _____ power per 1000 feet of altitude.
   a. 1%
   b. 3%
   c. 5%
   d. 6%

7. One cylinder of an automotive four-stroke cycle engine completes a cycle every _____ .
   a. 90 degrees
   b. 180 degrees
   c. 360 degrees
   d. 720 degrees

8. How many rotations of the crankshaft are required to complete each stroke of a four-stroke cycle engine?
   a. One-fourth
   b. One-half
   c. One
   d. Two

9. A rotating force is called _____ .
   a. Horsepower
   b. Torque
   c. Combustion pressure
   d. Eccentric movement

10. When gasoline and air in any engine burn, about how much of the total energy in the fuel (gasoline) is available at the crankshaft of the engine?
    a. About 15% to 18%
    b. About 25%
    c. About 50%
    d. About 75% to 80%

Lubrication System Operation and Diagnosis

Objectives: After studying Chapter 3, the reader should be able to:

1. Explain engine oil ratings.
2. Describe how an oil pump and engine lubrication work.
3. Discuss how and when to change the oil and filter.
4. Explain how to inspect an oil pump for wear.

Engine oil is the lifeblood of any engine. The purposes of engine oil include the following:

1. Lubricating all moving parts to prevent wear
2. Helping to cool the engine
3. Helping to seal piston rings
4. Cleaning and holding dirt in suspension in the oil until it can be drained from the engine
5. Neutralizing acids that are formed as the result of the combustion process
6. Reducing friction
7. Preventing rust and corrosion

■ LUBRICATION PRINCIPLES

Lubrication between two moving surfaces results from an oil film that separates the surfaces and supports the load. If oil were put on a flat surface and a heavy block were pushed across the surface, the block would slide more easily than if it were pushed across a dry surface.

The reason for this is that a wedge-shape oil film is built up between the moving block and the surface, as illustrated in Figure 3–1.

The force required to push the block across a surface depends on the weight of the block, how fast it moves, and the **viscosity** of the oil. Viscosity is the oil's thickness or resistance to flow.

The principle just described is that of **hydrodynamic lubrication.** The prefix *hydro-* refers to liquids, as in hydraulics, and *dynamic* refers to moving materials. Hydrodynamic lubrication occurs when a wedge-shape film of lubricating oil develops between two surfaces that have relative motion between them. See Figure 3–2. When this film becomes so thin that the surface's high spots touch, it is called **boundary lubrication.**

The engine oil pressure system feeds a continuous supply of oil into the lightly loaded part of the bearing oil clearance. Hydrodynamic lubrication takes over as the shaft rotates in the bearing to produce a wedge-shape hydrodynamic oil film that is curved around the bearing. This film supports the bearing and reduces the

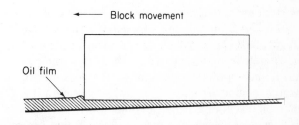

Figure 3–1 Wedge-shape oil film developed below a moving block.

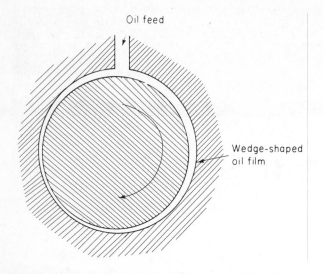

Figure 3–2 Wedge-shape oil film curved around a bearing journal.

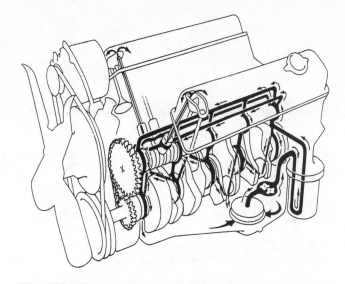

Figure 3–3 Typical V-8 engine lubrication system. Oil is stored in the oil pan (sump) and drawn into the oil pump and through the oil filter and on through the oil passages.

turning effort to a minimum when oil of the correct viscosity is used.

Most bearing wear occurs during the initial start-up. Wear continues until a hydrodynamic film is established.

■ ENGINE LUBRICATION SYSTEMS

The primary function of the engine lubrication system is to maintain a positive and continuous oil supply to the bearings. Engine oil pressure must be high enough to get the oil to the bearings with enough force to cause the oil flow that is required for proper cooling. Normal engine oil pressure range is from 10 to 60 psi (200 to 400 kPa) (10 psi per 1000 engine RPM). Conversely, hydrodynamic film pressures developed in the high-pressure areas of the engine bearings may be over 1000 psi (6900 kPa). The relatively low engine oil pressures obviously could not support these high bearing loads without hydrodynamic lubrication. See Figure 3–3.

■ PROPERTIES OF ENGINE OIL

The most important engine oil property is its thickness or viscosity. As mentioned, **viscosity** is the resistance to flow. As oil cools, it thickens. As oil heats, it gets thinner. Therefore, its viscosity changes with temperature. The oil must not be too thick at low temperatures to allow the engine to start. The lowest temperature at which oil will pour is called its **pour point.** An index of the change in viscosity between the cold and hot extremes is called the **viscosity index (VI).** All oils with a high viscosity index thin less with heat than do oils with a low viscosity index.

■ SAE RATING

Engine oils are sold with an **SAE (Society of Automotive Engineers)** grade number, which indicates the viscosity range into which the oil fits. Oils tested at 212°F (100°C) have a number with no letter following. For example, SAE 30 indicates that the oil has only been checked at 212°F (100°C). This oil's viscosity falls within the SAE 30 grade number range when the oil is hot. Oils tested at 0°F (–18°C) are rated with a number and the letter *W*, which means *winter* and indicates that the viscosity was tested at 0°F, such as SAE 20W. An SAE 5W-30 multigrade oil is one that meets the SAE 5W viscosity specification when cooled to 0°F (–18°C) and meets the SAE 30 viscosity specification when tested at 212°F (100°C).

Most vehicle manufacturers recommend the following multiviscosity engine oils:

- SAE 5W-30
- SAE 10W-30

An oil with a high viscosity has a higher resistance to flow and is thicker than a lower-viscosity oil. A thick oil is not necessarily a good oil and a thin oil is not necessarily a bad oil. Generally, the following items can be considered in the selection of an engine oil within the recommended viscosity range.

- Thinner oil
  1. Improved cold-engine starting
  2. Improved fuel economy
- Thicker oil
  1. Improved protection at higher temperatures
  2. Reduced fuel economy

Figure 3–4 API doughnut for SAE 10W-30, SJ engine oil. When compared to a reference oil, the "energy conserving" designation indicates a 1.1% better fuel economy for SAE 5W-30 oils and 0.5% better fuel economy for SAE 10W-30 oils.

■ API RATING

The **American Petroleum Institute (API),** working with the engine manufacturers and oil companies, has established an engine oil performance classification. Oils are tested and rated in production automotive engines. The oil container is printed with the API classification of the oil. The API performance or service classification and the SAE grade marking are the only information available to help determine which oil is satisfactory for use in an engine. See Figure 3–4 for a typical API oil container "doughnut."

Gasoline Engine Rating

In gasoline engine ratings, the letter *S* means *service*, but it can be remembered as being for use in *s*park ignition engines. The rating system is open ended so that newer, improved ratings can be readily added as necessary (the letter *I* is skipped to avoid confusion with the number one).

SA Straight mineral oil (no additives), not suitable for use in any engine

SB Nondetergent oil with additives to control wear and oil oxidation

SC Obsolete (1964)

SD Obsolete (1968)

SE Obsolete (1972)

SF Obsolete (1980)

SG Obsolete (1988)

SH Highest rating from 1993–1997

SJ Highest rating starting in 1997

NOTE: Older-model vehicles can use the newer, higher-rated engine oil classifications where older, now obsolete ratings were specified. Newly overhauled antique cars or engines also can use the newer, improved oils, as the appropriate SAE viscosity grade is used for the anticipated temperature range. The new oils have all the protection of the older oils, plus additional protection.

Diesel Engine Rating

Diesel classifications begin with the letter *C* which stands for *commercial*, but which can also be remembered as being for use in *c*ompression ignition or diesel engines.

CA   Obsolete

CB   Obsolete

CC   Obsolete

CD   Minimum rating for use in a diesel engine service

CE   Designed for certain turbocharged or supercharged heavy-duty diesel engine service

CF   For off-road indirect injected diesel engine service

CF-2 Two-stroke diesel engine service

CF-4 High-speed four-stroke cycle diesel engine service

CG-4 Severe-duty high-speed four-stroke diesel engine service

Why Is SAE 10W-30 Recommended Instead of SAE 10W-40?

Engine oils are manufactured in various viscosity grades. Vehicle manufacturers usually recommend that SAE 5W-30 and/or SAE 10W-30 be used. General Motors Corporation specifies that SAE 10W-40 not be used in any engine. These different viscosity grades are formulated by using a viscosity index improver, which is a polymer designed to induce thickening of a thin base oil at higher temperatures. For example, a 10W-30 oil starts as an SAE 10W oil, and viscosity index improver polymers are added to bring the high-temperature viscosity up to SAE 30 standards. These polymers react with heat to restrict the rate of flow of the oil at higher temperatures. The greater the amount of VI improver, the broader the viscosity range. For example, typical multiviscosity oils and the percentages of viscosity index improver that they use are as follows:

SAE 5W-30	7%–8% VI
SAE 10W-30	6%–8% VI
SAE 10W-40	12%–15% VI

Even though a 10W-40 oil will resist high-temperature thinning better than a 10W-30 oil, the increased amount of VI can contribute to some problems. As oil is used in an engine, it tends to thicken. This thickening occurs because of the following factors:

- *Oxidation*—When oil combines with oxygen, it becomes thicker.
- *Breakdown of polymer additives*—After 1000 to 2000 miles, the polymer additives can shear (break down) during use, which causes the oil to become thinner. The increased oxidation causes the oil to thicken and form sludge.

ILSAC OIL RATING

The **International Lubricant Standardization and Approval Committee (ILSAC)** developed an oil rating that consolidates the SAE viscosity rating and the API quality rating. If an engine oil meets the standards, a "star burst" symbol is displayed on the front of the oil container. If the star burst is present, the vehicle owner and technician know that the oil is suitable for use in almost any gasoline engine. See Figure 3–5. The original GF-1 (gasoline fueled) rating was updated to GF-2 in 1997 and GF-3 in 2000.

EUROPEAN OIL RATINGS

The **Association des Constructeurs European d'Automobiles (ACEA)** represents most of the

Figure 3–5 The International Lubricant Standardization and Approval Committee (ILSAC) star burst symbol. If this symbol is on the front of the container of oil, then it is acceptable for use in almost any gasoline engine.

Western European automobile and heavy-duty truck market. The organization uses different engines for testing than those used by API and SAE, and the requirements necessary to meet the ACEA standards are different yet generally correspond with most API ratings. ACEA standards tend to specify a minimum viscosity rating and certain volatility requirements not specified by API.

JAPANESE OIL RATINGS

The **Japanese Automobile Standards Organization (JASO)** also publishes oil standards. The JASO tests use small Japanese engines, and their ratings require more stringent valve train wear standards than other countries' oil ratings.

ENGINE OIL ADDITIVES

Additives are used in engine oils for three different reasons: (1) to replace some properties removed during refining, (2) to reinforce some of the oil's natural properties, and (3) to provide the oil with new properties it did not originally have. Oils from some petroleum oil fields require more and different additives than oils from other fields. Additives are usually classified according to the property they add to the oil.

- **Antioxidants** reduce the high-temperature contaminants. They prevent the formation of varnish on the parts, reduce bearing corrosion, and minimize particle formation.
- **Corrosion preventives** reduce acid formation that causes bearing corrosion.

- **Detergents** and **dispersants** prevent low-temperature sludge binders from forming and keep the sludge-forming particles finely divided. The finely divided particles will stay in suspension in the oil to be removed from the engine as the oil is removed at the next drain period.

  Extreme pressure and **antiwear additives** form a chemical film that prevents metal-to-metal seizure anytime boundary lubrication exists.

- **Viscosity index improvers** are used to reduce viscosity change as the oil temperature changes.
- **Pour point depressants** coat the wax crystals in the oil so that they will not stick together. The oil will then be able to flow at lower temperatures.

A number of other oil additives may be used to modify the oil to function better in the engine. These include rust preventives, metal deactivators, water repellents, emulsifiers, dyes, color stabilizers, odor control agents, and foam inhibitors.

Oil producers are careful to check the compatibility of the oil additives they use. A number of chemicals that will help each other can be used for each of the additive requirements. The balanced additives are called an **additive package.**

■ ENERGY-CONSERVING ENGINE OILS

For an engine oil to be classified as energy conserving, the oil must be able to meet the specifications of an ASTM engine test VI standard. The energy-conserving designation is only printed on containers of oil that have been tested and have shown to provide at least a 1.1% in fuel economy compared with a reference oil for SAE 5W-30 oils and at least 0.5% improvement for SAE 10W-30 oils.

■ OIL BRAND COMPATIBILITY

Many technicians and vehicle owners have their favorite brand of engine oil. The choice is often made as a result of marketing and advertising, as well as comments from friends, relatives, and technicians. If your brand of engine oil is not performing up to your expectations, then you may wish to change brands. For example, some owners experience lower oil pressure with a certain brand than they do with other brands with the same SAE viscosity rating.

Most experts agree that the oil changes are the most important regularly scheduled maintenance for an engine. It is also wise to check the oil level regularly and add oil when needed. According to SAE Standard J-357, all engine oils must be compatible with all other brands of engine oil. Therefore, any brand of engine oil can be used as long as it meets the viscosity and API standards recommended by the vehicle manufacturer. Even though many people prefer a particular brand, be assured that, according to API and SAE, any *major* brand-name engine oil can be used.

■ SYNTHETIC OIL

Synthetic engine oils have been available for years for military, commercial, and general public use. The term *synthetic* means that it is a manufactured product and not refined from a naturally occurring substance, as engine oil (petroleum base) is refined from crude oil. Synthetic oil is processed from several different base stocks using several different methods. The categories of chemical compounds generally usable for synthetic engine oil include the following:

- **Synthetic hydrocarbons** (usually polyalphaolefins such as Mobil 1)
- **Organic esters** (made by mixing an alcohol and an acid such as Castrol Syntec)
- **Polyglycols** such as polyalkaline glycol (PAG) oil used in R-134a air-conditioning systems

Various brand names of synthetic engine oil may be made from any one or a compatible combination of these types of chemical compounds. Some types of synthetic oil are not compatible with other types. Some synthetic oils are mixed with petroleum-base engine oils, but these must be labeled as a *blend.*

The major advantage of using synthetic engine oil is in its ability to remain fluid at very low temperatures. This characteristic of synthetic oil makes it popular in colder climates where cold-engine cranking is important.

The major disadvantage is cost. The cost of synthetic engine oils can be four or five times the cost of petroleum-base engine oils.

■ OIL TEMPERATURE

Excessive temperatures, either too low or too high, are harmful to any engine. If the oil is too cold, it could be too thick to flow through and lubricate all engine parts. If the oil is too hot, it could become too thin to provide the film strength necessary to prevent metal-to-metal contact and wear. Estimated oil temperature can be determined with the following formula:

$$\frac{\text{Estimated oil}}{\text{temperature}} = \frac{\text{Outside air}}{\text{temperature}} + 120°$$

For example,

$$\frac{90° \text{ outside air}}{\text{temperature}} + 120° = \frac{210° \text{ estimated}}{\text{oil temperature}}$$

During hard acceleration (or high-power demand activities such as trailer towing), the oil temperature will quickly increase. Oil temperature should not exceed 300°F (150°C).

■ OIL CHANGE INTERVALS

All vehicle and engine manufacturers recommend a maximum oil change interval. The recommended intervals are almost always expressed in terms of mileage or elapsed time (or hours of operation), whichever milestone is reached first.

Most vehicle manufacturers recommend an oil change interval of 7500 to 12,000 miles (12,000 to 19,000 kilometers) or every six months. If, however, *any one* of the conditions in the following list exists, the oil change interval recommendation drops to a more reasonable 2000 to 3000 miles (3000 to 5000 kilometers) or every three months. The important thing to remember is that these are recommended *maximum* intervals and they should be shortened substantially if any of the following operating conditions exists.

1. Operating in dusty areas
2. Towing a trailer
3. Short-trip driving, especially during cold weather (The definition of a short trip varies among manufacturers, but it is usually defined as 4 to 15 miles (6 to 24 kilometers) each time the engine is started.)
4. Operating in temperatures below freezing (32°F, 0°C)
5. Operating at idle speed for extended periods of time (such as normally occurs in police or taxi service)

TECH TIP

Follow the Seasons

Vehicle owners often forget when they last changed the oil. This is particularly true of the person who owns or is responsible for several vehicles. A helpful method for remembering when the oil should be changed is to change the oil at the start of each season of the year.

- Fall   (September 21)
- Winter   (December 21)
- Spring   (March 21)
- Summer   (June 21)

Remembering that the oil needs to be changed on these dates helps owners budget for the expense and the time needed.

Because most vehicles driven during cold weather are driven on short trips, most technicians and automotive experts recommend changing the oil every 2000 to 3000 miles or every two to three months, whichever occurs first.

■ OIL CHANGE PROCEDURE

The oil will drain more rapidly from a warm engine than from a cold one. In addition, the contaminants are more likely to be suspended in the oil immediately after running the engine. Position a drain pan under the drain plug; then remove the plug with care to avoid contact with hot oil.

CAUTION: Used engine oil has been determined to be harmful. Rubber gloves should be worn to protect the skin. If used engine oil gets on the skin, wash thoroughly with soap and water.

Allow the oil to drain freely so that the contaminants come out with the oil. It is not critically important to get every last drop of oil from the engine oil pan, because a quantity of used oil still remains in the engine oil passages and oil pump. While the engine oil is draining, the oil plug gasket should be examined. If it appears to be damaged, it should be replaced.

NOTE: Honda recommends that the oil drain plug gasket be replaced at every oil change on many of their vehicles. The aluminum sealing gasket does not seal once it has been tightened. Always follow the vehicle manufacturer's recommendations.

The Pick Trick

Removing an oil filter that is installed upside down can be a real mess. When this design filter is loosened, oil flows out from around the sealing gasket. To prevent this from happening, use a pick to poke a hole in the top of the filter, as shown in Figure 3–6. This small hole allows air to get into the filter, thereby allowing the oil to drain back into the engine rather than remain in the filter. After punching the hole in the filter, be sure to wait several minutes to allow time for the trapped oil to drain down into the engine before loosening the filter.

Figure 3–7 The round plastic cover is unscrewed to gain access to the paper oil filter element on this General Motors 3.5 DOHC, V-6.

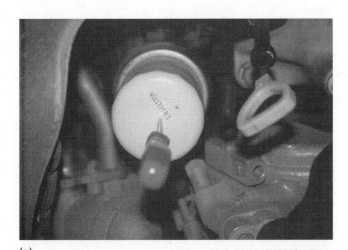

(a)

(b)

Figure 3–6 (a) A pick is pushed through the top of an oil filter that is positioned vertically. (b) When the pick is removed, a small hole allows air to get into the top of the filter which then allows the oil to drain out of the filter and back into the engine.

When the oil stops running and starts to drip, reinstall and tighten the drain plug. Replace the oil filter if that is to be done during this oil change. Refill the engine with the proper type, grade, and quantity of oil. Restart the engine and allow the engine to idle until it develops oil pressure; then check the engine for leaks, especially at the oil filter.

■ OIL FILTERS

The oil within the engine is pumped from the oil pan through the filter before it goes into the engine lubricating system passages. The oil filter can be either external or internal as shown in Figure 3–7. The filter is made from either closely packed cloth fibers or a porous paper. Large particles are trapped by the filter. Microscopic particles will flow through the filter pores. These particles are so small that they can flow through the bearing oil film and not touch the surfaces, so they do no damage.

Either the engine or the filter is provided with a **bypass** that will allow the oil to go around the filter element. The bypass allows the engine to be lubricated with dirty oil, rather than having no lubrication, if the filter becomes plugged. The oil also goes through the bypass when the oil is cold and thick. Most engine manufacturers recommend filter changes at every other oil change period. Correct oil filter selection includes using a filter with an internal bypass when the engine is not equipped with one. See Figure 3–8.

■ CHANGING OIL IN A TURBOCHARGED ENGINE

One of the most difficult jobs for engine oil is to lubricate the extremely hot bearings of a turbocharger. After a turbocharger has been in operation, it is always wise

Frequently Asked Question   ???

Why Change Oil if the Oil Filter Can Trap All the Dirt?

Many persons believe that oil filters will remove all dirt from the oil being circulated through the filtering material. Most oil filters will filter particles that are about 10 to 20 microns in size. A micron is one-millionth of a meter or 0.000039 inch. Most dirt and carbon particles that turn engine oil black are less than a micron in size. In other words, it takes about 3 million of these carbon particles to cover a pinhead. To help visualize the smallness of a micron, consider that a typical human hair is 60 microns in diameter. In fact, anything smaller than 40 microns is not visible to the human eye.

The dispersants added to engine oil prevent dirt from adhering together to form sludge. It is the same dispersant additive that prevents dirt from being filtered or removed by other means. If an oil filter could filter particles down to 1 micron, it would be so restrictive that the engine would not receive sufficient oil through the filter for lubrication. Oil recycling companies use special chemicals to break down the dispersants, which permit the dirt in the oil to combine into larger units that can be filtered or processed out of the oil.

Figure 3–8 Typical internal bypass valve used inside an oil filter.

TECH TIP

Every Friday?

A vehicle less than one year old came back to the dealer for some repair work. While writing the repair order, the service advisor noted that the vehicle had 88,000 miles on the odometer and was, therefore, out of warranty for the repair. Because the owner approved the repair anyway, the service advisor asked how he had accumulated so many miles in such a short time. The owner said that he was a traveling salesperson with a territory of "east of the Mississippi River."

Because the vehicle looked to be in new condition, the technician asked the salesperson how often he had the oil changed. The salesperson smiled and said proudly, "every Friday."

Many fleet vehicles put on over 2000 miles per week. How about changing their oil every week instead of by mileage?

to let the engine idle for about a minute to allow the turbocharger to slow down before shutting off the engine. This allows the turbo to keep receiving oil from the engine while it is still revolving fast.

However, just as with any engine, the greatest amount of wear occurs during start-up, especially following an oil change when the oil has been drained from the engine. Some technicians fill the new oil filter with new oil prior to installation to help the engine receive oil as rapidly as possible after starting.

A number of vehicle manufacturers also suggest that turbo-equipped engines be "primed" before starting. This means that the engine should be rotated without ignition so that it does not start, to allow the oil pump to pump oil to the bearings of the turbocharger before the engine starts.

On older vehicles, it is a simple process to disconnect the ignition coil wire from the distributor cap and ground it to prevent coil damage. After the ignition has been disconnected in this manner, simply crank the engine for 15 seconds. Some manufacturers recommend repeating the 15 seconds of cranking after a 30-second period to allow the starter motor to cool.

Many of today's vehicles are equipped with electronic fuel-injection and direct-fire distributorless ignition systems. These vehicles often require some time to disconnect either the ignition system or the fuel system to prevent the engine from starting.

There is one simple method that works on many fuel-injected vehicles. If the accelerator pedal is held down to the floor during cranking, then the engine computer senses the throttle position and reduces the amount of fuel injected into the engine. This mode of operation is often called the **clear-flood mode,** and during it, the computer limits the fuel delivery to such an extent that the engine should not start.

Therefore, to prime most late-model turbocharged engines, simply depress the accelerator to the floor and crank for 15 seconds. To start the engine, simply return the accelerator pedal to the idle position and crank the engine.

■ OIL PUMPS

All production automobile engines have a full-pressure oil system. The pressure is maintained by an oil pump. The oil is forced into the lubrication system under pressure. In most engines that use a distributor, the distributor drive gear meshes with a gear on the camshaft, as shown in Figure 3–9. The oil pump is driven from the

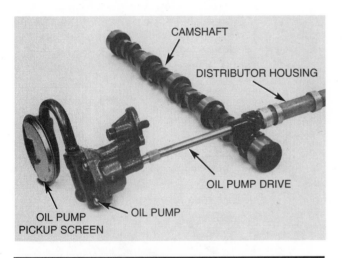

Figure 3–9 The oil pump is driven by an extension from the distributor drive gear on most engines.

end of the distributor shaft, often with a hexagon-shape shaft. Some engines have a short shaft gear that meshes with the cam gear to drive both the distributor and oil pump. With these drive methods, the pump turns at one-half engine speed. In other engines, the oil pump is driven by the front of the crankshaft, in a setup similar to that of an automatic transmission pump, so that it turns at the same speed as the crankshaft. Examples of a crankshaft-driven oil pump are shown in Figures 3–10 through 3–12.

Most automotive engines use one of two types of oil pumps: **gear** or **rotor** (Figure 3–13). All oil pumps are called **positive displacement pumps,** and each rotation of the pump delivers the same volume of oil; thus, everything that enters must exit. The gear-type oil pump consists of two spur gears in a close-fitting housing—one gear is driven while the other idles. As the gear teeth come out of mesh, they tend to leave a space, which is filled by oil drawn through the pump inlet. When the pump is pumping, oil is carried around the *outside* of each gear in the space between the gear teeth and the housing as shown in Figure 3–14. As the teeth mesh in the center, oil is forced from the teeth into an oil passage, thus producing oil pressure. The rotor-type oil pump consists essentially of a special lobe-shape gear meshing with the inside of a lobed rotor. The center lobed section is driven and the outer section idles. As the lobes separate, oil is drawn in just as it is drawn into gear-type pumps. As the pump rotates, it carries oil around and between the lobes. As the lobes mesh, they force the oil out from between them under pressure in the same manner as the gear-type pump. The pump is sized so that it will maintain a pressure of at least 10 psi (70 kPa) in the oil gallery when the engine is hot and idling. Pressure will increase by about 10 psi for each 1000 RPM as the engine speed increases, because the engine-driven pump also rotates faster.

Figure 3–10 Oil pump mounted in the front cover of the engine. The oil pump is driven by the crankshaft.

Figure 3–11 Geroter type of oil pump driven by the crankshaft.

Figure 3–12 A cutaway of an oil pump on a General Motors Northstar, V-8. The bolt for the harmonic balancer must be torqued properly because the clamp force of this bolt is what drives the oil pump.

Figure 3–13 Rotor-type oil pump (trachoid design) on the left and gear-type oil pump on the right.

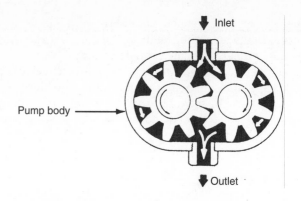

Figure 3–14 In a gear-type oil pump, the oil flows through the pump around the outside of each gear. This is an example of a positive displacement pump, wherein everything entering the pump must leave the pump.

Figure 3–15 Spring-loaded piston and ball-type oil pressure relief valve.

■ OIL PRESSURE REGULATION

In engines with a full-pressure lubricating system, maximum pressure is limited with a pressure relief valve. The relief valve (sometimes called the pressure regulating valve) is located at the outlet of the pump. The relief valve controls maximum pressure by bleeding off oil to the inlet side of the pump. See Figure 3–15. *The relief valve spring tension determines the maximum oil pressure.* If a pressure relief valve is not used, the engine oil pressure will continue to increase as the engine

speed increases. Maximum pressure is usually limited to the lowest pressure that will deliver enough lubricating oil to all engine parts that need to be lubricated. *Three to 6 gallons per minute are required to lubricate the engine.* The oil pump is made so that it is large enough to provide pressure at low engine speeds and small enough that it will not **cavitate** at high speed. Cavitation occurs when the pump tries to pull oil faster than it can flow from the pan to the pickup. When it cannot get enough oil, it will pull air. This puts air pockets or cavities in the oil stream. A pump is cavitating when it is pulling air or vapors.

NOTE: The reason for sheet-metal covers over the pickup screen is to prevent cavitation. Oil is trapped under the cover, which helps prevent the oil pump from drawing in air, especially during sudden stops or during rapid acceleration.

After the oil leaves the pump, it is delivered to the moving parts through drilled oil passages. See Figure 3–16. It needs no pressure after it reaches the parts that are to be lubricated. The oil film between the parts is developed and maintained by hydrodynamic lubrication. Excessive oil pressure requires more horsepower and provides no better lubrication than the minimum effective pressure.

■ FACTORS AFFECTING OIL PRESSURE

Oil pressure can only be produced when the oil pump has a capacity larger than all the "leaks" in the engine. The leaks are the clearances at end points of the lubrication system. The end points are at the edges of bearings, the rocker arms, the connecting rod spit holes, and

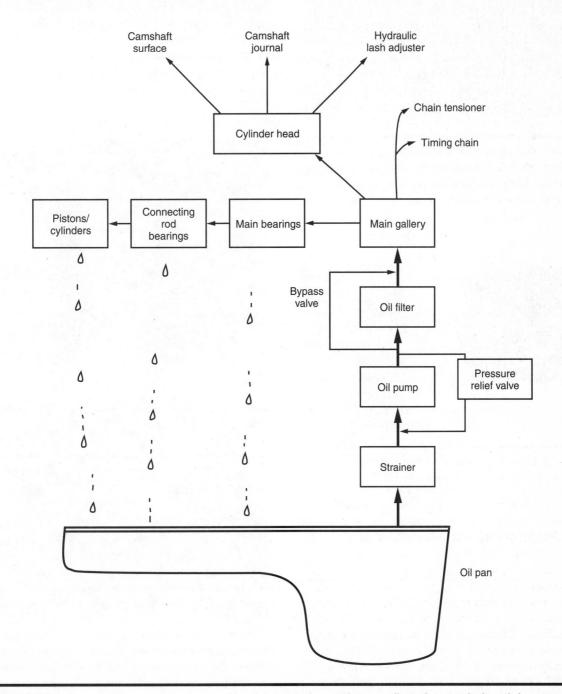

Figure 3–16 Oil flow through an engine starts at the oil pump pickup and eventually ends up with the oil dropping back into the oil pan.

so on. These clearances are designed into the engine and are necessary for its proper operation. As the engine parts wear and clearance becomes greater, more oil will leak out. The oil pump **capacity** must be great enough to supply extra oil for these leaks. The capacity of the oil pump results from its size, rotating speed, and physical condition. If the pump is rotating slowly as the engine is idling, oil pump capacity is low. *If the leaks are greater than the pump capacity, engine oil pressure is low.* As the engine speed increases, the pump capacity increases and the pump tries to force more oil out of the leaks. This causes the pressure to rise until it reaches the regulated maximum pressure.

The viscosity of the engine oil affects both the pump capacity and the oil leakage. Thin oil or oil of very low viscosity slips past the edges of the pump and flows freely from the leaks. Hot oil has a low viscosity, and therefore, a hot engine often has low oil pressure. Cold oil is more viscous (thicker) than hot oil. This results in higher pressures, even with the cold engine idling. High oil pressure occurs with a cold engine, because the oil relief valve must open further to release excess oil than is necessary with a hot engine. This larger opening increases the spring compression force, which in turn increases the oil pressure. Putting higher-viscosity oil in an engine will raise the engine oil pressure to the regulated setting of the relief valve at a lower engine speed.

■ OIL PUMP CHECKS

The cover is removed to check the condition of the oil pump. The gears and housing are examined for scoring. If the gears and housing are heavily scored, the entire pump should be replaced. If they are lightly scored, the clearances in the pump should be measured. These clearances include the space between the gears and housing, the space between the teeth of the two gears, and the space between the side of the gear and the pump cover. A feeler gauge is often used to make these measurements. Gauging plastic can be used to measure the space between the side of the gears and the cover. The oil pump should be replaced when excessive clearance or scoring is found. See Figures 3–17 and 3–18.

On most engines, the oil pump should be replaced as part of any engine work, especially if the cause for the repair is lack of lubrication.

> **NOTE:** The oil pump is the "garbage pit" of the entire engine. Any and all debris is often forced through the gears and housing of an oil pump.

See Figures 3–19 and 3–20 for examples of oil pump clearance checks. Always refer to the manufacturer's specifications when checking the oil pump for wear. Typical oil pump clearances include the following:

Figure 3–17 Badly worn oil pump, most likely caused by dirty or contaminated engine oil.

(a)

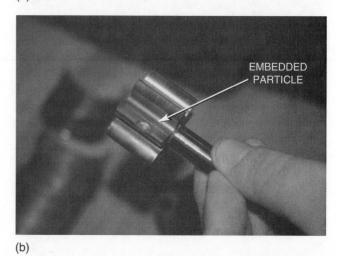

(b)

Figure 3–18 (a) A visual inspection indicated that this pump cover was worn. (b) An embedded particle of something was found on one of the pump gears making this pump worthless except for scrap metal.

Figure 3–19 Gear-type oil pump being checked for tooth clearance in the housing.

1. End plate clearance: 0.0015 inch (0.04 millimeter)
2. Side (rotor) clearance: 0.012 inch (0.30 millimeter)
3. Rotor tip clearance: 0.010 inch (0.25 millimeter)
4. Gear end play clearance: 0.004 inch (0.10 millimeter)

All parts should also be inspected closely for wear. Check the relief valve for scoring and check the condition of the spring. When installing the oil pump, coat the sealing surfaces with engine assembly lubricant. This lubricant helps draw oil from the oil pan on initial start-up.

■ OIL PASSAGES IN THE BLOCK

From the filter, oil goes through a drilled hole that intersects with a drilled main oil **gallery** or longitudinal header. This is a long hole drilled from the front of the block to the back. Inline engines use one oil gallery; V-type engines may use two or three galleries. One main gallery and two hydraulic valve lifter galleries used on a V-type engine can be seen in Figure 3–21. Passages drilled through the block bulkheads allow the oil to go from the main oil gallery to the main and cam bearings. In some engines, oil goes to the cam bearings first, and then to the main bearings.

It is important that the oil holes in the bearings match with the drilled passages in the bearing saddles so that the bearing can be properly lubricated. Over a long period of use, bearings will wear. This wear causes excess clearance. The excess clearance will allow too much oil to leak from the side of the bearing. When this happens, there will be little or no oil left for bearings located

Figure 3–20 Measuring the gear-to-cover clearance of an oil pump.

farther downstream in the lubricating system. This is a major cause of bearing failure. If a new bearing were installed in place of the oil-starved bearing, it, too, would fail unless the bearing having the excess clearance was also replaced.

■ VALVE TRAIN LUBRICATION

The oil gallery may intersect or have drilled passages to the valve lifter bores to lubricate the lifters. When hydraulic lifters are used, the oil pressure in the gallery keeps refilling them. On some engines, oil from the lifters goes up the center of a hollow pushrod to lubricate the pushrod ends, the rocker arm pivot, and the valve stem tip. In other engines, an oil passage is drilled from either the gallery or a cam bearing to the block deck, where it matches with a gasket hole and a hole drilled in the head to carry the oil to a rocker arm shaft. Some engines use an enlarged bolt hole to carry lubrication oil around the rocker shaft cap screw to the rocker arm shaft. This design is shown by a line drawing in Figure 3–22. Holes in the bottom of the rocker arm shaft allow lubrication of the rocker arm pivot. Mechanical loads on the valve train hold the rocker arm against the passage in the rocker arm shaft, as shown in Figure 3–23. This prevents excessive oil leakage from the rocker arm shaft. Often, holes are drilled in cast rocker arms to carry oil to the pushrod end and to the valve tip. Rocker arm assemblies need only a surface coating of oil, so the oil flow to the rocker assembly is minimized using restrictions or metered openings. The restriction or metering disk is in the lifter when the rocker assembly is lubricated through the pushrod. Cam journal holes that line up with oil passages are often used to meter oil to the rocker shafts.

Oil that seeps from the rocker assemblies is returned to the oil pan through drain holes. These oil

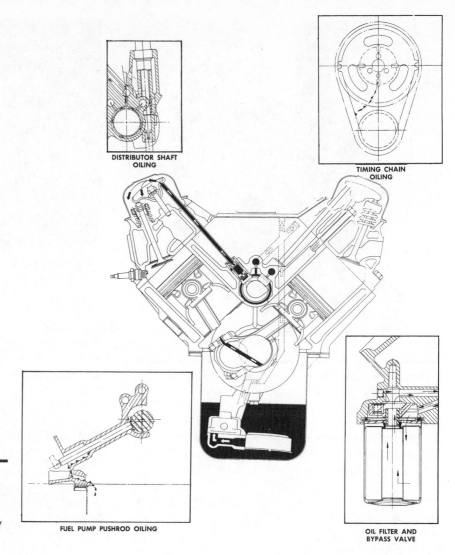

DISTRIBUTOR SHAFT
OILING

TIMING CHAIN
OILING

FUEL PUMP PUSHROD OILING

OIL FILTER AND
BYPASS VALVE

Figure 3–21 Lubricating system in a typical V-type engine. This engine has one main oil gallery directly above the camshaft and two lifter galleries. (*Courtesy of Chevrolet Motor Division, GMC*)

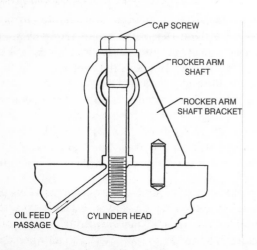

CAP SCREW

ROCKER ARM
SHAFT

ROCKER ARM
SHAFT BRACKET

OIL FEED
PASSAGE   CYLINDER HEAD

Figure 3–22 Clearance around the rocker shaft bracket cap screw makes a passage for oil to get into the rocker shaft. (*Courtesy of Dana Corporation*)

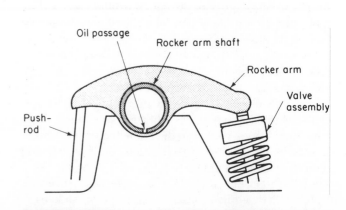

Oil passage   Rocker arm shaft

Rocker arm

Push-
rod

Valve
assembly

Figure 3–23 The rocker arm pivot is lubricated through the oil passage in the bottom of the rocker shaft. Other rocker arm styles are usually lubricated through a hollow pushrod.

WINDAGE TRAY

Figure 3–24 Windage tray attached between the crankshaft and the oil pan.

drain holes are often placed so that the oil drains on the camshaft or cam drive gears to lubricate them.

Some engines have means of directing a positive oil flow to the cam drive gears or chain. This may be a nozzle or a chamfer on a bearing parting surface that allows oil to spray on the loaded portion of the cam drive mechanism.

■ OIL PANS

As the vehicle accelerates, brakes, or turns rapidly, the oil tends to move around in the pan. Pan baffles and oil pan shapes are often used to keep the oil inlet under the oil at all times. As the crankshaft rotates, it acts like a fan and causes air within the crankcase to rotate with it. This can cause a strong draft on the oil, churning it so that air bubbles enter the oil, which then causes oil foaming. Oil with air will not lubricate like liquid oil, so oil foaming can cause bearings to fail. A baffle or **windage tray** is sometimes installed in engines to eliminate the oil-churning problem. This may be an added part, as shown in Figure 3–24, or it may be a part of the oil pan. Windage trays have the good side effect of reducing the amount of air disturbed by the crankshaft, so that less power is drained from the engine at high crankshaft speeds.

■ OIL COOLERS

Oil temperature must also be controlled on many high-performance or turbocharged engines. See Figure 3–25

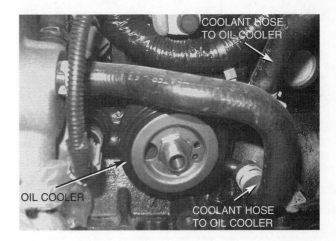

COOLANT HOSE TO OIL COOLER

OIL COOLER

COOLANT HOSE TO OIL COOLER

Figure 3–25 Typical engine oil cooler. Engine oil is cooled by passing coolant from the radiator through the auxiliary housing. The oil filter screws to the cooler.

for an example of an engine oil cooler used on a production high-performance engine. A larger-capacity oil pan also helps to control oil temperature. Coolant flows through the oil cooler to help warm the oil when the engine is cold and cool the oil when the engine is hot. Oil temperature should be above 212°F (100°C) to boil off any accumulated moisture, but it should not exceed about 280° to 300°F (138° to 148°C).

Check That Air Cleaner!

If oil is in the air cleaner, check the condition of the PCV valve and hoses

Frequently Asked Question ???

What Is Acceptable Oil Consumption?

There are a number of opinions regarding what is acceptable oil consumption. Most vehicle owners do not want their engine to use *any* oil between oil changes even if they do not change it more often than every 7500 miles (12,000 kilometers)! Engineers have improved machining operations and piston ring designs to help eliminate oil consumption.

Many stationary or industrial engines are not driven on the road; therefore, they do not accumulate miles, yet they still may consume excessive oil.

A general rule for "acceptable" oil consumption is that it should be about 0.002 to 0.004 pounds per horsepower per hour. To figure, use the following:

$$\frac{1.82 \times \text{Quarts used}}{\text{Operating hp} \times \text{Total hours}} = \text{lb/hp/hr}$$

Therefore, oil consumption is based on the amount of work an engine performs. Although the formula may not be usable for vehicle engines used for daily transportation, it may be usable by the marine or industrial engine builder. Generally, oil consumption that is greater than 1 quart for every 600 miles (1000 kilometers per liter) is considered to be excessive with a motor vehicle.

NOTE: A blocked or plugged PCV system is a major cause of high oil consumption and contributes to many oil leaks. Before expensive engine repairs are attempted, check the condition of the PCV system.

■ POSITIVE CRANKCASE VENTILATION

All engines remove blowby gases with **positive crankcase ventilation (PCV)** systems. This system pulls the crankcase vapors into the intake manifold. The vapors are sent to the cylinders with the intake charge to be burned in the combustion chamber. Under some operating conditions, the blowby gases are forced back through the inlet filter.

■ SUMMARY

1. Viscosity is the oil's thickness or resistance to flow.
2. Normal engine oil pump pressure ranges from 10 to 60 psi (200 to 400 kPa) or 10 psi for every 1000 engine RPM.
3. Hydrodynamic oil pressure around engine bearings is usually over 1000 psi (6900 kPa).
4. Most vehicle manufacturers recommend use of SAE 5W-30 or SAE 10W-30 engine oil.
5. Most vehicle manufacturers recommend changing the engine oil every six months or every 7500 miles (12,000 kilometers), whichever comes first. Most experts recommend changing the engine oil every 3000 miles (5000 kilometers) or every three months to help ensure long engine life.
6. The oil pump is driven directly by the crankshaft or by a gear or shaft from the camshaft.

■ REVIEW QUESTIONS

1. What causes a wedge-shape film to form in the oil?
2. What is hydrodynamic lubrication?
3. What is meant by the label "Energy Conserving"?
4. Explain why the oil filter is bypassed when the engine oil is cold and thick.
5. Explain why internal engine leakage affects oil pressure.
6. Explain the operation of the bypass valve located in the oil filter or oil filter adapter.
7. Describe how the oil flows from the oil pump, through the filter and main engine bearings, to the valve train.
8. What is the purpose of a windage tray?

■ ASE CERTIFICATION-TYPE QUESTIONS

1. Normal oil pump pressure in an engine is _____ .
   a. 3 to 7 psi
   b. 10 to 60 psi
   c. 100 to 150 psi
   d. 180 to 210 psi
2. Oil change intervals as specified by the vehicle manufacturer _____ .
   a. Are *maximum* time and mileage intervals
   b. Are *minimum* time and mileage intervals
   c. Only include miles driven between oil changes
   d. Generally only include time between oil changes

3. An SAE 10W-30 engine oil is _____ .
   a. An SAE oil 10 with VI additives
   b. An SAE oil 20 with VI additives
   c. An SAE oil 30 with VI additives
   d. An SAE oil 30 with detergent additives

4. As engine oil is used in an engine _____ .
   a. It becomes thinner as a result of chemical breakdown that occurs with age
   b. It becomes thicker because of oxidation, wear metals, and combustion by-products
   c. It becomes thicker because of temperature changes
   d. It becomes thinner because of oxidation, wear metals, and combustion by-products

5. Technician A says that the same engine oil should be used throughout an engine's entire service life. Technician B says that any engine oil of the correct API and SAE rating can be used because all engine oils are compatible. Which technician is correct?
   a. Technician A only
   b. Technician B only
   c. Both Technician A and B
   d. Neither Technician A nor B

6. Technician A says that some vehicle manufacturers recommend a diesel API grade and a gasoline grade for particular engines. Technician B says that an oil with the specified API rating *and* SAE viscosity rating should be used in an engine. Which technician is correct?
   a. Technician A only
   b. Technician B only
   c. Both Technician A and B
   d. Neither Technician A nor B

7. Two technicians are discussing oil filters. Technician A says that the oil will remain perfectly clean if just the oil filter is changed regularly. Technician B says that oil filters cannot filter particles smaller than the human eye can see. Which technician is correct?
   a. Technician A only
   b. Technician B only
   c. Both Technician A and B
   d. Neither Technician A nor B

8. Turbocharged engines have special engine oil needs such as _____ .
   a. Strict oil change intervals should be observed
   b. Oil of the proper API and SAE ratings should be used
   c. The turbocharger should be primed by cranking the engine before starting
   d. All of the above

9. A typical oil pump can pump how many gallons per minute?
   a. 3 to 6 gallons
   b. 6 to 10 gallons
   c. 10 to 60 gallons
   d. 50 to 100 gallons

10. In typical engine lubrication systems, what components are the last to receive oil and the first to suffer from a lack of oil or oil pressure?
   a. Main bearings
   b. Rod bearings
   c. Valve trains
   d. Oil filters

Starting and Charging System Operation and Diagnosis

Objectives: After studying Chapter 4, the reader should be able to:

1. List the precautions necessary when working with batteries.
2. Describe how to test a battery.
3. Explain how to safely charge a battery.
4. Describe how the cranking circuit works.
5. Describe how to perform cranking system testing procedures.
6. Discuss the various AC generator test procedures.

For any engine to start, it must be rotated. It is the purpose and function of the cranking circuit to create the necessary power and transfer it from the battery to the starter motor that rotates the engine.

Everything electrical in a vehicle is supplied with current from the battery. The battery is one of the most important parts of a vehicle.

All vehicles operate electrical components by taking current from the battery. It is the purpose and function of the charging system to keep the battery fully charged. The SAE standardized name for an alternator is the generator.

All electrical generators use the principle of electromagnetic induction to generate electrical power from mechanical power. Electromagnetic induction involves the generation of an electrical current in a conductor when the conductor is moved through a magnetic field.

■ PURPOSE OF A BATTERY

The primary purpose of an automotive battery is to provide a source of electrical power for starting and for electrical demands that exceed generator output. The battery also acts as a stabilizer to the voltage for the entire electrical system. The battery is a voltage stabilizer, because it acts as a reservoir where large amounts of current (amperes) can be removed quickly during starting and replaced gradually by the alternator during charging. The battery *must* be in good (serviceable) condition before the charging system and the cranking system can be tested.

■ HOW A BATTERY WORKS

A fully charged lead-acid battery has a positive plate of lead dioxide (peroxide) and a negative plate of lead surrounded by a sulfuric acid solution (electrolyte). The difference in potential (voltage) between lead peroxide and lead in acid is approximately 2.1 volts in each cell. See Figure 4–1.

During Discharging

The positive-plate lead dioxide (PbO_2) combines with the SO_4 from the electrolyte and releases its O_2 into the

Figure 4–1 Photo of a cutaway battery showing the connection of the cells to each other through the partition.

electrolyte, forming H_2O. The negative plate also combines with the SO_4 from the electrolyte and becomes **lead sulfate ($PbSO_4$)**. See Figure 4–2.

The Fully Discharged State

When the battery is fully discharged, both the positive and the negative plates are $PbSO_4$ (lead sulfate) and the electrolyte has become water (H_2O). It is usually impossible for a battery to become 100% discharged; however, as the battery is being discharged, the plates and electrolyte approach the completely dead situation.

> **CAUTION:** There is danger of freezing when a battery is discharged, because the electrolyte is mostly water.

During Charging

During charging, the sulfate (acid) leaves both the positive and the negative plates and returns to the electrolyte, where it becomes normal-strength sulfuric acid solution. The positive plate returns to lead dioxide (PbO_2) and the negative plate is again pure lead (Pb). See Figure 4–3.

■ SPECIFIC GRAVITY

The amount of sulfate in the electrolyte is determined by the electrolyte's **specific gravity.** Specific gravity is the ratio of the weight of a given volume of a liquid to the weight of an equal volume of water. In other words,

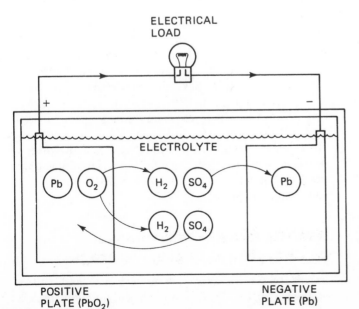

Figure 4–2 Chemical reaction for a lead-acid battery that is fully *charged* being discharged by the attached electrical load.

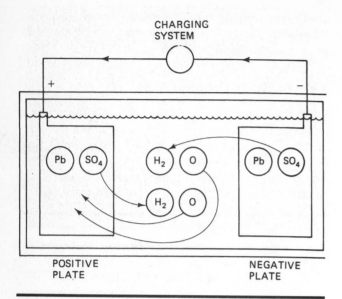

Figure 4–3 Chemical reaction for a lead-acid battery that is fully *discharged* being charged by the attached generator.

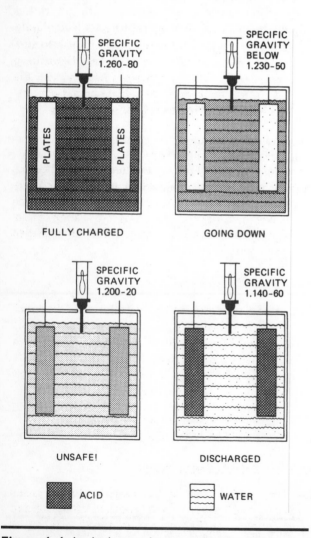

ACID

WATER

Figure 4–4 As the battery becomes discharged, the specific gravity of the battery acid decreases.

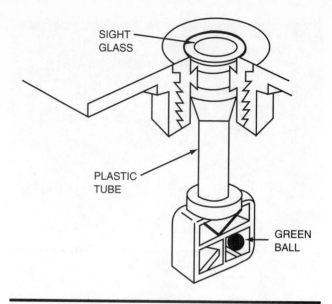

Figure 4–5 Typical battery charge indicator. If the specific gravity is low (battery discharged), the ball drops away from the reflective prism. When the battery is charged enough, the ball floats and reflects the color of the ball (usually green) back up through the sight glass and the sight glass is dark.

the more dense the material (liquid), the higher is its specific gravity. Pure water is the basis for this measurement and has a specific gravity of 1000 at 80°F. Pure sulfuric acid has a specific gravity of 1.835. The *correct* concentration of water and sulfuric acid (called *electrolyte*—64% water, 36% acid) is 1.260 to 1.280 at 80°F. The higher the battery's specific gravity, the more fully it is charged. See Figure 4–4.

Charge Indicators

Some batteries are equipped with a built-in state-of-charge indicator. This indicator is simply a small ball-type hydrometer that is installed in one cell. This hydrometer uses a plastic ball that floats if the electrolyte is dense enough (when the battery is about 65% charged). When the ball floats, it appears in the hydrometer's sight glass, changing its color. See Figures 4–5 and 4–6. Because the hydrometer is only testing one cell (out of six on a 12-volt battery), and because the hydrometer ball can easily stick in one position, it should not be trusted to give accurate information about a battery's state of charge.

Specific Gravity versus State of Charge and Battery Voltage

Values for specific gravity, state of charge, and battery voltage at 80°F (27°C) are given in the following table:

Figure 4–6 Cutaway of the battery showing the charge indicator. If the electrolyte level drops below the bottom of the prism, the sight glass shows clear (light). Most battery manufacturers warn that if the electrolyte level is low on a sealed battery, the battery must be replaced. Attempting to charge a battery that has low electrolyte level can cause a buildup of gases and possibly explosion.

Figure 4–7 This battery has a cranking amperes (CA) rating of 1000, which means that this battery is capable of supplying 1000 amperes to crank an engine for 30 seconds at a temperature of 32°F (0°C) at a minimum of 1.2 volts per cell (7.2 volts for a 12-volt battery).

Specific gravity	State of charge	Battery voltage (V)
1.265	Fully charged	12.6 or higher
1.225	75% charged	12.4
1.190	50% charged	12.2
1.155	25% charged	12.0
Lower than 1.120	Discharged	11.9 or lower

Battery Hold-Downs

All batteries must be attached securely to the vehicle to prevent battery damage. Normal vehicle vibrations can cause the active materials inside the battery to shed. Battery hold-down clamps or brackets help reduce vibration, which can greatly reduce the capacity and life of any battery.

■ BATTERY RATINGS

Batteries are rated according to the amount of current they can produce under specific conditions.

Cold-Cranking Amperes

Every automotive battery must be able to supply electrical power to crank the engine in cold weather and still provide voltage high enough to operate the ignition system for starting. The cold-cranking power of a battery is the number of amperes that can be supplied by a battery at 0°F (−18°C) for 30 seconds while the battery still maintains a voltage of 1.2 volts per cell or higher. This

means that the battery voltage would be 7.2 volts for a 12-volt battery and 3.6 volts for a 6-volt battery. The cold-cranking performance rating is called **cold-cranking amperes (CCA).** Try to purchase a battery with the highest CCA for the money. See vehicle manufacturers' specifications for recommended battery capacity.

Cranking Amperes

Cranking amperes (CA) are not the same as CCA, but are often advertised and labeled on batteries. The designation CA refers to the number of amperes that can be supplied by the battery at 32°F (0°C). This rating results in a higher number than the more stringent rating of CCA. See Figure 4–7.

Reserve Capacity

The **reserve capacity** rating for batteries is *the number of minutes* for which the battery can produce 25 amperes and still have a battery voltage of 1.75 volts per cell (10.5 volts for a 12-volt battery). This rating is actually a measurement of the time for which a vehicle can be driven in the event of a charging system failure.

■ BATTERY SERVICE

Safety Considerations

Batteries contain acid and release explosive gases (hydrogen and oxygen) during normal charging and discharging cycles. To help prevent physical injury or damage to the vehicle, always adhere to the following safety procedures:

Figure 4–8 A severely corroded battery terminal.

Figure 4–10 Carefully inspect all battery terminals for corrosion. This vehicle uses two positive battery cables connected at the battery using a long bolt. This is a common source of corrosion that can cause a starting (cranking) problem.

Figure 4–9 This battery cable was found to be corroded underneath. The corrosion had eaten through the insulation yet was not noticeable until it was carefully inspected. This cable should be replaced.

1. When working on any electrical component of a vehicle, disconnect the negative battery cable from the battery. When the negative cable is disconnected, all electrical circuits in the vehicle will be open, which will prevent accidental electrical contact between an electrical component and ground. Any electrical spark has the potential to cause explosion and personal injury.
2. Wear eye protection when working around any battery.
3. Wear protective clothing to avoid skin contact with battery acid.
4. Always adhere to all safety precautions as stated in the service procedures for the equipment used in battery service and testing.
5. Never smoke or use an open flame around any battery.

Battery Maintenance

Battery maintenance includes making certain that the battery case is clean and adding clean water, if necessary. Distilled water is recommended by all battery manufacturers, but if distilled water is not available, clean ordinary drinking water, low in mineral content, can be used. Because water is the only thing in a battery that is consumed, acid should never be added to a battery. Some of the water in the electrolyte escapes during the normal operation of charging and discharging, but the acid content of the electrolyte remains in the battery. Do not overfill a battery, because normal bubbling (gassing) of the electrolyte will cause the electrolyte to escape and start corrosion on the battery terminals, hold-down brackets, and battery tray. Fill batteries to the indicator that is approximately 1 1/2 inches (3.8 centimeters) from the top of the filler tube.

Battery cable connections should be checked and cleaned to prevent voltage drop at the connections. One common reason for an engine not starting is loose or corroded battery cable connections. See Figures 4–8, 4–9, and 4–10.

Battery Voltage Testing

Testing the battery voltage with a voltmeter is a simple method for determining the state of charge of any battery. The voltage of a battery does not necessarily indicate whether the battery can perform satisfactorily, but it does indicate to the technician more about the battery's condition than a simple visual inspection. A battery that "looks good" may not be good. This test is commonly called an **open-circuit battery voltage test,** because it is conducted with an open circuit—with no current flowing and no load applied to the battery.

1. If the battery has just been charged or the vehicle has recently been driven, it is necessary to remove the surface charge from the battery before testing. A surface charge is of higher-than-normal voltage that is only on the surface of the battery plates. The surface charge is quickly removed when the battery is loaded and therefore does not accurately represent the true state of charge of the battery.
2. To remove the surface charge, turn the headlights on high beam (brights) for 1 minute, then turn the headlights off and wait 2 minutes.
3. With the engine and all electrical accessories off, and the doors shut (to turn off the interior lights), connect a voltmeter to the battery posts. Connect the red positive lead to the positive post and the black negative lead to the negative post.

> **NOTE:** If the meter reads negative, the battery has been reverse charged (has reversed polarity) and should be replaced, or the meter has been connected incorrectly.

4. Read the voltmeter and compare the results with the following state-of-charge chart. The voltages shown are for a battery at or near room temperature (70° to 80°F) or (21° to 27°C). See Figure 4–11.

Battery voltage (V)	State of charge
12.6 or higher	100% charged
12.4	75% charged
12.2	50% charged
12.0	25% charged
11.9 or lower	Discharged

Battery Load Testing

One of the most accurate tests to determine the condition of any battery is the **load test.** Most automotive starting and charging testers use a carbon pile to create an electrical load on the battery. The amount of the load is determined by the original capacity of the battery being tested. The capacity is measured in cold-cranking amperes, which is the number of amperes that a battery can supply at 0°F (−18°C) for 30 seconds. An older type of battery rating is called the **ampere-hour rating.** *The proper electrical load to be used to test a battery is one-half the CCA rating or three times the ampere-hour rating, with a minimum 250-ampere load.* After the battery has been tested to be at least 75% charged by

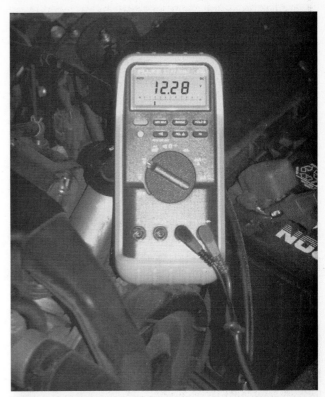

(a)

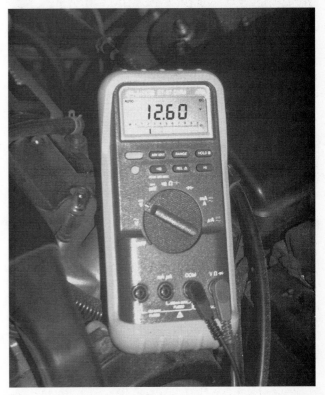

(b)

Figure 4–11 (a) Voltmeter showing the battery voltage after the headlights were on (engine off) for 1 minute. (b) Headlights were turned off and the battery voltage quickly recovered to indicate 12.6 volts.

observing the built-in hydrometer or by performing an open-circuit voltage test, a load test can be performed. Apply the load for a full 15 seconds and observe the voltmeter at the end of the 15-second period while the battery is still under load. A good battery should indicate above 9.6 V. Many battery manufacturers recommend performing the load test twice, using the first load period to remove the surface charge on the battery and the second test to provide a truer indication of the condition of the battery. Wait 30 seconds between tests to allow time for the battery to recover. See Figures 4–12 and 4–13.

Figure 4–12 A Bear Automotive starting and charging tester. This tester automatically loads the battery for 15 seconds to remove the surface charge, then waits 30 seconds to allow the battery to recover, then again loads the battery. The display indicates the status of the battery.

Figure 4–13 A Sun Electric VAT-40 (Volt Amp Tester, model 40) connected to a battery for load testing. The technician turns the load knob until the ammeter registers an amperage reading equal to one-half the battery's CCA rating. The load is maintained for 15 seconds, and the voltage of the battery should be higher than 9.6 volts at the end of the time period *with the load still applied.*

If the battery fails the load test, recharge the battery and retest. If a second failure occurs, replace the battery.

> **NOTE:** Some battery testers measure the capacitance of the battery to determine the state of charge and battery condition. Always follow the test equipment manufacturer's recommended test procedure.

Battery Charging

If the state of charge of a battery is low, it must be recharged. It is best to slow-charge any battery to prevent possible overheating damage to the battery. See Figure 4–14 for the recommended charging rate. *Remember, it may take eight hours or more to charge a fully discharged battery.* The initial charge rate should be about 35 amperes for 30 minutes to help start the charging process. Fast-charging a battery increases the temperature of the battery and can cause warping of the plates inside the battery. Fast-charging also increases the amount of gassing (release of hydrogen and oxygen), which can create a health and fire hazard. The battery temperature should not exceed 125°F (hot to the touch). *Most batteries should be charged at a rate equal to 1% of the battery's CCA rating.*

Fast charge: 15 amperes maximum
Slow charge: 5 amperes maximum

TECH TIP

It Could Happen to You!

The owner of a Toyota replaced the battery. After replacing the battery, the owner noted that the "airbag" amber warning lamp was lit and the radio was locked out. The owner had purchased the vehicle used from a dealer and did not know the four-digit security code needed to unlock the radio. Determined to fix it, the owner tried three four-digit numbers, hoping that one of them would work. However, after three tries, the radio became permanently disabled.

Frustrated, the owner went to a dealer. It cost over $300 to fix the problem. A special tool was required to reset the airbag lamp. The radio had to be removed and sent out of state to an authorized radio service center and then reinstalled into the vehicle.

Therefore, before disconnecting the battery, please check with the owner to be certain that the owner has the security code for a security-type radio. A "memory saver" may be needed to keep the radio powered when the battery is being disconnected. See Figure 4–15.

Figure 4–14 This battery charger is charging the battery at a 10-ampere rate. A slow rate such as this is easier on the battery than a fast charge that may overheat the battery and cause warpage of the plates inside the battery.

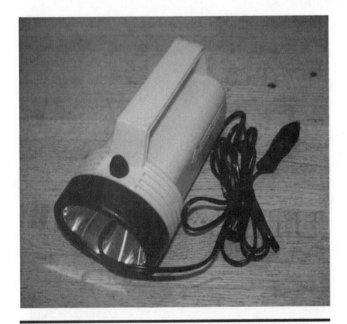

Figure 4–15 Here is a clever idea. This technician made a tool using an old lantern battery connected to a lighter plug to be used as a memory saver. The technician kept the lantern and simply connected the lighter plug pigtail to the lantern battery terminals. A lantern battery is better to use than a small 9-volt battery in case someone opens the door of the vehicle while the memory saver is plugged in. A small 9-volt battery would be quickly drained whereas the lantern battery has enough capacity to light the interior lights and still have enough charge to keep the memories alive.

■ JUMP STARTING

To jump-start another vehicle with a dead battery, connect good-quality copper jumper cables as indicated in

Frequently Asked Question   ???

Should Batteries Be Kept Off Concrete Floors?

All batteries should be stored in a cool, dry place when not in use. Many technicians have been warned not to store or place a battery on concrete. According to battery experts, it is the temperature difference between the top and the bottom of the battery that causes a difference in the voltage potential between the top (warmer section) and the bottom (colder section). It is this difference in temperature that causes self-discharge to occur. In fact, submarines cycle seawater around their batteries to keep all sections of the battery at the same temperature to help prevent self-discharge.

Therefore, always store or place batteries off the floor and in a location where the entire battery can be kept at the same temperature, avoiding extreme heat and freezing temperatures. Concrete cannot drain the battery directly, because the battery case is a very good electrical insulator.

Figure 4–16. The last connection made should always be on the engine block or an engine bracket as far from the battery as possible. It is normal for a spark to be created when the jumper cables finally complete the jumping circuit, and this spark could cause an explosion of the gases around the battery. Many newer vehicles have special ground connections built away from the battery just for the purpose of jump starting. Check the owner's manual or service manual for the exact location.

■ CRANKING CIRCUIT

The cranking circuit includes those mechanical and electrical components required to crank the engine for starting. In the early 1900s, the cranking force was the driver's arm. Modern cranking circuits include the following:

1. *Starter motor.* The starter is normally a 0.5 to 2.6-horsepower (0.4 to 2.0-kilowatt) electric motor. See Figure 4–17.
2. *Battery.* The battery must be of the correct capacity and be at least 75% charged to provide the necessary current and voltage for correct operation of the starter.
3. *Starter solenoid or relay.* The high current required by the starter must be able to be turned on and off. A large switch would be required if the current were controlled by the driver directly. Instead, a small

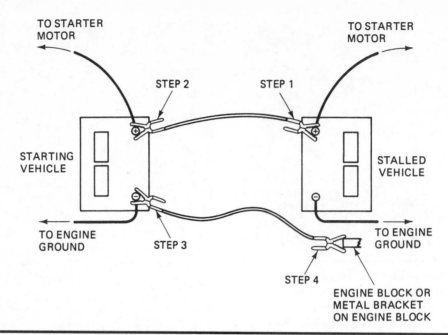

Figure 4–16 Jumper cable usage guide. Notice that the last electrical connection is made to the engine block or an engine bracket away from the battery to help prevent a spark that could occur causing harm to the disabled vehicle or to the person performing the jump starting.

Figure 4–17 Typical solenoid-operated starter.

TECH TIP ✔

Watch the Dome Light

When diagnosing any starter-related problem, open the door of the vehicle and observe the brightness of the dome or interior light(s).

- The brightness of any electrical lamp is proportional to the voltage.
- Normal operation of the starter results in a slight dimming of the dome light.
- If the light remains bright, the problem is usually an open circuit in the control circuit.
- If the light goes out or almost goes out, the problem is usually a shorted or grounded armature of field coils inside the starter or a defective battery.

current switch (ignition switch) operates a solenoid or relay that controls the high starter current.
4. *Starter drive.* The starter drive uses a small gear that contacts the engine flywheel gear and transmits starter motor power to rotate the engine.
5. *Ignition switch.* The ignition switch and safety control switches control the starter motor operation.
6. *Neutral safety (clutch switch).* This switch prevents the operation of the starter unless the gear selector is in park or neutral or the clutch pedal is depressed. See Figure 4–18.

■ STARTING SYSTEM TROUBLESHOOTING

The proper operation of the starting system depends on a good battery, good cables and connections, and a good starter motor. Because a starting problem can be caused by a defective component anywhere in the starting circuit, it is important to check for the proper operation of each part of the circuit to diagnose and repair the problem quickly.

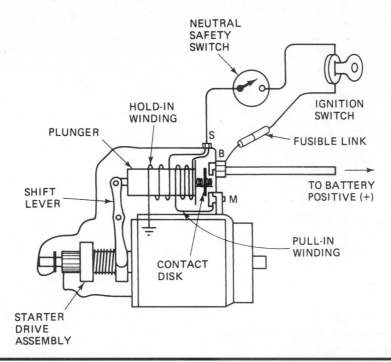

Figure 4–18 Wiring diagram of a typical starter solenoid. Notice that both the pull-in winding and the hold-in winding are energized when the ignition switch is first turned to the "start" position. As soon as the solenoid contact disk makes electrical contact with both the B and M terminals, the battery current is conducted to the starter motor.

TECH TIP ✔

Don't Hit That Starter!

In the past, it was common to see service technicians hitting a starter in their effort to diagnose a no-crank condition. Often the shock of the blow to the starter aligned or moved the brushes, armature, and bushings. Many times, the starter functioned after being hit—even if only for a short time.

However, most of today's starters use permanent-magnet (PM) fields, and the magnets can be easily broken if hit. A magnet that is broken becomes two weaker magnets. Some early PM starters used magnets that were glued or bonded to the field housing. If struck with a heavy tool, the magnets could be broken with parts of the magnet falling onto the armature and into the bearing pockets, making the starter impossible to repair or rebuild.

IMPORTANT: Starter remanufacturers state that the single most common cause of starter motor failure is low battery voltage. When battery voltage drops, additional current (amperes) must flow through the starter to maintain the balance of electrical power. Since electrical power is amperes times volts, a drop in battery voltage causes the increase in starter amperage draw.

TECH TIP ✔

Too Hot!

If a cable or connection is hot to the touch, there is electrical resistance in the cable or connection. The resistance changes electrical energy into heat energy. Therefore, if a voltmeter is not available, touch the battery cables and connections while cranking the engine. If any cable or connection is hot to the touch, it should be cleaned or replaced.

■ STARTER AMPERAGE TESTING

Before performing a starter amperage test, be certain that the battery is sufficiently charged (75% or more) and capable of supplying adequate starting current.

A starter amperage test should be performed when the starter fails to operate normally (is slow in cranking) or as part of a routine electrical system inspection. Some service manuals specify normal starter amperage for starter motors being tested on the vehicle; however, most service manuals only give the specifications for bench-testing a starter without a load applied. If exact specifications are not available, the following can be

Frequently Asked Question ???

Why Does a Weak Battery Cause an Increase in the Starter Current?

A starter motor requires a certain amount of *power* to start an engine. What is power? Power expressed in electrical terms is amperes times volts (Power = $I \times E$). The power required to start an engine remains the same even if the battery voltage decreases. For example:

Good battery	Weak battery
11.0 V during cranking	9.8 V during cranking
190 A	213 A
Power = 11.0 × 190	Power = 9.8 × 213
= 2090 W	= 2090 W

Notice that the power required for the starter motor to crank the engine is the same (2090 watts). However, the good battery can maintain 11.0 volts while supplying the necessary current for starter operation (190 amperes). A weak battery decreases in voltage while supplying the high current required for cranking. The *power* required by the starter to crank an engine is constant. If the battery voltage decreases, the amount of current must *increase* to compensate for the drop in voltage. Notice that the required current is increased from 190 amperes (good battery) to 213 amperes for the weak battery. Therefore, to get accurate test results, a battery that is known to be good and that is at least 75% charged should be used during starter testing.

used as general specifications for testing a starter on the vehicle.

4-cylinder engines = 150–185 amperes

6-cylinder engines = 160–200 amperes

8-cylinder engines = 185–250 amperes

Excessive current draw may indicate one or more of the following:

1. Low battery voltage (discharged or defective battery)
2. Binding of starter armature as a result of worn bushings
3. Oil too thick (viscosity too high) for weather conditions
4. Shorted or grounded starter windings or cables
5. Tight or seized engine

Also see the starter trouble diagnostic chart in Figure 4–19.

■ BENCH TESTING

Every starter should be tested before it is installed in a vehicle. The usual method includes clamping the starter in a vise to prevent rotation during operation and connecting heavy-gauge jumper wires (minimum 4 gauge) to a battery known to be good and the starter. The starter motor should rotate as fast as specifications indicate and not draw more than the free-spinning amperage permitted.

■ AC GENERATORS

How an AC Generator Works

A rotor inside an AC generator (also called an **alternator**) is turned by the engine through an accessory drive belt. The magnetic field of the rotor generates a current in the windings of the stator by electromagnetic induction. See Figures 4–20 and 4–21.

Most AC generators are designed to supply between 13.5 and 15.0 volts at 2000 engine RPM. Be sure to check the vehicle manufacturer's specifications. For example, most General Motors vehicles specify a charging voltage of 14.7 volts ± 0.5 (or between 14.2 and 15.2 volts).

Charging-system voltage tests should be performed on a vehicle with a battery at least 75% charged. If the battery is discharged (or defective), the charging voltage may be below specifications. To measure charging-system voltage, follow these steps:

1. Connect the voltmeter to the positive and negative terminals of the battery.
2. Set the meter to read DC volts.
3. Start the engine and raise to a fast idle (about 2000 RPM).
4. Read the voltmeter and compare with specifications. See Figure 4–22. If lower than specifications, charge the battery and test for excessive charging-circuit voltage drop before replacing the alternator.

HINT: If the voltmeter reading rises then becomes lower as the engine speed is increased, the generator drive (accessory drive) belt is loose or slipping.

AC Voltage Check

A good AC generator should *not* produce any AC voltage. It is the purpose of the diodes in the AC generator to rectify all AC voltage into DC voltage. The procedure to check for AC voltage includes the following steps:

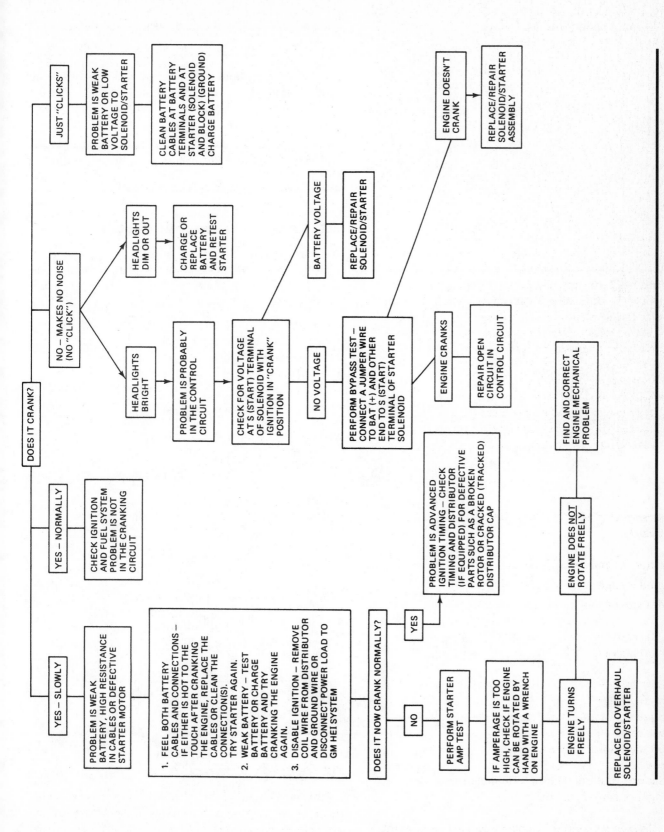

Figure 4–19 Starter trouble diagnostic chart.

Step 1 Set the digital meter to read AC volts.

Step 2 Start the engine and operate it at 2000 RPM (fast idle).

Step 3 Connect the voltmeter leads to the positive and negative battery terminals.

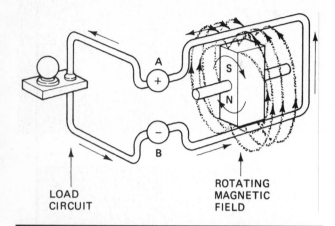

Figure 4–20 Magnetic lines of force cutting across a conductor induce a voltage and current in the conductor.

Step 4 Turn on the headlights to provide an electrical load on the AC generator.

> **NOTE:** A higher, more accurate reading can be obtained by touching the meter lead to the output terminal of the AC generator.

The results should be interrupted as follows: If the diodes are good, the voltmeter should read *less* than 0.4 volt AC. If the reading is over 0.5 volt AC, the rectifier diodes are defective.

> **NOTE:** This test will *not* test for a defective diode trio.

AC Generator Output Testing

A charging circuit may be able to produce correct charging-circuit voltage but not adequate amperage output. If in doubt about charging-system output, first check the condition of the AC generator drive belt. With

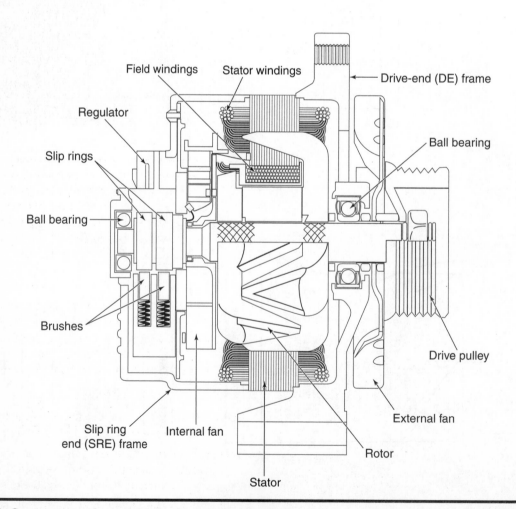

Figure 4–21 Cutaway view of a typical AC generator (alternator).

Figure 4–22 The digital multimeter should be set to read DC volts and the red lead connected to the battery positive (+) terminal and the black meter lead connected to the negative (−) battery terminal.

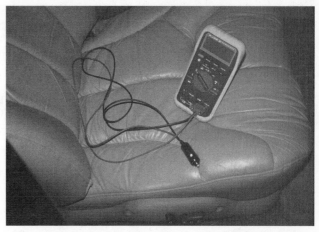

(a)

(b)

Figure 4–23 (a) A simple and easy-to-use tester can be made from a lighter plug and double banana plug that fits the COM and V terminals of most digital meters. (b) By plugging the lighter plug into the lighter, the charging circuit voltage can be easily measured.

TECH TIP ✔

The Lighter Plug Trick

Battery voltage measurements can be read through the lighter socket. See Figure 4–23. Simply construct a test tool using a lighter plug at one end of a length of two-conductor wire and the other end connected to a double banana plug. The double banana plug will fit most meters in the common (COM) terminal and the volt terminal of the meter.

TECH TIP ✔

Use a Test Light to Check for a Defective Fusible Link

Most AC generators (alternators) use a fusible link between the output terminal located on the slip-ring-end frame and the positive (+) terminal of the battery. If this fusible link is defective (blown), then the charging system will not operate. Many AC generators have been replaced repeatedly because of a blown fusible link that was not discovered until later. A quick and easy test to check if the fusible link is okay is to touch a test light to the output terminal. With the other end of the test light attached to a good ground, the fusible link is okay if the light lights. This test confirms that the circuit between the AC generator and the battery has continuity.

---

the engine off, attempt to rotate the fan of the AC generator by hand. Replace or tighten the drive belt if the AC generator fan can be rotated by hand. See Figures 4–24 and 4–25 for typical test equipment hookup.

The testing procedure for AC generator output is as follows:

Step 1 Connect the starting and charging test leads according to the manufacturer's instructions.

Step 2 Turn the ignition switch on (engine off) and observe the ammeter. This is the ignition circuit current, and it should be about 2 to 8 amperes.

Step 3 Start the engine and operate it at 2000 RPM (fast idle). Turn the load increase control slowly to

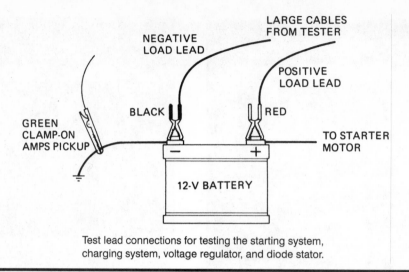

Test lead connections for testing the starting system, charging system, voltage regulator, and diode stator.

Figure 4–24 Typical hookup of a starting and charging tester.

Figure 4–25 When connecting an inductive ammeter probe, be certain that the pickup is over *all* wires. The probe will work equally well over either all positive or all negative cables, because all current leaving a battery must return.

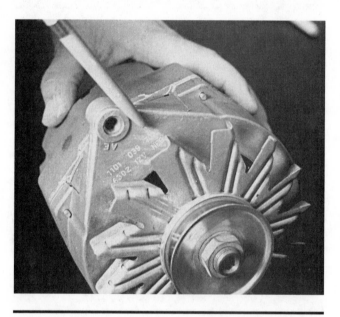

Figure 4–26 The amperage rating of most GM generators is stamped on the drive-end housing either facing the front (pulley side) or on top behind the small threaded mounting lug.

obtain the highest reading on the ammeter scale. Note the ampere reading.

Step 4 Total the amperes from steps 2 and 3. Results should be within 10% (or 15 amperes) of the rated output. Rated output may be stamped on the AC generator as shown in Figure 4–26.

If the AC generator output is not within 10% of its rated output, perform the same test as just described,

but this time bypass the voltage regulator and provide a full-field current to the rotor (field) of the AC generator.

> **NOTE:** When applying a load to the battery with a carbon pile tester during an AC generator output test, do not permit the battery voltage to drop below 12 volts. Most AC generators will produce their maximum output (in amperes) above 13 volts.

PHOTO SEQUENCE Accessory Drive Belt Replacement

PS 3–1 A special tool used to remove and replace most serpentine accessory drive belts. This tool comes with various sockets that fit a variety of vehicles.

PS 3–2 The tool attaches to the tensioner. The long handle provides leverage needed to remove the tension from the belt.

PS 3–3 By rotating the tensioner, the tension on the belt is removed.

PS 3–4 The belt can be easily removed after the tension has been removed.

PS 3–5 Installing a new serpentine accessory drive belt requires that force be maintained on the tool while the belt is routed onto all of the accessory pulleys. Most vehicles have a placard under the hood showing the correct routing of the accessory drive belt.

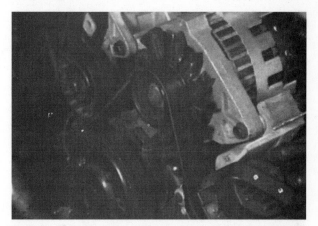

PS 3–6 After the belt is positioned over the pulleys, the tension can be removed from the tensioner and the tool removed. Start the engine and verify proper accessory drive belt installation.

PHOTO SEQUENCE Starting and Charging Voltmeter Test

PS 4–1 Prepare a digital multimeter to read volts by placing the red meter lead into the "VΩ" (red) input terminal and the black meter lead into the input terminal labeled "COM" as shown.

PS 4–2 Connect the red meter lead clip to the positive (+) terminal of the battery and connect the black meter lead clip to the negative (−) terminal of the battery.

PS 4–3 Turn the meter on and select DC volts.

PS 4–4 Turn the headlights on for about 1 minute to remove the surface charge from the battery.

PS 4–5 Watch the meter display with the headlights on. A good fully charged battery will indicate a slight drop in voltage such as shown here (12.44 volts). A weak or discharged battery will usually indicate a rapidly falling voltage reading when the headlights are first turned on.

PS 4–6 Turn off the headlights after about 1 minute or when the voltage reading stops rising.

Starting and Charging Voltmeter Test—continued

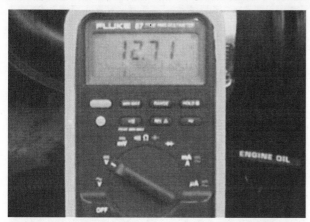

PS 4–7 The voltage should increase after the lights are turned off. Record the voltage when the reading stops increasing. A reading of 12.6 or higher indicates a fully charged 12-volt battery.

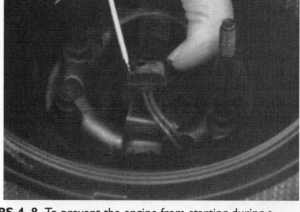

PS 4–8 To prevent the engine from starting during a cranking voltage part of the test, the fuel injector can be disconnected.

PS 4–9 Crank the engine using the ignition switch.

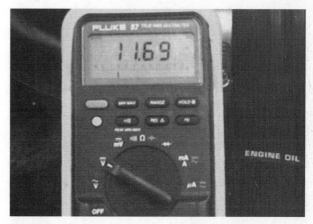

PS 4–10 Observe the voltmeter while cranking. A reading of about 9.6 volts indicates that the cranking circuit is okay.

Starting and Charging Voltmeter Test—continued

PS 4–11 Reconnect the fuel injector.

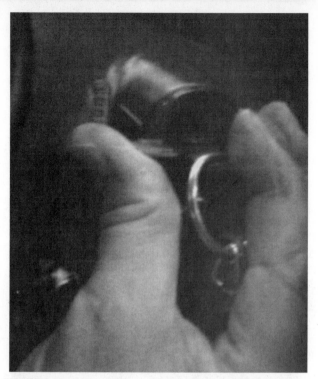

PS 4–12 Start and operate the engine at 2000 RPM (fast idle).

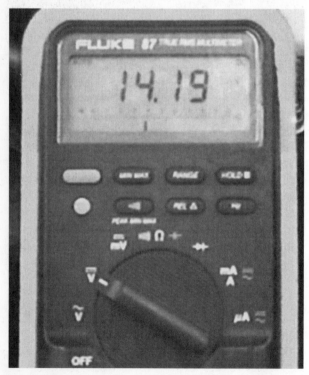

PS4–13 Observe the voltmeter. Acceptable charging system voltage should be between 13.5 and 15.0 volts.

PS 4–14 Turn the engine off and disconnect the meter leads. This test is complete.

PS 5–1 A typical Sun VAT-40 used to perform a battery load test. This type of tester uses a carbon pile to provide a connective path to load the battery, and therefore, is often called a carbon-pile tester.

PS 5–2 Start the test by connecting the large red clamp from the tester to the positive (+) terminal of the battery and the large black clamp to the negative (−) terminal of the battery.

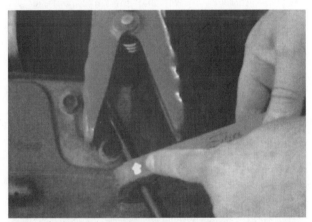

PS 5–3 Attach the inductive amp probe over the meter red tester lead wire. According to Sun Electric, the arrow on the probe should point toward the battery.

PS 5–4 Zero the ammeter by turning the zero adjust knob until the needle on the meter indicates zero.

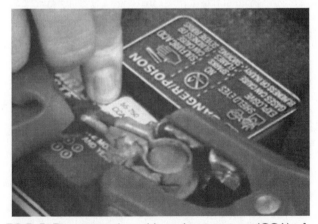

PS 5–5 Determine the cold-cranking amperes (CCA) of the battery. This rating is usually on a sticker on the battery case.

PS 5–6 Turn the load knob until the ammeter reading is one-half of the CCA rating of the battery. Maintain applying this load for 15 seconds. With the load still applied, observe the voltmeter reading at the end of the 15-second test. The battery voltage should be above 9.6 volts. Most vehicle manufacturers recommend that the test be repeated, often waiting a few minutes to allow the battery time to recover. The first load test is used to remove the surface charge.

PS 6–1 A Sun Electric VAT-40 is being used to measure the amount of current, in amperes, required to crank the engine.

PS 6–2 Attach the red clamp from the tester to the positive (+) terminal of the battery and the black clamp to the negative (−) terminal of the battery. Clamp the inductive ampere probe around either all of the wires from the positive terminal or over all of the wires from the negative terminal as shown.

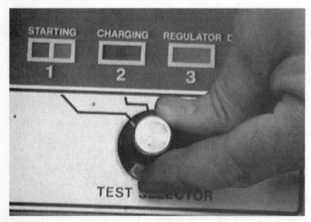

PS 6–3 Select "starting" with the test selector knob. This position indicates that the amperage should be read on the red-lettered scale and the voltage read on the green-lettered scale.

PS 6–4 Disable the ignition or the fuel system to prevent the engine from starting when the engine is being cranked. The "computer" fuse is being removed on this Chrysler vehicle to disable the fuel delivery system.

PS 6–5 Crank the engine and observe the ammeter reading.

PS 6–6 The starter on this vehicle equipped with a V-6 engine requires 120 amperes as displayed on the VAT-40 display. Disregard the first initial higher amperage reading. This starter motor is okay because the allowable starter amperage draw for most six-cylinder engines is 200 A or less.

PHOTO SEQUENCE   Generator (Alternator) Output Test

PS 7–1 A typical Sun Electric VAT-40 (volt/amp tester model 40) used to measure the output of an AC generator (alternator).

PS 7–2 Connect the large black clamp from the VAT-40 to the negative (−) terminal of the battery and the large red clamp to the positive (+) terminal of the battery.

PS 7–3 Attach the ammeter inductive probe to either the negative or positive vehicle battery cable whichever is most accessible. Be sure to clamp over *all* of the wires connecting to the battery terminal. In this case, the negative cable was selected because it was not possible to get all of the wiring leading from the positive battery terminal onto the ampere clamp.

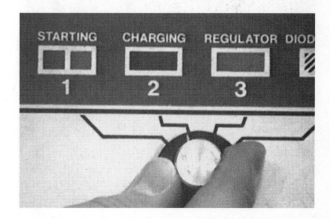

PS 7–4 Select "charging" on the VAT-40 unit.

PS 7–5 Start the engine. This reading (about 25 amperes as shown on the upper scale) represents the amount of current being produced by the generator at idle after a start. This does not represent the maximum output. To measure the maximum output, the battery must be loaded and the engine speed increased.

Generator (Alternator) Output Test—continued

PS 7–6 To measure the maximum AC generator (alternator) output, increase engine speed to 2000 RPM.

PS 7–7 With the engine operating at 2000 RPM, turn the load knob until the highest ampere reading is displayed.

PS 7–8 The output should be within 10% of its rated output. The specification for this vehicle was 90 amperes and output was measured at 92 amperes. If the output is lower than specifications, stop the engine and turn the ignition switch to the on (run) position (engine off) and observe the ammeter. This reading represents the amount of current consumed by the ignition system and any units being operated such as the blower motor when the engine was running. This amperage should be added to the amount measured above to determine the actual maximum generator output.

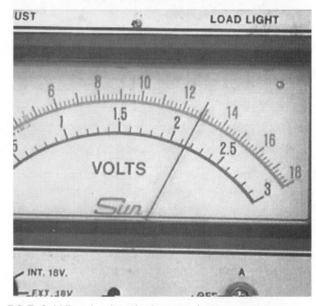

PS 7–9 When loading the battery during a generator output test, be sure to keep the voltage above 12 volts. Most charging systems produce the maximum output at about 13 volts as shown here during the test.

■ SUMMARY

1. When a battery is being discharged, the acid (SO_4) is leaving the electrolyte and being deposited on the plates. When the battery is being charged, the acid (SO_4) is forced off the plates and back into the electrolyte.

2. Batteries are rated according to CCA, CA, and reserve capacity.

3. All batteries should be securely attached to the vehicle with hold-down brackets to prevent vibration damage.

4. Batteries can be tested with a voltmeter to determine the state of charge. A battery load test loads the battery to one-half its CCA rating. A good battery should be able to maintain higher than 9.6 volts for the entire 15-second test period.

5. Proper operation of the starter motor depends on the battery being at least 75% charged and the battery cables being of the correct size (gauge) and having no more than a 0.2 voltage drop.

6. Voltage-drop testing includes cranking the engine, measuring the drop in voltage from the battery to the starter, and measuring the drop in voltage from the negative terminal of the battery to the engine block.

7. The cranking circuit should be tested for proper amperage draw.

8. Normal charging voltage (at 2000 engine RPM) is 13.5 to 15.0 volts.

9. The AC generator output is tested using a carbon pile tester connected to load the battery and measure the maximum amount of current being generated.

10. If more than 0.5 volt AC is measured at the output terminal of the battery, then the diode or stator is defective inside the AC generator.

■ REVIEW QUESTIONS

1. List the parts of the cranking circuit.

2. Explain why discharged batteries can freeze.

3. Identify the three battery rating methods.

4. Describe the results of a voltmeter test of a battery and its state of charge.

5. List the steps for performing a battery load test.

6. Discuss how to measure the amperage output of an AC generator.

7. Explain how testing can be used to determine whether a diode or stator is defective.

■ ASE CERTIFICATION-TYPE QUESTIONS

1. When a battery becomes completely discharged, both positive and negative plates become _____ and the electrolyte becomes _____ .
   a. H_2SO_4; Pb
   b. $PbSO_4$; H_2O
   c. PbO_2; H_2SO_4
   d. $PbSO_4$, H_2SO_4

2. A fully charged 12-volt battery should indicate _____ .
   a. 12.6 volts or higher
   b. A specific gravity of 1.265 or higher
   c. 12 volts
   d. Both a and b

3. A battery measures 12.4 volts after removing the surface charge. This battery is charged at what percent?
   a. 100%
   b. 75%
   c. 50%
   d. 25%

4. Reserve capacity for batteries means _____ .
   a. The number of *hours* the battery can supply 25 amperes and remain higher than 10.5 volts
   b. The number of *minutes* the battery can supply 25 amperes and remain higher than 10.5 volts
   c. The number of *minutes* the battery can supply 20 amperes and remain higher than 9.6 volts
   d. The number of *minutes* the battery can supply 10 amperes and remain higher than 9.6 volts

5. A battery high-rate discharge (load capacity) test is being performed on a 12-volt battery. Technician A says that a good battery should have a voltage reading of higher than 9.6 volts while under load at the end of the 15-second test. Technician B says that the battery should be discharged (loaded to two times its CCA rating). Which technician is correct?
   a. Technician A only
   b. Technician B only
   c. Both Technician A and B
   d. Neither Technician A nor B

6. When charging a maintenance-free (lead-calcium) battery, _____ .
   a. The initial charging rate should be about 35 amperes for 30 minutes
   b. The battery may not accept a charge for several hours, yet may still be a good (serviceable) battery
   c. The battery temperature should not exceed 125°F (hot to the touch)
   d. All of the above are correct

7. When jump-starting, _____ .
   a. The last connection should be the positive post of the dead battery
   b. The last connection should be the engine block of the dead vehicle
   c. The alternator must be disconnected on both vehicles
   d. Both a and c

8. Slow cranking by the starter can be caused by all *except* the following _____ .
   a. A low or discharged battery
   b. Corroded or dirty battery cables
   c. Engine mechanical problems
   d. An open neutral safety switch

9. A starter motor draws more amperage than specifications. Technician A says that the battery may be discharged. Technician B says that the starter may be defective. Which technician is correct?
   a. Technician A only
   b. Technician B only
   c. Both Technician A and B
   d. Neither Technician A nor B

10. An acceptable charging circuit voltage on a 12-volt system is _____ .
    a. 13.5 to 15.0 volts
    b. 12.6 to 15.6 volts
    c. 12 to 14 volts
    d. 14.9 to 16.1 volts

Ignition System Operation and Diagnosis

Objectives: After studying Chapter 5, the reader should be able to:

1. Describe how to check for spark using a spark tester.
2. Describe how a pickup coil, Hall effect switch, crankshaft position sensor, or optical distributors are used to trigger the ignition module.
3. Explain how to diagnose a no-start condition.
4. Describe the importance of proper ignition timing for best engine operation.

The ignition system includes those parts and wiring required to generate and distribute a high voltage to the spark plugs.

■ IGNITION SYSTEM OPERATION

The ignition system includes the components and wiring necessary to create and distribute a high voltage (up to 40,000 volts or more). All ignition systems apply voltage close to battery voltage to the positive side of the ignition coil and pulse the negative side to ground. When the negative coil lead is grounded, the primary (low voltage) circuit of the coil is completed and a magnetic field is created by the coil windings. When the circuit is opened, the magnetic field collapses and induces a high-voltage spark from the secondary winding of the ignition coil. Early ignition systems used a mechanically opened set of contact points to make and break the electrical connection to ground. Electronic ignition uses a sensor, such as a pickup coil or trigger, to signal an electronic module that makes and breaks the primary connection of the ignition coil.

> **NOTE: Distributor ignition (DI)** is the term specified by the Society of Automotive Engineers (SAE) for an ignition system that uses a distributor. **Electronic ignition (EI)** is the term specified by the Society of Automotive Engineers for an ignition system that does not use a distributor.

Ignition Coils

The heart of any ignition system is the **ignition coil.** The coil creates a high-voltage spark by electromagnetic induction. Many ignition coils contain two separate but electrically connected windings of copper wire. Other coils are true transformers in which the primary and secondary windings are not electrically connected. See Figure 5–1.

The center of an ignition coil contains a core of laminated soft iron (thin strips of soft iron). This core increases the magnetic strength of the coil. Surrounding the laminated core are approximately 20,000 turns of fine wire (approximately 42 gauge). These windings are called the **secondary coil windings.** Surrounding the secondary windings are approximately 150 turns of heavy wire (approximately 21 gauge). These windings are called the **primary coil windings.** In many coils,

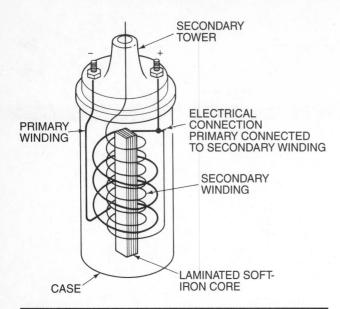

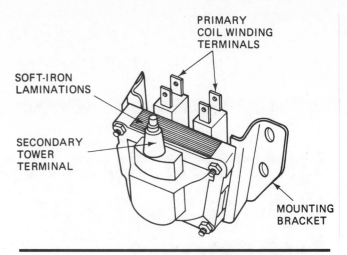

Figure 5–2 Typical air-cooled epoxy-filled E coil.

Figure 5–1 Internal construction of an oil-cooled ignition coil. Notice that the primary winding is electrically connected to the secondary winding. The polarity (positive or negative) of a coil is determined by the direction in which the coil is wound.

these windings are surrounded with a thin metal shield and insulating paper and placed in a metal container. Many coils contain oil to help cool the ignition coil. Other coil designs, such as those used on GM's **high-energy ignition (HEI)** systems, use an air-cooled, epoxy-sealed **E coil,** named for the *E* shape of the metal laminations inside the coil. See Figures 5–2 and 5–3.

How Ignition Coils Create 40,000 Volts

Current for the primary winding is supplied through the ignition switch to the positive terminal of the ignition coil. The negative terminal is connected to the ground return through an electronic ignition module (igniter).

If the primary circuit is completed, then current (approximately 3 to 8 amperes) can flow through the primary coil windings. This flow creates a strong magnetic field inside the coil. When the primary coil winding ground-return path connection is opened, the magnetic field collapses and induces a high-voltage (20,000 to 40,000 volts), low amperage (20 to 80 milliamperes) current in the secondary coil windings. This high-voltage pulse flows through the coil wire (if the vehicle is so equipped), distributor cap, rotor, and spark plug wires to the spark plugs. For each spark that occurs, the coil must be charged with a magnetic field and then discharged. The ignition components that regulate the current in the coil primary winding by turning it on and off are known collectively as the **primary ignition circuit.** The components necessary to create and distrib-

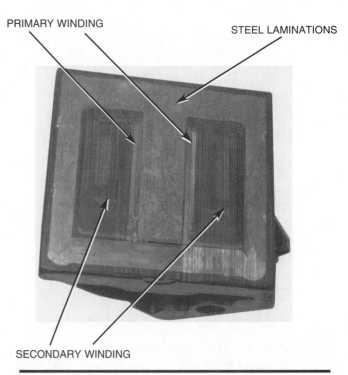

Figure 5–3 Cutaway of a General Motors Type II distributorless ignition coil. Note that the primary windings are inside of the secondary windings.

ute the high voltage produced in the secondary windings of the coil are called the **secondary ignition circuit.** See Figures 5–4 and 5–5.

■ PRIMARY CIRCUIT OPERATION

To get a spark out of an ignition coil, the primary coil circuit must be turned on and off. This primary circuit

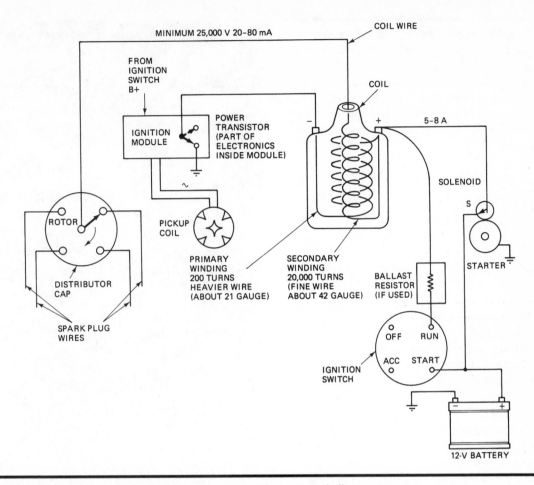

Figure 5–4 Typical primary and secondary electronic ignition using a ballast resistor and a distributor. To protect the ignition coil from overheating at lower engine speeds, many electronic ignitions do not use a ballast resistor, but rather electronic circuits within the module.

current is controlled by a **transistor** (electronic switch) inside the **ignition module (igniter)** that in turn is controlled by one of several devices, including:

- **Pickup coil (pulse generator).** Located inside the distributor, the pickup coil generates a varying voltage signal that triggers the transistor inside the module. See Figures 5–6 and 5–7 on pages 84 and 85. The pickup coil signal is also used by the computer for piston position information and engine speed (RPM).
- **Hall effect switch.** Located inside the distributor or near the crankshaft, most Hall effect sensors or switches take reference voltage to ground when triggered, producing a square wave. This sensor triggers the ignition module and computer as to piston position and engine speed (RPM). See Figures 5–8 and 5–9 on page 85.
- **Magnetic crankshaft position sensors.** These sensors use the changing strength of the magnetic field surrounding a coil of wire to signal the module and computer. This signal is used by the electronics

in the module and computer as to piston position and engine speed (RPM). See Figure 5–10 on page 86.
- **Optical sensors.** These sensors use light from a **light-emitting diode (LED)** and a **phototransistor** to signal the computer. An interrupter disc between the LED and the phototransistor has slits that allow the light from the LED to trigger the phototransistor on the other side of the disc. Most optical sensors (usually located inside the distributor) use two rows of slits to provide individual cylinder recognition (low resolution) and precise distributor angle recognition (high resolution) signals. See Figure 5–11 on page 87.

■ DIRECT-FIRE IGNITION SYSTEMS

Direct-fire ignition occurs without the use of a distributor—also called **distributorless ignition system (DIS)** or simply **EI.** Each end of the secondary winding

Figure 5–5 A typical General Motors HEI coil installed in the distributor cap. When the coil and/or distributor cap are replaced, always check that the ground clip is transferred from the old distributor cap to the new. Without proper grounding, coil damage is likely. There are two designs of HEI coils. One uses red and white wire as shown and the other design, which has reversed polarity, uses red and yellow wire for the coil primary.

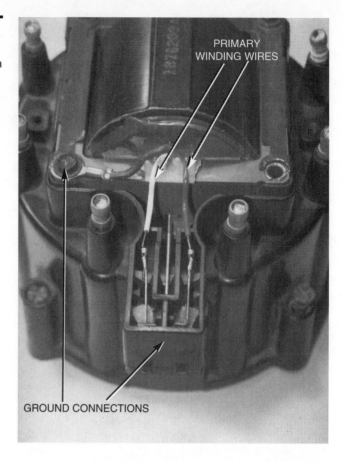

PRIMARY WINDING WIRES

GROUND CONNECTIONS

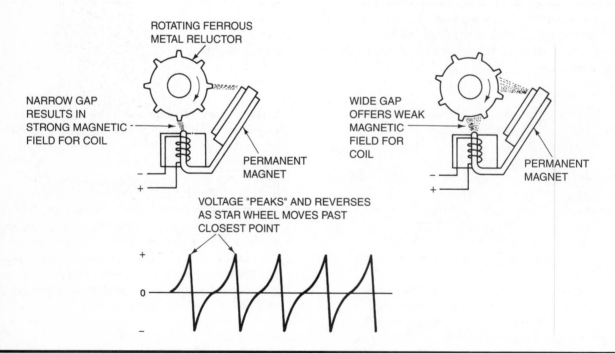

ROTATING FERROUS METAL RELUCTOR

NARROW GAP RESULTS IN STRONG MAGNETIC FIELD FOR COIL

PERMANENT MAGNET

WIDE GAP OFFERS WEAK MAGNETIC FIELD FOR COIL

PERMANENT MAGNET

VOLTAGE "PEAKS" AND REVERSES AS STAR WHEEL MOVES PAST CLOSEST POINT

Figure 5–6 Operation of a typical pulse generator (pickup coil). At the bottom is a line drawing of a typical scope pattern of the output voltage of a pickup coil. The module receives this voltage from the pickup coil and opens the ground circuit to the ignition coil when the voltage starts down from its peak (just as the reluctor teeth start moving away from the pickup coil).

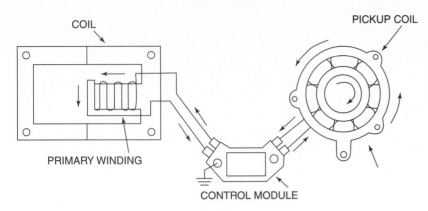

COIL

PRIMARY WINDING

PICKUP COIL

CONTROL MODULE

Figure 5–7 The varying voltage signal from the pickup coil triggers the ignition module. The ignition module grounds and ungrounds the primary winding of the ignition coil creating a high-voltage spark.

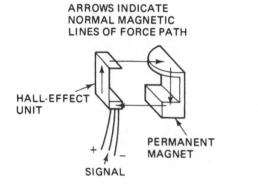

ARROWS INDICATE NORMAL MAGNETIC LINES OF FORCE PATH

HALL-EFFECT UNIT

PERMANENT MAGNET

+   –

SIGNAL

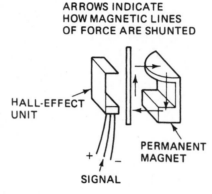

ARROWS INDICATE HOW MAGNETIC LINES OF FORCE ARE SHUNTED

HALL-EFFECT UNIT

PERMANENT MAGNET

+   –

SIGNAL

Figure 5–8 Hall effect switches use metallic shutters to shunt magnetic lines of force away from a silicon chip and related circuits. All Hall effect switches produce a square wave output for every accurate triggering.

TECH TIP ✔

Optical Distributors Do Not Like Light

Optical distributors use the light emitted from LEDs to trigger phototransistors. Most optical distributors use a shield between the distributor rotor and the optical interrupter ring. Sparks jump the gap from the rotor tip to the distributor cap inserts. The shield blocks the light of the electrical arc from interfering with the detection of the light from the LEDs.

If this shield is not replaced during service, the light signals are reduced and the engine may not operate correctly. This can be difficult to detect because nothing looks wrong during a visual inspection. Just remember that all optical distributors must be shielded between the rotor and the interrupter ring.

Figure 5–9 Shutter blade of a rotor as it passes between the sensing silicon chip and the permanent magnet.

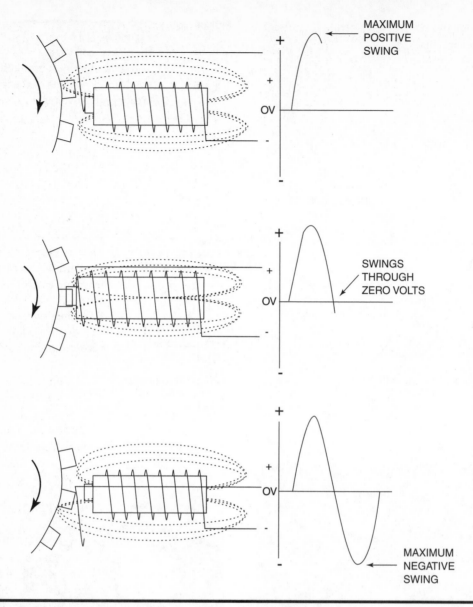

Figure 5–10 A magnetic sensor uses a permanent magnet surrounded by a coil of wire. The notches of the crankshaft (or camshaft) create a variable magnetic field strength around the coil. When a metallic section is close to the sensor, the magnetic field is stronger because metal is a better conductor of magnetic lines of force than air.

is connected to a cylinder exactly opposite the other in the firing order. See Figure 5–12 on page 88. This means that *both* spark plugs fire at the same time! When one cylinder (for example, 6) is on the compression stroke, the other cylinder (3) is on the exhaust stroke. The spark that occurs on the exhaust stroke is called the **waste spark,** because it does no useful work and is only used as a ground path for the secondary winding of the ignition coil. The voltage required to jump the spark plug gap on cylinder 3 (the exhaust stroke) is only 2 to 3 kilovolts and provides the *ground circuit* for the secondary coil circuit. The remaining coil energy is used by the cylinder on the compression stroke. One spark plug of each pair fires straight polarity and the other cylinder fires reverse polarity. Spark plug life is not greatly affected by the

NOTE: With a distributor-type ignition system, the coil has two air gaps to fire: one between the rotor tip and the distributor insert (not under compression forces) and the other in the gap at the firing tip of the spark plug (under compression forces). A DIS system also fires two gaps: one under compression (compression stroke plug) and one not under compression (exhaust stroke plug).

(a)

(b)

Figure 5–11 (a) An optical distributor on a Nissan 3.0 liter V-6 shown with the light shield removed. (b) A light shield being installed before the rotor is attached.

reverse polarity. If there is only one defective spark plug wire or spark plug, two cylinders may be affected.

Direct-fire ignitions require a sensor (usually a crankshaft sensor) to trigger the coils at the correct time. See Figure 5–13. The crankshaft sensor cannot be moved to adjust ignition timing, because it is nonadjustable.

■ COIL-ON-PLUG IGNITION

Coil-on-plug ignition uses one ignition coil for each spark plug. This system is also called **coil-by-plug** or **coil-near-plug ignition.** See Figure 5–14 on page 89. The coil-on-plug system eliminates the spark plug wires, which are often sources of **electromagnetic interference (EMI)** that can cause problems with some computer signals. The vehicle computer pulses the ground terminal of each coil at the proper time.

TECH TIP

The Tachometer Trick

When diagnosing a no-start or intermediate missing condition, check the operation of the tachometer. If the tachometer does not indicate engine speed (no-start condition) or drops toward zero (engine missing), then the problem is due to a defect in the *primary* ignition circuit. The tachometer gets its signal from the pulsing of the primary winding of the ignition coil. Components included in the primary circuit that could cause the tachometer to not work when the engine is cranking include:

- Pickup coil
- Crankshaft position sensor
- Ignition module (igniter)
- Coil primary wiring

If the vehicle is not equipped with a tachometer, connect a handheld tachometer to the negative terminal of the coil. Just remember,

No tachometer reading = Problem is in the primary ignition circuit

Tachometer reads OK = Problem is in the secondary ignition circuit or is a fuel-related problem

---

■ CHECKING FOR SPARK

In the event of a no-start condition, the first step should be to check for secondary voltage out of the ignition coil or to the spark plugs. If the engine is equipped with a separate ignition coil, then remove the coil wire from the center of the distributor cap, install a **spark tester,** and crank the engine. See the Tech Tip, "Always Use a Spark Tester." A good coil and ignition system should produce a blue spark at the spark tester. See Figure 5–15 on page 89.

If the ignition system being tested does not have a separate ignition coil, disconnect any spark plug wire from a spark plug and, while cranking the engine, test for spark available at the spark plug wire, again using a spark tester.

NOTE: An intermittent spark should be considered a no-spark condition.

CAUTION: Most distributorless (direct-fire) ignition (EI) systems can produce 40,000 volts or more with energy levels high enough to cause personal injury. Do not open the circuit of an electronic ignition secondary wire, because damage to the system (or to you) can occur.

Figure 5–12 A waste spark system fires one cylinder while its piston is on the compression stroke and into paired or companion cylinders while it is on the exhaust stroke. In a typical engine, it requires only about 2 to 3 kilovolts to fire the cylinder on the exhaust strokes. The remaining coil energy is available to fire the spark plug under compression (typically about 8 to 12 kilovolts).

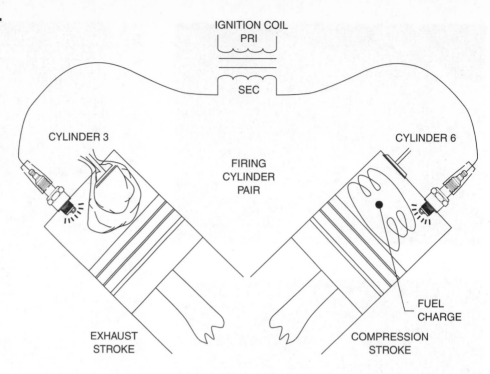

Figure 5–13 Typical Ford EDIS four-cylinder ignition system. The crankshaft sensor, called a variable-reluctance sensor (VRS), sends crankshaft position and speed information to the EDIS module. A modified signal is sent to the computer as a profile ignition pickup (PIP) signal. The PIP is used by the computer to calculate ignition timing, and the computer sends a signal back to the EDIS module as to when to fire the spark plug. This return signal is called the spark angle word (SAW) signal.

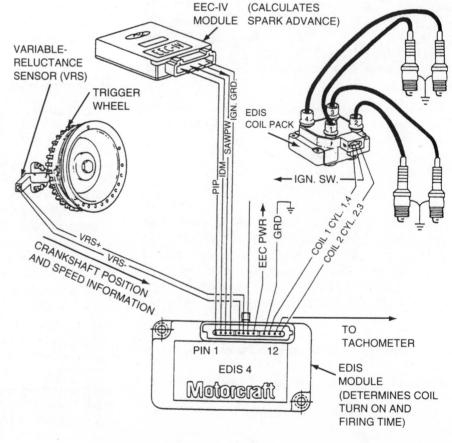

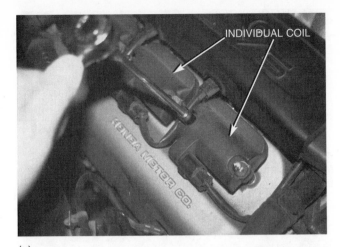

(a)

(b)

Figure 5–14 A coil-on-plug ignition system.

Figure 5–15 Using a spark tester on an engine with direct-fire (distributorless) ignition. The spark tester is grounded to the rocker cover stud. This is the recommended type of spark tester, with the center electrode recessed into the center insulator.

TECH TIP

Always Use a Spark Tester

A spark tester looks like a spark plug without a side electrode, with a gap between the center electrode and the grounded shell. The tester commonly has an alligator clip attached to the shell so that it can be clamped onto a good ground connection on the engine. A good ignition system should be able to cause a spark to jump this wide gap at atmospheric pressure. Without a spark tester, a technician might assume that the ignition system is okay because it can spark across a normal, grounded spark plug. The voltage required to fire a standard spark plug when it is out of the engine and not under pressure is about 3000 volts or less. An electronic ignition spark tester requires a minimum of 25,000 volts to jump the 3/4-inch gap. Therefore, never assume that the ignition system is okay because it fires a spark plug—always use a spark tester. *Remember that an intermittent spark across a spark tester should be interpreted as a no-spark condition.*

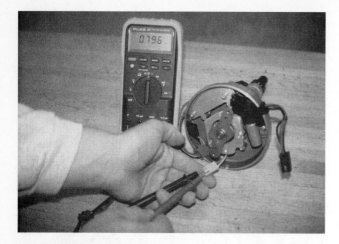

Figure 5–16 Measuring the resistance of an HEI pickup coil using a digital multimeter set to the ohms position. The reading on the face of the meter is 0.796 KΩ or 796 ohms right in the middle of the 500 to 1500-ohm specifications.

■ PICKUP COIL TESTING

The pickup coil, located under the distributor cap on many distributor ignition (DI) engines, can cause a no-spark condition if defective. The pickup coil must generate an AC voltage pulse signal to the ignition module so that the module can trigger the ignition coil.

A pickup coil contains a coil of wire, and the resistance of this coil should be within the range specified by the manufacturer. See Figure 5–16. Some common specifications include the following:

Manufacturer	Pickup coil resistance
General Motors	500 to 1500 ohms (white and green leads)
Ford	400 to 1000 ohms (orange and purple leads)
Chrysler	150 to 900 ohms (orange and black leads)

If the pickup coil resistance is not within the specified range, replace the pickup coil assembly.

The pickup coil can also be tested for proper voltage output. During cranking, most pickup coils should produce a minimum of 0.25 volt AC. This can be tested with the distributor out of the vehicle by rotating the distributor drive gear by hand.

■ DISTRIBUTOR CAP AND ROTOR INSPECTION

Inspect a distributor cap for a worn or cracked center carbon insert, excessive side insert wear, or corrosion, cracks, or carbon tracks; and check the towers for burn-

TECH TIP

Bad Plug Wire: Replace the Coil

When performing engine testing (such as a compression test), always ground the coil wire. Never allow the coil to discharge without a path to ground for the spark. High-energy electronic ignition systems can produce 40,000 volts or more of electrical pressure. If the spark cannot spark to ground, the coil energy can (and usually does) arc inside the coil itself, creating a low-resistance path to the primary windings or the steel laminations of the coil. See Figure 5–17. This low-resistance path is called a **track** and could cause an engine to miss under load even though all remaining component parts of the ignition system are functioning correctly. Often these tracks do not show up on any coil test, including most scopes. Because the track is a lower-resistance path to ground than normal, it requires that the ignition system be put under a load for it to be detected, and even then the problem (engine missing) may be intermittent.

Therefore, when disabling an ignition system, use one of the following procedures to prevent possible ignition coil damage:

1. Remove the power source wire from the ignition system to prevent any ignition operation.
2. On distributor-equipped engines, remove the secondary coil wire from the center of the distributor cap and connect a jumper wire between the disconnected coil wire and a good engine ground. (This ensures that the secondary coil energy will be safely grounded and prevents high-voltage coil damage.)

ing or corrosion by removing spark plug wires from the distributor cap one at a time. Remember, a defective distributor cap affects starting and engine performance, especially in high-moisture conditions. If a carbon track is detected, it is most likely the result of a high-resistance or open spark plug wire. Replacement of a distributor cap because of a carbon track without checking and replacing the defective spark plug wire(s) will often result in the new distributor cap failing in a short time.
See Figures 5–18 through 5–21.

TECH TIP

Look Before You Pry

Some distributor rotors are secured to the distributor shaft with a retaining screw, as shown in Figure 5–22. Serious damage can occur if excessive force is used to remove the rotor.

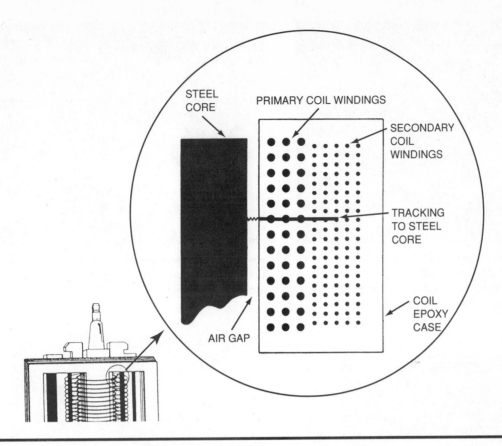

Figure 5–17 A track inside an ignition coil is not a short, but rather a low-resistance path or hole that has been burned through from the secondary wiring to the steel core.

Figure 5–18 Note where the high-voltage spark jumped through the plastic rotor to arc into the distributor shaft. Always check for a defective spark plug(s) whenever a defective distributor cap or rotor is discovered. If a spark cannot jump to a spark plug, then it tries to find a ground path wherever it can.

Figure 5–19 This distributor cap came off a GM V-8 engine that was starting and running okay. The only problem seemed to be a "snapping" noise heard in the distributor.

Figure 5–20 This rotor had arced through to the distributor shaft. The engine would not run above an idle speed and the spark from the coil could easily fire a spark tester.

Figure 5–21 Carbon track in a distributor cap. These faults are sometimes difficult to spot and can cause intermittent engine missing. The usual cause of a tracked distributor cap (or coil, if it is a distributorless ignition) is a defective (open) spark plug wire.

■ SPARK PLUG WIRE INSPECTION

Spark plug wires should be visually inspected for cuts or defective insulation and checked for resistance with an ohmmeter. Good spark plug wires should measure less than 10,000 ohms per foot of length. See Figures 5–23

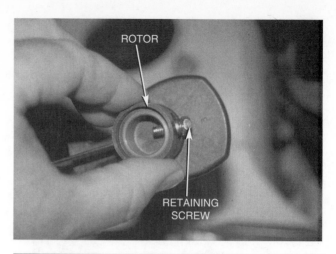

Figure 5–22 Some rotors are retained by a screw, so look before you pry.

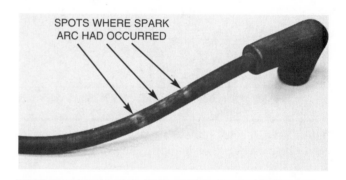

Figure 5–23 Careful visual inspection discovered this defective spark plug wire.

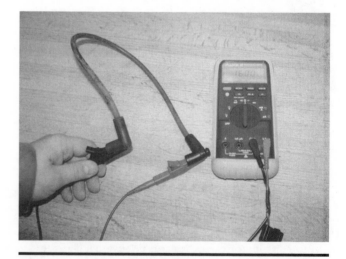

Figure 5–24 Measuring the resistance of a spark plug wire with a multimeter set to the ohms position. The reading of 16.03 KΩ (16,030 ohms) is okay because the wire is about 2 feet long. Maximum allowable resistance for a spark plug wire this long would be 20 KΩ (20,000 ohms).

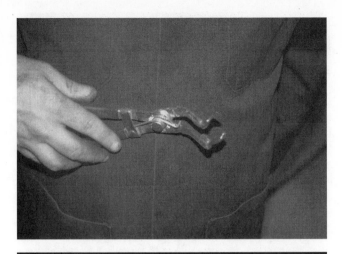

Figure 5–25 Spark plug wire boot pliers are a handy addition to any toolbox.

Figure 5–26 The firing order is usually cast or stamped on engines equipped with distributor ignition.

T E C H   T I P

Spark Plug Wire Pliers Are a Good Investment

Spark plug wires are often difficult to remove. Using good-quality spark plug wire pliers, such as shown in Figure 5–25, saves time and reduces the chance of doing harm to the wire during removal.

---

and 5–24. Faulty spark plug wire insulation can cause hard starting or no starting in damp weather conditions.

■ FIRING ORDER

Firing order refers to the order that the spark is distributed to the correct spark plug at the right time. The firing order of an engine is determined by crankshaft and camshaft design. The firing order is determined by the location of the spark plug wires in the distributor cap of an engine equipped with a distributor. The firing order is often cast into the intake manifold for easy references as shown in Figure 5–26. Most service manuals

CAUTION: Ford V-8s use two different firing orders depending on whether the engine is high output (HO) or standard. Using the incorrect firing order can cause the engine to backfire and could cause engine damage or personal injury. General Motors V-6s use different firing orders and different locations for #1 cylinder between the 60° V-6 and the 90° V-6. Using the incorrect firing order or cylinder number location chart could result in very poor engine operation if in fact it will start at all.

Figure 5–27 Many original-equipment spark plug wires are labeled as to the correct cylinder. Whenever replacing or reinstalling spark plug wires, be sure to place them into the specified position in the wiring loom to help prevent cross fire that can occur between two cylinders that fire next to each other in the firing order.

also show the firing order and the direction of the distributor rotor rotation as well as the location of the spark plug wires on the distributor cap. See Figure 5–27.

Firing order is also important for waste-spark-type distributorless (direct-fire) ignition systems. The spark plug wires can often be installed on the wrong coil pack which can create a no-start condition or very poor engine operation.

■ SPARK PLUG SERVICE

Spark plugs should be inspected when an engine performance problem occurs and should be replaced regularly to ensure proper ignition system performance.

Figure 5–28 A spark plug thread chaser is a low-cost tool that hopefully will not be used often, but its use is necessary to clean the threads before new spark plugs are installed.

Figure 5–29 Since 1991, General Motors engines have been equipped with slightly (1/8 in. or 3 mm) longer spark plugs. This requires that a longer spark plug socket be used to prevent the possibility of cracking a spark plug during installation. The longer socket is shown next to a normal 5/8-inch spark plug socket.

Many spark plugs have a service life of over 20,000 miles (32,000 kilometers). Platinum-tipped original-equipment spark plugs have a typical service life of 60,000 to 100,000 miles (100,000 to 160,000 kilometers). *Platinum-tipped spark plugs should not be regapped!* Using a gapping tool can break the platinum after it has been used in an engine.

Be certain that the engine is cool before removing spark plugs, especially on engines with aluminum cylinder heads. To help prevent dirt from getting into the cylinder of an engine while removing a spark plug, use compressed air or a brush to remove dirt from around the spark plug before removal. See Figures 5–28 and 5–29.

Spark Plug Inspection

Spark plugs are the windows to the inside of the combustion chamber. A thorough visual inspection of the spark plugs can often lead to the root cause of an engine performance problem. Two indications and their possible root causes include the following:

1. *Carbon fouling.* If the spark plug(s) has *dry black carbon* (soot), the usual causes include
   - Excessive idling
   - Slow-speed driving under light loads that keeps the spark plug temperatures too low to burn off the deposits
   - Over-rich air-fuel mixture
   - Weak ignition system output

2. *Oil fouling.* If the spark plug has *wet, oily* deposits with little electrode wear, oil may be getting into the combustion chamber from
   - Worn or broken piston rings
   - Defective or missing valve stem seals

NOTE: If the deposits are heavier on one side of the plug, the cause is usually due to excessive valve stem clearance or defective intake valve stem seals.

Inspect all spark plugs for wear by first checking the condition of the center electrode. As a spark plug wears, the center electrode becomes rounded. If the center electrode is rounded, higher ignition system voltage is required to fire the spark plug. See Figures 5–30 through 5–33. When installing spark plugs, always use the correct tightening torque to ensure proper heat transfer from the spark plug shell to the cylinder head. See the following table.

	Torque with Torque Wrench (in pound-foot)		Torque without Torque Wrench (in turns)	
Spark plug	Cast-iron head	Aluminum head	Cast-iron head	Aluminum head
Gasket				
14 mm	26–30	18–22	1/4	1/4
18 mm	32–38	28–34	1/4	1/4
Tapered seat				
14 mm				
	7–15	7–15	1/16 (snug)	1/16 (snug)
18 mm			1/16 (snug)	1/16 (snug)
	15–20	15–20		

TECH TIP

The Overheated Spark Plug Problem

A technician had a recurring problem with one spark plug on a customer's engine. About every three weeks the customer returned complaining of rough idle and reduced engine performance. Every time the technician discovered that the same spark plug had the center electrode burned almost completely away. After the spark plug was replaced each time, the engine ran correctly. After three times, the shop foreman advised the technician that a loose spark plug could be the cause of the problem.

The technician admitted that the spark plug was loose every time it was removed. A speck of dirt between the cylinder head and the spark plug on the tapered seat (conical seat) could also have caused the spark plug to run hot. (Most of the heat travels from the tip of a spark plug to the cylinder head.)

After making sure the spark plug was correctly tightened, the engine performed with no further problems. After returning the vehicle to the customer, the technician admitted to the shop foreman that the affected spark plug was in a difficult location to properly tighten and that the problem was due to the technician and not caused by the engine problem.

TECH TIP

Two-Finger Trick

To help prevent overtightening a spark plug when a torque wrench is not available, simply use two fingers on the ratchet handle. Even the strongest service technician cannot overtighten a spark plug by using only two fingers.

NOTE: General Motors does not recommend the use of antiseize compound on the threads of spark plugs being installed in an aluminum cylinder head. The reason is the spark plug will be tightened too much. This excessive tightening torque places the threaded portion of the spark plug too far into the combustion chamber where carbon can accumulate and result in the spark plugs being very difficult to remove. If antiseize compound is used on spark plug threads, reduce the tightening torque by 40%. Always follow the vehicle manufacturers' recommendations.

TECH TIP

Use Original-Equipment Manufacturer Spark Plugs

A technician at an independent service center replaced the spark plugs in a Pontiac with new Champion-brand spark plugs of the correct size, reach, and heat range. When the customer returned to pay his bill, he inquired as to the brand name of the replacement parts used for the tune-up. When told that Champion spark plugs were used, he stopped signing his name on the check he was writing. He said that he owned 1000 shares of General Motors stock and he owned two General Motors vehicles and he expected to have General Motors parts used in his General Motors vehicles. The service manager had the technician replace the spark plugs with AC-brand spark plugs, because this brand was used in the engine when the vehicle was new. Even though most spark plug manufacturers produce spark plugs that are correct for use in almost any engine, many customers prefer that original-brand—original-equipment manufacturer (OEM)—spark plugs be used in their engines.

Figure 5–30 Spark plug removed from an engine after a 500-mile race. Note the clipped side (ground) electrode. The electrode design and narrow (0.025 in.) gap are used to ensure that a spark occurs during extremely high engine speed operation. The color and condition of the spark plug indicate that near-perfect combustion has been occurring.

Figure 5–32 New spark plug that was fouled by a too-rich air-fuel mixture. The engine from which this spark plug came had a defective (stuck partially open) injector on this one cylinder only.

Figure 5–31 Typical worn spark plug. Notice the rounded center electrode. The deposits indicate that there may be an oil usage problem.

Figure 5–33 Typical worn spark plug showing gasoline- or oil-additive deposits.

■ IGNITION TIMING

Ignition timing is when the spark occurs in relation to piston position in the cylinder. Ignition timing should be checked and adjusted according to the manufacturer's specifications on vehicles that have adjustable ignition timing. Generally, for testing, engines must be at idle with the computer engine controls put into base timing. **Base timing** is the timing of the spark before the computer advances the timing. To be assured of the proper ignition timing, follow exactly the timing procedure indicated on the underhood emission decal.

> **NOTE:** Most older engines equipped with a vacuum advance must have the vacuum hose removed and plugged before they are checked for timing.

If the ignition timing is too far *advanced*—for example, if ignition timing is set at 12 degrees before top dead center (BTDC) instead of 8 degrees BTDC—the following symptoms may occur:

1. Engine ping or spark knock may be heard, especially while driving up a hill or during acceleration.
2. Cranking (starting) may be slow and jerky, especially when the engine is warm.
3. The engine may overheat.

If the ignition timing is too far *retarded*—for example, if ignition timing is set at 4 degrees BTDC instead of 8 degrees BTDC, the following symptoms may occur:

1. The engine may lack in power and performance.
2. The engine may require a long period of starter cranking before starting.
3. Poor fuel economy may result.
4. The engine may overheat.

Timing Light Connections

For checking or adjusting ignition timing, make the timing light connections as follows:

1. Connect the timing light battery leads to the vehicle battery: the red to the positive terminal and the black to the negative terminal.
2. Connect the timing light high-tension lead to the #1 spark plug cable. See Figure 5–34.

Determining the #1 Cylinder

The following will help in determining the #1 cylinder:

1. Four- or six-cylinder engines. On all inline four- and six-cylinder engines, the #1 cylinder is the *most forward* cylinder.

T E C H   T I P

"Turn the Key" Test

If the ignition timing is correct, a warm engine should start immediately when the ignition key is turned to the start position. If the engine cranks a long time before starting, the ignition timing may be retarded. If the engine cranks slowly, the ignition timing may be too far advanced. However, if the engine starts immediately, the ignition timing, although it may not be exactly set according to specification, is usually fairly close to specifications. When a starting problem is experienced, check the ignition timing first, before checking the fuel system or the cranking system for a possible problem. This procedure can be used to help diagnose a possible ignition timing problem quickly without tools or equipment.

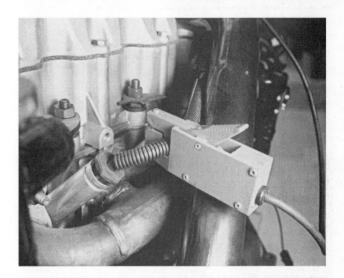

Figure 5–34 Inductive pickup for a timing light connected around cylinder #1 of a GM four-cylinder engine with a distributor. Even though the computer controls timing on most engines, the base (initial) timing can and should be checked and adjusted (if possible) as part of a thorough engine performance check.

2. V-6 or V-8 engines. Most V-type engines use the left-front (driver side) cylinder as the #1 cylinder, except for Ford engines and some Cadillacs, which use the right-front (passenger side) cylinder.
3. Sideways (transverse) engines. Most front-wheel-drive vehicles with engines installed sideways use the cylinder to the far right (passenger side) as the #1 cylinder [plug wire closest to the drive belt(s)].

Follow this rule of thumb: If the #1 cylinder is unknown for a given type of engine, it is the *most-forward* cylinder as viewed from above (except in Pontiac V-8 engines). See Figure 5–35 for typical #1 cylinder locations.

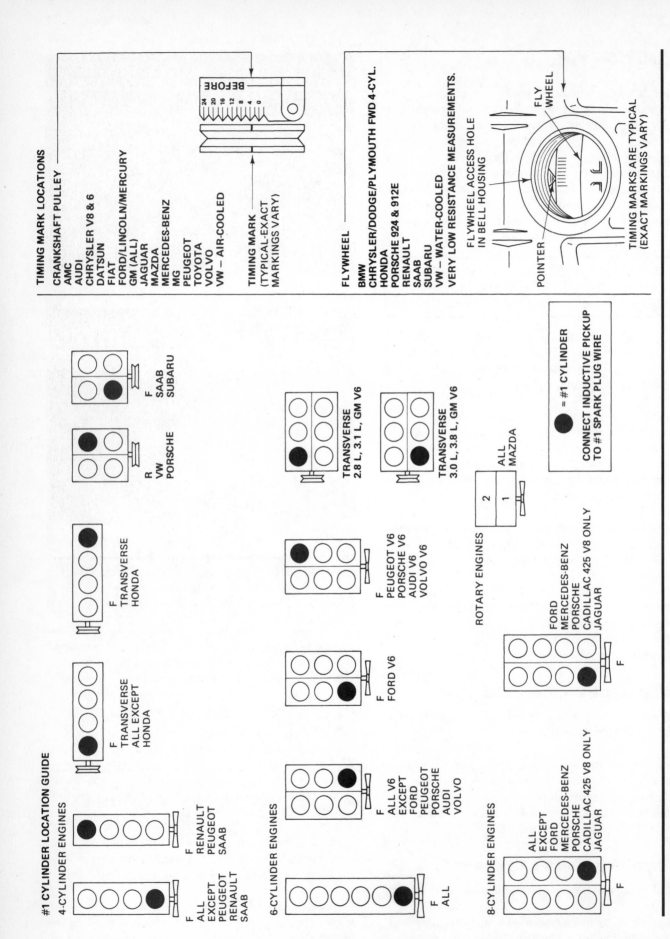

Figure 5-35 Cylinder #1 and timing mark location guide.

NOTE: Some engines are not timed off the #1 cylinder. For example, Jaguar inline 6-cylinder engines before 1988 used cylinder #6, but the cylinders were numbered from the bulkhead (firewall) forward. Therefore, #6 cylinder was the most-forward cylinder. International Harvester (Navistar) V-8s usually time off the #8 cylinder. Always check the specifications and procedures for the vehicle being tested.

HINT: If the #1 cylinder is difficult to reach, such as up against the bulkhead (firewall) or close to an exhaust manifold, simply use the opposite cylinder in the firing order (paired cylinder). The timing light will not know the difference and will indicate the correct position of the timing mark in relation to the pointer or degree mark.

Checking or Adjusting Ignition Timing

Follow these steps for checking or adjusting ignition timing:

1. Start the engine and adjust the speed to that specified for ignition timing.
2. With the timing light aimed at the stationary timing pointer, observe the position of the timing mark with the light flashing. Refer to the manufacturer's specifications on the underhood decal for the correct setting. See Figure 5–36.

NOTE: If the timing mark appears ahead of the pointer, in relation to the direction of crankshaft rotation, the timing is advanced. If the timing mark appears behind the pointer, in relation to the direction of crankshaft rotation, the timing is retarded.

3. To adjust timing, loosen the distributor locking bolt or nut and turn the distributor housing until the timing mark is in correct alignment. Turn the distributor housing in the direction of rotor rotation to retard the timing and against rotor rotation to advance the timing.
4. After adjusting the timing to specifications, carefully tighten the distributor locking bolt. It is sometimes

(a)

(b)

Figure 5–36 (a) Typical SPOUT connector as used on many Ford engines equipped with distributor ignition (DI). (b) The connector must be opened (disconnected) to check and/or adjust the ignition timing. On DIS/EDIS systems, the connector is called SPOUT/SAW (spark output/spark angle word).

necessary to readjust the timing after the initial setting, because the distributor may rotate slightly when the hold-down bolt is tightened.

NOTE: If the timing mark appears to be way off or if the engine runs poorly (worse) after correcting the timing, the outer ring of the harmonic balancer may have slipped and must be replaced.

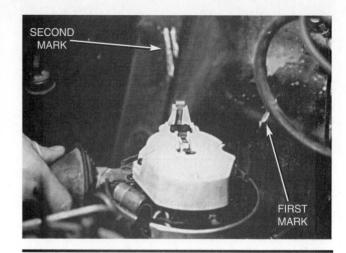

TECH TIP

Two Marks Are the Key to Success

Whenever a distributor is removed from an engine, always mark the direction the rotor is pointing to be assured that the distributor is reinstalled in the correct position. Because of the helical cut on the distributor drive gear, the rotor rotates as the distributor is being removed from the engine. To help reinstall a distributor without any problems, simply make another mark where the rotor is pointing just as the distributor is lifted out of the engine. Then to reinstall, simply line up the rotor to the second mark and lower the distributor into the engine. The rotor should then line up with the original mark as a double check. See Figure 5–37.

Figure 5–37 The first mark indicates the direction the rotor is pointing when the distributor is in the engine. The second mark indicates where the rotor is pointing just as it is pulled from the engine.

PS 8–1 The tools and supplies needed to test for a fault in the secondary ignition system include: spark plug boot removal pliers, spark tester, secondary ignition system voltage measuring tools, test light, short (2 inches long) pieces of 5/32 in. ID vacuum hose and protective gloves to avoid getting burned around the hot exhaust system.

PS 8–2 The first step in the diagnosis of the ignition system is to check for adequate voltage from the coil(s). Using a spark plug wire boot removal tool, carefully remove the spark plug wire from the spark plug.

PS 8–3 Attach a spark tester to the end of the spark plug wire and then clip the spark tester to a good engine ground. Start the engine and observe the spark tester. A spark should consistently jump the gap indicating that the system is capable of supplying at least 25,000 volts (25 kV).

PS 8–4 Engine faults as well as ignition system faults can often be detected by using a tester capable of measuring spark plug firing voltage such as this unit from Snap-On tools. Connect the ground clip to a good engine ground and clip the probe around a spark plug wire.

PS 8–5 Start the engine and rotate the thumb wheel until the red light emitting diode (LED) just flickers off and then read the firing voltage on the display. This cylinder shows about 12–13 kV with conventional firing. This reading is about normal (5 to 15 kV).

PS 8–6 This cylinder indicates a firing voltage of about 8 kV for the inverted spark on another cylinder. This cylinder is firing in the opposite polarity of the other cylinder (inverted). The firing voltage indicates a possible narrow gap or fouled spark plug.

PS 8–7 Another tester that can be used is one from OTC tools. To use this tester, connect the ground clip to a good engine ground and connect the test probe around a spark plug wire.

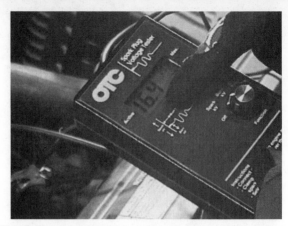

PS 8–8 Start the engine and select "spark kV." This is the voltage required to fire the spark plugs and this display indicates 16.4 kV. This is higher than normal and could be due to a high-resistance spark plug wire or a wide gap spark plug.

PS 8–9 Move the selector to read "burn kV" and the reading indicates 1.9 kV. This is the voltage necessary to keep the spark firing after it has been started. It should be less than 2 kV for most vehicles.

PS 8–10 Move the selector to "burn time" and the reading is 1.2 mS (milliseconds). This is the duration of the spark and it should be between 1 and 2 mS.

PS 8–11 Ground out a cylinder one at a time and observe if the engine speed or idle quality is affected. If one cylinder does not respond then this test can help pin-point a fault in a particular cylinder. Insert 2-inch lengths of vacuum hose between the coil tower and the spark plug wires. This test can also be performed on vehicles equipped with a distributor.

PS 8–12 Use a grounded test light and touch the section of rubber hose with the tip. The high voltage will travel though the test light to ground and not fire the spark plug. This is an easy test to perform that does not require expensive test equipment to perform and can be done quickly to help isolate a cylinder that has a fault.

PHOTO SEQUENCE   Ignition Timing

PS 9–1 The tools and equipment needed to check and adjust ignition timing include a timing light and wrenches or sockets and extension and ratchet necessary to reach and turn the distributor hold-down bolt or nut.

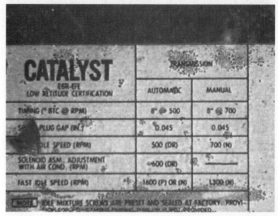

PS 9–2 Be sure to check the underhood decal or service manual for the correct ignition timing specification and procedure.

PS 9–3 Locate, clean, and mark the timing mark usually located on the harmonic balancer at the front of the engine. Use chalk, correction fluid, or paint to highlight the correct timing mark.

PS 9–4 Connect the power and ground leads of the timing light to the positive and negative terminals of the battery.

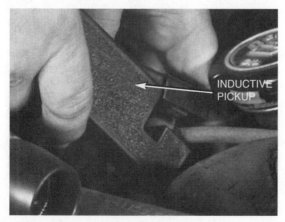

PS 9–5 Attach the inductive pickup of the timing light around the spark plug wire for #1 cylinder.

PS 9–6 The specified procedure for checking ignition timing on this 5.0 L, Ford V-8 is to locate and disconnect the spark output (SPOUT) connector. The connector is located near the distributor.

PS 9–7 Disconnect the end of the SPOUT connector. This connector opens the circuit between the distributor and the vehicle computer and puts the timing on base timing.

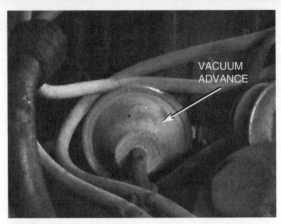

PS 9–8 On engines equipped with a vacuum advance mechanism, most timing procedures specify that the vacuum line to the distributor should be removed and plugged.

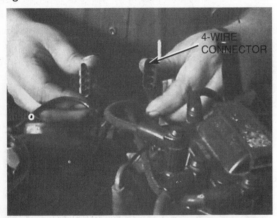

PS 9–9 The four-way electrical connector near the distributor should be disconnected on most GM vehicles equipped with a carburetor and a computer such as this mid-1980s Chevrolet V-8. Some GM engines are timed by first connecting terminals A and B at the data link connector (DLC). Always check for the correct procedure for the vehicle you are checking.

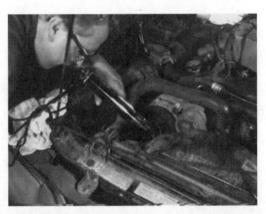

PS 9–10 Start the engine and point the timing light toward the timing marks. Be careful to avoid moving fan blades and pulleys.

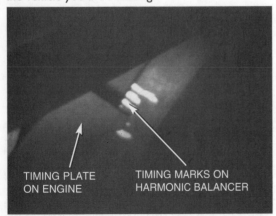

PS 9–11 A view of timing marks as shown when bright light (strobe light) flashes in timing with the firing of cylinder #1.

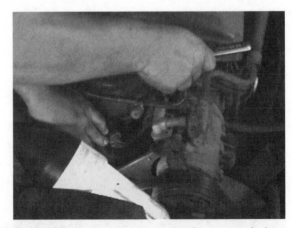

PS 9–12 If the timing is not correct (timing mark does not align with the specified mark), then use a wrench or socket and ratchet and extension to loosen the distributor hold-down bolt or nut. Special curved distributor wrenches are also available that help get to hard-to-reach distributor hold-down bolts.

PS 9–13 Do not remove the distributor hold-down bolt (nut), just loosen it enough so that the distributor can be turned.

PS 9–14 Here is the tricky part. While watching the timing mark, gently rotate the distributor until the correct timing is achieved. The distributor should be loose enough to allow it to be rotated yet not so loose that it will not stay where it is turned.

PS 9–15 After the timing has been set to the correct mark, gradually tighten the distributor hold-down bolt (nut). After tightening the distributor hold-down, double check that the timing is still correct because the timing could have changed as the distributor hold-down was tightened.

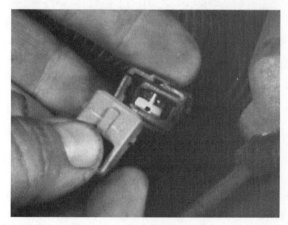

PS 9–16 Reconnect the SPOUT connector.

PS 9–17 Disconnect the timing light from #1 cylinder spark plug wire and the battery.

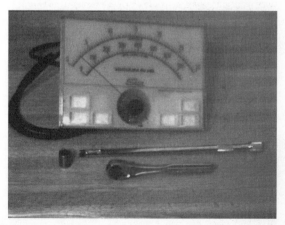

PS 9–18 A vacuum gauge can also be used to set the "approximate" timing. Sometimes, the harmonic balancer could be defective and the mark is no longer in the correct position on the timing mark or the engine timing plate could be missing.

PS 9–19 Start the vacuum timing procedure by connecting a vacuum gauge to a manifold vacuum source.

PS 9–20 Loosen the distributor hold-down bolt (nut). Do not disconnect the SPOUT or other connections. The best results using a vacuum gauge to set the timing are achieved by allowing the computer to control the timing.

PS 9–21 Start the engine and allow to run until the engine reaches normal operating temperature. Slowly rotate the distributor (advance) until the highest vacuum is observed on the vacuum gauge (19.5 in. Hg).

PS 9–22 After the highest vacuum reading is observed, rotate the distributor in the opposite direction (retard) until the vacuum gauge reads 2 in. Hg lower than the highest reading achieved in the previous step.

PS 9–23 When the vacuum gauge reads 2 in. Hg lower than the highest reading (17.5 in. Hg), tighten the distributor hold-down bolt (nut). While this method of setting timing is not accurate enough to assure lowest exhaust emissions, it is close enough to allow the engine to be run in an emergency without doing any harm to the engine.

PS 9–24 After completing the ignition timing sequence, double check that the distributor hold-down bolt is tight and reconnect all vacuum hoses and connectors that were disconnected during the procedure.

■ SUMMARY

1. All inductive ignition systems supply battery voltage to the positive side of the ignition coil and pulse the negative side of the coil on and off to ground to create a high-voltage spark.

2. If an ignition system uses a distributor, it is called a DI system, meaning distributor ignition.

3. If an ignition system does not use a distributor, it is called simply an EI system, meaning electronic ignition.

4. Always use a spark tester that requires at least 25 kilovolts (kV) to fire when checking for spark.

5. Ignition coils usually test at about 1 ohm across the primary winding and from 6000 to 30,000 ohms across the secondary winding.

6. A typical magnetic pickup coil should measure approximately in the middle of its specification for resistance and be able to produce an AC voltage of at *least* 0.25 volt while the engine is cranking.

7. An open spark plug wire can damage the ignition coil.

8. A thorough visual inspection should be performed of all ignition components when diagnosing an engine performance problem.

9. Platinum spark plugs should not be regapped after use in an engine.

■ REVIEW QUESTIONS

1. Explain how 12 volts from a battery can be changed to 40,000 volts for ignition.

2. Discuss how a magnetic sensor works.

3. Discuss how a Hall effect sensor works.

4. Explain why a spark tester should be used to check for spark rather than a standard spark plug.

5. Explain how to test a pickup coil for resistance and AC voltage output.

6. Discuss what harm can occur if the engine is cranked or run with an open (defective) spark plug wire.

■ ASE CERTIFICATION-TYPE QUESTIONS

1. The primary (low-voltage) ignition system must be working correctly before any spark occurs from a coil. Which component is *not* in the primary ignition circuit?
   a. Spark plug wiring
   b. Ignition module (igniter)
   c. Pickup coil (pulse generator)
   d. Ignition switch

2. The ignition module has direct control over the firing of the coil(s) of an electronic ignition system. Which component(s) triggers (controls) the module?
   a. Pickup coil
   b. Computer
   c. Crankshaft sensor
   d. All of the above

3. Distributorless (direct-fire) ignition systems can be triggered by a _____ .
   a. Hall effect sensor
   b. Magnetic sensor
   c. Spark sensor
   d. Either a or b

4. Engine damaging spark knock (detonation) can be caused if the ignition timing is:
   a. Advanced
   b. Retarded

5. Technician A says that a pickup coil (pulse generator) can be tested with an ohmmeter. Technician B says that ignition coils can be tested with an ohmmeter. Which technician is correct?
   a. Technician A only
   b. Technician B only
   c. Both Technician A and B
   d. Neither Technician A nor B

6. Typical primary coil resistance specifications usually range from _____ .
   a. 100 to 450 ohms
   b. 500 to 1500 ohms
   c. 1 to 3 ohms
   d. 6000 to 30,000 ohms

7. Typical secondary coil resistance specifications usually range from _____ .
   a. 100 to 450 ohms
   b. 500 to 1500 ohms
   c. 1 to 3 ohms
   d. 6000 to 30,000 ohms

8. Technician A says that an engine will not start and run without a pulse signal to the ignition module (igniter). Technician B says that one wire of any pickup coil must be grounded. Which technician is correct?
   a. Technician A only
   b. Technician B only
   c. Both Technician A and B
   d. Neither Technician A nor B

9. A 2-foot-long spark plug wire is being tested using an ohmmeter. The wire measures 7.86 KΩ (7.860 ohms). Technician A says the wire is okay. Technician B says that the wire should also be carefully inspected for cuts or tears in the insulation before being reinstalled on the engine. Which technician is correct?
   a. Technician A only
   b. Technician B only
   c. Both Technician A and B
   d. Neither Technician A nor B

10. A spark plug has dry, fluffy deposits. Technician A says that this is caused by the engine burning oil. Technician B says that the engine may be operating with a rich air-fuel mixture. Which technician is correct?
    a. Technician A only
    b. Technician B only
    c. Both Technician A and B
    d. Neither Technician A nor B

Fuel and Emission System Operation and Diagnosis

Objectives: After studying Chapter 6, the reader should be able to:

1. Discuss the properties of gasoline.
2. Describe how to select the proper grade of gasoline.
3. Explain how volatility affects driveability.
4. Describe how the PCV system operates and how to diagnose a fault with the system.
5. Describe how the evaporative emission control system works and how to test for its proper operation.
6. Discuss the purpose and function of the EGR system and how to diagnose EGR operational problems.
7. Explain how to test a catalytic converter for obstructions and operating efficiency.

The quality of the fuel any engine uses is very important to its proper operation and long life. If the fuel is not right for the air temperature or if the tendency of the fuel to evaporate is incorrect, severe driveability problems can result. An engine burns about 10,000 cubic feet of air (a box 10 feet × 10 feet × 100 feet) for every cubic foot of gasoline (about 7.5 gallons).

■ GASOLINE

Gasoline is a term used to describe a complex mixture of various hydrocarbons refined from crude petroleum oil for use as a fuel in engines. The word **petroleum** means "rock oil." The refinery where gasoline is produced removes undesirable ingredients such as paraffins and puts in additives such as octane improvers. Most gasoline is "blended" to meet the needs of the local climates and altitudes.

■ VOLATILITY

Volatility describes how easily the gasoline evaporates (forms a vapor). The definition of volatility assumes that the vapors will remain in the fuel tank or fuel line and will cause a certain pressure based on the temperature of the fuel.

Winter Blend

Reid vapor pressure (RVP) is the pressure of the vapor above the fuel when the fuel is at 100°F (38°C). Increased vapor pressure permits the engine to start in cold weather. Gasoline without air will not burn. Gasoline must be vaporized (mixed with air) to burn in an engine. Cold temperatures reduce the normal vaporization of gasoline; therefore, winter-blended gasoline is specially formulated to vaporize at lower temperatures for proper starting and driveability at low ambient temperatures. The **American Society for Testing and**

Materials (ASTM) standards for winter-blend gasoline allow volatility of up to 15 pounds per square inch RVP.

Summer Blend

At warm ambient temperatures, gasoline vaporizes easily. However, the fuel system (fuel-pump, carburetor, fuel-injector nozzles, etc.) is designed to operate with liquid gasoline. The volatility of summer-grade gasoline should be about 7.0 psi RVP. According to ASTM standards, the maximum RVP should be 10.5 psi for summer-blend gasoline.

■ VOLATILITY PROBLEMS

At higher temperatures, liquid gasoline can easily vaporize and this can cause **vapor lock.** Vapor lock is a *lean* condition caused by vaporized fuel in the fuel system. This vaporized fuel takes up space normally occupied by liquid fuel and prevents normal fuel-pump operation. Vapor lock is caused by bubbles that form in the fuel, preventing proper operation of the fuel-pump, carburetor, or fuel-injection system.

Bubbles in the fuel can be caused by heat or by sharp bends in the fuel system. Heat causes some of the fuel to evaporate, thereby causing bubbles. Sharp bends cause the fuel to be restricted at the bend. When the fuel flows past the bend, the fuel can expand to fill the space after the bend. This expansion drops the pressure, and bubbles form in the fuel lines. When the fuel is full of bubbles, the engine is not being supplied with enough fuel and the engine runs lean. A lean engine will stumble during acceleration, will run rough,

and may stall. Warm weather and alcohol-blended fuels both tend to increase vapor lock and engine performance problems.

If winter-blend gasoline (or high-RVP fuel) is used in an engine during warm weather, the following problems may occur:

- Rough idle
- Stalling
- Hesitation on acceleration
- Surging

■ NORMAL AND ABNORMAL COMBUSTION

The octane rating of gasoline is the measure of its antiknock properties. **Engine knock** (also called **detonation, spark knock,** or **ping**) is a metallic noise an engine makes, usually during acceleration, resulting from abnormal or uncontrolled combustion inside the cylinder.

Normal combustion occurs smoothly and progresses across the combustion chamber from the point of ignition. See Figure 6–1.

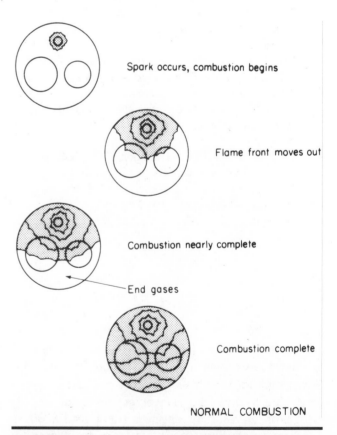

Figure 6–1 Flame front movement during normal combustion.

Normal combustion propagation is between 45 and 90 miles per hour (mph) (72 and 145 km/h). The speed of the flame front depends on air-fuel ratio, combustion chamber design (determining amount of turbulence), and temperature.

During periods of spark knock (detonation), the combustion speed increases by up to 10 times to near the speed of sound. The increased combustion speed also causes increased temperatures and pressures, which can damage pistons, gaskets, and cylinder heads. See Figures 6–2 through 6–4.

One of the first additives used in gasoline was **tetraethyl lead (TEL).** Tetraethyl lead was added to gasoline in the early 1920s to reduce the engine's tendency to knock. It was often called "ethyl" or "high test" gasoline. Tetraethyl lead is no longer available in pump gasoline.

Shortly after the introduction of tetraethyl lead as a fuel additive, the Society of Automotive Engineers established standards for the antiknock rating of gasoline.

With standardized fuel, the automobile manufacturers could produce engines that would operate knock free based on the quality of the available fuel.

The antiknock "standard" or basis of comparison was the knock-resistant hydrocarbon **isooctane,** chemically called trimethylpentane (C_8H_{18}), also known as 2-2-4 trimethylpentane. If a gasoline tested had the exact same antiknock characteristics as isooctane, it was rated as 100-octane gasoline. If the gasoline tested had only 85% of the antiknock properties of isooctane, it was rated as 85 octane. Remember, octane rating is only a comparison test.

In actual testing, a special single-cylinder engine called a **cooperative fuel research (CFR)** engine is used. A test fuel is compared in this engine with a known combination of isooctane (with an octane rating of 100) and another hydrocarbon called N-heptane (C_7H_{16}) (with an octane rating of zero). For example, if the knock resistance of a fuel is the same as that of a test fuel with a ratio of 9 parts isooctane to 1 part N-heptane, the unknown fuel has a rating of 90 octane.

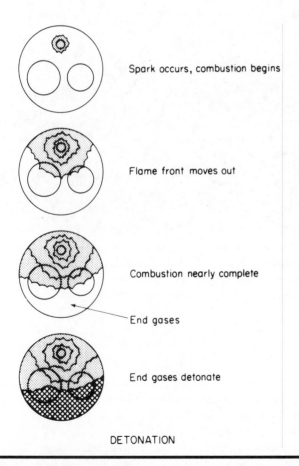

Spark occurs, combustion begins

Flame front moves out

Combustion nearly complete

End gases

End gases detonate

DETONATION

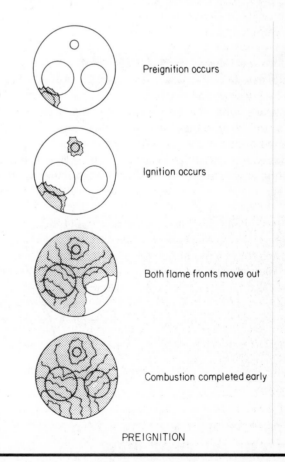

Preignition occurs

Ignition occurs

Both flame fronts move out

Combustion completed early

PREIGNITION

Figure 6–2 Flame front movement and end gas reaction during knock or detonation.

Figure 6–3 Flame front movement during preignition.

Figure 6–4 Abnormal combustion can quickly destroy an engine. Note how the higher-than-normal temperature melted the edge of the piston and softened the center. The excessive pressure created during the abnormal combustion then blew a hole in the top of this piston.

■ RESEARCH AND MOTOR METHODS OF OCTANE RATING

There are two basic methods used to rate gasoline for antiknock properties (octane rating): the research method and the motor method. Each uses a model of the special CFR single-cylinder engine. The research method and the motor method vary as to temperature of air, spark advance, and other parameters. The research method typically results in readings that are 6 to 10 "points" higher than those of the motor method. For example, a fuel with a research octane number (RON) of 93 might have a motor octane number (MON) of 85.

The octane rating posted on pumps in the United States is the average of the two methods and is referred to as (R + M)/2, meaning that, for the fuel used in the previous example, the rating posted on the pumps would be

$$\frac{RON + MON}{2} = \frac{93 + 85}{2} = 89$$

See Figures 6–5 and 6–6.

■ GASOLINE GRADES AND OCTANE NUMBER

The posted octane ratings on gasoline pumps is the rating achieved by the average of the research and the mo-

Knock Test		
Condition	Research	Motor
* Engine speed	600	900
Oil temperature	135	135
Coolant temperature	212	212
Intake humidity 9r/lb air	25–50	25–50
* Intake air temperature	125	100
* Mixture temperature	—	300
* Spark advance	13	varies with CR
Fuel/air ratio	adj for max knock	adj for max knock

Figure 6–5 Test parameters for research and motor methods. Notice that the research method results in less knock (higher octane reading) because the ignition timing is fixed, whereas the motor method varies the timing and has a higher engine speed than the speed used during the research test.

Figure 6–6 Engine and instruments used to check the octane rating of gasoline. The large meter in the center top of the console is called the knockmeter.

tor methods. Except in high-altitude areas, the grades and octane ratings are as follows:

Grades	Octane rating
Regular	87
Midgrade (also called Plus)	89
Premium	91 or higher

■ OXYGENATED FUELS

Oxygenated fuels contain oxygen in the molecule of the fuel itself. Examples of oxygenated fuels include methanol, ethanol, methyl tertiary butyl ether (MTBE), and ethyl tertiary butyl ether (ETBE). See Figure 6–7.

Oxygenated fuels are commonly used in high-altitude areas to reduce carbon monoxide (CO) emissions. The extra oxygen in the fuel itself is used to convert harmful CO into carbon dioxide CO_2. The extra oxygen in the fuel helps ensure that there is enough oxygen to convert all the CO into CO_2 during the combustion process in the engine or catalytic converter.

MTBE   Methyl tertiary butyl ether is manufactured by means of the chemical reaction of methanol and isobutylene. Unlike methanol, MTBE does not increase the volatility of the fuel, and it is not as sensitive to water as are other alcohols. The maximum allowable volume level, according to the EPA, is 15%. See Figure 6–8.

ETBE   Ethyl tertiary butyl ether is derived from ethanol. The maximum allowable volume level is 17.2%. The use of ETBE is the cause of much of the odor from the exhaust of vehicles using reformulated gasoline.

Ethanol   Ethyl alcohol is drinkable alcohol made from grain. Adding 10% ethanol (ethyl alcohol or grain alcohol) increases the (R + M)/2 octane rating by 3 points. The alcohol added to the base gasoline, however, also raises the volatility of the fuel about 1/2 psi. Most automobile manufacturers permit up to 10% ethanol if driveability problems are not experienced. The oxygen content of a 10% blend of ethanol in gasoline is 3.5% oxygen by weight. See Figure 6–9.

Methanol   Methyl alcohol is made from wood (wood alcohol), natural gas, or coal. Methanol is poisonous if consumed and tends to be more harmful to the materials in the fuel system and it tends to separate when combined with gasoline unless used with a cosolvent. A cosolvent is another substance (usually another alcohol) that is soluble in both methanol and gasoline and is used to reduce the tendency of the liquids to separate. Methanol can damage fuel system parts. Methanol is corrosive to lead (used as a coating of fuel tanks), aluminum, magnesium, and some plastics and rubber. Methanol can also cause rubber products (elastomers) to swell and soften. Methanol itself is 50% oxygen. Gasoline containing 5% methanol would have an oxygen content of 2.5% by weight.

Figure 6–8 This sign was on a fuel-pump in Pittsburgh, Pennsylvania. Not all gasoline that contains MTBE has such a sign—in fact, it is unusual to see one. MTBE is currently being phased out as an additive because of its effect on the groundwater supply in the event of an in-ground gasoline storage tank leak.

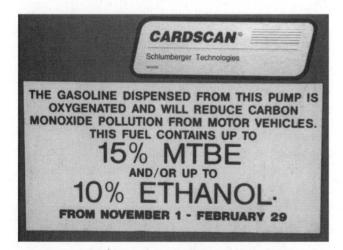

Figure 6–7 Not all fuel-pumps have a sign indicating whether the fuel is oxygenated. This sign was on a fuel-pump in Orem, Utah, elevation about 4500 feet (1400 m) and the use of oxygenated fuels in the winter months helps to reduce carbon monoxide (CO) exhaust emissions.

Figure 6–9 Note that the midgrade contains 10% ethanol, whereas the regular and the premium grade are listed as containing 100% pure gasoline.

> **CAUTION:** All alcohols can absorb water, and the alcohol-water mixture can separate from the gasoline and sink to the bottom of the fuel tank. This process is called **phase separation.** To help avoid engine performance problems, try to keep at least a quarter tank of fuel at all times, especially during seasons in which there is a wide temperature span between daytime highs and nighttime lows. These conditions can cause moisture to accumulate in the fuel tank as a result of condensation of the moisture in the air.

■ COMBUSTION CHEMISTRY

The combustion process involves the chemical combination of oxygen (O_2) from the air (about 21% of the atmosphere) with the hydrogen and carbon from the fuel. In a gasoline engine, a spark starts the combustion process, which takes about 3 milliseconds (ms) (0.003 second) to be completed inside the cylinder of an engine. The chemical reaction that takes place can be summarized as follows: hydrogen (H) plus carbon (C) plus oxygen (O_2) plus nitrogen plus spark equals heat plus water (H_2O) plus carbon monoxide (CO) plus carbon dioxide (CO_2) plus hydrocarbons (HC) plus oxides of nitrogen (NO_x) plus many other chemicals.

If the combustion process is complete, all of the gasoline (hydrocarbons) will be completely combined with all of the available oxygen. This total combination of all components of the fuel is referred to as being **stoichiometric.** The stoichiometric quantities for gasoline are 14.7 parts air for 1 part gasoline by weight. Different fuels have different stoichiometric proportions.

The heat produced by the combustion process is measured in BTUs. One BTU is the amount of heat required to raise one pound of water one Fahrenheit degree. The metric unit of heat is the calorie (cal). One calorie is the amount of heat required to raise the temperature of one gram (g) of water one Celsius degree.

Fuel	Heat energy (BTUs/gal)	Stoichiometric ratio
Gasoline	About 130,000	14.7:1
Ethanol alcohol	About 76,000	9.0:1
Methanol alcohol	About 60,000	6.4:1

■ VALVE RECESSION AND UNLEADED FUEL

Unleaded fuel has been available since the early 1970s and ever since that time there has been concern about valve problems related to using unleaded fuel. Without lead, the valve movement against the seat tears away tiny iron oxide particles during engine operation. The

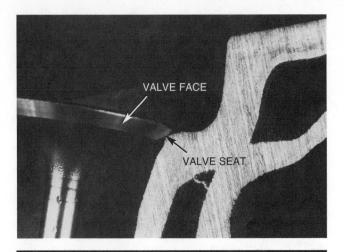

Figure 6–10 Using unleaded gasoline in an engine without hardened valve seats can cause valve seat erosion (wear). This wear may require years of driving before the valves will have to be ground and the seat restored or replaced.

valve movement causes these particles of iron oxide to act like valve grinding compound, cutting into the valve seat surface. As the valve seat is eroded, the valve recedes further into the cylinder head. See Figure 6–10.

Vehicle engines produced after 1971 for sale in the United States had to be able to operate on unleaded fuel. Most engine manufacturers started induction hardening of valve seats to help prevent valve recession. A summary of factors regarding unleaded fuel is as follows:

1. All vehicle engines built after the mid-1970s should have hardened valve seats (usually, just the exhaust seats). (Some light-duty and medium-duty truck engines may not have hardened seats if unleaded fuel was not required when the truck was manufactured.)
2. Many heavy-duty engines were manufactured using hardened valve seats *prior* to the mid-1970s.
3. Valve seat erosion is most likely to occur, or to be substantially increased, because of high engine speeds (RPM) and/or high engine loads, both of which create higher combustion chamber temperatures and pressures.
4. Generally a level of only 0.1 gram of tetraethyl lead per gallon is required to prevent valve seat recession.
5. Additives containing tetraethyl lead are generally not economically feasible because the amount of lead that can be sold cannot exceed 4.2 grams per gallon. Therefore, it would require an entire quart of additive per 10 gallons of unleaded fuel to bring the level to 0.1 gram per gallon.
6. Older-model and antique vehicles would probably not suffer valve damage from using unleaded fuel

for many years if the engines were not used for long periods at high RPM or under high loads. If and when the engine needed to be overhauled, hardened exhaust valve seats could be installed to prevent any future valve problems.

7. Engines with the highest risk of valve damage (recession) are those that are continuously operated at high engine speeds (RPM) and/or high engine loads. Typical examples of such engines would be those used in farm equipment, irrigation pumps, generators, or similar industry or mining applications. Whenever repairing or overhauling an engine used in continuous service, hardened valve seats should be installed.

■ REFORMULATED GASOLINE

To help reduce emissions, the gasoline refiners reformulate gasoline in the following manner:

1. *Reduce light compounds.* They eliminate butane, pentane, and propane, which have a low boiling point and evaporate easily. These unburned hydrocarbons (HCs) are released into the atmosphere during refueling and through the fuel tank vent system, contributing to smog formation.
2. *Reduce heavy compounds.* They eliminate heavy compounds with high boiling points such as aromatics and olefins. The purpose of this reduction is to reduce the amount of unburned HCs that goes to the catalytic converter.

■ GOVERNMENT TEST FUEL

Because of the variation of commercially available fuel, the federal government uses a standardized fuel for testing engines for emission and fuel economy. This standard fuel is **indolene** and it is used as a standard replacement for regular unleaded gasoline during these tests.

■ GENERAL GASOLINE RECOMMENDATIONS

The fuel used by an engine is a major expense in the operation cost of the vehicle. The proper operation of the engine depends on clean fuel of the proper octane rating and vapor pressure for the atmospheric conditions.

To help ensure proper engine operation and keep fuel costs to a minimum, follow these guidelines:

• Purchase fuel from a busy station. This helps ensure that the fuel is fresh and less likely to be contaminated with water or moisture.

• Keep the fuel tank above one-quarter full, especially during seasons in which the temperature rises and falls by more than 20 degrees between daytime highs and nighttime lows. This helps to reduce condensed moisture in the fuel tank and could prevent gas line freeze-up in freezing weather.

> **NOTE:** Gas line freeze-up occurs when the *water in the gasoline freezes and forms an ice blockage in the fuel line.*

• Do not purchase fuel with a higher octane rating fuel than is necessary. Try using premium high-octane fuel to check for operating differences. Most newer engines are equipped with a detonation (knock) sensor that signals the vehicle computer to retard the ignition timing when spark knock occurs. Therefore, an operating difference may not be noticeable to the driver when using a low-octane fuel, except for a decrease in power and fuel economy.
• Avoid using gasoline with alcohol in warm weather, even though many alcohol blends do not affect engine driveability. If warm-engine stumble, stalling, or rough idle occurs, change brands of gasoline.
• Do not purchase fuel from a retail outlet when a tanker truck is filling the underground tanks. During the refilling procedure, dirt, rust, and water may be stirred up in the underground tanks. This undesirable material may be pumped into your vehicle's fuel tank.
• Do not overfill the gas tank. After the nozzle "clicks off," add just enough fuel to round up to the next dime. Adding additional gasoline will cause the excess to be drawn into the charcoal canister. This can lead to engine flooding and excessive exhaust emissions. See Figure 6–11.

■ FUEL SYSTEM OPERATION

The fuel delivery system is designed to supply the carburetor(s) or fuel-injection system with clean fuel under pressure. The following are typical pressures for the carburetor-equipped engine (which usually uses a mechanical engine-driven fuel pump): 4 to 8 psi or 28 to 55 kilopascals (kPa) or 0.3 to 0.5 BAR (one BAR is equal to 14.7 psi). Fuel-pressure alone is not enough for proper engine operation. Sufficient fuel capacity (flow) should be at least 2 pints (1 liter) per minute (0.5 pint in 15 seconds).

All fuel must be filtered to prevent dirt and impurities from damaging the fuel system and/or engine. The first filter is inside the gas tank. This filter, commonly called the **fuel sock filter,** is usually not replaceable separately, since it is attached to the fuel-pump (if the pump is electric) and/or fuel gauge sending unit. A

Figure 6–11 Many gasoline service stations have signs posted warning customers to place plastic fuel containers on the ground while filling. If placed in a trunk or pickup truck bed equipped with a plastic liner, static electricity could build up during fueling and discharge from the container to the metal nozzle creating a spark and possible explosion. Some service stations have warning signs not to use cell phones while fueling to help avoid the possibility of an accidental spark creating a fire hazard.

replaceable fuel filter is usually located between the fuel tank and the inlet to the carburetor or fuel-injection system.

■ MECHANICAL FUEL-PUMP

Mechanical fuel-pumps are used on most vehicles equipped with a carburetor. Mechanical fuel-pumps are mounted on the engine itself and are operated by an eccentric or cam lobe at one-half engine (crankshaft) speed. The purpose of the pump is to draw fuel from the fuel tank and deliver the fuel to the carburetor. A typical mechanical fuel-pump consists of an actuating arm that contacts an eccentric driven by the camshaft or by a lobe on the camshaft itself. See Figure 6–12.

■ ELECTRONIC FUEL-INJECTION OPERATION

Electronic fuel-injection systems use the computer to control the operation of fuel injectors and other functions based on information sent to the computer from the various sensors. Most electronic fuel-injection systems share the following:

- **Electric fuel-pump**—usually located inside the fuel tank
- **Fuel-pump relay**—usually controlled by the computer
- **Fuel-pressure regulator**—mechanically operated, spring-loaded rubber diaphragm maintains proper fuel-pressure
- **Fuel-injector nozzle or nozzles**—located on or in the intake manifold

There are two types of electronic fuel-injection systems—a **throttle-body-injection (TBI)** type and a **port-injection** type. A TBI system delivers fuel from a nozzle(s) into the air above the throttle plate. See Figure 6–13. A port-injection design uses a nozzle for each cylinder and the fuel is squirted into the intake manifold about 2 to 3 inches (70 to 100 mm) from the intake valve. See Figure 6–14. Both types of electronic fuel injection require higher fuel-pump pressure than a carburetor does.

Testing Fuel-Pump Pressure

Most fuel-injection systems operate at either a low pressure of about 10 psi or a high pressure of between 35 and 45 psi.

	Normal Operating Pressure (psi)	Maximum Pump Pressure (psi)
Low-pressure TBI units	9–13	18–20
High-pressure TBI units	25–35	50–70
Port fuel-injection systems	35–45	70–90
Central port fuel injection (GM)	55–64	90–110

In both types of systems, maximum fuel-pump pressure is about double the normal operating pressure to ensure that a continuous flow of cool fuel is being supplied to the injector(s) to help prevent vapor from forming in the fuel system. Although vapor or foaming in a fuel system can greatly affect engine operation, the

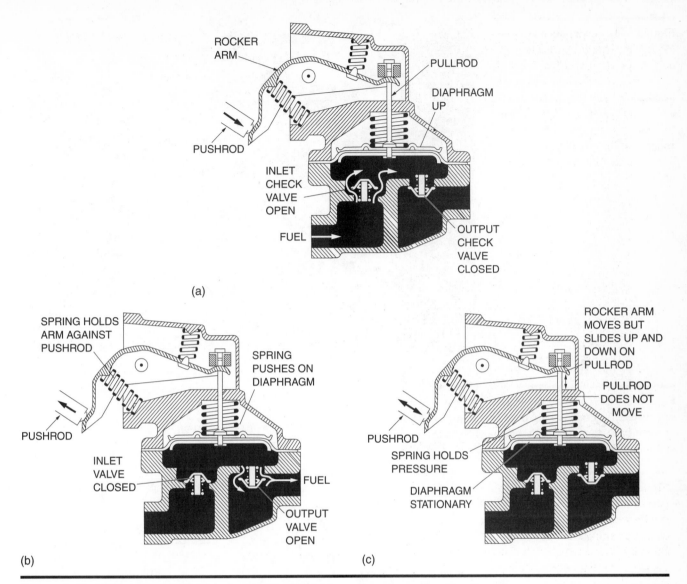

(a)

(b)

(c)

Figure 6–12 (a) Fuel is drawn through the inlet check valve into the pressure chamber of the pump as the diaphragm is moved upward. (b) When the pushrod moves inward, the pump spring pushes on the diaphragm and forces the fuel out the outlet check valve. (c) When the engine is at idle, the diaphragm remains in the upward position because the pump is capable of supplying far more fuel than the engine is able to consume at idle speed.

TECH TIP   ✔

The Ear Test

No, this is not a test of your hearing, but rather using your ear to check that the electric fuel-pump is operating. The electric fuel-pump inside the fuel tank is often difficult to hear running, especially in a noisy shop environment. A commonly used trick to better hear the pump is to use a funnel in the fuel filter neck. See Figure 6–15 on page 119.

cooling and lubricating flow of the fuel must be maintained to ensure the durability of injector nozzles.

To measure fuel-pump pressure, locate the Schrader valve (see Figure 6–16 on page 119). Attach a fuel-pressure gauge as shown in Figure 6–17 on page 119.

NOTE: Some vehicles, such as those with General Motors TBI fuel-injection systems, require a specific fuel-pressure gauge that connects to the fuel system. Always follow the manufacturers' recommendations and procedures.

Figure 6–13 Older-style General Motors throttle-body-injection unit. A special light called a *noid* (short for sole*noid*) light can be installed in the wiring connector and the engine cranked. If the light flashes, the computer is receiving an ignition (RPM) pulse and is capable of pulsing the injector nozzle.

Figure 6–14 A typical port-injection system squirts fuel into the low pressure (vacuum) of the intake manifold, about 3 inches (70 to 100 millimeters) from the intake valve.

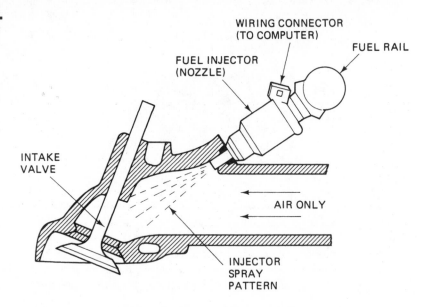

■ THROTTLE-BODY INJECTION

The throttle-body type of fuel injection uses one or two injectors (nozzles) to spray atomized fuel into a throttle body, which is similar to the base of a carburetor. The air and fuel mix in the throttle-body unit and flow as a mixture down the intake manifold to the intake valves.

Most throttle-body electronic fuel-injection units operate at a relatively low fuel-pump pressure of about 10 psi (9 to 13 psi). Some TBI units, however, operate at higher pressures of 30 to 40 psi. These are often called **high-pressure TBI** systems.

The throttle-body injection unit costs less to manufacture, because it only uses one or two injectors (noz-

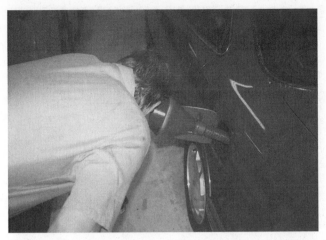

(a)

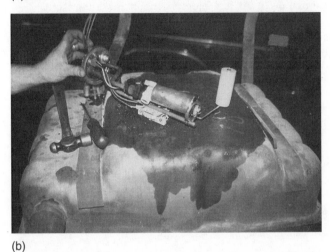

(b)

Figure 6–15 (a) Using a funnel to help hear if the electric fuel-pump inside the gas tank is working.
(b) If the pump is not running, check the wiring and current flow before going through the process of dropping the fuel tank to remove the pump.

Figure 6–16 Typical fuel-pressure test Schrader valve.

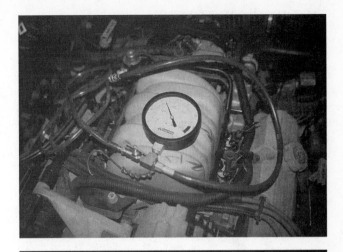

Figure 6–17 A fuel-pressure gauge connected to the fuel-pressure tap (Schrader valve) on a port-injected V-6 engine.

Figure 6–18 Typical TBI nozzle. Because fuel enters the nozzle at the bottom, this type of injector is often called a *bottom-feed* type.

zles), whereas port-injection systems require an injector for every cylinder plus the additional computer capabilities to control all the injectors. See Figures 6–18 and 6–19.

■ PORT FUEL INJECTION

Port-injection systems used on gasoline-powered engines inject a fine mist of fuel into the *intake manifold* just above the intake valve. The pressure in the intake manifold is below atmospheric pressure on a running engine, and the manifold is therefore a vacuum. Gasoline fuel injectors operate at a regulated pressure of approximately 35 to 45 psi (240 to 310 kPa).

The major advantage of using port injection instead of the simpler throttle-body injection is that the intake manifolds on port-injected engines contain only air, not a mixture of air and fuel. This allows the engine design engineer the opportunity to design long, "tuned"

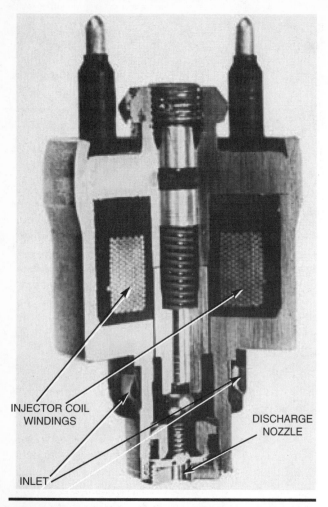

INJECTOR COIL
WINDINGS

DISCHARGE
NOZZLE

INLET

Figure 6–19 Cutaway of a typical TBI nozzle. Notice that the fuel enters the injector at the bottom.

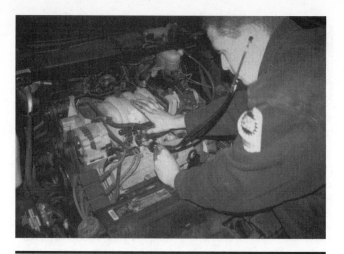

Figure 6–20 All fuel injectors should make the same sound with the engine running at idle speed. A lack of sound indicates a possible electrically open injector or a break in the wiring. A defective computer could also be the cause of a lack of clicking (pulsing) of the injectors.

T E C H T I P

Listen for the Clicks Test

A commonly used test for injector operation is to listen to the injector using a stethoscope with the engine operating at idle speed. See Figure 6–20. All injectors should produce the same clicking sound. If any injector sounds different from the others, further testing or replacement may be necessary.

---

intake-manifold runners that help the engine produce increased torque at low engine speeds. Most port fuel-injected engines use a vacuum hose connected to the fuel-pressure regulator. At idle, the pressure inside the intake manifold is low (high vacuum). Manifold vacuum is applied above the diaphragm inside the fuel-pressure regulator. This reduces the pressure exerted on the diaphragm and results in a lower (about 5 psi) fuel pressure applied to the injectors.

> **NOTE:** If gasoline drips out of the vacuum hose when removed from the fuel-pressure regulator, the regulator is defective and will require replacement.

> **NOTE:** Some vehicles do not use a vacuum-type fuel-pressure regulator. These vehicles use a regulator located inside the fuel tank that supplies a constant pressure of fuel to the fuel injectors. This type of system is called a **returnless** system, because there is no return line from the regulator back to the fuel tank.

Port Fuel-Injection System Diagnosis

To determine if a port fuel-injection system, including the fuel-pump, injectors, and fuel-pressure regulator, are operating okay, follow these steps:

1. Attach a fuel-pressure gauge to the Schrader valve on the fuel rail.
2. Turn the ignition key on or start the engine to build up the fuel-pump pressure (it should be about 35 to 45 psi).
3. Wait 20 minutes and observe the fuel-pressure retained in the fuel rail and note the psi. [The fuel-pressure should not drop more than 20 psi (140 kPa) in 20 minutes.] If the drop is less than 20 psi in 20 minutes, everything is okay. If the drop is *greater* than 20 psi in 20 minutes, there is a possible problem with:
   • The check valve in the fuel-pump
   • Leaking injectors
   • A defective (leaking) fuel-pressure regulator

TECH TIP ✔

Horsepower and Fuel Flow

To produce 1 horsepower, the engine must be supplied 1/2 pound of fuel per hour. Fuel injectors are rated in pounds per hour. For example, a V-8 engine equipped with 25 lb/hr fuel injectors could produce 50 horsepower per cylinder (per injector) or 400 horsepower. Even if the cylinder heads or block are modified to produce more horsepower, the limiting factor may be the injector flow rate.

The following are flow rates and resulting horsepower for a V-8 engine:

30 lb/hr: 60 hp per cylinder or 480 hp

35 lb/hr: 70 hp per cylinder or 560 hp

40 lb/hr: 80 hp per cylinder or 640 hp

Of course, injector flow rate is just one of many variables that affect power output. Installing larger injectors without other major engine modifications could decrease engine output and drastically increase exhaust emissions.

4. To determine which unit is defective, perform the following:
- Reenergize the electric fuel-pump.
- Clamp the fuel *supply* line, wait 10 minutes (see Caution box). If the pressure drop does not occur, replace the fuel-pump. If the pressure drop still occurs, continue with the next step.
- Repeat the pressure buildup of the electric pump and clamp the fuel return line. If the pressure drop time is now okay, replace the fuel-pressure regulator.
- If the pressure drop still occurs, one or more of the injectors is leaking. Remove the injectors with the fuel rail and hold over paper. Replace those injectors that drip one or more drops after 10 minutes with pressurized fuel.

CAUTION: Do not clamp plastic fuel lines. Connect shutoff valves to the fuel system to shut off supply and return lines. See Figure 6–21.

Testing for an Injector Pulse

One of the first checks that should be performed when diagnosing a no-start condition is whether the fuel injectors are being pulsed by the computer. Checking for proper pulsing of the injector is also important in diagnosing a weak or dead cylinder.

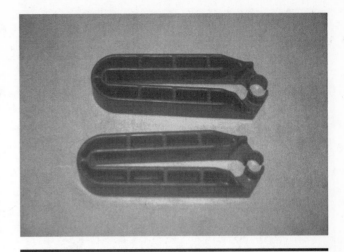

Figure 6–21 To service the fuel filter or fuel lines, a special tool may be necessary to disconnect the union of two sections of the plastic fuel line. These two sizes shown fit most General Motors applications.

A noid light is designed to electrically replace the injector in the circuit and to flash if the injector circuit is working correctly. See Figure 6–22. To use a noid light, disconnect the electrical connector at the fuel injector and plug the noid light into the injector harness connections. Crank or start the engine. The noid light should flash regularly.

NOTE: The term *noid* is simply an abbreviation of sole*noid*. Injectors use a movable iron core and are therefore a solenoid. Therefore, a noid light is a replacement for the solenoid (injector).

■ NEED FOR EMISSION CONTROLS

Air pollution has been a serious problem especially in the state of California since the 1960s. The common term used to describe air pollution is **smog,** a word that combines the two words *smo*ke and *fog*. See Figure 6–23 on page 123. Smog is formed in the atmosphere when sunlight combines with unburned fuel (hydrocarbon or HC) and oxides of nitrogen (NO_X) produced during the combustion process inside the cylinders of an engine. Smog is ground-level ozone (O_3), a strong irritant to the lungs and eyes.

NOTE: Although upper-atmospheric ozone is desirable because it blocks out harmful ultraviolet rays from the sun, ground-level ozone is considered to be unhealthy smog.

- **HC (unburned hydrocarbons).** Excessive HC emissions are controlled by the evaporative system

Diagnostic Story

The Quad Four Story

A service technician was diagnosing a rough-running condition on a General Motors Quad Four engine. The paper test indicated a cylinder miss. To help determine which cylinder was possibly causing the problem, the technician disconnected the fuel-injector connectors one at a time. When the injector was disconnected from cylinder #2, the engine did not change in the way it was running. A compression test indicated that the cylinder had good compression. The technician removed the ignition cover and used conventional spark plug wires to connect the coils to the spark plugs. The technician then connected short lengths of rubber vacuum hose to each of the sparks. The technician then touched each rubber hose with a grounded test light to ground out each cylinder. Again, cylinder #2 was found to be completely dead.

Then the technician made a mistake by assuming that the fault had to be a defective fuel injector. A replacement fuel injector did not solve the problem. Further testing of the injectors revealed that injector #3 was shorted. Because both injectors #2 and #3 share the same driver inside the computer, the injector that was shorted electrically required more current than the normal good injector. Because the computer driver circuit controls and limits current flow, the defective (shorted) injector would fire (squirt), whereas the good injector did not have enough current to work.

CAUTION: The use of fuel-injector cleaner may damage the electrical windings of the fuel injector. Gasoline flows over the copper coil windings of an injector to help keep it cool. If a strong solvent is used in the fuel, the varnish insulation on the coil may be damaged. As a result, the coil windings may short against each other, lowering the resistance of the injector.

(a)

(b)

Figure 6–22 (a) Noid lights are usually purchased as an assortment so that one is available for any type or size of injector wiring connector. (b) The connector is unplugged from the injector and a noid light is plugged into the injector connector. The noid light should flash when the engine is being cranked if the power circuit and the pulsing to ground by the computer are functioning okay.

(charcoal canister), the positive crankcase ventilation (PCV) system, the air-pump system, and the catalytic converter.
- **CO (carbon monoxide).** Excessive CO emissions are controlled by the PCV system, the air-pump system, and the catalytic converter.
- **NO_X (oxides of nitrogen).** Excessive NO_X emissions are controlled by the exhaust gas recirculation (EGR) system and the catalytic converter.

HINT: Exhaust emissions depend on the condition of the engine, ignition system, and fuel system as well as the proper operation of exhaust emission-control devices. Proper vehicle maintenance, including regular oil and oil filter, air, and fuel filter changes and other scheduled service, contributes to the ability of the engine to operate properly and produce the lowest possible emissions.

Figure 6–23 Smog is ground-level ozone that looks like either smoke or fog.

■ POSITIVE CRANKCASE VENTILATION SYSTEM

All engines remove blowby gases from the crankcase with a **positive crankcase ventilation (PCV)** system. This system pulls the crankcase vapors into the intake manifold and was first used on most vehicles in 1961 in California and nationally in 1963. The vapors are sent to the cylinders with the intake charge to be burned in the combustion chamber. Under some operating conditions, the blowby gases are forced back through the inlet filter. See Figure 6–24.

> **NOTE:** A blocked or plugged PCV system is a major cause of high oil consumption, and contributes to many oil leaks. Before expensive engine repairs are attempted, check the condition of the PCV system.

TECH TIP ✔

Check for Oil Leaks with the Engine Off

The owner of an older vehicle equipped with a V-6 engine complained to his technician that he smelled burning oil, but only *after* shutting off the engine. The technician found that the rocker cover gaskets were leaking. But why did the owner only notice the smell of hot oil when the engine was shut off? Because of the positive crankcase ventilation (PCV) system, engine vacuum tends to draw oil away from gasket surfaces. But when the engine stops, engine vacuum disappears and the oil remaining in the upper regions of the engine will tend to flow down and out through any opening. Therefore, a good technician should check an engine for oil leaks not only with the engine running but also shortly after shutdown.

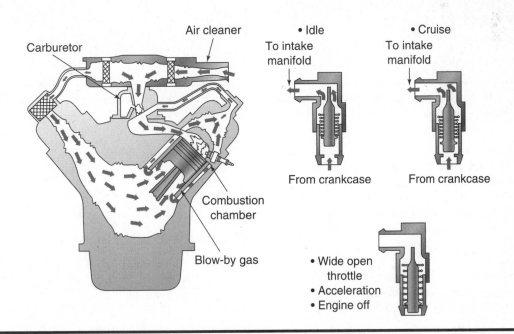

Figure 6–24 A positive crankcase ventilation (PCV) system includes a hose from the air cleaner assembly so that filtered air can be drawn into the crankcase. This filtered air is then drawn by engine vacuum through the PCV valve and into the intake manifold where the crankcase fumes are burned in the cylinder. The PCV valve controls and limits this flow of air and fumes into the engine and the valve shuts in the event of a backfire to prevent flames from entering the crankcase area. (*Courtesy of Chrysler Corporation*)

■ PCV SYSTEM PERFORMANCE CHECK

A properly operating positive crankcase ventilation system should be able to draw vapors from the crankcase and into the intake manifold. If the pipes, hoses, and PCV valve itself are not restricted, vacuum is applied to the crankcase. A slight vacuum is created in the crankcase (usually less than 1 in. Hg if measured at the dipstick) and is also applied to other areas of the engine. Oil drain back holes provide a path for oil to drain back into the oil pan. These holes also allow crankcase vacuum to be applied under the rocker covers and in the valley area of most V-type engines. There are several methods that can be used to test a PCV system.

The Rattle Test

The rattle test is performed by simply removing the PCV valve and shaking it in your hand. See Figure 6–25.

- If the PCV valve does *not* rattle, it is definitely defective and must be replaced.
- If the PCV valve *does* rattle, it does not necessarily mean that the PCV valve is good. All PCV valves contain springs that can become weaker with age and heating and cooling cycles. Replace any PCV valve with the *exact* replacement according to vehicle manufacturers' recommended intervals (usually every three years or 36,000 miles, or 60,000 km).

The 3 × 5 Card Test

Remove the oil-fill cap (where oil is added to the engine) and start the engine.

> **NOTE:** Use care on some overhead camshaft engines. With the engine running, oil may be sprayed from the open oil-fill opening.

Hold a 3 × 5 card over the opening (a dollar bill or any other piece of paper can be used for this test).

- If the PCV system, including the valve and hoses, is functioning correctly, the card should be held down on the oil-fill opening by the slight vacuum inside the crankcase.
- If the card will not stay, carefully inspect the PCV valve, hose(s), and manifold vacuum port for carbon buildup (restriction). Clean or replace as necessary.

> **NOTE:** On some four-cylinder engines, the 3 × 5 card may vibrate on the oil fill opening when the engine is running at idle speed. This is normal because of the time intervals between intake strokes on a four-cylinder engine.

Figure 6–25 A typical positive crankcase ventilation (PCV) valve. A defective or clogged PCV valve or hose can cause a rough idle or stalling problem. Because the airflow through the PCV valve accounts for about 20% of the air needed by the engine at idle, use of the incorrect valve for an application could have a severe effect on idle quality.

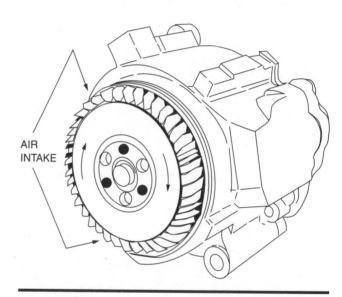

Figure 6–26 A typical belt-driven air pump. Air enters through the revolving fins. These fins act as a moving air filter because dirt is heavier than air and therefore the dirt in the air is deflected off the fins at the same time the air is drawn into the pump.

The Snap-Back Test

The proper operation of the PCV valve can be checked by placing a finger over the inlet hole in the valve when the engine is running and removing the finger rapidly. Repeat several times. The valve should "snap back." If the valve does not snap back, replace the valve.

■ AIR-PUMP SYSTEM

An air pump provides the air necessary for the oxidizing process inside the catalytic converter. See Figure 6–26.

> **NOTE:** This system is commonly called **AIR,** meaning **air-injection reaction.** Therefore, an AIR pump does pump air.

The computer controls the airflow from the pump by switching on and off various solenoid valves. When the engine is cold, the air pump output is directed to the exhaust manifold to help provide enough oxygen to convert HC (unburned gasoline) and CO (carbon monoxide) to H_2O (water) and CO_2 (carbon dioxide). When the engine becomes warm and operates in closed loop, the computer operates the air valves so as to direct the air pump output to the catalytic converter. When the vacuum rapidly increases above the normal idle level, as during rapid deceleration, the computer diverts the air pump output to the air cleaner assembly to silence the air. Diverting the air to the air cleaner prevents exhaust backfire during deceleration. See Figure 6–27. Three basic types of air pumps are the belt-driven air pump, the pulse air-driven air pump, and the electric motor-driven air pump. All air-pump systems use one-way check valves to allow air to flow into the exhaust manifold and to prevent the hot exhaust from flowing into the valves on the air pump itself.

> **NOTE:** These check valves commonly fail resulting in excessive exhaust emissions (CO especially). When the check valve fails, hot exhaust can travel up to and destroy the switching valve(s) and air pump itself.

Belt-Driven Air Pumps

The belt-driven air pump uses a centrifugal filter just behind the drive pulley. As the pump rotates, underhood air is drawn into the pump and slightly compressed. The air is then directed to

- The exhaust manifold when the engine is cold to help oxidize CO and HC into carbon dioxide (CO_2) and water vapor (H_2O)
- The catalytic converter on many models to help provide the extra oxygen needed for the efficient conversion of CO and HC into CO_2 and H_2O
- The air cleaner during deceleration or wide-open throttle (WOT) engine operation (see Figure 6–28)

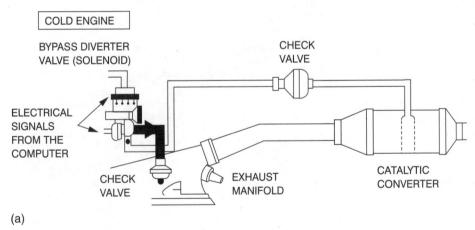

(a)

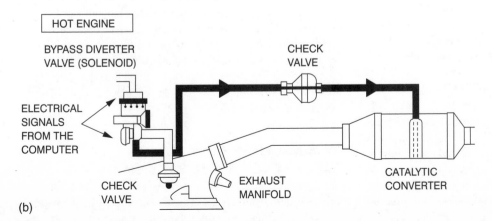

(b)

Figure 6–27 (a) When the engine is cold and before the oxygen sensor is hot enough to reach closed loop, the airflow is directed to the exhaust manifold(s) through one-way check valve(s). These valves keep exhaust gases from entering the switching solenoids and the air pump itself. (b) When the engine achieves closed loop, airflow from the pump is directed to the catalytic converter through a check valve.

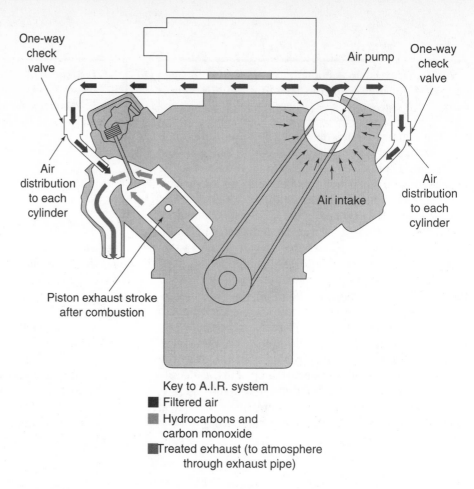

Figure 6–28 The air pump supplies air to the exhaust port of each cylinder. Unburned hydrocarbons (HCs) are oxidized into carbon dioxide (CO_2) and water (H_2O) and carbon monoxide (CO) is converted to carbon dioxide (CO_2).

One-way check valve

Air pump

One-way check valve

Air distribution to each cylinder

Air intake

Air distribution to each cylinder

Piston exhaust stroke after combustion

Key to A.I.R. system
■ Filtered air
■ Hydrocarbons and carbon monoxide
■ Treated exhaust (to atmosphere through exhaust pipe)

Electric Motor-Driven Air Pumps

An electric motor-driven air pump is usually used only during cold engine operation and is controlled by the vehicle computer.

Pulse Air-Driven Devices

The pulse air-driven air pump uses the exhaust system pulses to draw in the compressed air. See Figure 6–29.

■ EVAPORATIVE EMISSION CONTROL SYSTEM

The purpose of the **evaporative (EVAP)** emission control system is to trap and hold gasoline vapors. The charcoal canister is part of an entire system of hoses and valves called the **evaporative control system.** Before the early 1970s, most gasoline fumes were simply vented to the atmosphere.

Charcoal or carbon granules have a natural tendency to absorb gasoline fumes (vapors) because carbon attracts carbon. After being absorbed by the canister, the gasoline vapors are drawn by the engine vacuum back into the intake manifold to be burned (see Figures 6–30 and 6–31 on page 128). This process of drawing in vapors from the charcoal canister is called **purging.** How much should be purged, and when, is controlled by a vacuum valve or a computer-controlled solenoid.

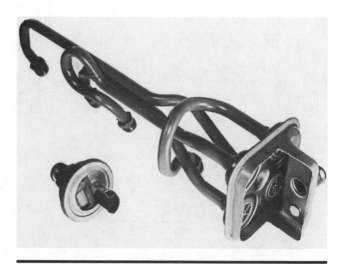

Figure 6–29 Cutaway of a pulse air-driven AIR device used on many older engines to deliver air to the exhaust port through the use of the exhaust pulses acting on a series of one-way check valves. Air from the air cleaner assembly moves through the system and into the exhaust port where the additional air helps reduce HC and CO exhaust emissions.

■ EXHAUST GAS RECIRCULATION SYSTEM

To reduce the emission of **oxides of nitrogen (NO_x)**, engines have been equipped with **exhaust gas**

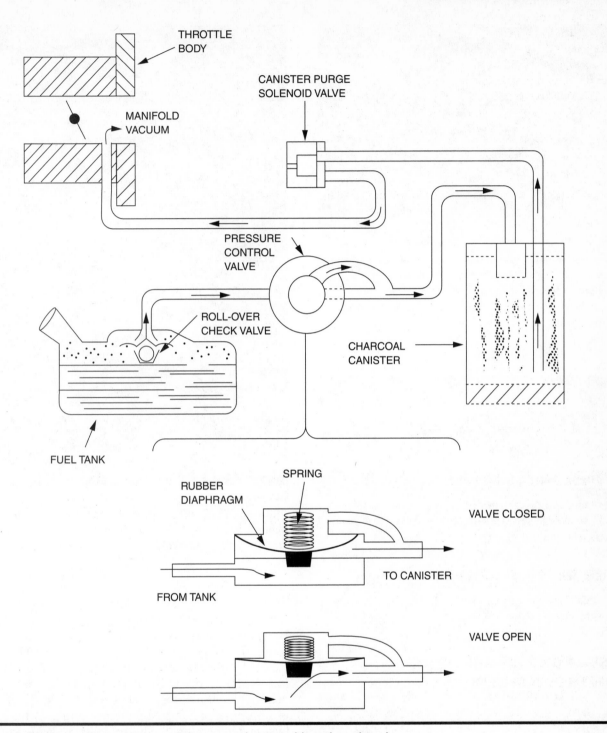

THROTTLE BODY

CANISTER PURGE SOLENOID VALVE

MANIFOLD VACUUM

PRESSURE CONTROL VALVE

ROLL-OVER CHECK VALVE

CHARCOAL CANISTER

FUEL TANK

RUBBER DIAPHRAGM

SPRING

VALVE CLOSED

FROM TANK

TO CANISTER

VALVE OPEN

Figure 6–30 A typical evaporative emission control system. Note that when the computer turns on the canister purge solenoid valve, manifold vacuum draws any stored vapors from the canister into the engine. Manifold vacuum also is applied to the pressure control valve and when this valve opens, fumes from the fuel tank are drawn into the charcoal canister and eventually into the engine. When the solenoid valve is turned off (or the engine stops and there is no manifold vacuum), the pressure control valve is spring loaded shut to keep vapors inside the fuel tank from escaping to the atmosphere.

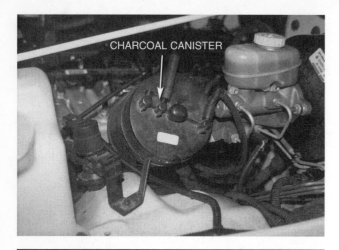

Figure 6–31 Charcoal canister as mounted under the hood of this Jeep. Not all charcoal canisters are this accessible; in fact, most are hidden away under the hood or in other locations on the vehicle.

Frequently Asked Question ???

When Filling My Fuel Tank, Why Should I Stop when the Pump Clicks Off?

Every fuel tank has an upper volume chamber that allows for expansion of the fuel when hot. The volume of the chamber is between 10% and 20% of the volume of the tank. For example, if a fuel tank had a capacity of 20 gallons, the expansion chamber volume would be from 2 to 4 gallons. A hose is attached at the top of the chamber and vented to the charcoal canister. If extra fuel is forced into this expansion volume, liquid gasoline can be drawn into the charcoal canister. This liquid fuel can saturate the canister and create an overly rich air-fuel mixture when the canister purge valve is opened during normal vehicle operation. This extra-rich air-fuel mixture can cause the vehicle to fail an exhaust emissions test, reduce fuel economy, and possibly damage the catalytic converter. To avoid problems, simply add fuel to the next dime's worth after the nozzle clicks off. This will ensure that the tank is full, yet not overfilled.

Figure 6–32 Typical vacuum-operated EGR valve. The operation of the valve is controlled by the computer by pulsing the EGR control solenoid on and off.

recirculation **(EGR)** valves. See Figure 6–32. From 1973 until recently, EGR valves were used on almost all vehicles. Because of the efficiency of computer-controlled fuel injection, some newer engines do not require an EGR system to meet emissions standards. Some engines use intake and exhaust valve overlap as a means of trapping some exhaust in the cylinder.

The EGR valve opens at speeds above idle on a warm engine. When open, the valve allows from 5% to 10% of the exhaust gas to enter the intake manifold. Here, the exhaust gas mixes with and takes the place of some intake charge. This leaves less room for the intake charge to enter the combustion chamber. The recirculated exhaust gas is **inert** (chemically inactive) and does not enter into the combustion process. The result is a lower peak combustion temperature. As the combustion temperature is lowered, the production of oxides of nitrogen is also reduced.

The EGR system has some means of interconnecting the exhaust and intake manifolds. See Figure 6–33. The interconnecting passage is controlled by the EGR valve. On V-type engines, the intake manifold crossover is used as a source of exhaust gas for the EGR system. A cast passage connects the exhaust crossover to the EGR valve. The gas is sent from the EGR valve to openings in the manifold. On inline-type engines, an external tube is generally used to carry exhaust gas to the EGR valve. This tube is often designed to be long so that the exhaust gas is cooled before it enters the EGR valve.

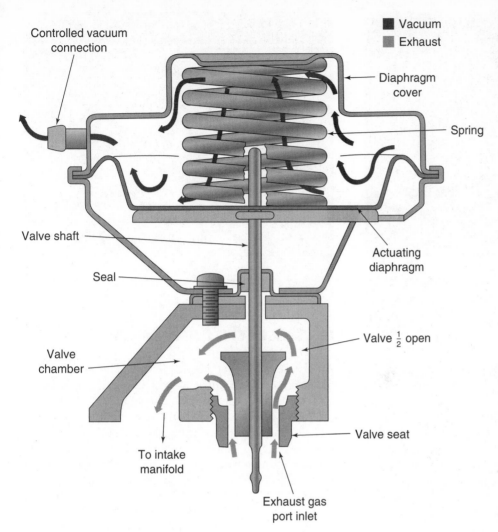

Controlled vacuum
connection

■ Vacuum
■ Exhaust

Diaphragm
cover

Spring

Valve shaft

Actuating
diaphragm

Seal

Valve ½ open

Valve
chamber

Valve seat

To intake
manifold

Exhaust gas
port inlet

Figure 6–33 When the EGR
valve opens, exhaust flows
through the valve and into
passages in the intake manifold.

Positive and Negative Back Pressure EGR Valves

Many EGR valves are designed with a small valve inside that bleeds off any applied vacuum and prevents the valve from opening. Some EGR valves require a positive back pressure in the exhaust system. This is called a **positive back pressure** EGR valve. At low engine speeds and light engine loads, the EGR system is not needed and the back pressure in it is also low. Without sufficient back pressure, the EGR valve does not open even though vacuum may be present at the EGR valve.

On each exhaust stroke, the engine emits an exhaust "pulse." Each pulse represents a positive pressure. Behind each pulse is a small area of low pressure. Some EGR valves react to this low pressure area by closing a small internal valve, which allows the EGR valve to be opened by vacuum. This type of EGR valve is called a **negative back pressure** EGR valve. The following conditions must occur:

1. Vacuum must be applied to the EGR valve itself. This is usually ported vacuum on older, carburetor-

equipped and some TBI fuel-injected systems. The vacuum source is often manifold vacuum and is controlled by the computer through a solenoid valve.
2. Exhaust back pressure must be present to close an internal valve inside the EGR to allow the vacuum to move the diaphragm.

Electronic EGR

Many engines since the mid-1990s have used computer-controlled solenoids or stepper motors (called linear EGR) to control the flow of exhaust into the intake manifold. See Figure 6–34 for an example of an assembly that uses three solenoids on a General Motors V-6 engine. The vehicle computer controls all three solenoids and can turn one, two, or three on as necessary to provide the exact amount of EGR needed.

A **linear EGR** valve is used on many engines and uses a stepper motor capable of being pulsed by the vehicle computer to deliver the exact amount of exhaust gas into the engine under all driving conditions. A feedback circuit allows the computer to deliver the exact

Figure 6–34 This General Motors 3800, V-6 uses three solenoids for EGR. A scan tool can be used to turn on each solenoid to check whether the valve is working and if the exhaust passages are capable of flowing enough exhaust to the intake manifold to affect engine operation when cycled.

position and will set a diagnostic trouble code (DTC) if the actual position is not within the acceptable range of commanded positions. A scan tool can be used to operate the valve to check its operation.

Diagnosing a Defective EGR Valve or System

If the EGR valve is not opening or the flow of the exhaust gas is restricted, then the following symptoms are likely:

- Ping (spark knock or detonation) during acceleration or during cruise (steady-speed driving)
- Excessive oxides of nitrogen (NO_x) exhaust emissions

If the EGR valve is stuck open or partially open, then the following symptoms are likely:

- Rough idle or frequent stalling
- Poor performance/low power

TECH TIP

Watch Out for Carbon Balls!

Exhaust gas recirculation (EGR) valves can get stuck partially open by a chunk of carbon. The EGR valve or solenoid will test as defective. When the valve (or solenoid) is removed, small chunks or balls of carbon often fall into the exhaust manifold passage. When the replacement valve is installed, the carbon balls can be drawn into the new valve again causing the engine to idle roughly or stall.

To help prevent this problem, start the engine with the EGR valve or solenoid removed. Any balls or chunks of carbon will be blown out of the passage by the exhaust. Stop the engine and install the replacement EGR valve or solenoid.

■ CATALYTIC CONVERTERS

An exhaust pipe is connected to the manifold or header to carry gases through a catalytic converter and then to the muffler or silencer. In single exhaust systems used on V-type engines, the exhaust pipe is designed to collect the exhaust gases from both manifolds using a Y-shaped design. Vehicles with dual exhaust systems have a complete exhaust system coming from each of the manifolds. In most cases, the exhaust pipe must be made up in several sections so that it can be assembled in the space available under the vehicle.

The **catalytic converter** is installed between the manifold and the muffler to help reduce exhaust emissions. The converter has a heat-resistant metal housing. See Figure 6–35. A bed of catalyst-coated pellets or a catalyst-coated honeycomb grid is inside the housing.

Catalytic Converter Operation

The converter contains small amounts of **rhodium, palladium,** and **platinum.** These elements act as **catalysts** (entities that start a chemical reaction without becoming a part of the chemical reaction). As the exhaust gas passes through the catalyst, oxides of nitrogen (NO_x) are chemically reduced (that is, nitrogen and oxygen are separated) in the first section of the catalytic converter. In the second section of the catalytic converter, most of the hydrocarbons and carbon monoxide remaining in the exhaust gas are oxidized to form harmless carbon dioxide (CO_2) and water vapor (H_2O). An air-injection system or pulse air system is used on some engines to supply additional air that may be needed in the oxidation process. See Figure 6–36. Since the early 1990s, many converters also contain **cerium,** an element that can store oxygen. The purpose of the cerium is to provide oxygen to the oxidation bed

Diagnostic Story

The Blazer Story

The owner of a Chevrolet Blazer equipped with a 4.3 L, V-6 engine complained that the engine would stumble and hesitate at times. Everything seemed to be functioning correctly, except that the service technician discovered a weak vacuum going to the EGR valve at idle. This vehicle was equipped with an EGR valve-control solenoid, called an **electronic vacuum regulator valve** or **EVRV** by General Motors Corporation. The computer pulses the solenoid to control the vacuum that regulates the operation of the EGR valve. The technician checked the service manual for details on how the system worked. The technician discovered that vacuum should be present at the EGR valve only when the gear selector indicates a drive gear (drive, low, re-

verse). Because the technician discovered the vacuum at the solenoid to be leaking, the solenoid was obviously defective and required replacement. After replacement of the solenoid (EVRV), the hesitation problem was solved.

> **NOTE:** The technician also discovered in the service manual that blower-type exhaust hoses should not be connected to the tailpipe on any vehicle while performing an inspection of the EGR system. The vacuum created by the system could cause false EGR valve operation to occur.

Diagnostic Story

I Was Only Trying to Help!

On a Friday, an experienced service technician found that the driveability performance problem with a Buick V-6 was a worn EGR valve. When vacuum was applied to the valve, the valve did not move at all. Additional vacuum from the hand-operated vacuum pump resulted in the valve popping all the way open. A new valve of the correct part number was not available until Monday, yet the customer wanted the vehicle back for a trip during the weekend.

To achieve acceptable driveability, the technician used a small hammer and deformed the top of the valve to limit the

travel of the EGR valve stem. The technician instructed the customer to return on Monday for the proper replacement valve.

The customer did return on Monday, but now accompanied by his lawyer. The engine had developed a hole in one of the pistons. The lawyer reminded the technician and the manager that an exhaust emission control device had been "modified." The result was the repair shop paid for a new engine and the technician learned to always repair the vehicle correctly or not at all.

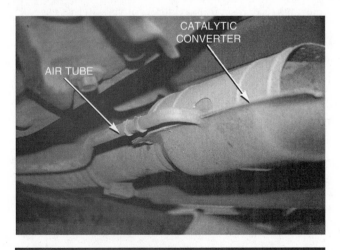

Figure 6–35 Typical catalytic converter. The small tube in the side of the converter comes from the air pump. The additional air from the air pump helps oxidize the exhaust into harmless H_2O (water) and CO_2 (carbon dioxide).

Figure 6–36 A cutaway of a three-way catalytic converter showing the air tube in the center of the reducing and oxidizing section of the converter. Note the small holes in the tube to distribute air from the AIR pump to the oxidizing rear section of the converter.

of the converter when the exhaust is rich and lacks enough oxygen for proper oxidation. When the exhaust is lean, the cerium absorbs the extra oxygen. The converter must have a varying rich-to-lean exhaust for proper operation:

- A rich exhaust is required for reduction—stripping the oxygen (O_2) from the nitrogen in NO_x.
- A lean exhaust is required to provide the oxygen necessary to oxidize HC and CO (combining oxygen with HC and CO to form H_2O and CO_2).

If the catalytic converter is not functioning correctly, check to see that the air-fuel mixture being supplied to the engine is correct and that the ignition system is free of defects.

The Tap Test

This simple test involves tapping (not pounding) on the catalytic converter using a rubber mallet. If the substrate inside the converter is broken, the converter will rattle when hit. If the converter rattles, a replacement converter is required. See Figure 6–37. See Chapter 8 for details on how to check for exhaust system restriction.

Figure 6–37 This catalytic converter blew up when gasoline from the excessively rich running engine ignited. Obviously, raw gasoline was trapped inside and all it needed was a spark. No further diagnosis of this converter is necessary.

Frequently Asked Question ???

Can a Catalytic Converter Be Defective without Being Clogged?

Yes. Catalytic converters can fail by being chemically damaged or poisoned without being mechanically clogged. Therefore, the catalytic converter should not only be tested for physical damage (clogging) by performing a back pressure or vacuum test and a rattle test but also for temperature rise, usually with a pyrometer or propane test, to check the efficiency of the converter.

Testing a Catalytic Converter for Temperature Rise

A properly working catalytic converter should be able to reduce NO_x exhaust emissions into nitrogen (N) and oxygen (O_2) and oxidize unburned hydrocarbon (HC) and carbon monoxide (CO) into harmless carbon dioxide (CO_2) and water vapor (H_2O). During these chemical processes, the catalytic converter should increase in temperature at least 10% if the converter is working properly. To test, operate the engine at 2500 RPM for at least two minutes to fully warm the converter. Measure the inlet and the outlet temperatures as shown in Figure 6–38.

NOTE: If the engine is extremely efficient, the converter may not have any excessive unburned hydrocarbons or carbon monoxide to convert! In this case, a spark plug wire could be grounded out using a vacuum hose and a test light to create some unburned hydrocarbon in the exhaust. Do not ground out a cylinder for longer than 10 seconds or the excessive amount of unburned hydrocarbon could overheat and damage the converter.

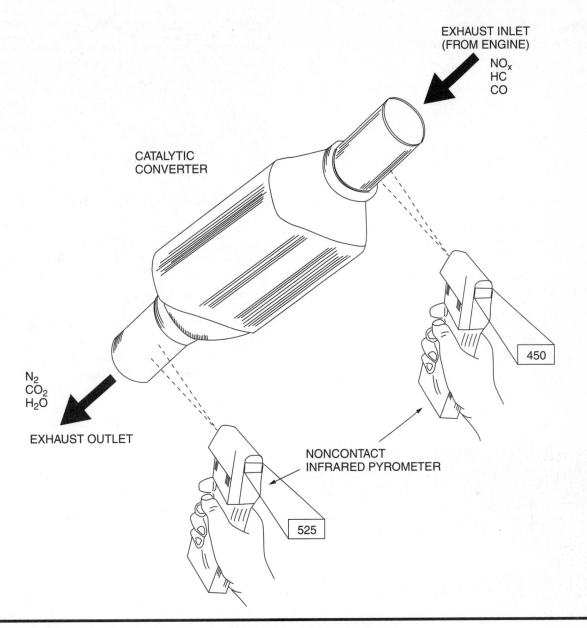

EXHAUST INLET
(FROM ENGINE)
NO_x
HC
CO

CATALYTIC
CONVERTER

450

N_2
CO_2
H_2O

EXHAUST OUTLET

NONCONTACT
INFRARED PYROMETER

525

Figure 6–38 The temperature of the outlet should be at least 10% hotter than the temperature of the inlet. This converter is very efficient. The inlet temperature is 450°F. Ten percent of 450°F is 45°F (45°F + 450°F = 495°F). In other words, the outlet temperature should be at least 495°F for the converter to be considered okay. In this case, the outlet temperature of 525°F is more than the minimum 10% increase in temperature. If the converter is not working at all, the inlet temperature will be hotter than the outlet temperature.

Catalytic Converter Replacement Guidelines

Because a catalytic converter is a major exhaust gas emission control device, the Environmental Protection Agency (EPA) has strict guidelines for its replacement, including:

- If a converter is replaced on a vehicle with less than 50,000 miles or the vehicle is less than five years old or 80,000/8 years, depending on the year of the vehicle, an original-equipment catalytic converter must be used as a replacement.
- The replacement converter must be of the same design as the original. If the original had an air-pump fitting, so must the replacement.
- The old converter must be kept for possible inspection by the authorities for 60 days.
- A form must be completed and signed by both the vehicle owner and a representative from the service facility. This form must state the cause of the converter failure, and must remain on file for two years.

NOTE: Just because new vehicles are covered by an exhaust emission warranty for five years or 50,000 miles (eight years or 80,000 miles from 1995), this should not be a factor. However, this law does prevent a service technician from installing a high-performance converter.

TECH TIP

Catalytic Converters Are Murdered

Catalytic converters start a chemical reaction but do not enter into the chemical reaction. Therefore, catalytic converters do not wear out and they do not die of old age. If a catalytic converter is found to be defective (nonfunctioning or clogged), look for the *root* cause. Remember this:

"Catalytic converters do not commit suicide—they're murdered."

Items that should be checked when a defective catalytic converter is discovered include all components of the ignition and fuel systems. Excessive unburned fuel can cause the catalytic converter to overheat and fail. The oxygen sensor must be working and fluctuating from 0.5 to 5 Hz (times per second) to provide the necessary air-fuel mixture variations for maximum catalytic converter efficiency.

PHOTO SEQUENCE Five-Gas Exhaust Analysis

PS10–1 A typical portable exhaust gas analyzer that is capable of measuring unburned hydrocarbons (HCs), carbon monoxide (CO), oxides of nitrogen (NO_x), carbon dioxide (CO_2), and oxygen (O_2).

PS10–2 After turning the unit on, most exhaust analyzers require a warm-up period.

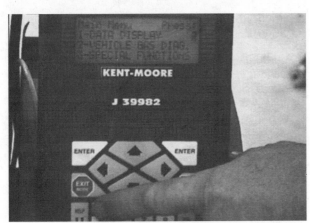

PS10–3 To test the exhaust of a vehicle, select "data display" from the main menu.

PS10–4 Select "gases/RPM/oil temp" from the data display menu.

PS10–5 Wait again! This is the reason why many service technicians turn on the exhaust gas analyzer at the beginning of each day and leave it on all day to avoid having to wait for the unit to become operational.

PS10–6 The unit is now able to display exhaust gas readings. It has been about 15 minutes from the time the unit was first turned on!

Five-Gas Exhaust Analysis—continued

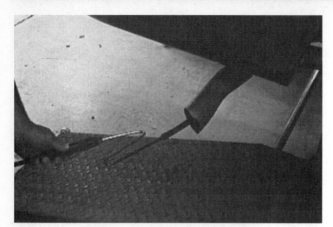

PS10–7 Insert the test probe into the tailpipe.

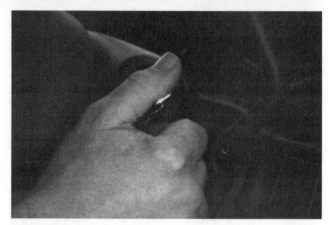

PS10–8 Start the engine.

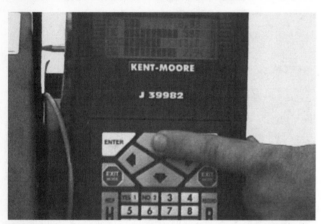

PS10–9 Use the up and down arrow keys to scroll up and down the data list to observe the gases. This unit can only display four of the five gases at a time. Because we are not concerned with NO_x when the engine is not going to be driven, this technician selected this display showing CO, HC, CO_2, and O_2.

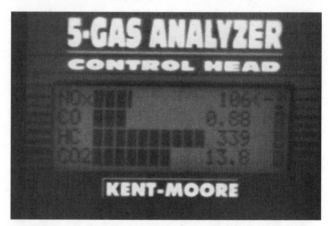

PS10–10 This display shows a typical engine at idle after a cold start. Notice the higher-than-normal HC reading.

PS10–11 To help get the engine, oxygen sensor, and catalytic converter up to operating temperature, operate the engine at 2000 RPM for several minutes.

PS10–12 After the engine has reached operating temperature, the HC readings are now 13 PPM—well within the normal allowable limit of less than 50 PPM.

PS11–1 A cutaway of a typical vacuum-operated exhaust gas recirculation (EGR) valve.

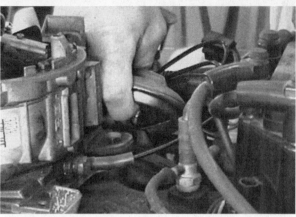

PS11–2 With the engine operating at idle speed, the engine should stall if the EGR valve is opened by hand. The technician should use a glove or shop cloth to prevent the possibility of being burned on the hot EGR valve.

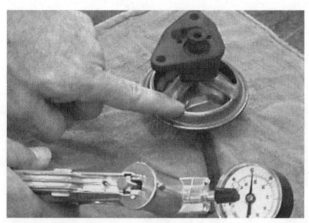

PS11–3 An EGR valve can also be tested off-vehicle by applying vacuum from a hand-operated vacuum pump. The diaphragm of the valve should move when vacuum is applied and the vacuum should hold if the valve is okay.

PS11–4 This is a negative back pressure EGR valve because the vacuum dropped to zero when shop air (compressed air) was blown over the end of the EGR valve pintle. A positive back pressure EGR valve would require the air pressure to close an internal valve to allow the valve to open when vacuum was applied to the diaphragm.

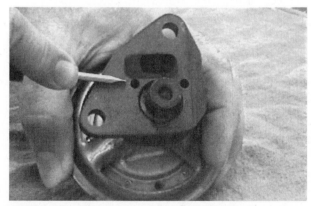

PS11–5 All EGR valve passages should be checked for carbon blockages that can prevent the valve from flowing enough exhaust gas to reduce NO_x exhaust emissions.

PS11–6 All EGR passages in the intake manifold should also be checked for carbon and cleaned out if restricted. Use a vacuum cleaner to help get all of the pieces of carbon out of the passages.

PHOTO SEQUENCE   Fuel-Pressure Regulator Test

A defective fuel-pressure regulator can cause a variety of engine performance problems, including stalling, rough idle, hesitation, lack of power, and poor fuel economy.

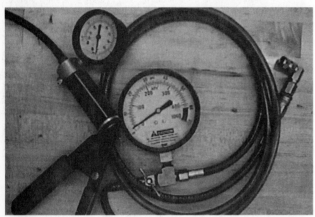

PS12–1 A hand-operated vacuum pump and a fuel-pressure gauge designed for fuel-injection systems are all that are needed to test the fuel-pressure regulator.

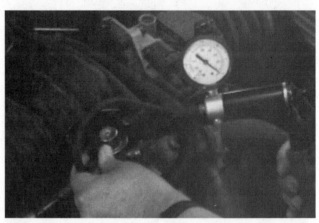

PS12–2 With the engine off, disconnect the vacuum hose from the fuel-pressure regulator and attach the hose from the hand-operated vacuum pump.

PS12–3 Operate the vacuum pump until about 20 in. Hg is applied to the regulator. Stop the vacuum pump and observe the vacuum gauge. The gauge reading should remain stationary and not drop. This particular test checks the condition of the rubber diaphragm inside the fuel-pressure regulator. If the vacuum gauge reading falls, the regulator is defective.

PS12–4 To test how the regulator can control fuel pressure, start by connecting a fuel-pressure gauge to the Schrader valve located near the fuel-pressure regulator.

Fuel-Pressure Regulator Test—continued

PS12–5 Cycle the ignition key to energize the fuel pump. The fuel-pressure gauge should increase when the pump is energized.

PS12–6 Start the engine.

PS12–7 The fuel-pressure gauge should now show a lower pressure because engine vacuum is being applied to the fuel-pressure regulator.

PS12–8 Disconnect and block the vacuum hose at the regulator. The fuel pressure should increase about 10 psi. This test confirms that the fuel-pressure regulator is capable of regulating fuel pressure with changes to engine intake manifold vacuum.

PS12–9 Reattach the vacuum hose to the fuel-pressure regulator. The pressure should decrease, again indicating that the regulator is capable of varying fuel pressure based on engine vacuum.

PS12–10 Turn the ignition off and carefully disconnect the pressure gauge holding a shop cloth around the fitting as the gauge is removed to catch any spilled fuel.

PHOTO SEQUENCE   Fuel-Injector Pressure Drop Balance Test

This test determines if all injectors are capable of flowing the same amount of fuel.

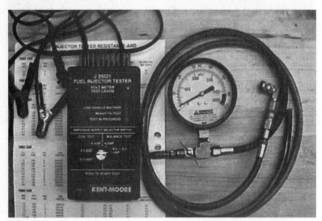

PS13–1 The equipment needed to perform this test includes a fuel-pressure gauge and injector pulse unit.

PS13–2 Start the test by connecting a fuel-pressure gauge to the fuel rail Schrader valve.

PS13–3 Attach the power leads of the pulse unit to the positive and negative terminals of the battery.

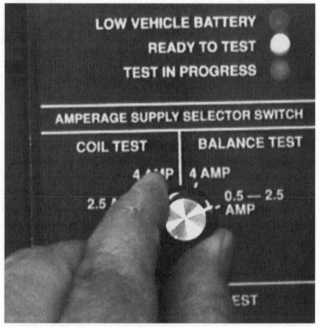

PS13–4 Be sure the "ready to use" light is on and select the proper setting as determined by the application guide that accompanies the tester.

Fuel-Injector Pressure Drop Balance Test—continued

PS13–5 Disconnect the injector connector and attach the connector from the balance tester.

PS13–6 Turn the ignition key on to energize the fuel pump and note the fuel-pressure reading.

PS13–7 Push the "start" button on the tester. The tester will pulse the injector on for exactly 500 ms (1/2 second).

PS13–8 Record the pressure reading on the fuel-pressure gauge after the injector has been pulsed. Repeat the test for the other injectors. All injectors should drop the pressure the same amount, within 1.5 psi (10 kPa) of each other. A clogged injector will drop the pressure less than a normal injector.

■ SUMMARY

1. Gasoline is a complex blend of hydrocarbons. Gasoline is blended for seasonal usage for the correct volatility for easy starting and maximum fuel economy under all driving conditions.

2. Winter-blend fuel used in a vehicle during warm weather can cause a rough idle and stalling because of the higher Reid vapor pressure (RVP) of winter-grade fuel.

3. Abnormal combustion (also called detonation or spark knock) increases both the temperature and the pressure inside the combustion chamber.

4. Most regular-grade gasoline today [using the (R + M)/2 rating method] is 87 octane, midgrade (plus) is 89, and premium grade is 91 or higher.

5. Oxygenated fuels usually contain alcohol or MTBE that includes oxygen in its content to lower CO exhaust emissions.

6. Gasoline should always be purchased from a busy station, and the tank should not be overfilled.

7. The positive crankcase ventilation (PCV) system pulls blowby gases and crankcase vapors into the intake manifold.

8. An AIR pump supplies air to the exhaust manifold when the engine is cold and to the catalytic converter when the engine achieves closed-loop operation.

9. The evaporative (EVAP) emission control system uses a charcoal (carbon) canister and various hoses and lines to trap and hold gasoline fumes and to prevent these fumes from escaping into the atmosphere.

10. The exhaust gas recirculation (EGR) system bleeds some inert exhaust gases into the combustion chamber to prevent the higher peak temperature that could occur. The main purpose and function of the EGR system is to reduce the formation of oxides of nitrogen (NO_x) exhaust emissions.

11. A catalytic converter is used in the exhaust system to start a chemical reaction among the exhaust gases but is not consumed by the reaction. Its function is to separate NO_x exhaust emissions into nitrogen (N) and oxygen (O_2). The other part of the converter is designed to oxidize hydrocarbons (HCs) and carbon monoxide (CO) into harmless CO_2 and H_2O (water vapor).

■ REVIEW QUESTIONS

1. Describe the difference between summer-blend and winter-blend gasoline.

2. Define Reid vapor pressure.

3. Describe the (R + M)/2 gasoline pump octane rating.

4. Define stoichiometric.

5. Describe how valves can recede into the head on engines using unleaded gasoline without hardened valve seats.

6. List three tests that can be performed to check the PCV system.

7. Describe how to test an AIR system using an exhaust gas analyzer.

8. List three methods that can be used to test an EGR valve and system.

9. Describe three tests that can be used to test the condition of a catalytic converter.

■ ASE CERTIFICATION-TYPE QUESTIONS

1. Winter-blend gasoline _____ .
   a. Vaporizes more easily than summer-blend gasoline
   b. Has a higher RVP
   c. Can cause engine driveability problems if used during warm weather
   d. All of the above

2. Technician A says that spark knock, ping, and detonation are different names for abnormal combustion. Technician B says that any abnormal combustion raises the temperature and pressure inside the combustion chamber and can cause severe engine damage. Which technician is correct?
   a. Technician A only
   b. Technician B only
   c. Both Technician A and B
   d. Neither Technician A nor B

3. Technician A says that the research octane number is higher than the motor octane number. Technician B says that the octane rating posted on fuel-pumps is an average of the two ratings. Which technician is correct?
   a. Technician A only
   b. Technician B only
   c. Both Technician A and B
   d. Neither Technician A nor B

4. Valve seat recession is most likely to occur with older engines *not* equipped with hardened valve seats if _____ .

   a. Driven at high speeds and with heavy loads

   b. Driven at slow speeds and with light loads

   c. Used at idle most or all of the time

   d. Both a and c

5. Two technicians are discussing positive crankcase ventilation (PCV) valves. Technician A says that if the valve rattles, it is good. Technician B says the PCV valve may still require replacement. Which technician is correct?

   a. Technician A only

   b. Technician B only

   c. Both Technician A and B

   d. Neither Technician A nor B

6. Technician A says that a defective one-way exhaust check valve could cause the air pump to fail. Technician B says that the air should stop flowing to the exhaust manifold when the engine is warm and operating in closed loop. Which technician is correct?

   a. Technician A only

   b. Technician B only

   c. Both Technician A and B

   d. Neither Technician A nor B

7. Technician A says that all engines built since 1973 are equipped with EGR valves. Technician B says a positive back pressure EGR valve will not hold vacuum if tested using a vacuum pump without the engine running. Which technician is correct?

   a. Technician A only

   b. Technician B only

   c. Both Technician A and B

   d. Neither Technician A nor B

8. Technician A says that a partially clogged EGR passage can cause the vehicle to fail due to excessive NO_x emissions. Technician B says the vehicle could fail for excessive CO if the EGR passage was clogged. Which technician is correct?

   a. Technician A only

   b. Technician B only

   c. Both Technician A and B

   d. Neither Technician A nor B

9. Technician A says the catalytic converter must be replaced if it rattles when tapped. Technician B says a catalytic converter can be defective and not working yet not be clogged. Which technician is correct?

   a. Technician A only

   b. Technician B only

   c. Both Technician A and B

   d. Neither Technician A nor B

10. Technician A says that a defective PCV valve could cause a rough idle. Technician B says that a defective EGR valve could cause a rough idle. Which technician is correct?

   a. Technician A only

   b. Technician B only

   c. Both Technician A and B

   d. Neither Technician A nor B

Cooling System Operation and Diagnosis

Objectives: After studying Chapter 7, the reader should be able to:

1. Describe how coolant flows through an engine.
2. Discuss the operation of the thermostat.
3. Explain the radiator pressure cap purpose and function.
4. Describe the various types of antifreezes and how to recycle and discard used coolant.
5. Discuss how to diagnose cooling system problems.

Satisfactory cooling system operation depends on the design and operating conditions of the system. The design is based on heat output of the engine, radiator size, type of coolant, size of water pump (coolant pump), type of fan, thermostat, and system pressure. Unfortunately, the cooling system is usually neglected until there is a problem. Proper routine maintenance can prevent problems.

■ COOLING SYSTEM PURPOSE AND FUNCTION

The cooling system must allow the engine to warm up to the required operating temperature as rapidly as possible and then maintain that temperature. It must be able to do this when the outside air temperature is as low as –30°F (–35°C) and as high as 110°F (45°C).

Peak combustion temperatures in the engine cycle run from 4000°F to 6000°F (2200°C to 3300°C). The combustion temperatures will *average* between 1200°F and 1700°F (650° and 925°C). Continued temperatures as high as this would weaken engine parts, so heat must be removed from the engine. The cooling system keeps the head and cylinder walls at a temperature that is within the range for maximum efficiency. See Figure 7–1.

■ LOW-TEMPERATURE ENGINE PROBLEMS

Engine operating temperatures must be above a minimum temperature for proper engine operation. When the temperature is too low, there is not enough heat to properly vaporize the fuel in the intake charge. As a result, extra fuel must be added to supply more volatile fuel to make a combustible mixture. The heavy, less volatile part of the gasoline does not vaporize, and so it remains as unburned liquid fuel. In addition, cool engine surfaces quench part of the combustion gases, leaving partially burned fuel as soot.

Gasoline combustion is a rapid oxidation process that releases heat as the hydrocarbon fuel chemically combines with oxygen from the air. *For each gallon of fuel used, moisture equal to a gallon of water is produced.* It is a part of this moisture that condenses and gets into the oil pan, along with unburned fuel and soot, and causes sludge formation. The condensed moisture

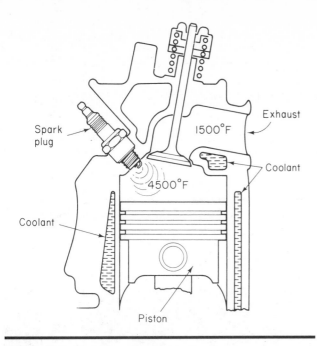

(a)

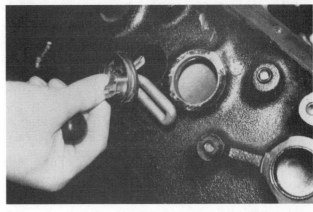

(b)

Figure 7–1 Typical combustion and exhaust temperatures.

Figure 7–2 (a) Loosening the screw that tightens the block heater element into the core plug opening in the side of the block. (b) Block heater element removed from block. The heater warms the coolant around the element, and the warm coolant rises, drawing cooler coolant up. As a result of this thermal circulation, all coolant surrounding the entire engine is warmed.

TECH TIP ✔

Overheating Can Be Expensive

A faulty cooling system seems to be a major cause of engine failure. Engine rebuilders often have nightmares about seeing their rebuilt engine placed back in service in a vehicle with a clogged radiator. Most engine technicians routinely replace the water pump and all hoses after an engine overhaul or repair. The radiator should also be checked for leaks and proper flow whenever the engine is repaired or replaced. Overheating is one of the most common causes of engine failure.

■ HIGH-TEMPERATURE ENGINE PROBLEMS

Maximum temperature limits are required to protect the engine. High temperatures will oxidize the engine oil. This breaks the oil down, producing hard carbon and varnish. If high temperatures are allowed to continue, the carbon that is produced will plug piston rings. The varnish will cause the hydraulic valve lifter plungers to stick. High temperatures always thin the oil. Metal-to-metal contact within the engine will occur when the oil is too thin. This will cause high friction, loss of power, and rapid wear of the parts. Thinned oil will also get into the combustion chamber by going past the piston rings and through valve guides to cause excessive oil consumption.

The combustion process is very sensitive to temperature. High coolant temperatures raise the combustion

combines with unburned hydrocarbons and additives to form carbonic acid, sulfuric acid, nitric acid, hydrobromic acid, and hydrochloric acid. These acids are responsible for engine wear by causing corrosion and rust within the engine. Rust occurs rapidly when the coolant temperature is below 130°F (55°C). Below 110°F (45°C), water from the combustion process will actually accumulate in the oil. High cylinder wall wear rates occur whenever the coolant temperature is below 150°F (65°C).

To reduce cold-engine problems and to help start engines in cold climates, most manufacturers offer block heaters as an option. These block heaters are plugged into household current (110 volts AC) and the heating element warms the coolant. See Figure 7–2.

Engine Temperature and Exhaust Emissions

Many areas of the United States and Canada have exhaust emission testing. Hydrocarbon (HC) emissions are simply unburned gasoline. To help reduce HC emissions and be able to pass emission tests, be sure that the engine is at normal operating temperature. Vehicle manufacturers' definition of "normal operating temperature" includes the following:

1. Upper radiator hose is hot and pressurized.
2. Electric cooling fan(s) cycles twice.

Be sure that the engine is operating at normal operating temperature before testing for exhaust emissions. For best results, the vehicle should be driven about *20 miles (32 kilometers)* to be certain that the catalytic converter and engine oil, as well as the coolant, are at normal temperature. This is particularly important in cold weather. Most drivers believe that their vehicle will "warm up" if allowed to idle until heat starts flowing from the heater. The heat from the heater comes from the coolant. Most manufacturers recommend that idling be limited to a maximum of 5 minutes and that the vehicle should be warmed up by driving slowly after just a minute or two to allow the oil pressure to build.

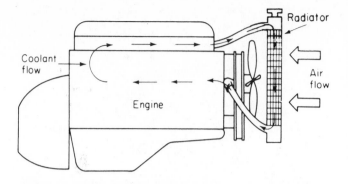

Figure 7–3 Coolant flow through an engine cooling system.

Figure 7–4 This block with the deck cut away shows the coolant passages surrounding the cylinders. Notice that coolant flows completely around and between the cylinders.

temperatures to a point that may cause detonation and preignition to occur. These are common forms of abnormal combustion. If they are allowed to continue for any period of time, the engine will be damaged.

■ COOLING SYSTEM DESIGN

Coolant flows through the engine, where it picks up heat. It then flows to the radiator, where the heat is given up to the outside air. The coolant continually recirculates through the cooling system, as illustrated in Figures 7–3 and 7–4. Its temperature rises as much as 15°F (8°C) as it goes through the engine; then it recools as it goes through the radiator. *The coolant flow rate may be as high as 1 gallon (4 liters) per minute for each horsepower the engine produces.*

Hot coolant comes out of the thermostat housing on the top of the engine. The engine coolant outlet is connected to the top of the radiator by the upper hose and clamps. The coolant in the radiator is cooled by air flowing through the radiator. As it cools, it moves from the top to the bottom of the radiator. Cool coolant leaves the lower radiator area through an outlet and lower hose, going into the inlet side of the water pump, where it is recirculated through the engine.

NOTE: Some newer engine designs such as Daimler-Chrysler's 4.7 L, V-8 and General Motors 4.8, 5.3, 5.7, and 6.0 L, V-8s place the thermostat on the inlet side of the water pump. As the cooled coolant hits the thermostat, the thermostat closes until the coolant temperature again causes it to open. Placing the thermostat in the inlet side of the water pump therefore reduces thermal cycling by reducing the rapid temperature changes that could cause stress in the engine, especially if aluminum heads are used with a cast-iron block.

Much of the cooling capacity of the cooling system is based on the functioning of the radiator. Radiators are designed for the maximum rate of heat transfer using minimum space. Cooling airflow through the radiator is aided by a belt- or electric motor-driven cooling fan.

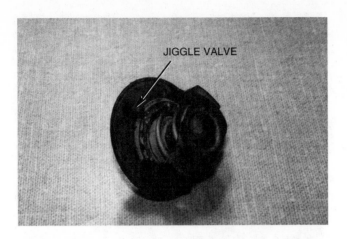

Figure 7–5 A typical automotive engine thermostat. This style of thermostat includes a small hole with a movable stopper called a **jiggle valve.** The jiggle valve moves and breaks up air pockets and allows air to escape the engine block and flow to the radiator. This helps prevent air from getting trapped in the engine, which could lead to overheating. The thermostat is usually installed with the jiggle valve up.

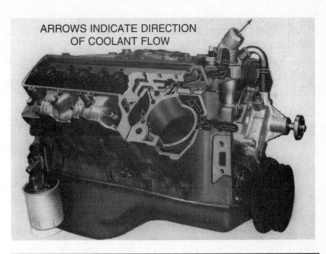

Figure 7–6 Typical coolant flow in a V-type engine.

■ THERMOSTAT TEMPERATURE CONTROL

There is a normal operating temperature range between low-temperature and high-temperature extremes. The thermostat controls the minimum normal temperature. The thermostat is a temperature-controlled valve placed at the engine coolant outlet. See Figure 7–5. An encapsulated wax-based plastic pellet heat sensor is located on the engine side of the thermostatic valve. As the engine warms, heat swells the heat sensor. A mechanical link, connected to the heat sensor, opens the thermostat valve. As the thermostat begins to open, it allows some coolant to flow to the radiator, where it is cooled. The remaining part of the coolant continues to flow through the bypass, thereby bypassing the thermostat and flowing back through the engine. See Figure 7–6. The rated temperature of the thermostat indicates the temperature at which the thermostat starts to open. The thermostat is fully open at about 20°F higher than its opening temperature. See the following examples.

Thermostat opening temperature	Starts to open	Fully open
180°F	180°F	200°F
195°F	195°F	215°F

If the radiator, water pump, and coolant passages are functioning correctly, the engine should always be operating within the opening and fully open temperature range of the thermostat. See Figure 7–7.

(a)

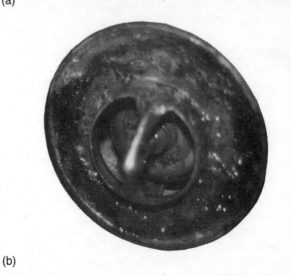

(b)

Figure 7–7 (a) Typical thermostat located in the intake manifold with the thermostat housing removed. (b) A thermostat that is stuck in the open position. This caused the engine to operate too cold and the vehicle failed an exhaust emission test because of this defect.

NOTE: A **bypass** around the closed thermostat allows a small part of the coolant to circulate within the engine during warm-up. It is a small passage that leads from the engine side of the thermostat to the inlet side of the water pump. It allows some coolant to bypass the thermostat even when the thermostat is open. The bypass may be cast or drilled into the engine and pump parts. See Figures 7–8 and 7–9. The bypass aids in uniform engine warm-up. Its operation eliminates hot spots and prevents the building of excessive coolant pressure in the engine when the thermostat is closed.

TECH TIP ✔

Do Not Take Out the Thermostat!

Some vehicle owners and technicians remove the thermostat in the cooling system to "cure" an overheating problem. In some cases, removing the thermostat can *cause* overheating—not stop overheating. This is true for three reasons:

1. Without a thermostat the coolant can flow more quickly through the radiator. The thermostat adds some restriction to the coolant flow, and therefore, keeps the coolant in the radiator longer. The presence of the thermostat thus ensures a greater reduction in the coolant temperature before it returns to the engine.
2. Heat transfer is greater with a greater difference between the coolant temperature and air temperature. Therefore, when coolant flow rate is increased (no thermostat), the temperature difference is reduced.
3. Without the restriction of the thermostat, much of the coolant flow often bypasses the radiator entirely and returns directly to the engine.

If overheating is a problem, removing the thermostat will usually not solve the problem. Remember, the thermostat controls the temperature of the engine coolant by opening at a certain temperature and closing when the temperature falls below the minimum rated temperature of the thermostat. If overheating occurs, two basic problems could be the cause:

1. The engine is producing too much heat for the cooling system to handle. For example, if the engine is running too lean or if the ignition timing is either excessively advanced or excessively retarded, overheating of the engine can result.
2. The cooling system has a malfunction or defect that prevents it from getting rid of its heat.

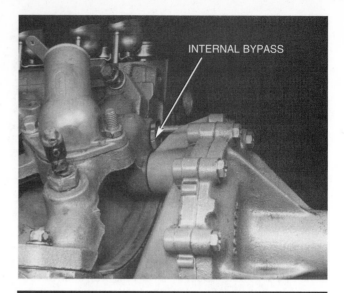

Figure 7–8 One type of cooling system internal bypass.

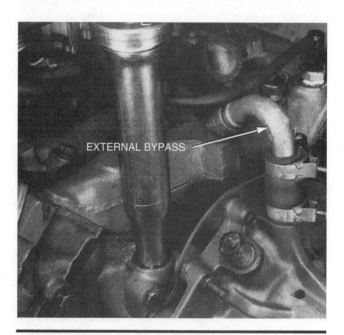

Figure 7–9 One type of cooling system external bypass.

■ TESTING THE THERMOSTAT

There are three basic methods that can be used to check the operation of the thermostat.

1. **Hot water method.** If the thermostat is removed from the vehicle and is closed, insert a 0.015-inch (0.4-millimeter) feeler gauge in the opening so that the thermostat will hang on the feeler gauge. The thermostat should then be suspended by the feeler gauge in a bath along with a thermometer. See Figure 7–10. The bath should be heated until the

Figure 7–10 Setup used to check the opening temperature of a thermostat.

Figure 7–11 Some thermostats are an integral part of the housing. This thermostat and radiator hose housing is serviced as an assembly. Some thermostats simply snap into the engine radiator fill tube underneath the pressure cap.

NOTE: If the temperature rises higher than 20°F (11°C) above the opening temperature of the thermostat, inspect the cooling system for a restriction or low coolant flow. A clogged radiator could also cause the excessive temperature rise.

---

thermostat opens enough to release and fall from the feeler gauge. The temperature of the bath when the thermostat falls is the opening temperature of the thermostat. If it is within 5°F (4°C) of the temperature stamped on the thermostat, the thermostat is satisfactory for use. If the temperature difference is greater, the thermostat should be replaced.

2. **Infrared pyrometer method.** An infrared pyrometer can be used to measure the temperature of the coolant near the thermostat. The area on the engine side of the thermostat should be at the highest temperature that exists in the engine. A properly operating cooling system should cause the pyrometer to read as follows:
   - As the engine warms, temperature reaches near thermostat opening temperature.
   - As the thermostat opens, temperature drops just as the thermostat opens, sending coolant to the radiator.
   - As the thermostat cycles, temperature should range between the opening temperature of the thermostat and 20°F (11°C) above the opening temperature.

3. **Scan tool method.** A scan tool can be used on many vehicles to read the actual temperature of the coolant as detected by the engine coolant temperature (ECT) sensor. Although the sensor or the wiring to and from the sensor may be defective, at least the scan tool can indicate what the computer "thinks" the engine coolant temperature is.

■ THERMOSTAT REPLACEMENT

An overheating engine may result from a faulty thermostat. An engine that does not get warm enough always indicates a faulty thermostat.

To replace the thermostat, coolant will have to be drained from the radiator drain petcock to lower the coolant level below the thermostat. It is not necessary to completely drain the system. The upper hose should be removed from the thermostat housing neck; then the housing must be removed to expose the thermostat. See Figure 7–11.

The gasket flanges of the engine and thermostat housing should be cleaned, and the gasket surface of the housing must be flat. The thermostat should be placed in

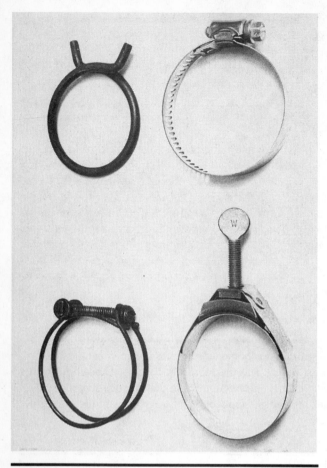

Figure 7–12 Types of hose clamps used on coolant hoses. Most replacement clamps are of the screw type. Hose clamps are sold by number. The higher the clamp number, the larger the clamp. Typical sizes include #10 or #12 for heater hoses and #24 to #30 for radiator hoses.

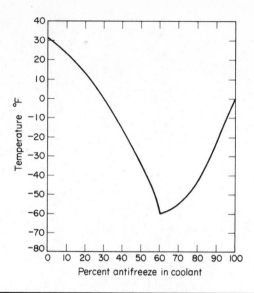

Figure 7–13 Graph showing the relationship of the freezing point of the coolant to the percentage of antifreeze used in the coolant.

the engine with the sensing pellet *toward* the engine. Make sure that the thermostat position is correct, and install the thermostat housing with a new gasket.

> **CAUTION:** Failure to set the thermostat into the recessed groove will cause the housing to become tilted when tightened. If this happens and the housing bolts are tightened, the housing will usually crack, creating a leak.

Then the upper hose should be installed and the system refilled. Install the proper size of radiator hose clamp. See Figure 7–12.

■ ANTIFREEZE

Water is able to absorb more heat per gallon than any other liquid coolant. Under standard conditions, water boils at 212°F (100°C) and freezes at 32°F (0°C). *When water freezes, it increases in volume about 9%.* The expansion of the freezing water can easily crack engine blocks, cylinder heads, and radiators. All manufacturers recommend the use of **ethylene glycol-based antifreeze** mixtures for protection against this problem.

A curve depicting freezing point as compared with the percentage of antifreeze mixture is shown in Figure 7–13. It should be noted that the freezing point increases as the antifreeze concentration is increased above 60%. The normal mixture is 50% antifreeze and 50% water. Ethylene glycol antifreezes contain anticorrosion additives, rust inhibitors, and water pump lubricants.

At the maximum level of protection, an ethylene glycol concentration of 60% will absorb about 85% as much heat as will water. Ethylene glycol-based antifreeze also has a higher boiling point than water. See Figure 7–14. If the coolant boils, it vaporizes and does not act as a cooling agent because it is not in liquid form and in contact with the cooling surfaces.

■ ORGANIC ADDITIVE TECHNOLOGY COOLANT

Organic additive technology (**OAT**) antifreeze coolant does not contain silicates or phosphates. This type of coolant is usually orange in color and was first developed by Havoline (called **DEX-COOL**) and used in General Motors vehicles starting in 1996. A newer variation of this technology is called **hybrid organic additive technology** (**HOAT**) and is similar to the OAT-type antifreeze as it uses additives that are not abrasive to water pumps, yet provide the correct pH.

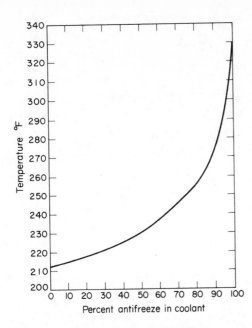

Figure 7–14 Graph showing how the boiling point of the coolant increases as the percentage of antifreeze in the coolant increases.

The pH of the coolant is usually above 11. A pH of 7 is neutral with lower numbers indicating an acidic solution and higher numbers indicating a caustic solution. If the pH is too high, the coolant can cause scaling and reduce the heat transfer ability of the coolant. If the pH is too low, the resulting acidic solution could cause corrosion of the engine components exposed to the coolant.

■ PROPYLENE GLYCOL ANTIFREEZE

Propylene glycol antifreeze is advertised as being safer and less toxic than ethylene glycol. Although propylene glycol is less poisonous to humans and animals, it can still be harmful if ingested.

> **NOTE:** Because ethylene glycol is sweet, animals are attracted to it and drink any coolant that is within reach. Ethylene glycol is often fatal if ingested.

Propylene glycol has freezing and boiling temperatures similar to those of ethylene glycol. It is when the two types of antifreezes are mixed that heat transfer reduction may occur. This is the reason why most vehicle manufacturers warn against using propylene glycol unless all existing coolant is thoroughly flushed from the system. Always check the vehicle manufacturer's recommendation before using propylene glycol antifreeze.

■ PHOSPHATE-FREE ANTIFREEZE

Volkswagen specifies phosphate-free antifreeze for use in any of its liquid-cooled engines. Volkswagen testing revealed that the phosphate additive tended to settle out of the coolant when used with high-mineral content (hard) water.

The phosphate-free antifreeze *does* tend to produce white chalky deposits although these do not cause any cooling system problems. Using antifreeze that contains phosphate will stop the formation of the chalky deposits but is not recommended by Volkswagen. However, there is a compromise: Using any good-quality antifreeze containing phosphate with distilled water should reduce problems associated with phosphate use, without requiring the purchase of the expensive phosphate-free formula.

■ ANTIFREEZE CAN FREEZE

Antifreeze and water mixture is an example wherein the freezing point differs from the freezing point of either pure antifreeze or pure water.

	Freezing point
Pure water	32°F (0°C)
Pure antifreeze*	0°F (–18°C)
50/50 mixture	–34°F (–37°C)
70% antifreeze/30% water	–84°F (–64°C)

*Pure antifreeze is usually 95% ethylene glycol, 2% to 3% water, and 2% to 3% additives. Depending on the exact percentage of water used, antifreeze as sold in containers freezes between –8°F and 8°F (–13°C and –22°C). Therefore, it is easiest just to remember that most antifreeze freezes at about 0°F (–18°C).

The boiling point of antifreeze and water is also a factor of mixture concentrations.

	Boiling point at sea level	Boiling point with 15 psi pressure cap
Pure water	212°F (100°C)	257°F (125°C)
50/50 mixture	218°F (103°C)	265°F (130°C)
70/30 mixture	225°F (107°C)	276°F (136°C)

■ HYDROMETER TESTING

Coolant can be checked using a coolant hydrometer. The hydrometer measures the density of the coolant. The higher the density, the more concentration of antifreeze in the water. Most coolant hydrometers read the freezing point and boiling point of the coolant. See Figure 7–15. If the engine is overheating and the hydrometer reading is near –50°F (–60°C), suspect that pure

Diagnostic Story

If 50% Is Good, 100% Must Be Better

A vehicle owner said that the cooling system of his vehicle would never freeze or rust. He said that he used 100% antifreeze (ethylene glycol) instead of a 50/50 mixture with water.

However, after the temperature dropped to −20°F (−29°C), the radiator froze and cracked. [Pure antifreeze freezes at about 0°F (−18°C).] After thawing, the radiator had to be repaired. The owner was lucky that the engine block did not also crack.

For best freeze protection with good heat transfer, use a 50/50 mixture of antifreeze and water. A 50/50 mixture of antifreeze and water is the best compromise between temperature protection and the heat transfer that is necessary for cooling system operation. Do not exceed 70% antifreeze (30% water). As the percentage of antifreeze increases, the boiling temperature increases, and freezing protection increases (up to 70% antifreeze), but the heat transfer performance of the mixture decreases.

Figure 7–15 Checking the freezing and boiling protection levels of the coolant using a hydrometer.

TECH TIP

Ignore the Windchill Factor

The windchill factor is a temperature that combines the actual temperature and the wind speed to determine the overall heat loss effect on open skin. Because it is the heat loss factor for open skin, the windchill temperature is *not* to be considered when determining antifreeze protection levels.

Although moving air does make it feel colder, the actual temperature is not changed by the wind and the engine coolant will not be affected by the windchill. Not convinced? Try this. Place a thermometer in a room and wait until a stable reading is obtained. Now turn on a fan and have the air blow across the thermometer. The temperature will not change.

CAUTION: Most vehicle manufacturers warn that antifreeze coolant should not be reused unless it is recycled and the additives restored.

100% antifreeze is present. For best results, the coolant should have a freezing point lower than −20°F and a boiling point above 234°F.

■ RECYCLING COOLANT

Coolant (antifreeze and water) should be recycled. Used coolant may contain heavy metals, such as lead, aluminum, and iron, which are absorbed by the coolant during its use in the engine.

Recycle machines filter out these metals and dirt and reinstall the depleted additives. The recycled coolant, restored to be like new, can be reinstalled into the vehicle.

■ DISPOSING OF USED COOLANT

Used coolant drained from vehicles can usually be disposed of by combining it with used engine oil. The equipment used for recycling the used engine oil can easily separate the coolant from the waste oil. Check with recycling companies authorized by local or state government for the exact method recommended for disposal in your area. See Figure 7–16.

Figure 7–16 Used antifreeze coolant should be kept separate and stored in a leak-proof container until it can be recycled or disposed of according to federal, state, and local laws. Note that the storage barrel is placed inside another container to catch any coolant that may spill out of the inside barrel.

Figure 7–18 Typical cross-flow radiator. *(Courtesy of Modine Manufacturing Company)*

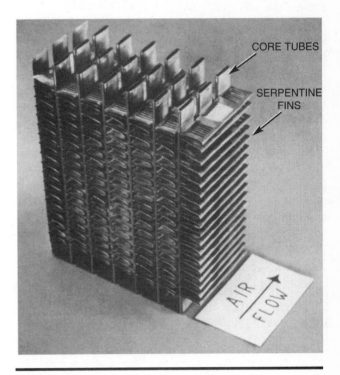

Figure 7–19 Section from a serpentine core radiator. *(Courtesy of Modine Manufacturing Company)*

Figure 7–17 An older style down-flow radiator. *(Courtesy of Dow Chemical Company)*

■ RADIATOR

Two types of radiator cores are in common use in domestic vehicles—the serpentine fin core and the plate fin core. In each of these types the coolant flows through oval-shape **core tubes.** Heat is transferred through the tube wall and soldered joint to **fins.** The fins are exposed to airflow, which removes heat from the radiator and carries it away. See Figures 7–17 through 7–20.

Older automobile radiators were made from yellow brass. Since the 1980s, most radiators have been made from aluminum. These materials are corrosion resistant, have good heat-transferring ability, and are easily formed.

Core tubes are made from 0.0045 to 0.012-inch (0.1 to 0.3-millimeter) sheet brass or aluminum, using the thinnest possible materials for each application. The metal is rolled into round tubes and the joints are sealed with a locking seam.

The main limitation of heat transfer in a cooling system is in the transfer from the radiator to the air. Heat transfers from the water to the fins as much as seven

Figure 7–20 Cutaway of a typical radiator showing restriction of tubes. Changing antifreeze frequently helps prevent this type of problem.

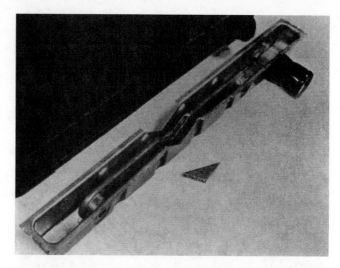

Figure 7–21 Cutaway showing an automatic transmission cooler passage inside the radiator. Air cools the coolant, which then cools the automatic transmission fluid that flows through the radiator. *(Courtesy of Dow Chemical Company)*

times faster than heat transfers from the fins to the air, assuming equal surface exposure. The radiator must be capable of removing an amount of heat energy approximately equal to the heat energy of the power produced by the engine. *Each horsepower is equivalent to 42 Btu (10,800 calories) per minute.* As the engine power is increased, the heat-removing requirement of the cooling system is also increased.

With a given frontal area, radiator capacity may be increased by increasing the core thickness, packing more material into the same volume, or both. The radiator capacity may also be increased by placing a shroud around the fan so that more air will be pulled through the radiator.

> **NOTE:** The lower air dam in the front of the vehicle is used to help direct the air through the radiator. If this air dam is broken or missing, the engine may overheat, especially during highway driving due to the reduced airflow through the radiator.

Radiator headers and tanks that close off the ends of the core were made of sheet brass 0.020 to 0.050 inch (0.5 to 1.25 millimeters) thick and now are made of molded plastic. When a transmission oil cooler is used in the radiator, it is placed in the outlet tank, where the coolant has the lowest temperature (Figure 7–21).

■ PRESSURE CAP

The filler neck is fitted with a pressure cap. The cap has a spring-loaded valve that closes the cooling system vent. This causes cooling pressure to build up to the pressure setting of the cap. At this point, the valve will release the excess pressure to prevent system damage. See Figure 7–22.

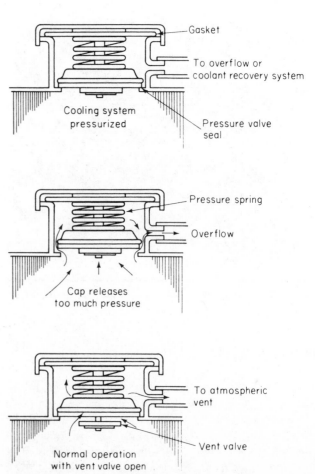

Figure 7–22 The operation of a typical pressure cap.

Engine cooling systems are pressurized to raise the boiling temperature of the coolant. *The boiling temperature will increase by approximately 3°F (1.6°C) for each pound of increase in pressure.* At standard atmospheric pressure, water will boil at 212°F (100°C). With a 15 psi (100 kPa) pressure cap, water will boil at 257°F (125°C), which is a maximum operating temperature for an engine.

The high coolant system temperature serves two functions.

1. It allows the engine to run at an efficient temperature, close to 200°F (93°C), with no danger of boiling the coolant.
2. The higher the coolant temperature, the more heat the cooling system can transfer. The heat transferred by the cooling system is proportional to the temperature difference between the coolant and the outside air. This characteristic has led to the design of small, high-pressure radiators that are capable of handling large quantities of heat. For proper cooling, the system must have the right pressure cap correctly installed. See Figure 7–23.

> **NOTE:** The proper operation of the pressure cap is especially important at high altitudes. The boiling point of water is lowered by about 1°F for every 550-foot increase in altitude. Therefore in Denver, Colorado (altitude 5280 feet), the boiling point of water is about 202°F, and at the top of Pike's Peak in Colorado (14,110 feet) water boils at 186°F.

■ METRIC RADIATOR CAPS

According to the *SAE Handbook*, all radiator caps must indicate their nominal (normal) pressure rating. Most original-equipment radiator caps are rated at about 14 to 16 psi (97 to 110 kPa).

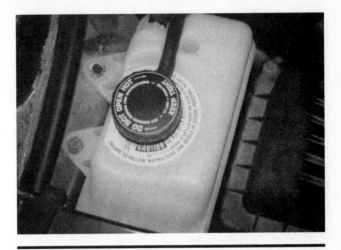

Figure 7–23 Some vehicles have the pressure cap on the reservoir bottle. This means that the expansion bottle is under the same pressure as the rest of the cooling system.

However, many vehicles manufactured in Japan or Europe have the radiator pressure indicated in a unit called a **bar.** One bar is the pressure of the atmosphere at sea level, or about 14.7 psi. The following conversion can be used when replacing a radiator cap to make certain it matches the pressure rating of the original.

Bar or atmospheres	Pounds per square inch (psi)
1.1	16
1.0	15
0.9	13
0.8	12
0.7	10
0.6	9
0.5	7

> **NOTE:** Many radiator repair shops use a 7-psi (0.5 -bar) radiator cap on a repaired radiator. A 7-psi cap can still provide boil protection of 21°F (3° × 7 psi = 21°F) above the boiling point of the coolant. For example, if the boiling point of the antifreeze coolant is 223°, 21° is added for the pressure cap, and boil-over will not occur until about 244° (223° + 21° = 244°). Even though this lower-pressure radiator cap does provide some protection and will also help protect the radiator repair, the coolant can still boil *before* the "hot" dash warning light comes on.

■ COOLANT RECOVERY SYSTEM

Excess pressure usually forces some coolant from the system through an overflow. Most cooling systems connect the overflow to a plastic reservoir to hold excess coolant while the system is hot. See Figure 7–24. When the system cools, the pressure in the cooling system is

Figure 7–24 Typical coolant recovery container.

reduced and a partial vacuum forms. This pulls the coolant from the plastic container back into the cooling system, keeping the system full. Because of this action, this system is called a **coolant recovery system.** The filler cap used on a coolant system without a coolant saver is fitted with a vacuum valve. This valve allows air to reenter the system as the system cools so that the radiator parts will not collapse under the partial vacuum.

■ PRESSURE TESTING

Pressure testing using a hand-operated pressure tester is a quick and easy cooling system test. The radiator cap is removed (engine cold!) and the tester attached in the place of the radiator cap. By operating the plunger on the pump, the entire cooling system is pressurized. See Figure 7–25.

> **CAUTION:** Do not pump up the pressure beyond that specified by the vehicle manufacturer. Most systems should not be pressurized beyond 14 psi (100 kPa). If a greater pressure is used, it may cause the water pump, radiator, heater core, or hoses to fail.

If the cooling system is free from leaks, the pressure should stay and not drop. If the pressure drops, look for evidence of leaks anywhere in the cooling system including:

- Heater hoses
- Radiator hoses
- Radiator
- Heat core
- Cylinder head
- Core plugs in the side of the block or cylinder head

(a)

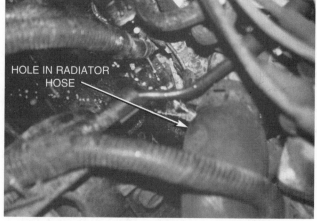

HOLE IN RADIATOR HOSE

(b)

Figure 7–25 (a) Using a hand-operated pressure tester to pressurize the entire cooling system. (b) Notice the coolant leaking out of a hole in the radiator hose. This is the reason why the owner of this minivan noticed a "hot coolant" smell.

Pressure testing should be performed whenever there is a leak or suspected leak. The pressure tester can also be used to test the radiator cap. An adapter is used to connect the pressure tester to the radiator cap. Replace any cap that will not hold pressure.

■ COOLANT DYE LEAK TESTING

One of the best methods to check for a coolant leak is to use a fluorescent dye in the coolant. Use a dye designed for coolant. Operate the vehicle with the dye in the coolant until the engine reaches normal operating temperature. Use a black light to inspect all areas of the cooling system. When there is a leak, it will be easy to spot because the dye in the coolant will be seen as bright green.

TECH TIP

Use Distilled Water in the Cooling System

Two technicians are discussing refilling the radiator after changing antifreeze. One technician says that distilled water is best to use because it does not contain minerals that can coat the passages of the cooling system. The other technician says that any water that is suitable to drink can be used in a cooling system. Both technicians are correct. If water contains minerals, however, it can leave deposits in the cooling system that could prevent proper heat transfer. Because the mineral content of most water is unknown, distilled water, which has no minerals, is better to use. Although the cost of distilled water must be considered, the amount of water required [usually about 2 gallons (8 liters) or less of water] makes the expense minor in comparison with the cost of radiator or cooling system failure.

Figure 7–26 Coolant flow through the impeller and scroll of a coolant pump for a V-type engine.

■ WATER PUMP OPERATION

The water pump (also called a coolant pump) is driven by a belt from the crankshaft or driven by the camshaft. Coolant recirculates from the radiator to the engine and back to the radiator. Low-temperature coolant leaves the radiator by the bottom outlet. It is pumped into the warm engine block, where it picks up some heat. From the block, the warm coolant flows to the hot cylinder head, where it picks up more heat.

> **NOTE:** Some engines use **reverse cooling.** This means that the coolant flows from the radiator to the cylinder head(s) before flowing to the engine block.

Water pumps are not positive displacement pumps. The water pump is a **centrifugal pump** that can move a large volume of coolant without increasing the pressure of the coolant. The pump pulls coolant in at the center of the **impeller.** Centrifugal force throws the coolant outward so that it is discharged at the impeller tips. This can be seen in Figure 7–26.

As engine speeds increase, more heat is produced by the engine and more cooling capacity is required. The pump impeller speed increases as the engine speed increases to provide extra coolant flow at the very time it is needed.

Coolant leaving the pump impeller is fed through a **scroll.** The scroll is a smoothly curved passage that changes the fluid flow direction with minimum loss in velocity. The scroll is connected to the front of the engine so as to direct the coolant into the engine block. On V-type engines, two outlets are used, one for each cylin-

der bank. Occasionally, diverters are necessary in the water pump scroll to equalize coolant flow between the cylinder banks of a V-type engine to equalize the cooling.

■ COOLANT FLOW IN THE ENGINE

Coolant flows through the engine in one of two ways—parallel or series. In the **parallel flow system,** coolant flows into the block under pressure and then crosses the gasket to the head through main coolant passages beside *each* cylinder. The gasket openings of a parallel system are shown in Figure 7–27. In the **series flow system,** the coolant flows around all the cylinders on each bank. All the coolant flows to the *rear* of the block, where large main coolant passages allow the coolant to flow across the gasket. Figure 7–28 shows the main coolant passages. The coolant then enters the rear of the heads. In the heads, the coolant flows forward to an

Frequently Asked Question   ???

How Much Coolant Can a Water Pump Pump?

A typical water pump can move a maximum of about 7500 gallons (28,000 liters) of coolant per hour, or recirculate the coolant in the engine over 20 times per minute. This means that a water pump could be used to empty a typical private swimming pool in an hour! The slower the engine speed, the less power is consumed by the water pump. However, even at 35 miles per hour (56 kilometers per hour), the typical water pump still moves about 2000 gallons (7500 liters) per hour or 1/2 gallon (2 liters) per second!

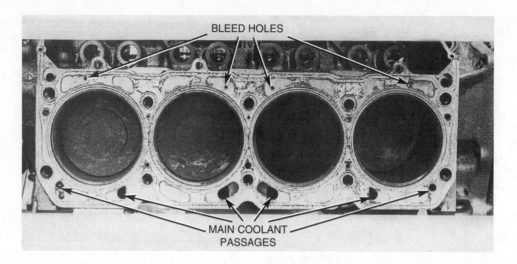

Figure 7–27 Gasket openings for a cooling system with a parallel type of flow.

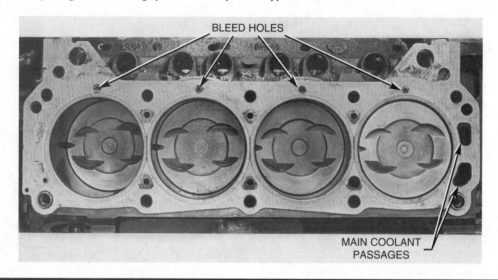

Figure 7–28 Gasket openings for a series-type cooling system.

outlet at the *highest point* in the engine cooling passage. This is usually located at the front of the engine. The outlet is either on the heads or in the intake manifold. Some engines use a combination of these two coolant flow systems and call it a **series-parallel coolant flow.** Any steam that develops will go directly to the top of the radiator. In series flow systems, **bleed holes** or **steam slits** in the gasket, block, and head perform the function of letting out the steam.

The coolant can also be directed through an oil filter adapter to help warm the engine oil when the engine is first started in cold weather as well as cool the engine oil when the oil is hot. See Figure 7–29.

■ WATER PUMP SERVICE

A worn impeller on a water pump can reduce the amount of coolant flow through the engine. See Figure

7–30. If the seal of the water pump fails, coolant will leak out of the hole as seen in Figure 7–31. The hole allows coolant to escape without getting trapped and forced into the water pump bearing assembly.

If the bearing is defective, the pump will usually be noisy and will have to be replaced. Before replacing a water pump that has failed because of a loose or noisy bearing, be sure to do all of the following:

1. Check belt tension
2. Check for bent fan
3. Check fan for balance

If the water pump drive belt is too tight, excessive force may be exerted against the pump bearing. If the cooling fan is bent or out of balance, the resulting vibration can damage the water pump bearing. See Figure 7–32.

Figure 7–29 An engine oil cooler. Coolant lines connect to the oil filter adapter to transfer heat from the hot engine oil to the cooling system. Because the coolant usually reaches operating temperature before the oil during cold weather, this cooler can also heat the cold engine oil so it reaches normal operating temperature quicker thereby helping to reduce engine wear.

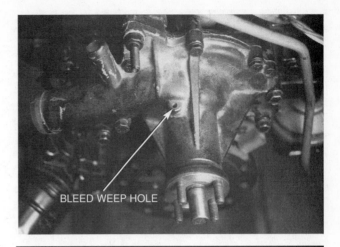

Figure 7–31 The bleed (weep) hole in the water pump allows coolant to leak out of the pump and not be forced into the bearing. If the bearing failed, more serious damage could result.

Figure 7–30 This severely corroded water pump could not circulate enough coolant to keep the engine cool. As a result, the engine overheated and blew a head gasket.

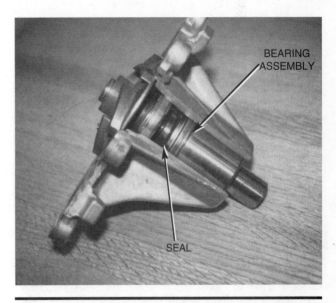

Figure 7–32 A cutaway of a typical water pump showing the long bearing assembly and the seal. The weep hole is located between the seal and the bearing. If the seal fails, then coolant flows out of the weep hole to prevent the coolant from damaging the bearing.

■ COOLING FANS

Air is forced across the radiator core by a cooling fan. On older engines used in rear-wheel-drive vehicles, it is attached to a fan hub that is pressed on the water pump shaft. See Figure 7–33. Most installations with rear-wheel drive and transverse engines drive the fan with an electric motor. See Figure 7–34.

The fan is designed to move enough air at the lowest fan speed to cool the engine when it is at its highest coolant temperature. The fan shroud is used to increase the cooling system efficiency. The horsepower required to drive the fan increases at a much faster rate than the

NOTE: Most electric cooling fans are computer controlled. To save energy, most cooling fans are turned off whenever the vehicle is traveling faster than 35 mph (55 km/h). The ram air from the vehicle's traveling at that speed should be enough to keep the radiator cool. Of course, if the computer senses that the temperature is still too high, the computer will turn on the cooling fan, to "high," if possible, in an attempt to cool the engine to avoid severe engine damage.

Diagnostic Story

The Heavy-Duty Water Pump Story

A rear-wheel-drive Chevrolet was returned to the dealer for a replacement water pump that was defective. Even though it was not covered by warranty, the owner wanted to be certain that a heavy-duty (HD) water pump was used as a replacement. The owner had purchased the vehicle new and had ordered a heavy-duty cooling system including a larger (thicker) radiator and an HD water pump.

When the technician went to the parts department to get an HD water pump, the parts person did not even look up the part number, but brought out a typical small-block Chevrolet V-8 water pump. The technician repeated the request for a "heavy-duty" pump as specified by the customer. Just to satisfy the technician, the parts manager showed the technician that the part number was the same for standard *and* HD pumps.

The technician said, "Then what did the customer get when the vehicle was purchased equipped with an HD water pump?" The parts manager said, "An HD water pump is driven by a slightly *smaller* pulley to turn the pump faster, and the drive pulley is not part of the pump."

> **NOTE:** This is one of the reasons why replacement drive belts are not always exactly the same length as the original. Replacement drive belts are designed to fit several applications and therefore, may be slightly longer or shorter than the original.

Figure 7–33 Typical water pump shaft and fan hub with the fan removed.

Figure 7–34 Typical electric cooling fan.

increase in fan speed. Higher fan speeds also increase fan noise. Fans with flexible plastic or flexible steel blades have been used. These fans have high blade angles that pull a high volume of air when turning at low speeds. As the fan speed increases, the fan blade angle flattens, reducing the horsepower required to rotate the blade at high speeds. See Figures 7–35 and 7–36.

■ THERMOSTATIC FANS

Since the early 1980s, most cooling fans have been computer-controlled electric motor units. On some rear-wheel-drive vehicles, a thermostatic cooling fan is driven by a belt from the crankshaft. It turns faster as the engine turns faster. Generally, the engine is required to produce more power at higher speeds. Therefore, the cooling system will also transfer more heat. Increased fan speed aids in the required cooling. Engine heat also becomes critical at low engine speeds in traffic where the vehicle moves slowly.

The thermal fan is designed so that it uses little power at high engine speeds and minimizes noise. The thermal fan has a **silicone coupling** fan drive mounted between the drive pulley and the fan.

> *HINT:* Whenever diagnosing an overheating problem, look carefully at the cooling fan. If silicone is leaking, then the fan may not be able to function correctly and should be replaced.

A second type of thermal fan has a **thermostatic spring** added to the silicone coupling fan drive. The thermostatic spring operates a valve that allows the fan to freewheel when the radiator is cold. As the radiator warms to about 150°F (65°C), the air hitting the thermostatic spring will cause the spring to change its shape. The new shape of the spring opens a valve that allows the drive to operate like the silicone coupling drive. When the engine is very cold, the fan may operate

Figure 7–35 Photo taken with high-speed flash showing the shape of flexible fan blades at low speed. Compare with Figure 7–36.

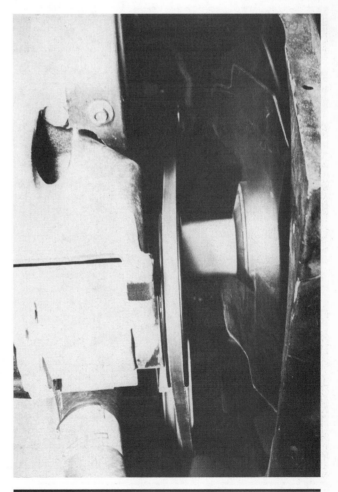

Figure 7–36 Same fan as shown in Figure 7–35, except at higher engine speed. Note the decrease in pitch of the fan blades.

at high speeds for a short time until the drive fluid warms slightly. The silicone fluid will then flow into a reservoir to let the fan speed drop to idle. See Figures 7–37 through 7–39.

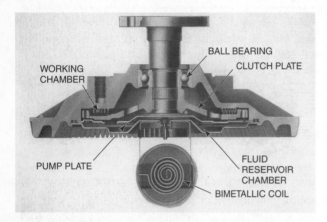

Figure 7–37 Sectional view of a thermostatic fan drive. *(Courtesy of Buick Motor Division, GMC)*

Figure 7–38 A cutaway of a viscous fan clutch showing the many grooves that are filled with viscous silicone fluid during operation.

■ HEATER CORE

Most of the heat absorbed from the engine by the cooling system is wasted. Some of this heat, however, is recovered by the vehicle heater. Heated coolant is passed through tubes in the small core of the heater. Air is passed across the heater fins and is then sent to the passenger compartment. In some vehicles, the heater and air conditioning work in series to maintain vehicle compartment temperature. See Figure 7–40.

■ HEATER PROBLEM DIAGNOSIS

When the vehicle's heater does not produce the desired amount of heat, many owners and technicians replace the thermostat before doing any other troubleshooting. It is true that a defective thermostat is the reason for the

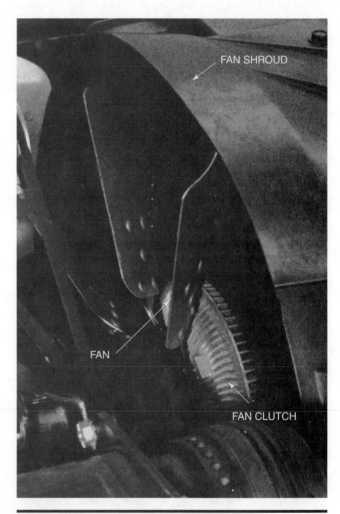

Figure 7–39 Note the relationship of the fan and fan shroud. At least 50% of the fan should be within the shroud to prevent overheating caused by under-the-hood air being drawn by the fan instead of outside air being drawn through the radiator.

Cause and Effect

A common cause of overheating is an inoperative cooling fan. Most front-wheel-drive vehicles and many rear-wheel-drive vehicles use electric motor–driven cooling fans. A fault in the cooling fan circuit often causes overheating during slow city-type driving.

Even slight overheating can soften or destroy rubber vacuum hoses and gaskets. The gaskets most prone to overheating damage are rocker cover (valve cover) and intake manifold gaskets. Gasket and/or vacuum hose failure often results in an air (vacuum) leak that leans the air-fuel mixture. The resulting lean mixture burns hotter in the cylinders and contributes to the overheating problem.

The vehicle computer can often compensate for a minor air leak (vacuum leak), but more severe leaks can lead to driveability problems, especially idle quality problems. If the leak is severe enough, a lean computer trouble code may be present. If a lean code is not set, the vehicle's computer may indicate a defective or out-of-range MAP sensor code in diagnostics.

Therefore, a typical severe engine problem can often be traced back to a simple, easily repaired, cooling system–related problem.

(a)

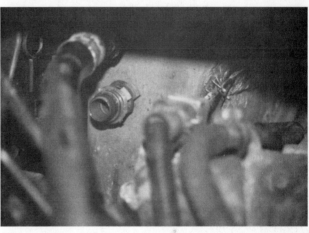

(b)

Figure 7–40 (a) Many vehicles today use quick connect-type fittings on the heater hose. (b) The outside of the heater core housing showing one hose removed. Carefully inspect and clean these connections to prevent a leak.

---

engine not to reach normal operating temperature. Many other causes besides a defective thermostat can result in lack of heat from the heater. To determine the exact cause, follow this procedure:

Step 1 After the engine has been operated, feel the upper radiator hose. If the engine is up to proper operating temperature, the upper radiator hose should be too hot for you to keep your hand on it. The hose should also be pressurized.

    a. If the hose is not hot enough, replace the thermostat.

    b. If the hose is not pressurized, test it. Replace the radiator pressure cap if it will not hold the specified pressure.

    c. If okay, see step 2.

Step 2 With the engine running, feel both heater hoses. (The heater should be set to the maximum heat position.) Both hoses should be too hot to hold. If both hoses are warm (not hot) or cool, check the heater control valve for proper operation. If one hose is hot and the other (return) is just warm or cool, remove both hoses from the heater core or engine and flush the heater core with water from a garden hose.

> **HINT:** Heat from the heater that "comes and goes" is most likely the result of low coolant level. Usually with the engine at idle, there is enough coolant flow through the heater; but at higher engine speeds the circulation of coolant through the heads and block prevents sufficient flow through the heater.

■ COOLANT TEMPERATURE WARNING LIGHT

Most vehicles are equipped with a heat sensor for the engine operating temperature. If the "hot" light comes on during driving (or the temperature gauge goes into the red danger zone), then the coolant temperature is about 250° to 258°F (120° to 126°C), which is still *below* the boiling point of the coolant (assuming a properly operating pressure cap and system). If this happens, follow these steps:

Step 1 Shut off the air conditioning and turn on the heater. The heater will help rid the engine of extra heat. Set the blower speed to high.

Step 2 If possible, shut the engine off and let it cool. (This may take over an hour.)

Step 3 Never remove the radiator cap when the engine is hot.

Step 4 Do *not* continue to drive with the hot light on, or serious damage to your engine could result.

Step 5 If the engine does not feel or smell hot, it is possible that the problem is a faulty hot light sensor or gauge. Continue to drive, but to be safe, stop occasionally and check for any evidence of overheating or coolant loss.

■ COMMON CAUSES OF OVERHEATING

Overheating can be caused by defects in the cooling system. Some common causes of overheating include

- Low coolant level
- Plugged, dirty, or blocked radiator
- Defective fan clutch or electric fan
- Incorrect ignition timing
- Low engine oil level
- Broken fan belt
- Defective radiator cap
- Dragging brakes
- Frozen coolant (in freezing weather)
- Defective thermostat
- Defective water pump (the impeller slipping on the shaft internally)

■ COOLING SYSTEM MAINTENANCE

The cooling system is one of the most maintenance-free systems in the engine. Normal maintenance involves an occasional check on the coolant level. It should also include a visual inspection for signs of coolant system leaks and for the condition of the coolant hoses and fan drive belts.

CAUTION: The coolant level should only be checked when the engine is cool. Removing the pressure cap from a hot engine will release the cooling system pressure while the coolant temperature is above its atmospheric boiling temperature. When the cap is removed, the pressure will instantly drop to atmospheric pressure level, causing the coolant to boil immediately. Vapors from the boiling liquid will blow coolant from the system. Coolant will be lost, and someone may be injured or burned by the high-temperature coolant that is blown out of the filler opening.

The coolant-antifreeze mixture is renewed at periodic intervals. Some vehicle manufacturers recommend that coolant system stop-leak pellets be installed whenever the coolant is changed. See Figure 7–41.

CAUTION: General Motors recommends the use of these stop-leak pellets in only certain engines. Using these pellets in some engines could cause a restriction in the cooling system and an overheating condition.

Diagnostic Story

Highway Overheating

A vehicle owner complained of an overheating vehicle, but the problem occurred only while driving at highway speeds. The vehicle, equipped with a General Motors QUAD 4, would run in a perfectly normal manner in city driving situations.

The technician flushed the cooling system and replaced the radiator cap and the water pump, thinking that restricted coolant flow was the cause of the problem. Further testing revealed coolant spray out of one cylinder when the engine was turned over by the starter with the spark plugs removed.

A new head gasket solved the problem. Obviously, the head gasket leak was not great enough to cause any problems until the engine speed and load created enough flow and heat to cause the coolant temperature to soar.

The technician also replaced the oxygen (O_2) sensor, because coolant contains silicone and silicates that often contaminate the sensor. The deteriorated oxygen sensor could have contributed to the problem.

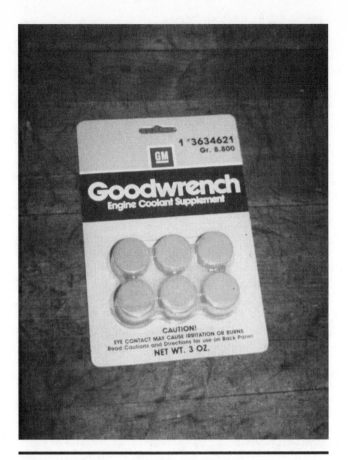

Figure 7–41 General Motors recommends that these stop-leak pellets be installed in the cooling system if the coolant is replaced on some engines, especially the Cadillac 4.1, 4.5, and 4.9 L, V-8s.

Drive belt condition and proper installation are important for the proper operation of the cooling system. See Figures 7–42 and 7–43.

■ FLUSH AND REFILL

Manufacturers recommend that a cooling system be flushed and that the antifreeze be replaced at specified intervals. Draining coolant when the engine is cool eliminates the danger of being injured by hot coolant. The radiator is drained by opening a petcock in the bottom tank, and the coolant in the block is drained into a suitable container by opening plugs located in the lower part of the cooling passage. See Figure 7–44.

Water should be run into the filler opening while the drains remain open. Flushing should be continued until only clear water comes from the system.

The volume of the cooling system must be determined. It is specified in the owner's handbook and in the engine service manual. The antifreeze quantity needed for the protection desired is shown on a chart that comes with the antifreeze. Open the bleeder valves and add the correct amount of the specified type of antifreeze followed by enough water to completely fill the system. See Figure 7–45. The coolant recovery reservoir should be filled to the "level-cold" mark with the correct antifreeze mixture.

■ BURPING THE SYSTEM

In most systems, small air pockets can occur. The engine must be thoroughly warmed to open the thermostat. This allows full coolant flow to remove the air pockets. The heater must also be turned to full heat.

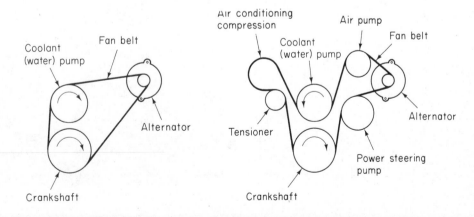

Figure 7–42 In the mid-1980s, many manufacturers started using serpentine belts. Older-model water pumps will bolt onto the engine, but the direction of rotation may be opposite. This could lead to overheating after the new pump is installed. If the wrong application of fan is installed, the blades of the fan will not be angled correctly to provide adequate airflow through the radiator.

Figure 7–43 Drive belt tension is critical for the proper operation of the water pump, as well as the generator (alternator), air-conditioning compressor, and other belt-driven accessories. A belt tension gauge should be used to make certain that accurate belt tension is achieved when replacing or retensioning any belt.

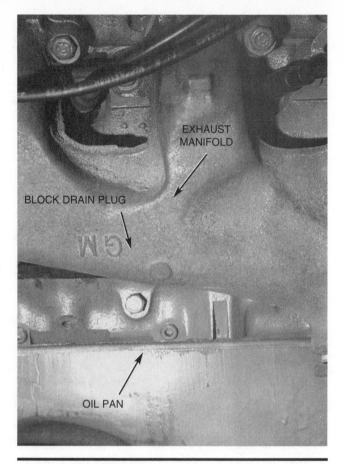

Figure 7–44 To thoroughly clean the cooling passages on the block, many technicians remove the block drain plugs and flush the block assembly separately from the rest of the cooling system.

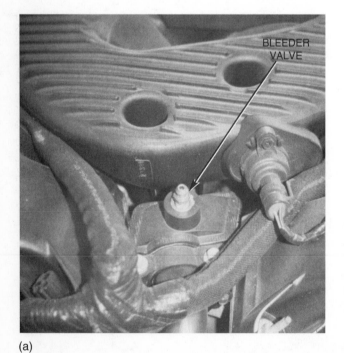

(a)

(b)

Figure 7–45 (a) DaimlerChrysler recommends that the bleeder valve be opened whenever refilling the cooling system. (b) DaimlerChrysler also recommends that a clear plastic hose (1/4″ ID) be attached to the bleeder valve and directed into a suitable container to keep from spilling coolant onto the ground and on the engine and to allow the technician to observe the flow of coolant for any remaining air bubbles.

> *HINT:* The cooling system will not function correctly if air is not released (burped) from the system after a refill. An easy method involves replacing the radiator cap after the refill, but only to the first locked position. Drive the vehicle for several minutes and check the radiator level. Without the radiator cap tightly sealed, no pressure will build in the cooling system, and driving the vehicle helps circulate the coolant enough to force all air pockets up and out of the radiator filler. Top off the radiator after burping and replace the radiator cap to the fully locked position. Failure to burp the cooling system to remove all the air will often result in lack of heat from the heater and may result in engine overheating.

■ HOSES

Coolant system hoses are critical to engine cooling. As the hoses get old, they become either soft or brittle and sometimes swell in diameter. Their condition depends on their material and on the engine service conditions. If a hose breaks while the engine is running, all coolant will be lost. A hose should be replaced anytime it appears to be abnormal.

> *HINT:* To make hose removal easier and to avoid possible damage to the radiator, use a utility knife and slit the hose lengthwise. Then simply peel the hose off.

Care should be taken to avoid bending the soft metal hose neck on the radiator. The hose neck should be cleaned before a new hose is slipped in place. The clamp is placed on the hose; then the hose is pushed fully over the neck. The hose should be cut so that the clamp is close to the bead on the neck. This is especially important on aluminum hose necks to avoid corrosion. When the hoses are in place and the drain petcock is closed, the cooling system can be refilled with the correct coolant mixture.

■ BACK FLUSHING A RADIATOR

Overheating problems may be caused by deposits that restrict coolant flow. These can often be loosened by **back flushing.** Back flushing requires the use of a special gun that mixes air with water. Low-pressure air is used so that it will not damage the cooling system. See Figure 7–46. Deposits will come out of the filler opening and out of the hose connected to the upper hose neck.

If, after flushing, some deposits still plug the radiator core, then the radiator will have to be removed and sent to a radiator repair shop for cleaning.

■ CLEANING THE RADIATOR EXTERIOR

Overheating can result from exterior radiator plugging as well as internal plugging. External plugging is caused by dirt and insects. This type of plugging can be seen if you look straight through the radiator while a light is held behind it. It is most likely to occur on off-road vehicles. The plugged exterior of the radiator core can usually be cleaned with water pressure from a hose. The water is aimed at the *engine side* of the radiator. The water should flow freely through the core at all locations. If this does not clean the core, the radiator should be removed for cleaning at a radiator shop.

TECH TIP

Quick and Easy Cooling System Problem Diagnosis

If overheating occurs in slow stop-and-go traffic, the usual cause is low airflow through the radiator. Check for airflow blockages or cooling fan malfunction. If overheating occurs at highway speeds, the cause is usually a radiator or coolant circulation problem. Check for a restricted or clogged radiator.

Figure 7–46 Setup to back flush a radiator.

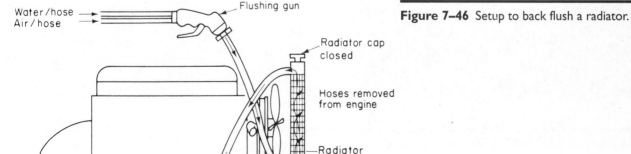

PHOTO SEQUENCE   Radiator Pressure Test

PS 14–1 This vehicle has an obvious coolant leak. The exact location or cause of the leak can be easily determined by performing a radiator pressure test.

PS 14–2 After the engine has been allowed to cool, the radiator cap is removed and inspected for any obvious faults. The filler neck of the radiator and the overflow hose are also inspected visually.

PS 14–3 The coolant recovery container should also be inspected. In this case, the level of coolant was found to be low in the coolant recovery container but okay in the radiator.

PS 14–4 An adapter is required to attach the radiator pressure tester to the radiator filler neck on this vehicle. The hand-operated pressure pump should be pumped until the pressure gauge indicates the same pressure as the rating on the pressure cap. The radiator cap was rated at 1.1 bar and because each bar is equal to 14.7 psi, the pressure tester was pumped until 16 psi registered on the gauge.

PS 14–5 The radiator cap itself can be tested by using an adapter and applying pressure to the cap using the pressure tester. In this case, the pressure cap failed to hold any pressure and was the cause for the coolant loss.

■ SUMMARY

1. The purpose and function of the cooling system is to maintain proper engine operating temperature.

2. The thermostat controls engine coolant temperature by opening at its rated opening temperature to allow coolant to flow through the radiator.

3. Antifreeze coolant is usually ethylene glycol based. Other coolants include propylene glycol and phosphate-free coolants.

4. Used coolant should be recycled whenever possible.

5. Coolant fans are designed to draw air through the radiator to aid in the heat transfer process, drawing the heat from the coolant and transferring it to the outside air through the radiator.

6. The cooling system should be tested for leaks using a hand-operated pressure pump.

7. The freezing and boiling temperature of the coolant can be tested using a hydrometer.

8. Proper cooling system maintenance usually calls for replacing the antifreeze coolant every two years or every 24,000 miles (36,000 kilometers).

■ REVIEW QUESTIONS

1. Explain why the normal operating coolant temperature is about 200° to 220°F (93° to 104°C).

2. Explain why a 50/50 mixture of antifreeze and water is commonly used as a coolant.

3. Explain the flow of coolant through the engine and radiator.

4. Why is a cooling system pressurized?

5. Describe the difference between a series and a parallel coolant flow system.

6. Explain the purpose of the coolant system bypass.

7. Describe how to perform a drain, flush, and refill procedure on a cooling system.

8. Explain the operation of a thermostatic cooling fan.

9. Describe how to diagnose a heater problem.

10. List 10 common causes of overheating.

■ ASE CERTIFICATION-TYPE QUESTIONS

1. Permanent antifreeze is mostly _____ .
   a. Methanol
   b. Glycerin
   c. Kerosene
   d. Ethylene glycol

2. As the percentage of antifreeze in the coolant increases, _____ .
   a. The freeze point decreases (up to a point)
   b. The boiling point decreases
   c. The heat transfer increases
   d. All of the above occurs

3. Heat transfer is improved from the coolant to the air when _____ .
   a. The temperature difference is great
   b. The temperature difference is small
   c. The coolant is 95% antifreeze
   d. Both a and c

4. A water pump is a positive displacement-type pump.
   a. True
   b. False

5. Water pumps _____ .
   a. Only work at idle and low speeds; the pump is disengaged at higher speeds
   b. Use engine oil as a lubricant and coolant
   c. Rotate at about the same speed as the engine
   d. Disengage during freezing weather to prevent radiator failure

6. The procedure that should be used when refilling an empty cooling system includes the following _____ .
   a. Determine capacity, then fill the cooling system halfway with antifreeze and the rest of the way with water
   b. Fill completely with antifreeze, but mix a 50/50 solution for the overflow bottle
   c. Fill the block and one-half of the radiator with 100% pure antifreeze and fill the rest of the radiator with water
   d. Fill the radiator with antifreeze, start the engine, drain the radiator, and refill with a 50/50 mixture of antifreeze and water

7. Which statement is *true* about thermostats?
   a. The temperature marked on the thermostat is the temperature at which the thermostat should be fully open.
   b. Thermostats often cause overheating.
   c. The temperature marked on the thermostat is the temperature at which the thermostat should start to open.
   d. Both a and b

8. Technician A says that the radiator should always be inspected for leaks and proper flow before installing a rebuilt engine. Technician B says that overheating during slow city driving can only be due to a defective electric cooling fan. Which technician is correct?
   a. Technician A only
   b. Technician B only
   c. Both Technician A and B
   d. Neither Technician A nor B

9. A customer complains that the heater works sometimes, but sometimes only cold air comes out while driving. Technician A says that the water pump is defective. Technician B says that the cooling system could be low on coolant. Which technician is correct?
   a. Technician A only
   b. Technician B only
   c. Both Technician A and B
   d. Neither Technician A nor B

10. The normal operating temperature (coolant temperature) of an engine equipped with a 195°F thermostat is
    a. 175° to 195°F
    b. 185° to 205°F
    c. 195° to 215°F
    d. 175° to 215°F

Engine Condition Diagnosis

Objectives: After studying Chapter 8, the reader should be able to:

1. List the visual checks to determine engine condition.
2. Discuss engine noise and its relation to engine condition.
3. Describe how to perform a dry and a wet compression test.
4. Explain how to perform a cylinder leakage test.
5. Discuss how to measure the amount of timing chain slack.
6. Describe how an oil sample analysis can be used to determine engine condition.

If there is an engine operation problem, then the cause could be any one of many items, including the engine itself. The condition of the engine should be tested anytime the operation of the engine is not satisfactory.

■ TYPICAL ENGINE-RELATED COMPLAINTS

Many driveability problems are *not* caused by mechanical engine problems. A thorough inspection and testing of the ignition and fuel systems should be performed before testing for mechanical engine problems.

Typical engine problem complaints include the following:

- Excessive oil consumption
- Engine misfiring
- Loss of power
- Smoke from the engine or exhaust
- Engine noise

TECH TIP

The Binder Clip Trick

It is important to use fender covers whenever working on an engine. The problem is few covers remain in place and they often become more of a hindrance than a help. A binder clip, available at most office supply stores, can be used to hold fender covers to the lip of the fender of most vehicles. See Figure 8–1. When clipped over the lip, the cover is securely attached and cannot be pulled loose. This method works with cloth and vinyl covers.

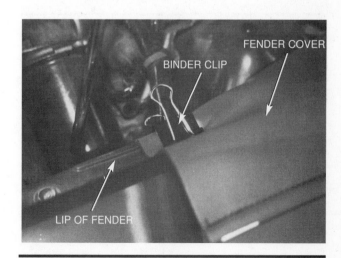

Figure 8–1 It is very important to use fender covers to protect the paint of the vehicle from being splashed with brake fluid. Use a binder clip, available at local office supply stores, to clip the fender cover to the lip of the fender, preventing the fender cover from slipping.

■ ENGINE SMOKE DIAGNOSIS

The color of engine exhaust smoke can indicate what engine problem might exist.

Typical Exhaust Smoke Color	Possible Causes
Blue	Blue exhaust indicates that the engine is burning oil. Oil is getting into the combustion chamber either past the piston rings or past the valve stem seals. Blue smoke only after start-up is usually due to defective valve stem seals. See Figure 8–2.
Black	Black exhaust smoke is due to excessive fuel being burned in the combustion chamber. Typical causes include a defective or misadjusted carburetor, leaking fuel injector, or excessive fuel-pump pressure.
White (steam)	White smoke or steam from the exhaust is normal during cold weather and represents condensed steam. Every engine creates about 1 gallon of water for each gallon of gasoline burned. If the steam from the exhaust is excessive, then water (coolant) is getting into the combustion chamber. Typical causes include a defective cylinder head gasket, a cracked cylinder head, or in severe cases a cracked block. See Figure 8–3.

NOTE: White smoke can also be created when automatic transmission fluid (ATF) is burned. A common source of ATF getting into the engine is through a defective vacuum modulator valve on the automatic transmission.

■ THE DRIVER IS YOUR BEST RESOURCE

The driver of the vehicle knows a lot about the vehicle and how it is driven. *Before* diagnosis is started, always ask the following questions:

- When did the problem first occur?
- Under what conditions does it occur?
  1. cold or hot?
  2. acceleration, cruise, or deceleration?
  3. At what distance?

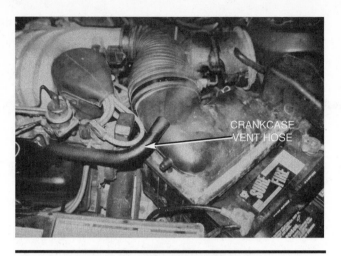

Figure 8–2 Blowby gases coming out of the crankcase vent hose. Excessive amounts of combustion gases flow past the piston rings and into the crankcase.

Figure 8–3 White steam is usually an indication of a blown (defective) cylinder head gasket that allows engine coolant to flow into the combustion chamber where it is turned to steam.

After the nature and scope of the problem are determined, the complaint should be verified before further diagnostic tests are performed.

■ VISUAL CHECKS

The first and most important "test" that can be performed is a careful visual inspection.

Oil Level and Condition

The first area for visual inspection is oil level and condition.

1. Oil level—oil should be to the proper level
2. Oil condition
   a. Using a match or lighter, try to light the oil on the dipstick; if the oil flames up, gasoline is present in the engine oil.
   b. Drip some of the engine oil from the dipstick onto the hot exhaust manifold. If the oil bubbles or boils, there is coolant (water) in the oil.
   c. Check for grittiness by rubbing the oil between your fingers.

Coolant Level and Condition

Most mechanical engine problems are caused by over-heating. The proper operation of the cooling system is critical to the life of any engine.

> **NOTE:** Check the coolant level in the radiator only if the radiator is cool. If the radiator is hot and the radiator cap is removed, the drop in pressure above the coolant will cause the coolant to boil immediately and can cause severe burns when the coolant explosively expands upward and outward from the radiator opening.

1. The coolant level in the coolant recovery container should be within the limits indicated on the overflow bottle. If this level is too low or the coolant recovery container is empty, then check the level of coolant in the radiator (only when cool) and also check the operation of the pressure cap.
2. The coolant should be checked with a hydrometer for boiling and freezing temperature. This test indicates if the concentration of the antifreeze is sufficient for proper protection.
3. Pressure test the cooling system and look for leakage. Coolant leakage will often cause
   a. A grayish white stain
   b. A rusty color stain
   c. Dye stains from antifreeze (usually greenish)
4. Check for cool areas of the radiator indicating clogged sections.
5. Check operation and condition of the fan clutch, fan, and coolant pump drive belt.

> **NOTE:** Check Chapter 7 for further information on the operation of the cooling system and diagnosis of related problems.

The Paper Test

A soundly running engine should produce even and steady exhaust at the tailpipe. Using a piece of paper (even a dollar bill works) or a 3×5 card, hold it within 1 inch (2.5 centimeters) of the tailpipe with the engine run-

---

TECH TIP ✔

What's Leaking?

The color of the leaks observed under a vehicle can help the technician determine and correct the cause. Some leaks, such as condensate (water) from the air-conditioning system, are normal, whereas a brake fluid leak is very dangerous. The following are colors of common leaks:

Sooty black	Engine oil
Yellow, green, blue, or orange	Antifreeze (coolant)
Red	Automatic transmission fluid
Murky brown	Brake or power steering fluid or very neglected antifreeze (coolant)
Clear	Air-conditioning condensate (water) (normal)

---

ning at idle. See Figure 8–4. The paper should blow out evenly without "puffing." If the paper is drawn *toward* the tailpipe at times, the valves in one or more cylinders could be burned. Other reasons why the paper might be sucked toward the tailpipe include the following:

1. The engine could be misfiring because of a lean condition that could occur normally when the engine is cold.
2. Pulsing of the paper toward the tailpipe could also be caused by a hole in the exhaust system. If exhaust escapes through a hole in the exhaust system, air could be drawn—in the intervals between the exhaust puffs—from the tailpipe to the hole in the exhaust, causing the paper to be drawn toward the tailpipe.
3. Ignition fault causing misfire.

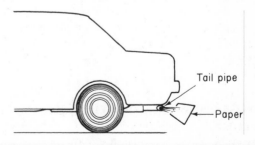

Figure 8–4 The paper test involves holding a piece of paper near the tailpipe of an idling engine. A good engine should produce even outward puffs of exhaust. If the paper is sucked in toward the tailpipe, a burned valve is a possibility.

Oil Leaks

Oil leaks can lead to severe engine damage if the resulting low oil level is not corrected. Besides causing an oily mess where the vehicle is parked, the oil leak can cause blue smoke to occur under the hood as leaking oil drips on the exhaust system. *Finding* the location of the oil leak can often be difficult. See Figures 8–5 and 8–6. To help find the source of oil leaks follow these steps:

Step 1 Clean the engine or area around the suspected oil leak. Use a high-powered hot water spray to wash the engine. A coin-operated car wash could also be used. While the engine is running, spray the entire engine and the engine compartment. Avoid letting the water come into direct contact with the air inlet and ignition distributor or ignition coil(s).

> **HINT:** If the engine starts to run rough or stalls when the engine gets wet, then the secondary ignition wires (spark plug wires) or distributor cap may be defective or have weak insulation. Be certain to wipe all wires and the distributor cap dry with a soft, dry cloth if the engine stalls.

An alternative method is to spray a degreaser on the engine, then start and run the engine until warm. Engine heat helps the degreaser penetrate the grease and dirt. Use a water hose to rinse off the engine and engine compartment.

Step 2 If the oil leak is not visible or oil seems to be coming from "everywhere," use a white talcum powder. The leaking oil will show as a dark area on the white powder. See the Tech Tip, "The Foot Powder Spray Trick."

Step 3 Fluorescent dye can be added to the engine oil. Add about 1/2 oz (15 cc) of dye per 5 quarts of engine oil. Start the engine and allow it to run about 10 minutes to thoroughly mix the dye throughout the engine. A black light can then be shown around every suspected oil leak location. The black light will easily show all oil leak locations because the dye will show as a bright yellow/green area.

■ ENGINE NOISE DIAGNOSIS

An engine knocking noise is often difficult to diagnose. Several items that can cause a deep engine knock include:

- **Valves clicking** because of lack of oil to the lifters. This noise is most noticeable at idle when the oil pressure is the lowest. See Figure 8–7.

Figure 8–5 Typical valve (rocker cover) gasket leak. Always check the *highest* and *most forward* parts of the engine that are wet when attempting to find a fluid leak.

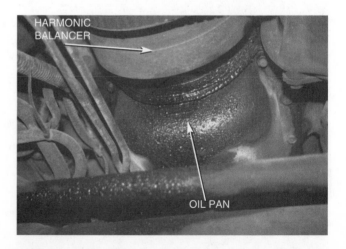

HARMONIC BALANCER

OIL PAN

Figure 8–6 Oil leak at the front of the engine could be from the front seal, oil pan gasket, or timing chain cover gasket.

Figure 8–8 Typical drive plate (flex plate) as used on the principal end of an engine using an automatic transmission.

Figure 8–7 Pushrod worn through a rocker arm.

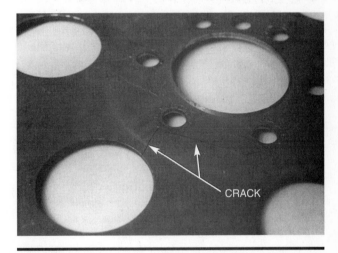

Figure 8–9 Cracked drive (flex) plate. The noise this plate made was similar to a rod bearing knocking noise.

- **Torque converter** attaching bolts or nuts loose on the flex plate. This noise is most noticeable at idle or when there is no load on the engine.
- **Cracked flex plate.** The noise of a cracked flex plate is often mistaken for a rod or main bearing noise. See Figures 8–8 and 8–9.
- **Loose or defective drive belts.** If an accessory drive belt is loose or defective, the flopping noise often sounds similar to a bearing knock. See Figure 8–10.
- **Piston pin knock.** This knocking noise is usually not affected by load on the cylinder. If the clearance is too great, a double knock noise is heard when the engine idles. If all cylinders are grounded out one at a time and the noise does not change, a defective piston pin could be the cause.
- **Piston slap.** A piston slap is usually caused by an undersize or improperly shaped piston or oversize cylinder bore. A piston slap is most noticeable when the engine is cold and tends to decrease or stop making noise as the piston expands during engine operation.

- **Timing chain noise.** An excessively loose timing chain can cause a severe knocking noise when the chain hits the timing chain cover. This noise can often sound like a rod bearing knock.
- **Heat riser noise.** A loose (worn) or defective heat riser valve in the exhaust can make a knocking noise similar to a bearing noise. Even a vacuum-controlled heat riser [also called an **early fuel evaporation (EFE)** valve] can make a knocking noise, especially under load, as the result of slight vacuum variations

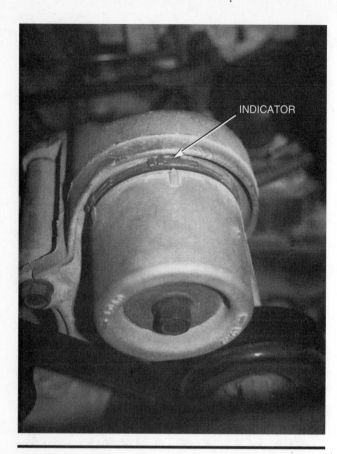

INDICATOR

Figure 8–10 An accessory drive belt tensioner. Most tensioners have a mark that indicates normal operating location. If the belt has stretched, this indicator mark will be outside of the normal range. Anything wrong with the belt or the tensioner can cause noise.

applied to the actuator diaphragm. To eliminate the heat riser as a possible cause, remove the vacuum hose to the actuator or retain the thermostatic valve with a wire or other suitable means.

- **Rod bearing noise.** The noise from a defective rod bearing is usually load sensitive and changes in intensity as the load on the engine increases and decreases. A rod bearing failure can often be detected by grounding out the spark plugs a cylinder at a time. If the knocking noise decreases or is eliminated when a particular cylinder is grounded, then the grounded cylinder is the one from which the noise is originating.
- **Main bearing knock.** A main bearing knock often cannot be isolated to a particular cylinder. The sound can vary in intensity and may disappear at times depending on engine load. See Figure 8–11.

Regardless of the type of loud knocking noise, after the external causes of the knocking noise have been eliminated, the engine should be disassembled and carefully inspected to determine the exact cause.

Typical Noises	Possible Causes
Clicking noise—like the clicking of a ballpoint pen	1. Loose spark plug 2. Loose accessory mount (for air-conditioning compressor, alternator, power steering pump, etc.) 3. Loose rocker arm 4. Worn rocker arm pedestal 5. Fuel pump (broken mechanical fuel pump return spring) 6. Worn camshaft 7. Exhaust leak 8. Ping (detonation)
Clacking noise—like tapping on metal	1. Worn piston pin 2. Broken piston 3. Excessive valve clearance 4. Timing chain hitting cover
Knock—like knocking on a door	1. Rod bearing(s) 2. Main bearing(s) 3. Thrust bearing(s) 4. Loose torque converter 5. Cracked flex plate (drive plate)
Rattle—like a baby rattle	1. Manifold heat control valve 2. Broken harmonic balancer 3. Loose accessory mounts 4. Loose accessory drive belt or tensioner
Clatter—like rolling marbles	1. Rod bearings 2. Piston pin 3. Loose timing chain
Whine—like an electric motor running	1. Alternator bearing 2. Drive belt 3. Power steering 4. Belt noise (accessory or timing)
Clunk—like a door closing	1. Engine mount 2. Drive axle shaft U-joint or constant velocity (CV) joint

TECH TIP

Engine Noise and Cost

A light, ticking noise often heard at one-half engine speed and associated with valve train noise is a less serious problem than many deep-sounding knocking noises. Generally, the deeper the sound of the engine noise, the more the owner will have to pay for repairs. A light "tick tick tick," though often not cheap, is usually far less expensive than a deep "knock knock knock" from the engine.

Figure 8–11 Typical worn serpentine accessory drive belt. A defective or worn belt can cause a variety of noises, including squealing and severe knocking similar to a main bearing knock, if glazed or loose.

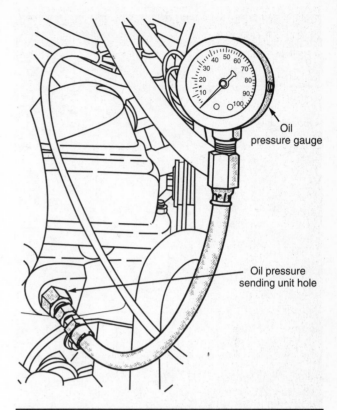

Figure 8–12 To measure engine oil pressure, remove the oil pressure sending (sender) unit usually located near the oil filter. Screw the pressure gauge into the oil pressure sending unit hole.

■ OIL PRESSURE TESTING

Proper oil pressure is very important for the operation of any engine. *Low oil pressure can cause engine wear, and engine wear can cause low oil pressure.*

If main and rod bearings are worn, oil pressure is reduced because of leakage of the oil around the bearings. See Chapter 13 for details on the oil pump and the lubrication system. Oil pressure testing is usually performed with the following steps:

Step 1 Operate the engine until normal operating temperature is achieved.

Step 2 With the engine off, remove the oil pressure sending unit or sender, usually located near the oil filter. Thread an oil pressure gauge into the threaded hole. See Figure 8–12.

HINT: An oil pressure gauge can be made from another gauge, such as an old air-conditioning gauge no longer used for air-conditioning work, and a flexible brake hose. The threads are often the same as those used for the oil pressure sending unit.

Step 3 Start the engine and observe the gauge. Record the oil pressure at idle and at 2500 RPM.

Most vehicle manufacturers recommend a minimum oil pressure of 10 psi per 1000 RPM. Therefore, at 2500 RPM, the oil pressure should be at least 25 psi. Always compare your test results with the manufacturer's recommended oil pressure.

Besides engine bearing wear, other possible causes for low oil pressure include:

- Low oil level
- Diluted oil
- Stuck oil pressure relief valve

■ OIL PRESSURE WARNING LAMP

The red oil pressure warning lamp in the dash usually lights when the oil pressure is less than 4 to 7 psi, depending on vehicle and engine. The oil light should not be on during driving. If the oil warning lamp is on, stop the engine immediately. Always confirm oil pressure with a reliable mechanical gauge before performing engine repairs. The sending unit or circuit may be defective.

TECH TIP

Use the KISS Test Method

Engine testing is done to find the cause of an engine problem. All the simple things should be tested first. Just remember KISS—"keep it simple, stupid." A loose alternator belt or loose bolts on a torque converter can sound just like a lifter or rod bearing. A loose spark plug can make the engine perform as if it had a burned valve. Some simple items that can cause serious problems include the following:

Oil Burning

- Low oil level
- Oil dilution caused by a leaking fuel pump (leaks gasoline and thins the oil)
- Clogged PCV valve or system, causing blowby and oil to be blown into the air cleaner
- Dirty oil that has not been changed for a long time [(Change the oil and drive for about 1000 miles (1600 kilometers) and change the oil and filter again.)]

Noises

- Loose torque-to-flex plate bolts (or nuts), causing a loud knocking noise

> **HINT:** Often this problem will cause noise only at idle; the noise tends to disappear during driving or when the engine is under load.

- A defective fuel pump, which may cause ticking, lifter-type noise (may not affect pump operation if only the lever return spring is broken). (Use a stethoscope to isolate the noise.)
- A loose and/or defective drive belt, which may cause a rod or main bearing knocking noise. (A loose or broken mount for the alternator, power steering pump, or air-conditioning compressor can also cause a knocking noise.)

■ OIL ANALYSIS

Most large fleets and transit operations use oil analysis data as part of their normal preventive maintenance program. Oil analysis involves getting a sample of the engine's crankcase oil and sending it to a local or regional laboratory for analysis. The results can show mechanical engine problems before there is any other indication. Many engines have been "saved" by oil analysis. The engine can be removed and disassembled to correct faults found by the oil analysis before serious and expensive engine damage occurs. Some truck and bus companies use oil analysis not only to spot trouble early, but also to

Figure 8–13 A commercially available oil analysis kit. The price of the kit includes a sample bottle, the mailing address to send the sample, and the oil analysis.

determine the maximum acceptable oil drain interval. To find a laboratory to perform oil analysis, look in the telephone yellow pages under "laboratories" or "testing laboratories" in larger cities. See Figure 8–13.

■ GETTING THE SAMPLE

For the most accurate test results, the oil sample should be from a *warm* engine. The recommended procedure is to begin to drain the oil in the usual way by removing the drain plug. To prevent getting residue from the bottom of the oil pan, allow oil to drain for several seconds before placing the sample container into the oil stream. An alternate method is to siphon oil from the crankcase, from the oil filler tube, or from the crankcase vent passages. A 4-oz. (120-cc) sample should be large enough for the testing laboratory.

■ STUDYING THE RESULTS

When the oil sample results are returned from the testing laboratory, they must be studied carefully to determine if any corrective action needs to be performed on the engine, or if the results are normal given the engine's hours, miles, and conditions of operation. Although some laboratories explain the test results, many laboratories do *not* interpret the test results for you. Most testing laboratories want the following information included with the sample to help them and you determine the results:

1. Total miles (kilometers) on the vehicle
2. Miles since the last oil change (oil life miles)
3. Engine description (gasoline, diesel, etc.)
4. Viscosity of oil originally

Following are the items measured during a typical oil sample test and a brief explanation of the meaning of the results.

Viscosity Increase

If viscosity is higher (thicker) than the original grade, this usually means that oxidation of the oil has occurred. Excessive oxidation can be caused by the following:

- Overheating due to weak cooling system function
- Aeration (air mixed into the oil) due to oil being stirred up by moving engine parts (This commonly occurs if the oil level is below recommended level.)
- Presence of small metal particles, which normally come from engine wear (These small metal particles act as a catalyst that speed the chemical reaction between oxygen and the engine oil, causing the oil to thicken.)

Other products of oxidation include sludge, gum, varnish, lacquer, carbon deposits, and acidic compounds. Maximum allowable viscosity is generally considered to be 30% thicker than the original. If thickening is greater than 30%, careful inspection should be made of the engine cooling system. Corrective action should be performed as necessary, and the engine oil and filter should be replaced. The engine and vehicle use should be carefully monitored to ensure that severe oxidation does not reoccur.

Viscosity Decrease

Most testing laboratories consider a decrease in viscosity (oil becoming thinner) to be the result of fuel dilution. A maximum allowable fuel dilution of 3% of the volume is generally accepted. Fuel dilution results in thin oil and an increase in engine wear rates. A high level of fuel dilution may be due to the following:

- Short driving cycles (especially during cold weather)
- A defective thermostat (stuck open), which could prevent the engine from reaching normal operating temperatures

- A defective choke (carburetor) or coolant temperature sensor
- A clogged exhaust gas passage under the intake (inlet) manifold
- A defective heat riser or control unit affecting intake (inlet) air temperature
- A defective carburetor float or power circuit, or a defective injector nozzle
- A clogged air filter or closed air inlet

Moisture

The contamination of engine oil by moisture (water) can result in poor lubrication and sludge formation. Normal readings are considered to be less than 0.05%. Readings higher than 2% are considered to be excessive by most testing laboratories.

A high level of moisture in the engine oil can be due to the following:

- A leaking head gasket
- A cracked block
- A cracked head
- A clogged PCV valve and/or hoses
- An inoperative crankcase breather
- Short driving cycles
- Extended oil change intervals

Antifreeze

Engine oil contaminated with antifreeze (ethylene glycol) can congeal. If the oil congeals, it is too thick to flow through the engine and lubricate properly. Possible causes of antifreeze in engine oil include the following:

- A cracked cylinder head
- A leaking head gasket
- A cracked block
- Sabotage

Iron

Iron (chemical symbol Fe) is a major wear metal. Almost every oil sample will contain some iron, measured in parts per million (PPM), as the result of normal wear.

- Normal iron content: 50 to 250 PPM
- Abnormal iron content: 250 to 350 PPM
- Excessive iron content: over 350 PPM

Iron in the oil can come from wear and rusting of:

- Rocker arms or pivot shaft
- Cylinders or cylinder sleeve
- Camshaft
- Valve guides
- Timing gear and/or chain
- Crankshaft
- Rings

- Oil pump
- Lifters
- Fuel pump rocker and/or fulcrum

Aluminum

Aluminum (Al) is also a wear metal and is measured in parts per million (PPM).

- Normal aluminum content: 5 to 25 PPM
- Abnormal aluminum content: 30 PPM
- Excessive aluminum content: over 40 PPM

     Aluminum can originate from:

- Pistons
- Rod and/or main bearings
- Camshaft bearings
- Fuel pump

Copper

Copper (Cu) is another wear metal measured in parts per million (PPM).

- Normal copper content: 5 to 25 PPM
- Abnormal copper content: 100 PPM
- Excessive copper content: over 300 PPM

     Copper can originate from:

- Bearings
- Bushings (such as distributor, fuel pump, or oil pump)

Tin

Tin (Sn) may be found in the oil. It is another wear metal measured in parts per million (PPM).

- Normal tin content: 0 to 1 PPM
- Abnormal tin content: 5 to 10 PPM
- Excessive tin content: over 15 PPM

     Tin can originate from:

- Piston coating
- Bearings

    The usual source of tin is the piston coating commonly plated on aluminum pistons, but tin can also come from bearings.

Chrome

The oil may contain chrome (Cr) wear metal. It is measured in parts per million (PPM) and originates almost exclusively from chrome piston rings. Some engines do not use chrome rings, and therefore no chrome should be found

in the oil sample of these engines. Most heavy-duty diesel engines use chrome rings, and the amount of chrome found in the oil sample indicates ring wear.

- Normal chrome content: 5 to 25 PPM
- Abnormal chrome content: 30 PPM
- Excessive chrome content: 40 PPM

Silicon

Silicon (Si) is basically dirt or sand. Silicon is the most common substance on earth. More than one-fourth of the earth's crust is silicon. The word *silicone* is often confused with *silicon*. [*Silicone* is a term used to describe a large number of compounds wherein silicon replaces carbon in an organic substance for increased stability and resistance to extremes in temperature. Therefore, silicones (with an *e* at the end of the word) can be oils, greases, resins, and synthetic rubber.]

- Normal silicon content: 5 to 25 PPM
- Abnormal silicon content: 30 PPM
- Excessive silicon content: 40 PPM

■ COMPRESSION TEST

Testing an engine for proper compression is one of the fundamental engine diagnostic tests that can be performed. For smooth engine operation, all cylinders must have equal compression. An engine can lose compression by leakage of air through one or more of only three routes:

- Intake or exhaust valve
- Piston rings (or piston, if there is a hole)
- Cylinder head gasket

    For best results, the engine should be warmed to normal operating temperature before testing. An accurate compression test should be performed as follows:

Step 1 Remove all spark plugs. This allows the engine to be cranked to an even speed. Be sure to label all spark plug wires.

> **CAUTION:** Disable the ignition system by disconnecting the primary leads from the ignition coil or module or by grounding the coil wire after removing it from the center of the distributor cap. Also disable the fuel-injection system to prevent the squirting of fuel into the cylinder.

Step 2 Block open the throttle and choke (if the vehicle is so equipped). This permits the maximum amount of air to be drawn into the engine. This step also ensures consistent compression test results.

Step 3 Thread a compression gauge into one spark plug hole and crank the engine. See Figure 8–14. Continue cranking the engine through *four* compression strokes. Each compression stroke makes a puffing sound.

> **HINT:** Note the reading on the compression gauge after the first puff. This reading should be at least one-half the final reading. For example, if the final, highest reading is 150 psi, then the reading after the first puff should be higher than 75 psi. A low first-puff reading indicates possible weak pistons. Release the pressure on the gauge and repeat for the other cylinder rings.

Step 4 Record the highest readings and compare the results. Most vehicle manufacturers specify the minimum compression reading and the maximum allowable variation among cylinders. Most manufacturers specify a maximum difference of 20% between the highest reading and the lowest reading. For example:

If the high reading is   150 psi
Subtract 20%   −30 psi
Lowest allowable compression is 120 psi

> **HINT:** To make the math quick and easy, think of 10% of 150, which is 15 (move the decimal point to the left one place). Now double it: $15 \times 2 = 30$. This represents 20%.

> **NOTE:** During cranking, the oil pump cannot maintain normal oil pressure. Extended engine cranking, such as that which occurs during a compression test, can cause hydraulic lifters to collapse. When the engine starts, loud valve clicking noises may be heard. This should be considered normal after performing a compression test, and the noise should stop after the vehicle has been driven a short distance.

■ WET COMPRESSION TEST

If the compression test reading indicates low compression on one or more cylinders, add three squirts of oil to the cylinder and retest. This is called a **wet compression test,** when oil is used to help seal around the piston rings.

Figure 8–14 Typical compression gauge being used to check the compression on a V-8 engine. For best results, all the spark plugs should be removed to ensure consistent cranking speed.

> **CAUTION:** Do not use more oil than three squirts from a hand-operated oil squirt can. Too much oil can cause a hydrostatic lock, which can damage or break pistons or connecting rods or even crack a cylinder head.

TECH TIP

The Hose Trick

Installing spark plugs can be made easier by using a rubber hose on the end of the spark plug. The hose can be a vacuum hose, fuel line, or even an old spark plug wire end. See Figure 8–15. The hose makes it easy to start the threads of the spark plug into the cylinder head. After starting the threads, continue to thread the spark plug for several turns. Using the hose eliminates the chance of cross-threading the plug. This is especially important when installing spark plugs in aluminum cylinder heads.

Perform the compression test again and observe the results. If the first-puff readings greatly improve and the readings are much higher than without the oil, the cause of the low compression is worn or defective piston rings. If the compression readings increase only slightly (or not at all), then the cause of the low compression is usually defective valves. See Figure 8–16.

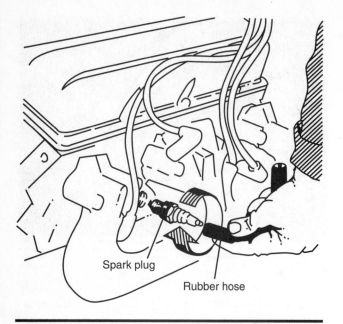

Figure 8–15 Use a vacuum or fuel line hose over the spark plug to install it without danger of cross-threading the cylinder head.

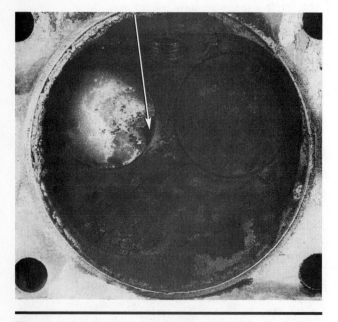

Figure 8–16 Badly burned exhaust valve. A compression test could have detected a problem, and a cylinder leakage test (leak-down test) could have been used to determine the exact problem.

■ RUNNING COMPRESSION TEST

The compression test is commonly used to help determine engine condition. A compression test is usually performed with the engine cranking.

What is the RPM of a cranking engine? An engine idles at about 600 to 900 RPM, and the starter motor obviously cannot crank the engine as fast as the engine idles. Most manufacturers' specifications require the engine to crank at 80 to 250 cranking RPM. Therefore, a check of an en-

gine's compression at cranking speed determines the condition of an engine that does not run at such low speeds.

But what should be the compression of a running engine? Some would think that the compression would be substantially higher, because the valve overlap of the cam is more effective at higher engine speeds which would tend to increase the compression.

Actually, the compression pressure of a running engine is much *lower* than cranking compression pressure. This results from the volumetric efficiency. The engine is revolving faster, and therefore, there is less *time* for air to enter the combustion chamber. With less air to compress, the compression pressure is lower. Typically, the higher the engine RPM, the lower the running compression. For most engines, the value ranges are as follows:

- Compression during cranking: 125 to 160 psi
- Compression at idle: 60 to 90 psi
- Compression at 2000 RPM: 30 to 60 psi

As with cranking compression, the running compression of all cylinders should be equal. Therefore, a problem is not likely to be detected by single compression values, but by *variations* in running compression values among the cylinders. Broken valve springs, worn valve guides, bent pushrods, and worn cam lobes are some items that would be indicated by a low running compression test reading on one or more cylinders.

Performing a Running Compression Test

To perform a running compression test, remove just one spark plug at a time. With one spark plug removed from the engine, use a jumper wire to *ground* the spark plug wire to a good engine ground. This prevents possible ignition coil damage. Start the engine, push the pressure release on the gauge, and read the compression. Increase the engine speed to about 2000 RPM and push the pressure release on the gauge again. Read the gauge. Stop the engine, reattach the spark plug wire, and repeat the test for each of the remaining cylinders. Just like the cranking compression test, the running compression test can inform a technician of the *relative* compression of all the cylinders.

■ CYLINDER LEAKAGE TEST

One of the best tests that can be used to determine engine condition is the cylinder leakage test. This test involves injecting air under pressure into the cylinders one at a time. The amount and location of any escaping air helps the technician determine the condition of the engine. The air is put into the cylinder through a cylinder leakage gauge into the spark plug hole. See Figures 8–17 and 8–18.

Figure 8–17 Typical cylinder leakage tester. The percentage of air escaping the cylinder is read on the gauge. An engine in good condition should not leak more than 20% of the air being forced into the cylinder.

Step 1 For best results, the engine should be at normal operating temperature (upper radiator hose hot and pressurized).

Step 2 The cylinder being tested must be at top dead center (TDC) of the compression stroke.

> **NOTE:** The greatest amount of wear occurs at the top of the cylinder because of the heat generated near the top of the cylinders. The piston ring flex also adds to the wear at the top of the cylinder.

Step 3 Calibrate the cylinder leakage unit as per manufacturer's instructions.

Step 4 Inject air into the cylinders one at a time, rotating the engine as necessitated by firing order to test each cylinder at TDC on the compression stroke.

Figure 8–18 A handheld portable cylinder leakage gauge. These relatively low-cost testers are available at most automotive parts stores or from tool trucks that visit dealerships and automotive service facilities.

Step 5 Evaluate the results:

Less than 10% leakage: good

Less than 20% leakage: acceptable

Less than 30% leakage: poor

More than 30% leakage: definite problem

> **HINT:** If leakage seems unacceptably high, repeat the test, being certain that it is being performed correctly and that the cylinder being tested is at TDC on the compression stroke.

Step 6 Check the source of air leakage.

   a. If air is heard escaping from the oil filler cap, the *piston rings* are worn or broken.

   b. If air is observed bubbling out of the radiator, there is a possible blown *head gasket* or cracked *cylinder head*.

   c. If air is heard coming from the carburetor or air inlet on fuel-injection-equipped engines, there is a defective intake valve(s).

   d. If air is heard coming from the tailpipe, there is a defective *exhaust valve(s)*.

■ CYLINDER POWER BALANCE TEST

Most large engine analyzers have a cylinder power balance feature. The purpose of a cylinder balance test is to determine if all cylinders are contributing power equally. It determines this by shorting out one cylinder at a time. If the engine speed (RPM) does not drop as much for one cylinder as for other cylinders of the same engine, then the shorted cylinder must be weaker than the other cylinders. For example:

Cylinder number	RPM drop when ignition is shorted
1	75
2	70
3	15
4	65
5	75
6	70

Cylinder #3 is the weak cylinder.

NOTE: Most automotive test equipment uses automatic means for testing cylinder balance. Be certain to correctly identify the offending cylinder. Cylinder #3 as identified by the equipment may be the third cylinder in the firing order instead of the actual cylinder #3.

■ POWER BALANCE TEST PROCEDURE

When point-type ignition was used on all vehicles, the common method for determining which, if any, cylinder was weak was to remove a spark plug wire from one spark plug at a time while watching a tachometer and a vacuum gauge. This method is not recommended on any vehicle with any type of electronic ignition. If any of the spark plug wires are removed from a spark plug with the engine running, the ignition coil tries to supply increasing levels of voltage attempting to jump the increasing gap as the plug wires are removed. This high voltage could easily track the ignition coil or damage the ignition module or both.

The acceptable method of canceling cylinders, which will work on all types of ignition systems, including distributorless, is to *ground* the secondary current for each cylinder. See Figure 8–19. The cylinder with the least RPM drop is the cylinder not producing its share of power.

■ VACUUM TESTING

Vacuum is pressure below atmospheric pressure and is measured in **inches** (or millimeters) **of Mercury (Hg).** An engine in good mechanical condition will run with high manifold vacuum. Manifold vacuum is developed by the pistons as they move down on the intake stroke to draw the charge from the carburetor and intake manifold. Air to refill the manifold comes past the throttle plate into the manifold. Vacuum will increase anytime the engine turns faster or has better cylinder sealing while the throttle plate remains in a fixed position. Manifold vacuum will decrease when the engine turns more

Figure 8–19 Using a vacuum hose and a test light to ground one cylinder at a time on a distributorless ignition system. This works on all types of ignition systems and provides a method for grounding out one cylinder at a time without fear of damaging any component.

slowly or when the cylinders no longer do an efficient job of pumping.

Cranking Vacuum Test

Measuring the amount of manifold vacuum during cranking is a quick and easy test to determine if the piston rings and valves are properly sealing. (For accurate results, the engine should be warm and the throttle closed.)

Step 1 Disable the ignition.

Step 2 Connect the vacuum gauge to a manifold vacuum source.

Step 3 Crank the engine while observing the vacuum gauge.

Cranking vacuum should be higher than 2.5 inches of mercury. (Normal cranking vacuum is 3 to 6 inches Hg.) If it is lower than 2.5 inches Hg, then the following could be the cause:

- Too slow a cranking speed
- Worn piston rings
- Leaking valves
- Excessive amounts of air bypassing the throttle plate (This could give a false low vacuum reading. Common sources include a throttle plate partially open or a high-performance camshaft with excessive overlap.)

Idle Vacuum Test

An engine in proper condition should idle with a steady vacuum between 17 and 21 inches Hg. See Figure 8–20.

> **NOTE:** Engine vacuum readings vary with altitude. A reduction of 1 inch Hg per 1000 feet (300 meters) of altitude should be subtracted from the expected values if testing a vehicle above 1000 feet (300 meters).

Low and Steady Vacuum

If the vacuum is lower than normal, yet the gauge reading is steady, the most common causes include

- Retarded ignition timing
- Retarded cam timing (check timing chain for excessive slack or timing belt for proper installation)

Fluctuating Vacuum

If the needle drops, then returns to a normal reading, then drops again, and again returns, then this indicates a sticking valve. A common cause of sticking valves is lack of lubrication of the valve stems.

> **HINT:** A common trick that some technicians use is to squirt some automatic transmission fluid (ATF) down the carburetor or into the air inlet of a warm engine. Often the idle quality improves and normal vacuum gauge readings are restored. The use of ATF does create excessive exhaust smoke for a short time, but it should not harm oxygen sensors or catalytic converters.
>
> If the vacuum gauge fluctuates above and below a center point, burned valves or weak valve springs may be indicated. If the fluctuation is slow and steady, unequal fuel mixture could be the cause.

■ EXHAUST RESTRICTION TEST

If the exhaust system is restricted, the engine will be low on power, yet smooth. Common causes of restricted exhaust include the following:

- Clogged catalytic converter. Always check the ignition system for faults that could cause excessive amounts of unburned fuel to be exhausted. Excessive unburned fuel can overheat the catalytic converter and cause the beads or structure of the converter to fuse together, creating the restriction. A defective fuel delivery system could also cause excessive unburned fuel being dumped into the converter.
- Clogged or restricted muffler. This can cause low power. Often a defective catalytic converter will shed

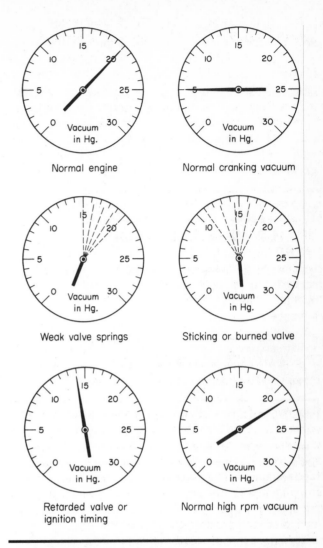

Figure 8–20 Vacuum gauge as a diagnostic tool. Connect a vacuum gauge to a manifold vacuum source (a port that has vacuum at idle).

particles that can clog a muffler. Broken internal baffles can also restrict exhaust flow.
- Damaged or defective piping. This can reduce the power of any engine. Some exhaust pipe is constructed with double walls, and the inside pipe can collapse and form a restriction that is not visible on the outside of the exhaust pipe.

■ TESTING BACK PRESSURE WITH A VACUUM GAUGE

A vacuum gauge can be used to measure manifold vacuum at a high idle (2000 to 2500 RPM). If the exhaust system is restricted, pressure increases in the exhaust system. This pressure is called **back pressure.** Manifold vacuum will drop gradually if the engine is kept at a constant speed if the exhaust is restricted.

The reason the vacuum will drop is that all exhaust leaving the engine at the higher engine speed cannot get through the restriction. After a short time (within one minute), the exhaust tends to "pile up" above the restriction and eventually remains in the cylinder of the engine at the end of the exhaust stroke. Therefore, at the beginning of the intake stroke, when the piston traveling downward should be lowering the pressure (raising the vacuum) in the intake manifold, the extra exhaust in the cylinder *lowers* the normal vacuum. If the exhaust restriction is severe enough, the vehicle can become undriveable because cylinder filling cannot occur except at idle.

■ TESTING BACK PRESSURE WITH A PRESSURE GAUGE

Exhaust system back pressure can be measured directly by installing a pressure gauge into an exhaust opening. This can be accomplished in one of the following ways:

- With an oxygen sensor. Remove the inside of an old discarded oxygen sensor and thread in an adapter to convert to a vacuum or pressure gauge.

> **NOTE:** An adapter can be easily made by inserting a metal tube or pipe. A short section of brake line works great. The pipe can be brazed to the oxygen sensor housing or it can be glued in with epoxy. An 18-millimeter compression gauge adapter can also be adapted to fit into the oxygen sensor opening. See Figure 8–21.

- With the exhaust gas recirculation (EGR) valve. Remove the EGR valve and fabricate a plate to connect to a pressure gauge.
- With the air-injection reaction (AIR) check valve. Remove the check valve from the exhaust tubes leading down to the exhaust manifold. Use a rubber cone with a tube inside to seal against the exhaust tube. Connect the tube to a pressure gauge.

At idle, the maximum back pressure should be less than 1.5 psi (10 kPa), and it should be less than 2.5 psi (15 kPa) at 2500 RPM.

■ TIMING CHAIN SLACK DIAGNOSIS

Engines with high mileage often have timing chains with slack that is excessive for proper operation. As the timing chain stretches, the cam retards in relation to the position of the crankshaft and pistons. Because the camshaft operates the valves, this also causes the valves to open and close later in the stroke than they were designed to do. (This discussion does *not* involve

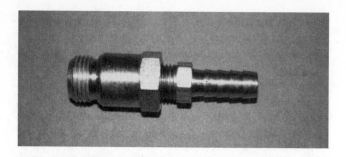

Figure 8–21 A back pressure testing tool can be assembled by using an 18-mm air-holding fitting and a 1/4-inch male barb fitting. Most oxygen sensors use an 18-mm thread and the barb fitting can be used to attach a rubber hose leading to a pressure gauge. Both of these low-cost parts are available at most automotive parts stores.

engines equipped with timing *belts*.) This retarded or late closing of the intake valve and late closing of the exhaust valve tends to lower available power at low speeds. However, the retarded cam timing does tend to slightly improve high-engine speed performance. A typical comment from an owner of a vehicle with excessive timing chain stretch is that the engine performs best after "getting it going faster."

To determine the condition of a timing chain, follow this simple procedure:

Step 1 With the ignition off, rotate the engine by hand clockwise as viewed from the front or belt end (nonprincipal end) until the timing mark aligns with top dead center (TDC).

> **NOTE:** Do not turn the engine counterclockwise if turned past TDC! This will loosen the tension on the chain, and the results of the test will not be accurate. If the engine is accidentally turned beyond TDC, continue clockwise rotation until the timing mark once again lines up with TDC.

Step 2 Remove the distributor cap.

Step 3 Slowly rotate the engine counterclockwise as viewed from the front of the engine (nonprincipal end) while observing for any movement of the distributor rotor.

Step 4 As soon as the rotor starts to move, note the distance of the timing mark from TDC.

A distance of less than 5 degrees is normal and acceptable, especially for a high-mileage engine. A distance of 5 to 8 degrees is acceptable for a high-mileage engine, but not acceptable for a low-mileage engine. Very little change in the operation of the engine would be noticed if the timing chain were replaced. If the distance is over 8 degrees, the timing chain definitely re-

Diagnostic Story

The Right Noise—Wrong Repair

A technician diagnosed a tapping noise heard at idle on a small V-8 engine to be a noisy (defective) hydraulic lifter. The noise was heard in the cam-lifter area with a stethoscope at one-half engine speed. Because this was typical valve train noise, the technician removed the intake manifold and carefully inspected all valve train components. All hydraulic valve lifters looked and tested good and were replaced back in their original locations. The camshaft was carefully inspected. Finding no obvious problem, the technician reassembled the engine. After the engine was restarted, the noise was still present.

This time the technician listened intently and everywhere for the noise. The noise was the loudest at the fuel pump. The fuel pump was replaced (it had a broken rocker arm return spring), and the noise was eliminated. The fuel pump operated off of the camshaft. The broken rocker arm return spring did not affect the operation of the fuel pump, but it did create noise that was transmitted through the engine along the camshaft.

Figure 8–22 Checking ignition timing with a timing light. If the timing mark moves back and forth, suspect a worn timing chain or gears, or a distributor problem (if the vehicle is so equipped).

Figure 8–23 Excessive timing chain wear was observed on a Ford V-8 (over 10 degrees of slack). After replacing the timing chain, the real cause of the slack was finally discovered—a worn distributor gear.

■ EXHAUST ANALYSIS AND COMBUSTION EFFICIENCY

A popular method of engine analysis involves the use of four-gas exhaust analysis equipment. See Figure 8–24. The four gases analyzed and their significance are as follows:

Hydrocarbons

Hydrocarbons (HCs) are unburned gasoline and are measured in parts per million (PPM). A correctly operating engine should burn (oxidize) almost all of the gasoline; therefore, very little unburned gasoline should be present in the exhaust. Acceptable levels of HCs are 50 PPM or less. High levels of HCs could be due to excessive oil consumption caused by weak piston rings or worn valve guides. The most common cause of

quires replacement for proper engine operation and to prevent severe engine damage that could occur if the timing chain and/or gear should fail during engine operation. See Figures 8–22 and 8–23.

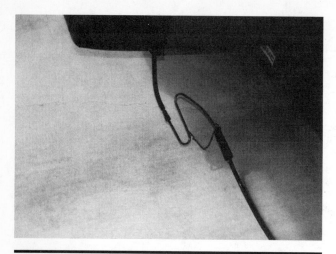

Figure 8–24 A typical partial stream sample type of exhaust probe used to measure exhaust gases in parts per million (PPM) or percentages (%).

excessive HC emissions is a fault in the ignition system. Items that should be checked include

- Spark plugs
- Spark plug wires
- Distributor cap and rotor (if the vehicle is so equipped)
- Ignition timing
- Ignition coil

Carbon Monoxide

Carbon monoxide (CO) is unstable and will easily combine with any oxygen to form stable carbon dioxide (CO_2). The fact that CO combines with oxygen is the reason that CO is a poisonous gas (in the lungs, it combines with oxygen to form CO_2 and deprives the brain of oxygen). CO levels of a properly operating engine should be less than 0.5%. High levels of CO can be caused by clogged or restricted crankcase ventilation devices such as PCV valve, hose(s), and tubes. Other items that might cause excessive CO include:

- Clogged air filter
- Incorrect idle speed
- Too-high fuel pump pressure
- Any other items that can cause a rich condition

Carbon Dioxide

Carbon dioxide (CO_2) is the result of oxygen in the engine combining with the carbon of the gasoline. An acceptable level of CO_2 is between 12% and 15%. A high reading indicates an efficiently operating engine. If the

Diagnostic Story

Horrible, Loud Sound from the Engine Compartment

The owner of a Dodge minivan complained that the vehicle made a horrible sound whenever accelerating. A visual inspection revealed that an engine mount had broken and allowed the engine to rock toward the rear of the engine compartment during acceleration, then flop back when the acceleration was released. A replacement motor mount solved the noise problem and the customer was happy that it was not as serious as it sounded. See Figure 8–25.

CO_2 level is low, the mixture may be either too rich or too lean.

Oxygen

The last of the four gases is oxygen (O_2). There is about 21% oxygen in the atmosphere, and most of this oxygen should be "used up" during the combustion process to oxidize all of the hydrogen and carbon (hydrocarbons) in the gasoline. Levels of O_2 should be very low (about 0.5%). High levels of O_2, especially at idle, could be due to an exhaust system leak.

NOTE: Adding 10% alcohol to gasoline provides additional oxygen to the fuel and will result in lower levels of CO and higher levels of O_2 in the exhaust.

■ DIAGNOSING HEAD GASKET FAILURE

Several items can be used to help diagnose a head gasket failure:

- *Exhaust gas analyzer.* With the radiator cap removed, place the probe from the exhaust analyzer above the radiator filler neck. If the HC reading increases, the exhaust (unburned hydrocarbons) is getting into the coolant from the combustion chamber.
- *Chemical test.* A chemical tester using blue paper is also available. The paper turns yellow if combustion gases are present in the coolant.
- *Bubbles in the coolant.* Remove the coolant pump belt to prevent pump operation. Remove the radiator cap and start the engine. If bubbles appear in the coolant before it begins to boil, a defective head gasket or cracked cylinder head is indicated.

(a)

(b)

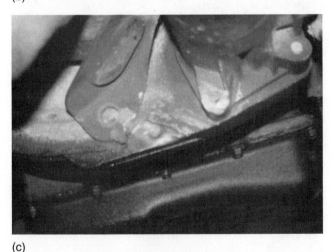

(c)

Figure 8–25 (a) A view of the engine with the transmission in park—note its location in the engine compartment. (b) The same vehicle with the transmission in drive with the driver depressing the brake pedal while gradually accelerating the engine. Note how far the engine has moved. (c) A view of the broken bracket on the lower engine mount.

- *Excessive exhaust steam.* If excessive water or steam is observed coming from the tailpipe, this means that coolant is getting into the combustion chamber from a defective head gasket or a cracked head. If there is leakage between cylinders, the engine usually misfires and a power balancer test and/or compression test can be used to confirm the problem.

If any of the preceding indicators of head gasket failure occur, remove the cylinder head(s) and check all of the following:

1. Head gasket
2. Sealing surfaces—for warpage
3. Castings—for cracks

HINT: A leaking thermal vacuum valve can cause symptoms similar to those of a defective head gasket. Most thermal vacuum valves thread into a coolant passage, and they often leak only after they get hot.

■ DASH WARNING LIGHTS

Most vehicles are equipped with several dash warning lights often called "telltale" or "idiot" lights. These lights are often the only warning a driver receives that there may be engine problems. A summary of typical dash warning lights and their meanings follows.

Oil (Engine) Light

The red oil light indicates that the engine oil pressure is too low [usually lights when oil pressure is 3 to 7 psi (20 to 50 kPa)]. Normal oil pressure should be 10 to 60 psi (70 to 400 kPa) or 10 psi per 1000 engine RPM.

When this light comes on, the driver should shut off the engine immediately and check the oil level. If the oil level is okay, then there is a possible serious engine problem or a possible defective oil pressure sending (sender) unit. The automotive technician should always check the oil pressure using a reliable mechanical oil pressure gauge if low oil pressure is suspected.

NOTE: Some automobile manufacturers combine the dash warning lights for oil pressure and coolant temperature into one light, usually labeled "engine." Therefore, when the engine light comes on, the technician should check for possible coolant temperature and/or oil pressure problems.

Coolant Temperature Light

Most vehicles are equipped with a coolant temperature gauge or dash warning light. The warning light may be labeled "coolant," "hot," or "temperature." If the coolant temperature warning light comes on during driving, this usually indicates that the coolant temperature is above a safe level, or above about 250°F (120°C). Normal coolant temperature should be about 200° to 220°F (90° to 105°C).

If the coolant temperature light comes on during driving, the following steps should be followed to prevent possible engine damage:

1. Turn off the air conditioning and turn on the heater. The heater will help get rid of some of the heat in the cooling system.
2. Raise the engine speed in neutral or park to increase the circulation of coolant through the radiator.
3. If possible, turn the engine off and allow it to cool (this may take over an hour).
4. Do not continue driving with the coolant temperature light on (or the gauge reading in the red warning section or above 260°F) or serious engine damage may result.

NOTE: If the engine does not feel or smell hot, it is possible that the problem is a faulty coolant temperature sensor or gauge.

Charge Light

The red charge warning light indicates that the charging system is not operating. The charge light may also be labeled "gen" or "alt" (alternator). Because most batteries are capable of supplying the electrical needs of the vehicle for a short time, it is not necessary to stop the engine if this warning light comes on.

If, however, the charging system is not repaired or serviced, the engine will eventually cease running because the ignition system, which ignites the spark plugs, requires a certain level of voltage to operate (usually a minimum of 9 volts).

Computer Warning Light

Most vehicles with an engine control computer use dash warning lights to warn the driver that some computer sensor, actuator, or engine parameter is not within acceptable range.

The computer dash warning light called a malfunction indicator lamp (MIL) is usually orange in color and indicates a less than serious problem, whereas some computer warning lights may be red, indicating more serious engine problems. For example, some computer systems monitor oil pressure versus engine RPM, battery voltage, and coolant temperature. The computer warning lights might be labeled

Check Engine

Check Engine Soon

Check Engine Now

Power Loss

Power Limited

If an orange engine computer light comes on, continue driving and check for any stored trouble codes as per the vehicle manufacturer's procedures. If a *red* engine computer light comes on, it is best to stop the engine and check all vital engine systems before continuing operation. Follow the manufacturer's recommended procedures for determining the cause and corrective action required.

Emission Reminder Light

Many vehicles are equipped with an emission light notifying the driver that some emission-related service is required. Some manufacturers use a mechanical sign (flag) that covers a part of the odometer when the designated mileage occurs.

The need for an emission light depends upon the ability of the manufacturer to certify the engine's emission control systems. If corrective action is required to maintain the emission standards, then the driver must be notified at the appropriate mileage intervals. A service manual should be consulted whenever the emission indicator is encountered to determine what corrective action should be taken to maintain acceptable emission levels to determine the exact method to follow to reset the emission indicator.

NOTE: The emission light and the engine light are often confusing to drivers. Before attempting service work, make certain that the service is appropriate for the warning light.

TECH TIP

The Quick and Easy Decarbonizing Trick

Carbon is a by-product of combustion. Carbon deposits accumulate in the combustion chamber and on the backsides of both intake and exhaust valves. These carbon deposits can build up on valves and valve guides, causing hesitation, rough idle, and even stalling problems. Carbon deposits can coat the combustion chamber and tops of pistons, causing an increase in compression and an increase in nitrogen (NO_x) emissions.

No chemical can dissolve carbon, but decarbonizing an engine can be as easy as the following:

Step 1 Pour a can of **top engine cleaner** into a container such as a large coffee can. Fill the top engine cleaner can with water and add that to the coffee can, creating a 50/50 mix of cleaner and water.

> **NOTE:** The cleaner disperses and penetrates through the carbon, and the water in the mixture turns to steam in the combustion chamber to force the carbon off of internal engine parts.

Step 2 Start and run the engine until it reaches normal operating temperature. Connect one end of a length of 5/32-inch ID vacuum hose to a manifold vacuum port close to the throttle plate and place the other end into the coffee can with the cleaner-water mixture.

Step 3 Operate the engine at a fast idle (2500 RPM) until all the cleaner-water mixture is drawn into the engine. Stop the engine.

Step 4 Allow the cleaner to work for about one hour and then start the engine. Drive the vehicle aggressively to blow out the loosened carbon deposits. Repeat if necessary.

PS 15–1 Always use a vacuum "T" at the end of the vacuum gauge to make sure that the gauge is measuring the engine as it is normally operating. The gauge being used is from an old engine analyzer.

PS 15–2 Locate a good manifold vacuum source. A common location that is often easy to access is the vacuum line at the fuel-pressure regulator.

PS 15–3 Be sure all vacuum hoses fit snugly onto the fittings.

PS 15–4 Start the engine and observe the vacuum gauge. The vacuum at idle (engine warm) should be 17 to 21 in. Hg (at sea level) and steady. This reading of slightly over 20 in. Hg indicates that the condition of the engine is sound.

PS 15–5 An ignition misfire will often cause the vacuum gauge needle to occasionally drop less than 1 in. Hg. A test light is being used to ground out a spark plug wire to show how a vacuum gauge reacts to an ignition misfire. (By attaching a 2-inch length of vacuum hose between the coil and a plug wire, a test light is used to ground out the spark.)

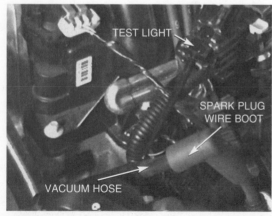

PS 15–6 Notice that the vacuum gauge reads about 1 in. Hg lower than normal every time the plug was grounded.

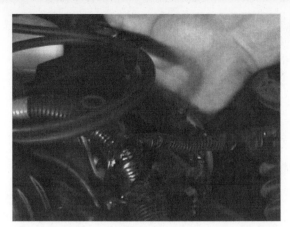

PS 15–7 An engine mechanical fault such as a sticking valve or broken valve spring will cause the vacuum gauge to drop more than 1 in. Hg and fluctuate. A low vacuum reading can also be caused by a restricted intake or exhaust system. Placing a hand partially over the intake throttle plate causes the vacuum to decrease.

PS 15–8 A lower than normal reading is usually a result of retarded ignition or valve timing. A misadjusted distributor or a worn (stretched) timing chain can cause both the valve and the ignition timing to be retarded. An incorrectly installed timing belt could also cause the vacuum to be steady, but lower than normal.

PS 15–9 Rapidly accelerating the engine (or driving the vehicle at wide-open throttle) should cause the vacuum gauge to read zero.

PS 15–10 If greater than 1 in. Hg of vacuum is observed during rapid acceleration, look for a restricted intake system.

PS 15–11 During deceleration, the vacuum should increase above the idle reading. Just remember that a vacuum gauge senses engine load. Light load (such as deceleration) is indicated by a high vacuum reading whereas a heavy load (much as driving at wide-open throttle) results in a very low or zero reading.

PS 15–12 After testing, be sure to reinstall the vacuum connector at the fuel pressure regulator and keep the T fitting attached to the hose of the vacuum gauge for future use.

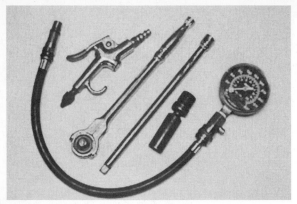

PS 16–1 The tools and equipment needed to perform a compression test include a compression gauge, an air nozzle, and the socket ratchets and extensions that may be necessary to remove the spark plugs from the engine.

PS 16–2 To prevent ignition and fuel-injection operation while the engine is being cranked, remove both the fuel-injection fuse and the ignition fuse. If the fuses cannot be removed, disconnect the wiring connectors for the injectors and the ignition system.

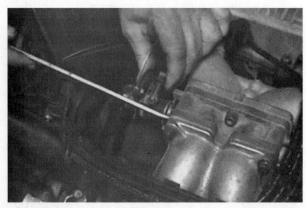

PS 16–3 Block open the throttle (and choke, if the engine is equipped with a carburetor). Here a screwdriver is being used to wedge the throttle linkage open. Keeping the throttle open ensures that enough air will be drawn into the engine so that the compression test results will be accurate.

PS 16–4 Before removing the spark plugs, use an air nozzle to blow away any dirt that may be around the spark plug. This step helps prevent debris from getting into the engine when the spark plugs are removed.

PS 16–5 Remove all of the spark plugs. Be sure to mark the spark plug wires so that they can be reinstalled onto the correct spark plugs after the compression test has been performed.

PS 16–6 Select the proper adapter for the compression gauge. The threads on the adapter should match those on the spark plug.

PS 16–7 If necessary, connect a battery charger to the battery before starting the compression test. It is important that consistent cranking speed be available for each cylinder being tested.

PS 16–8 Have an assistant use the ignition key to crank the engine while you are observing the compression gauge. Make a note of the reading on the gauge after the first "puff," which indicates the first compression stroke that occurred on that cylinder as the engine was being rotated. An engine with good piston rings should indicate at least one-half the final reading on the first puff. If the first puff reading is low and the reading gradually increases with each puff, weak or worn piston rings may be indicated.

PS 16–9 After the engine has been cranked for four "puffs," stop cranking the engine and observe the compression gauge.

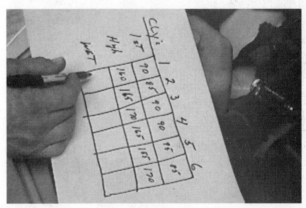

PS 16–10 Record the first puff and this final reading for each cylinder. The final readings should all be within 20% of each other.

PS 16–11 If a cylinder(s) is lower than most of the others, use an oil can and squirt two squirts of engine oil into the cylinder and repeat the compression test. This is called performing a wet compression test.

PS 16–12 If the gauge reading is now much higher than the first test results, then the cause of the low compression is due to worn or defective piston rings. The oil in the cylinder temporarily seals the rings which causes the higher reading.

PHOTO SEQUENCE   Cylinder Leakage Test

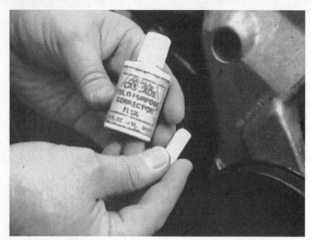

PS 17–1 Chalk and/or correction fluid can be used to highlight the timing marks.

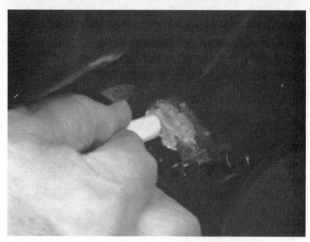

PS 17–2 Rub the timing mark with chalk. Tape the chalk to a stick if necessary to reach the timing mark.

PS 17–3 Wipe off the excess chalk from the timing mark. The chalk remaining in the low places makes reading the marks easier.

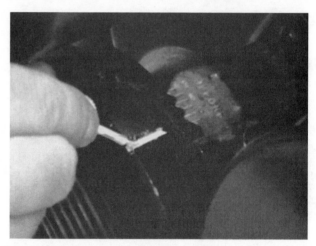

PS 17–4 Use correction fluid (or chalk) to highlight the timing mark on the harmonic balancer.

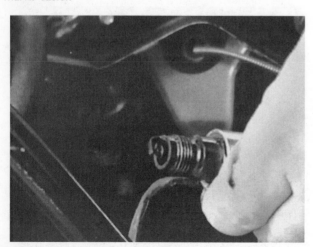

PS 17–5 Remove the spark plugs and note their condition. This spark plug is gasoline fouled and could be the cause of poor engine operation.

PS 17–6 Connect a cylinder leak tester to a shop air (compressed air) hose.

Cylinder Leakage Test—continued

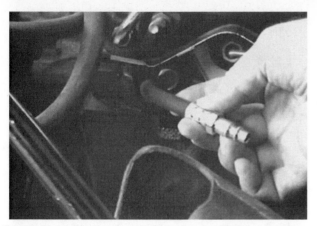

PS 17–7 Install the tester hose into the spark plug hole. Rotate the engine until the cylinder is at the top dead center compression as indicated by the timing mark. Starting at cylinder #1 makes rotating to the next cylinder easier.

PS 17–8 After calibrating the gauge and connecting the hose to the tester, the needle indicates the percentage (%) of the air that is leaking out of the cylinder. In this case, the percentage is extremely high indicating that there is a problem with this cylinder.

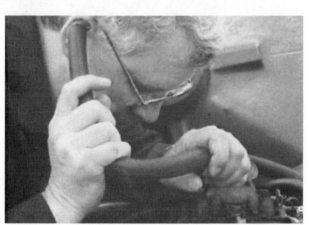

PS 17–9 Use a rubber heater hose to listen for air escaping. In this case, air was heard coming from the carburetor. A burned or bent intake valve or other valve train problem is the likely cause.

PS 17–10 Seeing air bubbles in the radiator or hearing air escaping from the radiator would indicate a blown head gasket, cracked cylinder head, or cracked block.

PS 17–11 If air is heard escaping from the oil-fill opening, then the piston rings are weak or broken. A hole in a piston would create a high leakage rate and would be heard at the oil-fill opening.

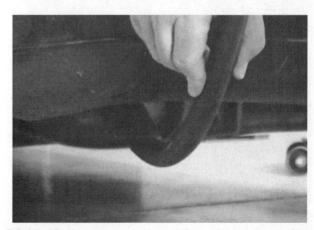

PS 17–12 If air is heard escaping from the tailpipe, a burned or stuck open exhaust valve is the most likely cause. Repeat the test for each cylinder.

PHOTO SEQUENCE   Oil Pressure Measurement

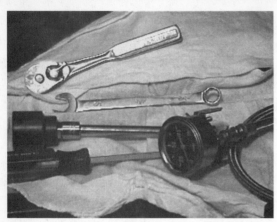

PS 18–1 The tools needed to measure engine oil pressure include an oil pressure gauge, oil pressure sending unit socket, and a ratchet with an extension.

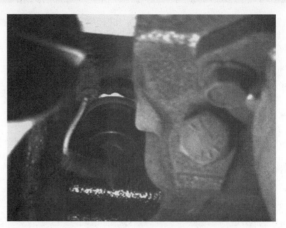

PS 18–2 To measure the oil pressure, the oil pressure warning sending unit has to be located. On this Lincoln, the oil pressure sending unit is located near the oil filter with one wire attached that leads to the dash warning light.

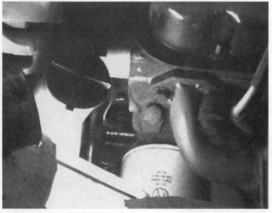

PS 18–3 To gain access to the oil pressure sending unit, the air cleaner housing duct was removed.

PS 18–4 Be sure the ignition is off before using an oil pressure sending unit socket (or a 1 1/16-in., six-point socket) to remove the oil pressure sending unit.

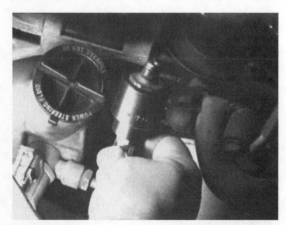

PS 18–5 The original sending unit had sealant around the threads to prevent oil from leaking from around the threads.

PS 18–6 Attach the threaded end of the oil pressure gauge into the threaded opening where the oil pressure sending unit was removed.

Oil Pressure Measurement—continued

PS 18–7 Be sure that the gauge is out of the way of any moving parts and then start the engine.

PS 18–8 Observe the oil pressure gauge. This is normal oil pressure for a cold engine. Normal oil pressure should be about 10 psi per 1000 RPM.

PS 18–9 After allowing the engine to reach normal operating temperature and observing that the oil pressure is within the normal range at idle and at higher engine speeds, the ignition key can be turned off.

PS 18–10 Remove the oil pressure gauge assembly.

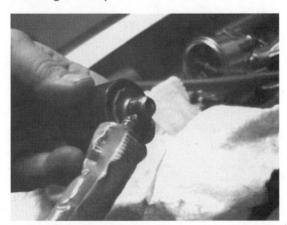

PS 18–11 Apply sealant to the threads of the oil pressure sending unit. Most vehicle manufacturers warn against using Teflon® tape because the threads can cut through the tape and cause strips of the tape to travel through the oil system possibly causing a partial blockage which can create a major engine mechanical fault.

PS 18–12 After threading the oil pressure sending unit back into the block, reattach the sending unit wire. Start the engine and check for leaks.

■ SUMMARY

1. The first step in diagnosing engine condition is to perform a thorough visual inspection, including a check of oil and coolant levels and condition.
2. Oil leaks can be found by using a white powder or a fluorescent dye and a black light.
3. Many engine-related problems make a characteristic noise.
4. Oil analysis by an engineering laboratory can reveal engine problems by measuring the amount of dissolved metals in the oil.
5. A compression test can be used to test the condition of valves and piston rings.
6. A cylinder leakage test fills the cylinder with compressed air, and the gauge indicates the percentage of leakage.
7. A cylinder balance test indicates whether all cylinders are working.
8. Testing engine vacuum is another procedure that can help the service technician determine engine condition.
9. If the timing chain has worn and stretched, the engine cannot produce normal power.
10. Exhaust analysis testing is another diagnostic tool that can tell the service technician whether the engine is performing correctly and efficiently.

■ REVIEW QUESTIONS

1. Describe four visual checks that should be performed on an engine if a mechanical malfunction is suspected.
2. List three simple items that could cause excessive oil consumption.
3. List three simple items that could cause engine noises.
4. Explain what could be wrong with an engine if the oil analysis report came back from a testing laboratory with the following information:

Silicon: 35 PPM
Copper: 57 PPM
Tin: 1 PPM
Chrome: 8 PPM
Aluminum: 31 PPM
Iron: 303 PPM
Fuel dilution: none
Antifreeze: none
Moisture content: zero

5. Describe how to perform a compression test and how to determine what is wrong with an engine based on a compression test result.
6. Describe the cylinder leakage test.
7. Explain how a technician can safely ground out one cylinder at a time without damage to the electronics of the vehicle.
8. Describe how a vacuum gauge would indicate if the valves were sticking in their guides.
9. Describe the test procedure for determining if the exhaust system is restricted (clogged) using a vacuum gauge.

■ ASE CERTIFICATION-TYPE QUESTIONS

1. Technician A says that the paper test could detect a burned valve. Technician B says that a grayish white stain could be a coolant leak. Which technician is correct?
   a. Technician A only
   b. Technician B only
   c. Both Technician A and B
   d. Neither Technician A nor B

2. Two technicians are discussing oil leaks. Technician A says that an oil leak can be found using a fluorescent dye in the oil with a black light to check for leaks. Technician B says that a white spray powder can be used to locate oil leaks. Which technician is correct?
   a. Technician A only
   b. Technician B only
   c. Both Technician A and B
   d. Neither Technician A nor B

3. An increase in viscosity can be due to _____.
   a. Wear metals in the oil
   b. Fuel dilution of the oil
   c. A clogged air filter
   d. All of the above

4. Antifreeze in the engine oil can cause _____ .
   a. The oil to become thinner (decrease viscosity)
   b. The oil to become thicker (increase viscosity)
   c. The oil to congeal
   d. Both b and c

5. A smoothly operating engine depends on
_____ .
   a. High compression on most cylinders
   b. Equal compression between cylinders
   c. Cylinder compression levels above 100 psi (700 kPa) and within 70 psi (500 kPa) of each other
   d. Compression levels below 100 psi (700 kPa) on most cylinders

6. A good reading for a cylinder leakage test would be
_____ .
   a. Within 20% between cylinders
   b. All cylinders below 20% leakage
   c. All cylinders above 20% leakage
   d. All cylinders above 70% leakage and within 7% of each other

7. Technician A says that during a power balance test, the cylinder that causes the biggest RPM drop is the weak cylinder. Technician B says that if one spark plug wire is grounded out and the engine speed does not drop, a weak or dead cylinder is indicated. Which technician is correct?
   a. Technician A only
   b. Technician B only
   c. Both Technician A and B
   d. Neither Technician A nor B

8. _Cranking_ vacuum should be _____ .
   a. 2.5 inches Hg or higher
   b. Over 25 inches Hg
   c. 17 to 21 inches Hg
   d. 6 to 16 inches Hg

9. Technician A says that a worn (stretched) timing chain and worn gears will cause the valve and ignition timing to be retarded. Technician B says that if the timing chain slack is over 8 degrees, the timing chain and gears should be replaced. Which technician is correct?
   a. Technician A only
   b. Technician B only
   c. Both Technician A and B
   d. Neither Technician A nor B

10. The low oil pressure warning light usually comes on
_____ .
   a. Whenever an oil change is required
   b. Whenever oil pressure drops dangerously low (3 to 7 psi)
   c. Whenever the oil filter bypass valve opens
   d. Whenever the oil filter antidrain back valve opens

Engine Removal and Disassembly

The decision to repair an engine should be based on all the information about the engine that is available to the service technician. In some cases, the engine might not be worth repairing. It is the responsibility of the technician to discuss the advantages and disadvantages of the different repair options with the customer. The customer, who is paying for the repair, must make the final decision on the reconditioning procedure to be used. The decision will be based on the recommendation of the service technician.

■ COMPONENT REPAIR

Most customers want to spend the least amount of money, so they only have the faulty component repaired. If a part fails, it may only be the result of the faulty part. An example of this would be a failed timing sprocket and chain. The problem will be corrected when a new timing sprocket and chain are installed. On the other hand, a part may have failed because some other part was not working correctly. An example of this would be a rocker arm pivot that was badly scored

because it did not get proper lubrication. Perhaps the lubrication was restricted by a faulty metering valve inside the hydraulic lifter. If only the rocker arm and pivot were replaced, the new rocker arm and pivot would soon fail because the lifter problem was not also repaired. Figure 9–1 shows a rocker arm and pivot from an engine on which this was done. The service technician should explain to the customer why the part failed and suggest different repairs that could be made to keep the part from failing again.

■ VALVE JOB

Failure of a valve to seal on the seat is one of the most common cases of premature failure, and future, engine problems. When there is a leak between the valve and

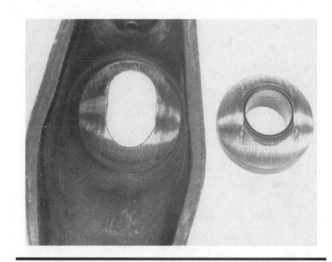

Figure 9–1 Scoring of rocker arm and pivot caused by loss of lubrication. This problem is most commonly found on cylinders nearest the EGR valve. The extra heat of the exhaust passages in this area can overheat the oil, causing deposits that clog oil passages.

the seat, the combustion pressure is lowered. This will reduce both engine economy and power. The high-pressure combustion gases escaping between the leaking valve and seat will burn the valve face, and this, in turn, increases the leakage. The tops of the pistons are visible once the head is removed for a valve job. Their condition may indicate that the pistons should also be serviced.

Failure of a valve to seal on the seat can result from abnormal combustion, incorrect valve lash, valve stem deposits, abusive engine operation, and so on. Valve leakage is corrected by doing a **valve job.** This does not necessarily correct the malfunction that caused the valve to leak. Stopping valve leakage improves manifold vacuum. The greater manifold vacuum may draw the oil past worn piston rings and into the combustion chamber during the intake stroke, causing oil consumption to increase. See Figure 9–2.

Figure 9–2 An alternative to performing a valve job is to purchase remanufactured heads. The photo shows finished head assemblies as found on the showroom floor of an engine remanufacturer. The top three numbers indicate engine size in cubic inches, and the bottom three numbers are the last three numbers of the casting number.

■ MINOR OVERHAUL

In this discussion, engine overhaul includes both a ring and a valve job. New connecting rod bearings are usually installed during an overhaul. Sometimes, this type of reconditioning is called a **minor overhaul.** A minor overhaul can usually be done without removing the engine from the chassis. It does require removal of both the head and the oil pan. The overhaul is usually done when the engine lacks power, has poor fuel economy, uses an excessive amount of oil, produces visible tailpipe emissions, runs rough, or is hard to start. It is still only a repair procedure. Many worn parts remain in the engine. Other engine problems may be noticed after the oil pan is removed and the piston and rod assemblies are taken out. The customer should be informed about any other engine problem so that the service the engine requires can be authorized. In the high performance industry, this procedure is called **freshening the engine.**

■ MAJOR OVERHAUL

A complete engine reconditioning job is called rebuilding. Sometimes, this type of reconditioning is called a **major overhaul.** To rebuild the engine, the engine must be removed from the chassis and be completely disassembled. All serviceable parts are reconditioned to either new or service standards. All bearings, gaskets, and seals are replaced. When the reconditioning is done properly, a rebuilt engine should operate as long as a new engine.

A special form of precision engine rebuilding is called **blueprinting.** Blueprinting is usually done to give the engine maximum performance. The clearances are all set near the maximum specifications and combustion chambers are adjusted to minimum and equal volumes. All servicing details are done with extreme care. The engine is carefully balanced. Blueprinting requires skilled and detailed labor and so is very expensive.

The vehicle is out of service while the engine is being rebuilt. This is inconvenient for some customers and very expensive for others. Because of the total cost, the customer might decide to replace the engine instead of having it rebuilt.

■ SHORT BLOCK

The quickest way to get a vehicle back in service is to exchange the faulty engine for a different one. In an older vehicle, the engine may be replaced with a used engine from a salvage yard. In some cases, only a reconditioned block, including the crankshaft, rods, and pistons, is used. This replacement assembly is called a

short block. The original heads and valve train are reconditioned and used on the short block.

■ FITTED BLOCK

A **fitted block** is a reconditioned block with pistons only. The individual pistons are selected for proper clearance for each cylinder. A fitted block is generally not the preferred unit to purchase because the block does *not* contain the following components:

- Crankshaft and bearings
- Connecting rods and bearings
- Camshaft and bearings

■ LONG BLOCK

The replacement assembly is called a **long block** when the reconditioned assembly includes the heads and valve train. Many automotive machine shops maintain a stock of short and long blocks of popular engines. Usually, the original engine parts, called the **core,** are exchanged for the reconditioned assembly. The core parts are reconditioned by the automotive machine shop and put back in stock for the next customer. See Figure 9–3.

■ REMANUFACTURED ENGINES

Some engines are **remanufactured.** The engine cores are completely disassembled, and each serviceable part is reconditioned with specialized machinery. Engines are then assembled on an engine assembly line similar

Figure 9–3 Shipping area of a major regional engine remanufacturer. Note that each engine is bolted to a wooden pallet and covered in a plastic bag for shipment. Cores can be shipped back to the plant on the same wooden pallet.

to the original manufacturer's assembly line. The parts that are assembled together as an engine have not come out of the same engine. The remanufactured engine usually has new pistons, valves, and lifters, together with other parts that are normally replaced in a rebuilt engine. All clearances and fits in the remanufactured engine are the same as in a new engine. A remanufactured engine should give service as good as that of a new engine, and it will cost about half as much. Remanufactured engines usually carry a warranty. This means that they will be replaced if they fail during the period of the warranty. They may even cost less than a rebuilt engine, because much of the reconditioning is done by specialized machines rather than by expensive skilled labor.

■ ENGINE REMOVAL

The engine exterior and the engine compartment should be cleaned before work is begun. A clean engine is easier to work on; and the cleaning not only helps to keep dirt out of the engine, but also minimizes accidental damage from slipping tools.

- **Disconnect the negative cable** and remove the battery from the vehicle if it could interfere with the removal of the engine. Remove the hood and store it on fender covers placed on the top of the vehicle, where it is least likely to be damaged.
- **Drain the coolant** from the radiator and the engine block to minimize the chance of coolant getting into the cylinders when the head is removed.
- **Disconnect the exhaust system**—On some engines, it may be easier to remove the exhaust manifold(s) from the cylinder head(s), whereas on others, it may be easier to disconnect the exhaust pipe from the manifold(s).
- **Label everything**—Tape can be marked with the proper location of each item so that all items can be easily replaced during engine assembly.
- **Disconnect all coolant hoses** and the transmission oil cooler lines from the radiator. Remove the

T E C H T I P

A Picture Is Worth a Thousand Words

Take pictures with a Polaroid camera, digital camera, or a video camcorder of the engine being serviced. These pictures will be worth their weight in gold when it comes time to reassemble or reinstall the engine. It is very difficult for anyone to remember the *exact* location of every bracket, wire, and hose. Referring back to the photos of the engine before work was started will help you restore the vehicle to like-new condition.

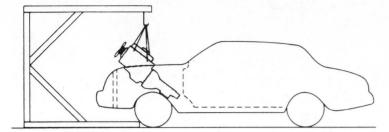

Figure 9–4 An engine must be tipped as it is pulled from the chassis.

Figure 9–5 When removing just the engine from a front-wheel-drive vehicle, the transaxle must be supported. Shown here is a typical fixture that can be used to hold the engine if the transaxle is removed or to hold the transaxle if the engine is removed.

radiator and have it checked and cleaned while it is out of the chassis.

- **Recover the air-conditioning refrigerant if necessary.** Set the air-conditioning compressor aside and remove the condenser if necessary.

There are two ways to remove the engine.

1. The engine can be lifted out of the chassis with the transmission/transaxle attached.
2. The transmission/transaxle can be separated from the engine and left in the chassis.

The method to be used must be determined before the engine is removed from the vehicle.

Under the vehicle, the driveshaft (propeller shaft) or half shafts are removed and the exhaust pipes disconnected. In some installations, it may be necessary to loosen the steering linkage idler arm to give clearance. The transmission controls, speedometer cable, and clutch linkages are disconnected and tagged.

A sling, either a chain or lift cable, is attached to the manifold or head cap screws on top of the engine. A hoist is attached to the sling and snugged to take most of the weight. This leaves the engine resting on the mounts. (Most engines use three mounts, one on each side and one at the back of the transmission or at the front of the engine.) The rear cross-member is removed, and on rear-wheel-drive vehicles, the transmission is lowered. The hoist is tightened to lift the engine. The engine will have to nose up as it is removed. The front of the engine must come almost straight up as the transmission slides from under the floor pan, as illustrated in Figure 9–4. The engine and transmission are hoisted free of the automobile, swung clear, and lowered on an open floor area.

NOTE: The engine is lowered and removed from underneath on many front-wheel-drive vehicles. See Figures 9–5 through 9–10 on pages 205–207.

Figure 9–6 This front-wheel-drive engine was dropped out of the bottom of the vehicle along with the cradle (subframe) and transaxle as an assembly.

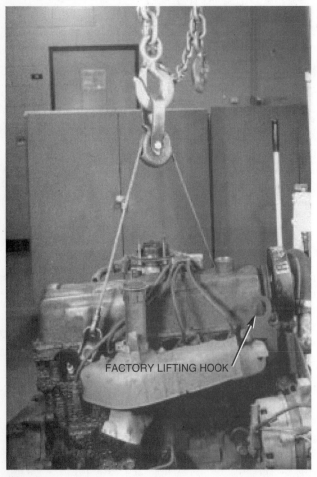

(a)

(b)

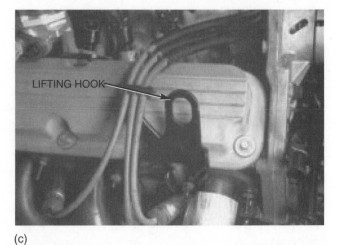

(c)

Figure 9–7 (a) Notice how this four-cylinder Ford engine is well balanced on the hoist. (b) Factory hook on rear (bell housing end) of the engine. (c) Factory hook on the front (accessory drive end) of the engine. These factory hooks are usually well placed for balance and ease of use, because the factory uses them while installing the engine in the vehicle. Time and labor are saved by not removing them after the engine is installed.

Figure 9–8 The transmission should be supported when the engine is removed. This engine was removed because all of the oil leaked out after the wrong oil filter was used during an oil change and the engine had to be replaced.

Figure 9–9 Look for bent, damaged, or broken parts as the engine is being removed from the vehicle. This broken engine mount could cause excessive engine movement and driveline stress.

■ ENGINE DISASSEMBLY

The following disassembly procedure applies primarily to pushrod engines. The procedure will have to be modified somewhat when working on overhead cam engines. Engines should be cold before disassembly to minimize the chance of warpage.

Removal of the rocker arm covers gives the first opportunity to see inside a part of the engine. See Figure

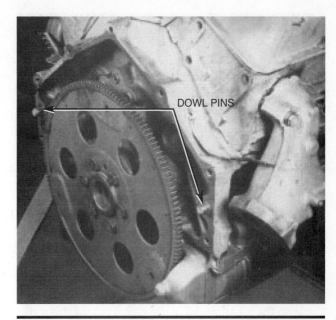

Figure 9–10 Be certain not to damage these alignment dowel pins when removing or reinstalling a transmission. These dowel pins are critical for the proper alignment of the engine transmission assembly.

Figure 9–11 Typical deposits inside a valve cover.

9–11. Make a good visual examination of this area to identify and determine the cause of any abnormal condition. Examine the rocker arms, valve springs, and valve tips for obvious defects.

Remove the manifold hold-down cap screws and nuts, and lift off the manifold. If the gaskets are stuck, a flat blade, such as that of a putty knife, can be worked alongside of the gaskets to loosen them. Care must be taken to avoid damaging the parting surface as the gasket is loosened. When the manifold and lifter valley cover are off of V-type engines, the technician has another opportunity to examine the interior of the engine. On some V-type engines, it is possible to see the condition of the cam at the bottom of the lifter valley.

Figure 9–12 The top of the piston is completely gone on this engine. The parts were found in the oil pan.

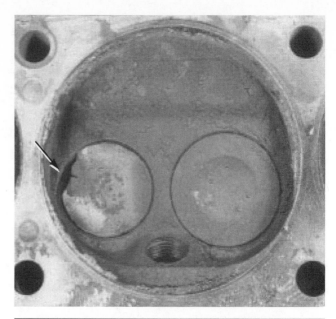

Figure 9–13 Notice the badly burned exhaust valve.

With the manifold off of the V-type engine, note any obvious abnormal conditions, loosen the rocker arms, and remove the pushrods. The usual practice is to leave the lifters in place when doing only a valve job. The lifters can be removed at this time if they are causing the problem or if the engine valve train is to be serviced.

Remove the head cap screws and lift the head from the block deck. If the head gasket is stuck, carefully pry the head to loosen the gasket.

CAUTION: Aluminum cylinder heads often warp upward in the center of the head. Loosening the center head bolts first will tend to increase the warpage, especially if the head is being removed to replace a head gasket because of overheating. Always follow the torque table backward, starting with the highest-number bolt and working toward the lowest number. In other words, always loosen fasteners starting at the end or outside of the component and work toward the inside or center of the component.

Special care should be taken to pry only on edges of the head that will not break. Parting surfaces should *not* be scratched. Scratched or burred surfaces will lead to leaks in the repaired engine.

The combustion chamber is exposed when the head is removed. The combustion chamber pocket in the head and the top of the piston should be given a thorough visual examination. See Figures 9–12 and 9–13. A normal combustion chamber is coated with a layer of hard, light-colored deposits. If the combustion chamber has been running too hot, the deposits will be very thin and white colored. Also see Figure 9–14.

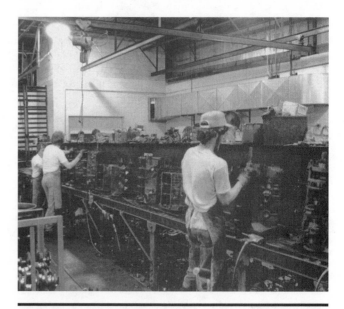

Figure 9–14 Engine disassembly on a conveyor line at a large regional engine remanufacturer. This remanufacturer can completely remanufacture about 200 engines a day.

■ REMOVING THE CYLINDER RIDGE

The ridge above the top ring must be removed before the piston and connecting rod assembly is removed. Cylinder wear leaves an upper ridge. Ridge removal is necessary to avoid catching a ring on the ridge and breaking the piston as pictured in Figure 9–15. The ridge is removed with a cutting tool that is fed into the

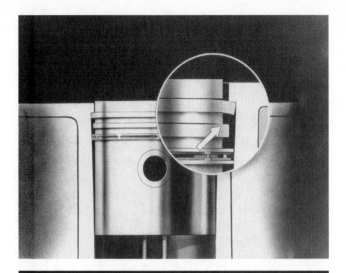

Figure 9–15 If the ridge at the top of a cylinder is not removed, the piston could break when pushed out of the cylinder during disassembly. *(Courtesy of Sealed Power)*

metal ridge. A guide on the tool prevents accidental cutting below the ridge. The ridge reaming job should be done carefully with frequent checks of the work so that no more material than necessary is removed. One type of ridge reamer is shown in Figures 9–16 and 9–17.

CAUTION: Some vehicle manufacturers warn not to use a punch or an electric pencil on powdered metal connection rods.

■ PISTON REMOVAL

The connecting rod caps should be marked (numbered). If not, be sure to use an electric pencil or a permanent marker to number the connecting rods. See Figure 9–18.

Rotate the engine until the piston that is to be removed is at top dead center (TDC). Remove connecting rod nuts from the rod so that the rod cap with its bearing half can be removed. Fit the rod bolts with protectors to keep the bolt threads from damaging the crankshaft journals, and remove the piston and rod assemblies.

■ PISTON CONDITION

Normal piston wear shows up as even wear on the thrust surfaces of the piston. The wear is from the top to the bottom in the center of the thrust surfaces, as

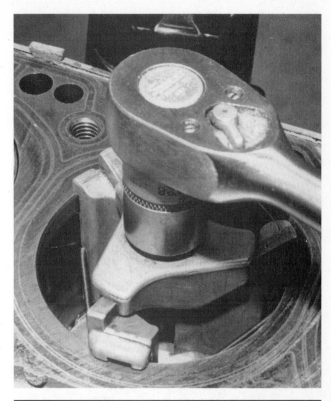

Figure 9–16 Ridge being removed with one type of ridge reamer before the piston assemblies are removed from the engine.

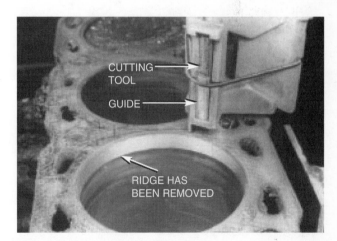

Figure 9–17 Ridge reamer and cylinder after ridge has been removed. Remanufacturers do not remove the cylinder ridge because all remanufactured engines are bored oversize and receive replacement pistons.

shown in Figure 9–19. The top ring should be slightly loose in the groove. This type of piston can usually be reconditioned for additional useful service.

Figure 9–18 Notice the numbers on the connecting rods and main bearing caps. If the main bearing caps and rod caps are not marked at the factory, they should be marked before the engine is disassembled.

Figure 9–20 Piston burned as a result of detonation. The owner of this engine was operating the vehicle without mufflers and did not hear the engine-damaging spark knock. (The ignition was set too far advanced.)

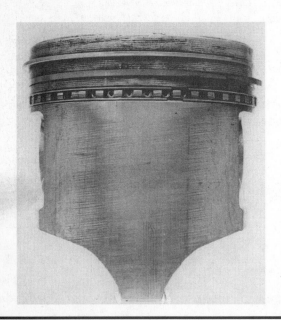

Figure 9–19 Normal piston thrust surface wear. This piston could be reconditioned to give further service.

Heat Damage

Holes in pistons, burned areas, severely damaged ring lands, and scoring are obviously abnormal conditions. The exact nature of the abnormal condition should be determined. This is necessary so that the cause can be corrected.

Combustion knock or detonation will burn the edge of the piston from the head down, in behind the rings, as pictured in Figures 9–20 and 9–21. This burning usually occurs at a point far from the spark plug, where the hot end gases rapidly release their heat energy during detonation. High temperature softens the piston, allowing combustion pressure to burn through, usually near

Figure 9–21 This high performance engine used for drag racing suffered from detonation that destroyed this piston.

Figure 9–22 Hole burned through the head of a piston as a result of preignition.

Figure 9–23 Scuffed piston skirt caused by overheating and lubrication breakdown.

Figure 9–24 Piston ring scuffing caused by overheating.

Figure 9–25 Piston rings stuck in their grooves with hard carbon.

the middle of the piston head, as shown in Figure 9–22. The piston metal will often show some spattering.

Another form of heat damage is scuffing, similar to that pictured in Figure 9–23. This happens when excess heat causes the piston to expand until it becomes tight in the cylinder bore. The lubricant is thinned from the heat and it is squeezed from the cylinder wall. This causes metal-to-metal contact. Excessive heat can come from a malfunctioning cooling system, as well as from abnormal combustion.

Piston rings may get hot spots on their face from a lack of lubrication, from high combustion tempera-tures, or from ineffective cooling systems. Metal from the ring hot spots will transfer to the cylinder wall, scuffing the ring and piston (Figure 9–24).

Worn piston rings allow hot combustion gases to blow by the piston. The worn rings will also allow oil to come up from the crankcase to the combustion cham-ber. Hot combustion gases meet the oil in the area of the rings, where the heat will partially burn the oil. This produces hard carbon around the rings, causing them to stick in the grooves, as shown in Figure 9–25. If this is the only piston problem, it can be corrected by cleaning.

Corrosion Damage

Low operating temperatures will produce a corrosive mixture in the oil. Coolant leakage into the combustion chamber increases the rate of corrosion. Corrosion produces mottled gray pits on the aluminum piston. Low operating temperatures are caused by short-trip driving or by a faulty or missing cooling system ther-mostat.

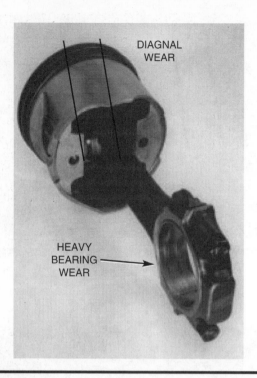

Figure 9–26 Angled piston skirt wear caused by a misaligned (twisted) connecting rod.

Figure 9–27 Piston damage when a pin lock ring came out.

Mechanical Damage

Piston damage can result from mechanical problems. Connecting rod misalignment and twist will show up as a diagonal thrust surface wear pattern across the piston skirt, which indicates that the piston is not operating straight in the cylinder (Figure 9–26). This means that the rings are not running squarely on the walls, so they cannot seal properly.

> **NOTE:** If there is diagonal wear on the piston, the connecting rod *must* be reconditioned. See Chapter 17 for details.

Piston damage can come from the loss of a piston pin lock ring. The lock will come out if the lock grooves are damaged or if the lock ring is weak. It will also come out if the rod is bent so that a side load is placed on the piston pin, forcing it against the lock ring. The piston and possibly the cylinder will be badly damaged as the lock ring slides between them. A new piston will be required when this type of damage occurs, as shown in Figure 9–27.

Pistons can crack, usually on the skirt or near the piston pin boss. Cracks generally occur at high mileage, because of overloading or because the pistons were improperly designed. A typical piston skirt crack is shown in Figure 9–28.

Figure 9–28 Cracked piston.

Dirt entering the engine greatly increases the amount of wear. Dirt will scratch and wear the face of the piston rings and wear the side of the ring and groove. Dirt will come in with the air through a leaking air filter element or through an air leak. Dirt in the oil will cause abnormal wear on the piston skirts, the sides of the ring groove, and the oil ring. A badly worn piston ring and groove are shown in Figure 9–29.

Figure 9–29 Badly worn piston ring and piston ring groove.

Figure 9–30 Piston lands damaged because of broken rings.

Figure 9–31 Puller being used to pull the vibration damper from the crankshaft.

Figure 9–32 Worn timing chain on a high-mileage engine. Notice that the timing chain could "jump a tooth" at the bottom of the smaller crankshaft gear where the chain is in contact with fewer teeth. Notice also that the technician placed all of the bolts back in the block after removal of the part. This procedure helps protect against lost or damaged bolts and nuts.

These loads may break the rings, which generally causes excessive piston land damage similar to that shown in Figure 9–30.

■ ROTATING ENGINE ASSEMBLY REMOVAL

The next step in disassembly is to remove the water pump and the crankshaft **vibration damper** (also called a **harmonic balancer**). The bolt and washer that hold the damper are removed. The damper should be removed only with a threaded puller similar to the one in Figure 9–31. If a hook-type puller is used around the edge of the damper, it may pull the damper ring from the hub. If this happens, the damper assembly will have to be replaced with a new assembly. With the damper assembly off, the timing cover can be removed, exposing the timing gear or timing chain. Examine these parts for excessive wear and looseness. A worn timing chain on a high-mileage engine is shown in Figure 9–32. Bolted cam sprockets can be removed to free the timing chain. On some engines this will require removal of the crankshaft gear at the same time. Pressed-on gears and sprockets are removed from the shaft *only* if they are faulty. They are removed after the camshaft is removed from the block. It is necessary to remove the camshaft thrust plate retaining screws when they are used.

Camshaft Removal

The camshaft can be removed at this time, or it can be removed after the crankshaft is out. It must be carefully eased from the engine to avoid damaging the cam bearings or cam lobes. This is done most easily with the front of the engine pointing up. Bearing surfaces are soft and scratch easily, and the cam lobes are hard and chip easily.

Crankshaft Removal

The main bearing caps should be checked for position markings before they are removed. They have been machined in place and will not fit perfectly in any other location. After marking, they can be removed to free the crankshaft. When the crankshaft is removed, the main bearing caps and bearings are reinstalled on the block to reduce the chance of damage to the caps.

Block Inspection

After the pistons and crankshaft have been removed, carefully inspect the block for obvious structure defects such as a cracked block as in Figure 9–33. Further detailed inspection should be completed after the components have been cleaned.

■ CYLINDER HEAD DISASSEMBLY

After the heads are removed and placed on the bench, the valves are removed. A C-type valve spring compressor, similar to the one in Figure 9–34, is used to free the **valve keepers (locks)**. The valve spring compressor is air powered in production shops where valve jobs are being done on a regular basis. Mechanical valve spring compressors are used where valve work is done only occasionally. After the valve keeper (lock) is removed, the compressor is released to free the valve retainer and spring. See Figure 9–35. The spring assemblies are lifted from the head together with any spacers being used under the valve spring. Here, the parts should be kept in order to aid in diagnosing the exact cause of any malfunction that shows up. The valve tip edge and keeper (lock) area should be lightly filed or stoned, as shown in Figure 9–36, to remove any burrs *before* sliding the valve from the head. Burrs will scratch the valve guide.

When all valves are removed following the same procedure, the valve springs, retainers, keepers (locks), guides, and seats should be given another visual examination. Any obvious faults should be noted. Parts that are obviously not repairable should be marked and set aside for later reference and fault diagnosis. See Figures 9–37 and 9–38. See Chapters 13 and 14 for valve and cylinder head service procedures.

Figure 9–33 This cracked block was discovered when the piston was removed. There is no need to do further work on this block because this crack cannot be repaired and the block has to be scraped.

Figure 9–34 A valve spring compressor being used to remove the valve locks (keepers).

TECH TIP

Hollander Interchange Manual

Most salvage businesses that deal with wrecked vehicles use the reference book, *Hollander Interchange Manual*. In this yearly publication, every vehicle part is given a number. If a part or component, such as an engine or engine accessory, from one vehicle has the same Hollander number as that from another vehicle, then the parts are interchangeable. See Figure 9–39.

TECH TIP

Mark It To Be Safe

Whenever you disassemble anything, it is always wise to mark the location of parts, bolts, hoses, and other items that could be incorrectly assembled. Remember, the first part removed will be the last part that is assembled. If you think you will remember where everything goes—forget it! It just does not happen in the real world.

One popular trick is to use correction fluid to mark the location of parts before they are removed. See Figure 9–40. Most of these products are alcohol or water based, dry quickly, and usually contain a brush in the cap for easy use.

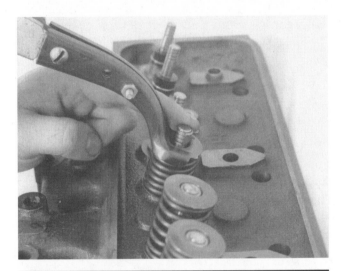

Figure 9–35 When using a valve spring compressor, it is best to use a magnet to help remove and hold the valve locks (keepers). When reinstalling, many technicians use grease to hold the locks (keepers) in place while releasing the spring pressure.

Figure 9–37 After removing this intake valve, it became obvious why this engine has been running poorly and using oil. The valve stem seals have been allowing engine oil into the combustion chamber and the valve stems have a severe buildup of carbon that can cause the engine to hesitate during acceleration.

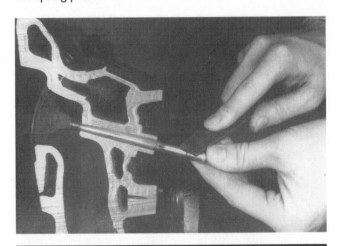

Figure 9–36 Always remove the burrs from around the valve lock grooves and tip before removing the valves from the head. The burrs could damage the guides if not removed. Spraying carburetor cleaner between the valve and valve guide also helps in valve removal.

OPENING FROM COMBUSTION CHAMBER TO COOLANT PASSAGE

Figure 9–38 This defective cylinder head was discovered as soon as the head was removed. The repair on this engine will be more extensive than the replacement of the head gasket that the tests seemed to indicate was at fault.

Figure 9–39 *Hollander Interchange Manuals* are available for both domestic and imported vehicles.

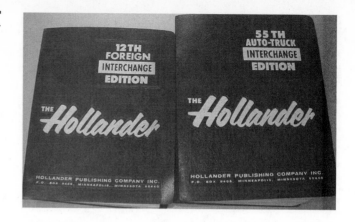

■ SUMMARY

1. A repair, valve job, overhaul, and entire engine replacement are some of the solution options for an engine failure.

2. A short block is the block assembly with pistons and crankshaft. A long block also includes the cylinder head(s).

3. The factory lifting hooks should be used when hoisting an engine.

4. Cylinder heads should only be removed when the engine is cold. Also always follow the torque table backward, starting with the highest-number head bolt and working toward the lowest number. This procedure helps prevent cylinder head warpage.

5. The ridge at the top of the cylinder should be removed before removing the piston(s) from the cylinder.

6. The connecting rod and main bearing caps should be marked before removing to ensure that they can be reinstalled in the exact same location when the engine is reassembled.

7. The tip of the valve stem should be filed before removing valves from the cylinder head to help prevent damage to the valve guide.

■ REVIEW QUESTIONS

1. Describe what a valve job includes.

2. Explain the differences between a minor and a major overhaul.

3. What does blueprinting an engine mean?

4. When should the factory-installed lifting hooks be used?

5. What is the purpose of the tapered dowel pins on the rear of most engine blocks?

6. Explain why the cylinder bore should be measured for taper and out-of-round before continuing with an engine disassembly.

Figure 9–40 Correction fluid is easy to use to mark parts before disassembly.

7. State two reasons for the removal of the ridge at the top of the cylinder.

8. Explain why the burrs must be removed from valves before removing the valves from the cylinder head.

■ ASE CERTIFICATION-TYPE QUESTIONS

1. A valve job involves _____ .
   a. Removing and replacing the cylinder head(s)
   b. Grinding the valve to prevent valve leakage
   c. Replacing any worn or damaged parts as needed
   d. All of the above

2. Blueprinting means _____ .
   a. The same as a minor overhaul
   b. The same as a major overhaul
   c. An overhaul with all parts equally matched
   d. Painting the engine blue after an overhaul

3. A long block can be made from a short block with the addition of _____ .
   a. Cylinder heads and valve train
   b. Intake and exhaust manifolds
   c. Oil pump, oil pan, and timing chain cover
   d. Fuel pump, carburetor, and air cleaner assembly

4. Lifting hooks are often installed at the factory because _____ .
   a. They make removing the engine easier for the technician
   b. They are used to install the engine at the factory
   c. They are part of the engine and should not be removed
   d. They make servicing the top of the engine easier for the technician

5. With the rocker cover (valve cover) removed, the technician can inspect all items *except* _____ .
   a. Combustion chamber deposits
   b. Rocker arms and valve spring
   c. Camshaft (overhead camshaft engine only)
   d. Valve stems and pushrods (overhead valve engines only)

6. After the oil pan (sump) is removed, the technician should inspect _____ .
   a. The oil pump and pickup screen
   b. To make certain that all rod and main bearings are numbered or marked
   c. The valve lifters (tappets) for wear
   d. Both a and b

7. The ridge at the top of the cylinder _____ .
   a. Is caused by wear at the top of the cylinder by the rings
   b. Represents a failure of the top piston ring to correctly seal against the cylinder wall
   c. Should not be removed before removing pistons except when reboring the cylinders
   d. Means that a crankshaft with an incorrect stroke was installed in the engine

8. Before the timing chain can be inspected and removed, the following component(s) must be removed _____ .
   a. Rocker cover (valve cover)
   b. Vibration damper
   c. Cylinder head(s)
   d. Intake manifold (V-type engines only)

9. Before the valves are removed from the cylinder head, what operations need to be completed?
   a. Remove valve keepers (locks) (keepers)
   b. Remove cylinder head(s) from the engine
   c. Remove burrs from the stem of the valve(s)
   d. All of the above

10. Technician A says that a minor overhaul can often be done with the engine remaining in the vehicle. Technician B says that a core is required for most remanufactured engines. Which technician is correct?
   a. Technician A only
   b. Technician B only
   c. Both Technician A and B
   d. Neither Technician A nor B

Engine Cleaning, Crack Detection, and Repair

Objectives: After studying Chapter 10, the reader should be able to:

1. List the types of engine cleaning methods.
2. Describe how to chemically clean parts.
3. Discuss how high temperatures can be used to clean engine parts.
4. List the various methods that can be used to check engine parts for cracks.
5. Describe crack repair procedures.

> ### TECH TIP
>
> **The Wax Trick**
>
> Before the engine block can be thoroughly cleaned, all oil gallery plugs must be removed. A popular trick of the trade involves heating the plug (not the surrounding metal) with an oxyacetylene torch. The heat tends to expand the plug and make it tighter in the block. Do not overheat. See Figure 10–1.
>
> As the plug is cooling, touch the plug with paraffin wax (beeswax or candle wax may be used). See Figure 10–2. The wax will be drawn down around the threads of the plug by capillary attraction as the plug cools and contracts. After being allowed to cool, the plug is easily removed.

The purpose of any cleaning procedure is to restore like-new appearance. The soft plugs or core plugs will have to be removed to thoroughly clean the cooling passages in the block and head. See the Tech Tip, "The Wax Trick."

■ MECHANICAL CLEANING

Mechanical cleaning involves scraping, brushing, and abrasive blasting. It should, therefore, be used very carefully on soft metals. Heavy deposits that remain after chemical cleaning will have to be removed by mechanical cleaning.

The most frequently used type of scraper is a **putty knife.** See Figure 10–3. The blade of the putty knife is pushed under the deposit to free it from the surface. The blade works best on flat surfaces such as gasket surfaces and the piston head. The broad blade of the putty knife prevents it from scratching the surface as it is used to clean the parts.

Wire brushes can be used on uneven surfaces. A hand wire brush can be used on the exterior of the block and on the head. A round wire brush used with a hand drill motor does a good job of cleaning the combustion chamber and parts of the head. A wire wheel can be used to clean the valves. See Figures 10–4 and 10–5.

Figure 10–1 Heating oil gallery plugs on a small Chevrolet V-8 block.

Figure 10–2 Applying the wax to the heated plug. Notice the wax vapors. This indicates that the plug is still slightly too hot. The wax needs to be liquid (not a vapor) to flow down around the threads of the plug.

Figure 10–3 Mechanical cleaning means using scrapers and similar tools to physically remove carbon and deposits.

Figure 10–4 Cleaning the combustion chamber with a rotary wire brush.

> *CAUTION:* Do not use a steel wire brush on aluminum parts! Steel is harder than aluminum and will remove some of the aluminum from the surface during cleaning.

■ CHEMICAL CLEANERS

Cleaning chemicals applied to the parts will mix with and dissolve the deposits. The chemicals loosen the deposits so that they can be brushed or rinsed from the surface. A deposit is said to be **soluble** when it can be dissolved with a chemical or solvent.

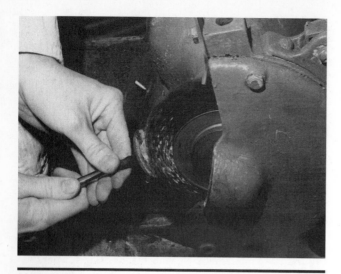

Figure 10–5 Cleaning carbon from a valve with a rotating wire wheel.

Most chemical cleaners used for cleaning carbon-type deposits are a strong soap, or **caustic material.** A value called **pH,** measured on a scale from 1 to 14, is used to indicate the amount of chemical activity. The term *pH* is from the French word *pouvoir hydrogine,* meaning "hydrogen power." Pure water is neutral. On the pH scale, water is pH 7. Caustic materials have pH numbers from 8 through 14. The higher the number, the stronger the caustic action will be. **Acid materials** have pH numbers from 6 through 1. The lower the number, the stronger the acid action will be. Caustic materials and acid materials neutralize each other, such as when baking soda (a caustic) is used to clean the outside of the battery (an acid surface). The caustic baking soda neutralizes any sulfuric acid that has been spilled or splashed on the outside of the battery.

CAUTION: Whenever working with chemicals, eye protection must be used.

■ SOLVENT-BASED CLEANING

Chemical cleaning can involve a spray washer or a soak in a cold or hot tank. The cleaning solution is usually solvent based, with a medium pH rating of between 10 and 12. Most chemical solutions also contain silicates to protect the metal (aluminum) against corrosion. Strong caustics do an excellent job on cast-iron items but are often too corrosive for aluminum parts. Aluminum cleaners include mineral spirit solvents and alkaline detergents.

CAUTION: When cleaning aluminum cylinder heads, blocks, or other engine components, be certain that the chemicals used are "aluminum safe." Many chemicals that are not aluminum safe may turn the aluminum metal black. Try to explain that to a customer!

■ WATER-BASED CHEMICAL CLEANING

Because of environmental concerns, most chemical cleaning is now performed using water-based solutions (or **aqueous based**). Most aqueous-based chemicals are silicate based and are mixed with water. Aqueous-based solutions can be sprayed or used in a tank for soaking parts. Aluminum heads and blocks usually require overnight soaking with the temperature of the solution kept at about 190°F (90°C). For best results, the cleaning solution should be agitated.

■ SPRAY WASHING

A spray washer directs streams of liquid through numerous high-pressure nozzles to dislodge dirt and grime on an engine surface. The force of the liquid hitting the surface, combined with the chemical action of the cleaning solution, produces a clean surface. Spray washing is typically performed in an enclosed washer (like a dishwasher), where parts are rotated on a washer turntable.

Spray washing is faster than soaking. A typical washer cycle is less than 30 minutes per load, compared with 8 or more hours for soaking. Most spray washers use an aqueous-based cleaning solution heated to 160° to 180°F (70° to 80°C) with foam suppressants. High-volume remanufacturers use industrial dishwashing machines to clean the disassembled engines' component parts. See Figure 10–6.

■ STEAM CLEANING

Steam cleaners are a special class of sprayers. Steam vapor is mixed with high-pressure water and sprayed on the parts. The heat of the steam and the propellant force of the high-pressure water combine to do the cleaning. Steam cleaning must be used with extreme care. Usually, a caustic cleaner is added to the steam and water to aid in the cleaning. This mixture is so active that it will damage and even remove paint, so painted surfaces must be protected from the spray. Engines are often steam cleaned before they are removed from the chassis.

Figure 10–6 Load of crankshafts being placed into a huge chemical cleaning system at a large engine remanufacturing plant.

■ THERMAL CLEANING

Thermal cleaning uses heat to vaporize and char dirt into a dry, powdery ash. Thermal cleaning is best suited for cleaning cast iron, where temperatures as high as 800°F (425°C) are used, whereas aluminum should not be heated to over 600°F (315°C).

The major advantages of thermal cleaning include the following:

1. This process cleans inside and outside of the casting or part.
2. The waste generated is nonhazardous and provides easy disposal.

However, the heat in the oven usually discolors the metal and leaves it looking dull. Additional cleaning with a shot blaster is usually necessary to restore proper appearance.

A **pyrolytic** (high-temperature) oven cleans engine parts by decomposing dirt, grease, and gaskets with heat, in a manner similar to that of a self-cleaning oven. This method of engine part cleaning is becoming the most popular because there is no hazardous waste associated with it. Labor costs are also reduced because the operator does not need to be present during the actual cleaning operation. See Figure 10–7.

■ COLD TANK CLEANING

The cold soak tank is used to remove grease and carbon. The disassembled parts are placed in the tank so that they are *completely* covered with the chemical cleaning solution. After a soaking period, the parts are

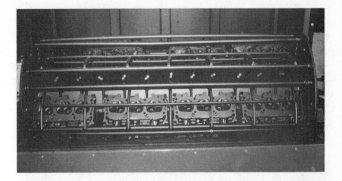

Figure 10–7 Cylinder heads being cleaned in a pyrolytic oven. The term *pyrolytic* refers to the heating of organic compounds to very high temperatures. All that remains after cleaning is a fine dust. Most remanufacturers and rebuilders are using this type of equipment because of the absence of associated hazardous materials.

removed and rinsed until the milky appearance of the emulsion is gone. The parts are then dried with compressed air. The clean, dry parts are usually given a very light coating of clean oil to prevent rusting. Carburetor cleaner, purchased with a basket in a bucket, is one of the most common types of cold soak agents in the automotive shop. Usually, the chemical will have water over its surface to prevent evaporation of the chemical. This water is called a **hydroseal.**

Parts washers are often used in place of the soaking tanks. The parts are moved back and forth through the cleaning solution, or the cleaning solution is pumped over the parts. This movement, called **agitation,** keeps fresh cleaning solution moving past the soil to help it loosen. The parts washer is usually equipped with a safety cover held open with a low-temperature **fusible link.** If a fire occurs, the fusible link will melt and the cover will drop closed to snuff the fire out.

■ HOT TANK CLEANING

The hot soak tank (Figure 10–8) is used for cleaning heavy organic deposits and rust from iron and steel parts. Caustic cleaning solution used in the hot soak tank is kept near 200°F (93°C) for rapid cleaning action. The solution must be inhibited when aluminum is to be cleaned. After the deposits have been loosened, the parts are removed from the tank and rinsed with hot water or steam cleaned. The hot parts will dry rapidly. They must be given a light coating of oil to prevent rusting.

HINT: **Fogging oil** from a spray can does an excellent job of coating metal parts to keep them from rusting.

Figure 10–9 Bead blasting a cylinder head.

Figure 10–8 Hot spray washer is similar to an industrial dish washer.

■ VAPOR CLEANING

Vapor cleaning is popular in some automotive service shops. The parts to be cleaned are suspended in hot vapors above a perchloroethylene solution. The vapors of the solution loosen the soil from the metal so that it can be blown, wiped, or rinsed from the surface.

■ ULTRASONIC CLEANING

Ultrasonic cleaning is used to clean small parts that must be absolutely clean. Hydraulic lifters and diesel injectors are examples of these parts. The disassembled parts are placed in a tank of cleaning solution. The solution is vibrated at ultrasonic speeds to loosen all the soil from the parts. The soil goes into the solution or falls to the bottom of the tank.

■ VIBRATORY CLEANING

This vibratory method of cleaning is best suited for small parts. Parts are loaded into a vibrating bin with small, odd-shape ceramic or steel pieces, called **media,** with a cleaning solution of mineral spirits or water-based detergents. Detergents usually contain a lubricant additive to help the media pieces slide around more freely. The movement of the vibrating solution and the scrubbing action of the media do an excellent job of cleaning metal.

■ BLASTERS

Cleaning cast-iron or aluminum engine parts with solvents or heat usually requires another operation to achieve a uniform surface finish. Blasting the parts with steel, cast-iron, aluminum, or stainless steel shot, or glass beads is a simple way to achieve a matte or satin surface finish on the engine parts. See Figure 10–9. To keep the shot or beads from sticking, the parts must be dry without a trace of oil or grease prior to blasting. This means that blasting is the second cleaning method, after the part has been precleaned in a tank, spray washer, or oven.

Some blasting is done automatically in an airless shot blasting machine. Another method is to hard blast parts in a sealed cabinet.

> *CAUTION:* Glass beads often remain in internal passages of engine parts, where they can come loose and travel through the cylinders when the engine is started. Among other places, these small, but destructive, beads can easily be trapped under the oil baffles of rocker covers, and in oil pans and piston ring grooves. To help prevent the glass beads from sticking, make sure that the parts being cleaned are free of grease and dirt and completely *dry.*

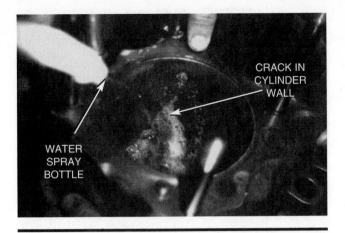

Figure 10–10 To make sure that the mark observed in the cylinder wall was a crack, compressed air was forced into the cooling jacket while soapy water was sprayed on the cylinder wall. Bubbles confirmed that the mark was indeed a crack.

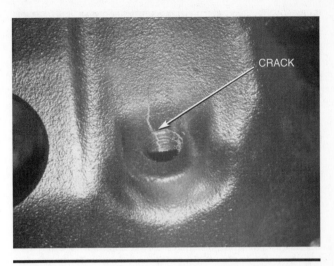

Figure 10–11 This crack in a vintage Ford 289, V-8 block was likely caused by the technician using excessive force trying to remove the plug in the block. The technician should have used heat and wax to not only make the job easier but also to prevent damaging a block.

■ VISUAL INSPECTION

After the parts have been thoroughly cleaned, they should be reexamined for defects. A magnifying glass is helpful in finding these defects. Critical parts of a performance engine should be checked for cracks using specialized magnetic or penetration inspection equipment. Internal parts such as pistons, connecting rods, and crankshafts that have cracks should be replaced. Cracks in the block and heads can often be repaired. These repair procedures are described in a later section. See Figure 10–10.

■ MAGNETIC CRACK INSPECTION

Checking for cracks using a magnetic field is commonly called Magnafluxing, which is a brand name. Cracks in engine blocks, cylinder heads, crankshafts, and other engine components are sometimes difficult to find during a normal visual inspection. This is the reason why all remanufacturers and most engine builders use a crack detection procedure on all critical engine parts.

Magnetic flux testing is the method most often used on steel and iron components. A metal engine part (such as a cast-iron cylinder head) is connected to a large electromagnet. Magnetic lines of force are easily conducted through the iron part. The magnetic lines of force are more concentrated on the edges of a crack. A fine iron powder can then be applied to the part being tested, and the powder will be attracted to the strong magnetic concentration around the crack. See Figures 10–11 through 10–14.

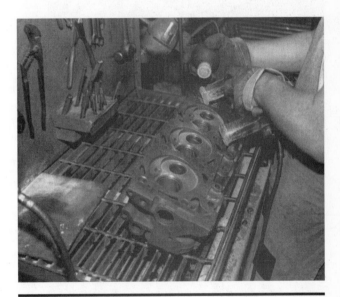

Figure 10–12 Magnetic crack inspection being performed at a large engine remanufacturing plant.

■ DYE PENETRANT TESTING

Dye penetrant testing is primarily used on pistons and other parts constructed of aluminum or other nonmagnetic material. A dark red penetrating chemical is first sprayed on the component being tested. After cleaning, a white powder is sprayed over the test area. If a crack is present, the red dye will stain the white powder. Even though this method will also work on iron and steel (magnetic) parts, it is normally used only on nonmagnetic parts, because magnetic methods do not work on these parts.

Figure 10–13 The white iron powder tends to concentrate on the edges of cracks. This photo shows a crack through an exhaust seat of a cylinder head.

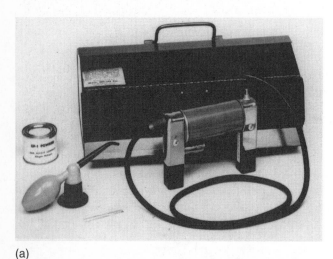

(a)

(b)

Figure 10–14 (a) Magnetic crack inspection equipment. (b) How a block crack in a cylinder looks after the fine iron powder is used. (*Courtesy of George Olcott Company*)

Figure 10–15 Pressure testing a Chevrolet V-8 block using *hot* water. Cylinder heads are also pressure tested using similar equipment. The hot water tends to expand the metal parts, and minor leaks are found more easily than if cold water were used to pressure test the component.

■ FLUORESCENT PENETRANT TESTING

Fluorescent penetrant requires a black light to be seen and can be used on iron, steel, or aluminum parts. This method is commonly called **Zyglo,** which is a trademark of the Magnaflux Corporation. Any cracks show up as bright lines when viewed with a black light.

■ PRESSURE TESTING

Cylinder heads and blocks are often pressure tested with air and checked for leaks. All coolant passages are blocked with rubber plugs or gaskets, and compressed air is applied to the water jacket(s). The head or block is lowered into water. Air bubbles indicate a leak. For more accurate results, the water should be heated. The hot water expands the casting by about the same amount as in an operating engine.

An alternative method involves running heated water with a dye through the cylinder or block. Any leaks indicate a crack. See Figures 10–15 through 10–17.

■ CRACK REPAIR

Cracks in the engine block can cause coolant to flow into the oil or oil into the coolant. A cracked block can also cause coolant to leak externally from a crack that goes through to a coolant passage. Cracks in the head

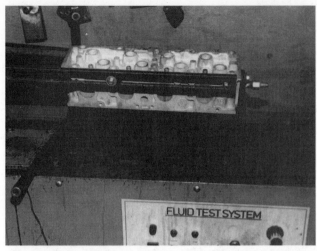

(a)

(b)

Figure 10–16 Aluminum cylinder head being checked for
cracks in the coolant passages.
(a) Head is being supported in preparation for testing.
(b) Compressed air is put into the cylinder head while it is
underwater, and the water is checked for bubbles from
cracks in the casting.

Figure 10–17 A cylinder head is under water and being
pressure tested using compressed air. Note that the air
bubbles indicate a crack.

Figure 10–18 After cleaning and before machining
operations are begun, carefully inspect for hidden cracks or
other damage. Crack detection methods should *always* be
used before restoring any engine casting such as cylinder
heads.

will allow coolant to leak into the engine, or they will allow combustion gases to leak into the coolant. Cracks
across the valve seat cause hot spots on the valve. The
hot spots will burn the valve face. A head with a crack
will either have to be replaced or have the crack repaired. Cracked heads are shown in Figure 10–18. Two
methods of crack repair are commonly used: welding
and plugging.

NOTE: A hole can be drilled at each end of the crack
to keep it from extending further. This step is sometimes called **stop drilling.** Cracks that do not cross
oil passages, bolt holes, or seal surfaces can sometimes be left unrepaired if stopped.

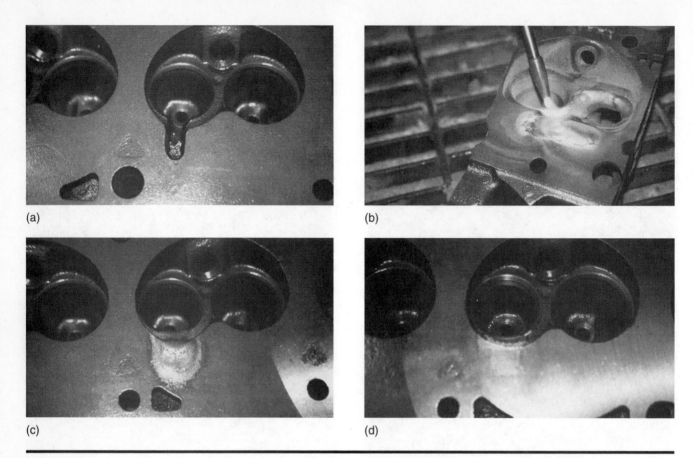

(a)

(b)

(c)

(d)

Figure 10–19 (a) Before welding, the crack is ground out using a carbide grinder. (b) Here the technician is practicing using the special cast-iron welding torch before welding the cracked cylinder head. (c) The finished welded crack before final machining. (d) The finished cylinder head after the crack has been repaired using welding.

■ CRACK WELDING CAST IRON

It takes a great deal of skill to weld cast iron. The cast iron does not puddle or flow as steel does when it is heated. Heavy cast parts, such as the head and block, conduct heat away from the weld so fast that it is difficult to get the part hot enough to melt the iron for welding. When it does melt, a crack will often develop next to the edge of the weld bead. Welding can be satisfactorily done when the entire cast part is heated red hot.

One new method shown in Figure 10–19 uses a special torch to weld cast iron.

■ CRACK WELDING ALUMINUM

Cracks in aluminum can be welded using a Heli-arc® or similar welder that is specially designed to weld aluminum. See Figure 10–20. The crack should be cut or burned out before welding begins. The old valve seat insert should be removed if the crack is in or near the combustion chamber.

Figure 10–20 This cylinder head is being repaired. Cracks were found in this Ford Escort cylinder head, and the material around the cracks has been cut out (note the missing exhaust valve seats). The failed area will be welded and remachined. After welding, the head will be stress relieved and straightened before final machining.

■ CRACK PLUGGING

In the process of crack plugging, the crack is closed using interlocking tapered plugs. The ends of the crack are center punched and drilled with the proper size of tap drill for the plugs. The hole is reamed with a tapered reamer (Figure 10–21). The hole is then tapped to give full threads (Figure 10–22). The plug is coated with sealer; then it is tightened into the hole (Figure 10–23). The plug is sawed about one-fourth of the way through; then it is broken off. The saw slot controls the breaking point (Figure 10–24). If the plug should break below the surface, it will have to be drilled out and a new plug installed. The plug should go to the full depth or thickness of the cast metal. After the first plug is installed on each end, a new hole is drilled with the tap drill so that it cuts into the edge of the first plug. This new hole is reamed and tapped, and a plug is inserted as before. The plug should fit about one-fourth of the way into the first plug to lock it into place (Figure 10–25). Interlocking plugs are placed along the entire crack, alternating slightly from side to side. The exposed ends of the plugs are peened over with a hammer to help secure them in place. The surface of the plugs is ground or filed down nearly to the gasket surface. The plugs are ground down to the original surface in the combustion chamber and at the ports, using a hand grinder. The gasket surface of the head must be resurfaced after the crack has been repaired. See Figure 10–26 for an example of cylinder head repair using plugs.

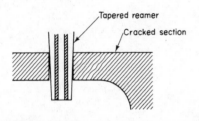

Figure 10–21 Reaming a hole for a tapered plug.

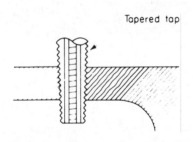

Figure 10–22 Tapping a tapered hole for a plug.

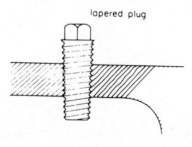

Figure 10–23 Screwing a tapered plug in the hole.

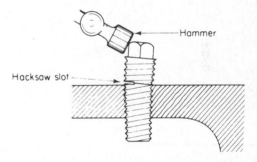

Figure 10–24 Cutting the plug with a hacksaw.

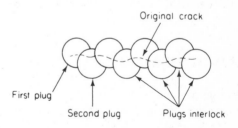

Figure 10–25 Interlocking plugs.

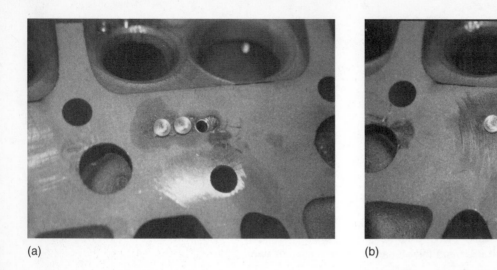

(a)

(b)

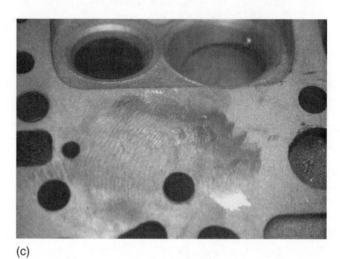

(c)

Figure 10–26 (a) A hole is drilled and tapped for the plugs. (b) The plugs are installed. (c) After final machining, the cylinder head can be returned to useful service.

PHOTO SEQUENCE   Checking For Cracks

PS 19–1 A strong electromagnet can be used to check a cast-iron cylinder head for cracks. The cylinder head should be thoroughly cleaned and placed on a work surface that gives good visibility.

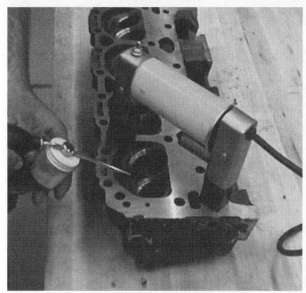

PS 19–2 Turn the electromagnet on using the switch at the top and spray a fine iron powder between the poles of the magnet. The magnetic lines of force are more concentrated on the edges of a crack and the iron powder will be attracted to the strong magnetic concentration around the crack.

PS 19–3 Pay particular attention to the area around and between the valve seats.

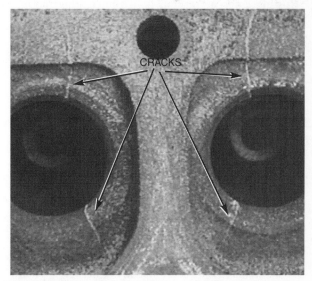

PS 19–4 This cylinder head has cracks running from two valve seats. This cylinder head will either have to be replaced or repaired.

■ SUMMARY

1. Mechanical cleaning is used to remove deposits using scrapers or wire brushes.

2. Steel wire brushes should never be used to clean aluminum parts.

3. Most chemical cleaners are a strong soap called a caustic material.

4. Always use aluminum-safe chemicals when cleaning aluminum parts or components.

5. Thermal cleaning is done in a pyrolytic oven in temperatures as high as 800°F (425°C) to turn grease and dirt into harmless ash deposits.

6. Blasters use metal shot or glass beads to clean parts. All metal shot or glass beads must be cleaned from the part so as not to cause engine problems.

7. All parts should be checked for cracks using magnetic, dye penetrant, fluorescent penetrant, or pressure testing methods.

8. Cracks can be repaired by welding or by plugging.

■ REVIEW QUESTIONS

1. Describe five methods that could be used to clean engines or engine parts.

2. Explain magnetic crack inspection, dye penetrant testing, and fluorescent penetrant testing methods and where each can be used.

3. Explain why the use of blasters using metal shot or glass beads requires that the parts be cleaned before and after being blasted clean.

■ ASE CERTIFICATION-TYPE QUESTIONS

1. A solvent is _____ .
   a. Pure water
   b. A type of bead used in bead blasting parts
   c. A chemical that can mix with and dissolve deposits
   d. A type of wire brush used to remove deposits

2. Cleaning chemicals are usually either a caustic material or an acid material. Which of the following statements is true?
   a. Both caustics and acids have a pH of 7 if rated according to distilled water.
   b. An acid is lower than 7 and a caustic is higher than 7 on the pH scale.
   c. An acid is higher than 7 and a caustic is lower than 7 on the pH scale.
   d. Pure water is a 1 and a strong acid is a 14 on the pH scale.

3. Many cleaning methods involve chemicals that are hazardous to use and expensive to dispose of after use. The least hazardous method is generally considered to be the _____ .
   a. Pyrolytic oven
   b. Hot vapor tank
   c. Hot soak tank
   d. Cold soak tank

4. Magnetic crack inspection _____ .
   a. Uses a red dye to detect cracks in aluminum
   b. Uses a black light to detect cracks in iron parts
   c. Uses a fine iron powder to detect cracks in iron parts
   d. Uses a magnet to remove cracks from iron parts

5. Technician A says that the fluorescent penetrant test method can be used to detect cracks in iron, steel, or aluminum parts. Technician B says that the dye penetrant test can only be used with aluminum parts. Which technician is correct?
   a. Technician A only
   b. Technician B only
   c. Both Technician A and B
   d. Neither Technician A nor B

6. Technician A says that engine parts should be cleaned before a thorough test can be done to detect cracks. Technician B says that pressure testing can be used to find cracks in blocks or cylinder heads. Which technician is correct?
   a. Technician A only
   b. Technician B only
   c. Both Technician A and B
   d. Neither Technician A nor B

7. Cast-iron cylinder heads and blocks can be welded if cracked.
   a. True
   b. False

8. Aluminum cylinder heads and blocks can be welded if cracked.
   a. True
   b. False

9. Drilling a hole at each end of a crack _____ .
   a. Stops the crack from getting larger
   b. Allows room for the weld to expand
   c. Allows the technician a method for determining how deep the crack goes into the cylinder head or block
   d. Relieves stress in the cylinder head or block

10. Tapered pins used to repair cracks should be used _____ .
   a. Only on cast-iron heads or blocks
   b. Only on aluminum heads or blocks
   c. Along with welding to repair a crack
   d. Instead of welding in cast iron

Engine Measuring and Math

The purpose of any engine repair is to restore the engine to factory specification tolerance. Every engine repair procedure involves measuring. The service technician must measure twice.

- The original engine components must be measured to see if correction is necessary to restore the engine to factory specifications.
- The replacement parts and finished machined areas must be measured to ensure proper dimension before the engine is assembled.

■ MICROMETER

A micrometer is the most used measuring instrument in engine service and repair. See Figure 11–1. The **thimble** rotates over the **barrel** on a screw that has 40 threads per inch. Every revolution of the thimble moves the spindle 0.025 inch. The thimble is graduated into 25 equally spaced lines; therefore, each line represents 0.001 inch. Every micrometer should be checked for calibration on a regular basis. See Figure 11–2.

■ CRANKSHAFT MEASUREMENT

Even though the connecting rod journals and the main bearing journals are usually different sizes, they both can and should be measured for out-of-round and taper. See Figure 11–3.

Out-of-Round

A journal should be measured in at least two positions across the diameter and every 120 degrees around the journal as shown in Figure 11–4 for an example of the six readings. Calculate the out-of-round measurement by subtracting the lowest reading from the highest reading for both A and B positions.

Position A: 2.0000 – 1.9995 = 0.0005 inch

Position B: 2.0000 – 1.9989 = 0.0011 inch

The maximum out-of-round measurement occurs in position A (0.0011 inch), which is the measurement that should be used to compare with factory specifications to determine if any machining will be necessary.

Taper

To determine the taper of the journal, compare the readings in the same place between A and B positions and

Figure 11–1 Typical micrometers used for dimensional inspection.

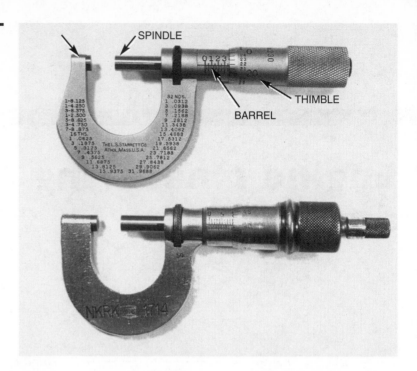

Figure 11–2 All micrometers should be checked and calibrated as needed using a gauge rod.

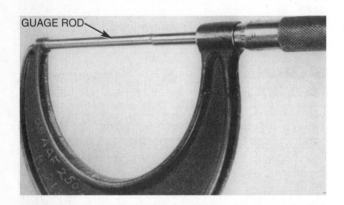

subtract the lower readings from the higher reading. For example:

Position A		Position B	
2.0000	–	2.0000	= 0.0000
1.9999	–	1.9999	= 0.0000
1.9995	–	1.9989	= 0.0006

Use 0.006 inch as the taper for the journal and compare with factory specifications.

Camshaft Measurement

The journal of the camshaft(s) can also be measured using a micrometer and compared with factory specifications for taper and out-of-round. See Figure 11-5.

Figure 11–3 Using a micrometer to measure the connecting rod journal for out-of-round and taper.

NOTE: On overhead valve (pushrod) engines, the camshaft journal diameter often decreases slightly toward the rear of the engine. Overhead camshaft engines usually have the same journal diameter.

The lift can also be measured with a micrometer and compared with factory specifications as shown in Figure 11–6.

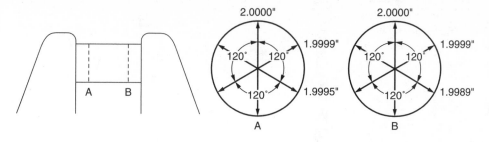

(a)

Figure 11–4 Crankshaft journal measurements. Each journal should be measured in at least six locations; in position A and position B at 120-degree intervals around the journal.

Figure 11–5 Camshaft journals should be measured in three locations, 120-degrees apart, to check for out-of-round.

Figure 11–6 Checking camshaft for wear by measuring the lobe height with a micrometer.

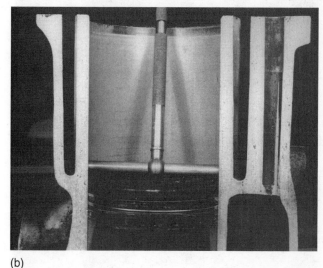

(b)

Figure 11–7 When the head is first removed, the cylinder taper and out-of-round should be checked below the ridge (a) and above the piston when it is at the bottom of the stroke (b).

■ TELESCOPIC GAUGE

A telescopic gauge is used with a micrometer to measure the inside diameter of a hole or bore.

Cylinder Bore

The cylinder bore can be measured by inserting a telescopic gauge into the bore and rotating the handle lock to allow the arms of the gauge to contact the inside bore of the cylinder. Tighten the handle lock and remove the gauge from the cylinder. Use a micrometer to measure the telescopic gauge. See Figures 11–7 and 11–8. A telescopic gauge can also be used to measure the following:

- Camshaft bearing (see Figure 11–9)
- Main bearing bore (housing bore) measurement
- Connecting rod bore measurement

Figure 11–8 Most of the cylinder wear is on the top inch just below the cylinder ridge. This wear is due to the heat and combustion pressures that occur when the piston is near the top of the cylinder. (*Courtesy of Dana Corp.*)

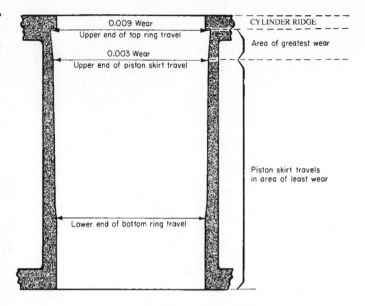

(a)

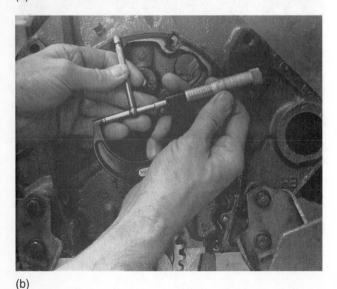

(b)

Figure 11–9 (a) A telescopic gauge being used to measure the inside diameter (ID) of a camshaft bearing. (b) An outside micrometer is used to measure the telescopic gauge.

■ SMALL-HOLE GAUGE

A small-hole gauge (also called a **split-ball gauge**) is used with a micrometer to measure the inside diameter of small holes such as a valve guide in a cylinder head. See Figures 11–10 and 11–11.

■ VERNIER DIAL CALIPER

A vernier dial caliper is normally used to measure the outside diameter or length of a component such as a piston diameter or crankshaft and camshaft bearing journal diameter. See Figures 11–12 and 11–13 on page 236.

Frequently Asked Question **???**

What Is the Difference Between the Word Gage and Gauge?

The word *gauge* means "measurement or dimension to a standard of reference." The word *gauge* can also be spelled *gage*. Therefore, in most cases, the words mean the same.

INTERESTING NOTE: One vehicle manufacturing representative told me that *gage* was used rather than *gauge* because even though it is the second acceptable spelling of the word, it is correct and it saved the company a lot of money in printing costs because the word *gage* has one less letter! One letter multiplied by millions of vehicles with gauges on the dash and the word *gauge* used in service manuals adds up to a big savings to the manufacturer.

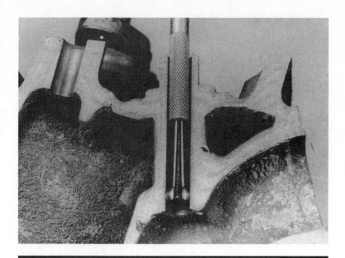

Figure 11–10 Cutaway of a valve guide with a hole gauge adjusted to the hole diameter.

Figure 11–11 The outside of a hole gauge being measured with a micrometer.

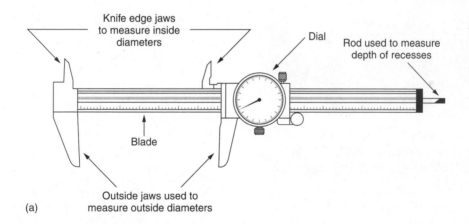

Knife edge jaws to measure inside diameters

Dial

Rod used to measure depth of recesses

Blade

(a)

Outside jaws used to measure outside diameters

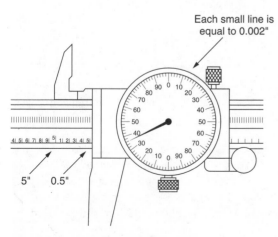

Each small line is equal to 0.002"

5"   0.5"

(b)

Add reading on blade (5.5") to reading on dial (0.036") to get final total measurement (5.536")

Figure 11–12 (a) A typical vernier dial caliper. This is a very useful measuring tool for automotive engine work because it is capable of measuring inside and outside measurements. (b) To read a vernier dial caliper, simply add the reading on the blade to the reading on the dial.

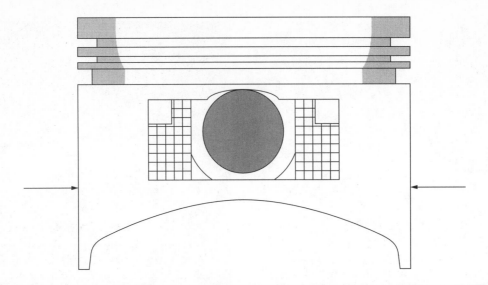

Figure 11–13 Most vehicle manufacturers specify that the diameter of the piston be measured below the piston pin. The piston diameter should be measured perpendicular (90°) to the piston pin as shown.

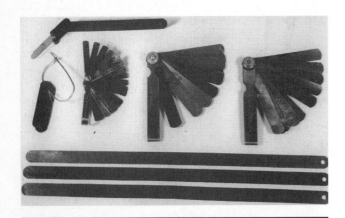

Figure 11–14 A group of feeler gauges (also known as thickness gauges), used to measure between two parts. The long gauges on the bottom are used to measure the piston-to-cylinder wall clearance.

■ FEELER GAUGE

A feeler gauge (also known as a thickness gauge) is an accurately manufactured strip of metal that is used to determine the gap or clearance between two components. See Figure 11–14. A feeler gauge can be used to check the following:

- Piston ring gap—see Figures 11–15 and 11–16
- Piston ring side clearance—see Figure 11–17
- Piston to cylinder wall clearance—see Figure 11–18 on page 238
- Connecting rod side clearance—see Figure 11–19 on page 238

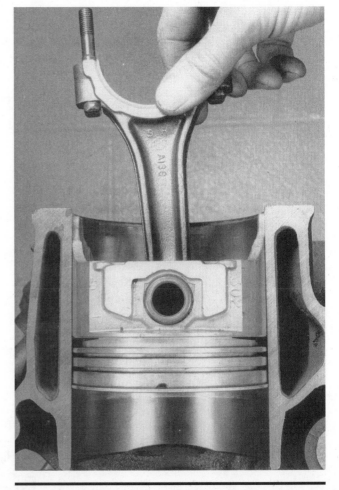

Figure 11–15 The side clearance of the piston ring is checked with a feeler gauge.

Figure 11–17 Position of the notch at the front of the piston, and the connecting rod numbers.

■ DIAL BORE GAUGE

A dial bore gauge is an expensive, but important, gauge used to measure cylinder taper and out-of-round as well as main bearing (block housing) bore for taper and out-of-round. See Figures 11–24 through 11–26 on page 240. A dial bore gauge has to be adjusted to a dimension such as the factory specifications, then the reading on the dial bore gauge indicates plus (+) or minus (−) readings from the predetermined dimension. This is why a dial bore is best used to measure taper and out-of-round because it shows the difference in cylinder or bore rather than an actual measurement.

■ ENGINE MATH AND FORMULAS

Engine Displacement

The formula to calculate the displacement of an engine is basically the formula for determining the volume of a cylinder multiplied by the number of cylinders. However, it seems somewhat confusing, because the formula has been publicized in many different forms. Regardless of the method used, the results will be the same. The easiest and most commonly used formula is

Bore × Bore × Stroke × 0.7854 × Number of cylinders = Cubic inch displacement (CID).

For example, take a six-cylinder engine where

Bore = 4.000 inches
Stroke = 3.000 inches

Applying the formula,

4.000 inches × 4.000 inches × 3.000 inches × 0.7854 × 6 = 226 cubic inches

Figure 11–16 A piston is used to push the ring squarely into the cylinder.

■ STRAIGHTEDGE

A straightedge is a precision ground metal measuring gauge that is used to check the flatness of engine components when used with a feeler gauge. A straightedge is used to check the flatness of the following:

• Cylinder heads—see Figure 11–20 on page 239
• Cylinder block deck—see Figure 11–21 on page 239
• Straightness of the main bearing bores (saddles)—see Figure 11–22 on page 239

■ DIAL INDICATOR

A dial indicator is a precision measuring instrument used to measure crankshaft end play, crankshaft runout, and valve guide wear. See Figure 11–23 on page 239.

Figure 11–18 Measuring the clearance between the piston and the cylinder wall with a strip feeler gauge. There are no rings on the piston when this measurement is made.

Figure 11–19 The connecting rod side clearance is measured with a feeler gauge.

Cubic Inches to Cubic Centimeters

- 1 cubic inch = 16.4 cubic centimeters
- 1000 cc = 1 liter
- 1 liter = 61 cubic inches

To convert 226 cubic inches to cubic centimeters (cc), use the formula: $226 \times 16.4 = cc$

$$226 = 3706 \text{ cc or } 3.7 \text{ liters}$$

Engine Size if Bored or Stroked

If an engine is bored, material is removed from the cylinder walls and a larger piston is installed. The displacement and compression ratio are both increased when the engine is bored.

A stock six-cylinder engine (like the one used in the previous displacement example) with a bore of 4.000 inches and a stroke of 3.000 inches has a displacement of 226 cubic inches. If the engine is bored to 0.060 inch oversize, the size of the bore now becomes 4.060 inches.

The formula for displacement in cubic inches remains the same except that 4.060 is substituted for 4.000.

Cubic inch displacement = Bore × Bore × Stroke × 0.7854 × Number of cylinders
4.060 inches × 4.060 inches × 3.000 inches × 0.7854 × 6 = 233 cubic inches = 3818 cc

If the bore remains the same and the stroke is increased by changing the crankshaft, the cubic inch dis-

(a)

(b)

Figure 11–20 (a) Checking the head for warping. This head should not vary by over 0.002 inch in any 6-inch length and not by more than 0.004 inch overall. (Rule of thumb: no more than 0.001 inch per cylinder.) (b) Do not forget to check diagonally for twist. The same specifications apply. Always use a true straightedge.

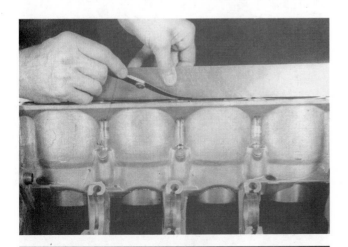

Figure 11–21 Check the level of the deck of a block with a straightedge. A good-quality straightedge should be accurate to 0.0002 inch (0.2 or two-tenths of a thousandth of an inch).

Figure 11–22 Checking alignment of main bearing saddles with a straightedge and a feeler gauge.

Figure 11–23 Using a dial indicator to check the crankshaft end play. Note the use of a pry bar to move the crankshaft while watching the dial indicator.

placement will increase and the compression ratio will also increase. If the stroke is increased 1/8 inch (0.125 inch), keeping the same stock bore, the new displacement will be calculated as follows:

Cubic inch displacement = Bore × Bore × Stroke × 0.7854 × Number of cylinders
4.000 inches × 4.000 inches × 3.125 inches × 0.7854 × 6 = 236 cubic inches = 3867 cc

If the engine is both bored and stroked (bored 0.060 inch, stroked 0.125 inch), the resultant displacement will be

4.060 inches × 4.060 inches × 3.125 inches × 0.7854 × 6 = 243 cubic inches = 3982 cc

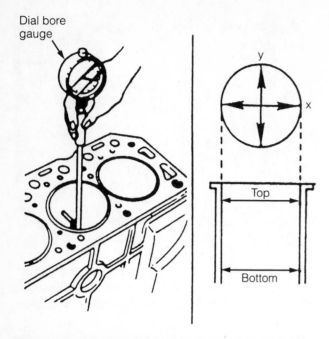

Figure 11–24 Checking the cylinder using a dial bore gauge. First, measure the top of the cylinder at 90 degrees from the crankshaft centerline. This is the "X" diameter. Then measure the diameter at the top of the cylinder in line with the crankshaft. This is the "Y" diameter. Subtracting the Y dimension from the X dimension will give the amount by which the cylinder is out-of-round. Measure the cylinder diameter at 90 degrees from the crankshaft centerline at the bottom of the cylinder. Subtract this measurement from the X diameter to calculate cylinder taper.

Figure 11–25 Using a dial bore gauge to check a cylinder for taper and out-of-round.

Compression Ratio

Compression ratio is the ratio of the volume in the cylinder with the piston at bottom dead center divided by the volume in the cylinder with the piston at top dead center. During routine engine remanufacturing, the following machining operations are performed:

1. Cylinders are bored oversize and larger-diameter pistons are installed. Boring the cylinder increases displacement and compression ratio because the cylinder volume is increased and combustion chamber volume remains the same, resulting in more air being squeezed into the same volume.
2. Block top surfaces are refinished. This machining operation is called "decking the block" and increases the compression ratio because it results in the cylinder heads being down closer to the tops of the pistons.
3. Cylinder head(s) are resurfaced, which also increases the compression ratio.

Figure 11–26 Using a dial bore gauge to measure the main bearing (block housing) bores for taper and out-of-round.

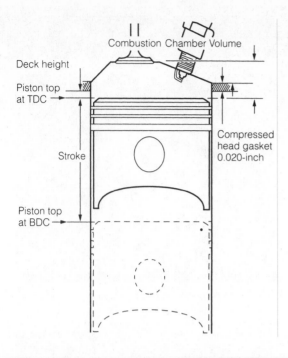

Figure 11–27 Combustion chamber volume is the volume above the piston with the piston at top dead center.

> **NOTE:** To avoid raising the compression ratio beyond stock rating, most remanufacturers use replacement pistons that are 0.015 inch to 0.020 inch shorter than usual.

To calculate the exact compression ratio of the engine, exact measurements must be made of the bore, stroke, and combustion chamber volume. See Figure 11–27.

$$\text{Compression ratio} = \frac{(PV + DV + GV + CV)}{(DV + GV + CV)}$$

where PV = Piston volume

DV = Deck clearance volume (volume in cylinder above piston at TDC)

GV = Head gasket volume = Bore × Bore × 0.7854 × Thickness of gasket

CV = Combustion chamber volume (if measured in cubic centimeters, divide by 16.386 to convert to cubic inches)

For example: What is the compression ratio of a 350-cubic-inch Chevrolet V-8 if the only change was to install 62-cubic-centimeter instead of 74-cubic-centimeter heads?

Bore = 4.000 inches

Stroke = 3.480 inches

Number of cylinders = 8

CV = 74 cc = 4.52 cubic inches = 62 cc = 3.78 cubic inches

GV = Bore × Bore × 0.7854 × Thickness of compressed gasket = 4.000 inches × 4.000 inches × 0.7854 × 0.020 inch = 0.87 cubic inches

To keep the math easier and to illustrate just the effect of changing combustion chamber volume, it is assumed that flat-top pistons are being used with zero deck clearance volume.

> **NOTE:** This is almost never the situation, but is assumed here to simplify the calculation.

PV = Bore × Bore × Stroke × 0.7854
   = 4.000 inches × 4.000 inches × 3.48 inches × 0.7854
   = 43.73 cubic inches

$$CR = \frac{(PV + DV + GV + CV)}{DV + GV + CV} = \frac{(43.73 + 0 + 0.87 + 4.52)}{0 + 0.87 + 4.52}$$

$$= \frac{49.12}{5.39} = 9.1:1$$

With 62-cubic-centimeter (3.78-cubic-inch) heads,

$$CR = \frac{(PV + DV + GV + CV)}{(DV + GV + CV)} = \frac{(43.73 + 0 + 0.87 + 3.78)}{(0 + 0.87 + 3.78)}$$

$$\frac{48.38}{4.65} = 10.4:1$$

The compression ratio was increased from 9.1:1 to 10.4:1 by just changing cylinder heads from 74 cubic centimeters to 62 cubic centimeters. Because 10.4:1 compression is usually *not* recommended for use with today's gasoline, this change should only be done for racing purposes when expensive fuel or fuel additives will be used.

PHOTO SEQUENCE   Micrometer Usage

PS 20–1   This large wooden mock-up shows the use of a micrometer. The fixed part is called the barrel.

PS 20–2   The movable portion of the micrometer is called the thimble or sleeve.

PS 20–3   To read a micrometer, the numbers on the barrel represent 0.025-inch lines with numbers every 0.100 inch.

PS 20–4   The thimble has 25 markings that represent 0.001 inch each.

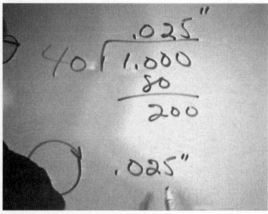

PS 20–5   The thimble has 40 threads per inch. Therefore, one rotation of the thimble moves it along the barrel 0.025 inch (40 into 1.000 inch equals 0.025 inch).

PS 20–6   To read a micrometer therefore involves both reading the lines on the barrel and adding the lines on the thimble.

Micrometer Usage—continued

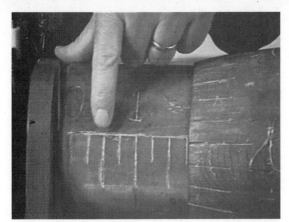

PS 20–7 On the barrel, each rotation of the thimble is represented by one line. Each line represents 0.025 inch. Four lines represent 0.025 × 4 = 0.100 and is marked with a "1" representing one hundred thousandth of an inch.

PS 20–8 This reading shows one line (0.025″) plus a zero on the thimble indicating that the thimble has rotated one complete turn beyond 0.025 inch. The second line on the barrel is barely visible. This reading is 0.050 inch.

PS 20–9 By rotating the thimble just one-thousandth of an inch, the new reading is 0.051 inch (two lines on the barrel at 0.025 each = 0.050 plus 0.001 or the thimble = 0.051 inch).

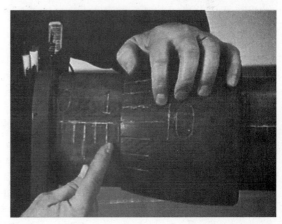

PS 20–10 The thimble has been rotated enough turns so that the "1" shows on the barrel, meaning 0.100 inch (100 thousandths) plus another line indicating another 0.025 (25 thousandths) plus another 0.010 inch (10 thousandths) on the thimble. This reading is therefore 0.135 inch (100 + 25 + 10 = 135).

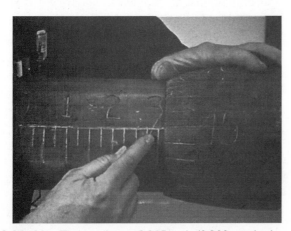

PS 20–11 This reading is 0.315 inch (0.300 on the barrel plus 0.015 inch on the thimble).

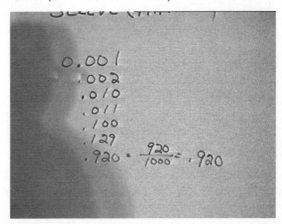

PS 20–12 One-thousandth of an inch is written as 0.001 inch whereas nine hundred twenty (920) thousandths of an inch is written as 0.920 inch.

■ SUMMARY

1. A micrometer can measure 0.001 inch by using a thimble that has 40 threads per inch. Each rotation of the thimble moves the thimble 0.025 inch. The circumference of the thimble is graduated into 25 marks each representing 0.001 inch.

2. A micrometer is used to check the diameter of a crankshaft journal as well as the taper and out-of-round.

3. A camshaft bearing and lobe can be measured using a micrometer.

4. A telescopic gauge is used with a micrometer to measure the inside of a hole or bore, such as the big end of a connecting rod or a cylinder bore.

5. A small-hole gauge (also called a split-ball gauge) is used with a micrometer to measure small holes such as the inside diameter of a valve guide in a cylinder head.

6. A vernier dial caliper is used to measure the outside diameter of components such as pistons or crankshaft bearing journals.

7. A feeler gauge (also called a thickness gauge) is used to measure the gap or clearance between two components such as piston ring gap, piston ring side clearance, and connecting rod side clearance. A feeler gauge is also used with a precision straightedge to measure flatness of blocks and cylinder heads.

8. A dial indicator and dial bore gauge are used to measure differences in a component such as crankshaft end play (dial indicator) or cylinder taper (dial bore gauge).

9. Engine displacement is determined by the formula: Bore × Bore × Stroke × 0.7854 × Number of cylinders.

10. Compression ratio is the ratio of the volume of a cylinder with the piston at bottom dead center (BDC) to the volume of the cylinder with the piston at top dead center (TDC).

■ REVIEW QUESTIONS

1. Explain how a micrometer is read.

2. Describe how to check a crankshaft journal for out-of-round and taper.

3. List engine components that can be measured with the help of a telescopic gauge.

4. List the gaps or clearances that can be measured using a feeler (thickness) gauge.

5. Explain why a dial bore gauge has to be set to a dimension before using.

6. What is the formula for determining displacement?

7. How many cubic inches are in a 3.0 L, V-6?

■ ASE CERTIFICATION-TYPE QUESTIONS

1. The threaded movable part that rotates on a micrometer is called the _____ .
   a. Barrel
   b. Thimble
   c. Spindle
   d. Anvil

2. To check a crankshaft journal for taper, the journal should be measured in at least how many locations?
   a. One
   b. Two
   c. Four
   d. Six

3. To check a crankshaft journal for out-of-round, the journal should be measured in at least how many locations?
   a. Two
   b. Four
   c. Six
   d. Eight

4. A telescopic gauge can be used to measure a cylinder bore if what other measuring device is used to measure the telescopic gauge?
   a. Micrometer
   b. Feeler gauge
   c. Straightedge
   d. Dial indicator

5. To directly measure the diameter of a valve guide in a cylinder head, use a micrometer and a _____.
   a. Telescopic gauge
   b. Feeler gauge
   c. Small-hole gauge
   d. Dial indicator

6. Which of the following *cannot* be measured using a feeler gauge?
   a. Valve guide clearance
   b. Piston ring gap
   c. Piston ring side clearance
   d. Connecting rod side clearance

7. Which of the following *cannot* be measured using a straightedge and a feeler gauge?
   a. Cylinder head flatness
   b. Block deck flatness
   c. Straightness of the main bearing bores
   d. Straightness of the cylinder bore

8. Which measuring gauge needs to be set up (adjusted) to a fixed dimension before use?
   a. Dial indicator
   b. Dial bore gauge
   c. Vernier dial gauge
   d. Micrometer

9. An eight-cylinder engine with a bore of 4.000 inches and a stroke of 3.000 inches has a displacement of:
   a. 226 cubic inches
   b. 302 cubic inches
   c. 350 cubic inches
   d. 383 cubic inches

10. An engine has been bored 0.030 inch oversize. The cylinder heads were not machined and the stroke of the crankshaft was not changed. Technician A says that the compression ratio will be higher than before the repair. Technician B says that the compression will be lower than before the repair. Which technician is correct?
    a. Technician A only
    b. Technician B only
    c. Both Technician A and B
    d. Neither Technician A nor B

Intake and Exhaust Manifolds

Objectives: After studying Chapter 12, the reader should be able to:

1. Discuss the purpose and function of intake manifolds.
2. Explain the differences between carburetor manifolds and port-injection manifolds.
3. Describe the operation of the exhaust gas recirculation system in the intake manifold.
4. List the materials used in exhaust manifolds and exhaust systems.
5. Discuss the operation of the heat riser and the need for manifold heating.

The term *manifold* means "from one to many or many to one." The *intake manifold* (also called *inlet manifold*) is used to distribute the air-fuel mixture from one source (the air filter) or distribute it to all of the cylinders. The exhaust manifold collects the exhaust from many cylinders and combines it into one outlet.

Smooth operation can only occur when each combustion chamber produces the same pressure, as does every other chamber in the engine. For this to be achieved, each cylinder must receive a charge exactly like the charge going into the other cylinders in quality and quantity. The charges must have the same physical properties and the same air-fuel mixture.

Air coming into an engine will flow through the carburetor or injector throttle body. *All air entering an engine must be filtered.* See Figure 12–1.

NOTE: If an engine is operated without an air filter, the rate of engine wear is increased almost 10 times!

Frequently Asked Question ???

What Does this Tube Do?

A frequently asked question is what is the purpose of the odd-shape tube attached to the inlet duct between the air filter and the throttle body as seen in Figure 12–2? The tube shape is designed to dampen out certain resonant frequencies that can occur at certain engine speeds. The length and shape of this tube are designed to absorb shock waves that are created in the air intake system and to provide a reservoir for the air that will then be released into the airstream during cycles of lower pressure. The overall effect of these resonance tubes is to reduce the noise of the air entering the engine.

■ CARBURETOR AND THROTTLE-BODY INJECTION INTAKE MANIFOLDS

A carburetor and throttle-body fuel injector force finely divided droplets of liquid fuel into the incoming air to form a combustible air-fuel mixture. See Figure 12–3 for an example of a typical throttle-body injection (TBI) unit. These droplets start to evaporate as soon as they leave the carburetor or throttle body injector nozzles. With a carburetor engine operating at its highest level of volumetric efficiency, about 60% of the fuel will evapo-

(a)

(b)

Figure 12–1 (a) Note the discovery as the air filter housing was opened during service on a Pontiac Bonneville. The nuts were obviously deposited by squirrels (or some other animal). (b) Not only was the housing filled with nuts, but also this air filter was extremely dirty indicating that this vehicle had not been serviced for a long time.

Figure 12–2 A resonance tube, called a Helmholtz resonator, is used on the intake duct between the air filter and the throttle body to reduce air intake noise during engine acceleration.

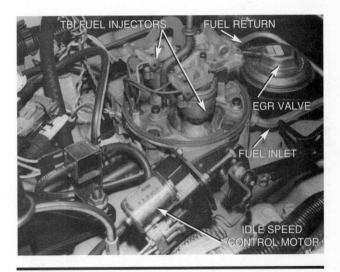

Figure 12–3 A typical throttle-body injection (TBI) unit. This TBI uses two injectors. Most V-6 and V-8 engines require two throttle-body injectors, whereas four-cylinder engines use one injector.

rate by the time the intake charge reaches the combustion chamber. This means that there will be some liquid droplets in the charge as it flows through the manifold. *The droplets stay in the charge as long as the charge flows at high velocities.* At maximum horsepower, these velocities may reach 300 feet per second. Separation of the droplets from the charge as it passes through the manifold occurs when the velocity drops below 50 feet per second. Intake charge velocities at idle speeds are often below this value. When separation occurs—at low engine speeds—extra fuel must be supplied to the charge in order to have a combustible mixture reach the combustion chamber.

Manifold sizes represent a compromise. They must have a cross section large enough to allow charge flow for maximum power. The cross section must be small enough that the flow velocities of the charge will be high enough to keep the fuel droplets in suspension. This is required so that equal mixtures reach each cylinder. Manifold cross-sectional size is one reason why engines designed especially for racing will not run at low engine speeds. Racing manifolds must be large enough to reach maximum horsepower. This size, however, allows the charge to move slowly, and the fuel will separate from the charge at low engine speeds. Fuel separation leads to poor accelerator response. Standard passenger vehicle engines are primarily designed for economy during light-load, partial-throttle operation. Their manifolds, therefore, have a much smaller cross-sectional area than do those of racing engines. This small size will help keep flow velocities of the charge high throughout the normal operating speed range of the engine.

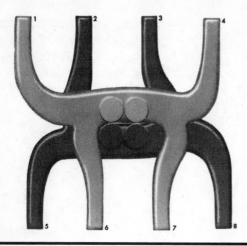

Figure 12–4 One side of a carburetor (or one injector of a dual throttle-body fuel-injector system) supplies fuel to one-half of the cylinders, which corresponds to every other cylinder in the firing order. *(Courtesy of Ford Motor Company).*

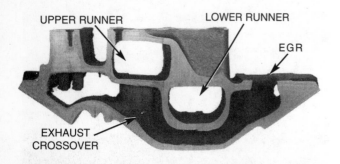

Figure 12–5 Most dual-plane intake manifolds use runners on two levels to provide as equal a distance as possible between the throttle plate and intake valve of all cylinders. The two levels also result in smaller runners for higher mixture velocity and improved throttle response.

In a four-stroke cycle, the intake stroke is approximately one-fourth of the cycle. Four cylinders can, therefore, be attached to the same carburetor when the cylinders are timed so that each cylinder takes a different quarter of the 720-degree four-stroke cycle. This principle is also used in V-type automotive engines. In these engines, the intake manifold is divided into two sections or branches with runners on two levels. This style of intake manifold is said to have a **180-degree** or **dual-plane** design. See Figures 12–4 and 12–5. Using this design, relatively long runners can be fit between the heads. Successively firing cylinders are fed alternately from the upper and lower runners, so the runner design must match the cylinder firing order. If the carburetor feeds all cylinders from one open plenum, it is said to have a **360-degree** or **single-plane** design.

In the tuned runners, the length is designed to take advantage of the natural pressure wave that occurs in a gas column. The pressure wave reaches the cylinder at

Figure 12–6 In the late 1950s, Chrysler Corporation produced some high performance engines that used two, four-barrel carburetors on a long "cross ram" intake manifold. The long runners of the intake manifold help create a ram effect especially at low engine speeds to help increase engine torque. These intake manifolds were so long that they had to be removed from the engine to gain access to the spark plugs.

the exact instant that the intake valve is open. This allows the charge to enter the cylinder with a supercharging or ram effect. The effect of intake manifold tuning is illustrated in Figure 12–6. On V-8 engines using four-barrel carburetors, the primary barrels are often placed approximately on the center of the runners to improve low-range and mid-range performance. See Figure 12–7. The primary barrels of the carburetor are in constant use. Sharp bends tend to increase fuel separation, as shown in Figure 12–8. The air, having less mass, is able to make turns much more quickly than the heavy fuel droplets. Rough interior runner surfaces add a drag and turbulence to the charge.

Main intake runners have cross-sectional areas of approximately 0.008 square inch per engine cubic inch of displacement. Branch runners have cross-sectional areas of approximately 0.006 square inche per cubic inch of displacement. Ribs and guide vanes, such as those that can be seen in Figure 12–9 on page 250, are often positioned in the floor of the manifold runners. They aid in equal distribution of the intake charge to the cylinders, even when some of the fuel remains in liquid form. It is just as important for the fuel to have equal distribution as it is for the air to have equal distribution.

■ OPEN AND CLOSED INTAKE MANIFOLDS

Two general intake manifold designs are used on modern V-type engines. The first type of manifold is an **open-type manifold.** Runners go through the open-type branches. Lifter valley covers are needed on engines using open-type manifolds. In some engines, the lifter valley covers are an extension of the intake manifold gasket. Figure 12–11 on page 250 shows a typical open-type intake manifold.

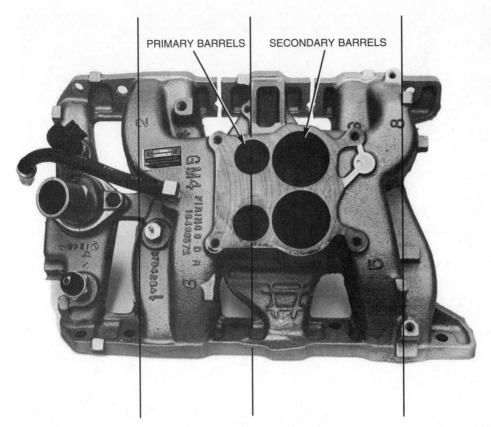

PRIMARY BARRELS   SECONDARY BARRELS

Figure 12–7 Primary barrels of the carburetor fit on the intake manifold bores near the center of the manifold.

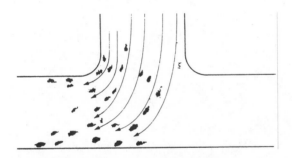

Figure 12–8 Heavy fuel droplets separate as they flow around an abrupt bend in an intake manifold.

The second type of intake manifold is a **closed-type manifold.** It is used on V-type engines as illustrated in Figure 12–12 on page 251. This manifold has cast metal between the runners. It is used as a lifter valley cover and a manifold.

Closed-type manifolds on V-type engines have the exhaust crossover located just above the lifter valley, where engine oil could contact the hot surface. Hot exhaust in the crossover would heat the oil that lands on the surface of the crossover. This would cause coking. **Coking** is the heating of oil until a solid residue remains. Eventually, the coking will contaminate the oil, which, in turn, would lead to the need for frequent oil changes. Therefore, **shields** are put in engines to keep the oil from hitting these hot surfaces. A sheet-metal deflector may be fastened to the lifter valley side of the intake manifold to keep the oil from the hot crossover. This is shown in the sectional view in Figure 12–13 on page 251.

TECH TIP

Every Other Cylinder

All engines of four or more cylinders are furnished fuel according to firing order. The intake manifold on a V-type engine is designed so that each side of the carburetor or TBI unit supplies the air-fuel mixture to every other cylinder in the *firing order* for each barrel (venturi) of the carburetor or throttle-body fuel-injection unit. It is easy to determine which cylinders are fed an air-fuel mixture from the same side of a carburetor or throttle-body injector unit.

Step 1 Write out the cylinder numbers in their firing order: 1 6 5 4 3 2

Step 2 Mark every other cylinder in the firing order: <u>1</u> 6 <u>5</u> 4 <u>3</u> 2

The marked cylinders share the same side of the carburetor, and the unmarked cylinders share the other side of the carburetor.

NOTE: Most V-6 engines are split so that the left bank of cylinders is on one runner and the right bank is on the other runner. Most V-8s have two cylinders on each side of the engine sharing a barrel with two cylinders of the opposite bank. See Figure 12–10.

Figure 12–9 Guide vanes in the floor of a typical intake manifold. These vanes or ribs help to create turbulence in the manifold to help keep the fuel in the airstream. If the flow of the air-fuel mixture is allowed to slow, the heavier fuel tends to drop to the bottom of the manifold floor.

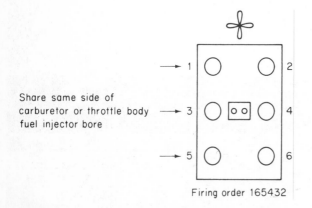

Share same side of carburetor or throttle body fuel injector bore

Firing order 165432

Figure 12–10 Many V-6 engines that use a carburetor or a throttle-body type of fuel injection use an intake manifold that is designed so that each side of the carburetor or TBI unit feeds fuel to every other cylinder in the firing order. This usually means that on a V-6, one entire side of the engine shares the same side of the carburetor. A vacuum leak on one side usually results in a very rough idle because of this design.

CAUTION: Be certain to remove and thoroughly clean under the heat shield. Trapped dirt and carbon can easily be dislodged when the engine is reassembled. This debris can do serious damage to new engine bearings and all other engine parts. Some engines have a large single-piece manifold gasket to do the job of deflecting oil from the crossover (Figure 12–14).

Figure 12–11 Open-type intake manifold on a V-type engine. The runners on this manifold are on a single plane.

■ MANIFOLD HEAT

Heat is required in the manifold so that liquid fuel in the charge will evaporate as the charge travels from the carburetor to the combustion chamber. When heat is taken from the air in the intake charge by fuel evaporation, the charge temperature is lowered. Additional fuel will not evaporate from the cooled charge as rapidly as it would from a warm charge. Additional heat is supplied to the charge when it is needed. The added heat gives good fuel evaporation for smooth engine operation when the engine is cold. An intake charge temperature range of about 100° to 130°F (38° to 55°C) is necessary to give

Figure 12–12 Closed-type intake manifold on a V-type engine. Notice that the aluminum intake manifold extends over the cylinder heads and actually provides a rail for the valve covers. Sealing of this type of manifold is critical for proper operation and prevention of fluid and air leaks.

Figure 12–13 The finger points to a sheet-metal deflector oil shield fastened to the lifter valley side of the intake manifold. This shield protects the engine oil from the high temperature of the crossover exhaust passage through the manifold.

TECH TIP ✔

The Glue and Antiseize Compound Trick

A common problem with using aluminum intake manifolds on a V-type cast-iron engine is that the gasket often fails. Aluminum expands at twice the rate of cast iron (0.0012 inch per 100°F for aluminum versus 0.0006 inch per 100°F for cast iron). As a result, when the engine gets warm, the intake manifold expands and tends to move upward, sliding over the surface of the cast-iron cylinder heads.

To help prevent premature intake manifold gasket failure, use a contact adhesive to glue the gasket to the cast-iron head. This helps hold the gasket in place for easier installation and prevents movement of the gasket against the cast iron. Then, before installing the aluminum intake manifold, coat the gasket and/or the sealing surface of the intake manifold with antiseize compound. This will allow movement without damage to the gasket.

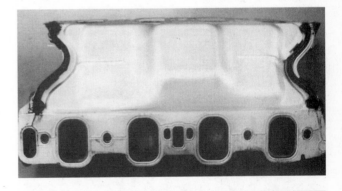

Figure 12–14 Single-piece intake manifold gasket that serves as an oil shield.

---

good fuel evaporation. In most current engines, heat is supplied to the intake manifold during low-temperature operation by a system known as a **thermostatic air cleaner (TAC).** Heat is picked up from around the exhaust manifold and routed to the air cleaner inlet. A thermostatically controlled bimetallic switch adjusts a **vacuum motor.** It controls the amount of heated air used. Parts of this system are shown in Figure 12–15. Another thermostatic valve, called a **heat riser,** directs exhaust gases against the intake manifold directly below the carburetor. On V-type engines, exhaust gas is routed through a passage called an exhaust **heat crossover.** Part of the exhaust gas is directed against

the intake manifold directly under the throttle body. This can be seen in Figure 12–16.

> **NOTE:** Port fuel-injected engines do not require an exhaust heat crossover because there is no fuel in the air flowing through the intake runner.

On some emission-controlled engines, the heat riser valve is operated by a vacuum diaphragm actuator assembly controlled by a temperature-sensitive valve. This system is called **early fuel evaporation (EFE).** A typical EFE valve is shown in Figure 12–17.

When the engine gets fully warmed up, the heat riser valve directs the exhaust gas away from the intake manifold and crossover. The exhaust gas is sent directly out through the exhaust system.

Some engines use the coolant to supply heat to the charge mixture. Warm coolant is allowed to flow through a passage below the intake runners. Heat from the engine

Figure 12–15 Typical carburetor air inlet preheat temperature regulator. If the preheat tube is defective or missing, serious cold-engine driveability problems occur. Most throttle-body fuel-injection systems also use preheated air during the warm-up period. *(Courtesy of Chevrolet Motor Division, General Motors Corporation)*

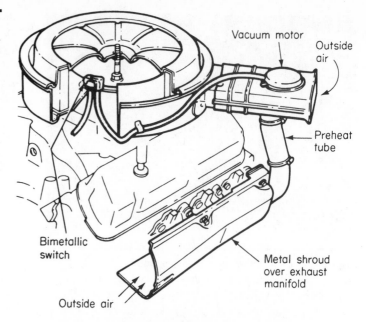

Figure 12–16 Exhaust heat crossover on a V-type engine intake manifold. If this passage becomes clogged with carbon, the engine will perform poorly during the warm-up period and prevent the choke from opening on carburetor-equipped engines. *(Courtesy of Chevrolet Motor Division, General Motors Corporation)*

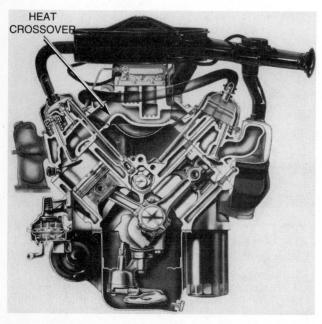

coolant is not available until the engine begins to warm up. Engine coolant is always used to provide intake manifold heat on an inline engine when the intake and exhaust manifolds are on opposite sides of the head. An example of these manifolds on a head is shown in Figure 12–18. Manifolds on V-type engines often contain a coolant passage. It connects the cooling system between the V heads. This passage provides a common cooling outlet for the engine cooling system at the thermostat.

Figure 12–17 Typical early fuel evaporation (EFE) system. Manifold vacuum is applied to the actuator through a thermo vacuum switch located in a cooling system passage near the thermostat. When the valve is closed, the exhaust is forced through the cylinder head, under the intake manifold, through the opposite cylinder head passage, and out through the left-side exhaust manifold.

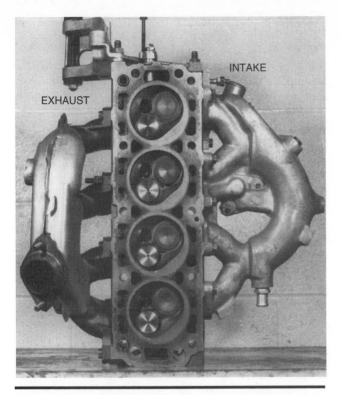

Figure 12–18 Head of an engine with the intake and exhaust manifolds on opposite sides of the head. This is called a cross-flow head.

■ CHOKE HEAT

The carburetor is designed with a choke to provide an excessively rich charge mixture for starting. Without the choke, there would not be enough of the volatile part of the fuel to make a combustible mixture. There are two additional problems.

- First, the intake charge velocity is low during cranking, allowing the fuel to separate from the air.
- Second, no extra heat is available for fuel evaporation before the engine starts. Most chokes are automatic. They are closed by a temperature-sensing thermostatic spring. In some applications, heat is carried to the thermostatic spring through a tube from a heat chamber called a **stove.** The choke heat stove is often located in the exhaust manifold where it can pick up exhaust heat. An insulated tube carries warm air from the choke heat stove to the sensing spring on the carburetor. The intake manifold shown in Figure 12–19 has the choke heat stove. In this location, the stove is heated by exhaust at the exhaust heat crossover in the intake manifold. Some applications place the heat-sensing choke spring directly in the stove well. A link connects the choke spring with the carburetor choke plate.

Figure 12–19 A choke heat stove gets hot because exhaust gases flow through the intake manifold passage under the carburetor. The choke is heated by the drawing of filtered air through this heat stove and to the choke housing.

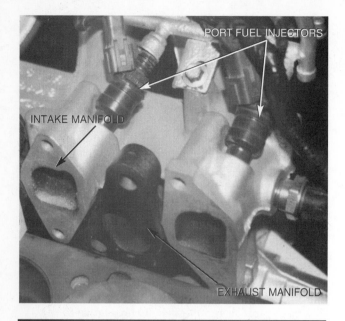

Figure 12–20 An inline engine with part of the cylinder head cut away showing the locations of the fuel injectors in the intake manifold.

■ PORT-INJECTION INTAKE MANIFOLDS

The size and shape of port fuel-injected engine intake manifolds can be optimized because the only thing in the manifold is air. The fuel injection is located in the intake manifold about 3 inches (70 to 100 mm) from the intake valve. See Figure 12–20. Therefore, the runner length and shape are designed for tuning only. There is no need to keep an air-fuel mixture homogenized throughout its trip from the carburetor or TBI unit to the intake valve.

- Long runners build low-RPM torque.
- Shorter runners provide maximum high-RPM power.

TECH TIP

The Aluminum Epoxy Trick

Often, aluminum intake manifolds are corroded around the coolant passages. Rather than replacing the manifold, simply apply an 80% aluminum epoxy to fill the pitted area. Be sure that the area to be repaired is thoroughly cleaned, and mix the epoxy according to the manufacturer's instructions. The epoxy can be applied with a putty knife or other similar tool. After the epoxy has hardened, the area can be surfaced as usual. Epoxy can also be used to repair pitted coolant pumps.

Some engines with four valve heads utilize a dual or variable intake runner design. At lower engine speeds, long intake runners provide low-speed torque. At higher engine speeds, shorter intake runners are opened by means of a computer-controlled valve to increase high-speed power. See Figures 12–21 and 12–22 on page 256.

■ PLASTIC INTAKE MANIFOLDS

Most thermoplastic intake manifolds are molded from fiberglass-reinforced nylon. The plastic manifolds can be cast or injected molded. Some manifolds are molded in two parts and bonded together. Plastic intake manifolds are lighter than aluminum manifolds and can better insulate engine heat from the fuel injectors.

Plastic intake manifolds have smoother interior surfaces than do other types of manifolds, resulting in greater airflow. See Figures 12–23 and 12–24 on page 256.

■ EXHAUST GAS RECIRCULATION

To reduce the emission of oxides of nitrogen (NO_x), engines have been equipped with **exhaust gas recirculation (EGR)** valves. From 1973 until recently, they were used on almost all vehicles. Because of the efficiency of computer-controlled fuel injection, some newer engines do not require an EGR system to meet emission standards. Some engines use intake and exhaust valve overlap as a means of trapping some exhaust in the cylinder. The EGR valve opens at speeds above idle on a warm engine. When open, the valve allows a small portion of the exhaust gas (5% to 10%) to enter the intake mani-

TECH TIP

The Snake Trick

The EGR passages on many intake manifolds become clogged with carbon. This reduces the flow of exhaust and reduces the amount of exhaust gases in the cylinders. This can cause spark knock (detonation) and increase emissions of oxides of nitrogen (NO_x) (especially important in areas with enhanced exhaust emissions testing).

To quickly and easily remove carbon from exhaust passages, cut a length of about 1 foot (30 cm) from stranded wire such as garage door guide wire or from an old vehicle speedometer cable. Flare the end and place the wire-end-first into the passage. Set the drill on reverse. Turn the drill on, and the wire will pull its way through the passage, cleaning the carbon as it goes, just like a snake in a drainpipe.

(a)

(b)

(c)

(d)

Figure 12–21 (a) Tuned intake manifold design as used on a port fuel-injected engine. The intake manifold can be designed with these long tubes to add low-speed torque because the only thing inside the manifold is air. (b) Four-valve head intake manifold showing two different-length intake runners. (c) Tuned intake runner for a port fuel-injected four-cylinder engine. (d) Tuned intake runners for a port fuel-injected V-6.

fold. Here, the exhaust gas mixes with and takes the place of some of the intake charge. This leaves less room for the intake charge to enter the combustion chamber. The recirculated exhaust gas is inert and does *not* enter into the combustion process. The result is a lower peak combustion temperature. As the combustion temperature is lowered, the production of oxides of nitrogen is also reduced.

The EGR system has some means of interconnecting the exhaust and intake manifolds. The interconnecting passage is controlled by the EGR valve. On V-type engines, the intake manifold crossover is used as a source of exhaust gas for the EGR system. A cast passage connects the exhaust crossover to the EGR valve. The gas is sent from the EGR valve to openings below the carburetor. On inline-type engines, an ex-

ternal tube is generally used to carry exhaust gas to the EGR valve. This tube is often designed to be long so that the exhaust gas is cooled before it enters the EGR valve. Figure 12–25 on page 257 shows a typical long EGR tube. The EGR valve is usually attached to an adapter between the carburetor and intake manifold. Here, it can release the exhaust gas directly into the intake manifold runner.

■ INTAKE MANIFOLD GASKETS

Like heads, manifolds are torqued with high clamping loads. As a result, manifold gaskets used on older engines have the same types of construction and require the same fit and surface finish as do head gaskets.

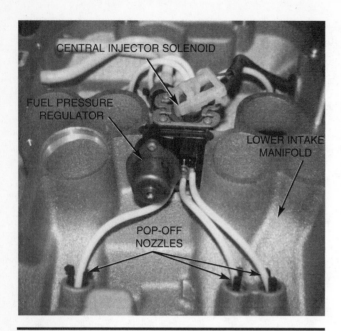

Figure 12–22 The lower intake manifold used on a Chevrolet pickup truck engine. This central port-injection system uses one central injector with plastic lines leading to individual pop-off-type injectors near each cylinder.

Figure 12–23 This DaimlerChrysler V-6 engine uses an intake manifold tuning valve that is controlled by the engine computer to switch where the air is directed through the passages of the manifold to allow the engine to produce the most torque possible at every engine speed.

Some older V-type engines use a large metal pan-type intake manifold gasket. It goes between the lifter valley and the bottom of the manifold. Its purpose is to keep oil from splashing on the bottom of the exhaust crossover in the manifold. The latest intake manifold gasket designs have synthetic rubber O-ring types of beads molded on a plastic, fiber, or steel carrier. See Figure 12–26.

Figure 12–24 This prototype inline six-cylinder engine uses long plastic manifold runners to help the engine produce maximum torque at low engine speeds without hurting high engine speed power.

■ TURBOCHARGING

A turbocharged (exhaust driven) system is designed to provide a pressure greater than atmospheric pressure in the intake manifold. This increased pressure forces additional amounts of air and fuel into the combustion chamber over what would normally be forced in by atmospheric pressure. This increased charge increases engine power. The amount of "boost" (or pressure in the intake manifold) is measured in pounds per square inch, in **inches of mercury** (in. Hg), in **bars,** or in **atmospheres.**

1 atmosphere = 14.7 psi

1 atmosphere = 30 in. Hg

1 atmosphere = 1.0 bar

1 bar = 14.7 psi

The higher the level of boost (pressure), the greater the horsepower potential. However, other factors must be considered when increasing boost pressure:

1. As boost pressure increases, the temperature of the air also increases.
2. As the temperature of the air increases, combustion temperatures also increase, which increases the possibility of detonation.
3. Power can be increased by cooling the compressed air after it leaves the turbocharger. *The power can be increased about 1% per 10°F by which the air is cooled.* A typical cooling device is called an intercooler and is similar to a radiator, wherein outside air can pass through, cooling the pressurized heated air.

Figure 12–25 EGR tube used to supply and cool the exhaust gas to the EGR valve.

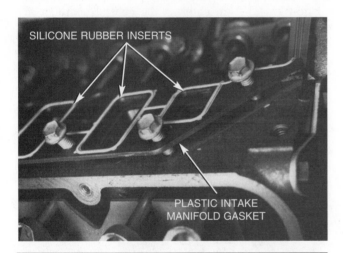

Figure 12–26 Many engines today use reusable intake manifold gaskets. Before reusing a gasket, check the vehicle manufacturer's recommended procedure and recommendations.

4. As boost pressure increases, combustion temperature and pressures increase, which if not limited, can do severe engine damage. The maximum exhaust gas temperature must be 1550°F (840°C). Higher temperatures decrease the durability of the turbocharger *and* the engine. See Figure 12–27.

■ WASTEGATE OPERATION

To prevent severe engine damage, most turbocharger systems use a wastegate. A wastegate is a valve similar to a door that can open and close. If the valve is closed, all exhaust travels to the turbocharger. When a predetermined amount of boost pressure develops in the intake manifold, the wastegate valve is opened. As the valve opens, the exhaust flows directly out the exhaust system, bypassing the turbocharger. With less exhaust

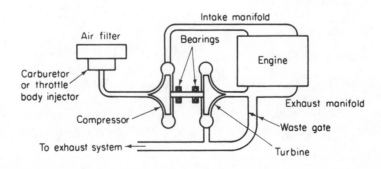

Figure 12–27 Typical turbocharger operation.

flowing across the vanes of the turbocharger, the turbocharger decreases in speed and boost pressure is reduced. When the boost pressure drops, the wastegate valve can then close to direct the exhaust over the turbocharger vanes and again allow the boost pressure to rise. This is a continuous process of wastegate operation to control boost pressure.

The wastegate is the pressure control valve of a turbocharger system. The wastegate is usually controlled by the onboard computer. The **manifold absolute pressure (MAP) sensor** is the most important sensor used by the computer to control the wastegate. The computer usually controls a vacuum valve, which operates the wastegate valve. See Figures 12–28 and 12–29.

■ TURBOCHARGER FAILURES

When turbochargers fail to function correctly, a drop in power is noticed. To restore proper operation, the turbocharger must be rebuilt, repaired, or replaced. It is not possible to simply remove the turbocharger and seal any openings—and still maintain decent driveability. Bearing failure is a common cause of turbocharger failure, and replacement bearings are usually only available to rebuilders. Another common turbocharger problem is excessive and continuous oil consumption resulting in blue exhaust smoke. Turbochargers use small rings similar to piston rings on the shaft to prevent exhaust (combustion gases) from entering the central bearing. Because there are no seals to keep oil in, usual causes of excessive oil consumption include the following:

1. A plugged positive crankcase ventilation (PCV) system resulting in excessive crankcase pressures forcing oil into the air inlet. This failure is not related to the turbocharger, but the turbocharger is often blamed.

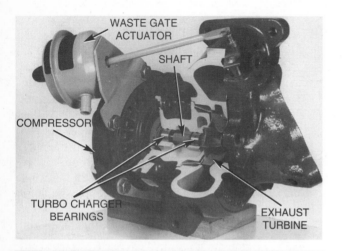

Figure 12–28 Turbocharger cutaway showing internal parts. The wastegate is used to limit maximum boost pressure and is usually controlled by the engine computer.

Figure 12–29 Typical turbocharger installation. The wastegate is computer controlled based on input signals regarding engine RPM, coolant temperatures, MAP, and other variables.

2. A clogged air filter, which causes a low-pressure area in the inlet, which can draw oil past the turbo shaft rings and into the intake manifold.

3. A clogged oil return (drain) line from the turbocharger to the oil pan (sump), which can cause the engine oil pressure to force oil past the turbocharger's shaft rings and into the intake *and* exhaust manifolds. Obviously, oil being forced into both the intake and exhaust would create lots of smoke.

■ SUPERCHARGING

A supercharging system is an engine-driven system designed to provide pressure greater than atmospheric pressure in the intake manifold. See Figure 12–30. Supercharging has some advantages and disadvantages as compared with turbocharging.

Advantages	Disadvantages
1. Gives instantaneous throttle response (no lag)	**1.** Takes power from the engine
2. Involves less plumbing (no connections to the exhaust system)	**2.** Drains power from the engine continuously

■ BOOST IS THE RESULT OF RESTRICTION

Boost pressure of a turbocharger (or supercharger) is commonly measured in pounds per square inch. If a cylinder head is restricted because of small valves and ports, the turbocharger will quickly provide boost. Boost results when the air being forced into the cylin-

Figure 12–30 Cutaway of a Roots-type, positive displacement-type supercharger. The air is drawn from the top and flows outward and down between the rotors and the housing, where the air is trapped and compressed.

der heads cannot flow into the cylinders fast enough and "piles up" in the intake manifold, increasing boost pressure. If an engine had large valves and ports, the turbocharger could provide a much greater *amount* of air into the engine at the same boost pressure as an identical engine with smaller valves and ports.

■ EXHAUST MANIFOLD DESIGN

The exhaust manifold is designed to collect high-temperature spent gases from the head exhaust ports. The hot gases are sent to an exhaust pipe, then to a catalytic converter, to the muffler, to a resonator, and on to the tailpipe, where they are vented to the atmosphere. This must be done with the least possible amount of restriction or back pressure while keeping the exhaust noise at a minimum.

Exhaust gas temperature will vary according to the power produced by the engine. The manifold must be designed to operate at both engine idle and continuous full power. Under full-power conditions, the exhaust manifold will become red-hot, causing a great deal of expansion.

> **NOTE:** The temperature of an exhaust manifold can exceed 1500°F (815°C).

At idle, the exhaust manifold is just warm, causing little expansion. After casting, the manifold may be annealed. **Annealing** is a heat-treating process that takes out the brittle hardening of the casting to reduce the chance of cracking from the temperature changes. During vehicle operation, manifold temperatures usually reach the high-temperature extremes. Most exhaust manifolds are made from cast iron to withstand extreme and rapid temperature changes. The manifold is bolted to the head in a way that will allow expansion and contraction. In some cases, hollow-headed bolts are used to maintain a gas-tight seal while still allowing normal expansion and contraction.

The exhaust manifold is designed to allow the free flow of exhaust gas. Some manifolds use internal cast-rib deflectors or dividers to guide the exhaust gases toward the outlet as smoothly as possible. Figure 12–31 shows two types of exhaust manifolds that fit inline engines.

Some exhaust manifolds are designed to go above the spark plug, whereas others are designed to go below. The spark plug and carefully routed ignition wires are usually shielded from the exhaust heat with sheet-metal deflectors. Typical deflectors can be seen in Figure 12–32.

Exhaust systems are especially designed for the engine-chassis combination. The exhaust system length, pipe size, and silencer are designed, where possible, to make use of the tuning effect of the gas column

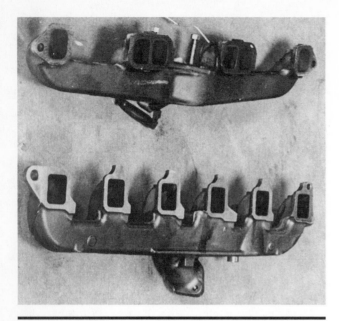

Figure 12–31 The top exhaust manifold has Siamese runners. The bottom exhaust manifold has separate runners for each cylinder.

Figure 12–32 Example of heat deflector shields placed between the exhaust manifold and the spark plugs and plug wires. Even high-temperature-resistant silicone jacket spark plug wires cannot withstand the high exhaust manifold temperatures.

resonating within the exhaust system. Tuning occurs when the exhaust pulses from the cylinders are emptied into the manifold between the pulses of other cylinders. See Figure 12–33.

■ EXHAUST MANIFOLD GASKETS

Exhaust heat will expand the manifold more than it will the head. It causes the exhaust manifold to slide on the

Figure 12–33 Original-equipment (OE) type of tubular steel exhaust manifold.

How Can a Cracked Exhaust Manifold Affect Engine Performance?

A crack in an exhaust manifold will not only allow exhaust gases to escape and cause noise but the crack can also allow air to enter the exhaust manifold. See Figure 12–34. Exhaust flows from the cylinders as individual puffs or pressure pulses. Behind each of these pressure pulses, a low pressure (below atmospheric pressure) is created. Outside air at atmospheric pressure is then drawn into the exhaust manifold through the crack. This outside air contains 21% oxygen and is measured by the oxygen sensor (O2S). The air passing the O2S signals the engine computer that the engine is operating too lean (excess oxygen) and the computer, not knowing that the lean indicator is false, adds additional fuel to the engine. The result is that the engine will be operating richer (more fuel than normal) and spark plugs could become fouled causing poor engine operation.

sealing surface of the head. The heat also causes thermal stress. When the manifold is removed from the engine for service, the stress is relieved and this may cause the manifold to warp slightly. Exhaust manifold gaskets are included in gasket sets to seal slightly warped exhaust manifolds. These gaskets *should* be used, even if the engine did not originally use exhaust manifold gaskets. When a perforated core exhaust manifold gasket has facing on one side only, put the facing side against the head and put the manifold against the perforated metal core. The manifold can slide on the metal of the gasket just as it slid on the sealing surface of the head.

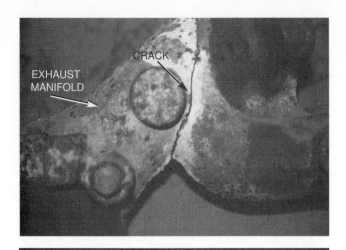

Figure 12–34 A crack in an exhaust manifold is often not this visible. A crack in the exhaust manifold upstream of the oxygen sensor can fool the sensor and affect engine operation.

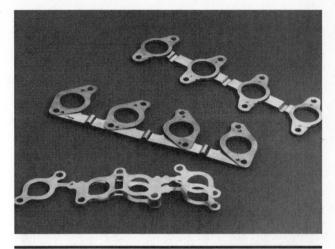

Figure 12–35 Typical exhaust manifold gaskets. Note how they are laminated to allow the exhaust manifold to expand and contract due to heating and cooling.

Gaskets are used on new engines with tubing- or header-type exhaust manifolds. The gaskets often include heat shields to keep exhaust heat from the spark plugs and spark plug cables. They may have several layers of steel for high-temperature sealing. The layers are spot welded together. Some are embossed where special sealing is needed. See Figure 12–35. Many new engines do not use gaskets with cast exhaust manifolds. The flat surface of the new cast-iron exhaust manifold fits tightly against the flat surface of the new head.

Figure 12–36 An exhaust manifold spreader tool is a tool that is absolutely necessary to use when reinstalling exhaust manifolds. When they are removed from the engine, they tend to warp slightly even though the engine is allowed to cool before being removed. The spreader tool allows the technician to line up the bolt holes without doing any harm to the manifold.

■ HOW HEADERS WORK

On many engines, a welded steel tubing **header** is used instead of a cast-iron exhaust manifold. Use of the lightweight header allows a smooth, nearly ideal exhaust manifold design that will handle the large volume of exhaust gas produced when the engine is operating at high speeds.

Headers work in two ways:

1. Headers reduce exhaust system restriction. With a lower level of restriction, the exhaust can leave the engine more easily, requiring less power from the engine to push the exhaust out through the exhaust system.
2. Immediately after an exhaust pulse leaves an exhaust port, there is a lower pressure in the cylinder. **Tuned** headers are designed to combine individual exhaust pulses into one larger pulse, with a corresponding lower pressure behind the pulse. This low pressure is less than atmospheric pressure. This lower pressure actually helps to draw more air-fuel mixture into the cylinder.

TECH TIP ✔

The Correct Tools Save Time

When cast-iron exhaust manifolds are removed, the stresses built up in the manifolds often cause the manifolds to twist or bend. This distortion even occurs when the exhaust manifolds have been allowed to cool before removal. Attempting to reinstall distorted exhaust manifolds is often a time-consuming and frustrating exercise.

However, special spreading jacks can be used to force the manifold back into position so that the fasteners can be lined up with the cylinder head. See Figure 12–36.

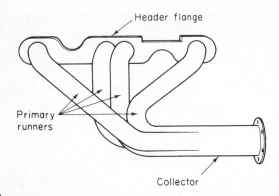

(a)

(b)

Figure 12–37 (a) Equal-length header exhaust manifold. (b) Factory tri-Y type of tubular exhaust manifolds.

This "reverse supercharging" works best at a certain level of engine RPM. This RPM level is based on primary tube and collector length. The longer the primary tube and collector, the lower the engine RPM level at which the header "works." Some headers use an adjustable collector. Use the shortest collector for high-RPM and the longest for lower-RPM benefits. Regardless of header design or lengths, the benefits only become measurable at higher engine speeds (generally over 3500 RPM, depending on engine design). See Figure 12–37.

For low- to medium-RPM power and torque:

1. The primary runner should be long (34 to 38 inches is typical long primary runner length).
2. The collector should also be long (12 to 15 inches is typical collector length for lower-engine speed torque and power).

For higher-RPM power and torque, the primary runner diameter should be increased and the length of tubes decreased. The collector can be shorter or made adjustable to tune in maximum torque at the desired engine speed.

> **NOTE:** Header configuration is just one of many engine tuning factors that should be considered in the designing of an engine system. Other related factors include cam, cam timing, intake runner sizes, engine size, and compression. A change in one factor will usually influence the needs in all other areas.

Headers are working properly when the exhaust makes a **rapping** sound. With most headers used for street driving, the exhaust will generally start to rap at about 3500 RPM and will continue rapping until about 5000 RPM. At the higher RPM, the exhaust pulses are no longer able to reinforce each other; therefore, the reverse supercharging effect of the headers is reduced. However, the headers still provide a lower level of exhaust restriction than do most exhaust manifolds.

Because of the reduced exhaust back pressure, the EGR valve may not function correctly, resulting in spark knock, if header exhaust is added. Also, not all engine computers can compensate correctly for the changes in intake manifold pressure or the changed position of the oxygen sensor when headers are installed.

> **CAUTION:** Federal, state, provincial, or local laws may prohibit the installing of header-type exhaust manifolds on vehicles operating on public streets and highways.

■ HEAT RISERS

A heat riser is used on carburetor-equipped engines and some throttle fuel-injected engines. The purpose of the heat riser is to divert some exhaust to warm the intake manifold. The extra heat that this provides improves cold-engine driveability. If the heat riser were to become stuck in the open position (no heat to the intake manifold), the engine could idle roughly, stall, or hesitate during acceleration. If the heat riser were to become stuck in the closed position (constant heat to the intake manifold), the engine would operate correctly when cold, but there could be spark knock (ping) or stalling when the engine was warm. On some inline engines, the intake manifold is attached to the exhaust manifold. The heat riser valve is located at this attachment point as shown in Figure 12–38. On V-type engines, the heat riser valve partially blocks one exhaust manifold exit, increasing the exhaust pressure in the exhaust manifold on that side of the engine. This forces the exhaust gases to flow through the intake manifold exhaust heat crossover passage to the opposite exhaust manifold.

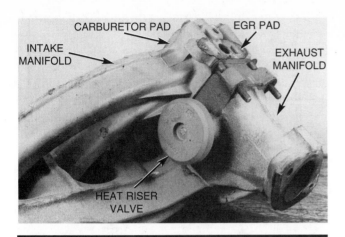

Figure 12–38 Heat riser at the junction of the intake and exhaust manifold.

■ CATALYTIC CONVERTERS

An exhaust pipe is connected to the manifold or header to carry the gases through a catalytic converter and then to the muffler or silencer. In single exhaust systems used on V-type engines, the exhaust pipe is designed to collect the exhaust gases from both manifolds using a Y-shape design. Vehicles with dual exhaust systems have a complete exhaust system coming from each of the manifolds. In most cases, the exhaust pipe must be made of several parts in order for it to be assembled in the space available under the vehicle.

The catalytic converter is installed between the manifold and muffler to help reduce exhaust emissions. The converter has a heat-resistant metal housing. See Figure 12–39. A bed of catalyst-coated pellets or a catalyst-coated honeycomb grid is inside the housing. See Figures 12–40 and 12–41. As the exhaust gas passes through the catalyst, oxides of nitrogen (NO_x) are chemically reduced (nitrogen and oxygen separated) in the first section of the catalytic converter. In the second section of the catalytic converter, most of the hydrocarbons and carbon monoxide remaining in the exhaust gas are oxidized to form harmless carbon dioxide (CO_2) and water vapor (H_2O). An air-injection system or pulse air system is used on some engines to supply additional air that may be needed in the oxidation process See Figure 12-42.

Figure 12–39 Typical catalytic converter. The small tube into the side of the converter comes from the air pump. The additional air from the air pump helps oxidize the exhaust into harmless H_2O (water) and CO_2 (carbon dioxide).

Figure 12–40 Bead-type catalytic converter.

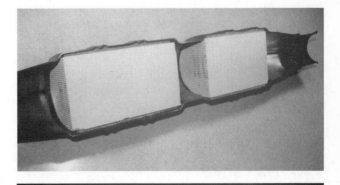

Figure 12–41 Cutaway of a three-way monolithic catalytic converter.

Figure 12–42 Cutaway of defective (clogged) catalytic converter.

■ MUFFLERS

When the exhaust valve opens, it rapidly releases high-pressure gas. This sends a strong air pressure wave through the atmosphere, which produces a sound we call an explosion. It is the same sound produced when the high-pressure gases from burned gunpowder are released from a gun. In an engine, the pulses are released one after another. The explosions come so fast that they blend together in a steady roar.

Sound is air vibration. When the vibrations are large, the sound is loud. The muffler catches the large bursts of high-pressure exhaust gas from the cylinder, smoothing out the pressure pulses and allowing them to be released at an even and constant rate. It does this through the use of perforated tubes within the muffler chamber. The smooth-flowing gases are released to the tailpipe. In this way, the muffler silences engine exhaust noise. Sometimes resonators are used in the exhaust system. They provide additional expansion space at critical points in the exhaust system to smooth out the exhaust gas flow. A cutaway muffler is pictured in Figure 12–43.

Most mufflers have a larger inlet diameter than outlet diameter. As the exhaust enters the muffler, it expands and cools. The cooler exhaust is more dense and occupies less volume. The diameter of the outlet of the muffler and the diameter of the tailpipe can be reduced with no decrease in efficiency.

Frequently Asked Question ???

Why Is There a Hole in My Muffler?

Many mufflers are equipped with a small hole in the lower rear part to drain accumulated water. About 1 gallon of water is produced in the form of steam for each gallon of gasoline burned. The water vapor often condenses on the cooler surfaces of the exhaust system unless the vehicle has been driven long enough to fully warm the muffler above the boiling point of water [212°F (100°C)]. See Figure 12–44.

HIGH PERFORMANCE TIP

More Airflow—More Power

One of the most popular high performance modifications is to replace the factory original air filter and air filter housing with a low-restriction unit as shown in Figure 12–45. The installation of one of these aftermarket filters not only increases power, but also increases air induction noise, which many drivers prefer. The aftermarket filter housing, however, may not be able to effectively prevent water from being drawn into the engine if the vehicle is traveling through deep water.

Just remember that almost every modification that increases performance has a negative effect on some other part of the vehicle, or else the manufacturer would include the change at the factory.

Figure 12–43 Muffler cutaway shows the interior.

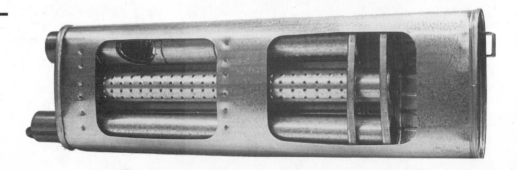

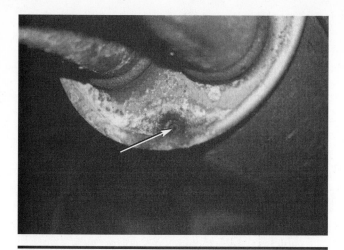

Figure 12–44 Hole in the muffler allows condensed water to escape.

Figure 12–45 A high performance aftermarket air filter often can increase the airflow into the engine for more power.

The tailpipe carries the exhaust gases from the muffler to the air, away from the vehicle. In most cases, the tailpipe exit is at the rear of the vehicle, below the rear bumper. In some cases, the exhaust is released at the side of the vehicle, just ahead of or just behind the rear wheel.

The muffler and tailpipe are supported with brackets called **hangers.** The hangers are made of rubberized fabric with metal ends that hold the muffler and tail pipe in position so that they do not touch any metal part. This helps to isolate the exhaust noise from the rest of the vehicle.

■ SUMMARY

1. All air entering an engine must be filtered.
2. Engines that use carburetors or throttle-body injection units are equipped with intake manifolds that keep the airflow speed through the manifold to 50 to 300 feet per second.
3. Intake manifolds are of either dual-plane (180-degree) or single-plane (360-degree) design.
4. Most intake manifolds have an EGR valve that regulates the amount of recirculated exhaust that enters the engine to reduce NO_x emissions.
5. Exhaust manifolds can be made from cast iron or stainless steel.
6. The exhaust system also contains a catalytic converter, exhaust pipes, and muffler. The entire exhaust system is supported by rubber hangers that isolate the noise and vibration of the exhaust from the rest of the vehicle.

■ REVIEW QUESTIONS

1. Why is it necessary to have intake charge velocities of about 50 feet per second?
2. Why can fuel-injected engines use larger (and longer) intake manifolds and still operate at low engine speed?
3. What is a tuned runner in an intake manifold?
4. Name three ways in which heat is added to the intake charge of a carburetor-equipped engine.
5. Why is it necessary to keep the engine oil off of the surface of the exhaust crossover passage in the intake manifold?
6. How does a muffler quiet exhaust noise?

■ ASE CERTIFICATION-TYPE QUESTIONS

1. Intake charge velocity has to be _____ to prevent fuel droplet separation.
   a. 25 feet per second
   b. 50 feet per second
   c. 100 feet per second
   d. 300 feet per second

2. The intake manifold of a port fuel-injected engine _____ .
   a. Uses a dual heat riser
   b. Contains a leaner air-fuel mixture than does the intake manifold of a carburetor system
   c. Contains only fuel (gasoline)
   d. Contains only air

3. With dual-plane intake manifold, _____ .
   a. Successively firing cylinders are at different levels (sections) of the manifold
   b. All left-side cylinders receive air-fuel mixture from the left side of the carburetor or throttle-body injection unit
   c. The intake runners are all of different lengths
   d. The manifold uses an exhaust passage

4. A heated air intake system is usually necessary for proper cold-engine driveability *except* _____ .
   a. On one- or two-barrel carburetor systems
   b. On four-barrel carburetor systems
   c. On port fuel-injection systems
   d. On throttle-body fuel-injection systems

5. Another name for a heat riser type of valve that directs exhaust under the carburetor through a passage in the intake manifold is _____ .
   a. Heated air inlet system
   b. Early fuel evaporation valve
   c. Thermo vacuum switch (valve)
   d. Exhaust gas recirculation valve

6. The purpose of the sheet-metal shield used on the lifter side of a V-type intake manifold is _____ .
   a. To protect the oil from burning on the exhaust crossover passage
   b. To protect the manifold from the hot engine oil
   c. To help keep the air-fuel charge cooler by keeping the hot engine oil off the bottom of the manifold
   d. To provide lubrication to the heat riser valve

7. Technician A says that a vacuum leak (air leak) on one cylinder of a V-type engine can affect another cylinder sharing the same intake manifold runner. Technician B says that some intake manifolds are designed to increase engine torque by providing a ram air effect. Which technician is correct?
   a. Technician A only
   b. Technician B only
   c. Both Technician A and B
   d. Neither Technician A nor B

8. Technician A says that header-type exhaust manifolds produce less back pressure than do most cast-iron exhaust manifolds. Technician B says that only cast-iron exhaust manifolds are used on production vehicles. Which technician is correct?
   a. Technician A only
   b. Technician B only
   c. Both Technician A and B
   d. Neither Technician A nor B

9. Which type of system uses exhaust heat to spin a turbine that turns an impeller to force additional air into the intake manifold?
   a. Supercharger
   b. Turbocharger
   c. Exhaust gas recirculation
   d. Heat riser

10. Technician A says that a crack in the exhaust manifold can cause a driveability problem because the air that leaks into the exhaust can give the oxygen sensor (O2S) a false reading. Technician B says that an exhaust leak can affect the operation of a turbocharger. Which technician is correct?
    a. Technician A only
    b. Technician B only
    c. Both Technician A and B
    d. Neither Technician A nor B

Cylinder Head and Valve Guide Service

Cylinder heads are the most frequently serviced engine components. The highest temperatures and pressures in the entire engine are located in the combustion chamber. Its valves must open and close thousands of times each time the engine is operated.

Combustion chambers of modern automotive overhead valve engines are of two basic types. One is the nonturbulent hemispherical chamber and the other is the turbulent wedge chamber.

■ HEMISPHERICAL COMBUSTION CHAMBER

In nonturbulent hemispherical combustion chambers, the charge is inducted through widely slanted valves. The charge is compressed and then ignited from a centrally located spark plug (Figures 13–1 and 13–2). The spark plug is as close as possible to all edges of the combustion chamber. Combustion radiates out from the

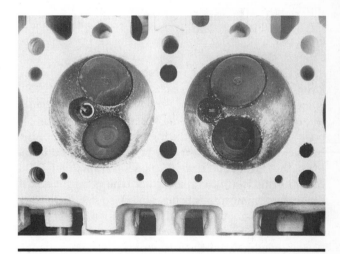

Figure 13–1 Hemispherical combustion chamber with a two-valve head.

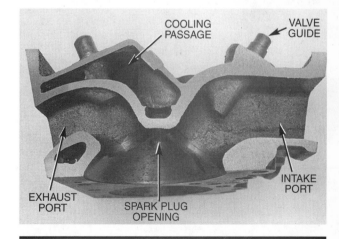

Figure 13–2 Sectional view of a hemispherical combustion chamber.

spark plug, completely burning in the shortest possible time. This tends to reduce the formation of NO_x. The end gases ahead of the flame front have little time to react, so knock is reduced. The rapidly burning charge in the hemispherical combustion chamber causes pressure to rise very rapidly.

Hemispherical combustion chambers are usually fully machined to form the hemispherical shape. This is an expensive operation that increases the cost of the engine.

WEDGE COMBUSTION CHAMBER

The wedge-shape combustion chamber is designed to produce smooth, uniform burning by controlling the rate of combustion. A sectional view of a wedge-shape combustion chamber is shown in Figure 13–3. In wedge-shape combustion chambers, the charge is inducted through parallel valves. As the piston nears the top of the compression stroke, it moves to a position that is close to a low or flat portion of the head. The gases are squeezed from between the piston and this head surface area. This area is called a **squish** or **quench area.** The gases squeezed from the squish area produce turbulence within the charge. *The turbulence thoroughly mixes the air and fuel in the charge.* The spark plug is positioned so as to be in the highly turbulent part of the charge. Ignition is followed by smooth and rapid burning of the turbulent charge. The combustion flame front radiates out from the spark plug. The end gases that would burn abnormally remain in the squish area. Here the end gases are cooled and they do not react, because this area is squeezed to be very thin, less than 0.100 inch (2.5 millimeters), when the piston is at the top center.

The combustion chamber is designed to meet specific engine and fuel requirements. Turbulent combustion chambers usually remain as cast in the head, with no machining being done. See Figure 13–4.

SURFACE QUENCHING

Unburned hydrocarbon emission from engines needs to be reduced to levels as low as possible. The charge adjacent to the combustion chamber surface, which is from 0.002 to 0.020 inch (0.005 to 0.050 millimeter) thick, does not burn. The temperature of the combustion chamber surface is lower than the temperature required for combustion. This cools the part of the charge that is next to the surface to a temperature below its burning temperature. The combustion flame goes out, which leaves unburned hydrocarbons. These unburned hydrocarbons are expelled with the burned gases on the exhaust stroke. Combustion chamber surface quenching is one of the major causes of unburned hydrocarbons in the exhaust gas.

Figure 13–4 Cutaway of a Chevrolet V-8 engine showing the wedge-shape combustion chamber.

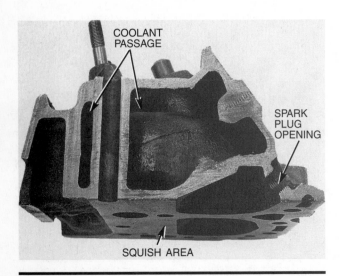

Figure 13–3 Sectional view of a wedge-shape combustion chamber.

NOTE: This unburned gasoline (HC) is a major exhaust emission. The quench volume is reduced by operating the engine at normal operating temperatures. Therefore, a defective thermostat can cause excessive HC exhaust emissions as a result of the quenching of the air-fuel vapors on the colder-than-normal cylinder head or cylinder walls.

Combustion chambers having a low surface area for their volume, such as the hemispherical combustion chamber, produce low levels of unburned hydrocarbons. The wedge combustion chamber, which has a relatively high surface area-to-volume ratio, produces high levels of unburned hydrocarbons.

New designs use cast combustion chambers rather than having expensive machined chambers. These chambers are referred to as **polyspherical, hemi-wedge, kidney shape,** and **pentroof.** All cylinder head designs try to place the spark plug in an ideal location for best combustion as shown in Figure 13–5.

■ STRATIFIED CHARGE COMBUSTION CHAMBER

The stratified engine gets its name from the layers or strata of different air-fuel mixtures that are formed within the swirling charge. Some of the layers have a rich air-fuel mixture, whereas others have a lean mixture. The overall stratified charge has a very lean air-fuel mixture.

A rich air-fuel mixture is easier to ignite with a spark plug than is a lean air-fuel mixture. For this reason, a rich stratum surrounds the spark plug. When a hot flame develops in this rich stratum after ignition, it puts both heat and pressure on the lean remaining charge. The lean part of the charge will then burn.

Two types of stratified charge designs have been used in production engines. One has a carburetor and uses two combustion chambers, a main chamber and a

prechamber. The other injects fuel into the swirling air near the end of the compression stroke. The spark plug is located near the injector, where it is surrounded by a rich fuel mixture. See Figures 13–6 and 13–7.

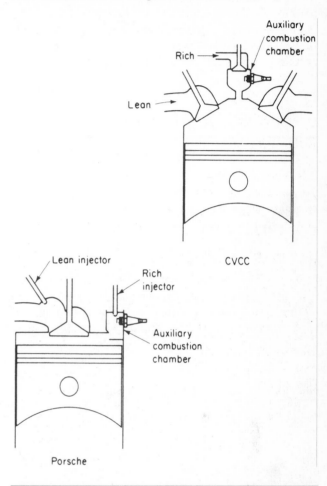

Figure 13–6 Line drawings showing the principle of two stratified charge combustion chambers.

Figure 13–7 Honda CVCC (compound vortex combustion chamber) cylinder head with one auxiliary valve partially removed.

Figure 13–5 Chevrolet V-8 angled plug cylinder head. Note that the spring seats have been machined for larger-diameter valve springs and the screw-in type of rocker arm studs. The angled spark plug places the plug in a location that helps combustion.

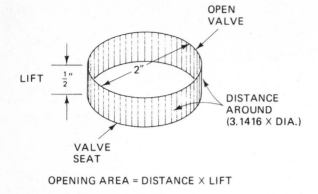

Figure 13–8 Method for measuring the valve opening space.

■ MULTIPLE-VALVE COMBUSTION CHAMBER

The power that any engine produces is directly related to the amount of air-fuel mixture that is ignited in the cylinder. Increasing cylinder displacement is a common method of increasing engine power. Turbocharging and supercharging also increase engine power, but these increase engine cost as well.

Adding more than two valves per cylinder permits more gas to flow into and out of the engine with greater velocity without excessive valve duration. **Valve duration** is the number of degrees by which the crankshaft rotates when the valve is off the valve seat. Increased valve duration increases valve overlap. The valve overlap occurs when both valves are off their seats at the end of the exhaust stroke and at the beginning of the intake stroke. At lower engine speeds, the gases can move back and forth between the open valves. Therefore, the greater valve duration hurts low engine speed performance and driveability, but it allows for more air-fuel mixture to enter the engine for better high-speed power.

The maximum amount of gas moving through the opening area of a valve depends on the distance around the valve and the degree to which it lifts open. See Figure 13–8. The normal opening lift is about 25% of the valve head diameter. For example, if the intake valve is 2.00 inches in diameter, the normal amount of lift off the seat (not cam lobe height) is 25% of 2.00 inches or 1/2 (0.500) inch. But the amount of air-fuel mixture that can enter a cylinder depends on the total area around the valve and not just the amount of lift. The distance around a valve is calculated by the equation pi × D (3.1416 × Valve diameter). See Figures 13–9 and 13–10.

More total area under the valve is possible when two smaller valves are used rather than one larger valve at the same valve lift. The smaller valves allow smooth low-speed operation (because of increased velocity of the mixture as it enters the cylinder as a result of smaller intake ports). Good high-speed performance is

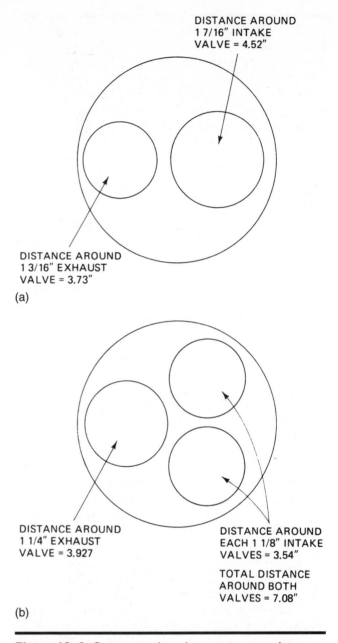

Figure 13–9 Comparing the valve opening areas between a two- and three-valve combustion chamber when the valves are open.

also possible because of the increased valve area and lighter-weight valves. See Figure 13–11.

When four valves are used, either the combustion chamber has a pentroof design, with each pair of valves in line (Figure 13–12), or it is hemispherical, with each valve on its own axis (Figure 13–13). Four valves on the pentroof design will be operated with dual overhead camshafts or with single overhead camshafts and rocker arms. Four valves in the hemispherical combustion chamber need a complex valve operating assembly, usually from a single overhead camshaft. When four valves are used, it is possible to place the spark plug at

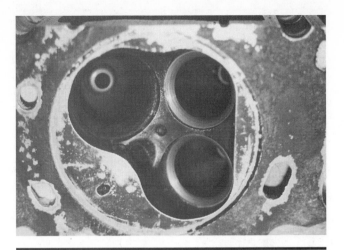

Figure 13–10 A typical three-valve cylinder head. The two smaller valves are intake valves and the one larger valve is the exhaust valve.

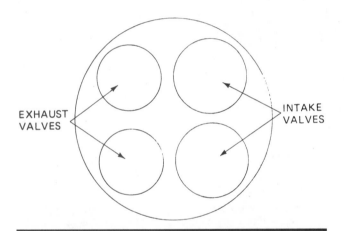

Figure 13–11 Typical four-valve head. The total area of opening of two small intake valves and two smaller exhaust valves is greater than the area of a two-valve head using much larger valves. The smaller valves also permit the use of smaller intake runners for better low-speed engine response.

the center of the combustion chamber. This is the best spark plug location for fast-burning combustion.

■ FOUR-VALVE HEAD

A four-valve cylinder head allows greater air and fuel flow than does a two-valve head of the same size. This additional air and fuel produces more heat and helps multivalve engines produce more power. However, the area around the exhaust valves often overheats, especially when the engine is operating at or near peak power levels. This heat buildup between the exhaust valves can cause the valves to burn or can cause softening and erosion of the area between the valve seats.

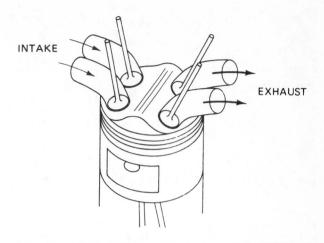

Figure 13–12 Four valves in a pentroof combustion chamber.

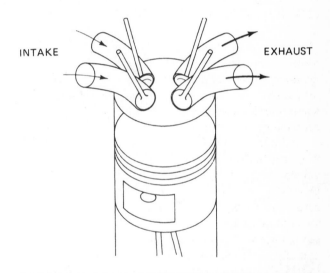

Figure 13–13 Four valves in a hemispherical combustion chamber.

HIGH PERFORMANCE TIP

Horsepower Is Airflow

To get more power from an engine, more air needs to be drawn into the combustion chamber. One way to achieve more airflow is to increase the valve and port size of the cylinder heads along with a change in camshaft lift and duration to match the cylinder heads. One popular, but expensive, method is to replace the stock cylinder heads with high performance cast-iron or aluminum cylinder heads such as shown in Figure 13–14.

All four-valve heads should be carefully inspected for cracks or other cylinder head damage between the exhaust valves.

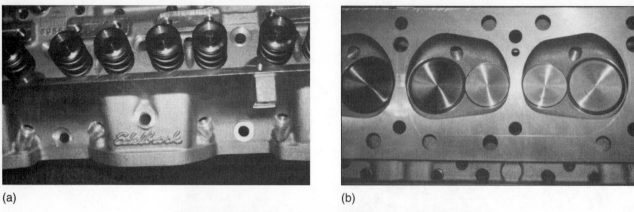

(a)

(b)

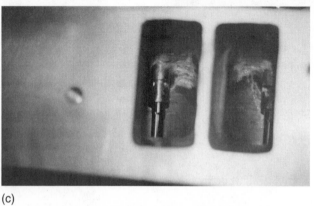

(c)

Figure 13–14 (a) A high performance aftermarket aluminum cylinder head. (b) The valves are larger than the stock cast-iron cylinder head. (c) The ports are also straighter and larger than the stock cast-iron cylinder heads, requiring that a special intake manifold be used with these aluminum heads.

■ INTAKE AND EXHAUST PORTS

The part of the intake or exhaust system passage that is cast in the cylinder head is called a **port.** Ports lead from the manifolds to the valves. The most desirable port shape is not always possible because of space requirements in the head. Space is required for the head bolt bosses, valve guides, cooling passages, and pushrod openings. Inline engines may have both intake and exhaust ports located on the same side of the engine. Often, two cylinders share the same port because of the restricted space available. Shared ports are called **siamese ports.** See Figure 13–15. Each cylinder uses the port at a different time. Larger ports and better breathing are possible in engines that have the intake port on one side of the head and the exhaust port on the opposite side. This type of head is said to have a **cross-flow** head design. The cross-flow head shown in Figure 13–16 allows the valve to be located and angled so as to permit most efficient engine breathing. It also allows the spark plug to be placed near the center of the combustion chamber. All V-type engines have the cross-flow head design.

Figure 13–15 Close-up view of a siamese exhaust port.

The flow of gases is often different than one might think. At times a restricting hump (Figure 13–17) within a port may actually increase the airflow capacity of the port. It does this by redirecting the flow to an area of the port that is large enough to handle the flow.

Figure 13–16 Typical two-valve cross-flow cylinder head. The intake manifold is on the right side and the exhaust manifold is on the left side.

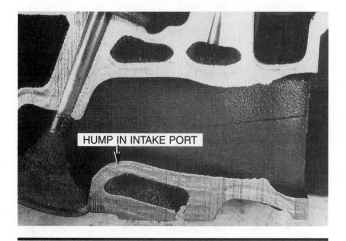

HUMP IN INTAKE PORT

Figure 13–17 A hump in the intake port that actually increases the airflow capacity of the port.

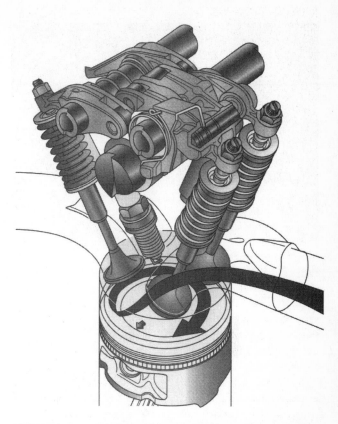

Figure 13–18 The intake manifold design and combustion chamber design both work together to cause the air-fuel mixture to swirl as it enters the combustion chamber.

Modifications in the field, such as **porting** or **relieving,** would result in restricting the flow of such a carefully designed port.

The intake port in a cylinder head designed for use with a carburetor or throttle-body-type fuel injection is relatively long, whereas the exhaust port is short. The long intake port wall is heated by coolant flowing through the head. The heat aids in vaporizing the fuel in the intake charge. The exhaust port is short so that the least amount of exhaust heat is transferred to the engine coolant. On engines designed for use with port fuel injection, the cylinder head ports are designed to help promote swirl in the combustion chamber as shown in Figure 13–18.

HIGH PERFORMANCE TIP

Sneaky Acid Porting

Some classifications of motor sports racing forbid any porting (enlarging) of the cylinder head ports.

If the cylinder head is ported using a grinder, the surface is smooth and does not resemble the as-cut appearance of a stock cylinder head, so some racers use acid to enlarge the ports of cast-iron cylinder heads. The appearance after the acid treatment is the same rough casting look of a completely stock cylinder head. See Figure 13–19. It just goes to show that the old saying may be right: "There are two types of racers—cheaters and losers."

■ CYLINDER HEAD COOLANT PASSAGES

The engine is designed so that coolant will flow from the coolest portion of the engine to the warmest portion. The water pump takes the coolant from the radiator. The coolant is pumped into the block, where it is di-

Figure 13–19 The top cylinder head is stock and the bottom cylinder head has been ported using two different methods. The first inch from the gasket surface has been ground using a grinder to make the opening in the cylinder head match the intake manifold. The rest of the port between the valve and the gasket surfaces has been enlarged using acid. This acid treatment is a common "trick" used to increase the flow characteristics of a stock class cylinder head. The acid treatment gives the same rough cast-like surface as a completely stock cylinder head.

rected all around the cylinders. The coolant then flows upward through the gasket to the cooling passages cast into the cylinder head. The heated coolant is collected at a common point and returned to the radiator to be cooled and recycled.

> **NOTE:** Reversed-flow cooling systems, such as that used on the Chevrolet LT1 V-8, send the coolant from the radiator to the cylinder heads first. This results in a cooler cylinder head and allows for more spark advance without engine-damaging detonation.

Typical coolant passages in a head are shown in Figure 13–20.

There are relatively large holes in the gasket surface of the head leading to the head cooling passages. The large holes are necessary to support the cooling passage core through these openings while the head is being cast. After casting, the core is broken up and removed through these same openings. Core support openings to the outside of the engine are closed with expansion plugs or soft plugs. These plugs are often mistakenly called freeze plugs. The openings between the head and the block are usually too large for the correct coolant flow. When the openings are too large, the head gasket performs an important coolant flow function. Special-size holes are made in the gasket. These holes correct the coolant flow rate at each opening. Therefore, it is important that the head gasket be installed

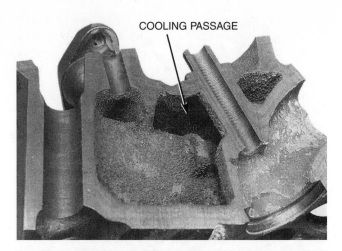

Figure 13–20 Coolant passages can be seen in this section of a cylinder head.

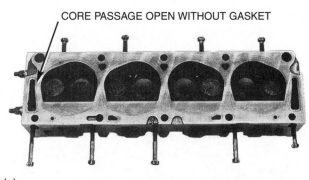

(a)

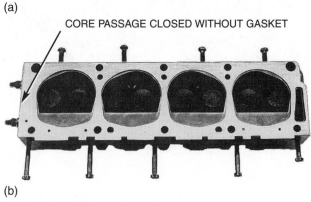

(b)

Figure 13–21 Coolant flow control. (a) Head core passages open without a gasket. (b) Gasket covering the left-hand core passage opening.

correctly for proper engine cooling. A head gasket with special-size holes to cover the head openings is shown in Figure 13–21.

Carefully located openings, or deflectors, may be designed into the head. They direct the coolant toward a portion of the head where localized heat must be removed. Usually, this is in the area of the exhaust valve. Some of the deflectors are cast in the cooling passages.

Figure 13–22 Before any camshaft can be removed, the followers or lifters must be removed. Notice how the valve has to be compressed slightly to remove the camshaft followers from the overhead camshaft engine.

Figure 13–23 Special valve spring compressors are often necessary to use on multiple valve heads such as this 2.7 L DaimlerChrysler V-6.

■ LUBRICATING OVERHEAD VALVES

Lubricating oil is delivered to the overhead valve mechanism, either through the valve pushrods or through drilled passages in the head and block casting. There are special openings in the head gasket to allow the oil to pass between the block and head without leaking. After the oil passes through the valve mechanisms, it returns to the oil pan through oil return passages. Some engines have drilled oil return holes, but most engines have large cast holes that allow the oil to return freely to the engine oil pan. The cast holes are large and do not easily become plugged.

> **NOTE:** Many aluminum cylinder heads have smaller than normal drain-back holes. If an engine has excessive oil consumption, check the drain holes before removing the engine.

■ REMOVING THE OVERHEAD CAMSHAFT

The overhead camshaft will have either one-piece bearings in a solid bearing support or split bearings and a bearing cap. When one-piece bearings are used, the valve springs will have to be compressed with a fixture or the finger follower will have to be removed before the camshaft can be pulled out endwise. When bearing caps are used, they should be loosened alternately so that bending loads are not placed on either the cam or bearing caps (Figure 13–22).

■ DISASSEMBLY OF THE CYLINDER HEAD

As discussed in Chapter 9, the cylinder head should be disassembled, cleaned, and checked for cracks or damage before performing any service work. Many aluminum cylinder heads, especially those with overhead camshafts and multiple valves, require special valve spring compressors as shown in Figures 13–23 and 13–24. Cleaning an aluminum head should only be done with tools and procedures that will not harm the cylinder head or gasket surface.

- Use a wooden or plastic scraper to remove old gaskets (never use a metal scraper to avoid nicking or damaging aluminum cylinder head surfaces).
- Use bristle discs as shown in Figure 13–25. Do not use fibrous discs. Some vehicle manufacturers warn that the small fibers that come off the discs during the operation can fall into small threaded holes and cause an assembly problem because the small fibers cannot always be removed during the cylinder head cleaning process.

■ CYLINDER HEAD RECONDITIONING SEQUENCE

Although not all cylinder heads require all service operations, cylinder heads should be reconditioned using the following sequence.

1. Disassemble and thoroughly clean the heads (see Chapter 9).

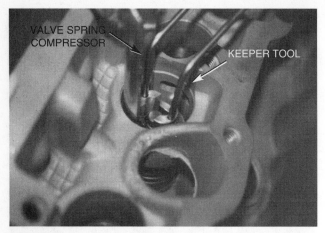

(a)

(b)

Figure 13–24 (a) As the valve spring is being compressed, use a magnet or a special tool to grasp and remove the valve keepers. (b) This simple tool makes removing and installing valve keepers quick and easy.

2. Check for cracks and repair as necessary (see Chapter 10).
3. Check the surface that contacts the engine block and machine if necessary.
4. Check valve guides and replace or service as necessary.
5. Grind valves and reinstall them in the cylinder head with new valve stem seals (see Chapter 14).

■ CYLINDER HEAD RESURFACING

All valve train components that are to be reused must be kept together. As wear occurs, parts become worn together. Pushrods can be kept labeled if stuck through a cardboard box as shown in Figure 13–26. Be sure to keep the top part of the pushrod at the top. Intake and

Figure 13–25 Bristle-type cleaning discs are used with an air-powered die grinder to remove gasket material. The green disc (on the right) has a 50-grit abrasive embedded in the plastic bristles and is designed for use on cast-iron parts. The yellow disc (in the middle) contains 80-grit abrasive and may be used on aluminum parts; however, most vehicle manufacturers recommend that only the white disc (on the left) with 120-grit abrasive be used on aluminum engine parts.

Figure 13–26 Individual parts become worn together; therefore, cardboard is a crude but effective material to use to keep all valve train parts together and labeled exactly as they came from the engine.

exhaust valve springs are different and must be kept with the correct valve.

The surface must be thoroughly cleaned and inspected as follows:

Step 1 After removing the old gasket material, use a file and draw it across the surface of the head to remove any small burrs. See Figure 13–27.

Figure 13–27 After scraping the gasket surface with a scraper, use a file and **draw** across the surface. When a file is drawn across the head sideways, little (if any) material is removed, but burrs and other surface imperfections are removed or highlighted.

Frequently Asked Question ???

What Is a Seasoned Engine?

A new engine is machined and assembled within a few hours after the heads and block are cast from melted iron. Newly cast parts have internal stresses within the metal. The stress results from the different thickness of the metal sections in the head. Forces from combustion in the engine, plus continued heating and cooling, gradually relieve these stresses. By the time the engine has accumulated 20,000 to 30,000 miles (32,000 to 48,000 kilometers), the stresses have been completely relieved. This is why some engine rebuilders prefer to work with used heads and blocks that are stress relieved. Used engines are often called **seasoned** because of the reduced stress and movement these components have as compared with new parts. The head will usually have some warpage when the engine is disassembled.

Step 2 The head should be checked in five planes as shown in Figure 13–28.

Checking the cylinder head gasket surface in five planes checks the head for **warpage, distortion, bend,** and **twist.**

These defects are determined by trying to slide a 0.004-inch (0.10-millimeter) feeler gauge under a straightedge held against the head surface.

> **NOTE:** The cylinder head surface that mates with the top deck of the block is often called the **fire deck.**

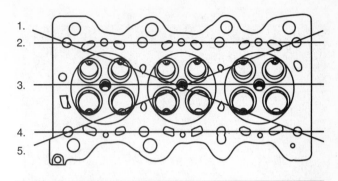

Figure 13–28 Cylinder heads should be checked in five planes for warpage, distortion, bend, or twist.

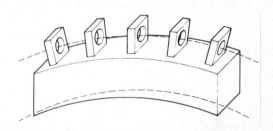

Figure 13–29 Warped overhead camshaft cylinder head. If the gasket surface is machined to be flat, the camshaft bearings will still not be in proper alignment. The solution is to straighten the cylinder head or to align bore the cam tunnel because the head is actually D-shaped.

The head should not vary by over 0.002 inch (0.05 millimeter) in any 6-inch (15-centimeter) length, or by more than 0.004 inch overall. Always check the manufacturer's recommended specifications.

> **NOTE:** Always check the cylinder head thickness and specifications to be sure that material can be safely removed from the surface. Some manufacturers do not recommend *any* machining, but rather require cylinder head replacement if cylinder head surface flatness is not within specifications.

■ ALUMINUM CYLINDER HEAD STRAIGHTENING

Aluminum expands at about twice the rate of cast iron when heated. Aluminum cylinder heads used on cast-iron blocks can warp and/or crack if they are overheated. The expanding cylinder head first hits the head bolts. Further expansion of the head causes the head to expand upward and bow in the center. If a warped (bowed) cylinder head is resurfaced, the stresses of expansion are still present, and if the cylinder head uses an overhead camshaft, further problems exist. With a D-shaped cylinder head (see Figure 13–29), the camshaft

Figure 13–30 Cylinder head straightening is very important on heads such as this one with the cam bearing cut as part of the head assembly.

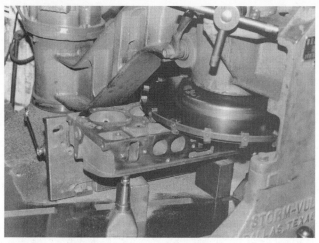

(a)

(b)

Figure 13–31 (a) Milling-type resurfacer machining the gasket surface of a cylinder head. (b) Grinder-type resurfacer.

centerline bearing supports must also be restored. To restore the straightness of the cam-bearing bore (sometimes called the **cam tunnel**), align boring and/or honing may be necessary. See Figure 13–30.

The best approach to restore a warped aluminum cylinder head (especially an overhead camshaft head) is to relieve the stress that has caused the warpage *and* to straighten the head before machining.

Step 1 Determine the amount of warpage with a straightedge and thickness (feeler) gauge. Cut shim stock (thin strips of metal) to one-half of the amount of the warpage. Place shims of this thickness under each end of the head.

Step 2 Tighten the center of the cylinder head down on a strong, flat base. A 2-inch-thick piece of steel that is 8 inches wide by 20 inches long makes a good support for the gasket surface of the cylinder head (use antiseize compound on the bolt thread to help in bolt removal).

Step 3 Place the head and base in an oven for 5 hours at 500°F (260°C). Turn the oven off and leave the assembly in the oven.

NOTE: If the temperature is too high, the valve seat inserts may fall out of the head! At 500°F, a typical valve seat will still be held into the aluminum head with a 0.002-inch interference fit based on calculations of thermal expansion of the aluminum head and steel insert.

Allow the head to cool in the oven for 4 or 5 hours to relieve any stress in the aluminum from the heating process. For best results, the cooling process should be

allowed to occur overnight. Several cylinder heads can be "cooked" together.

If the cylinder head is still warped, the heating and cooling process can be repeated. After the head is straightened and the stress relieved, the gasket surface (fire deck) can be machined in the usual manner. To prevent possible camshaft bore misalignment problems, do not machine more than 0.010 to 0.015 inch (0.25 to 0.38 millimeter) from the head gasket surface.

■ RESURFACING METHODS

Two common resurfacing methods are used: milling and grinding. A **milling** type of resurfacer uses metal-cutting tool bits fastened in a disk. The disk is the rotating work head of the mill. This can be seen in Figure 13–31. The surface **grinder** type uses a large-diameter abrasive wheel. Both types of resurfacing can be done with table-type and precision-type surfacers. With a table-type surfacer, the head or block is passed over the cutting head that extends slightly above a worktable.

The abrasive wheel is dressed before grinding begins. The wheel head is adjusted to just touch the surface. At this point, the feed is calibrated to zero. This is necessary so that the operator knows exactly the size of the cut being made. Light cuts are taken. The abrasive wheel cuts are limited to 0.005 inch (0.015 millimeter). The abrasive wheel surface should be wire brushed after each five passes, and the wheel should be redressed after grinding each 0.100 inch (2.50 millimeters). The mill-type cutting wheel can remove up to 0.030 inch (0.075 millimeter) on each pass. A special mill-cutting tool or a dull grinding wheel is used when aluminum heads are being resurfaced.

NOTE: Resurfacing the cylinder head changes the compression ratio of the engine by about 1/10 point per 0.010 inch of removed material. For example, the compression ratio would be increased from 9.0:1 to 9.2:1 if 0.020 inch were removed from a typical cylinder head.

■ SURFACE FINISH

The surface finish of a reconditioned part is as important as the size of the part. Surface finish is measured in units called microinches (abbreviated **μ in**). The symbol in front of the inch abbreviation is the Greek letter *mu*. One microinch equals 0.000001 inch [(0.025 micrometer (μm)]. The finish classification in microinches gives the distance between the highest peak and the deepest valley. The usual method of expressing surface finish is by the **arithmetic average roughness height, (RA),** that is, the average of the distances of all peaks and valleys from the mean (average) line. Surface finish is measured using a machine with a diamond stylus. See Figure 13–32.

Another classification of surface finish, which is becoming obsolete, is called the **root-mean-square (RMS).** The RMS is a slightly higher number and can be obtained by multiplying RA × 1.11.

Typical surface finish roughness recommendations for cast-iron and aluminum cylinder heads and blocks include the following:

Cast Iron

Maximum:	110 RA (125 RMS) (Rough surfaces can limit gasket movement and conformity.)
Minimum:	30 RA (33 RMS) (Smoother surfaces increase the tendency of the gasket to flow and *reduce* gasket sealing ability.)
Recommended range:	60 to 100 RA (65 to 110 RMS)

Aluminum

Maximum:	60 RA (65 RMS)
Minimum:	30 RA (33 RMS)
Recommended range:	50 to 60 RA (55 to 65 RMS)

The rougher the surface is, the higher the microinch finish measurement will be. Typical preferred microinch finish standards for other engine components include the following:

Crank and rod journal: 10 to 14 RA (12 to 15 RMS)

Honed cylinder: 18 to 32 RA (20 to 35 RMS)

Connecting rod big end: 45 to 72 RA (50 to 80 RMS)

■ CORRECTING INTAKE MANIFOLD ALIGNMENT

The intake manifold of a V-type engine may no longer fit correctly after the gasket surfaces of the heads are ground. The ports and the assembly bolt holes may no longer match. The intake manifold surface must be resurfaced to remove enough metal to rematch the ports and bolt holes. The amount of metal that must be removed depends on the angle between the head gasket surface and the intake manifold gasket surface. Figure 13–33 shows how this is calculated. Automotive machine shops doing head resurfacing have tables that specify the exact amount of metal to be removed. It is usually necessary to remove some metal from both the front and the back gasket surface of closed-type intake manifolds used on V-type engines. This is necessary to provide a good gasket seal that will prevent oil leakage from the lifter valley.

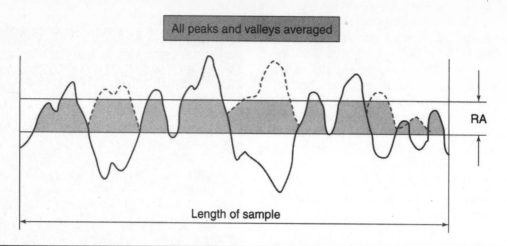

All peaks and valleys averaged

RA

Length of sample

Figure 13–32 A graph showing a typical rough surface as would be viewed through a magnifying glass. RA is an abbreviation indicating the average height of all peaks and valleys.

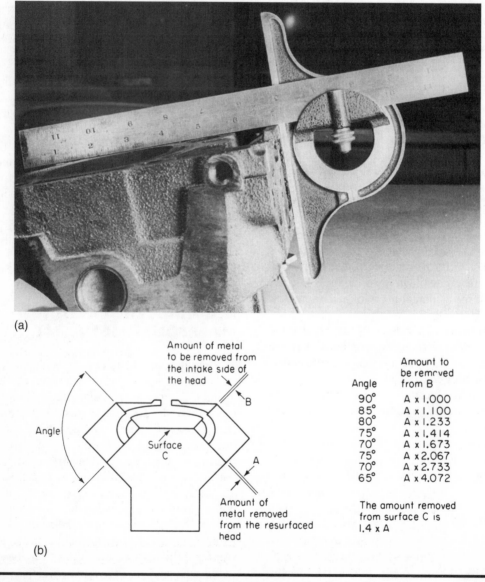

(a)

Amount of metal to be removed from the intake side of the head

B

Angle

Surface C

A

Amount of metal removed from the resurfaced head

Angle	Amount to be removed from B
90°	A x 1.000
85°	A x 1.100
80°	A x 1.233
75°	A x 1.414
70°	A x 1.673
75°	A x 2.067
70°	A x 2.733
65°	A x 4.072

The amount removed from surface C is 1.4 x A

(b)

Figure 13–33 (a) Measuring the angle between the intake manifold and the head gasket surface. (b) The material that must be removed for a good manifold fit.

Figure 13–34 Scuffed valve guide.

TECH TIP

Tight Is Not Always Right

Many engine manufacturers specify a valve stem-to-valve guide clearance of 0.001 to 0.003 inch (0.025 to 0.076 millimeter). However, some vehicles, especially those equipped with aluminum cylinder heads, may specify a much greater clearance. For example, many Chrysler 2.2-liter and 2.5-liter engines have a specified valve stem-to-valve guide clearance of 0.003 to 0.005 inch (0.076 to 0.127 millimeter). This amount of clearance feels loose to those technicians accustomed to normal valve stem clearance specifications. While this large amount of clearance may seem excessive, remember that the valve stem increases in diameter as the engine warms up. Therefore, the *operating* clearance is smaller than the clearance measured at room temperature. Always double-check factory specifications before replacing a valve guide for excessive wear.

CAUTION: Do not remove any more material than is necessary to restore a flat cylinder head-to-block surface. Some manufacturers limit *total* material that can be removed from block deck and cylinder head to 0.008 inch (0.2 millimeter). Removal of material from the cylinder head of an overhead camshaft engine shortens the distance between the camshaft and the crankshaft. This causes the valve timing to be *retarded* unless a special copper spacer shim is placed between the block deck and the gasket to restore proper crankshaft-to-camshaft centerline dimension.

■ VALVE GUIDES

The valve guide supports the valve stem so that the valve face will remain perfectly centered, or **concentric,** with the valve seat. The valve guide is generally **integral** with the head casting for better heat transfer and for lower manufacturing costs. **Valve guide inserts** are always used where the valve stem and head materials are not compatible.

No matter how good the valves or seats are, they cannot operate properly if the valve guide is not accurate. In use, the valve operating mechanism pushes the valve tip sideways. This is the major cause of valve stem and guide wear. The valve normally rotates a little each time it is opened to keep wear even all around the stem. The valve guide, on the other hand, always has the wear in the same place. See Figure 13–34. This causes both the top and bottom ends of the guide to wear until the guide has an oval or egg shape. The valve guide does not have to be measured if the valve feels sloppy in the guide; it obviously requires reconditioning. A guide

must be reconditioned to match the valve that is to be used in that valve guide.

■ VALVE STEM-TO-GUIDE CLEARANCE

Engine manufacturers usually recommend the following valve stem-to-valve guide clearances.

- Intake valve: 0.001 to 0.003 inch (0.025 to 0.075 millimeter)
- Exhaust valve: 0.002 to 0.004 inch (0.05 to 0.10 millimeter)

Be sure to check the exact specifications for the engine being serviced. The exhaust valve clearance is greater than the intake valve clearance because the exhaust valve runs hotter and therefore expands more than the intake valve.

Excessive valve stem-to-guide clearance can cause excessive oil consumption. The intake valve guide is exposed to manifold vacuum that can draw oil from the top of the cylinder head down into the combustion chamber. In this situation, valves can also run hotter than usual, because much of the heat in the valve is transferred to the cylinder head through the valve guide.

HINT: A human hair is about 0.002 inch (0.05 millimeter) in diameter. Therefore, the typical clearance between a valve stem and the valve guide is only the thickness of a human hair.

Figure 13–35 (a), (b), and (c) A cutaway head is used to show how a small-hole gauge is used to measure the taper and wear of a valve guide. (d) After it is adjusted to the valve guide size, the small-hole gauge is measured with an outside micrometer.

■ MEASURING VALVE GUIDES FOR WEAR

Valves should be measured for stem wear before valve guides are measured. The valve guide is measured in the middle with a small-hole gauge. The gauge size is checked with a micrometer. The guide is then checked at each end. This is shown using a cutaway valve guide in Figure 13–35. The expanded part of the ball should be placed crosswise to the engine where the greatest amount of valve guide wear exists. The dimension of the valve stem diameter is subtracted from the dimension of the valve guide diameter. If the clearance exceeds the specified clearance, then the valve guide will have to be reconditioned.

Valve stem-to-guide clearance can also be checked using a dial indicator (gauge) to measure the amount of movement of the valve when lifted off the valve seat.

See Figure 13–36. The valve stem should also be measured as shown in Figure 13–37.

■ OVERSIZE STEM VALVES

Most domestic automobile manufacturers that have integral valve guides in their engines recommend reaming worn valve guides and installing new valves with **oversize (OS) stems.** When a valve guide is worn, the valve stem is also likely to be worn. In this case, new valves are required. If new valves are used, they can just as well have oversize stems as standard stems. Typically, available sizes include 0.003, 0.005, 0.015, and 0.030 inch **OS**. The valve guide is reamed or honed to the correct size to fit the oversize stem of the new valve. Figure 13–38 shows a reamer in a valve guide. The resulting clearance of the valve stem in the guide is the same as

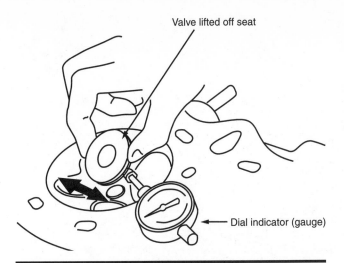

Valve lifted off seat

Dial indicator (gauge)

Figure 13–36 Measuring valve stem-to-guide clearance with a dial indicator while rocking the stem in the direction of normal thrust. The reading on the dial indicator should be compared with specifications, because it does not give the stem-to-guide clearance directly. The usual conversion factor is to record the reading on the dial indicator and divide by 2 to obtain the valve guide clearance. The valve is usually lifted off its seat to its maximum operating lift.

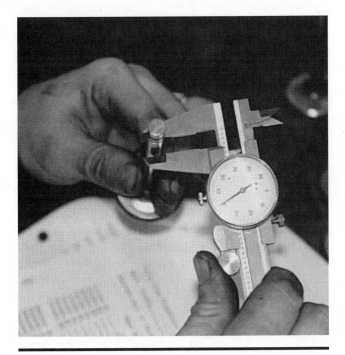

Figure 13–37 Using a vernier dial caliper to measure the valve stem diameter of a valve. Subtract the diameter of the valve stem from the inside diameter of the valve guide to determine the valve guide clearance.

the original clearance. The oil clearance and the heat transfer properties of the original valve and guide are not changed when new valves with oversize stems are installed.

Figure 13–38 Reaming a valve guide to be oversize. This permits the use of new valves with oversize stem diameters. Many remanufacturers use this method to save the money and time involved in replacing or knurling valve guides and grinding old valves.

> **NOTE:** Many remanufacturers of cylinder heads use oversize valve stems to simplify production.

■ VALVE GUIDE KNURLING

In the process known as **valve guide knurling,** a tool is rotated as it is driven into the guide. The tool *displaces* the metal to reduce the hole diameter of the guide. Knurling is ideally suited to engines with integral valve guides (guides that are part of the cylinder head and are nonremovable). It is recommended that knurling not be used to correct wear exceeding 0.006 inch (0.15 millimeter). In the displacing process, the knurling tool pushes a small tapered wheel or dull threading tool into the wall of the guide hole. This makes a groove in the wall of the guide without removing any metal, as pictured in Figures 13–39 and 13–40. The metal piles up along the edge of the groove just as dirt would pile up along the edge of a tire track as the tire rolled through soft dirt. (The dirt would be displaced from under the wheel to form a small ridge alongside the tire track.)

The knurling tool is driven by an electric drill by an attached speed reducer that slows the rotating speed of the knurling tool. The reamers that accompany the knurling set will ream just enough to provide the correct valve stem clearance for commercial reconditioning standards. The valve guides are honed to size in the precision shop when precise fits are desired. Clearances of knurled valve guides are usually one-half of the new valve guide clearances. Such small clearance can be used because knurling leaves so many small oil rings down the length of the guide for lubrication.

Figure 13–39 Knurling tool being used in a valve guide. After the knurling tool displaces the metal inside the guide, a reamer is run through the guide to produce a restored, serviceable valve guide.

Figure 13–40 Sectional view of a knurled valve guide.

■ VALVE GUIDE REPLACEMENT

When an engine is designed with replaceable valve guides, their replacement is always recommended when the valve assembly is being reconditioned. The original valve guide height should be measured before the guide is removed so that the new guide can be properly positioned.

After the valve guide height is measured, the worn guide is pressed from the head with a properly fitting *driver*. Figure 13–41 shows how the driver is used to remove and replace valve guides. The driver has a stem to fit the guide opening and a shoulder that pushes on the end of the guide. If the guide has a flange, care should be taken to make sure that the guide is pushed out from the correct end, usually from the port side and toward the rocker arm side. The new guide is pressed into the guide bore using the same driver. Make sure that the guide is pressed to the correct depth. After the guides are replaced, they are reamed or honed to proper inside diameter.

Replacement valve guides can also be installed to repair worn integral guides. Both cast-iron and bronze guides are available. See Figure 13–42 on page 286. Three common valve guide sizes are as follows:

5/16 or 0.313 inch

11/32 or 0.343 inch

3/8 or 0.375 inch

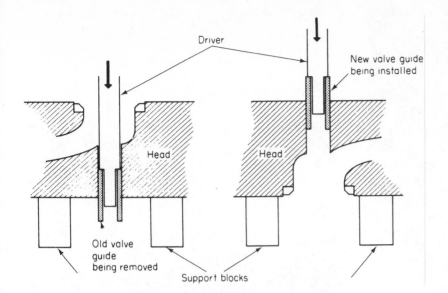

Figure 13–41 Valve guide replacement procedure.

■ VALVE GUIDE INSERTS

When the integral valve guide is badly worn, it can be reconditioned using an insert. This repair method is usually preferred in heavy-duty and high-speed engines. Two types of guide inserts are commonly used for guide repair: a **thin-walled bronze alloy sleeve bushing** and a **spiral bronze alloy bushing.** The thin-walled bronze sleeve bushings are also called **bronze guide liners.** The valve guide rebuilding kit used to install each of these bushings includes all of the reamers, installing sleeves, broaches, burnishing tools, and cutoff tools that are needed to install and properly size the bushings.

The valve guide must be bored to a large enough size to accept the thin-walled insert sleeve. The boring tool is held in alignment by a rugged fixture. One type is

TECH TIP ✔

Right Side Up

When replacing valve guides, it is important that the recommended procedures be followed. Most manufacturers specify that replaceable guides be driven from the combustion chamber side toward the rocker arm side. For example, big block Chevrolet V-8 heads (396, 402, 427, and 454 cubic inches) have a 0.004-inch (0.05-millimeter) taper (small end toward the combustion chamber).

Other manufacturers, however, may recommend driving the old guide from the rocker arm side to prevent any carbon buildup on the guide from damaging the guide bore. Always consult the manufacturer's recommended procedures before attempting to replace a valve guide.

shown in Figure 13–43 on page 287. Depending on the make of the equipment, the boring fixture is aligned with the valve guide hole, the valve seat, or the head gasket surface. First, the boring fixture is properly aligned. The guide is then bored, making a hole somewhat smaller than the insert sleeve that will be used. The bored hole is reamed to make a precise smooth hole that is still slightly smaller than the insert sleeve. The insert sleeve is installed with a press fit that holds it in the guide. The press fit also helps to maintain normal heat transfer from the valve to the head. The thin-walled insert sleeve is held in an installing sleeve. A driver is used to press the insert from the installing sleeve into the guide. A broach is then pressed through the insert sleeve to firmly seat it in the guide. The broach is designed to put a knurl in the guide to aid in lubrication. The insert sleeve is then trimmed to the valve guide length. Finally, the insert sleeve is reamed or honed to provide the required valve stem clearance. A very close clearance of 0.0005 inch (one-half of one thousandth of an inch) (0.013 millimeter) is usually used with the bronze thin-walled insert sleeve. See Figures 13–44 and 13–45 on pages 287–288.

■ SPIRAL BRONZE INSERT BUSHINGS

The spiral bronze alloy insert bushing is screwed into a thread that is put in the valve guide. The tap used to put cut threads in the valve guide has a long pilot ahead of the thread-cutting portion of the tap. This aids in restoring the original guide alignment. The long pilot is placed in the guide from the valve seat end. A power driver is attached to the end of the pilot that extends from the spring end of the valve guide. The threads are cut in the guide from the seat end toward the spring end as the power driver turns the tap, pulling it toward the driver.

(a)

(b)

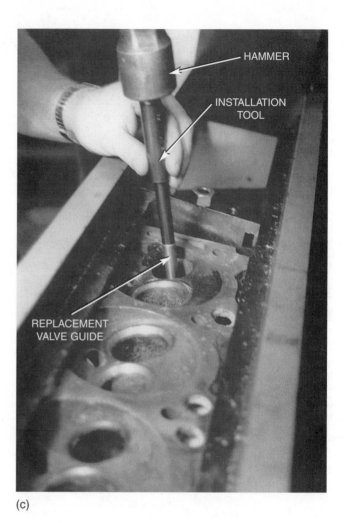

(c)

Figure 13–42 (a) Drilling out old valve guide in preparation for replacing the guide. (b) Reaming the hole after drilling. (c) Replacement guide being driven into the cylinder head.

The tap is stopped before it comes out of the guide, and the power driver is removed. The thread is carefully completed by hand to avoid breaking either the end of the guide or the tap. An installed spiral bronze insert bushing can be seen in Figure 13–46 on page 288.

The spiral bronze bushing is tightened on an inserting tool. This holds it securely in the wound-up position so that it can be screwed into the spring end of the guide. It is screwed in until the bottom of the bushing is flush with the seat end of the guide. The holding tool is removed, and the bushing material is trimmed to one coil *above* the spring end of the guide. The end of the bushing is temporarily secured with a plastic serrated bushing retainer and a worm gear clamp. This holds the bushing in place as a broach is driven through the bushing to firmly seat it in the threads. The bushing is reamed or honed to size before the temporary bushing retainer is removed. The final step is to trim the end of the bushing with a special cutoff tool that is included in the bushing installation tool set. This type of spiral bronze bushing can be removed by using a pick to free the end of the bushing. It can then be stripped out and a

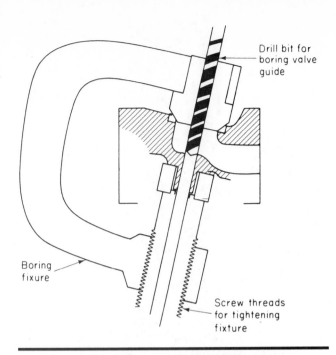

Figure 13–43 Type of fixture required to bore the valve guide to be oversize to accept a thin-walled insert sleeve.

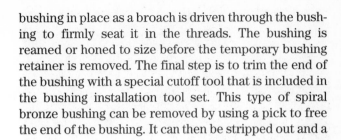

(b)

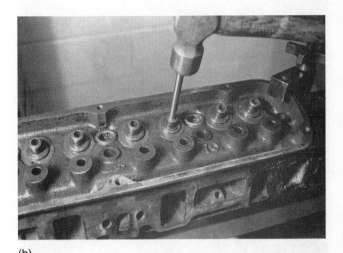

(c)

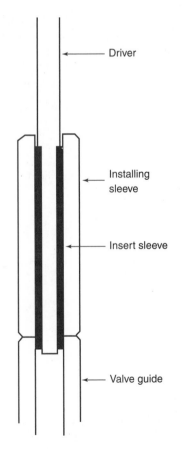

(a)

(d)

Figure 13–44 (a) The valve guide thin-walled insert being pushed into the valve guide from the installing sleeve. (b) Burnishing a thin-walled bronze liner. (c) Reaming a bronze guide liner (thin-walled bronze sleeve). (d) Finished installation. Bronze guides wear many times longer than cast-iron guides.

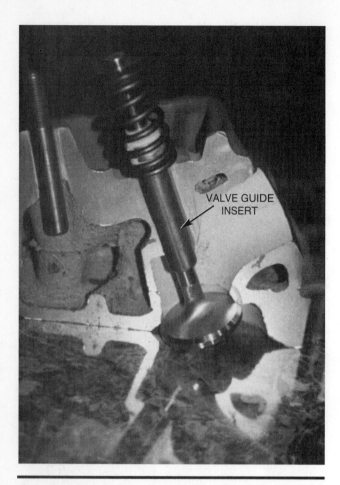

Figure 13–45 A cutaway cylinder head showing a bronze guide liner.

Figure 13–46 Installed spiral bronze insert bushing.

new bushing inserted in the original threads in the guide hole. New threads do not have to be put in the guide. The spiral bushing design has natural spiral grooves to hold oil for lubrication. The valve stem clearances are the same as those used for knurling and for the thin-walled insert (about one-half of the standard recommended clearance).

PHOTO SEQUENCE   Installing Replacement Valve Guides

PS 21–1 The first step when replacing valve guides is to square the cylinder head and secure it on the holding fixture.

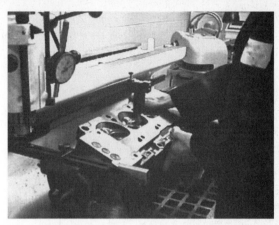

PS 21–2 After the cylinder head has been installed on the holding fixture, level the head using a bubble level inserted in the valve guide.

PS 21–3 The first step is to drill and ream out the original integral valve guide. Here a combination drill and reamer is doing this in one operation and should be performed dry without using any lubricant.

PS 21–4 A close-up view of the drill/reamer used to prepare the valve guide before installing the thin-wall bronze guides.

PS 21–5 Before installing the thin-wall bronze guide, lubricate the guides with bronze guide lubricant.

PS 21–6 Sometimes it is desirable to remove the sharp edge left by the drilling/reaming process. Here the edge of a tapered punch is being used to taper the opening to the guide slightly so that the bronze thin-wall guide can be easily inserted.

Installing Replacement Valve Guides—continued

PS 21–7 Installing the thin-wall bronze guide insert.

PS 21–8 Using an installer to force the thin-wall bronze guide fully into the guide from the combustion chamber side of the head.

PS 21–9 The thin-wall bronze guide insert is longer than the guide and protrudes out of the top of the original guide.

PS 21–10 The top of the thin-wall bronze guide insert is then trimmed to the same level as the original integral guide.

■ SUMMARY

1. The most commonly used combustion chamber types include hemispherical, wedge, and pentroof.
2. Coolant and lubricating openings and passages are located throughout most cylinder heads.
3. Cylinder head reconditioning should start with cleaning and repairing, if needed, followed by resurfacing of valves and, finally, grinding of valves and seats.
4. Cylinder head resurfacing machines include grinders and milling machines.
5. Valve guides should be checked for wear using a ball gauge or a dial indicator. Typical valve stem-to-guide clearance is 0.001 to 0.003 inch for intake valves and 0.002 to 0.004 inch for exhaust valves.
6. Valve guide repair options include use of oversize stem valves, replacement valve guides, valve guide inserts, and knurling of the original valve guide.

■ REVIEW QUESTIONS

1. What forms the top and bottom of the combustion chamber?
2. What are the advantages of a hemispherical combustion chamber?
3. What are the advantages of a wedge combustion chamber?
4. What is meant by the term *cross-flow head?*
5. What is a siamese port?
6. Why are intake valves larger than exhaust valves?
7. What are the advantages of using four valves per cylinder?

■ ASE CERTIFICATION-TYPE QUESTIONS

1. Hemispherical combustion chambers _____ .
   a. Create a turbulent air-fuel charge
   b. Always use four valves per cylinder
   c. Are nonturbulent
   d. Use inline (parallel) valves

2. For lowest hydrocarbon emissions, the engine design feature used is _____ .
   a. Low combustion chamber surface area-to-volume ratio
   b. High combustion chamber surface area-to-volume ratio
   c. Noncentrally mounted spark plug
   d. Increased (as much as possible) quench area

3. To help ensure proper engine cooling, the cylinder head design features used on most engines are _____ .
   a. Long exhaust ports and short intake ports
   b. Short exhaust ports and long intake ports

   c. Large exhaust crossover passages
   d. Coolant passages restricted by head gaskets

4. The gasket surface of a cylinder head, as measured with a straightedge, should have a maximum variation of _____ .
   a. 0.002 inch in any 6-inch length or 0.004 inch overall
   b. 0.001 inch in any 6-inch length or 0.004 inch overall
   c. 0.020 inch in any 10-inch length or 0.020 inch overall
   d. 0.004 inch in any 10-inch length or 0.008 inch overall

5. A warped aluminum cylinder head can be restored to useful service by _____ .
   a. Grinding the gasket surface and then align honing the camshaft bore
   b. Heating it in an oven at 500°F with shims under each end, allowing it to cool, and then machining it
   c. Heating it to 500°F for 5 hours and cooling it rapidly before final machining
   d. Machining the gasket surface to one-half of the warped amount and then heating the head in an oven and allowing it to cool slowly

6. Most vehicle manufacturers recommend repairing integral guides using _____ .
   a. OS stem valves
   b. Knurling
   c. Replacement valve guides
   d. Valve guide inserts

7. Typical valve stem-to-valve guide clearance is _____ .
   a. 0.030 to 0.045 inch (0.8 to 0.10 millimeter)
   b. 0.015 to 0.020 inch (0.4 to 0.5 millimeter)
   c. 0.005 to 0.010 inch (0.13 to 0.25 millimeter)
   d. 0.001 to 0.004 inch (0.03 to 0.01 millimeter)

8. What other engine component may have to be machined if the cylinder heads are machined on a V-type engine?
   a. Exhaust manifold
   b. Intake manifold
   c. Block deck
   d. Distributor mount (if the vehicle is so equipped)

9. Which operation should be performed first?
   a. Resurfacing the head
   b. Installing replacement guides

10. Which statement is true about surface finish?
    a. Cast-iron surfaces should be smoother than aluminum surfaces.
    b. The rougher the surface, the higher the microinch finish measurement.
    c. The smoother the surface, the higher the microinch finish measurement.
    d. A cylinder head should be a lot smoother than a crankshaft journal.

Valve and Seat Service

Valves need to be reconditioned more often than any other engine part.

■ INTAKE AND EXHAUST VALVES

Automotive engine valves are of a **poppet valve** design. The valve is opened by means of a valve train that is operated by a cam. The cam is timed to the piston position and crankshaft cycle. The valve is closed by one or more springs.

Typical valves are shown in Figure 14–1. Intake valves control the inlet of cool, low-pressure induction charges. Exhaust valves handle hot, high-pressure exhaust gases. This means that exhaust valves are exposed to more severe operating conditions. They are, therefore, made from much higher-quality materials than the intake valves. This makes them more expensive.

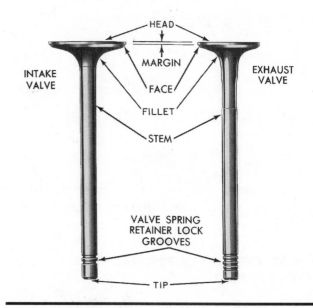

Figure 14–1 Identification of valve parts. (*Courtesy of Chrysler Corporation*)

The guide is centered over the **valve seat** so that the **valve face** and seat make a gas-tight fit. The face and seat will have an angle of 30 degrees or 45 degrees. These are the nominal angles. Actual service angles might be a degree or two different from these. Most engines use a nominal 45-degree valve and seat angle. A **valve spring** holds the valve against the seat. The valve **keepers** (also called **locks**) secure the spring **retainer** to the stem of the valve. For valve removal, it is necessary to compress the spring and remove the valve keeper. Then the spring, valve seals, and valve can be removed from the head. A typical valve assembly is shown in Figure 14–2.

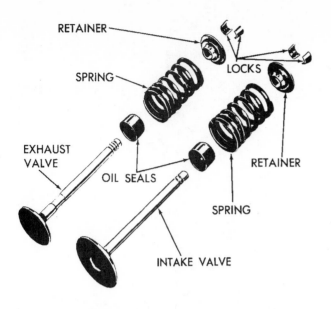

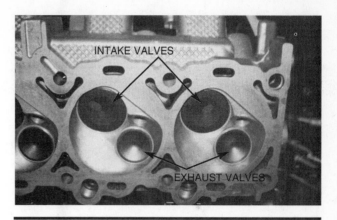

Figure 14–3 The intake valve is larger than the exhaust valve because the intake charge is being drawn into the combustion chamber at a low speed due to differences in pressure between atmospheric pressure and the pressure (vacuum) inside the cylinder. The exhaust is actually pushed out by the piston and, therefore, the size of the valve does not need to be as large leaving more room in the cylinder head for the larger intake valve.

Figure 14–2 Identification and relationship of valve components. Note the different valve locks (keepers) used on the exhaust valve as compared with the intake valve. The oil seals shown are also called umbrella-type valve stem seals. (*Courtesy of Chrysler Corporation*)

■ VALVE SIZE RELATIONSHIPS

Extensive testing has shown that a normal relationship exists between the different dimensions of valves. Engines with cylinder bores that measure from 3 to 8 inches (80 to 200 millimeters) will have intake valves that measure approximately 45% of the bore size. The exhaust valve size is approximately 38% of the cylinder bore size. The intake valve must be larger than the exhaust valve to handle the same mass of gas. The larger intake valve controls low-velocity, low-density gases. The exhaust valve, on the other hand, controls high-velocity, high-pressure, denser gases. These gases can be handled by a smaller valve. Exhaust valve heads are, therefore, approximately 85% of the size of intake valve heads. See Figure 14–3. For satisfactory operation, valve head diameter is nearly 115% of the valve port diameter. The valve must be large enough to close over

the port. The extent to which the valve opens, called **valve lift,** is close to 25% of the valve diameter.

■ VALVE DESIGN

Poppet valve heads may be of various designs, from a **rigid valve** to an **elastic valve,** as shown in Figure 14–4. The rigid valve is strong, holds its shape, and conducts heat readily. It also causes less valve recession. Unfortunately, it is more likely to leak and burn than other valve head types. The elastic valve, on the other hand, is able to conform to valve seat shape. This allows it to seal easily, but it runs hot and the flexing to conform may cause it to break. A popular shape is one with a small cup in the top of the valve head. It offers a reasonable weight, good strength, and good heat transfer at a slight cost penalty. Elastic valve heads are more likely to be found on intake valves, and rigid, on exhaust valves.

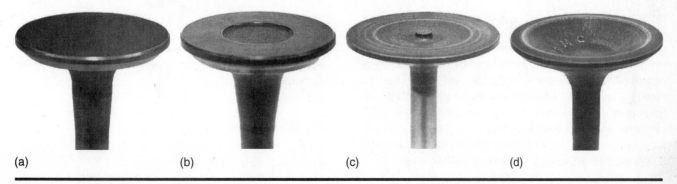

(a) (b) (c) (d)

Figure 14–4 Valve head types, from rigid (a) to elastic (d).

■ VALVE MATERIALS

Alloys used in exhaust valve materials are largely of chromium for oxidation resistance, with small amounts of nickel, manganese, and nitrogen added. Heat-treating is used whenever it is necessary to produce special valve properties. Some exhaust valves are manufactured from two different materials when a one-piece design cannot meet the desired hardness and corrosion resistance specifications. The joint cannot be seen after valves have been used. The valve heads are made from special alloys that can operate at high temperatures, have physical strength, resist lead oxide corrosion, and have indentation resistance. These heads are welded to stems that have good wear resistance properties. Figure 14–5 shows an inertia welded valve before final machining. In severe applications, facing alloys such as stellite are welded to the valve face and valve tip. Stellite is an alloy of nickel, chromium, and tungsten and is nonmagnetic. The valve is aluminized where corrosion may be a problem. Aluminized valve facing reduces valve recession when unleaded gasoline is used. Aluminum oxide forms to separate the valve steel from the cast-iron seat to keep the face metal from sticking.

■ SODIUM-FILLED VALVES

Some heavy-duty applications use hollow stem exhaust valves that are partially filled with metallic sodium. An unfilled hollow valve stem is shown in Figure 14–6. The sodium in the valve becomes a liquid at operating temperatures. As it splashes back and forth in the valve stem, the sodium transfers heat from the valve head to the valve stem. The heat goes through the valve guide into the coolant. In general, a one-piece valve design using properly selected materials will provide satisfactory service for automotive engines.

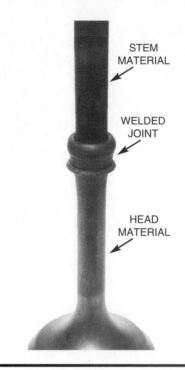

STEM MATERIAL

WELDED JOINT

HEAD MATERIAL

Figure 14–5 Inertia welded valve stem and head before machining.

Figure 14–6 Hollow valve stem. (*Courtesy of Sealed Power Corporation*)

■ VALVE SEATS

The valve face closes against a valve seat to seal the combustion chamber. The seat is generally formed as part of the cast-iron head of automotive engines, and is

Figure 14–7 Sectional view of valve assembly showing integral valve seat and valve guide.

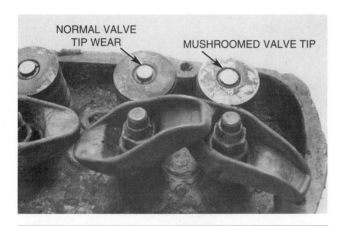

Figure 14–8 Mushroomed valve tip may indicate other valve train damage, such as excessive valve clearance (lash).

Figure 14–9 Badly burned exhaust valve.

Figure 14–10 Valve face burning.

called an **integral seat.** The seats are usually induction hardened so that unleaded gasoline can be used. This minimizes valve recession as the engine operates. Valve recession is the wearing away of the seat, so that the valve seats further into the head. Insert seats are used in applications for which corrosion and wear resistance are critical. Insert seats and guides are always required in aluminum heads. It should be noted that the exhaust valve seat runs as much as 180°F (100°C) *cooler* in aluminum heads than in cast-iron heads. Insert seats are also used as a salvage measure in the reconditioning of integral automotive engine valve seats that have been badly damaged. Typical integral valve seats and guides can be seen in Figure 14–7.

Valve seat distortion is a major cause of premature valve failure. Valve seat distortion may be temporary as the result of pressure and thermal stress or it may become permanent as the result of mechanical stress. Stress is a force put on a part that tries to change its shape.

■ VALVE INSPECTION

Careful inspection of the cylinder and valves can often reveal the root cause of failure. Excessive valve lash (clearance) can cause the top of the valve to be pounded until it becomes mushroomed as shown in Figure 14–8. Valve face burning (Figures 14–9 and 14–10) and valve face **guttering** (Figure 14–11) result from poor seating that allows the high-temperature and high-pressure combustion gases to leak between the valve and seat. Poor seating results from too small a valve lash, hard carbon deposits, valve stem deposits, excessive valve stem-to-guide clearances, or out-of-square valve guide and seat. A valve lash that is too small can result from improper valve lash adjustments on solid lifter engines. It can also result from misadjustments on a valve train using hydraulic lifters. The clearance will

Figure 14-11 Valve face guttering.

Figure 14-13 Valve face peening.

Figure 14-12 Typical intake valve seat wear. Also notice the excessive deposits on the valve. These deposits not only reduce the amount of air and fuel flow into the engine, but can also cause hesitation by absorbing fuel instead of allowing the fuel into the combustion chamber.

also be reduced as a result of valve head cupping or valve face and seat wear. Figure 14-12 shows typical intake valve and seat wear.

Hard carbon deposits are loosened from the combustion chamber. Sometimes, these flaking deposits stick between the valve face and seat to hold the valve slightly off its seat. This reduces valve cooling through the seat and allows some of the combustion gases to escape. Continued pounding on hard carbon particles gives the valve face a **peened** appearance, pictured in Figure 14-13.

Fuel and oil on the hot valve will break down to become hard carbon and varnish deposits that build up on the valve stem. Heavy valve stem deposits are shown in Figure 14-14. These deposits cause the valve to stick in

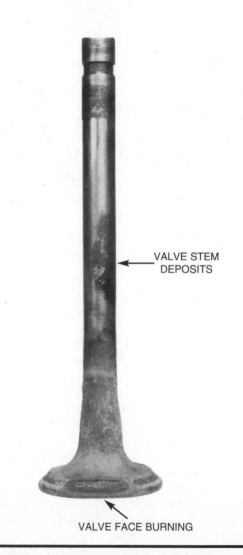

VALVE STEM DEPOSITS

VALVE FACE BURNING

Figure 14-14 Valve stem with heavy deposits and valve face burning.

Figure 14–15 Intake valve with heavy deposits.

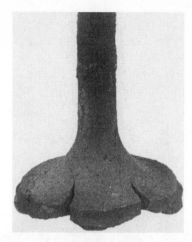

Figure 14–16 Badly guttered valve face.

Figure 14–17 Hoop stress cracks in a valve head.

the guide so that the valve does not completely close on the seat and therefore cause the valve face to burn. This is one of the most common causes of valve face burning.

If there is a large clearance between the valve stem and guide or faulty valve stem seals, too much oil will go down the stem. This will increase deposits, as shown on the intake valve in Figure 14–15. In addition, a large valve guide clearance will allow the valve to cock or lean sideways, especially with the effect of the rocker arm action. Continued cocking keeps the valve from seating properly and causes it to leak, burning the valve face.

Sometimes, the cylinder head will warp slightly as the head is tightened to the block deck during assembly. In other cases, heating and cooling will cause warpage. When head warpage causes valve guide and seat misalignment, the valve cannot seat properly and it will leak, burning the valve face.

Excessive Temperatures

High valve temperature occurs when the valve does not seat properly; however, it can occur regardless. Cooling system passages in the head may be partially blocked by faulty casting or by deposits built up from the coolant. A corroded head gasket will change the coolant flow. This can cause overheating when the coolant is allowed to flow to the wrong places. Extremely high temperatures are also produced by preignition and by detonation. These are forms of abnormal combustion. Both of these produce a very rapid increase in temperature that can cause uneven heating. The rapid increase in temperature will give a **thermal shock** to the valve. A thermal shock is a sudden change in temperature. The shock will often cause radial cracks in the valve. The cracks will allow the combustion gases to escape and gutter the valve

face. A badly guttered valve face is shown in Figure 14–16. If the radial cracks intersect, a pie-shape piece will break away from the valve head. A thermal shock can also result from rapid cycling of the engine from full throttle to closed throttle and back again. Valves with hard metal facings have special problems. Excess heat causes the base metal to expand more than the hoop of the hard face metal. The hard face metal hoop is stressed until it cracks. The crack allows gases to gutter the base metal, as shown in Figure 14–17.

High engine speeds require high gas velocities. The high-velocity exhaust gases hit on the valve stem and tend to erode or wear away the metal mechanically. The gases are also corrosive, so the valve stem will tend to corrode. Corrosion removes the metal chemically. The corrosion rate doubles for each 25°F (14°C) increase in temperature. Erosion and corrosion of the valve stem cause **necking** which weakens the stem and leads to breakage. Necking is shown in Figure 14–18.

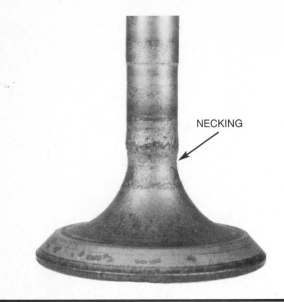

Figure 14–18 Necked valve stem.

Figure 14–19 Valve head broken from the stem.

Figure 14–20 Broken piston caused by a valve breaking from the stem.

Figure 14–21 Everything in the valve train has to be working correctly or an engine can be destroyed. The valve in this engine separated from the retainer at high engine speed, turned around in the cylinder, and punctured the piston.

Misaligned Valve Seats

When the valve-to-seat alignment is improper, the valve head must twist to seat each time the valve closes. If twisting or bending becomes excessive, it fatigues the stem, and the valve head will break from the stem. An example of this can be seen in Figure 14–19. The break appears as lines arching around a starting point. The head of the valve usually damages the piston when it gets trapped between the piston and the cylinder head.

High-Velocity Seating

High-velocity seating is indicated by excessive valve face wear, valve seat recession, and impact failure. It can be caused by excessive lash in mechanical lifters and by collapsed hydraulic lifters. Lash allows the valve to hit the seat without the effects of the cam ramp to ease the valve onto its seat. Excessive lash may also be caused by wear of parts, such as the cam, lifter base, pushrod ends, rocker arm pivot, and valve tip. Weak or broken valve springs allow the valves to float away from

the cam lobes so that the valves are uncontrolled as they hit the seat. The normal tendency of hydraulic lifters is to pump up under valve float conditions, and this reduces valve impact damage.

Impact breakage may occur under the valve head or at the valve keeper grooves. The break lines radiate from the starting point. Impact breakage may also cause the valve head to fall into the combustion chamber. In most cases, it will ruin the piston before the engine can be stopped, as pictured in Figures 14–20 and 14–21.

High Mileage

Excessive wear of the valve stem (Figure 14–22), guide, face, and seat is the result of high mileage. The affected

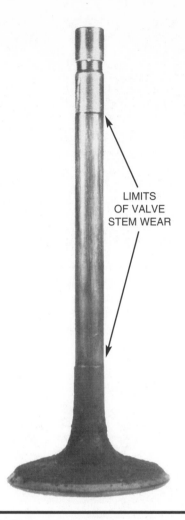

Figure 14–22 High-mileage valve stem wear.

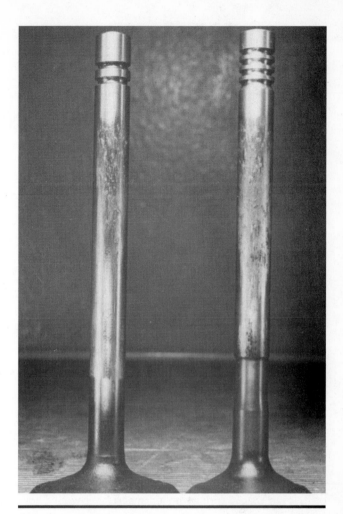

Figure 14–23 Valve stems scuffed as a result of loss of valve train lubrication.

valves usually have a great buildup of deposits. The valves will, however, still be seating, and they will show no sign of cracking or burning.

When the valve stems do not have enough lubricant, they **scuff.** In scuffing, the valve stem temporarily welds to the guide when the valve is closed. The weld breaks as the valve is forced to open. Welded metal tears from the guide and sticks to the valve stem. An example of valve stem scuffing is shown in Figure 14–23. The metal knobs on the valve stem scratch the valve guide as it operates. This also scuffs the valve guide. In a short time, the valve will stick in the guide and not close. This will stop combustion in that cylinder. Both valve and valve guide will have to be replaced.

Often, valve tips become damaged. This damage can be seen before the valves are removed from the head. Some valve tip problems are caused by rapid rotation as the valve is being opened. This causes circles on the valve tip. Still other valves do not rotate at all. These valves wear in the direction of the rocker arm or finger follower movement. Examples of excessive valve tip wear can be seen in Figure 14–24.

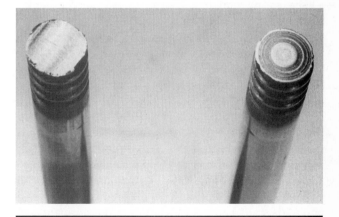

Figure 14–24 Excessive valve tip wear.

■ VALVE SPRINGS

A valve spring holds the valve against the seat when the valve is not being opened. One end of the valve spring is seated against the head. The other end of the spring is

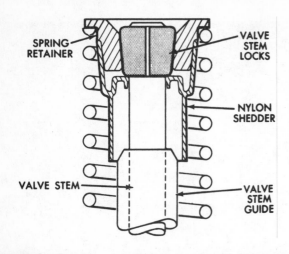

Figure 14–25 Parts of the valve keepers (locks) and retainer assembly.

Figure 14–26 Valve spring types (*left to right*): coil spring with equally spaced coils; spring with damper inside spring coil; closely spaced spring with a damper; taper wound coil spring.

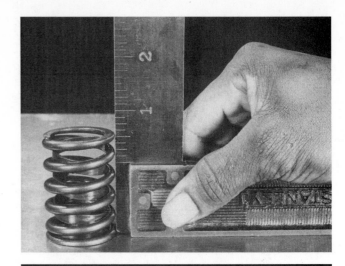

Figure 14–27 Determining the squareness of a valve spring with a square on a flat surface. The spring should be replaced if more than 1/16 inch (1.6 millimeters) is measured between the top of the spring and the square.

Figure 14–28 Out-of-square valve spring. This spring should not be tested further, but should be replaced. A distorted valve spring exerts side loads on the valve, which often causes excessive valve guide wear.

attached under compression to the valve stem through a valve spring retainer and a valve spring keeper (lock), as shown in Figure 14–25.

Valves usually have a single inexpensive valve spring. The springs are generally made of chromium vanadium alloy steel. When one spring cannot control the valve, other devices are added. Variable-rate springs add spring force when the valve is in its open position. This is accomplished by using closely spaced coils on the cylinder head end of the spring. The closely spaced coils also tend to dampen vibrations that may exist in an equally wound coil spring. The damper helps to reduce valve seat wear. Some valve springs use a flat coiled damper inside the spring. This eliminates spring surge and adds some valve spring tension. The normal valve spring winds up as it is compressed. This causes a small but important turning motion as the valve closes on the seat. The turning motion helps to keep the wear even around the valve face. Figure 14–26 illustrates typical valve springs.

Multiple valve springs are used where large lifts are required and a single spring does not have enough strength to control the valve. Multiple valve springs gen-

erally have their coils wound in opposite directions. This is done to control valve spring surge and to prevent excessive valve rotation. **Valve spring surge** is the tendency of a valve spring to vibrate.

■ VALVE SPRING INSPECTION

Valve springs close the valves after they have been opened by the cam. They must close squarely to form a tight seal and to prevent valve stem and guide wear. It is necessary, therefore, that the springs be square and have the proper amount of closing force. The valve springs are checked for squareness by rotating them on a flat surface with a square held against the side. They should be within 1/16 inch or 1.6 millimeters of being square, as shown in Figure 14–27. Only the springs that are square should be checked to determine their compressed force. See Figure 14–28. Out-of-square springs

Figure 14–29 One popular type of valve spring tester used to measure the compressed force of valve springs. Specifications usually include (1) free height (height without being compressed), (2) pressure at installed height *with valve closed,* and (3) pressure *with valve open* the maximum amount and height to specifications.

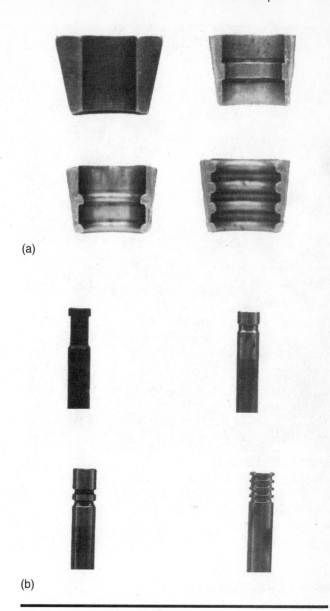

Figure 14–30 Valve split lock types (a) and stem grooves (b).

will have to be replaced. The surge damper should be *removed* from the valve spring when the spring force is being checked. A valve spring scale is used to measure the valve spring force. One popular type, shown in Figure 14–29, measures the spring force directly. Another type uses a torque wrench on a lever system to measure the valve spring force. Valve springs are checked for the following:

1. Free height (without being compressed) [should be within 1/16 (0.060) inch]
2. Pressure with valve closed and height as per specifications
3. Pressure with valve open and height as per specifications

Most specifications allow for variations of plus or minus 10% from the published figures.

■ VALVE KEEPERS

A valve keeper (lock) is used on the end of the valve stem to retain the spring. The inside surface of the split keeper uses a variety of grooves or beads. The design depends on the holding requirements. The outside of the split keeper fits into a cone-shape seat in the center of the valve spring retainer (see Figure 14–30).

Figure 14–31 Notice that there is no gap between the keepers on this DaimlerChrysler 4.7 L, V-8. As a result, the valve is free to rotate because the retainer applies a force holding the keepers in place but not tight against the stem of the valve.

■ VALVE ROTATORS

Some retainers have built-in devices called valve rotators. They cause the valve to rotate in a controlled manner as it is opened. The purposes and functions of valve rotators include the following:

- Help prevent carbon buildup from forming
- Reduce hot spots on the valves by constantly turning them
- Help to even out the wear on the valve face and seat
- Improve valve guide lubrication

The two types of valve rotators are free and positive.

- **Free rotators**—The free rotators simply take the pressure off the valve to allow engine vibration to rotate the valve. See Figure 14–31.
- **Positive rotators**—The opening of the valve forces the valve to rotate. One type of positive rotator uses small steel balls and slight ramps. Each ball moves down its ramp to turn the rotor sections as the valve

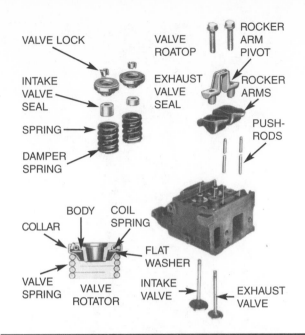

Figure 14–32 Parts of a valve assembly showing the location of the valve rotator. (*Courtesy of Oldsmobile Division, GMC*)

opens. A second type uses a coil spring. The spring lies down as the valve opens. This action turns the rotator body in relation to the collar. Valve rotors are only used when it is desirable to increase the valve service life, because rotors cost more than plain retainers. See Figures 14–32 and 14–33.

■ VALVE RECONDITIONING PROCEDURE

Valve reconditioning is usually performed using the following sequence:

Step 1 The valve stem is lightly ground and chamfered. This step helps to ensure that the valve will rest in the **collet** (holder of the valve stem during valve grinding) of the valve grinder correctly. This process is often called **truing** the valve tip.

> **NOTE:** Some engine machinists also grind the stem of the valve using a centerless grinder as shown in Figure 14–34.

Step 2 The face of the valve is ground using a valve grinder.

Step 3 The valve seat is ground in the head. (The seat must be matched to the valve that will be used in that position.)

Step 4 Installed height and valve stem height are checked and corrected as necessary.

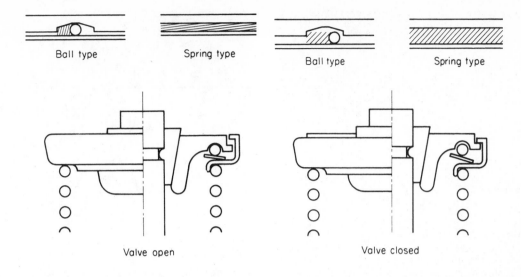

Figure 14–33 Types of valve rotator operation. Ball-type operation is on the left and spring-type operation is on the right.

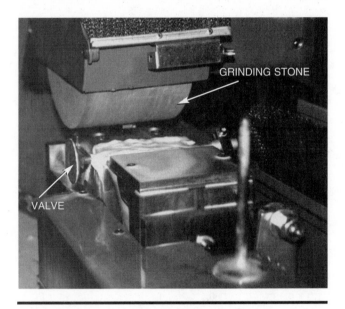

Figure 14–34 A centerless grinder being used to machine the stem of a valve.

Step 5 After a thorough cleaning, the cylinder head should be assembled with new valve stem seals installed.

The rest of the chapter discusses valve face and seat reconditioning and cylinder head reassembly.

■ VALVE FACE GRINDING

Each valve grinder operates somewhat differently. The operation manual that comes with the grinder should be followed for lubrication, adjustment, and specific operating procedures. The general procedures given in

HIGH PERFORMANCE TIP

Grinding the Valves for More Power

A normal "valve job" includes grinding the face of the valve to clean up any pits and grinding the valve stems to restore the proper stem height. However, a little more airflow in and out of the cylinder head can be accomplished by performing two more simple grinding operations.

- Use the valve grinder and adjust to 30 degrees (for a 45-degree valve) and grind a transition between the valve face and the valve stem area of the valve. While this step may reduce some desirable swirling of the air-fuel mixture at lower engine speeds, it also helps increase cylinder filling, especially at times when the valve is not fully open.
- Chamfer or round the head of the valve between the top of the valve and the margin on the side. By rounding this surface, additional airflow into the cylinder is achieved. See Figure 14–35.

the following paragraphs apply to all valve grinding equipment.

CAUTION: Safety glasses should *always* be worn for valve and seat reconditioning work. During grinding operations, fine hot chips fly from the grinding stones.

The face of the valve is ground on a **valve grinder.** Before starting, the tip of the valve should be lightly

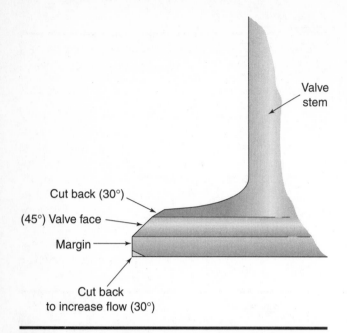

Figure 14–35 After grinding the 45-degree face angle, additional airflow into the engine can be accomplished by grinding a transition between the face angle and the stem, plus by angling or rounding the transition between the margin and the top of the valve.

Figure 14–36 Valve in a fixture to grind the valve tip.

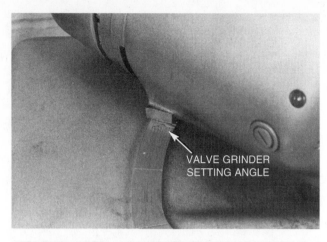

Figure 14–37 Valve grinder set to the recommended angle to refinish a valve face. In this case, the angle is set to 44 degrees to provide a 1-degree interference angle between the valve face and the 45-degree valve seat angle.

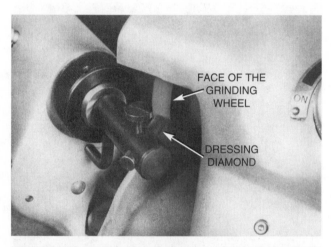

Figure 14–38 Dressing the face of the grinding wheel with a diamond dressing tool. This operation helps ensure a good-quality valve face finish.

ground and chamfered. Many valve grinders use the end of the valve to center the valve while grinding. If the tip of the valve is not square with the stem, the face of the valve may be ground improperly. See Figure 14–36. After grinding the tip, set the grinder head at the **valve face angle** as specified by the vehicle manufacturer (Figure 14–37). The grinding stone is **dressed** with a special diamond tool to remove any roughness from the stone surface (Figure 14–38). The valve stem is clamped

in the work head as close to the fillet under the valve head as possible to prevent vibrations. The work head motor is turned on to rotate the valve. The wheel head motor is turned on to rotate the grinding wheel. The coolant flow is adjusted to flush the material away, but not so much that it splashes (Figure 14–39). The rotating grinding wheel is fed slowly to the rotating valve face. Light grinding is done as the valve is moved back and forth across the grinding wheel face. The valve is never moved off the edge of the grinding wheel. It is ground only enough to clean the face (Figure 14–40). The margin of the exhaust valve should be over 0.030 inch (0.8 millimeter) when grinding is complete (Figure 14–41).

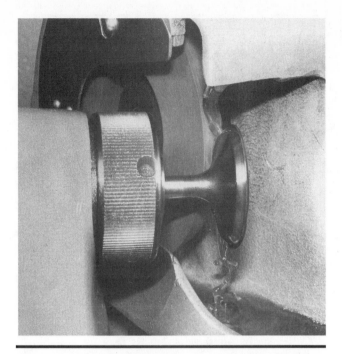

Figure 14–39 Grinding the face of a valve. Note the use of cutting oil to lubricate and cool the grinding operation.

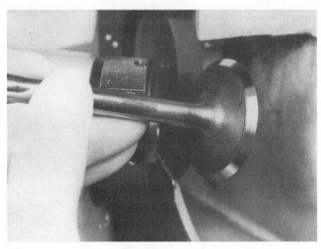

(a)

(b)

Figure 14–40 (a) Finished valve face after grinding. Do not remove any more material than is necessary. (b) A valve that is bent. Notice how the grinding stone only removed material from about one-half of the valve face. This valve should be replaced.

NOTE: To help visualize a 0.030-inch margin, note that this dimension is about 1/32 inch or the thickness of an American dime.

Intake valves can usually perform satisfactorily with a margin less than 0.030 inch. Some vehicle manufacturers even allow intake valves to be used if they have at least a 0.005 inch margin. Always check the engine manufacturer's specifications for the cylinder being serviced. Aluminized valves will lose their corrosion resistance properties when ground. For satisfactory service, aluminized valves must be replaced if they require refacing.

Figure 14–42 shows the refacing of a valve using a lathe.

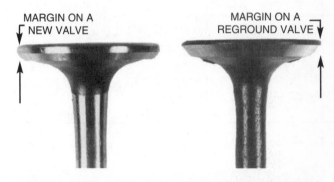

Figure 14–41 The difference in the margin on a new and a used valve head. The margin should be greater than 0.030 inch (0.8 millimeter) (about 1/32 inch or the thickness of an American dime). The thicker the margin is, the longer the valve will last.

Figure 14–42 Refacing a valve on a lathe using a special silicon carbide tool bit. The valve face is smoother than it would have been if the valve had been refaced with a stone.

TECH TIP ✔

Valve Seat Recession and Engine Performance

If unleaded fuel is used in an engine without hardened valve seats, valve seat recession is likely to occur in time. Without removing the cylinder heads, how can a technician identify valve seat recession?

As the valve seat wears up into the cylinder head, the valve itself also seats higher in the head. As this wear occurs, the valve lash *decreases*. If hydraulic lifters are used on the engine, this wear will go undetected until the reduction in valve clearance finally removes all clearance (bottoms out) in the lifter. When this occurs, the valve does not seat fully, and compression, power, and fuel economy are drastically reduced. With the valve not closing completely, the valve cannot release its heat and will burn or begin to melt. If the valve burns, the engine will miss and not idle smoothly.

If solid lifters are used on the engine, the decrease in valve clearance will first show up as a rough idle only when the engine is hot. As the valve seat recedes farther into the head, low power, rough idle, poor performance, and lower fuel economy will be noticed sooner than if the engine were equipped with hydraulic lifters.

To summarize, refer to the following symptoms as valve seat recession occurs.

1. Valve lash (clearance) decreases (valves are *not* noisy).
2. The engine idles roughly when hot as a result of reduced valve clearance.
3. Missing occurs, and the engine exhibits low power and poor fuel economy, along with a rough idle, as the valve seat recedes farther into the head.
4. As valves burn, the engine continues to run poorly; the symptoms include difficulty in starting (hot and cold engine), backfiring, and low engine power.

HINT: If valve lash is adjustable, valve burning can be prevented by adjusting the valve lash regularly. Remember, as the seat recedes, the valve itself recedes, which decreases the valve clearance. Many technicians do not think to adjust valves unless they are noisy. If, during the valve adjustment procedure, a *decrease* in valve lash is noticed, then valve seat recession could be occurring.

■ VALVE SEAT RECONDITIONING

The valve seats are reconditioned after the head has been resurfaced and the valve guides have been resized. The final valve seat width and position are checked with the valve that is to be used on the seat being reconditioned.

Valve seats will have a normal seat angle of either 45 degrees or 30 degrees. Narrow 45-degree valve seats will crush carbon deposits to prevent buildup of deposits on the seat. The valve will therefore close tightly on the seat. While the valve is closed on the seat, the valve heat will transfer to the seat and cylinder head. The 30-degree valve seat is more likely to burn than a 45-degree seat because some deposits can build up to keep the valve from seating properly. The 30-degree valve seat will, however, allow more gas flow than a 45-degree valve seat when both are opened to the same amount of lift. See Figure 14–43. This is especially true with valve lifts of less than 1/4 inch (6 millimeters). The 30-degree valve seat is also less likely to have valve seat

Figure 14–43 Relationship of the valve seating angles to the opening size with same amount of valve lift. Note that the 30-degree valve angle results in more flow past the valve than is seen with a 45-degree valve.

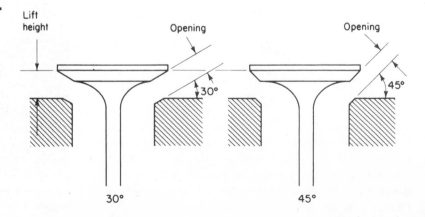

recession than is a 45-degree seat. Generally, when 30-degree valve seats are used, they are used on the cooler-operating intake valves rather than on hot exhaust valves.

The valve seats are only resurfaced enough to remove all pits and grooves and to correct any seat runout. As metal is removed from the seat, the seat is lowered into the head (Figure 14–44). This causes the valve to be located farther into the head when it is closed on the seat. The result of this is that the valve tip extends out farther from the valve guide. The valve being low in the head also tends to restrict the amount of valve opening. This will reduce the flow of gases through the opened valve. The reduced flow of gases, in turn, will reduce the maximum power the engine can produce.

Ideally, the valve face and valve seat should have exactly the same angle. This is impossible, especially on exhaust valves, because the valve head becomes much hotter than the seat and so the valve expands more than the seat. This expansion causes the hot valve to contact the seat in a different place on the valve than it did when it was cold.

Interference Angle

As a result of its shape, the valve does not expand evenly when heated. This uneven expansion also affects the way in which the hot valve contacts the seat. In valve and valve seat reconditioning, the valve is often ground with a face angle 1 degree less than the seat angle to compensate for the change in hot seating. This is illustrated in Figure 14–45. The angle between the valve face and seat is called an **interference angle.** It makes

a positive seal at the combustion chamber edge of the seat when the engine is first started after a valve job. As the engine operates, the valve will peen itself on the seat. In a short time, it will make a matched seal. After a few thousand miles, the valve will have formed its own seat, as pictured in Figure 14–46. The interference angle has another benefit. The valve and seat are reconditioned with different machines. Each machine must have its angle set before it is used for reconditioning. It is nearly impossible to set the exact same angles on both valve and seat reconditioning machines. Making an interference angle will ensure sure that any slight

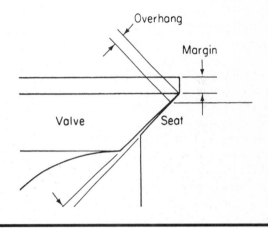

Figure 14–45 An interference angle gives the valve a tight-line seal at the combustion chamber edge of the seat.

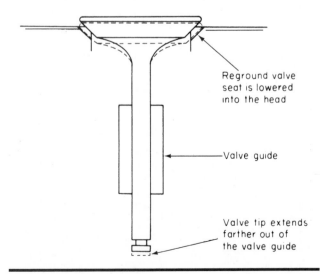

Figure 14–44 The valve seat is lowered into the cylinder head when ground. This places the valve tip further from the valve guide toward the rocker arm side of the cylinder head.

Figure 14–46 Typical valve-to-seat fit after engine use.

angle difference favors a tight seal at the combustion chamber edge of the valve seat when the valve servicing has been completed.

Valve Seat Width

As the valve seats are resurfaced, their widths increase. The resurfaced seats must be narrowed to make the seat width correct and to position the seat properly on the valve face. The normal automotive seat is from 1/16 to 3/32 inch (1.5 to 2.5 millimeters) wide. There should be at least 1/32 inch (0.8 millimeter) of the ground valve face extending above the seat. This is called **overhang**. The fit of a typical reconditioned valve and seat is shown in Figure 14–47. Some manufacturers recommend having the valve seat contact the middle of the valve face. In all cases, the valve seat width and the contact with the valve face should comply with the manufacturer's specifications.

For many years, most valve seats have been reconditioned with grinding wheels. Valve seat cutters are gradually becoming popular for reconditioning seats. The cutters will rapidly produce a good commercial-quality valve seat. See Figures 14–48 and 14–49.

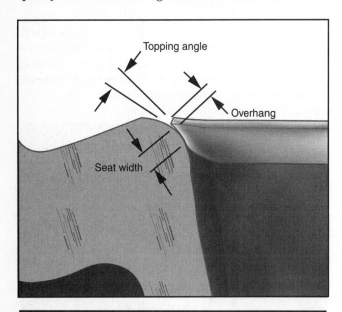

Figure 14–47 Fit of a typical reconditioned valve and seat.

Figure 14–48 Seat cutter on the left and valve seat grinding stone on the right.

■ VALVE GUIDE PILOTS

Valve seat reconditioning equipment uses a pilot in the valve guide to align the stone holder or cutter. Two types of pilots are used: tapered and expandable. Examples of these are pictured in Figure 14–50. **Tapered pilots** locate themselves in the least-worn section of the guide. They are made in standard sizes and in oversize increments of 0.001 inch, usually up to 0.004 inch oversize. The largest pilot that will fit into the guide is used for valve seat reconditioning. This type of pilot restores the seat to be as close to the original position as possible when used with worn valve guides.

Two types of **expandable pilots** are used with seating equipment. One type expands in the center of the guide to fit like a tapered pilot. Another expands to

Figure 14–49 Seat cutter. *Never* rotate a seat cutter counterclockwise! The replaceable cutters will last a long time if treated with care, including avoiding excessive force and maintaining proper operating direction.

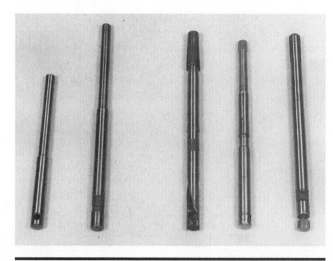

Figure 14–50 The two pilots on the left are of a solid tapered type. The three pilots on the right are adjustable (expandable) types.

contact the ends of the guide where there has been the greatest wear. The valve itself will align in the same way as the pilot.

> **NOTE:** If the guide is not reconditioned, the valve will match the seat when an expandable pilot is used.

The pilot and guide should be thoroughly cleaned. A guide cleaner as shown in Figures 14–51 and 14–52 that is rotated by a drill motor does a good job of cleaning the guide. The pilot is placed in the guide to act as an aligned support or pilot for the seat reconditioning tools. An expandable pilot is shown in a cutaway valve guide in Figure 14–53.

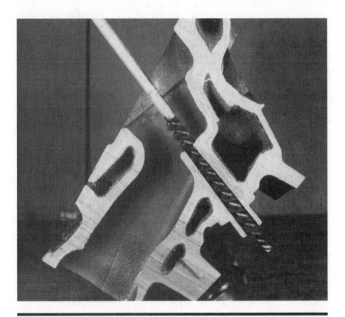

Figure 14–51 Sectioned head showing how a brush valve guide cleaner is used.

Figure 14–52 Using a valve guide brush with an electric drill. This cleaning of the valve guides is very important for proper valve seat reconditioning.

■ VALVE SEAT GRINDING STONES

Three basic types of grinding stones are used. All are used dry. A **roughing stone** is used to rapidly remove large amounts of seat metal. This would be necessary on a badly pitted seat or when installing new valve seat inserts. The roughing stone is sometimes called a seat **forming stone.** After the seat forming stone is used, a **finishing stone** is used to put the proper finish on the seat. The finishing stone is also used to recondition cast-iron seats that are only slightly worn. **Hard seat stones** are used on hard stellite exhaust seat inserts.

> **NOTE:** Stellite is a nonmagnetic hard alloy used for valve seats in heavy-duty applications.

The stone diameter and face angle must be correct. See Figure 14–54. The diameter of the stone must be larger than the valve head, but it must be small enough that it does not contact the edge of the combustion chamber. The angle of the grinding surface of the stone must be correct for the seat. When an interference angle is used with reground valves, it is common practice to use a seat with the standard seat angle. The interference angle is ground on the valve face. In some cases, such as with an aluminized valve, the valve has the standard angle and the seat is ground to give the interference angle. The required seat angle must be determined *before* the seat grinding stone is dressed.

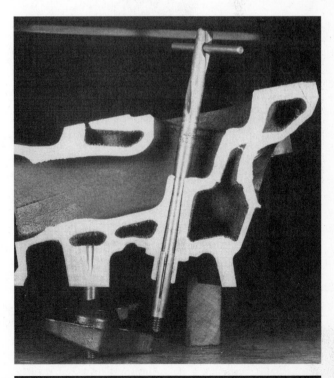

Figure 14–53 Expandable pilot shown in the valve guide of a sectioned head to illustrate how the pilot fits.

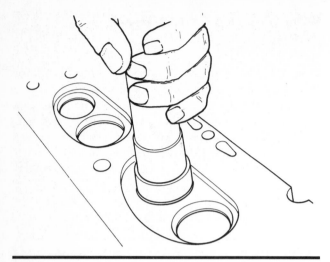

Figure 14–54 Properly fitting valve seat grinding stone.

Figure 14–55 Tip of a diamond dressing tool.

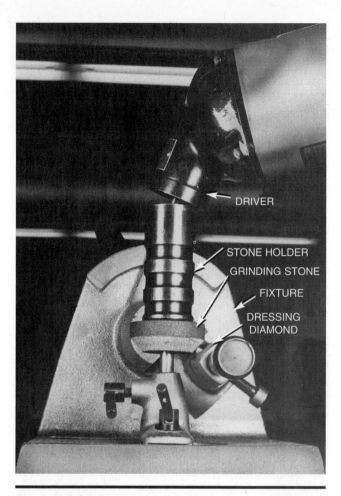

Figure 14–56 Typical assembly for dressing a valve seat grinding stone.

■ DRESSING THE GRINDING STONE

The selected grinding stone is installed on the stone holder. A drop of oil is placed on the spindle of the dressing fixture, and the assembly is placed on the spindle. The dressing tool diamond (Figure 14–55) is adjusted so that it extends 3/8 inch or less from its support. The valve seat angle is adjusted on the fixture. The driver for the seating tool is placed in the top of the stone holder. This assembly is shown in Figure 14–56. The holder and grinding stone assembly is rotated with the driver. The diamond is adjusted so that it just touches the stone face. The diamond dressing tool is moved slowly across the face of the spinning stone, taking a very light cut. Dressing the stone in this way will give it a clean, sharp cutting surface. It is necessary to redress the stone each time a stone is placed on a holder, at the beginning of each valve job, and any time the stone is not cutting smoothly and cleanly while grinding valve seats. See Figure 14–57.

■ VALVE SEAT GRINDING

It is a good practice to clean each valve seat before grinding. This keeps the soil from filling the grinding stone. The pilot is then placed in the valve guide. A drop of oil is placed on the end of the pilot to lubricate the holder. The holder, with the dressed grinding stone, is placed over the pilot. The driver should be supported so that no driver weight is on the holder. This allows the stone abrasive and the metal chips to fly out from between the stone and seat to give fast, smooth grinding. Grinding is done in short bursts, allowing the seating stone to rotate for approximately 10 turns. See Figure 14–58. The holder and stone should be lifted from the seat between each grinding burst to check the condition of the seat. The finished seat should be bright and

Figure 14–57 Dressing a seat grinding stone. Notice the grinding stone material being removed by the diamond-tip dressing tool.

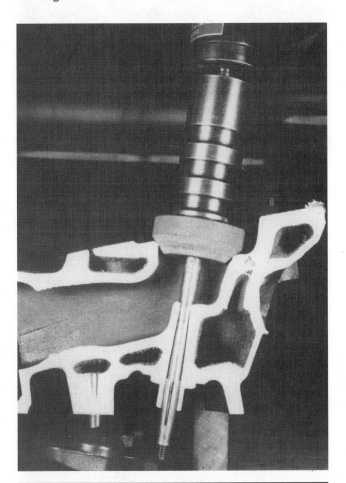

Figure 14–58 Typical setup for grinding a valve seat shown on a cutaway head.

Figure 14–59 Finished valve seat shown on a cutaway head.

smooth across the entire surface, with no pits or roughness remaining (Figure 14–59).

Some of the induction hardness from the exhaust valve seat will sometimes extend over into the intake seat. It may be necessary to apply a slight pressure on the driver toward the hardened spot to form a concentric seat. The seat is checked with a dial gauge to make sure that it is concentric within 0.002 inch (0.05 millimeter) before the seat is finished (Figure 14–60). The dial gauge measurement of the valve seat is very important. The maximum acceptable variation is 0.002 inch. This reading gives the **total indicator runout (TIR)** of the valve seat.

■ NARROWING THE VALVE SEAT

The valve seat becomes wider as it is ground. It is therefore necessary to narrow the seat so that it will contact the valve properly. The seat is **topped** with a grinding stone dressed to 15 degrees less than the seat angle. Topping lowers the top edge of the seat. The amount of topping required can best be checked by measuring the maximum valve face diameter using dividers (Figure 14–61). The dividers are then adjusted to a setting 1/16 inch smaller to give the minimum valve face overhang. The seat is checked with the dividers as shown in Figure 14–62 or measured (Figure 14–63), then topped with short grinding bursts, as required, to equal the diameter set on the dividers. The seat width is then measured (Figure 14–64). If it is too wide, the seat must be **throated** with a stone with a 60-degree angle. This removes metal from the port side of the seat, raising the lower edge of the seat. Throating is done with short grinding bursts until the correct seat width is achieved. Throating and topping angles are illustrated in Figure 14–65 on page 313. Generally accepted seat widths are as follows:

Figure 14–60 Typical dial indicator type of micrometer for measuring valve seat concentricity.

Figure 14–61 Measuring the maximum valve face diameter with dividers.

- For intake valves: 1/16 inch or 0.0625 inch (about the thickness of a nickel) (1.5 millimeters)
- For exhaust valves: 3/32 inch or 0.0938 inch (about the thickness of a dime and a nickel together) (2.4 millimeters)

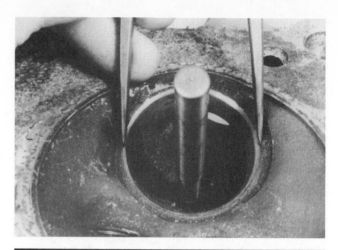

Figure 14–62 Checking the maximum valve seat diameter with the dividers adjusted to be 1/16 inch less than the maximum valve face diameter.

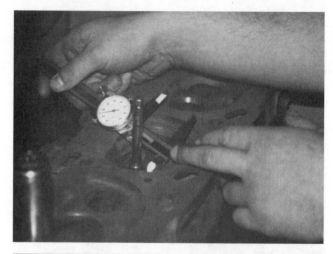

Figure 14–63 The seat width can be measured directly by using a vernier dial caliper.

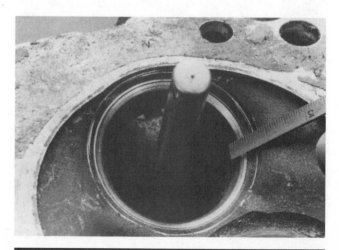

Figure 14–64 Measuring the valve seat width.

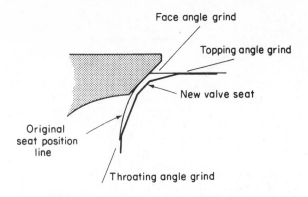

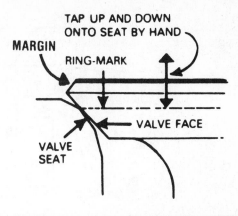

Figure 14-65 Throating and topping angles used to adjust the new valve seat width and contact location on the valve face. Unless otherwise specified, the contact width should be 1/16 inch for intake valves and 3/32 inch for exhaust valves.

Figure 14-67 Relationship of a valve seat and face. (*Courtesy of Neway*)

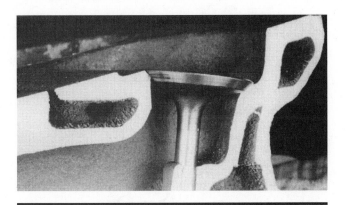

Figure 14-66 On this cutaway head, the location of the valve seat is shown where the ink from the felt-tip pen has transferred from the seat to the valve face. Prussian blue can also be used instead of a felt-tip marker.

The completed seat must be checked with the valve that is to be used on the seat. This can be done by marking across the valve face at four or five places with a felt-tip marker. The valve is then inserted in the guide so that the valve face contacts the seat. The valve is rotated 20 to 30 degrees and then removed. The location of the seat contact on the valve is observed where the felt-tip marking has been rubbed off from the valve. Valve seating can be seen in Figures 14–66 and 14–67. Valve seat grinding is complete when each of the valve seats has been properly ground, topped, and throated.

To summarize:

- Using a 30-degree topping stone (for a 45-degree seat) *lowers* the upper outer edge and narrows the seat.
- Using a 60-degree throating stone *raises* the lower inner edge and narrows the seat.
- Using a 45-degree stone *widens* the seat.

■ VALVE SEAT CUTTERS

Some automotive service technicians prefer to use valve seat cutters rather than valve seat grinders. See Figure 14–68. The valve seats can be reconditioned to commercial standards in much less time when using the cutters rather than the grinders. A number of cutting blades are secured at the correct seat angle in the cutting head of this valve seat reconditioning tool. The cutter angle usually includes the interference angle so that new valves with standard valve face angles can be used without grinding the new valve face. The cutters do not require dressing as stones do. The cutting head assembly is placed on a pilot in the same way that the grinding stone holder is used. The cutter is rotated by hand or by using a special speed reduction motor. Only metal chips are produced. The finished seat is checked for concentricity and fit against the valve face using the felt-tip marker method previously described.

■ VALVE SEAT TESTING

After the valves have been refaced and the guides and valve seats have been resurfaced, the valves should be inspected for proper sealing and to make certain that the valve seat is concentric with the valve face. Several methods that are often used to check valve face-to-seat concentricity and valve seating include the following:

1. Vacuum testing can be done by applying vacuum to the intake and/or exhaust port using a tight rubber seal and a vacuum pump. A good valve face-to-seat seal is indicated by the maintaining of at least 28 inches Hg of vacuum. This method also tests for leakage around the valve guides. Put some engine oil around the guides; if vacuum increases, valve guides may have excessive clearance.

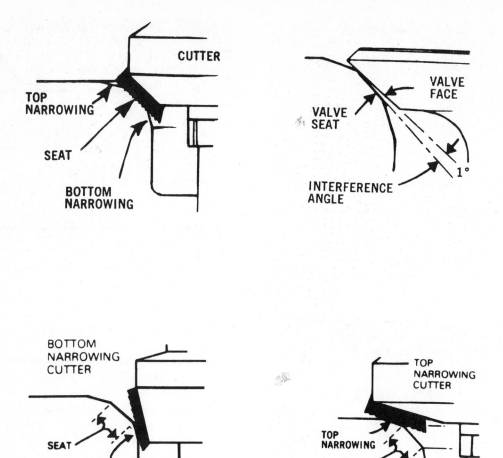

Figure 14–68 Using a valve seat cutter to cut a three-angle seat. Some seat cutters can cut all three angles at the same time. (*Courtesy of Neway*)

Figure 14–69 Testing for leakage past the valves by injecting compressed air into the combustion chamber through the spark plug hole. To prevent leakage at the head gasket surface, the cylinder head is placed on a foam rubber pad.

2. The ports or chamber can be filled with mineral spirits or some other suitable fluid. A good seal should not leak fluid for at least 45 seconds.
3. Valve seating can be checked by applying air pressure to the combustion chamber and checking for air leakage past the valve seat. See Figure 14–69.

■ VALVE SEAT REPLACEMENT

Valve seats need to be replaced if they are cracked or if they are burned or eroded too much to be reseated. A badly eroded valve seat is shown in Figure 14–70. It may not be possible to determine whether a valve seat needs to be replaced before an attempt is made to recondition the valve seat. Valve seat replacement is accomplished by using a pilot in the valve guide. This means that the valve guide must be reconditioned *before* the seat can

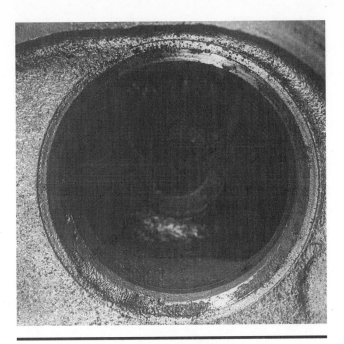

Figure 14–70 Badly eroded valve seat.

Figure 14–71 Valve seats are available in many different sizes and materials for almost every engine whether it be for normal daily use or high performance racing applications.

be replaced. Damaged **insert valve seats** are removed and the old seat counter bore is cleaned to accept a new oversize seat insert. Damaged integral valve seats must be counter bored to make a place for the new insert seat.

The old insert seat is removed by one of several methods. A small pry bar can be used to snap the seat from the counter bore. It is sometimes easier to do this if the old seat is drilled to weaken it. Be careful not to drill into the head material. Sometimes, an expandable hook-type puller is used to remove the seat insert. See the Tech Tip, "The MIG Welder Seat Removal Trick." The seat counter bore must be cleaned before the new, oversize seat is installed. The replacement inserts have a 0.002- to 0.003-inch (0.05- to 0.07-millimeter) interference fit in the counter bore. The counter bores are cleaned and properly sized, using the same equipment described in the following paragraph for installing replacement seats in place of faulty integral valve seats.

Cracked or badly burned integral valve seats can often be replaced to salvage the head. All head cracks are

repaired *before* the old integral seat is removed. The replacement seat is selected first. It must have the correct inside and outside diameters and it must have the correct thickness. Manufacturers of replacement valve seats supply tables that specify the proper seat insert to be used. If an insert is being replaced, the new insert must be of the same type of material as the original insert or better. Insert exhaust valve seats operate at temperatures that are 100° to 150°F (56° to 83°C) hotter than those of integral seats which are up to 900°F (480°C). Upgraded valve and valve seat materials are required to give the same service life as that of the original seats. Removable valve seats are available in different materials including:

- cast iron
- stainless steel
- nickel cobalt
- powdered metal (PM) (See Figure 14–71.)

A counter bore cutting tool is selected that will cut the correct diameter for the outside of the insert. The diameter of the bore is smaller than the outside diameter of the seat insert. The cutting tool is positioned securely in the tool holder so that it will cut the counter bore at the correct diameter. The tool holder is attached to the size of pilot that fits the valve guide. The tool holder feed mechanism is screwed together so that it has enough threads to properly feed the cutter into the head. This assembly is placed in the valve guide so that the cutting tool rests on the seat that is to be removed.

The new insert is placed between the support fixture and the stop ring. The stop ring is adjusted against the new insert so that cutting will stop when the counter bore reaches the depth of the new insert. See Figure 14–72. The boring tool is turned by hand or with

---

TECH TIP

The MIG Welder Seat Removal Trick

A quick and easy method to remove insert valve seats is to use a **microwire inert gas (MIG)** welder. After the valve has been removed, use the MIG welder and lay a welding bead around the seat area of the insert. As the weld cools, it shrinks and allows the insert to be easily removed from the cylinder head.

Figure 14–72 Adjusting the cutting tool stop ring with the new valve insert as a guide.

Figure 14–73 Seat cutting tool boring out the old eroded valve seat.

a reduction gear motor drive. It cuts until the stop ring reaches the fixture. See Figure 14–73. The support fixture and the tool holder are removed. The pilot and the correct size of adapter are placed on the driving tool. Ideally, the seats should be cooled with dry ice to cause them to shrink. Each insert should be left in the dry ice until it is to be installed. This will allow it to be installed with little chance of metal being sheared from the counter bore. Sheared chips could become jammed under the insert, keeping it from seating properly. The chilled seat is placed on the counter bore. The driver with a pilot is then quickly placed in the valve guide so that the seat will be driven squarely into the counter bore. The driver is hit with a heavy hammer to seat the insert, as shown in Figure 14–74. Heavy blows are used to start the insert, and lighter blows are used as the seat reaches the bottom of the counter bore. It serves no purpose to hit the driver after the insert is seated in the bottom of the counter bore. The installed valve seat insert is peened in place by running a peening tool around the metal on the outside of the seat. The peened metal is slightly displaced over the edge of the insert to help hold it in place. A fully installed seat insert is

shown in Figure 14–75. Seats are formed on the replacement inserts using the same procedures described for reconditioning valve seats.

■ VALVE STEM HEIGHT

Valve stem height is a different measurement from installed height. See Figure 14–76. Valve stem height is important to maintain for all engines, but especially for overhead camshaft engines. When the valve seat and the valve face are ground, the valve stem extends deeper into the combustion chamber and extends higher or further into the cylinder head.

The valve is put in the head, and the length of the tip is measured. The tip is ground to shorten the valve stem

---

TECH TIP

Use the Recommended Specifications

A technician replaced valve seat inserts in an aluminum cylinder head. The *factory* specification called for a 0.002-inch interference fit (the insert should be 0.002 inch larger in diameter than the seat pocket in the cylinder head). Shortly after the engine is started, the seat fell out, ruining the engine.

The technician should have used the interference fit specification supplied with the replacement seat insert. Interference fit specifications depend on the type of material used to make the insert. Some inserts for aluminum heads require as much as 0.007-inch interference fit. Always refer to the specification from the manufacturer of the valve inserts when replacing valve seats in aluminum cylinder heads.

(a)

Figure 14–74 (a) Seating the new chilled insert in the counter bore by hitting the driver with a heavy hammer. (b) Interference fit for valve inserts (hard cast or wrought inserts).

(b)

Outside diameter (in.)	Insert depth (in.)	Interference fit (in.)
0–1	$0-\frac{1}{4}$	0.001 – 0.003
1–2	$\frac{1}{4}-\frac{3}{8}$	0.002 – 0.004
2–3	$\frac{3}{8}-\frac{9}{16}$	0.003 – 0.005
3–4	$\frac{9}{16}-1$	0.004 – 0.006

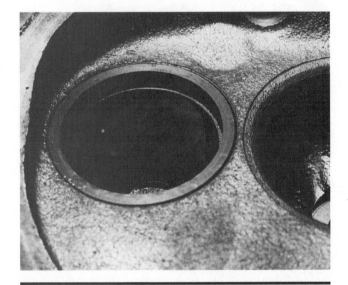

Figure 14–75 Fully installed valve seat insert.

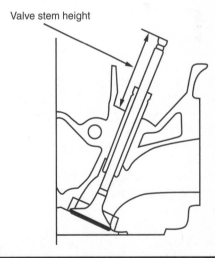

Valve stem height

Figure 14–76 Valve stem height is measured from the spring seat to the tip of the valve after the valve seat and valve face have been refinished. If the valve stem height is too high, up to 0.020 inch can be ground from the tips of most valves.

length to compensate for the valve face and seat grinding. The valve will not close if the valve tip extends too far from the valve guide on engines that have hydraulic lifters and nonadjustable rocker arms. If the valve is too long, the tip may be ground by as much as 0.020 inch (0.50 millimeter) to reduce its length. If more grinding is

required, the valve must be replaced. If it is too short, the valve face or seat may be reground, within limits, to allow the valve to seat deeper. Where excessive valve face and seat grinding has been done, shims can be placed under the rocker shaft on some engines as a repair to provide correct hydraulic lifter plunger centering. These shims must have the required lubrication holes to allow oil to enter the shaft.

■ CHECKING INSTALLED HEIGHT

When the valves and/or valve seats have been machined, the valve projects farther than before on the rocker arm side of the head. (The valve face is slightly recessed into the combustion chamber side of the head.) The valve spring tension is, therefore, reduced because the spring is not as compressed as it was originally. To restore original valve spring tension, special valve spring spacers, inserts, or shims are installed under the valve springs. These shims are usually called **valve spring inserts (VSI).** Valve spring inserts are generally available in three different thicknesses:

- 0.015 inch (0.38 millimeter): Used for balancing valve spring pressure
- 0.030 inch (0.75 millimeter): Generally used for new springs on cylinder heads that have had the valve seats ground and valves refaced
- 0.060 inch (1.5 millimeters): Necessary to bring assembled height to specifications (These thicker inserts may be required if the seats have been resurfaced more than one time.)

Step 1 To determine the exact thickness of insert to install, measure the valve spring height (as installed in the head). See Figure 14–77.

Step 2 If the installed height is greater than specifications, select the insert (shim) that brings the installed height to within specifications. See Figure 14–78.

■ VALVE STEM SEALS

Leakage past the valve guides is a major oil consumption problem in any overhead valve (or overhead cam) engine. A high vacuum exists in the intake port, as shown in Figure 14–79. Most engine manufacturers use valve stem seals on the exhaust valve, because a weak vacuum in the exhaust port area can draw oil into the exhaust stream, as illustrated in Figure 14–80.

Valve stem seals are used on overhead valve engines to control the amount of oil used to lubricate the valve stem as it moves in the guide. The stem and guide will scuff if they do not have enough oil. Too much oil will cause excessive oil consumption and will cause heavy carbon deposits to build up on the spark plug nose and on the fillet of the valves.

Figure 14–77 Checking installed height with a steel rule. Measure from spring seat surface of cylinder head to bottom surface of valve spring retainer.

Types of Valve Stem Seals

- The **umbrella valve stem seal** holds tightly on the valve stem and moves up and down with the valve. Any oil that spills off the rocker arms is deflected out over the valve guide, much as water is deflected over an umbrella (Figure 14–81 on page 320). As a result, umbrella valve stem seals are often called **deflector valve stem seals.**
- **Positive valve stem seals** hold tightly around the valve guide, and the valve stem moves through the seal. The seal wipes the excess oil from the valve stem (Figures 14–82 and 14–83 on page 320).
- **O-ring valve stem seal** used on Chevrolet engines keeps oil from leaking between the valve stem and valve spring retainer. The oil is deflected over the retainer and shield (Figure 14–84 on page 320). The assembly controls oil like an umbrella-type oil seal. Both types of valve stem seals allow only the correct amount of oil to reach the valve guide to lubricate the valve stem. The rest of the oil flows back to the oil pan.

(a)

(b)

Figure 14–78 (a) Valve spring inserts (VSI) (also called shims) are installed between the cylinder head and valve spring to restore the valve to proper installed height. (b) The serrations of the valve spring insert should face toward the cylinder head. The purpose of the serrations is to allow air to flow between the insert and the head to help keep the spring cooler.

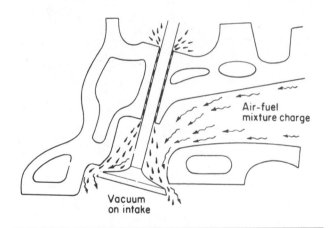

Figure 14–79 Engine vacuum can draw oil past the valve guides and into the combustion chamber. The use of valve stem seals limits the amount of oil that is drawn into the engine. If the seals are defective, excessive blue (oil) smoke is most often observed during engine start-up.

Valve Seal Materials

Valve stem seals are made from many different types of materials. They may be made from nylon or Teflon, but most valve stem seals are made from synthetic rubber. Three types of synthetic rubbers are in common use:

- **Nitrile (Nitril)**
- **Polyacrylate**
- **Viton**

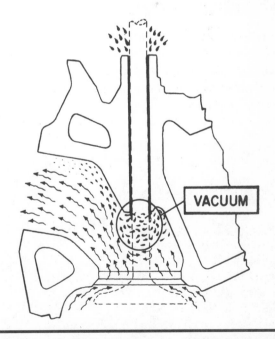

Figure 14–80 Engine oil can also be drawn past the exhaust valve guide because of a small vacuum created by the flow of exhaust gases. Any oil drawn past the guide would simply be forced out through the exhaust system and not enter the engine. Some engine manufacturers do not use valve stem seals on the exhaust valves. (*Courtesy of Dana Corporation*)

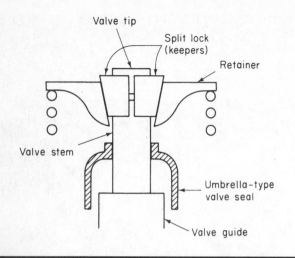

Figure 14–81 Location of umbrella-type valve stem oil seal. Note that the seal fits tightly on the valve stem and just covers the top of the valve guide.

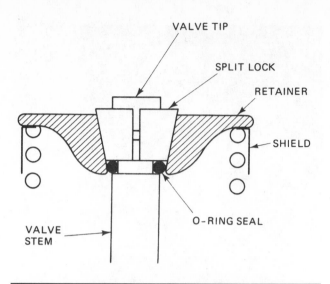

Figure 14–84 Chevrolet O-ring type of valve stem seal.

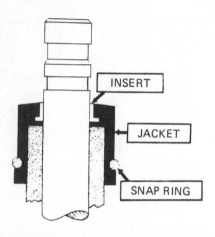

Figure 14–82 Positive-type valve stem oil seal. (*Courtesy of Dana Corporation*)

Figure 14–85 Poor-quality umbrella-type valve stem seal after several months of use. Note how heat has softened this seal and destroyed its sealing ability.

Figure 14–83 Positive-type valve stem seals come in a variety of sizes, designs, and materials to fill a wide range of engine applications.

Nitrile is the oldest valve stem seal material. It has a low cost and a low useful temperature. Engine temperatures have increased with increased emission controls and improved efficiencies, which made it necessary to use premium polyacrylate, even with its higher cost. In many cases, it is being retrofit to the older engines because it will last much longer than Nitrile. Diesel engines and engines used for racing, heavy trucks, and trailer towing, along with turbocharging, operate at still higher temperatures. These engines may require expensive Viton valve stem seals that operate at higher temperatures. See Figure 14–85.

Figure 14–86 The gaps between the halves of split locks (keepers) are necessary to ensure that the locks are properly seated in the grooves of the valve stem.

TECH TIP ✔

Don't Forget to Inspect the Keepers!

Valve keepers or locks are designed to retain the valve stem or keep it attached to the valve spring retainer under all operating conditions. The taper fit exerts the holding force. Before assembling the valves in the cylinder heads, place the split locks (keepers) in the groove(s) of the valve stem. There should be a slight gap between the keepers. If the keepers touch, they are not making full contact with the groove(s) of the valve stem. This could cause the keepers to release their grip on the valve at high engine speeds.

Using new valve keepers (split locks) is recommended, and every one should be inspected! Manufacturing flaws can create dimensions that are not to specifications, and a valve dropping at high engine speeds can result in destruction of the entire engine. See Figure 14–86.

It is interesting to note that an automotive service technician cannot tell the difference between these synthetic rubber valve stem seals if they have come out of the same mold for the same engine. Often suppliers that package gasket sets for sale at a low price will include low-temperature Nitrile, even when the engine needs higher-temperature polyacrylate. Your best chance of getting the correct valve stem seal material for an engine is to purchase gaskets and seals packaged by a major-brand gasket company.

■ INSTALLING THE VALVES

The cylinder head can be assembled after the head is thoroughly cleaned with soap and water to wash away

Figure 14–87 Setup needed to measure the combustion chamber volume in cubic centimeters (cc).

HIGH PERFORMANCE TIP ▐▐▐➡

"CC" The Heads for Best Performance

For best engine performance and smooth operation, all cylinders should have the same compression. To accurately measure the volume of the combustion chamber, a graduated burette is used with mineral spirits (or automatic transmission fluid) to measure the exact volume of the chamber in cubic centimeters (cc). See Figure 14–87.

---

any remaining grit and metal shavings from the valve grinding operation. Valves are assembled in the head, one at a time. The valve guide and stem are given a liberal coating of engine oil, and the valve is installed in its guide. Umbrella and positive valve stem seals are installed. Push umbrella seals down until they touch the valve guide. Use a plastic sleeve over the tip of the valve when installing positive seals. Make sure that the positive seal is fully seated on the valve guide and that it is square. Hold the valve against the seat as the valve spring seat or insert, valve spring, valve seals, and retainer are placed over the valve stem. One end of the valve spring compressor pushes on the retainer to compress the spring. The O-ring type of valve stem seal is installed in the lower groove. The valve keepers are installed while the valve spring is compressed. See Figure 14–88. Release the valve spring compressor slowly and carefully while making sure that the valve keepers seat properly between the valve stem grooves and the retainer. Each valve is assembled in the same manner. See Figures 14–89 and 14–90. Attach the hose from a vacuum pump to the top of the assembled valve. *A vacuum will hold if the O-ring type of valve stem seal is correctly installed*, as shown in Figure 14–91.

■ FLOW TESTING CYLINDER HEADS

Many specialty engines are tested for the amount of air that can flow through the ports and valves of the engine.

A flow bench is used to measure the amount of air [measured in cubic feet per minute (cfm)] that can flow through the valves at various valve openings.

After completion of the valve job and any port or combustion chamber work, weak valve springs are

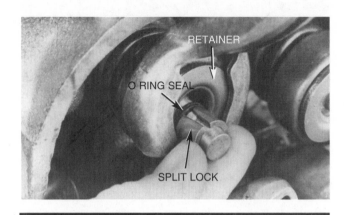

Figure 14–88 Proper installation of a typical Chevrolet O-ring valve stem seal and valve locks.

Figure 14–89 (a) Air-operated valve spring compressor being used to install valves. If the compressor compresses the valve spring too much, the O-ring valve stem seal may be knocked out of location when the compressor is released. (b) Putting grease on the split locks (keepers) helps to retain them when releasing pressure on the valve spring compressor to help prevent improper seating. (c) Valve after installation. Note the grease on the valve. The grease should be wiped off to prevent the possibility of certain greases clogging oil filters after the engine starts.

(a)

(b)

(c)

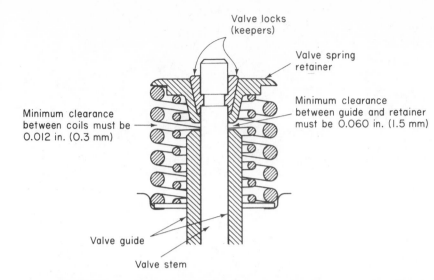

Valve locks (keepers)

Valve spring retainer

Minimum clearance between coils must be 0.012 in. (0.3 mm)

Minimum clearance between guide and retainer must be 0.060 in. (1.5 mm)

Valve guide

Valve stem

Figure 14–90 All valve springs should be checked for coil bind at maximum valve lift. The retainer can also hit the valve guide at high engine speeds if there is not sufficient clearance.

(a)

(b)

Figure 14–91 (a) A hand-operated vacuum pump is used to check the O-ring valve stem seals on this Chevrolet V-8 cylinder head. (b) A close-up showing the sealing cup over the retainer.

Figure 14–92 Cylinder head setup for flow testing. Note the weak valve springs that are strong enough to keep the valves shut, yet weak enough to permit the flow bench operator to vary the intake valve opening amount.

Figure 14–93 Modeling clay is installed around the port to duplicate the flow improvement characteristics of an intake manifold.

TECH TIP ✔

Do Not Simply Bolt on New Cylinder Heads

New assembled cylinder heads, whether aluminum or cast iron, are a popular engine buildup option. However, experience has shown that metal shavings and casting sand are often found inside the passages.

Before bolting on these "ready to install" heads, disassemble them and clean all passages. Often machine shavings are found under the valves. If this debris were to get into the engine, the results would be extreme wear or damage to the pistons, rings, block, and bearings. This cleaning may take several hours, but how much is your engine worth?

0.100" THICK SPACER (OPENS VALVE OFF SEAT)

TEST VALVE SPRINGS

Figure 14–94 By varying the thickness of the metal spacers, the flow bench operator can measure the airflow through the intake and exhaust ports and valves at various valve lifts.

---

installed temporarily. See Figure 14–92. Modeling clay is then temporarily applied around the ports to improve flow characteristics around the port area where the intake manifold would normally direct the flow into the port. See Figure 14–93.

Various thicknesses of metal spacers are placed between the cylinder head holding fixture and the valve stem. See Figure 14–94. Typical thicknesses used are 0.100 through 0.700 inch in 0.100-inch increments. The results are recorded on a work sheet. See Figure 14–95.

■ CYLINDER HEAD FLOW VERSUS HORSEPOWER

Most comprehensive engine machine shops have the equipment to measure the airflow through cylinder

head ports and valves. After the airflow through the open intake valve has been determined, a formula can be used to estimate horsepower. The following formula has proven to be a fairly accurate estimate of horsepower when compared with dynamometer testing after the engine is built.

NOTE: The first part of the formula is used to convert airflow measurement from a basis of being tested at 28 inches of water to that of being tested at 20 inches of water.

PRESSURE DROP ____28"____   NAME ____TEST INFO____

APPLICATION ____DART II IRON S.B/K.____

____IN = 2.055   Ex = 1.600____

3 ANGLE   GRIND ONLY

VALVE LIFT (in.)

	CYL. #	COMMENTS	R 0.100		R 0.200		R 0.300		R 0.400		R 0.500		R 0.600		R 0.700	
	IN		3	57.5	3	93.8	4	63.5	4	73.6	4	74.8	4	76.5	4	77.5
		CFM		88		144		189		219		223		228		231
	IN															
		CFM														
	IN															
A		CFM														
I	IN															
R		CFM														
F	EX		2	60.5	3	58.5	3	70.0	3	76.0	3	80.2	3	82.0	3	83.2
L		CFM		54		95		113		123		130		133		135
O	EX															
W		CFM														
	EX															
		CFM														
	EX															
		CFM														

Figure 14–95 Actual flow bench test work sheet. Note that the cylinder head was tested at up to 0.799 inch of lift!

Horsepower per cylinder =
Airflow at 28 inches of water × 0.598 × 0.43

For example, for a V-8 that measures 231 cfm of air-flow at 28 inches of water:

Horsepower =231 × 0.598 = 138 cfm at 20 inches of water × 0.43 = 59.4 hp per cylinder × 8 = 475 hp

CAUTION: Even though this formula has proven to be fairly accurate, there are too many variables in the design of any engine besides the airflow through the head for this formula to be accurate under all conditions.

PHOTO SEQUENCE Valve Seat Grinding

PS 22–1 To grind the valve seats in a cylinder head, the proper equipment and grinding stones must be available. On the left is a 45-degree stone for the valve seat angle. In the center is a 60-degree stone used to raise and narrow the valve seat. The 30-degree stone on the right is used to narrow and lower the valve seat as necessary.

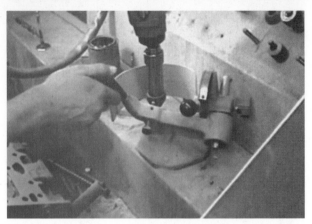

PS 22–2 Before grinding the seats, the stones should be "dressed" or cleaned using a diamond dressing tool. The stone is attached to a holding fixture which is rotated by the air-powered grinder. The technician is shown dressing the grinding stone on a 45-degree angle with a diamond tip.

PS 22–3 A pilot of the correct size is inserted into the valve guide. The pilot will keep the grinding stone in the center of the valve pocket so that a concentric valve seat will be ground.

PS 22–4 The grinding stone is turned by the high-speed, air-powered grinder. Use short bursts and avoid pressing down on the grinder.

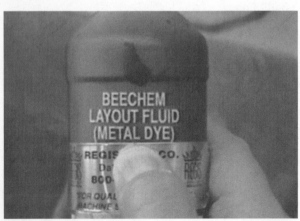

PS 22–5 This technician uses layout fluid to check the exact location where the valve contacts the seat. Prussian blue is also commonly used.

PS 22–6 A small felt ball is used to apply a thin coating of dye to the face of a valve.

PS 22–7 Some technicians use a felt-tip marker on the valve to check where it will contact the valve seat instead of using dye.

PS 22–8 After the dye is spread evenly over the valve face, the valve is placed into the guide and rotated by hand. Then the valve is removed from the grinder and examined. Notice that the seat is contacting the valve face in approximately the center of the face.

PS 22–9 The dye should be thoroughly cleaned from both the valve and the seat in the cylinder head.

PS 22–10 Some service technicians prefer to also use valve grinding compound between the valve seat and the valve face to lap the two surfaces for a better seal. Apply a thin coating of grinding compound on the face.

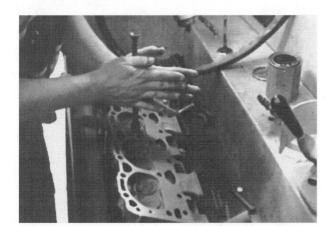

PS 22–11 Place the valve into the guide and use a suction cup stick to rotate the valve. The grinding compound between the valve face and the seat will help mate the two surfaces.

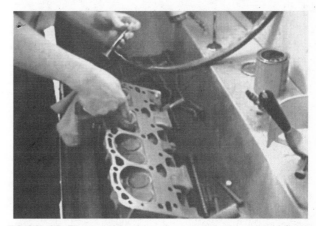

PS 22–12 Thoroughly clean the grinding compound from both the valve and the seat. This is a very important operation because leftover grinding compound could quickly cause excessive wear to all other parts of the engine.

PHOTO SEQUENCE   Grinding a Valve

PS 23–1 A typical valve grinding machine.

PS 23–2 The grinding stone should be dressed with a diamond dressing tool to be sure that the stone is square so as to provide smooth and accurate grinding of the valves.

PS 23–3 Before grinding the face of a valve, the tip of the stem should be chamfered so that the valve will seat properly in the collet during the grinding operation especially if using a Sioux valve grinder.

PS 23–4 Insert the valve into the collet. Try to keep the distance that the valve extends out to a minimum. Start the valve grinder and observe the valve face. If it wobbles, the stem is bent and the valve must be replaced.

Grinding a Valve—continued

PS 23–5 This particular valve grinding machine uses the side of the grinding stone to resurface the face angle on the valve.

PS 23–6 Coolant should be used on the valve to help wash away grit from the grinding operation and help keep the valve from getting hot.

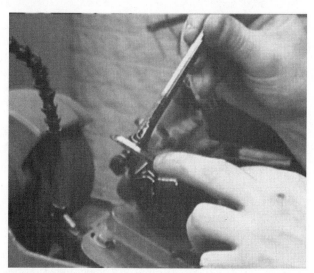

PS 23–7 Remove as little material as possible when grinding a valve. Check the face of the valve for a smooth surface. Also check that the margin is greater than the minimum specification.

PS 23–8 After grinding the face, remove one-half of the amount as removed from the face from the valve stem. This operation helps maintain the original valve stem height.

■ SUMMARY

1. The exhaust valve is about 85% of the size of the intake valve.

2. Valve springs should be kept with the valve at the time of disassembly and tested for squareness and proper spring force.

3. Free and positive are two types of valve rotators.

4. Valve grinding should start with truing the valve tip; then the face should be refinished. A pilot is placed into the valve guide to position the stone or cutter correctly for resurfacing the valve seat.

5. The installed height should be checked and corrected with valve spring inserts if needed.

6. Valve stem height should be checked and the top of the valve ground if necessary.

7. After a thorough cleaning, the cylinder head should be assembled using new valve stem seals.

■ REVIEW QUESTIONS

1. Why is valve guide reconditioning the first cylinder head servicing operation?

2. When is the valve tip ground? How do you know how much to remove from the tip?

3. What is an interference angle between the valve and the seat?

4. Describe the difference between cutting and grinding valve seats.

5. How is a valve seat insert installed?

6. How are the correct valve spring inserts (shims) selected and why are they used?

■ ASE CERTIFICATION-TYPE QUESTIONS

1. In a normally operating engine, intake and exhaust valves are opened by a cam and closed by the _____ .
   a. Rocker arms or cam follower
   b. Valve spring
   c. Lifters (tappets)
   d. Valve guide and/or pushrod

2. If an interference angle is machined on a valve or seat, this angle is usually _____ .
   a. 1 degree
   b. 0.005 degree
   c. 1 to 3 degrees
   d. 0.5 to 0.75 degree

3. Never remove more material from the tip of a valve than:
   a. 0.001 inch
   b. 0.002 inch
   c. 0.020 inch
   d. 0.050 inch

4. A valve should be discarded if the margin is less than _____ after refacing.
   a. 0.001 inch
   b. 0.006 inch
   c. 0.025 inch
   d. 0.060 inch

5. A valve seat should be concentric to the valve guide to a maximum TIR of _____ .
   a. 0.006 inch
   b. 0.004 inch
   c. 0.002 inch
   d. 0.00015 inch

6. To lower and narrow a valve seat that has been cut at a 45-degree angle, use a cutter or stone of what angle?
   a. 60 degrees
   b. 45 degrees
   c. 30 degrees
   d. 15 degrees

7. Valve spring inserts (shims) are designed to _____ .
   a. Increase installed height of the valve
   b. Decrease installed height of the valve
   c. Adjust the correct installed height
   d. Decrease valve spring pressure to compensate for decreased installed height

8. The proper relationship between intake and exhaust valve diameter is _____ .
   a. Intake valve size 85% of exhaust valve size
   b. Exhaust valve size 85% of intake valve size
   c. Exhaust valve size 38% of intake valve size
   d. Intake valve size 45% of exhaust valve size

9. Dampers (damper springs) are used inside some valve springs to _____ .
   a. Prevent valve spring surge
   b. Keep the valve spring attached to the valve
   c. Decrease valve spring pressure
   d. Retain valve stem seals

10. Umbrella-type valve stem seals _____ .
    a. Fit tightly onto the valve guide
    b. Fit on the valve face to prevent combustion leaks
    c. Fit tightly onto the valve stem
    d. Lock under the valve retainer

Camshaft and Valve Train Service

Objectives: After studying Chapter 15, the reader should be able to:

1. Describe how the camshaft and valve train function.
2. Discuss valve train noise and its causes.
3. Explain how to degree a camshaft.
4. Explain how a hydraulic lifter works.

The cam is driven by timing gears, chains, or belts located at the front of the engine. The gear or sprocket on the camshaft has twice as many teeth, or notches, as the one on the crankshaft. This results in two crankshaft turns for each turn of the camshaft. *The camshaft turns at one-half the crankshaft speed in all four-stroke cycle engines.*

■ CAMSHAFT FUNCTION

The camshaft's major function is to operate the valve train. Cam shape or **contour** is the major factor in determining the operating characteristics of the engine. The lobes on the camshaft open the valves against the pressure of the valve springs. The camshaft lobe changes rotary motion (camshaft) to linear motion (valves).

Cam lobe shape has more control over engine performance characteristics than any other single engine part. Engines identical in every way except cam lobe shape may have completely different operating charac-

teristics and performance. Two cam shapes for a small-block Chevrolet V-8 are shown in Figure 15–1.

The camshaft may also operate the following:

- Mechanical fuel pump
- Oil pump
- Distributor

■ CAMSHAFT LOCATION

Pushrod engines have the cam located in the block. See Figure 15–2. They are smaller and lighter than overhead cam engines. The camshaft is supported in the block by **camshaft bearings** and driven by the crankshaft with a gear or sprocket and chain drive.

Figure 15–1 Shape of two small-block Chevrolet V-8 cam lobes. A standard cam is on the left and a high performance cam is on the right.

Figure 15–2 Cutaway of a Chevrolet V-8 showing the valve train components.

Figure 15–3 Many overhead camshaft engines use a rubber plug (seal) on the end of the cylinder head to allow the camshaft to be removed. This seal is a common source of oil leaks and should be carefully inspected if an engine with an overhead camshaft has an oil leak.

(a)

(b)

Figure 15–4 (a) Here is what can happen if a roller lifter breaks loose from its retainer. The customer complained of "a little noise from the engine." (b) All engines equipped with roller lifters have some type of retainer for keeping the lifters from rotating.

■ CAMSHAFT PROBLEM DIAGNOSIS

A camshaft with a partially worn lobe is often difficult to diagnose. Sometimes a valve "tick tick tick" noise is heard if the cam lobe is worn. The ticking noise can be intermittent, which makes it harder to determine the cause. If the engine has an overhead camshaft (OHC), it is usually relatively easy to remove the cam cover and make a visual inspection of all cam lobes and the rest of the valve train. See Figure 15–3. In an overhead valve (OHV) engine, the camshaft is in the block, where easy visual inspection is not possible. See Figure 15–4 and the Tech Tip, "The Rotating Pushrod Test."

TECH TIP

The Rotating Pushrod Test

To quickly and easily test whether the camshaft is okay, observe if the pushrods are rotating when the engine is running. This test will work on any overhead valve pushrod engine that uses a flat-bottom lifter. Due to the slight angle on the cam lobe and lifter offset, the lifter (and pushrod) should rotate whenever the engine is running. To check, simply remove the rocker arm cover and observe the pushrods when the engine is running. If one or more pushrods is *not* rotating, this camshaft and/or the lifter for that particular valve is worn and needs to be replaced.

TECH TIP

The Tube Trick

Valve lifters are often difficult to remove because the ends of the lifters become mushroomed (enlarged) where they have contacted the camshaft. Varnish buildup can also prevent the lifters from being removed. Try this method:

Step 1 Raise the lifters upward as far away from the camshaft as possible.

Step 2 Slide in a thin plastic or cardboard tube with slots in place of the camshaft. See Figure 15–5.

Step 3 Push the lifters downward into the tube. Use a long magnet to retrieve the lifters from the end of the tube.

This trick will work on almost every engine that has the camshaft in the block. If the tube is made from plastic, it has to be thin plastic to allow it to flex slightly. The length of the lifters is greater than the diameter of the cam bearings. Therefore, the lifter has to be pushed downward into the tube slightly to allow the lifter room to fall over into the tube.

TECH TIP

Hot Lifter in 10 Minutes?

A technician working in a new-vehicle dealership discovered a noisy (defective) valve lifter on a Chevrolet small-block V-8. Another technician questioned how long it would take to replace the lifter and was told, "Less than an hour"! (The factory flat rate was much longer than one hour.) Ten minutes later the repair technician handed the questioning technician a hot lifter that had been removed from the engine. The lifter was removed by the following steps:

1. The rocker cover was removed.
2. The rocker arm and pushrod for the affected valve were removed.
3. The distributor was removed.
4. A strong magnet was fed through the distributor opening into the valley area of the engine. (If the valve lifter is not mushroomed or does not have varnish deposits, the defective lifter can be lifted up and out of the engine; remember, the technician was working on a new vehicle.)
5. A replacement lifter was attached to the magnet and fed down the distributor hole and over the lifter bore.
6. The pushrod was used to help guide the lifter into the lifter bore.

After the lifter preload was adjusted and the rocker cover was replaced, the vehicle was returned to the customer in less than one hour.

■ CAMSHAFT REMOVAL

If the engine is of an overhead valve design, the camshaft is usually located in the block above the crankshaft. The timing chain and gears (if the vehicle is so equipped) should be removed after the timing chain (gear) cover is removed. Loosen the rocker arms (or rocker arm shaft) and remove the pushrods.

> **NOTE:** Be sure to keep the pushrods and rocker arms together if they are to be reused.

Remove or lift up the lifters before carefully removing the camshaft. See the Tech Tip, "The Tube Trick."

■ CAMSHAFT DESIGN

The camshaft is a one-piece casting with lobes, bearing journals, drive flanges, and accessory gear blanks. The accessory drive gear is finished with a gear cutter. The lobes and journals are ground to the proper shape. The remaining portion of the camshaft surface is not machined. See Figure 15–6.

Figure 15–5 Instead of prying old lifters up and out of the engine block, use a plastic (or cardboard) tube in place of the camshaft and push the lifters down. Then use a magnet to pull the old lifters out of the tube.

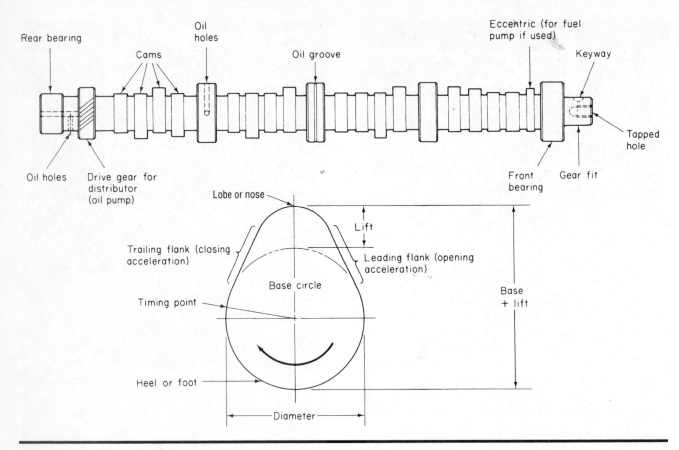

Figure 15-6 Cam and camshaft terms (nomenclature).

On pushrod engines, camshaft bearing journals must be larger than the cam lobe so that the camshaft can be installed in the engine through the cam bearings. Some overhead cam engines have bearing caps on the cam bearings. These cams can have large cam lobes with small bearing journals. Cam bearings on some engines are progressively smaller from the front journal to the rear. Other engines use the same size of camshaft bearing on all the journals.

Most automotive camshafts used with flat or convex-faced lifters are made from hardened alloy cast iron. It resists wear and provides the required strength. The very hardness of the camshaft causes it to be susceptible to chipping as the result of edge loading or careless handling.

Cast-iron camshafts have about the same hardness throughout. If reground, they should be recoated with a phosphate coating.

Steel camshafts are usually SAE 4160 or 4180 steel and are usually induction hardened. Induction hardening involves heating the camshaft to cherry red in an electric field (heating occurs by electrical induction). The heated camshaft is then dropped into oil. The rapid cooling hardens the surface. Camshafts can also be hardened by using the following:

- **Liquid nitriding**—hardens to 0.001 to 0.0015 inch of thickness
- **Gas nitriding**—hardens to 0.004 to 0.006 inch of thickness

Typical camshaft hardness should be 42 to 60 on the Rockwell "c" scale.

> **NOTE:** Rockwell is a type of hardness test, and the *c* represents the scale used. The higher the number, the harder the surface. The abbreviation *Rc60*, therefore, indicates Rockwell hardness of 60 as measured on the c scale.

If this outer hardness wears off, the lobes of the camshaft are easily worn until they are almost completely rounded, as shown in Figures 15–7 and 15–8.

■ COMPOSITE CAMSHAFTS

A composite camshaft uses a lightweight tubular shaft with hardened steel lobes press-fitted over the shaft. See Figure 15–9.

Figure 15–7 Worn camshaft with two lobes worn to the point of being almost round.

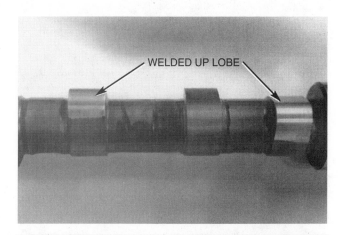

Figure 15–8 Worn camshaft that has been restored by welding the lobes and regrinding the original contour.

Figure 15–9 A composite camshaft is lighter in weight than a conventional camshaft made from cast iron.

The actual production of these camshafts involves placing the lobes over the tube shaft in the correct position. Then a steel ball is drawn through the hollow steel tube, expanding the tube and securely locking the cam lobes in position.

Figure 15–10 Hole through a camshaft bearing journal. The hole meters oil to a rocker shaft when it lines up with oil passages in the cam bearings.

■ CAMSHAFT LUBRICATION

Some engines transfer lubrication oil from the main oil gallery to the crankshaft around the camshaft journal or around the outside of the camshaft bearing. Cam bearing clearance is critical in these engines. If the clearance is too great, oil will leak out and the crankshaft bearings will not get enough oil. Other engines use drilled holes in the camshaft bearing journals to meter lubricating oil to the overhead rocker arm. Oil goes to the rocker arm each time the holes line up between the bearing oil gallery passage and the outlet passage to the rocker arm. Camshaft oil metering holes are shown in Figures 15–10 and 15–11.

■ FUEL-PUMP ECCENTRICS

An eccentric cam lobe for the fuel pump is often cast as part of the camshaft. The fuel pump is operated by this eccentric with a long pump arm or pushrod. Some engines use a steel cup type of eccentric that is bolted to the front of the cam drive gear. This allows a damaged fuel-pump eccentric to be replaced without replacing an entire camshaft. Typical fuel-pump eccentrics are identified on a number of camshafts pictured in Figure 15–12.

Figure 15–11 Damaged camshaft bearing support. This overhead camshaft engine overheated because of an electric cooling fan circuit failure. The cylinder head warped upward in the center, causing a binding of the camshaft in the bearing.

TECH TIP

Check the Camshaft and Then the Fuel Pump

Many mechanical fuel pumps operate off of a separate lobe on the camshaft. If this fuel-pump lobe becomes worn, the stroke of the fuel pump is reduced and the amount of fuel being supplied to the engine is reduced. The engine may experience a lack of power or cut out and miss under load. The problem can also be intermittent, depending on other factors. A worn fuel-pump cam lobe is often found on Ford 240- and 300-cubic-inch in-line six-cylinder engines. Some Ford Escort engines experience a worn fuel-pump *pushrod* and behave similarly to an engine with a worn fuel-pump cam lobe.

If a worn fuel-pump cam lobe is suspected, perform a fuel-pump capacity (volume) test. If the pump does not pump at least 1/2 pint in 15 seconds (1 pint in 30 seconds), then remove the pump and inspect for excessive cam lobe wear or fuel-pump pushrod wear before replacing the fuel pump.

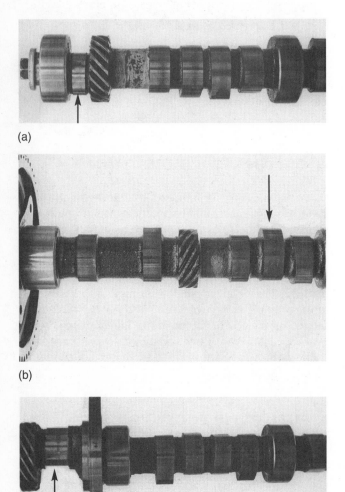

(a)

(b)

(c)

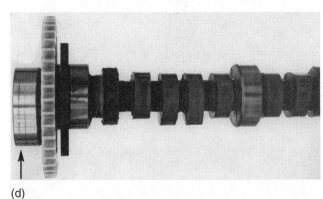

(d)

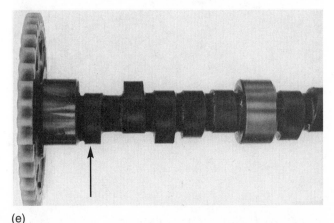

(e)

Figure 15–12 Typical fuel-pump eccentric locations on camshafts used in pushrod engines.

■ CAMSHAFT DRIVES

The camshaft is driven by the crankshaft through gears, sprockets and chains, or sprockets and timing belts. Timing chains are not as wide as timing belts, so engines with timing chains can be shorter. Timing chains often have tensioners (dampers) pressing on the unloaded side of the chain. The tensioner pad is a Nylatron molding that is filled with molybdenum disulfide to give it low friction. The tensioner is held against the chain by either a spring or hydraulic oil pressure (Figure 15–13). The gears or sprockets are keyed to their shafts so that they can be installed in only one position. The gears and sprockets are then indexed together by marks on the gear teeth or chain links. When the crankshaft and camshaft timing marks are properly lined up, the cam lobes are indexed to the crankshaft throws of each cylinder so that the valves will open and close correctly in relation to the piston position.

■ CAMSHAFT CHAIN DRIVES

The crankshaft gear or sprocket that drives the camshaft is usually made of sintered iron. When gears are used on the camshaft, the teeth must be made from a soft material to reduce noise. Usually, the whole gear is made of aluminum or fiber. When a chain and sprocket are used, the camshaft sprocket may be made of iron or it may have an aluminum hub with nylon teeth for noise reduction. Two types of timing chains are used.

1. **Silent chain type** (also known as a **flat-link type,** or **Morse type** for its original manufacturer). This type operates quietly but tends to stretch with use. See Figures 15–14 through 15–18 on pages 338–339.

> **NOTE:** When the timing chain stretches, the valve timing will be retarded and the engine will lack low-speed power. In some instances, the chain can wear through the timing chain cover and create an oil leak. See Chapter 8 for on-the-vehicle timing chain stretch diagnosis.

2. **Roller chain type.** This type is noisier but operates with less friction and stretches less than the silent type of chain. See Figure 15–19 on page 339.

Some four-cam engines use a two-stage camshaft drive system:

• Primary: From crankshaft to camshaft

• Secondary: From one camshaft to another

See Figure 15–20 on page 340.

■ CAMSHAFT BELT DRIVES

Many overhead camshaft engines use a timing belt rather than a chain. The belt is generally considered to be quieter, but it requires periodic replacement, usually every 60,000 miles (100,000 kilometers). Unless the engine is **free wheeling,** the piston can hit the valves if the belt breaks. See Figures 15–21 through 15–23 on pages 340–341.

■ CAMSHAFT TWISTING MOVEMENT

As the camshaft lobe pushes the lifter upward against the valve spring force, a backward twisting force is developed on the camshaft. After the lobe goes past its high point, the lifter moves down the backside of the lobe. This makes a forward twisting force (Figure 15–24 on page 341). This action produces an alternating torsion force forward, then backward, at each cam lobe. This alternating torsion force is multiplied by the number of cam lobes on the shaft. The camshaft must have sufficient strength to minimize torsion twist. It must also be tough enough to minimize fatigue from the alternating torsion forces.

■ CAM CHUCKING

Cam chucking is the movement of the camshaft *lengthwise in the engine during operation.* Each camshaft must have some means to control the shaft end thrust. Two methods are in common usage. One method is to use a **thrust plate** between the camshaft drive gear or sprocket and a flange on the camshaft (Figures 15–25 and 15–26 on page 342). This thrust plate is attached to the engine block with cap screws. In a few camshafts, a button, spring, or retainer that contacts the timing cover limits forward motion of the camshaft. See Figure 15–27 on page 342.

■ LIFTER ROTATION

Most valve trains use a spherical (curved) lifter face that slides against the cam lobe. This produces a surface on the lifter face that is slightly convex, by about 0.002 inch. The lifter also contacts the lobe at a point that is slightly off center. This produces a small turning force on the lifter to cause some lifter rotation for even wear. In operation, there is a wide line of contact between the lifter and the high point of the cam lobe. These are the highest loads that are produced in an engine. The lifter contact on the top of the cam lobe can be seen in Figures 15–28 and 15–29 on pages 342–343. This surface is the most critical lubrication point in an engine.

TENSIONER HELD
WITH A SPRING

(a)

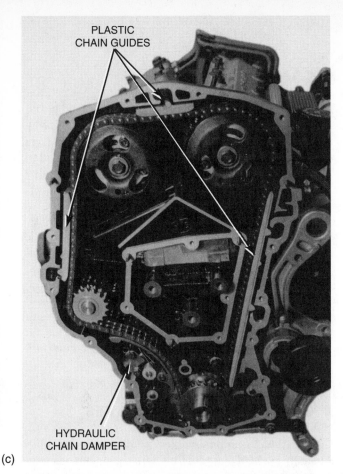

PLASTIC
CHAIN GUIDES

HYDRAULIC
CHAIN DAMPER

(c)

TENSIONER HELD WITH
OIL PRESSURE

(b)

Figure 15–13 (a) A spring-loaded timing chain tensioner (also called a damper). (b) Most overhead camshaft engines use an hydraulic tensioner. (c) Hydraulic tensioners use engine oil pressure to keep tension on the chain. A ratchet mechanism in the tensioner maintains some tension on the chain when the engine is shut off and oil pressure is zero. This design helps reduce noise when the engine starts and before oil pressure is again applied to the tensioner.

Figure 15–14 Two types of sprockets that can be used on the same engine. A cast-iron sprocket is on the left, and an aluminum nylon sprocket is on the right.

Figure 15–15 Close-up view of two types of timing chains. A silent chain is on the left, and a roller chain is on the right.

Figure 15–16 Excessively worn timing gear and chain.

Figure 15–18 Excessively worn timing chain guide. The metal guide finally broke into two pieces, making a lot of noise.

Figure 15–19 Various styles of timing chains. The three chains on the left represent different styles of silent or flat-link chain. The roller chain on the right is much longer because it drives two overhead camshafts. Sound tests have determined that a silent (flat-link or Morse style) chain is as much as 8 decibels quieter than a roller chain on the same engine.

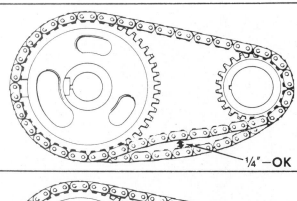

1/4"—OK

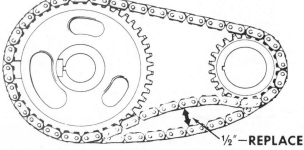

1/2"—REPLACE

Figure 15–17 The industry standard for when to replace a timing chain and gears is when 1/2 inch (13 millimeters) or more of slack is measured in the chain. However, it is best to replace the timing chain and gear anytime the camshaft is replaced or the engine is disassembled for repair or overhaul. (*Courtesy of Sealed Power Corporation*)

Roller Lifter Cam Wear

After any engine equipped with roller lifters is run for a short time, it will wear a path on the camshaft. The path traveled by the roller over the cam causes the area to have a mirrorlike appearance. The area on both sides of this shiny path retains the dull finish of the original camshaft.

This wear pattern is often mistakenly assumed to be abnormal, and as a result, the camshaft and lifters are sometimes needlessly replaced. To avoid replacing good parts or not replacing worn parts, always carefully measure all engine parts.

Figure 15–21 Notice the teeth missing from this timing belt. This belt broke at 88,000 miles because the owner failed to replace it at the recommended interval of 60,000 miles.

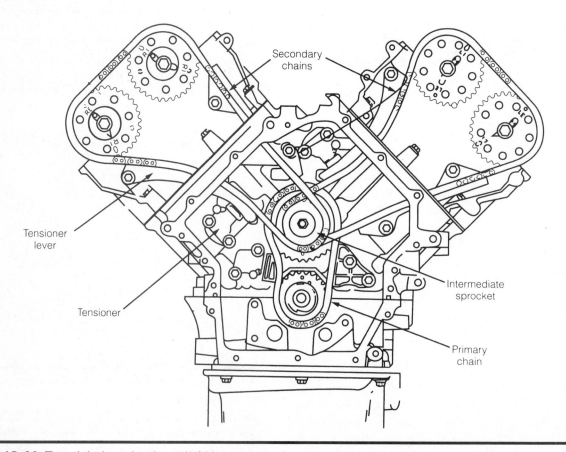

Figure 15–20 Typical dual overhead camshaft V-type engine that uses one primary timing chain and two secondary chains.

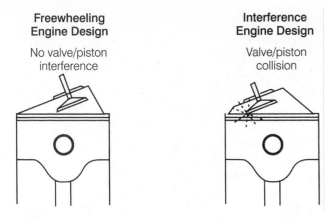

(a)

Figure 15–22 Many engines are of the interference design. If the timing belt (or chain) breaks, the piston still moves up and down in the cylinder while the valves remain stationary. With a freewheeling design, nothing is damaged, but in an interference engine, the valves are often bent.

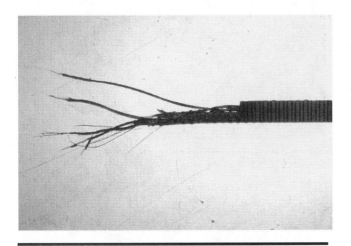

(b)

Figure 15–23 This timing belt broke because an oil leak from one of the camshaft seals caused oil to get into and weaken the belt. Most experts recommend replacing all engine seals in the front of the engine anytime a timing belt is replaced. If the timing belt travels over the water pump, the water pump should also be replaced as a precaution.

■ CAMSHAFT LIFT

The **lift** of the cam is usually expressed in decimal inches and represents the distance that the valve is lifted off the valve seat. The higher the lift, the more air and fuel that can theoretically enter the engine. The more air and fuel burned in an engine, the greater the power potential of the engine. The amount of lift of a camshaft is often different for the intake and exhaust valves. If the specifications vary, the camshaft is called

(c)

Figure 15–24 Lifter contact on the cam lobe. (a) The cam lobe is beginning to lift the lifter. (b) The lifter is fully raised. (c) The lifter is lowering.

Figure 15–25 Thrust plate controlling the camshaft end thrust on an overhead camshaft engine.

Figure 15–26 Typical thrust plate between the cam gear and a flange on the camshaft. Note the hole in the fiber composition gear to provide access to the thrust plate bolts.

Figure 15–27 Some engines use a spring-loaded button to help control cam chucking ("walking").

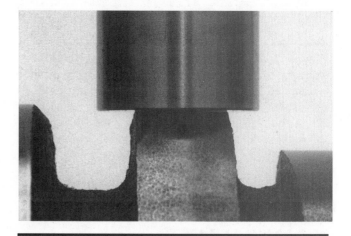

Figure 15–28 Typical lifter contact on the top of the cam lobe.

asymmetrical. If the lift is the same, the cam is called **symmetrical.** However, when the amount of lift increases, so do the forces on the camshaft and the rest of the valve train. Generally, a camshaft with a lift of over 0.500 inch (1.3 centimeters) is unsuitable for street operation except for use in engines that are over 400 cubic inches (6.0 liters).

The lift specifications at the valve face assume the use of the stock rocker arm ratio. If nonstock rocker arms with a higher ratio are installed (for example, 1.6:1 rockers replacing the stock 1.5:1 rocker arms), the lift at the valve is increased. Also, because the rocker arm rotation covers a greater distance at the pivot of the rocker arm, the rocker arm can hit the edge of the valve retainer.

■ ROCKER ARMS

A rocker arm reverses the upward movement of the pushrod to produce a downward movement on the tip of the valve. Engine designers make good use of the rocker

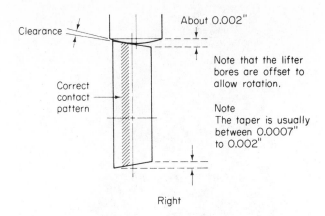

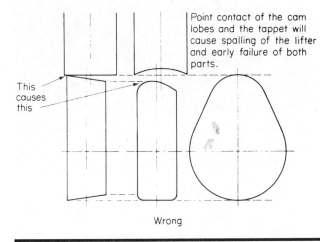

Most late model automotive cams are tapered to provide lifter rotation. The lifters have a spherical grind so that they do not ride on the edge of the cam lobe.
This contact spreads the load of the valve train against more of the lobe face.

Figure 15–29 New lifters should always be used with a new camshaft. If worn lifters are used on a new camshaft, edge wear on the cam lobes will quickly wear the camshaft. *(Courtesy of Sealed Power Corporation)*

arm. It is designed to reduce the travel of the cam follower or lifter and pushrod while maintaining the required valve lift. This is done by using a rocker arm ratio of approximately 1.5:1, as shown in Figure 15–30. For a given amount of lift on the pushrod, the valve will open to 1.5 times the pushrod lift distance. This ratio allows the camshaft to be small, so the engine can be smaller. It also results in lower lobe-to-lifter rubbing speeds.

> **CAUTION:** Using rocker arms with a higher ratio than stock can also cause the valve spring to compress too much and actually bind. Valve spring bind **(coil bind)** occurs when the valve spring is compressed to the point where there is no clearance in the spring. (It is completely compressed.) When coil bind occurs in a running engine, bent pushrods, broken rocker arms, or other valve train damage can result.

Rocker arms may be cast, forged, or stamped. Forged rocker arms are the strongest, but they require expensive manufacturing operations. Rocker arms may have bushings or bearings installed to reduce friction and increase durability. Cast rocker arms cost less to make and do not usually use bushings, but they do require several machining operations. They are not as strong as forged rocker arms but are satisfactory for

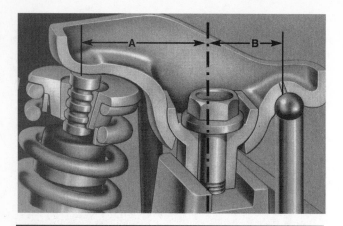

Figure 15–30 A 1.5:1 ratio rocker arm means that dimension A is 1.5 times the length of B. Therefore, if the pushrod is moved up 0.400 inch by the camshaft lobe, the valve will be pushed down (opened) 0.400 inch × 1.5, or 0.600 inch.

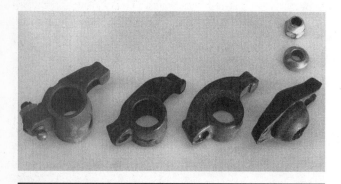

Figure 15–31 Typical cast rocker arm types.

Figure 15–32 Typical stamped rocker arm types.

passenger vehicle service. Typical cast rocker arms are shown in Figure 15–31.

Stamped rocker arms (Figure 15–32) are the least expensive type to manufacture. They are lightweight and very strong. Two general types are in use:

1. Those that operate on a ball or cylindrical pivot
2. Those that operate on a shaft

Figure 15–33 Overhead cam operating directly on top of the bucket-type cam follower.

The ball and cylindrical pivot types are lubricated through hollow pushrods. The shaft type is lubricated through oil passages that travel from the block, through the head and into the shaft, and then to the rocker arms.

Overhead camshaft engines use several methods for opening the valves:

1. One type opens the valves directly with a **cam follower** or **bucket** (Figure 15–33).
2. The second type uses a **finger follower** that provides an opening ratio similar to that of a rocker arm (Figures 15–34 through 15–36). Finger followers open the valves by approximately 1 1/2 times the cam lift. The pivot point of the finger follower may have a mechanical adjustment or it may have an automatic hydraulic adjustment.
3. A third type moves the rocker arm directly through a hydraulic lifter (Figure 15–37).
4. Some newer engines have the hydraulic adjustment in the rocker arm and are commonly called **hydraulic lash adjusters** (**HLA**). See Figure 15–38 on page 346.

All engines have some method for keeping the rocker arm correctly positioned over the valve tip. Rocker arms are held in position on rocker shafts with

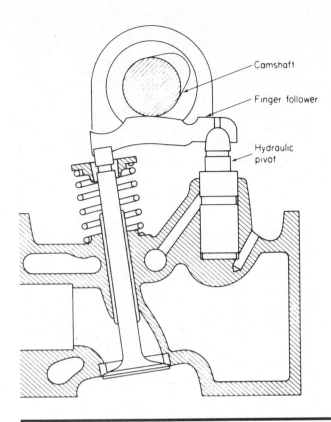

Figure 15-34 Overhead cam operating on a finger follower. A hydraulic pivot is on the right end of the finger follower. The finger follower operates the valve on the left.

Figure 15-35 Roller-type rocker arm (finger follower) used with an overhead cam.

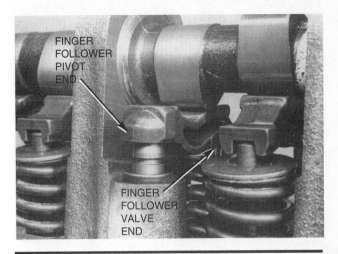

Figure 15-36 Finger follower held in place over the valve tip with a slot.

Figure 15-37 The overhead cam operates the rocker arm through a hydraulic lifter.

■ PUSHRODS

Pushrods are designed to be as light as possible and still maintain their strength. They may be either solid or hollow. If they are to be used as passages for oil to lubricate rocker arms, they *must* be hollow. Pushrods use a convex ball on the lower end that seats in the lifter. The rocker arm end is also a convex ball, unless there is an adjustment screw in the pushrod end of the rocker arm. In this case, the rocker arm end of the pushrod has a concave socket. It mates with the convex ball on the adjustment

springs and spacers. This can be seen in Figure 15-39. The rocker shaft keeps the rocker arms from twisting. Cylindrical pivots hold the rocker arm in position and keep it from twisting.

TECH TIP

Rocker Arm Shafts Can Cause Sticking Valves

As oil oxidizes, it forms a varnish. Varnish buildup is particularly common on hot upper portions of the engine, such as rocker arm shafts. The varnish restricts clean oil from getting into and lubricating the rocker arms. The cam lobe can easily *force* the valves open, but the valve springs often do not exert enough force to fully close the valves. The result is an engine miss, which may be intermittent. Worn valve guides and/or weak valve springs can also cause occasional rough idle, uneven running, or missing.

TECH TIP

Hollow Pushrod Dirt

Many engine rebuilders and remanufacturers do not reuse old hollow pushrods. Dirt, carbon, and other debris are difficult to thoroughly clean from inside a hollow pushrod. When an engine is run with used pushrods, the trapped particles can be dislodged and ruin new bearings and other new engine parts.

Figure 15-40 Types of pushrod ends.

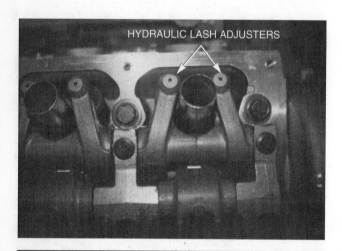

Figure 15-38 These hydraulic lash adjusters (HLA) are found on DaimlerChrysler 3.2 and 3.5 L, V-6 engines.

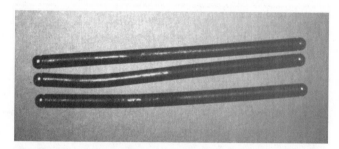

Figure 15-41 It was easy to see that these pushrods needed to be replaced because they became bent when the timing chain broke.

screw in the rocker arm. Pushrod end types are shown in Figure 15-40. All pushrods should be rolled on a flat surface to check for straightness. See Figure 15-41.

■ PUSHROD LENGTH

The tolerance in the valve train allows for some machining of engine parts without the need to change pushrod length. However, if one or more of the following changes have been made to an engine, a different pushrod length may be necessary:

Figure 15-39 The rocker arms are held in position by the spring and the rocker shaft on this high performance engine.

- Block deck height machined
- Cylinder head deck height machined
- Camshaft base circle size reduced

Figure 15–42 Stamped plate held in place under the rocker pivot stud.

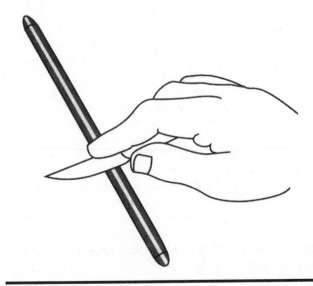

Figure 15–43 Hardened pushrods should be used in any engine that uses pushrod guides (plates). To determine if the pushrod is hardened, simply try to scratch the side of the pushrod with a pocketknife.

- Valve length increased
- Lifter design changed

■ CAMSHAFT DURATION

Camshaft duration is the number of degrees of crankshaft rotation for which the valve is lifted off the seat. The specifications for duration can be different for the intake valves and the exhaust valves. If the durations of the intake and exhaust valves are different from each other, the cam is called asymmetrical. The specification for duration can be expressed by several different methods, which must be considered when comparing one cam with another. The three most commonly used methods are as follows:

1. *Duration of valve opening at zero lash (clearance).* If a hydraulic lifter is used, the lash is zero. If a solid lifter is used, this method of expression refers to the duration of the opening of the valve after the specified clearance (lash) has been closed.
2. *Duration at 0.050-inch lifter (tappet) lift.* Because this specification method eliminates all valve lash clearances and compensates for lifter (tappet) styles, it is the preferred method to use when comparing one camshaft with another. Another method used to specify duration of some factory camshafts is to specify crankshaft duration at 0.010-inch lifter lift. The important point to remember is that the technician must be sure to use equivalent specification methods when comparing or selecting camshafts.

> **NOTE:** Fractions of a degree are commonly expressed in units called minutes (′). **Sixty minutes equal one degree.** For example, 45′ = 3/4°, 30′ = 1/2°, and 15′ = 1/4°.

3. **SAE camshaft specifications.** The valve timing and valve overlap are expressed in the number of degrees of crankshaft rotation for which the valves are off their seats. SAE's recommended practice is to measure all valve events at 0.006-inch (0.15-millimeter) valve lift. This method differs from the usual method used by vehicle or camshaft manufacturers. Whenever comparing valve timing events, be certain that the exact same methods are used on all camshafts being compared.

■ VALVE OVERLAP

Another camshaft specification is the number of degrees of overlap. **Camshaft overlap** is the number of

Figure 15–44 Graphic representation of a typical camshaft showing the relationship between the intake and exhaust valves.

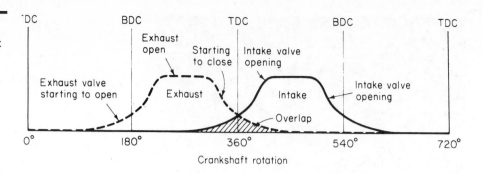

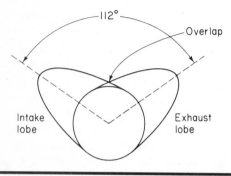

Figure 15–45 As the lobe center angle decreases, the overlap increases, with no other changes in the lobe profile lift and duration.

degrees of crankshaft rotation between the exhaust and intake strokes for which both valves are off their seats.

- A lower amount of overlap results in smoother idle and low-engine speed operation, but it also means that a lower amount of power is available at higher engine speeds.
- A greater valve overlap causes rougher engine idle, with decreased power at low speeds, but it means that high-speed power is improved.

For example: A camshaft with 50 degrees (or less) of overlap may be used in an engine in which low-speed torque and smooth idle qualities are desired. Engines used with overdrive automatic transmissions benefit from the low-speed torque and fuel economy benefits of a small-overlap cam. A camshaft with 100 degrees of overlap is more suitable for use with a manual transmission, with which high-RPM power is desired. An engine equipped with a camshaft with over 100 degrees of overlap tends to idle roughly and exhibit poorer low-engine speed response and lowered fuel economy. See Figure 15–44.

The valve overlap is the number of degrees for which both valves are open near TDC. In the previous example, the intake valve starts to open at 19 degrees. The exhaust valve is also open during this upward movement of the piston on the exhaust stroke. The exhaust valve is open until 22 degrees ATDC.

To determine overlap, total the number of degrees for which the intake valve is open BTDC (19 degrees) and the number of degrees for which the exhaust valve is open ATDC (22 degrees):

$$\text{Valve overlap} = 19° + 22° = 41°$$

■ LOBE CENTERS

Another camshaft specification that creates some confusion is the angle of the centerlines of the intake and exhaust lobes. This separation between the centerlines of the intake and exhaust lobes is called **lobe separation** or **lobe spread** and is measured in degrees. See Figure 15–45.

Two camshafts with identical lift and duration can vary greatly in operation because of variation in the angle between the lobe centerlines.

1. The smaller the angle between the lobe centerlines, the greater the amount of overlap. For example, 108 degrees is a narrower lobe center angle.
2. The larger the angle between the lobe centerlines, the less the amount of overlap. For example, 114 degrees is a wider lobe center angle.

NOTE: Some engines that are equipped with dual overhead camshafts and four valves per cylinder use a different camshaft profile for each of the intake and exhaust valves. For example, one intake valve for each cylinder could have a cam profile designed for maximum low-speed torque. The other intake valve for each cylinder could be designed for higher-engine speed power. This results in an engine that is able to produce a high torque over a broad engine speed range.

■ HOW TO DETERMINE LOBE CENTER ANGLE

To find the degree of separation between intake and exhaust lobes of a cam, use the following formula:

(Intake duration + Exhaust duration)/4 – Overlap/2 = Number of degrees of separation

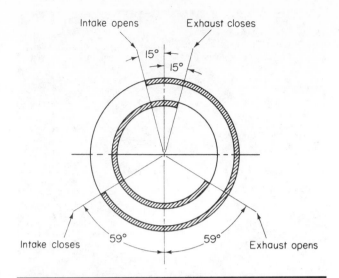

Figure 15–46 Typical cam timing diagram.

See Figure 15–46 for a typical camshaft valve timing diagram.

The lobe separation angle can be determined by transferring the intake and exhaust duration and overlap into the formula as follows:

Intake duration $= 15° + 59° + 180° = 254°$
Exhaust duration $= 59° + 15° + 180° = 254°$
Overlap $= 15° + 15° = 30°$

$$\left(\frac{254 + 254}{4}\right) - \frac{30°}{2} = \frac{504}{4} - \frac{30°}{2} = 127° - 15° = 112°$$

■ CAM TIMING SPECIFICATIONS

Cam timing specifications are stated in terms of the angle of the crankshaft in relation to top dead center (TDC) or bottom dead center (BDC) when the valves open and close.

■ INTAKE VALVE

The intake valves should open slightly before the piston reaches TDC and starts down on the intake stroke. This ensures that the valve is fully open when the piston travels downward on the intake stroke. The flow through a partially open valve (especially a valve ground at 45 degrees instead of 30 degrees) is greatly reduced as compared with that when the valve is in its fully open position. The intake valve closes after the piston reaches BDC because the air-fuel mixture has inertia, or the tendency of matter to remain in motion. Even after the piston stops traveling downward on the intake stroke and starts upward on the compression stroke, the inertia of the air-fuel mixture can still be used to draw in additional charge.

Typical intake valve specifications are to open at 19 degrees BTDC and close at 46 degrees after bottom dead center (ABDC).

■ EXHAUST VALVE

The exhaust valve opens while the piston is traveling down on the power stroke, before the piston starts up on the exhaust stroke. Opening the exhaust valve before the piston starts up on the exhaust stroke ensures that the combustion pressure is released and the exhaust valve is mostly open when the piston does start up. The exhaust valve does not close until after the piston has traveled past TDC and is starting down on the intake stroke. Because of inertia of the exhaust, some of the burned gases continue to flow out the exhaust valve after the piston is past TDC. This can leave a partial vacuum in the combustion chamber to start pulling in the fresh charge.

Typical exhaust valve specifications are to open at 49 degrees before bottom dead center (BBDC) and close at 22 degrees after top dead center (ATDC).

■ CAM TIMING CHART

During the four strokes of a four-stroke-cycle gasoline engine, the crankshaft revolves 720 degrees [it makes two complete revolutions ($2 \times 360° = 720°$)]. Camshaft specifications are given in crankshaft degrees. In the example in Figure 15–47, the intake valve starts to open at 39 degrees BTDC, remains open through the entire 180 degrees of the intake stroke, and does not close until 71 degrees ATDC. Therefore, the duration of the intake valve is 39 degrees + 180 degrees + 71 degrees, or 290 degrees.

The exhaust valve of the example camshaft opens at 78 degrees BBDC and closes at 47 degrees ATDC. When the exhaust valve specifications are added to the intake valve specifications in the diagram, the overlap period is easily observed. The overlap in the example is 39 degrees + 47 degrees, or 86 degrees. The duration of the exhaust valve opening is 78 degrees + 180 degrees + 47 degrees, or 305 degrees. Because the specifications of this camshaft indicate close to and over 300 degrees of duration, this camshaft should only be used where power is more important than fuel economy.

The usual method of drawing a camshaft timing diagram is in a circle illustrating two revolutions (720 degrees) of the crankshaft. See Figure 15–48 for an example of a typical camshaft timing diagram for a camshaft with the same specifications as the one illustrated in Figure 15–47.

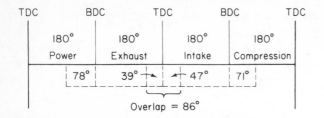

Figure 15–47 Typical high performance camshaft specifications on a straight-line graph. Intake valve duration = 39° + 180° + 71° = 290°. Exhaust valve duration = 78° + 180° + 47° = 305°. Because intake and exhaust valve specifications are different, the camshaft grind is called asymmetrical.

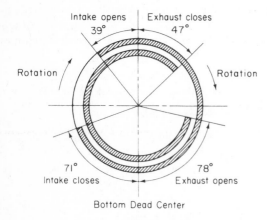

This valve timing diagram shows two revolutions (720°) of the crankshaft

Figure 15–48 Typical camshaft valve timing diagram with the same specifications as those shown in Figure 15–47.

■ MEASURING AND REGRINDING CAMSHAFTS

All camshafts should be checked for straightness by placing them on a V block and measuring the cam bearings for runout by using a dial indicator. The maximum **total indicator runout** (**TIR**) should be less than 0.002 inch (0.05 millimeter). See Figure 15–49.

Worn camshafts can be restored to original lift and duration by one of two methods:

1. If the camshaft is not excessively worn (less than 0.030 inch), the lobes can be reground by decreasing the diameter of the base circle, restoring the original lift and duration. See Figures 15–50 and 15–51.
2. If the cam lobe wear is excessive, the lobes can be welded and reground back to their original specifications.

NOTE: According to major engine remanufacturers, only about 35% of camshafts can be reground. Therefore, about two-thirds of the camshafts received in engine cores are excessively worn and must be replaced.

Figure 15–49 A cam shaft being checked for total indicator runout as it is being rotated on V blocks using a dial indicator.

■ INSTALLING THE CAMSHAFT

When the camshaft is installed, the lobes must be coated with a special lubricant that contains molydisulfide. This special lube helps to ensure proper initial lubrication to the critical cam lobe sections of the camshaft. Many manufacturers recommend multiviscosity engine oil such as SAE 5W-30 or SAE 10W-30. Some camshaft manufacturers recommend using straight SAE 30 or SAE 40 engine oil and not a multiviscosity oil for the first oil fill. Some manufacturers also recommend the use of an antiwear additive such as **zinc dithiophosphate** (**ZDP**). See Figure 15–52.

NOTE: Most camshafts are coated at the factory with a polycrystalline-structure chemical treatment. This coating is typically manganese phosphate and gives the camshaft a dull black appearance. The purpose of this treatment is to absorb and hold oil to help ensure lubrication during the break-in period. Under a microscope, this surface treatment looks like the surface of a golf ball.

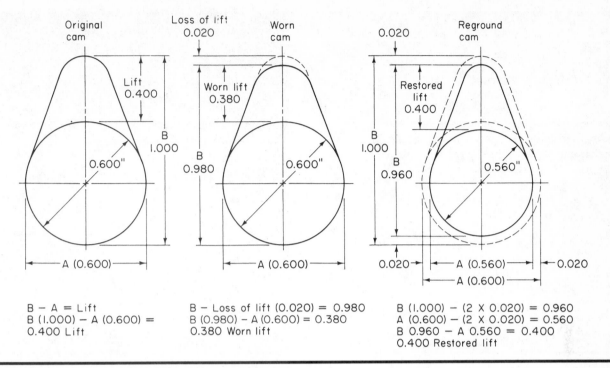

Original
cam

Lift
0.400

B
1.000

0.600"

A (0.600)

B − A = Lift
B (1.000) − A (0.600) =
0.400 Lift

Loss of lift
0.020

Worn
cam

Worn lift
0.380

B
0.980

0.600"

A (0.600)

B − Loss of lift (0.020) = 0.980
B (0.980) − A (0.600) = 0.380
0.380 Worn lift

0.020

Reground
cam

Restored
lift
0.400

B
1.000

B
0.960

0.560"

0.020 → A (0.560) ← 0.020
A (0.600)

B (1.000) − (2 X 0.020) = 0.960
A (0.600) − (2 X 0.020) = 0.560
B 0.960 − A 0.560 = 0.400
0.400 Restored lift

Figure 15–50 A worn camshaft lobe can be restored to its original lift by grinding the base circle smaller.

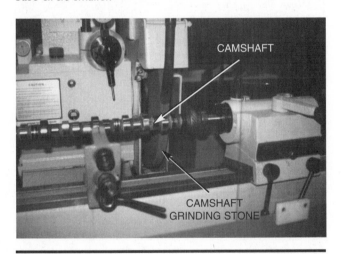

CAMSHAFT

CAMSHAFT
GRINDING STONE

Figure 15–51 A camshaft being ground on a camshaft grinding machine.

The camshaft must be broken in by maintaining engine speed above 1500 RPM for the first 10 minutes of engine operation. If the engine speed is decreased to idle (about 600 RPM), the lifter (tappet) will be in contact with and exerting force *on* the lobe of the cam for a longer period of time than occurs at higher engine speeds. The pressure and volume of oil supplied to the camshaft area are also increased at the higher engine speeds. Therefore, to ensure long camshaft and lifter life, make certain that the engine will start quickly after reassembly to prevent long cranking periods and subsequent low engine speeds after a new camshaft and lifters have been installed. Whenever repairing an engine, follow these rules regarding camshaft and lifters:

Figure 15–52 Special lubricant such as this one from General Motors is required to be used on the lobes of the camshaft and the bottom of the flat-bottomed lifters.

TECH TIP

TOO BIG = TOO BAD

A common mistake of beginning engine builders is to install a camshaft with too much duration for the size of the engine. This extended duration of valve opening results in a rough idle and low manifold vacuum, which causes carburetor metering problems and lack of low-speed power.

For example, a hydraulic cam with a duration greater than 225 degrees at 0.050-inch lift for a 350-cubic-inch engine will usually not be suitable for street driving. **Seat duration** is the number of degrees of crankshaft rotation that the valve is off the seat.

Common usage	Seat duration	Lift	Duration at 0.050 inch	Characteristics
Street	246°–254°	0.400	192°–199°	Smooth idle, power idle to 4500 RPM
Street	262°	0.432	207°	Broad power range, smooth idle, power idle to 4800 RPM
Street	266°	0.441	211°	Good idle for 350-cubic-inch engines, power idle to 5200 RPM
Street/drag strip	272°	0.454	217°	Lope idle, power idle to 5500 RPM
Street/race track	290°	0.500	239°	Shaky idle, power idle to 5500–6500 RPM

1. When installing a new camshaft, always install new valve lifters (tappets).
2. When installing new lifters, if the original cam is not excessively worn and if the pushrods all rotate with the original camshaft, the camshaft may be reused.

NOTE: Some manufacturers recommend that a new camshaft always be installed when replacing valve lifters.

3. *Never* use a hydraulic camshaft with solid lifters or hydraulic lifters with a solid lifter camshaft.
4. New lifters will be more compatible if the bottom part of the lifter that contacts the cam is polished with #600 grit sandpaper.

NOTE: Many molydisulfide greases can start to clog oil filters within 20 minutes after starting the engine. Most engine rebuilders recommend changing the oil and filter after 1/2 hour of running time.

■ DEGREEING THE CAMSHAFT

The purpose of degreeing the camshaft in the engine is to locate the valve action exactly as the camshaft manufacturers intended. The method most often recommended by camshaft manufacturers is the **intake lobe centerline method.** This method determines the exact centerline of the intake lobe and compares it to the specifications supplied with the replacement camshaft. On an overhead valve engine, the camshaft is usually degreed after the crankshaft piston and camshaft are installed and before the cylinder heads are installed. To determine the centerline of the intake

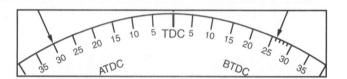

Figure 15–53 Degree wheel indicating where the piston stopped near top dead center. By splitting the difference between the two readings, the true TDC (28 degrees) can be located on the degree wheel.

lobe, follow these steps using a degree wheel mounted on the crankshaft:

Step 1 Locate the exact top dead center. Install a degree wheel and bring the #1 cylinder piston close to TDC. Install a piston stop. (A piston stop is any object attached to the block that can act as a solid mechanical stop to prevent the piston from reaching the top of the cylinder.) Turn the engine clockwise until the piston *gently* hits the stop.

CAUTION: Do not use the starter motor to rotate the engine. Use a special wrench on the flywheel or the front of the crankshaft.

Record the reading on the degree wheel, and then turn the engine in the opposite direction until it stops again and record that number. Figure 15–53 indicates a reading of 30 degrees ATDC and 26 degrees BTDC. Add the two readings together and divide by two (30° + 26° = 56° ÷ 2 = 28°). Move the degree wheel until it is 28 degrees and the engine has stopped rotating in either direction. Now TDC on the degree wheel is exactly at top dead center.

(a)

(b)

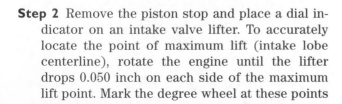

DEGREE WHEEL

(c)

Figure 15–54 (a) Photo showing the setup required to degree a camshaft. (b) Close-up of the pointer and the degree wheel. (c) The dial indicator is used to find exact top dead center.

Step 2 Remove the piston stop and place a dial indicator on an intake valve lifter. To accurately locate the point of maximum lift (intake lobe centerline), rotate the engine until the lifter drops 0.050 inch on each side of the maximum lift point. Mark the degree wheel at these points on either side of the maximum lift point. Now count the degrees between these two points and mark the halfway point. This halfway point represents the **intake centerline.** This point is often located between 100 degrees and 110 degrees. See Figure 15–54.

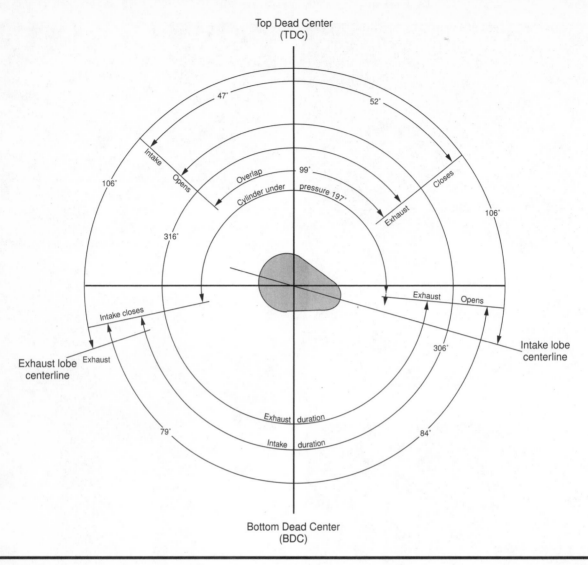

Figure 15–55 Typical valve timing diagram showing the intake lobe centerline at 106 degrees ATDC.

Step 3 Now that both TDC and intake centerline have been marked, compare the actual intake centerline with the specification. For example, if the actual intake centerline is 106 degrees and the camshaft specification indicates 106 degrees, then the camshaft is installed *straight up*. See Figure 15–55. If the actual reading is 104 degrees, the camshaft is advanced by 2 degrees. If the actual reading is 108 degrees, the camshaft is retarded by 2 degrees.

Advanced Cam Timing

If the camshaft is slightly ahead of the crankshaft, the camshaft is called *advanced*. An advanced camshaft (maximum of 4 degrees) results in more low-speed torque with a slight decrease in high-speed power. Some aftermarket camshaft manufacturers design about a 4-degree advance into their timing gears or camshaft. This permits the use of a camshaft with more

TECH TIP

Valve-to-Piston Clearance Versus Cam Timing

If the cam timing is *advanced* (relative to the crankshaft), the intake valve-to-piston clearance is *reduced*. If the cam timing is *retarded*, the exhaust valve-to-piston clearance is *reduced*.

This is true because the intake valve lags behind the motion of the piston on the intake stroke, whereas the piston "chases" the exhaust valve on the exhaust stroke. See Figure 15–56.

Figure 15–56 Modeling clay was used to determine valve-to-piston clearance. Most manufacturers recommend a minimum of 0.070 inch (1.8 millimeters). The clay is cut with a knife and the thickness of the clay is measured to determine the static (engine not running) clearance. The clearance decreases as the speed of the engine increases because of valve timing variations and connecting rod stretch.

Figure 15–57 The bottom of a lifter should be convex and *not* concave, as is the bottom of this worn lifter. Using worn lifters with a new camshaft can cause excessive camshaft wear on the edges of the cam.

lift and duration, yet still provides the smooth idle and low-speed responses of a milder camshaft.

Retarded Cam Timing

If the camshaft is slightly behind the crankshaft, the camshaft is called *retarded*. A retarded camshaft (maximum of 4 degrees) results in more high-speed power at the expense of low-speed torque.

If the measured values are different from specifications, special offset pins or keys are available to relocate the cam gear by the proper amount. Some manufacturers can provide adjustable cam timing sprockets for overhead cam engines.

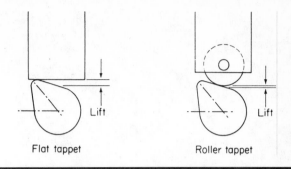

Figure 15–58 Note the difference in the amount of lift for a flat lifter (tappet) versus a roller lifter at the same cam angle. *Never* use a camshaft designed for roller tappets with flat tappets, or roller tappets on a camshaft designed for flat tappets.

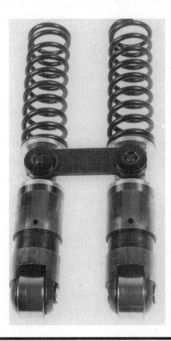

Figure 15–59 Typical aftermarket roller lifters (tappets). Note how the two lifters are mechanically connected to prevent lifter rotation. If a roller lifter rotated, it would be quickly destroyed by the camshaft.

■ LIFTERS OR TAPPETS

Valve lifters or tappets follow the contour or shape of the camshaft lobe. This arrangement changes the cam motion to a reciprocating motion in the valve train. Most older-style lifters have a relatively flat surface that slides on the cam. See Figure 15–57. Some lifters, however, are designed with a roller to follow the cam contour. Roller lifters are used primarily in production engines to reduce valve train friction (by up to 8%). This friction reduction can increase fuel economy and help to offset the greater manufacturing cost. All roller lifters must use a retainer to prevent lifter rotation. The retainer ensures that the roller is kept in line with the cam. If the retainer broke, the roller lifter could turn, destroying both the lifter and the camshaft. See Figures 15–58 through 15–60.

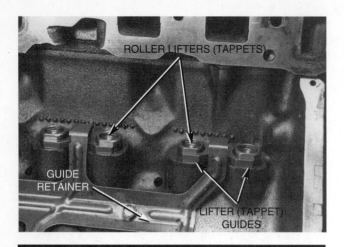

Figure 15–60 All roller lifters (tappets) must be prevented from rotating during engine operation. Note the stamped steel retainers used to hold guide plates on this V-6 engine.

Valve train clearance is also called **valve lash.** Valve train clearance must not be excessive, or it will cause noise or result in premature failure. Two methods are commonly used to make the necessary valve clearance adjustments. One involves a **solid valve lifter** with a mechanical adjustment, and the other involves a lifter with an automatic hydraulic adjustment built into the lifter body called a **hydraulic valve lifter.**

■ SOLID LIFTERS

Overhead valve engines with mechanical lifters have an adjustment screw at the pushrod end of the rocker arm or an adjustment nut at the ball pivot. Adjustable pushrods are available for some specific applications.

Valve trains using solid lifters must run with some clearance to ensure positive valve closure, regardless of the engine temperature. This clearance is matched by a gradual rise in the cam contour called a **ramp.** (Hydraulic lifter camshafts do not have this ramp.) The ramp will take up the clearance before the valve begins to open. The camshaft lobe also has a closing ramp to ensure quiet operation.

A lifter is solid in the sense that it transfers motion directly from the cam to the pushrod or valve. Its physical construction is that of a lightweight cylinder, either hollow or with a small-diameter center section and full-diameter ends. In some types that transfer oil through the pushrod, the external appearance is the same as for hydraulic lifters. See Figure 15–61.

■ HYDRAULIC LIFTERS

A hydraulic lifter consists primarily of a hollow cylinder body enclosing a closely fit hollow plunger, a check valve, and a pushrod cup. Lifters that feed oil up through the pushrod have a metering disk or restrictor valve located under the pushrod cup. Engine oil under pressure is fed through an engine passage to the exterior lifter body. An undercut portion allows the oil under pressure to surround the lifter body. Oil under pressure goes through holes in the undercut section into the center of the plunger. From there, it goes down through the check valve to a clearance space between the bottom of the plunger and the interior bottom of the lifter body. It fills this space with oil at engine pressure. Slight leakage allowance is designed into the lifter so that the air can bleed out and the lifter can leak down if it should become overfilled. The operating principle of a hydraulic lifter is shown in Figures 15–62 and 15–63 on pages 357–358.

The pushrod fits into a cup in the top, open end of the lifter plunger. Holes in the pushrod cup, pushrod end, and hollow pushrod allow oil to transfer from the lifter piston center, past a metering disk or restrictor valve, and up through the pushrod to the rocker arm. Oil leaving the rocker arm lubricates the rocker arm assembly.

As the cam starts to push the lifter against the valve train, the oil below the lifter plunger is squeezed and tries to return to the lifter plunger center. A lifter check valve, either ball or disk type, traps the oil below the lifter plunger. This hydraulically locks the operating length of the lifter. The hydraulic lifter then opens the engine valve as would a solid lifter. When the lifter returns to the base circle of the cam, engine oil pressure again works to replace any oil that may have leaked out of the lifter.

Figure 15–61 Typical solid valve lifters. The external appearance of the two lifters on the right is the same as that of a hydraulic lifter. The lifter on the far right is disassembled to show the internal parts required to control oil flow to the pushrod.

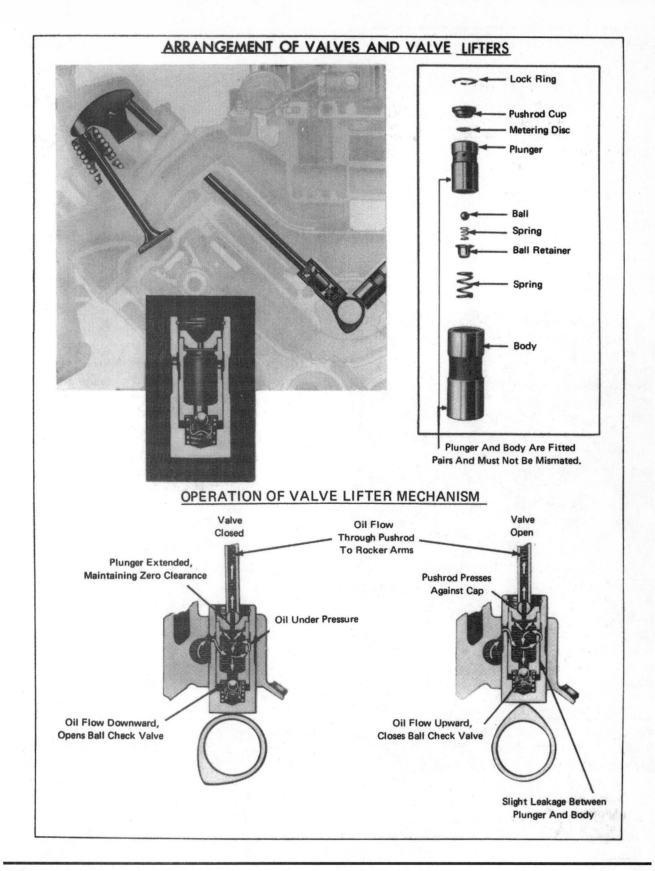

Figure 15–62 Operating principle of hydraulic lifters. *(Courtesy of Cadillac Motor Car Division, General Motors Corporation)*

Figure 15–63 Parts of two styles of hydraulic valve lifter (tappet).

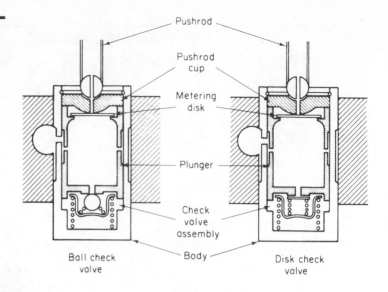

Figure 15–64 (a) Typical overhead camshaft four-cylinder engine using hydraulic lifters and followers. (b) Same engine with one follower and one lifter removed.

(a)

(b)

The hydraulic lifter's job is to take up all clearance in the valve train. Occasionally, engines are run at excessive speeds. This tends to throw the valve open, causing **valve float.** During valve float, clearance exists in the valve train. The hydraulic lifter will take up this clearance as it is designed to do. When this occurs, it will keep the valve from closing on the seat. This is called **pump-up.** Pump-up will not occur when the engine is operated in the speed range for which it is designed.

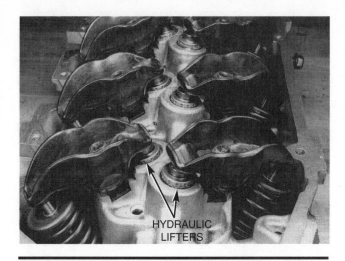

Figure 15–65 This four-cylinder overhead cam engine uses rocker arms that are moved upward by the hydraulic lifters. The camshaft is in the cylinder head under the lifters.

Many overhead camshaft engines use a hydraulic lifter. See Figures 15–64 through 15–66 for examples of various styles and types of hydraulic lifters used on overhead camshaft engines.

■ LIFTER PRELOAD

Lifter preload is actually the distance between the pushrod seat inside the lifter and the snap ring of the lifter when the lifter is resting on the base circle (or heel) of the cam and the valve is closed. This distance should be about 0.020 to 0.045 inch. On engines with adjustable rocker arms, this distance or preload is determined by turning the rocker arm adjusting nut one-quarter to one full turn after zero lash (clearance) is determined. See Figure 15–67 on page 361. Tightening this adjusting nut further can cause the pushrod to bottom in the lifter. If the engine is rotated with the pushrod bottomed out, bent valves or bent or damaged pushrods, rocker arms, or rocker arm studs can result.

Engines that have been rebuilt or repaired and that do not use adjustable rocker arms are particularly at risk for damage. If any of the following operations have been preformed, lifter preload *must* be determined:

• Regrinding the camshaft (reduces base circle dimensions)
• Milling or resurfacing cylinder heads
• Milling or resurfacing block deck
• Grinding valves and/or facing valve stems
• Changing to a head gasket thinner or thicker than the original

Most lifters can accept a total variation in the entire valve train of about 0.080 to 0.180 inch. To determine lifter preload, rotate the engine until the valve being tested is resting on the base circle of the cam. For example, with the valve cover off and rotating the engine in the normal operating direction, watch the exhaust valve start to open. This means that the intake valve for that cylinder is resting on the base circle (heel) of the cam. Apply pressure down on the lifter. Wait several minutes for the lifter to bleed down. Measure the distance between rocker arm and valve stem. If the proper clearance is not obtained (generally between 0.020 and 0.045 inch), the following may need to be done to get the proper clearance:

1. Install longer or shorter pushrods. Manufacturers produce pushrods in various lengths. Some are available in lengths up to 0.100 inch longer or shorter than stock.
2. Install adjustable pushrods or rocker arms if possible.
3. Shim or grind rocker stands or shafts.

> **NOTE:** Shim rocker arm supports to three-fifths of the measurement removed from the cylinder head (1.5:1 rocker ratio). For example, if 0.030 inch is removed from a cylinder head, shim the rocker arm to 0.030 inch times 3/5, or 0.018 inch.

■ DETERMINING LIFTER PRELOAD

The process of adjusting valves that use hydraulic valve lifters involves making certain that the lifter has the specified preload. A properly adjusted valve train should position the lifter in the center of its travel dimension.

The procedure for a valve train with *adjustable* rocker arms is as follows:

1. Rotate the engine clockwise as viewed from the nonprincipal or belt end (normal direction of rotation) until the exhaust lifter starts to move up.
2. Adjust the intake valve to zero lash (no preload) and then one-half turn more.
3. Rotate the engine until the intake valve is almost completely closed. Adjust the exhaust valve to zero lash and then one-half turn more.
4. Continue with this procedure for each cylinder until all the valves are correctly adjusted.

If the valve train uses *nonadjustable* rocker arms, the lifter preload must still be determined. The lifter preload *must* be measured if any or all of the following procedures have been performed on the engine:

• Head(s) milled
• Block decked
• Valves ground
• Any other machining operation that could change the valve train measurement

(a)

(b)

(c)

(d)

(e)

CAMSHAFT
FOR EXHAUST
VALVES

CAMSHAFT
FOR INTAKE
VALVE

CAMSHAFT
COVER

CAMSHAFT BEARINGS

CAMSHAFT
HOUSING

HYDRAULIC
LIFTERS

Figure 15–66 (a) A dual overhead camshaft inline four-cylinder engine. This engine has a cast-iron block with aluminum cylinder head and cam support housings (covers). (b) Removing the top of the camshaft housing shows that the camshaft bearings are a machined segment of the cover. (c) Removing the bottom section of the camshaft housing reveals the valves. The hydraulic lifters are still in the housing being removed. (d) With the camshaft removed, the tops of the hydraulic lifters are visible. (e) Camshaft housing showing one hydraulic lifter removed.

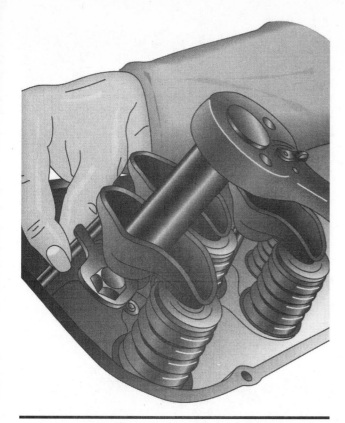

Figure 15–67 Adjusting a hydraulic lifter by tightening the rocker arm adjusting nut.

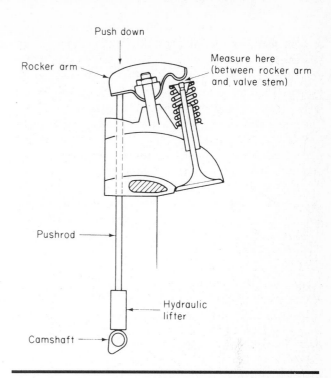

Figure 15–68 Procedure for determining proper lifter travel.

Shorter (or longer) replacement pushrods may be required to produce the correct lifter preload. Some engine manufacturers recommend using thin metal shims under the rocker arm supports if needed.

> **CAUTION:** If shims are used under the rocker arm supports, be sure that the shim has the required oil holes.

■ DETERMINING PROPER LIFTER TRAVEL

To determine if shimming or use of replacement pushrods of different lengths is required, use the following procedure:

1. With the valve cover removed, rotate the engine until the valve lifter being tested is resting on the base circle of the camshaft.
2. Depress the pushrod into the lifter with steady pressure. This should cause the lifter to bleed down until the pushrod bottoms out in the lifter bore.
3. Measure clearance (lash) between the rocker arm tip and the stem of the valve. This measurement

varies according to manufacturer and engine design, but it usually ranges from 0.020 to 0.080 inch. See Figure 15–68. Always consult exact manufacturer's specifications before taking any corrective measures.

If the measurement is not within acceptable range, select the proper-length pushrods to achieve the proper lifter travel dimension and preload.

> **NOTE:** Some engines use several different pushrod lengths depending on exact build date! Block casting numbers may be the same, but the engines may require different internal parts. Check with the manufacturer's specifications in the factory service manual for proper interchangeable parts.

■ VALVE NOISE DIAGNOSIS

Valve lifters are often noisy, especially at engine start-up. When the engine is off, some valves are open. The valve spring pressure forces the inner plunger to leak down (oil is forced out of the lifter). Therefore, many vehicle manufacturers consider valve ticking at one-half engine speed after start-up to be normal, especially if the engine is quiet after 10 to 30 seconds. Be sure that the engine is equipped with the correct oil filter, and that the filter has an internal check valve. If in doubt, use an original-equipment oil filter. If all of the valves are noisy, check the oil level. If low, the oil may have been **aerated** (air mixed with the oil), which would prevent proper operation of the hydraulic lifter. Low oil pressure can also cause all valves to be noisy. The oil level being too high can also cause noisy valve lifters. The connecting rods create foam as they rotate through the oil. This foam can travel through the oiling systems to the lifters. The foam in the lifters prevents normal operation and allows the valves to make noise.

If the valves are abnormally noisy, remove the rocker arm cover and use a stethoscope to determine which valves or valve train parts may be causing the noise. Check for all of the following items:

- Worn camshaft lobe
- Dirty, stuck, or worn lifters
- Worn rocker arm (if the vehicle is so equipped)
- Worn or bent pushrods (if the vehicle is so equipped)
- Broken or weak valve springs
- Sticking or warped valves

■ MECHANICAL LIFTER SERVICE

Mechanical lifters, like hydraulic lifters, should be replaced if the camshaft is replaced. If the lifters are to be reused, they *must* be kept in order and reinstalled in the exact positions in which they were originally used in the engine. All lifters should be cleaned and carefully inspected. If the base of the lifter is dished (concave), the lifter should be replaced.

> **NOTE:** Regrinding of valve lifter bases is generally not recommended because the hardened areas of the lifter can be ground through.

As with any lifter, new or used, the bore clearance should be checked.

■ HYDRAULIC LIFTER SERVICE

Hydraulic lifter service begins with a thorough visual inspection. Compare the lifter wear with the corresponding lobe on the camshaft. *All lifters should be replaced during a major engine overhaul or a camshaft replacement.*

Vehicle manufacturers usually recommend that, because of their high cost, hydraulic roller lifters be checked for wear, disassembled, and cleaned rather than being replaced. Any other hydraulic lifter that is to be reused should also be disassembled and cleaned using the following steps:

Step 1 Select a clean work area and tray for the disassembled parts. See Figure 15–69.

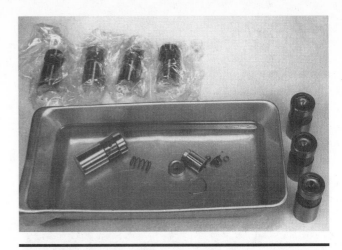

Figure 15–69 Cleaning a disassembled hydraulic lifter (tappet) in clean petroleum solvent. After cleaning and reassembly, all hydraulic lifters should be checked for proper leak-down rate using a special fluid and tester.

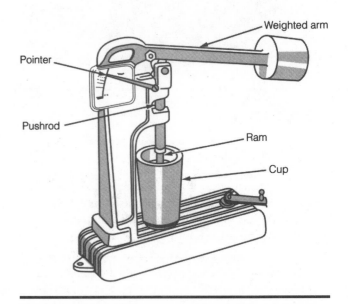

Figure 15–70 Typical hydraulic lifter leak-down tester.

Step 2 Disassemble the lifters and keep all parts in order.

Step 3 Clean all parts and reassemble. Always use a lintless cloth because lint can affect lifter operation.

Step 4 Test leak-down rate using a leak-down tester and special-viscosity fluid. See Figure 15–70.

   a. Measure the time required for the fluid to pass between the inner and outer body of the lifter.

   b. The time it takes for the lifter to collapse under a given weight should be longer than 10 seconds and less than 90 seconds.

   c. Check the service manual for the exact leak-down time for your vehicle. The average time for leak-down is 20 to 40 seconds.

■ HYDRAULIC VALVE LIFTER INSTALLATION

Most vehicle manufacturers recommend installing lifters *without* filling or pumping the lifter full of oil. If the lifter is filled with oil during engine start-up, the lifter may not be able to bleed down quickly enough and the valves may be kept open. Not only will the engine not operate correctly with the valves held open, but the piston could hit the open valves, causing serious engine damage. Most manufacturers usually specify that the lifter be lubricated. Roller hydraulic lifters can be lubricated with engine oil, whereas flat lifters require that engine assembly lube or extreme pressure (EP) grease be applied to the base.

■ BLEEDING HYDRAULIC LIFTERS

Air trapped inside a hydraulic valve lifter can be easily bled by simply operating the engine at a fast idle (2500 RPM). Normal oil flow through the lifters will allow all air inside the lifter to be bled out.

> **NOTE:** Some engines, such as many Nissan overhead camshaft engines, *must* have the air removed from the lifter before installation. This is accomplished by submerging the lifter in a container of engine oil and using a straightened paper clip to depress the oil passage check ball.

Consult a service manual if in doubt about the bleeding procedure for the vehicle being serviced. See Figure 15–71 for an example of the special tool needed to bleed out the air on hydraulic lash adjusters (HLA) used on a DaimlerChrysler 3.2 to 3.5 L, V-6 overhead camshaft.

NEEDLE TOOL

HYDRAULIC LASH ADJUSTER

Figure 15–71 A special tool that has a small needlelike probe is used to bleed air from the hydraulic lash adjuster (HLA).

PHOTO SEQUENCE Valve Adjustment

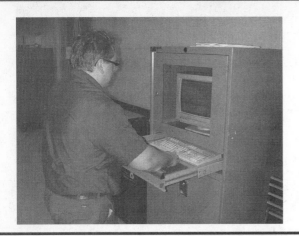

PS 24–1 Before starting the process of adjusting the valves, look up the specifications and exact procedures. The technician is checking this information from a computer CD-ROM-based information system.

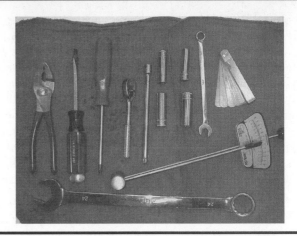

PS 24–2 The tools necessary to adjust the valves on an engine with adjustable rocker arms include basic hand tools, feeler gauge, and a torque wrench.

PS 24–3 An overall view of the four-cylinder engine that is due for a scheduled valve adjustment according to the vehicle manufacturer's recommendations.

PS 24–4 Start the valve adjustment procedure by first disconnecting and labeling, if necessary, all vacuum lines that need to be removed to gain access to the valve cover.

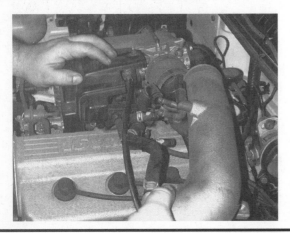

PS 24–5 The air intake tube is being removed from the throttle body.

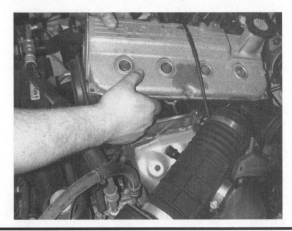

PS 24–6 With all vacuum lines and the intake tube removed, the valve cover can be removed after removing all retaining bolts.

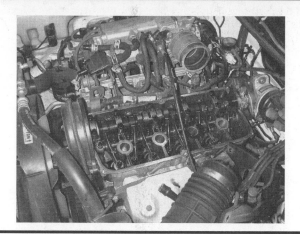

PS 24–7 Notice how clean the engine appears. This is a testament of proper maintenance and regular oil changes by the owner.

PS 24–8 To help locate how far the engine is being rotated, the technician is removing the distributor cap to be able to observe the position of the rotor.

TIMING MARKS

PS 24–9 The engine is rotated until the timing marks on the front of the crankshaft line up with zero degrees—top dead center (TDC)—with both valves closed on #1 cylinder.

PS 24–10 With the rocker arms contacting the base circle of the cam, insert a feeler gauge of the specified thickness between the camshaft and the rocker arm. There should be a slight drag on the feeler gauge if the clearance is the same as the thickness of the feeler gauge.

PS 24–11 If the valve clearance (lash) is not correct, loosen the retaining nut and turn the valve adjusting screw with a screwdriver to achieve the proper clearance.

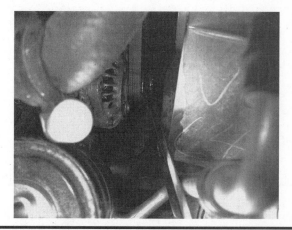

PS 24–12 After adjusting the valves that are closed, rotate the engine one full rotation until the engine timing marks again align. To rotate the engine, the technician is using a wrench on the generator (alternator) drive pulley.

PS 24–13 The engine is rotated until the timing marks again align indicating that the companion cylinder will now be in position for valve clearance measurement.

PS 24–14 On some engines, it is necessary to watch the direction the rotor is pointing to help determine how far to rotate the engine. Always follow the vehicle manufacturer's recommended procedure.

PS 24–15 The exhaust valves often have a greater clearance (lash) than the intake valves. Here the service technician is using a feeler gauge that is one-thousandth thinner and another one-thousandth thicker than the specified clearance as a double-check that the clearance is correct.

PS 24–16 Adjusting a valve takes both hands—one to hold the wrench to loosen and tighten the lock nut and one to turn the adjusting screw. Always double-check the clearance after an adjustment is made.

PS 24–17 After all valves have been properly measured and adjusted as necessary, start the reassembly process by replacing all gaskets and seals as specified by the vehicle manufacturer.

PS 24–18 Reinstall the valve cover being careful to not pinch a wire or vacuum hose between the cover and the cylinder head.

Valve Adjustment—continued

PS 24–19 Use a torque wrench and torque the valve cover retaining bolts to factory specifications.

PS 24–20 Reinstall the distributor cap.

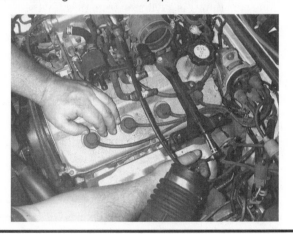

PS 24–21 Reinstall the spark plug wires and all brackets that were removed to gain access to the valve cover.

PS 24–22 Reconnect all vacuum and air hoses and tubes. Replace with new any vacuum hoses that are brittle or swollen.

PS 24–23 Be sure that the clips are properly installed. Start the engine and check for proper operation.

PS 24–24 Double-check for any oil or vacuum leaks after starting the engine.

■ SUMMARY

1. The camshaft rotates at one-half the crankshaft speed.

2. The pushrods should be rotating while the engine is running if the camshaft and lifters are okay.

3. On overhead valve engines, the camshaft is usually placed in the block above the crankshaft. The lobes of the camshaft are usually lubricated by splash lubrication.

4. Silent chains are quieter than roller chains but tend to stretch with use.

5. Cam chucking is the movement of the camshaft lengthwise in the engine during operation.

6. The lift of a cam is usually expressed in decimal inches and represents the distance that the valve is lifted off the valve seat.

7. In many engines, camshaft lift is transferred to the tip of the valve stem to open the valve by the use of a rocker arm or follower.

8. Pushrods transfer camshaft motion upward from the camshaft to the rocker arm.

9. Camshaft duration is the number of degrees of crankshaft rotation for which the valve is lifted off the seat.

10. Valve overlap is the number of crankshaft degrees for which both valves are open.

11. Camshafts should be installed according to the manufacturer's recommended procedures. Flat lifter camshafts should be thoroughly lubricated with extreme pressure lubricant.

12. If a new camshaft is installed, new lifters should also be installed.

■ REVIEW QUESTIONS

1. What puts thrust loads on a camshaft?

2. When is steel used as the camshaft material?

3. Explain why the lift and duration and lobe center dimension determine the power characteristics of the engine.

4. Explain lobe centerline.

5. List the various coatings that can be used on camshafts to harden and protect against wear.

6. Describe the operation of a hydraulic lifter.

7. Describe how to determine if the hydraulic lifter preload is correct.

■ ASE CERTIFICATION-TYPE QUESTIONS

1. The camshaft makes _____ for every revolution of the crankshaft.
   a. One-quarter revolution
   b. One-half revolution
   c. One revolution
   d. Two revolutions

2. Valve lifters rotate during operation because of the _____ of the camshaft.
   a. Taper of the lobe
   b. Thrust plate
   c. Chain tensioner
   d. Bearings

3. If lift and duration remain constant and the lobe center angle decreases, _____ .
   a. The valve overlap decreases
   b. The effective lift increases
   c. The effective duration increases
   d. The valve overlap increases

4. If a camshaft is reground, _____ .
   a. The base circle is reduced
   b. The original lift is maintained
   c. The original duration is maintained
   d. All of the above occur

5. If the cam timing is advanced from the stock setting, _____ .
   a. The intake valve-to-piston clearance is increased
   b. The intake valve-to-piston clearance is decreased
   c. The exhaust valve-to-piston clearance is decreased
   d. Both a and c occur
   e. All of the above occur

6. Typical lifter preload is _____ .
   a. 0.001 to 0.003 inch
   b. 0.005 to 0.010 inch
   c. 0.020 to 0.045 inch
   d. 0.080 to 0.180 inch

7. A DOHC V-6 has _____ camshaft(s)?
   a. 4
   b. 3
   c. 2
   d. 1

8. The intake valve opens at 39 degrees BTDC and closes at 71 degrees ABDC. The exhaust valve opens at 78 degrees BBDC and closes at 47 degrees ATDC.
   a. Intake valve duration is 110 degrees.
   b. Exhaust valve duration is 125 degrees.
   c. Overlap is 86 degrees.
   d. Both a and b.

9. Hydraulic valve lifters can make a ticking noise when the engine is running if _____ .
   a. The valve lash is too close
   b. The valve lash is too loose
   c. The lobe centerlines over 110 degrees
   d. Both a and c occur

10. Most camshafts are coated with _____ at the factory to add wear resistance.
    a. SAE 80W-90 gear lube
    b. SAE 5W-30 engine oil
    c. A phosphate coating
    d. Beeswax or candle wax

Engine Block Construction and Service

Objectives: After studying Chapter 16, the reader should be able to:

1. Describe the types of engine blocks and how they are manufactured.
2. List the machining operations required on most engine blocks.
3. Explain how the surface finish is achieved inside a cylinder bore.
4. List the steps necessary to prepare an engine block for assembly.

The engine block, which is the supporting structure for the entire engine, is made from gray cast iron or from cast or die-cast aluminum alloy. The gray color is a result of the 3% carbon in the form of graphite in the cast iron. The liquid cast iron is poured into a mold. The carbon in the cast iron allows for easy machining, often without coolant. The graphite in the cast iron also has lubricating properties. Newer blocks use thinner walls to reduce weight. Cast iron is strong for its weight and usually is magnetic. All other engine parts are mounted on or in the block. This large casting supports the crankshaft and camshaft and holds all the parts in alignment. Blocks are often of the **monoblock** design, which means that the cylinder, water jacket, main bearing supports (saddles), and oil passages are all cast as one structure for strength and quietness. Large-diameter holes in the block casting form the cylinders to guide the pistons. The cylinder holes are called bores, because they are made by a machining process called boring. Combustion pressure loads are carried from the head to the crankshaft bearings through the block structure. The block has webs, walls, and drilled passages to contain the coolant and lubricating oil and to keep them separated from each other. See Figure 16–1. Mounting pads or lugs on the block transfer the engine torque reaction to the vehicle frame through attached engine mounts. A large mounting surface at the rear of the engine block is used for fastening a bell housing or transmission.

The cylinder head(s) attach to the block. The attaching joints are sealed so that they do not leak. Gaskets are used in the joints to take up differences that are created by machining irregularities and that result from different pressures and temperatures.

■ BLOCK MANUFACTURING

Cast-iron cylinder block casting technology continues to be improved. The trend is to make blocks with larger cores, using fewer individual pieces. Oil-sand cores, shown in Figure 16–2, are forms that shape the internal openings and passages in the engine block. Before casting, the cores are supported within a core box. The core box also has a liner to shape the outside of the block.

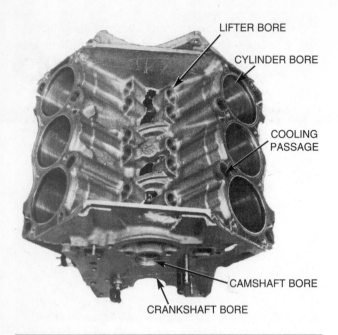

Figure 16-1 Typical V-type engine block.

Special alloy cast iron is poured into the box. It flows between the cores and the core box liner. As the cast iron cools, the core breaks up. When the cast iron has hardened, it is removed from the core box, and the pieces of sand core are removed through the openings in the block by vigorously shaking the casting. These openings in the block are plugged with **core plugs.** Core plugs are also called **freeze plugs** or **frost plugs.** Although the name infers that the plugs would be pushed outward if the coolant in the passages were to freeze, seldom do they work in this way.

One way to keep the engine weight as low as possible is to make the block with minimum wall thickness. The cast iron used with thin-wall casting techniques has higher nickel content and is harder than the cast iron previously used. Engine designers have used foundry techniques to make engines lightweight by making the cast-iron block walls and bulkheads only as heavy as necessary to support their required loads. They have omitted as much material as possible from the lifter gallery area. They have even designed small oil filters so that the attachment point size could be reduced.

■ CASTING NUMBERS

Whenever an engine part such as a block is cast, a number is put into the mold to identify the casting. See Figure 16–3. These casting numbers can be used to check dimensions such as the cubic-inch displacement and other information such as year of manufacture. Sometimes changes are made to the mold, yet the casting number is not changed. Most often the casting number is the best piece of identifying information that the service technician can use.

■ BLOCK MACHINING

After cooling and thorough cleaning, the block casting goes to the machining line. The top, bottom, and end surfaces are cleaned and semifinished with a **broach.** A broach is a large slab with several cutting teeth. Each tooth cuts a little more than the preceding tooth. It is somewhat like a large, coarse, contoured file. One pass of the broach will smooth both cylinder decks and the lifter valley cover rail. A second pass will smooth the up-

(a)

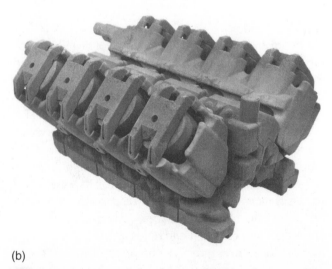

(b)

Figure 16–2 Casting cores. (a) Separate cores. (b) Assembled cores. *(Courtesy of Central Foundry Division, GMC)*

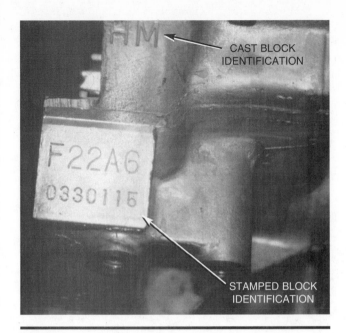

Figure 16–3 Engine block identification can be either cast or stamped or both.

per main bearing bores and the oil pan rail. The ends of the block may be finished with a third broach. Some of these surfaces are completed with the broach operation; others need to be finished with a mill, a final broach, or a boring operation. Broaching leaves straight lines across the surface, whereas milling leaves curved lines.

The cylinders are bored and honed in a number of operations until they have the required size and finish.

Figure 16–4 shows a part of a block production line. A slight notch or **scallop** is cut into the edge of the cylinder on some engines using very large valves (Figure 16–5). All drilling and thread tapping is accomplished on the block line.

■ ALUMINUM BLOCKS

Aluminum is used for some cylinder blocks and is non-magnetic and light weight. Aluminum blocks may have one of several different types of cylinder walls:

- Cast-aluminum blocks may have steel cylinder liners (Saturn, Northstar, and Ford modular V-8s and V-6s). The cast-iron cylinder sleeves are either cast into the aluminum block during manufacturing or pressed into the aluminum block. These sleeves are not in contact with the coolant passages and are called **dry cylinder sleeves.** See Figure 16–6.
- Another aluminum block design has the block die cast from silicon-aluminum alloy with no cylinder liners. Pistons with zinc-copper–hard iron coatings are used in these aluminum bores (Porsche 944 engines). See Figure 16–7.
- Some engines have die-cast aluminum blocks with replaceable cast-iron cylinder sleeves. The sleeves are sealed at the block deck and at their base. Coolant flows around the cylinder sleeve, so this type of sleeve is called a **wet cylinder sleeve** (Cadillac 4.1, 4.5, and 4.9L V-8 engines).

Figure 16–4 One section of an engine production line. *(Courtesy of Greenlee Brothers and Company)*

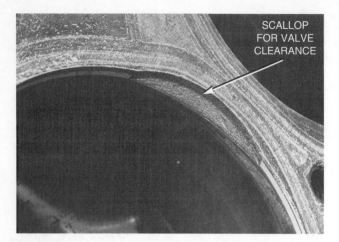

Figure 16-5 Scallop on the upper edge of the cylinder for valve clearance.

Figure 16-6 Cast-iron cylinder liners are either cast or press-fit into an aluminum block.

Figure 16-7 Four-cylinder block die-cast from silicon-aluminum alloy with no cylinder liners. Several manufacturers use this method to produce strong yet lightweight engine blocks. *(Courtesy of Chevrolet Motor Division, GMC)*

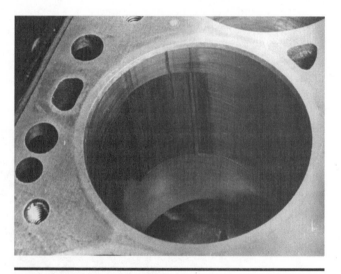

Figure 16-8 Cylinder wall scored as the result of a broken piston ring.

Cast-iron main bearing caps are used with aluminum blocks to give the required strength.

■ BLOCK CONDITION INSPECTION

Block faults occur in the cylinder wall, cooling system, and shaft bore alignment, and as broken parts. All other engine parts depend on the block for support, alignment, and operating climate.

Cylinder wall wear of this type is shown in Figure 16-8, one of the most noticeable abnormal block conditions. Cylinder walls, in normal use, have a smooth glaze from smoothing effects of the piston and rings during operation.

Sometimes the connecting rod is allowed to strike the bottom edge of the cylinder as the piston and rod assembly are removed or installed. This will nick the bottom edge of the cylinder and raise sharp points. If these points are not removed, they will scratch the piston skirt of the reconditioned engine. See Chapter 10 for details on block cleaning and crack detection.

■ LOWER ENGINE BLOCK DESIGN

The engine block consists primarily of the cylinders with a web or bulkhead to support the crankshaft and head attachments. The rest of the block consists of a water jacket, a lifter chamber, and mounting flanges. In most engine designs, each main bearing bulkhead supports both a cam bearing and a main bearing. The bulkhead is well ribbed to support and distribute loads applied to it. This gives the block structural rigidity and beam stiffness throughout its useful life.

Two types of lower block designs are in use. The first type is called **shallow skirt block.** The shallow skirt block is the smaller and lighter of the two engine block types (Figure 16–9). It has the least amount of cast iron, which makes it a small, compact, lightweight block. Cov-

ers, such as the oil pan and timing cover, are largely lightweight aluminum die-castings or sheet-steel stampings. The base of this block is close to the crankshaft centerline. This block base is called the **oil pan rail.**

The second type of block is called a **deep skirt block.** In this type, the deep skirt extends the oil pan rail well below the crankshaft centerline. The deep skirt block improves the stiffness of the entire engine (Figure 16–10). When used on a V-type engine, it is often called a "Y" block because it is shaped like the letter *Y*. It provides a wider surface on which to attach the bell housing. This greater rigidity ensures smooth, quiet engine operation and durability. The deep skirt must be wide enough to clear the connecting rods as they swing through the block, and therefore, a large oil capacity is provided with its use.

■ THE BLOCK DECK

The cylinder head is fastened to the top surface of the block. This surface is called the **block deck.** The deck has a smooth surface to seal *against* the head gasket. Bolt holes are positioned around the cylinders to form an even holding pattern. Four, five, or six head bolts are used around each cylinder in automobile engines. These bolt holes go into reinforced areas within the block that carry the combustion pressure load to the main bearing bulkheads. Additional holes in the block are used to transfer coolant and oil as seen in Figure 16–11.

■ CYLINDER SKIRTS

The cylinders may be of a **skirtless** design, flush with the interior top of the crankcase (Figure 16–12), or they

Figure 16–9 Typical shallow skirt block with the oil pan rail surface close to the crankshaft centerline. The block pictured here is upside down on a workbench.

Figure 16–10 Typical deep skirt block with the oil pan rail surface that extends well below the crankshaft centerline. The block pictured here is upside down on a workbench.

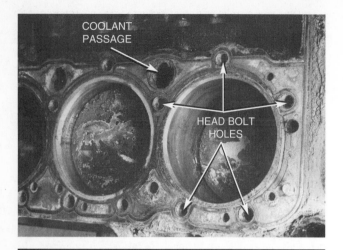

Figure 16–11 Head bolt holes and coolant passages are easily identified after removing the cylinder head(s).

Figure 16–13 Cylinder skirt that extends below the interior top of the crankcase.

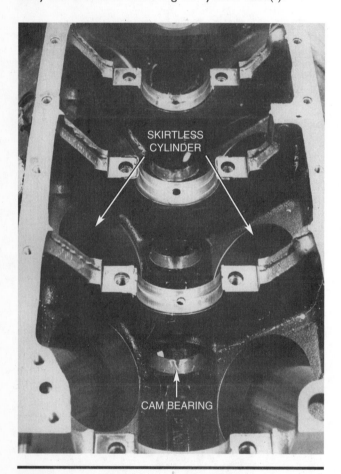

Figure 16–12 Skirtless cylinder that is flush with the interior of the top of the crankcase.

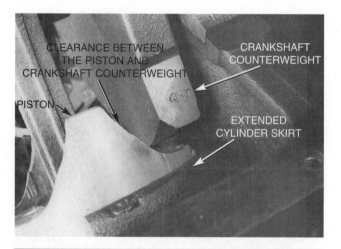

Figure 16–14 The piston comes very close to the crankshaft counterweight when it is at the bottom of the stroke on an engine that has a short connecting rod.

may have a skirt that extends into the crankcase (Figure 16–13). **Extended skirt** cylinders are used on engines with short connecting rods. In these engines, the pistons move very close to the crankshaft. The cylinder skirt must go as low as possible to support the piston when it is at the lowest point in its stroke. This can be

seen in Figure 16–14. The extended cylinder skirt allows the engine to be designed with a low overall engine height, because the engine has a small block size for its displacement.

Figure 16–15 Coolant passages surrounding the cylinders.

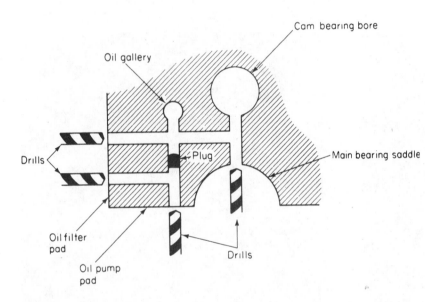

Figure 16–16 Typical oil hole drilling in the main bearing web.

COOLING PASSAGES

Cylinders are surrounded by cooling passages. These coolant passages around the cylinders are often called the **cooling jacket** (Figure 16–15). In most skirtless cylinder designs, the cooling passages extend nearly to the bottom of the cylinder. In extended skirt cylinder designs, the cooling passages are limited to the upper portion of the cylinder.

LUBRICATING PASSAGES

An engine block has many oil holes that carry lubricating oil to the required locations. During manufacture, all oil holes, called the **oil gallery,** are drilled from outside the block. When a curved passage is needed, intersecting drilled holes are used. In some engines, plugs are placed in the oil holes to direct oil to another point before it comes back to the original hole, on the opposite side of the plug as shown in Figure 16–16. After oil holes are drilled, the unneeded open ends may be capped by pipe plugs, steel balls, or cup-type soft plugs, often called **oil gallery plugs** (see Figure 16–17). These end plugs in the oil passages can be a source of oil leakage in operating engines.

MAIN BEARING CAPS

The main bearing caps are cast separately from the block. They are machined and then installed on the block for a final bore finishing operation. With caps installed, the main bearing bores and cam bearing bores are machined to the correct size and alignment. On some engines, these bores are honed to a very fine finish and exact size.

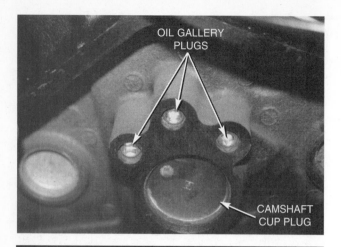

Figure 16–17 Typical oil gallery plugs on the rear of a Chevrolet small-block V-8 engine.

Figure 16–18 Small-block Chevrolet block. Note the left-hand dipstick hole and a pad cast for a right-hand dipstick.

TECH TIP

What Does LHD Mean?

The abbreviation LHD means **left-hand dipstick,** which is commonly used by rebuilders and remanufacturers in their literature in describing Chevrolet small-block V-8 engines. Before about 1980, most small-block Chevrolet V-8s used an oil dipstick pad on the left side (driver's side) of the engine block. Starting in about 1980, when oxygen sensors were first used on this engine, the dipstick was relocated to the right side of the block.

Therefore, to be assured of ordering or delivering the correct engine, knowing the dipstick location is critical. An LHD block cannot be used with the exhaust manifold setup that includes the oxygen sensor without major re-fitting or the installing of a different style of oil pan that includes a provision for an oil dipstick. Engine blocks with the dipstick pad cast on the right side are, therefore, coded as right-hand dipstick (RHD) engines.

> *NOTE:* Some blocks cast around the year 1980 are cast with both right- and left-hand oil dipstick pads, but only one is drilled for the dipstick tube. See Figure 16–18.

Figure 16–19 Standard two-bolt main bearing cap.

Main bearing caps are not interchangeable or reversible, because they are individually finished in place. Main bearing caps may have cast numbers indicating their position on the block. If not, they should be marked.

Standard production engines usually use two bolts to hold the main bearing cap in place (Figure 16–19). Heavy-duty and high performance engines often use additional main bearing support bolts. A four-bolt, and even six-bolt, main cap can be of a cross-bolted design

in a deep skirt block or of a parallel design in a shallow skirt block (Figure 16–20). Many smaller high-speed engines use a cast-iron **girdle** or main bearing support as shown in Figure 16–21. Remember that the expansion force of the combustion chamber gases will try to push the head off the top and the crankshaft off the bottom of the block. The engine is held together with the head bolts and main bearing cap bolts screwed into bolt

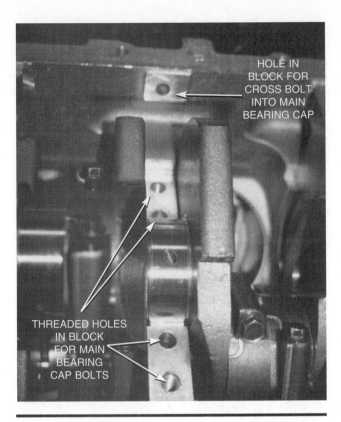

Figure 16–20 This Chevrolet LS-1, V-8 engine uses four parallel main bearing cap bolts plus two cross-bolted from the side of the block.

Figure 16–21 This engine uses a cast-iron girdle that attaches to all main bearings and ties them all together to form a solid and rigid support for the crankshaft.

bosses and ribs in the block. The **bosses** are enlarged areas of the block that surround the openings. The extra bolts on the main bearing cap help to support the crankshaft when there are high combustion pressures and mechanical loads, especially during high-engine speed operation. See Figure 16–22.

■ ENGINE BLOCK SERVICE

The engine block is the foundation of the engine. All parts of the block must be of the correct size and they must be aligned. The parts must also have the proper finishes if the engine is to function dependably for a normal service life. Blueprinting is the reconditioning of all the critical surfaces and dimensions so that the block is actually like new.

After a thorough cleaning, the block should be inspected for cracks or other flaws before machine work begins. If the block is in serviceable condition, the block should be prepared in the following sequence:

Operation 1 Align boring or honing main bearing saddles and caps

Operation 2 Machining the block deck surface parallel to the crankshaft

Operation 3 Cylinder boring and honing

■ MAIN BEARING HOUSING BORE ALIGNMENT

The main bearing journals of a straight crankshaft are in alignment. If the main bearing housing bores in the block are not in alignment, the crankshaft will bend as it rotates. This will lead to premature bearing failure and it could lead to a broken crankshaft. The original stress in the block casting is gradually relieved as the block is used. Some slight warpage may occur as the stress is relieved. In addition, the continued pounding caused by combustion will usually cause some stretch in the main bearing caps. See Figures 16–23 and 16–24. Realigning and resizing the main bearing bores in the block is a procedure called **align boring** or **align honing.**

A number of different types of equipment are used to align the main bearing housing bores in the block. Some are simple fixtures that clamp on the block, whereas others place the block in a large production align boring or align honing machine. The align boring tool is a cutting tool, similar to a lathe tool. Honing uses

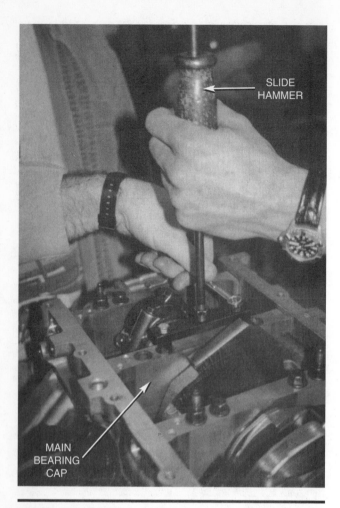

Figure 16–22 All main bearing caps should fit snugly in the block. A slide hammer is being used here to remove a main bearing cap after the bolts have been removed.

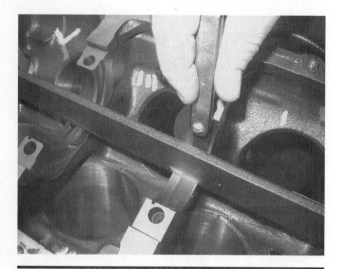

Figure 16–23 Checking alignment of main bearing saddles with a straightedge and a feeler gauge.

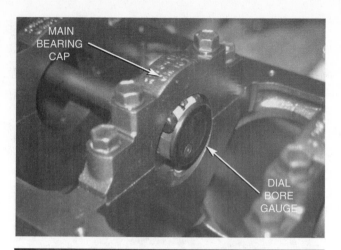

Figure 16–24 Before align honing (or boring), each main housing bore must be measured. A dial bore gauge is the tool of choice, because it is set to read the diameter of the housing bore, and the dial will indicate plus or minus readings from the specifications.

a stone instead of a cutting tool and produces a finer finish than does align boring.

The same general steps are followed in align boring, regardless of the type of equipment used.

Step 1 A small amount of metal is removed from the main bearing cap parting surfaces. Figure 16–25 shows one method used to do this. It is necessary that about 0.015 inch (0.38 millimeter) be removed when an align boring cutting tool is used. Only 0.002 inch (0.05 millimeter) needs to be removed in align honing.

Step 2 The resurfaced main bearing caps are torqued in place on the block.

Step 3 The main bearing housing bores are checked to determine exactly where metal must be removed to align the bores. The align boring tool is adjusted at each main bearing housing bore to cut the correct diameter. A typical align boring fixture is shown in Figure 16–26.

> **NOTE:** One dimension that is critical in all engines is the spacing between the cam bearing centerline and the crankshaft centerline. This must be maintained to have the proper cam drive gear mesh or the proper timing chain tension. If this dimension is not correct, it will lead to faulty timing and to premature failure of the cam drive. See Figure 16–27 on page 380.

Step 4 The align hone fits through all the main bearing housing bores at the same time. The align hone is stroked back and forth through the bearing bores to properly size them, as shown in Figure 16–28 on page 380. It takes individual instruction and practice to develop a touch and the skill necessary to properly align main bearing bores in the block.

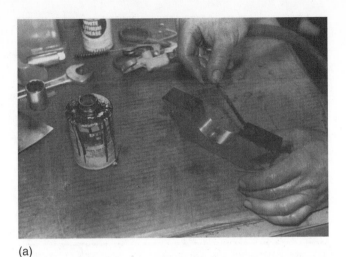

(a)

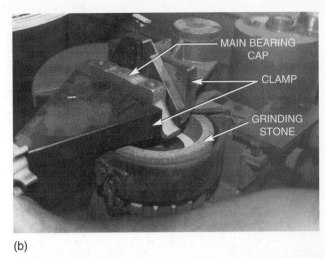

MAIN BEARING CAP

CLAMP

GRINDING STONE

(b)

Figure 16–25 (a) In preparation for align honing, the main bearing caps are coated with machinist bluing dye. Because less than 0.001 inch is to be removed from the bearing cap, the machinist wants to be certain that the material is removed equally. (b) One type of fixture is used here to remove a small amount of metal from a bearing cap.

Figure 16–26 Align boring the main bearing bores of a large industrial engine.

Step 5 The block and oil passages must be thoroughly cleaned after align boring to remove all abrasives and metal chips. The machined surfaces are coated with oil to prevent rusting until the block is finally cleaned for assembly.

■ MACHINING THE DECK SURFACE OF THE BLOCK

An engine should have the same combustion chamber size in each cylinder. For this to occur, each piston must come up an equal distance from the block deck. The con-

necting rods are attached to the rod bearing journals of the crankshaft. Pistons are attached to the connecting rods. As the crankshaft rotates, the pistons come to the top of the stroke. When all parts are sized equally, all the pistons will come up to the same level. This can only happen if the block deck is parallel to the main bearing bores. See Figures 16–29 through 16–31 on pages 380–381.

The block deck must be resurfaced in a surfacing machine that can control the amount of metal removed when it is necessary to match the size of the combustion chambers. This procedure is called **decking the block.** The block is set up on a bar located in the main bearing saddles, or set up on the oil pan rails of the block. The bar is parallel to the direction of cutting head movement. The

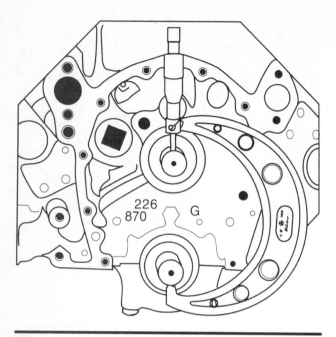

Figure 16–27 Special setup to measure the centerline distance between the crankshaft and camshaft. During align boring, material is removed from the saddle area of the block, placing the crankshaft closer to the camshaft.

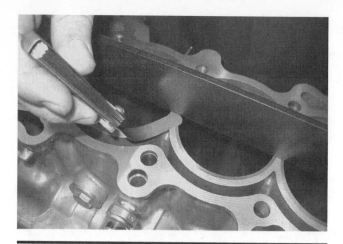

Figure 16–29 Check the level of the deck of a block with a straightedge. A good-quality straightedge should be accurate to 0.0002 inch (0.2 or two-tenths of a thousandth of an inch).

block is leveled sideways, and then the deck is resurfaced in the same manner as the head is resurfaced. Figure 16–32 on page 382 shows a block deck being resurfaced by grinding. Also see Figure 16–33 on page 382. The surface finish should be 60 to 100 Ra (65 to 110 RMS) for cast iron and 50 to 60 Ra (55 to 65 RMS) for aluminum block decks to be assured of a proper head gasket surface. See Chapter 13 for additional information on surface finish.

■ CYLINDER BORING

Cylinders should be measured across the engine (perpendicular to the crankshaft), where the greatest wear occurs. Most wear will be found just below the ridge, and the least amount of wear will occur below the lowest ring travel. See Figures 16–34 and 16–35 on pages 382–383. Most cylinders are serviceable if:

- Maximum of 0.003 inch (0.076 millimeter) out of round
- No more than 0.005 inch (0.127 millimeter) taper
- Have no deep scratches in the cylinder wall

Figure 16–28 Align honing the main bearing bores.

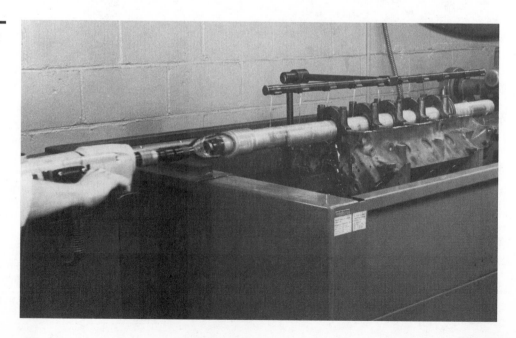

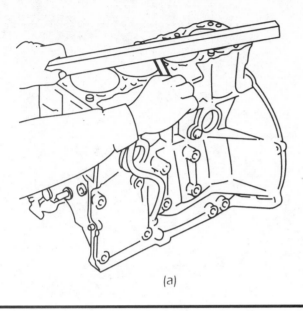

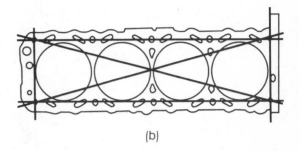

(a)

(b)

Figure 16–30 (a) Checking the flatness of the block deck surface using a straightedge and a feeler gauge. (b) To be sure that the top of the block is flat, check the block in six places as shown.

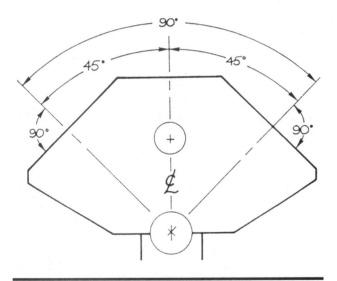

Figure 16–31 Machining a V-8 block helps to ensure that the deck surfaces are exactly 90 degrees from each other and that the block is square.

NOTE: Always check the specifications for the engine being surfaced. For example, the General Motors 5.7L, LS-1, V-8 has a maximum out-of-round of only 0.0003 (3/10 of one thousandth of an inch)!

The most effective way to correct excessive cylinder out-of-round, taper, or scoring is to **rebore** the cylinder. The rebored cylinder requires the use of a new, oversize piston.

Frequently Asked Question   **???**

How Do I Determine What Oversize Bore Is Needed?

An easy way to calculate oversize piston size is to determine the amount of taper, double it, and add 0.010 inch (Taper $\times$ 2 + 0.010 in. = OS piston). Common oversize measurements include 0.020 inch, 0.030 inch, 0.040 inch, and 0.060 inch. Use caution when boring for an oversize measurement larger than 0.030 inch.

The maximum bore oversize is determined by two things: the cylinder wall thickness and the size of the available oversize pistons. If in doubt as to the amount of overbore that is possible without causing structural weakness, an ultrasonic test should be performed on the block to determine the thickness of the cylinder walls. See Figure 16–36 on page 383. All cylinders should be tested. Variation in cylinder wall thickness occurs because of core shifting (moving) during the casting of the block. For best results, cylinders should be rebored to the smallest size possible.

HINT: The pistons that will be used should always be in hand *before* the cylinders are rebored. The cylinders are then bored and honed to match the exact size of the pistons.

Figure 16–32 Block deck being resurfaced with a grinder.

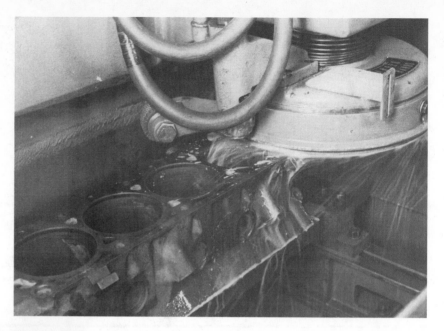

Figure 16–33 Typical abrasive grit stones. A fine grit stone is on the left and a coarse grit stone is on the right.

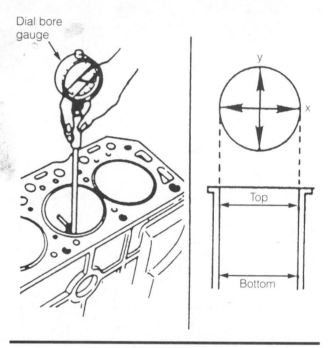

Dial bore gauge

Figure 16–34 Checking the cylinder using a dial bore gauge. First, measure the top of the cylinder at 90 degrees from the crankshaft centerline. This is the "X" diameter. Then, measure the diameter at the top of the cylinder in line with the crankshaft. This is the "Y" diameter. Subtracting the Y dimension from the X dimension will give the amount by which the cylinder is out-of-round. Measure the cylinder diameter at 90 degrees from the crankshaft centerline at the bottom of the cylinder. Subtract this measurement from the X diameter to calculate cylinder taper.

The cylinder must be perpendicular to the crankshaft for normal bearing and piston life. If the block deck has been aligned with the crankshaft, it can be used to align the cylinders. Portable cylinder boring bars are clamped to the block deck. Heavy-duty production boring machines support the block on the main bearing bores.

Main bearing caps should be torqued in place when cylinders are being rebored. In precision boring, a torque plate is also bolted on in place of the cylinder head while boring cylinders. In this way, distortion is

kept to a minimum. The general procedure used for reboring cylinders is to set the boring bar up so that it is perpendicular to the crankshaft. It must be located over the center of the cylinder. The cylinder center is found

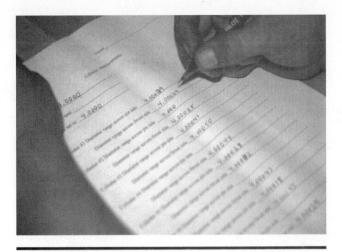

Figure 16–35 The wise technician measures and records all engine measurements before any machining is done to the block.

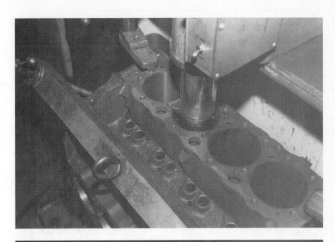

Figure 16–37 Production cylinder boring machine set up to begin boring a cylinder of a small-block Chevrolet V-8 engine.

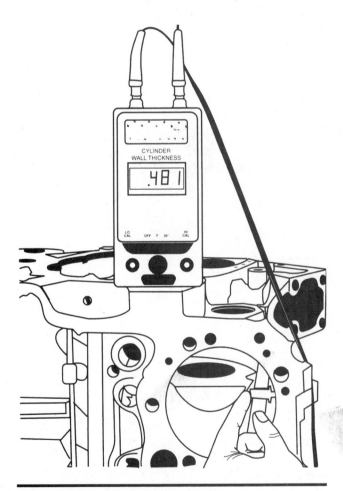

Figure 16–36 Ultrasonic testing can be used to determine the thickness of the cylinder walls. In this example, the thickness of the cast iron is 0.481 inch.

Figure 16–38 Four-cylinder automotive engine being bored two cylinders at a time at a large engine remanufacturing plant. Note that the block is being indexed off of the side rails instead of from the saddles. Oil pan side rails, saddles, and the block deck should all be parallel surfaces.

by installing centering pins in the bar. The bar is lowered so that the centering pins are located near the bottom of the cylinder, where the least wear has occurred. This lo-

cates the boring bar over the original cylinder center. Once the boring bar is centered, the boring machine is clamped in place to hold it securely. This will allow the cylinder to be rebored on the original centerline, regardless of the amount of cylinder wear. See Figures 16–37 and 16–38. A sharp, properly ground cutting tool is installed and adjusted to the desired dimension. Rough cuts remove a great deal of metal on each pass of the cutting tool. The surface of a rough cut is pictured in Figure 16–39. The rough cut is followed by a fine cut that

Figure 16–39 Finish of the cylinder surface after a rough cut has been made. *(Courtesy of Dana Corporation)*

Figure 16–40 Finish of the cylinder surface after a fine cut is made. *(Courtesy of Dana Corporation)*

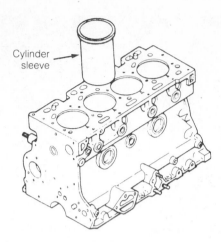

Figure 16–41 A sleeve can be used to save a block that is excessively worn. First the cylinder is bored to be slightly (about 0.003 inch) smaller than the outside diameter of the sleeve, and then the block is heated (to about 200°F) and the sleeve cooled in ice. The sleeve is then pressed into the block to form a new cylinder wall surface.

Figure 16–42 A typical cylinder sleeve.

produces a much smoother and more accurate finish, as shown in Figure 16–40. Different-shape tool bits are used for rough and finish boring. The cutting tools are resharpened before each cylinder is bored to accurately control the bore diameter and the surface finish. The last cut is made to produce a diameter that is at least 0.002 inch (0.05 millimeter) smaller than the required diameter. The cylinder wall is then finished by honing. Honing produces the required cylinder diameter and surface finish. Each cylinder is honed to give the correct clearance for the piston that is to operate in that cylinder.

■ SLEEVING THE CYLINDER

Sometimes, cylinders have a gouge so deep that it will not clean up when the cylinder is rebored to the maxi-

mum size. This could happen if the piston pin moved endways and rubbed on the cylinder wall. Cylinder blocks with deep gouges can be salvaged by **sleeving** the cylinder. This is done by boring the cylinder to a dimension that is greatly oversize to almost match the outside diameter of the cylinder sleeve. The sleeve is pressed into the rebored block; then the center of the sleeve is bored to the diameter required by the piston. The cylinder can be sized to use a standard-size piston when it is sleeved. See Figures 16–41 and 16–42.

■ CYLINDER HONING

It is important to have the proper surface finish on the cylinder wall for the rings to seat against. Some ring

Figure 16–43 Cutaway showing a spring-loaded deglazing hone in position for honing.

Figure 16–45 Cutaway engine shown with a sizing hone in position for honing.

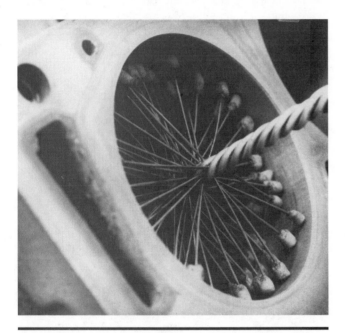

Figure 16–44 Brush (ball) type of deglazing hone in position for honing a cylinder.

Figure 16–46 Chevrolet small-block V-8 being honed after boring. Note that the main bearing caps are installed and torqued during both the boring and the honing operations to help prevent block distortion.

manufacturers recommend breaking the hard surface glaze on the cylinder wall with a hone before installing new piston rings. When honing is not required, no time is needed for honing or for cleanup. This reduces the reconditioning cost for the engine.

The cylinder wall should be honed to straighten the cylinder when the wall is wavy or scuffed. If honing is being done with the crankshaft remaining in the block, the crankshaft should be protected to keep honing chips from getting on the shaft.

Two types of hones are used for cylinder service.

- A **deglazing hone** removes the hard surface glaze remaining in the cylinder. It is a flexible hone that follows the shape of the cylinder wall, even when

the wall is wavy. It cannot be used to straighten the cylinder. A spring-loaded deglazing hone is shown in Figure 16–43. A **brush-type** (**ball type**) deglazing hone is shown in Figure 16–44.

- A **sizing hone** can be used to straighten the cylinder. Its honing stones are held in a rigid fixture with an expanding mechanism to control the size of the hone. The sizing hone can be used to straighten the cylinder taper by honing the lower cylinder diameter more than the upper diameter. As it rotates, the sizing hone only cuts the high spots so that cylinder out-of-round is also reduced. The cylinder wall surface finish is about the same when the cylinder is refinished with either type of hone. See Figures 16–45 and 16–46.

The hone is stroked up and down in the cylinder as it rotates. This produces a **crosshatch finish** on the

TECH TIP ✔

Always Use Torque Plates

Torque plates are thick metal plates that are bolted to the cylinder block to duplicate the forces on the block that occur when the cylinder head is installed. Even though not all machine shops use torque plates during the boring operation, the use of torque plates during the final dimensional honing operation is very beneficial. Without torque plates, cylinders can become out-of-round (up to 0.003 inch) and distorted when the cylinder heads are installed and torqued down. Even though the use of torque plates does not eliminate all distortion, their use helps to ensure a truer cylinder dimension. See Figure 16–47.

TECH TIP ✔

Bore to Size, Hone for Clearance

Many engine rebuilders and remanufacturers bore the cylinders to the exact size of the oversize pistons that are to be used. After the block is bored to a standard oversize measurement, the cylinder is honed. The rigid hone stones, along with an experienced operator, can increase the bore size by 0.001 to 0.003 inch (1 to 3 thousandths of an inch) for the typical clearance needed between the piston and the cylinder walls.

For example:

Actual piston diameter = 4.028 in.
Bore diameter = 4.028 in.
Diameter after honing = 4.030 in.
Amount removed by honing = 0.002 in

> **NOTE:** The minimum amount recommended to be removed by honing is 0.002 inch to remove the fractured metal in the cylinder wall caused by boring.

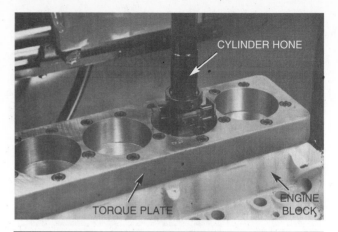

Figure 16–47 Honing a cylinder with a torque plate installed. The torque plate is bolted to the block and torqued so that it simulates the forces that act on the block when the cylinder head is installed. Therefore, the cylinder is machined to be true and straight when it is operating with the cylinder heads attached.

Figure 16–48 Typical finished honed cylinder. Note the crosshatch pattern necessary to ensure proper lubrication and wear in the piston rings.

cylinder wall. A typical honed cylinder is pictured in Figure 16–48. The angle of the crosshatch should be between 20 and 60 degrees. Higher angles are produced when the hone is stroked more rapidly in the cylinder.

■ CYLINDER SURFACE FINISH

The size of the abrasive particles in the grinding and honing stones controls the surface finish. The size of the abrasive is called the **grit size.** The abrasive is sifted through a screen mesh to sort out the grit size. A coarse-mesh screen has few wires in each square inch, so large pieces can fall through the screen. A fine-mesh screen has many wires in each square inch so that only small pieces can fall through. The screen is used to separate the different grit sizes. The grit size is the number of wires in each square inch of the mesh. A low-numbered grit has large pieces of abrasive material; a high-numbered grit has small pieces of abrasive material. The higher the grit number being used, the smoother the surface finish will be. A given grit size will produce the same finish as long as the cutting pressure

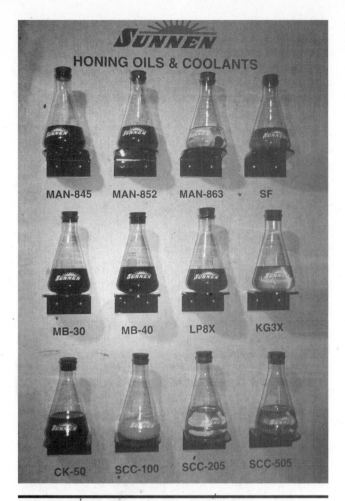

Figure 16–49 An assortment of the various honing oils and coolants available. Always use the correct oil or coolant as specified by the equipment manufacturer.

Figure 16–50 Each cylinder should be checked with a dial bore gauge often during the honing process to ensure that the cylinders are within the desired limits for taper and out-of-round.

is constant. With the same grit size, light cutting pressure produces fine finishes, and heavy cutting pressure produces rough finishes.

The surface finish should match the surface required for the type of piston rings to be used. See Chapter 17 for details on piston rings. Typical grit and surface finish standards include the following:

- Chrome—#180 grit (25 to 35 microinches)
- Cast iron—#200 grit (20 to 30 microinches)
- Moly—#220 grit (18 to 25 microinches)

NOTE: The correct honing oil and/or coolant is critical to proper operation of the honing equipment and to the quality of the finished cylinders. See Figure 16–49 for the many different examples of honing oil and coolants that one equipment manufacturer has available.

The hone is placed in the cylinder. Before the drive motor is turned on, the hone is moved up and down in the cylinder to get the feel of the stroke length needed. The end of the hone should just break out of the cylinder bore on each end. The hone must *not* be pulled from the top of the cylinder while it is rotating. Also, it must not be pushed so low in the cylinder that it hits the main bearing web or crankshaft. The sizing hone is adjusted to give a solid drag at the lower end of the stroke. The hone drive motor is turned on and stroking begins immediately. Stroking continues until the sound of the drag is reduced. The hone drive motor is turned off while it is still stroking. Stroking is stopped as the rotation of the hone stops. After rotation stops, the hone is collapsed and removed from the cylinder. The cylinder is examined to check the bore size and finish of the wall. If more honing is needed, the cylinder is again coated with honing oil and the cylinder is honed again. The finished cylinder should be within 0.0005 inch (0.013 millimeter) on both out-of-round and taper measurements. See Figure 16–50.

Figure 16–51 To achieve a finer surface finish, use a soft hone that is made from nylon bristles with impregnated abrasive. This hone is ideal for engines using low tension piston rings and provides a smooth surface that allows the rings to seal immediately.

■ PLATEAU HONING

Plateau honing is a two-step machining operation that reduces cylinder and piston ring wear. The first step involves a rough stone that cuts a crosshatch pattern on the cylinder walls 0.0025 to 0.0030 inch deep (2 1/2 to 3 thousandths of an inch) (0.06 to 0.07 millimeter). A second honing operation uses a relatively soft stone to remove the sharp tops of the grooves left by the first, rough hone. See Figures 16–51 and 16–52. The smooth, final hone provides grooves in which engine oil can stay to lubricate piston rings.

It is not unusual to remove the cylinder head of an engine with over 100,000 miles (160,000 kilometers) and observe the hone marks still on the cylinder walls. Wet and dry sleeves are also plateau honed in some engines.

■ CYLINDER CLEANING

After the cylinders have been honed and before the block is cleaned, use a sandpaper cone to chamfer the top edge of the cylinder as shown in Figure 16–53. Cleaning the honed cylinder wall is an important part of the honing process. If any grit remains on the cylinder wall, it will rapidly wear the piston rings. This wear will cause premature failure of the reconditioning job. Degreasing and decarbonizing procedures will only remove the honing oil. They will *not* remove the abrasive. The best way to clean the honed cylinders is to scrub the cylinder wall with a brush using a mixture of soap or detergent and water. See Figure 16–54. The block is scrubbed until it is absolutely clean. This can be determined by wiping the cylinder wall with a clean cloth. The cloth will pick up no soil when the cylinder wall is clean.

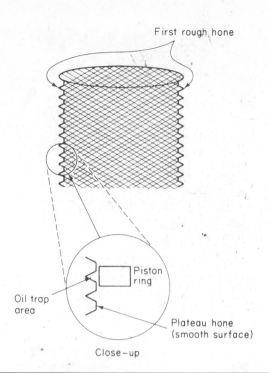

Figure 16–52 Plateau honing involves honing the cylinder with a coarse stone and then using a finer hone to flatten off the sharp peaks left from the coarse stone (forming a plateau).

Figure 16–53 The operator is using a tapered sandpaper cone to chamfer the sharp edges at the top of the cylinders after boring, honing, and decking of the block. This operation is necessary to prevent damage to piston rings during installation of pistons.

■ BLOCK DETAILING

Before the engine block can be assembled, a final detailed cleaning should be performed.

Figure 16–54 The best way to clean cylinders that have to be machined is to use soap (detergent) and water and thoroughly clean with a large washing brush.

Figure 16–55 All oil galleries should be cleaned using soap (detergent) and water and a long oil gallery cleaning brush.

1. All oil passages (galleries) should be cleaned by running a long bottle-type brush through all holes in the block as shown in Figure 16–55.
2. All tapped holes should be chamfered and cleaned with the correct size of tap to remove any dirt and burrs. See Figures 16–56 and 16–57.
3. Coat the newly cleaned block with fogging oil to prevent rust. Cover the block with a large plastic bag to keep out dirt until it is time to assemble the engine.

Figure 16–56 All bolt holes should be cleaned using a bottoming tap.

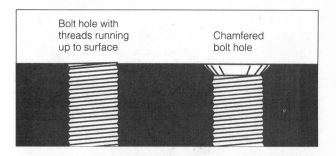

Figure 16–57 All bolt holes should be chamfered at the top to prevent the attaching bolts from pulling threads at the top surface.

PHOTO SEQUENCE   Cylinder Measurement and Honing

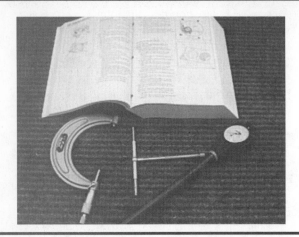

PS 25–1 The tools and equipment needed to hone the cylinder include the service manual for engine block specifications, a dial bore gauge, along with a telescoping gauge and outside micrometer to accurately measure the cylinder bore.

PS 25–2 Start the honing process by carefully lowering the engine block into the cylinder hone bay. Use a nylon strap to support and hoist the block to avoid causing harm to the machined surfaces of the block that may occur if a metal chain were used.

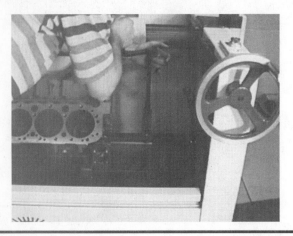

PS 25–3 Clamping the block to the holding fixture.

PS 25–4 After the block has been securely attached to the holding fixture, the hone has to be adjusted for the bore diameter. The technician is gauging the shims for the honing head.

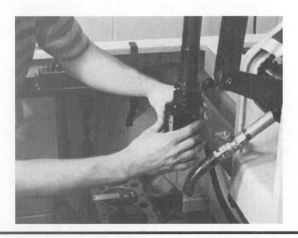

PS 25–5 After gauging the honing head, the shims are installed in the honing head.

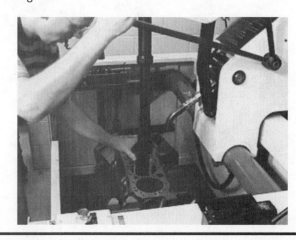

PS 25–6 After the honing head has been shimmed, it is lowered into the cylinder.

Cylinder Measurement and Honing—continued

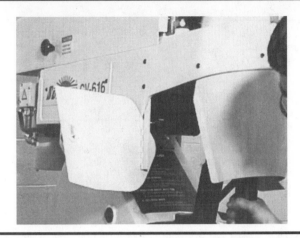

PS 25–7 After installing the honing head into the cylinder, the top limit of the stroke has to be set. Notice the safety shield is open.

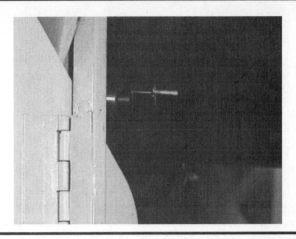

PS 25–8 When the marks align, the honing head is at the top of the stroke.

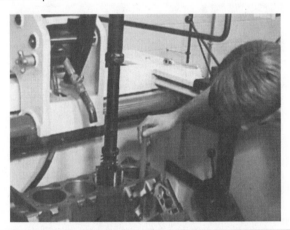

PS 25–9 The next step in the cylinder honing process is to use a hook ruler to measure the length of the cylinder.

PS 25–10 After determining the length of the cylinder, the stroke length is set.

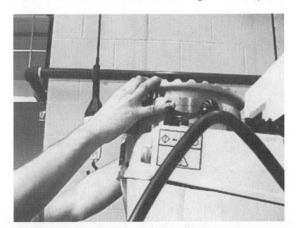

PS 25–11 Setting the "crown" for stock removal. This adjusts the pressure of the honing stone against the cylinder walls.

PS 25–12 The honing operation is started after all adjustments and settings have been performed.

Cylinder Measurement and Honing—continued

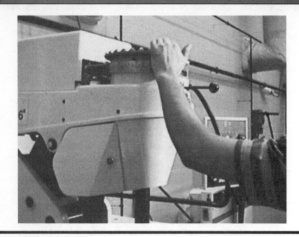

PS 25–13 The crown may need adjustment for the correct honing pressure.

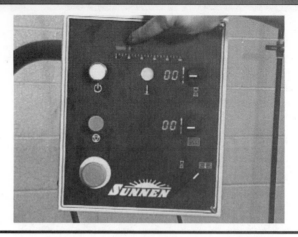

PS 25–14 The bar graph indicates honing pressure. For a rough cut, the pressure should be set to 60% to 80% and to 20% to 40% for a finish cut.

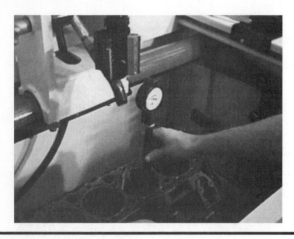

PS 25–15 After honing for a short time, it is important to check the cylinder for proper dimension using a dial bore gauge.

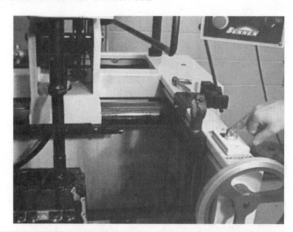

PS 25–16 It is often necessary to change the amount of time the hone stays in a certain area. For example, a dwell button is pushed to achieve greater stock removal at the bottom of the cylinder.

PS 25–17 The finish cylinder hone should have the characteristic 60-degree crosshatch pattern as shown.

PS 25–18 Finish honing should be performed using a torque plate. Using a finish honing stone results in a round cylinder with a plateau hone surface and correct surface finish.

PHOTO SEQUENCE   Main Bearing Housing Bore Align Honing

PS 26–1 Before align honing the main bearing bores, the main bearing caps are installed and torqued to factory specifications. A dial bore gauge is then used to determine the variation in diameter in the original housing bores.

PS 26–2 The dial bore gauge is also used to check for taper and out-of-round of each bore.

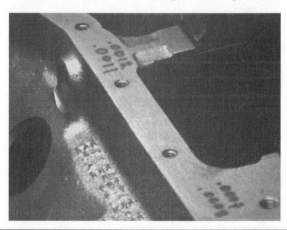

PS 26–3 The machinist wrote the variation in the bore housing on the rail of the block using a felt-tip marker for easy reference.

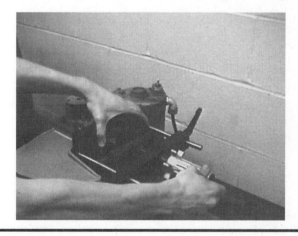

PS 26–4 After all main bearing bores have been measured and recorded, the main bearing caps are removed from the engine and placed on a cap grinder to remove material from the main bearing cap.

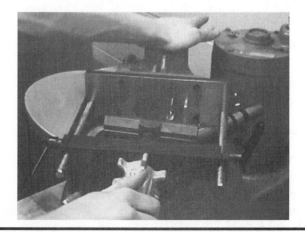

PS 26–5 The cap is first placed flat and clamped tight into the vise and then the side of the cap is ground.

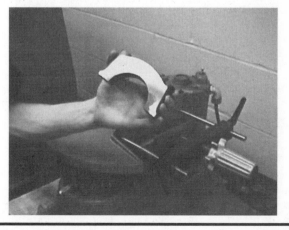

PS 26–6 Grinding the side of the cap first ensures that the cap is clamped into the vise squarely.

Main Bearing Housing Bore Align Honing—continued

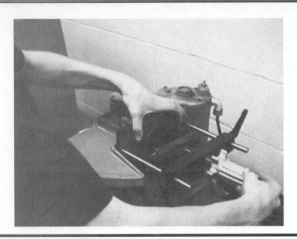

PS 26–7 After the side of the bearing cap is ground, it is then placed vertically in the vise with the machined surface of the main bearing cap against the flat surface of the holding fixture.

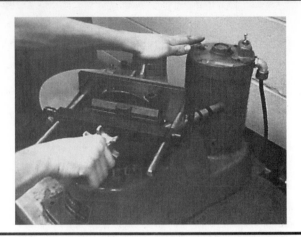

PS 26–8 A small amount of material is ground from the mating surface of the main bearing cap. The amount removed should be the same for each cap.

PS 26–9 The cap grinder is being adjusted for the amount of material to be removed from the main bearing cap.

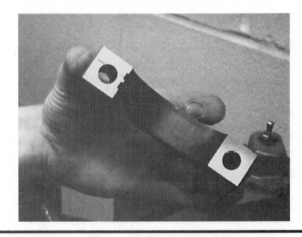

PS 26–10 The finished cap shows that the entire surface of the end of the cap has been ground. This procedure is repeated for all main bearing caps.

PS 26–11 Before reassembling the bearing caps onto the engine block, use a file to remove any sharp edges from the saddle area that could interfere with the proper joining of the bearing caps in the block.

PS 26–12 After the caps have been ground and before they are installed on the block, a file is used to remove any burrs from the sharp edges created by the grinding operating.

Main Bearing Housing Bore Align Honing—continued

PS 26–13 To be sure that everything is clean, all oil passages are blown out using compressed air.

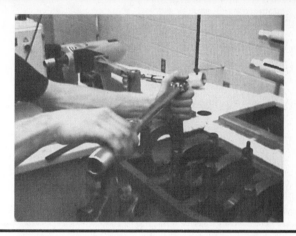

PS 26–14 After everything has been deburred and cleaned, the main bearing caps are reinstalled onto the block and torqued to factory specifications.

PS 26–15 The main bearing bores are again measured using a dial bore gauge to make sure that each is the same size. If necessary, a cap may have to be removed and additional material ground from the mating surface to achieve the proper diameter.

PS 26–16 The aligned hone is now installed and adjusted for proper tension.

PS 26–17 The main bearing bores are then honed round by using a large electric motor to drive the honing stones through the bores.

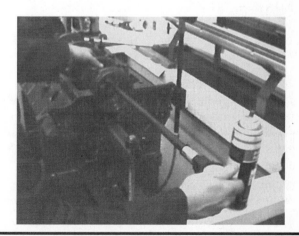

PS 26–18 The dimension of the main bearing bores should be checked after performing the honing process.

PHOTO SEQUENCE Decking a Block

PS 27–1 Before the deck surface of the block can be machined, it has to be precisely located onto the surfacer mounts by aligning the main bearing bores on a 2 inch diameter ground shaft. On the shaft are two bearing **pucks** that are specifically sized for each engine. These pucks are aligned with the front and rear main bearing bores.

PS 27–2 After attaching the main bearing caps over the pucks, the engine block is leveled by rotating the jack screw mechanism. Note the bubble level on the deck surface.

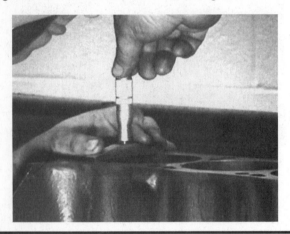

PS 27–3 To determine the deck height, a depth micrometer is being used to measure the distance between the deck surface and the ground shaft.

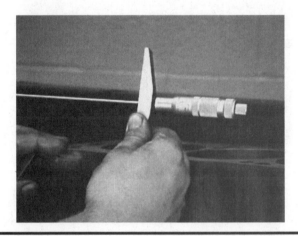

PS 27–4 Because the supporting shaft is exactly 2 inches in diameter, the deck height is determined by adding 1 inch to the measurement obtained on the micrometer. This is the exact distance from the deck surface to the centerline of the main bearing bores.

■ SUMMARY

1. Engine blocks are either cast iron or aluminum.

2. Cores are used inside a mold to form water jackets and cylinder bores. After the cast iron has cooled, the block is shaken, which breaks up the cores so that they fall out of openings in the side of the block. Core plugs are used to fill the holes.

3. Aluminum blocks normally use cast-iron cylinder liners. Some engines use cylinder sleeves that are in contact with the coolant and are called wet cylinder sleeves.

4. The block deck is the surface to which the cylinder head attaches. This surface must be flat and true for proper engine operation.

5. Main bearing caps should be installed and torqued to specification before any machining is performed on the block.

6. The first machining operation is align boring or honing, followed by machining the block deck surface, followed by cylinder boring and honing.

7. The cylinder should be bored to the same size as the piston diameter and then honed to the amount of cylinder bore-to-piston clearance specified.

8. All bolt holes should be chamfered and cleaned with a tap.

Decking a Block—continued

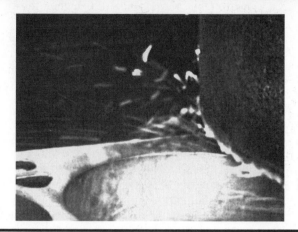

PS 27–5 After the block has been securely attached, leveled, and measured, the deck surface can be ground. A typical pass across the deck surface will remove about 0.001 inch to 0.0015 inch.

PS 27–6 It is wise to double-check the deck height especially if more than one cut is required to straighten the top of the block surface.

PS 27–7 A typical block may require 0.004 to 0.006 inches be removed from the deck surface to eliminate any warpage or waviness.

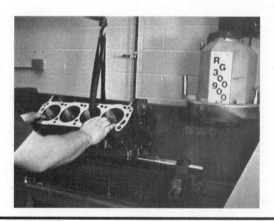

PS 27–8 After both deck surfaces have been machined and checked, the block can be removed from the attachment using an engine hoist equipped with a nylon strap to prevent damaging the machined surfaces of the block.

■ REVIEW QUESTIONS

1. How is #1 cylinder determined by looking at the block of a V-type engine?

2. Explain the difference between a shallow skirt and a deep skirt on a V block.

3. Explain why core plugs are named as such.

4. What is a broach and where is it used in the manufacturing process?

5. Describe the difference between a two-bolt and a four-bolt main engine block.

6. What is the difference between align boring and align honing?

7. What does "decking the block" mean?

8. Explain what microinch finish means.

9. What is the difference between deglazing and honing a cylinder?

10. What is the best method to use to clean an engine block after honing?

■ ASE CERTIFICATION-TYPE QUESTIONS

1. Cylinder #1 is generally _____ .
   a. The most forward cylinder [closest to the accessory drive belt(s)]
   b. The first one in the firing order
   c. The cylinder farthest from the principal end
   d. All of the above

2. A shallow skirt block _____ .
   a. Has the oil pan rail below the centerline of the crankshaft
   b. Has the oil pan rail above the centerline of the crankshaft
   c. Has the oil pan rail close to the centerline of the crankshaft
   d. Has a more shallow oil pan (sump) than other engine types

3. The block deck is the _____ .
   a. Bottom (pan rail) of the block
   b. Top surface of the block
   c. Valley surface of a V-type engine
   d. Area where the engine mounts are attached to the block

4. A broach is _____ .
   a. A type of boring machine
   b. A type of casting technique
   c. A machining process that uses a large slab with a number of cutting teeth
   d. A type of honing machine used on production engines only

5. Which engine block machining process should be done first when reconditioning?
   a. Cylinder boring
   b. Decking the block
   c. Honing the cylinders
   d. Align boring (honing)

6. The standard measurement for surface finish is the microinch root-mean-square. Which of the following is correct?
   a. The rougher the surface, the higher the microinch finish measurement.
   b. The smoother the surface, the higher the microinch finish measurement.
   c. The rougher the surface, the lower the microinch finish measurement.
   d. Both b and c.

7. Sleeving a cylinder means _____ .
   a. Plating the inner walls of the cylinder with a different metal, such as nickel
   b. Boring the cylinder to be oversize and installing a cast-iron sleeve to restore the cylinder to the original diameter
   c. Boring the cylinder to be 0.020 to 0.060 inch oversize to accept oversize pistons
   d. Using a hone to finish the cylinder after boring

8. For honing a cylinder for moly piston rings, a _____ grit hone should be used.
   a. #150
   b. #180
   c. #220
   d. #280

9. After decking, boring, and honing an engine block, what other metal-removing operation should be performed?
   a. Align honing the main bearing caps and saddles
   b. Chamfering the cylinder bores and bolt holes
   c. Broaching the timing chain cover surface
   d. Filing the oil pan rails flat

10. The minimum amount of material that is recommended to be removed from the cylinder after boring is _____ .
    a. 0.010 inch
    b. 0.008 inch
    c. 0.002 inch
    d. 0.001 inch

Pistons, Rings, and Connecting Rods

Objectives: After studying Chapter 17, the reader should be able to:

1. Describe the purpose and function of pistons, rings, and connecting rods.
2. Explain how pistons and rods are constructed and what to look for during an inspection.
3. Discuss connecting rod reconditioning procedures.
4. Explain how piston rings operate and how to install them on a piston.

All engine power is developed by burning fuel in the presence of air in the combustion chamber. Heat from the combustion causes the burned gas to increase in pressure. The force of this pressure is converted into useful work through the piston, connecting rod, and crankshaft.

■ PURPOSE AND FUNCTION OF PISTONS, RINGS, AND CONNECTING RODS

The **piston** forms a movable bottom to the combustion chamber. It is attached to the connecting rod with a **piston pin** or **wrist pin.** See Figure 17–1. The piston pin is allowed to have a rocking movement because of a swivel joint at the piston end of the connecting rod. The connecting rod is connected to a part of the crankshaft called a **crank throw, crankpin,** or **connecting rod bearing journal.** This provides another swivel joint.

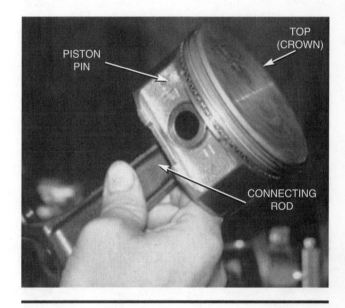

Figure 17–1 A piston and connecting rod assembly.

The center of the crank throw is the amount by which the large end of the connecting rod is offset from the crankshaft main bearing centerline. This dimension of the crankshaft determines the stroke of the engine.

NOTE: The stroke is the distance from the center of the main bearing journal to the center of the connecting rod journal times two.

Piston rings seal the small space between the piston and cylinder wall, keeping the pressure above the piston. When the pressure builds up in the combustion chamber, it pushes on the piston. The piston, in turn, pushes on the piston pin and upper end of the connecting rod. The lower end of the connecting rod pushes on the crank throw. This provides the force to turn the crankshaft. As the crankshaft turns, it develops inertia. *Inertia is the force that causes the crankshaft to continue rotating.* This action will bring the piston back to its original position, where it will be ready for the next power stroke. While the engine is running, the combustion cycle keeps repeating as the piston reciprocates (moves up and down) and the crankshaft rotates.

■ PISTON AND ROD REMOVAL

After the oil pan and cylinder head(s) have been removed, the piston and rod can be removed by the following steps

Step #1 The rod and caps should be checked for markings that identify their location. *If the rod and caps are not marked, they should be marked before disassembly.* If number stamps are not available, punch marks, as shown in Figure 17–2, can be used.

> **CAUTION:** Powdered metal connecting rods should only be marked with an electric etching pencil or a permanent marker to avoid damage to the rod. See Figure 17–3.

Step #2 The crankshaft is turned until the piston is at the bottom of its stroke. This places the connecting rod nuts or cap screws where they are easily accessible. They are removed, and the rod cap is taken off. This may require light tapping on the connecting rod bolts with a soft-faced hammer.

Step #3 Protectors should be placed over the rod bolt threads to protect the threads and the surface of the crankshaft journal. The piston and rod assembly is pushed out, care being taken to avoid hitting the bottom edge of the cylinder with the rod.

> **NOTE:** If the cylinder is hit, it will raise a burr. If the burr is not removed, it will score the piston after the engine is reassembled and run, as shown in Figure 17–4.

The rod caps should be reattached to the rod after the assembly has been removed from the cylinder. The rod caps are not interchangeable between rods. The assembly must be handled carefully. They should be

Figure 17–2 Punch marks on connecting rod and rod cap to identify their location in the engine.

Figure 17–3 Powdered metal connecting rods can be identified by their smooth appearance.

Figure 17–4 A piston skirt that was scored by a burr raised by hitting the bottom of the cylinder skirt with the connecting rod as it was being removed.

placed on a parts stand so that they do not strike each other. The aluminum piston can be easily scratched or nicked.

> **NOTE:** See Chapter 9 for ridge reaming procedures to be used before removing pistons from a high-mileage engine.

The rings are carefully removed from the piston to avoid damage to either the piston or the ring. The best way to remove them is to use a **piston ring expanding tool.**

■ PISTON DESIGN

When the engine is running, the piston starts at the top of the cylinder. As it moves downward, it accelerates until it reaches a maximum velocity slightly before it is halfway down. The piston comes to a stop at the bottom of the cylinder at 180 degrees of crankshaft rotation. During the next 180 degrees of crankshaft rotation, the piston moves upward. It accelerates to reach a maximum velocity slightly above the halfway point and then comes to a stop at the top of the stroke. Thus, the piston starts, accelerates, and stops twice in each crankshaft revolution.

> **NOTE:** A typical piston in an engine at 4000 RPM accelerates from 0 to 60 miles per hour (97 kilometers per hour) in about 0.004 seconds (4 milliseconds) as it descends about halfway down the cylinder.

This reciprocating action of the piston produces large **inertia forces.** Inertia is the force that causes a part that is stopped to stay stopped or a part that is in motion to stay in motion. The lighter the piston can be made, the less inertia force that is developed. Less inertia will allow higher engine operating speeds. For this reason, pistons are made to be as light as possible while still having the strength that is needed.

The piston operates with its head exposed to the hot combustion gases, whereas the skirt contacts the relatively cool cylinder wall. This results in a temperature difference of about 275°F (147°C) between the top and bottom of the piston. The temperature difference between cast and forged pistons is shown in Figure 17–5.

Aluminum alloy has proven to be the best material for making pistons. Good design has been able to provide sufficient engine displacement with a small external engine size. This is done by keeping the height of the piston to a bare minimum and bringing it close to the crankshaft at the bottom of the stroke, as shown in Figure 17–6. This piston must still have enough strength to support combustion pressure and reciprocating loads. It must also have enough piston skirt to guide it straight in the bore. In addition, the piston must have heat expansion control for quiet, long-life operation. Finally, it holds the piston rings perpendicular to the cylinder wall so that they can seal properly.

TECH TIP ☑

Piston Weight Is Important!

All pistons in an engine should weigh the same to help ensure a balanced engine. Piston weight becomes a factor when changing pistons. Most aluminum pistons range in weight from 10 to 30 ounces (280 to 850 grams) (1 oz = 28.35 grams). *A typical paper clip weighs 1 gram.* If the cylinder has been bored, larger replacement pistons are obviously required. If the replacement pistons weigh more, this puts additional inertia loads on the rod bearings. Therefore, to help prevent rod bearing failure on an overhauled engine, the replacement pistons should not weigh more than the original pistons.

> **CAUTION:** Some less-expensive replacement cast pistons or high performance forged pistons are much heavier than the stock pistons, even in the stock bore size. This means that the crankshaft may need heavy metal added to the counterweights of the crankshaft for the engine to be balanced.

For the same reason, if one piston is being replaced, all pistons should be replaced or at least checked and corrected to ensure the same weight.

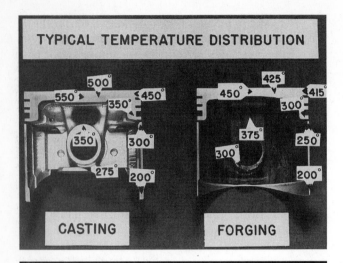

Figure 17–5 Differences in temperature within pistons operated under the same conditions. *(Courtesy of TRW)*

■ PISTON HEADS

Because the piston head forms a portion of the combustion chamber, its shape is very important to the combustion process. Generally, low-cost, low performance engines have **flat-top** pistons. Some of these flat-top pistons come so close to the cylinder head that **recesses** are cut in the piston top for valve clearance. Pistons used in high-powered engines may have raised domes or **pop-ups** on the piston heads. These are used to increase the compression ratio. Pistons used in other engines may be provided with a depression or a **dish.** The varying depths of the dish provide different compression ratios required by different engine models. Several piston head shapes are shown in Figure 17–7.

> **NOTE:** Newer engines do not use valve reliefs because this requires that the thickness of the top of the piston be increased to provide the necessary strength. The thicker the top of the piston, the lower down from the top the top piston ring. To reduce unburned hydrocarbon (HC) exhaust emissions, engineers attempt to place the top piston ring as close to the top of the piston as possible to prevent the unburned fuel from being trapped (and not burned) between the top of the piston and the top of the top piston ring.

Recesses machined or cast into the tops of the pistons for valve clearance are commonly called **eyebrows, valve reliefs,** or **valve pockets.** The depth of the eyebrows has a major effect on the compression ratio and is necessary to provide clearance for the valves if the timing belt of an overhead camshaft engine

Figure 17–6 The piston is very close to the crankshaft counterweight when the piston is at the bottom of the stroke. The piston has a slipper skirt when the connecting rod is short, as shown here.

should break. Without the eyebrows, the pistons could hit the valves near TDC if the valves are not operating (closing) because of nonrotation of the camshaft. If an engine is designed not to have the pistons hitting the valves, the engine is called **freewheeling.** For example, the Ford Escort engine was changed in the mid-1980s to a freewheeling design by machining deeper eyebrows into the tops of the pistons. Before this change, if the timing belt broke, serious engine damage resulted, because the pistons would still move up and down a few times while the valves did not change position. When the pistons hit the valves, the pistons could be cracked, which in turn could crack the block, besides damaging the rods and bending valves.

The piston head must have enough strength to support combustion pressures. Ribs are often used on the underside of the head to maintain strength while at the same time reducing material to lighten the piston. These ribs are also used as cooling fins to transfer some of the piston heat to the engine oil. Typical ribs on the underside of the piston can be seen in Figure 17–8.

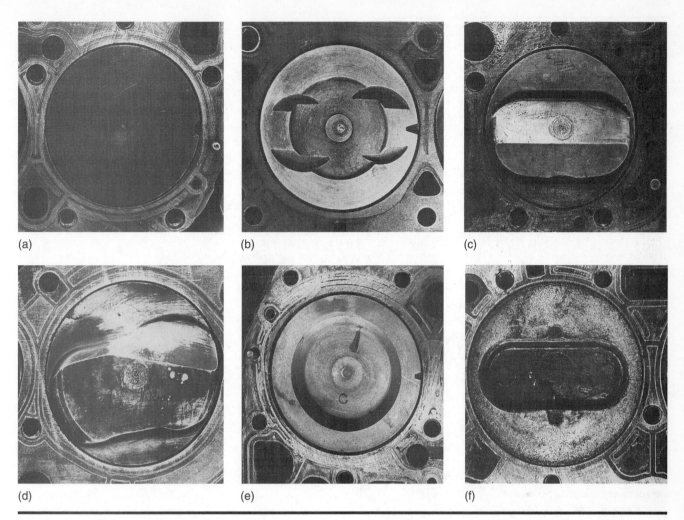

Figure 17–7 Piston head shapes: (a) flat, (b) recessed, (c and d) pop-up, and (e and f) dished.

Figure 17–8 Ribs on the underside of the piston.

RIBS

■ PISTON RING GROOVES

Piston ring **grooves** are located between the piston head and skirt. The width of the grooves, the width of the **lands** between the ring grooves, and the number of rings are major factors in determining minimum piston height. The outside diameter of the lands is about 0.020 to 0.040 inch (0.5 to 1.0 millimeter) smaller than the **skirt** diameter. See Figure 17–9. Some pistons for heavy-duty engines have oil ring grooves located on the piston skirt below the piston pin. Most engines use two compression rings and one oil control ring. They are all located above the piston pin.

> **NOTE:** Some engines, such as the Honda high-fuel economy engine, use pistons with two rings: one compression ring and one oil ring.

Cylinder sealing is possible because of accurate machining and fitting procedures. The piston ring groove must be deep enough to prevent the ring from hitting

Figure 17–9 Piston skirt cam shape. *(Courtesy of Chrysler Corporation)*

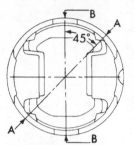

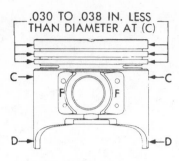

THE ELLIPTICAL SHAPE OF THE PISTON SKIRT SHOULD BE .010 TO .012 IN. LESS AT DIAMETER (A) THAN ACROSS THE THRUST FACES AT DIAMETER (B). MEASUREMENT IS MADE 1/8 IN. BELOW LOWER RING GROOVE

DIAMETERS AT (C) AND (D) CAN BE EQUAL OR DIAMETER AT (D) CAN BE .0015 IN. GREATER THAN (C)

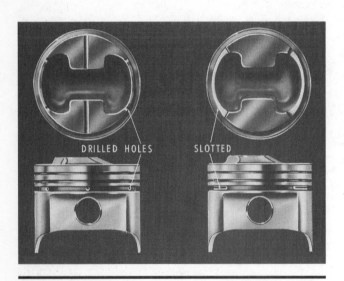

Figure 17–10 Oil ring groove venting using drilled holes and slots. *(Courtesy of Chevrolet Motor Division, GMC)*

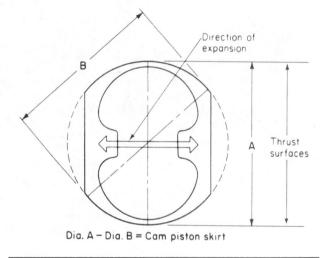

Dia. A – Dia. B = Cam piston skirt

Figure 17–11 Piston cam shape. The largest diameter is across the thrust surfaces and perpendicular to the piston pin (lettered *A*).

the base of the groove when the ring is pressed in so that it is flat with the land face. This is called **back spacing.** This groove depth becomes critical for some piston ring expander designs. These expanders wedge between the back of the ring and the base of the groove. The sides of the groove must be square and flat so that the side of the piston ring will seal on the side of the groove. Oil ring grooves are vented in the base so that oil scraped from the cylinder wall can flow through the vents to the crankcase. This venting is done through drilled holes or slots, as shown in Figure 17–10.

■ CAM GROUND PISTONS

Aluminum pistons expand when they get hot. A method of expansion control was devised using a **cam ground** piston skirt. With this design, the piston thrust surfaces

closely fit the cylinder, and the piston pin boss diameter is fitted loosely. As the cam ground piston is heated, it expands along the piston pin so that it becomes nearly round at its normal operating temperatures. A cam ground piston skirt is illustrated in Figure 17–11.

■ PISTON HEAD SIZE

The top or head of the piston is smaller in diameter than the rest of the piston. The top of the piston is exposed to the most heat and therefore tends to expand more than the rest of the piston. Most pistons have horizontal separation **slots** that act as **heat dams.** These slots reduce heat transfer from the hot piston head to the lower skirt. This, in turn, keeps the skirt temperature lower so that there will be less skirt expansion. Because the slot is placed in the oil ring groove, it can be used for oil drain-back and expansion control. Some engines are built with a slot below the piston pin. This isolates the lower skirt from piston pin boss deflections caused by stress that occurs on the power stroke. The lower skirt can better maintain its size. These heat dam slots can be seen in Figures 17–12 and 17–13.

■ PISTON STRUT INSERTS

A major development in expansion control occurred when the piston aluminum was cast around two stiff steel **struts.** The struts are not chemically bonded to the aluminum, nor do they add any strength to the piston. There is only a mechanical bond between the steel and aluminum. The bimetallic action of this strut in the aluminum forces the piston to bow outward along the

piston pin. This keeps the piston skirt thrust surfaces from expanding more than the cast-iron cylinder in which the piston operates. Pistons with steel strut inserts allow good piston-to-cylinder wall clearance at normal temperatures. At the same time, they allow the cold operating clearance to be as small as 0.0005 inch (one-half thousandth of an inch) (0.0127 millimeter). This small clearance will prevent cold piston slap and noise. A typical piston expansion control strut is visible in Figure 17–14.

With newer engines, the number and thickness of the piston rings have decreased and the cast-aluminum piston skirt has been reduced to a minimum by using an open-type **slipper skirt.** Examples of the slipper skirt piston are shown in Figures 17–15 and 17–16.

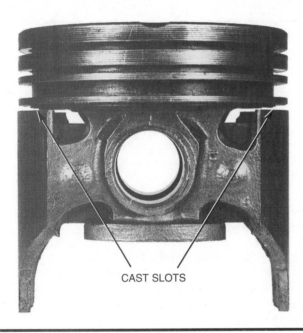

CAST SLOTS

Figure 17–12 Cast heat dam slots just below the oil ring grooves.

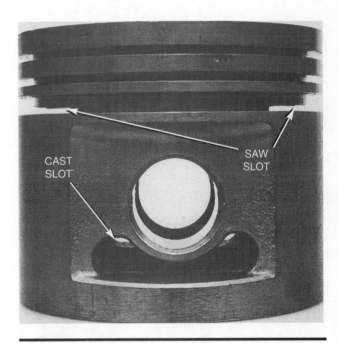

CAST SLOT

SAW SLOT

Figure 17–13 Sawed heat dam slot in the bottom of the oil ring groove and a cast slot below the piston pin.

Figure 17–14 Action of the steel strut to help control expansion of the piston as it gets hot.

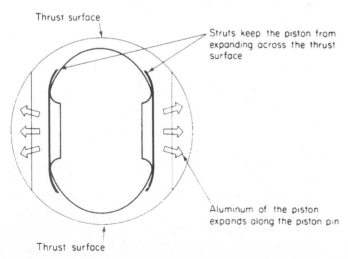

Thrust surface

Struts keep the piston from expanding across the thrust surface

Aluminum of the piston expands along the piston pin

Thrust surface

Figure 17–15 Two sectional views of a slipper-skirt-type piston that uses a steel expansion strut.

Figure 17–16 Piston from a dual overhead camshaft engine with four valves per cylinder. This high-revving engine (redline at 7500 RPM) uses a short skirt piston and thin, low-friction piston rings.

■ HYPEREUTECTIC PISTONS

A standard cast-aluminum piston contains about 9% to 12% silicon and is called a eutectic piston. To add strength, the silicon content is increased to about 16%, and the resulting piston is called a **hypereutectic** piston. Other advantages of a hypereutectic piston are its 25% weight reduction and lower expansion rate. The disadvantage of hypereutectic pistons is their higher cost, because they are more difficult to cast and machine.

Hypereutectic pistons are commonly used in the aftermarket and as original equipment in many turbocharged and supercharged engines.

■ FORGED PISTONS

High performance engines need pistons with added strength. They use impact-extruded forged pistons whose design falls between that of the two extremes of heavy-duty and automotive pistons. Figure 17–17 shows a forged aluminum piston with a trunk skirt.

■ PISTON SKIRT FINISH

For maximum life, the piston skirt surface finish is important. Older piston designs used turned grooves or waves that were 0.0005 inch (0.0125 millimeter) deep on the surface of some piston skirts, which produced a finish that would carry oil for lubrication. See Figure 17–18. A thin tin-plated surface (approximately 0.00005 inch or 0.00125 millimeter thick) is also used on some aluminum pistons to help reduce scuffing and scoring during occasional periods of minimum lubrication. The piston skirt normally rides on a film of lubricating oil. Anytime the oil film is lacking, metal-to-metal contact will occur, which starts piston scuffing. See Figure 17–19 for an example of a piston coated with a moly graphite coating to reduce scuffing.

Figure 17–19 A moly graphite coating on the skirt of this piston from a General Motors 3800 V-6 engine helps prevent piston scuffing when the engine is cold.

Figure 17–17 Grain flow lines can be seen in this forged aluminum piston with a trunk skirt.

■ PISTON BALANCE

Pistons used in older engines are provided with **enlarged pads** or skirt flanges (Figure 17–20) that are used for controlling piston weight. Material is removed from the surface of these pads by the manufacturer as

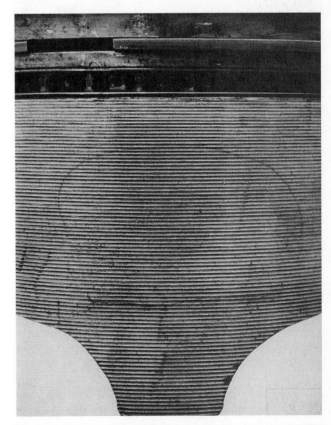

Figure 17–18 Typical piston skirt surfaces in common use.

Figure 17–20 Typical location of pads used to balance pistons.

the last machining operation to bring the piston within the correct weight tolerances.

■ PISTON SERVICE

When engine servicing equipment is not available, the repairable piston and rod assemblies are taken to the automotive machine shop for reconditioning. See Figures 17–21 through 17–24. The pistons are removed from the rods using a special fixture shown in Figure 17–25. After cleaning, the skirts of the used pistons should be resized, and a spacer is placed in the top of the upper ring grooves.

As the piston goes rapidly up and down in the cylinder, it tosses the rings to the top and to the bottom of the ring grooves. The pounding of each ring in its groove gradually increases the piston ring side clearance. Material is worn from both the ring and the groove. The greater the side clearance, the faster the wear becomes.

The upper ring groove can be reconditioned on industrial engines when the groove has worn by more than 0.005 inch (0.125 millimeter). To correct the ring groove clearance, the top ring groove is machined to be 0.025 inch (0.625 millimeter) wider than the standard groove. One type of tool used for this is shown in Figure 17–26 on page 410. A steel ring groove spacer is placed above the new piston ring in the reconditioned ring groove to return the ring side clearance to the standard dimension, as shown in Figure 17–27 on page 410. Industrial engine pistons can also be knurled to expand their skirts. See Figure 17–28 on page 410.

■ PISTON PINS

Piston pins are used to attach the piston to the connecting rod. Piston pins are also known as **gudgeon pins** (a British term). The piston pin transfers the force produced by combustion chamber pressures and piston inertia to the connecting rod. The piston pin is made from high-quality steel in the shape of a tube to make it both strong and light. Sometimes, the interior hole of the piston pin is tapered, so it is large at the ends and small in the middle of the pin. This gives the pin strength that is proportional to the location of the load placed on it. A double-taper hole such as this is more expensive to

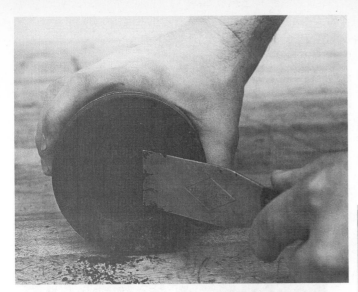

Figure 17–22 Ring groove cleaner being used to remove carbon from the bottom of the piston ring grooves. Care must be used to prevent enlarging the grooves by scraping away any aluminum.

Figure 17–24 Measuring a piston ring groove. Even the grooves of new replacement pistons should be measured to ensure that the proper-size piston rings are used.

Figure 17–21 The first step to be performed if the pistons are not being replaced is to thoroughly clean them, starting with scraping off encrusted deposits. Chemical or ultrasonic cleaning may also be necessary.

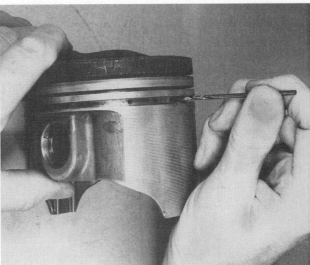

Figure 17–23 Complete piston cleaning includes cleaning the oil groove vent holes.

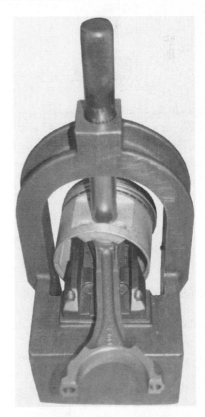

Figure 17–25 A press used to remove the connecting rod from the piston.

Figure 17–26 One type of piston ring groove reconditioner.

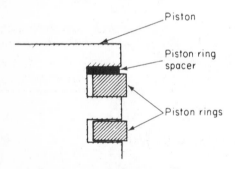

Figure 17–27 Ring groove spacer placed above the new upper ring in the reconditioned ring groove.

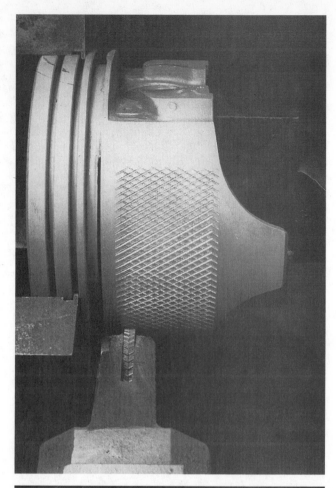

Figure 17–28 Knurling the piston skirt of an industrial engine to expand the skirt restoring the diameter of the piston.

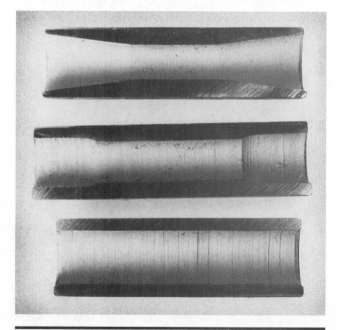

Figure 17–29 Cross-sectioned piston pins. Notice that the top two are taper bored to provide greater thickness (and strength) where the loads are highest.

manufacture, so it is used only where its weight advantage merits the extra cost. See Figure 17–29.

■ PISTON PIN OFFSET

The piston pin holes are not centered in the piston. They are located toward the **major thrust surface,** approximately 0.062 inch (1.57 millimeters) from the piston centerline, as shown in Figure 17–30.

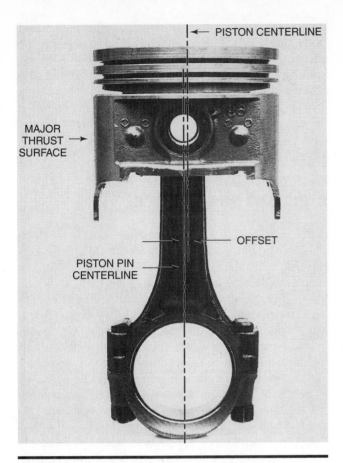

PISTON CENTERLINE

MAJOR
THRUST →
SURFACE

OFFSET

PISTON PIN
CENTERLINE

Figure 17–30 Piston pin is offset toward the major thrust surface.

NOTE: The major thrust side is the side of the cylinder to which the rod points during the power stroke.

Pin offset is designed to reduce piston slap and the noise that can result as the large end of the connecting rod crosses over top dead center.

The minor thrust side of the piston head has a greater area than does the major side. This is caused by the pin offset. As the piston moves up in the cylinder on the compression stroke, it rides against the minor thrust surface. When compression pressure becomes high enough, the greater head area on the minor side causes the piston to cock slightly in the cylinder. This keeps the *top* of the minor thrust surface on the cylinder. It forces the *bottom* of the major thrust surface to contact the cylinder wall. As the piston approaches top center, both thrust surfaces are in contact with the cylinder wall. When the crankshaft crosses over top center, the force on the connecting rod moves the entire piston toward the major thrust surface. The lower portion of the major thrust surface has already been in contact with the cylinder wall. The rest of the piston skirt slips into full contact just after the crossover point, thereby controlling piston slap. This action is illustrated in Figure 17–31.

Offsetting the piston toward the minor thrust surface would provide a better mechanical advantage. It also would cause less piston-to-cylinder friction. For these reasons, the offset is often placed toward the minor thrust surface in racing engines. Noise and durability are not as important in racing engines as is maximum performance.

NOTE: Not all piston pins are offset. In fact, many engines operate without the offset to help reduce friction and improve power and fuel economy.

■ PISTON PIN FIT

The finish and size of piston pins are closely controlled. Piston pins have a smooth mirrorlike finish. Their size is held to tens of thousandths of an inch so that exact

Figure 17–31 Effect of piston pin offset as it controls piston slap.

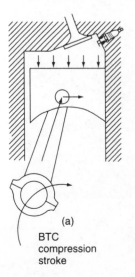

(a)

BTC
compression
stroke

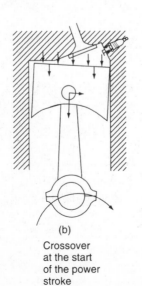

(b)

Crossover
at the start
of the power
stroke

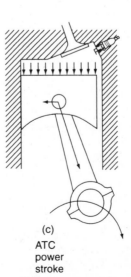

(c)

ATC
power
stroke

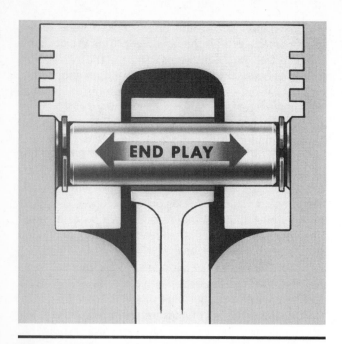

Figure 17–32 Full-floating piston pin retained by a lock ring on each end of the piston pin.

fits can be maintained. If the piston pin is loose in the piston or in the connecting rod, it will make a rattling sound while the engine is running. If the piston pin is too tight in the piston, it will restrict piston expansion along the pin diameter. This will lead to piston scuffing. Normal piston pin clearances range from 0.0005 to 0.0007 inch (0.0126 to 0.0180 millimeter).

PISTON PIN RETAINING METHODS

Full Floating

It is necessary to retain or hold piston pins so that they stay centered in the piston. If piston pins are not retained, they will move endwise and groove the cylinder wall. The piston pin may be **full floating,** with some type of stop located at each end.

Full-floating piston pins in automotive engines are retained by **lock rings** located in grooves in the piston pin hole at the ends of the piston pin (Figures 17–32 and 17–33). Some engines use aluminum or plastic plugs in both ends of the piston pin. These plugs touch the cylinder wall without scoring, to hold the piston pin centered in the piston.

Interference Fit

The modern method of retaining the piston pin in the connecting rod is to make the connecting rod hole slightly smaller than the piston pin. The pin is installed by heating the rod to expand the hole or by pressing the pin into the rod. This retaining method will securely hold the pin. See Figure 17–34. This press or shrink fit is called an **interference fit.** Care must be taken to have the correct hole sizes, and the pin must be centered in the connecting rod. The interference fit method is the least expensive to use. It is, therefore, used in the majority of engines.

PISTON PIN SERVICE

Piston pins do not normally become loose enough to cause a knock or tapping sound until the engine has very high mileage. The noise that a loose piston pin makes is a **double knock.** The knock is twice as fast as would be expected because the double knock occurs when the piston stops at the top and is starting downward again. Automotive machine shops may install oversize piston pins when reconditioning piston and rod assemblies. Once the connecting rod eye is honed to be oversize, an oversize piston pin must be used.

Both the piston and the small eye of the connecting rod are honed with precision equipment that can control the hole surface finish and the hole size, within 0.0001 inch (one tenth of one thousandth of an inch!) (0.0025 millimeter), either larger or smaller than the diameter of the piston pin. The piston pin hole in the piston is sized to give a clearance of 0.0002 to 0.0005 inch (0.0006 to 0.0012 millimeter). A typical pin hone is shown in Figure 17–35.

Diagnostic Story

Big Problem, No Noise

Sometimes the piston pin can "walk" off the center of the piston and score the cylinder wall. This scoring is often not noticed because this type of wear does not create noise. Because the piston pin is below the piston rings, little combustion pressure is lost past the rings until the groove worn by the piston pin has worn the piston rings.

Troubleshooting the exact cause of the increased oil consumption is difficult because the damage done to the oil control rings by the groove usually affects only one cylinder.

Often, compression tests indicate good compression because the cylinder seals, especially at the top. More than one technician has been surprised to see the cylinder gouged by a piston pin when the cylinder head has been removed for service. In such a case, the cost of the engine repair immediately increases far beyond that of normal cylinder head service.

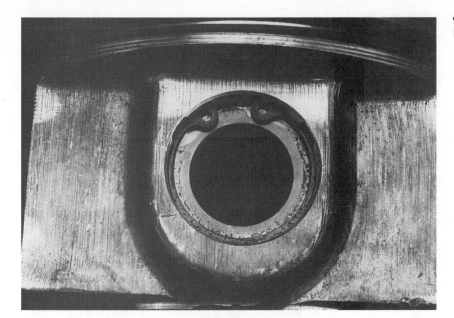

Figure 17–33 Piston pin lock ring.

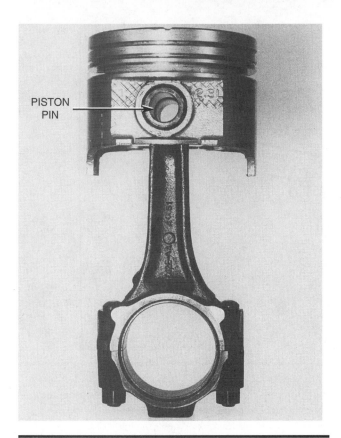

PISTON
PIN

Figure 17–34 Interference fit type of piston pin.

Figure 17–35 Honing a piston to fit an oversize piston pin.

■ PISTON RINGS

Piston rings serve two major functions in engines. They form a sliding combustion chamber seal that prevents the high-pressure combustion gases from leaking past the piston. They also keep engine oil from getting into the combustion chamber. In addition, the rings transfer some of the piston heat to the cylinder wall, where it is removed from the engine through the cooling system.

Piston rings are classified into two types: two **compression rings,** located toward the top of the piston, and one **oil control ring,** located below the compression rings. See Figure 17–36. The first piston rings were made with a simple rectangular cross section. This cross section was modified with tapers, chamfers, counter bores, slots, rails, and expanders. Piston ring materials have also changed from plain cast iron to materials such as pearlitic and nodular iron, as well as steel. **Ductile iron** is also used as a piston ring material in some automotive engines. See Figure 17–37.

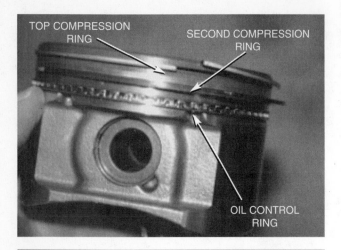

Figure 17–36 Most pistons use two compression rings and one oil control ring.

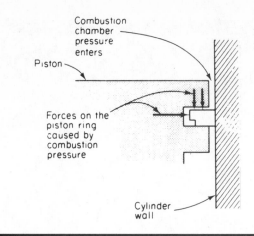

Figure 17–38 Combustion pressure forces the top piston ring downward and outward against the cylinder wall.

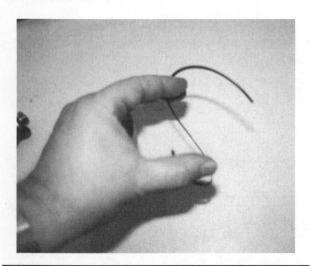

Figure 17–37 A ductile iron piston ring is very flexible and can be twisted without breaking.

Figure 17–39 The piston rings are slightly used, so only the line contact shows. The upper, barrel-faced ring has line contact in the center. The second, taper-faced ring has line contact along the lower edge of the ring.

■ COMPRESSION RINGS

A compression ring is designed to form a seal between the moving piston and the cylinder wall. This is necessary to get maximum power from the combustion pressure. At the same time, the compression ring must keep friction at a minimum. This is made possible by providing only enough static or built-in mechanical tension to hold the ring in contact with the cylinder wall during the intake stroke. Combustion chamber pressure during the compression, power, and exhaust strokes is applied to the top and back of the ring. This pressure will add the force on the ring that is required to seal the combustion chamber during these strokes. Figure 17–38 illustrates how the combustion chamber pressure adds force to the ring.

■ PISTON RING FORCES

The mechanical static tension of the ring results from the ring shape, material characteristics, and expanders used. Twist is used to provide **line contact** sealing on the cylinder wall and in the piston ring groove. The line contact can be seen on the slightly used rings pictured in Figure 17–39. Line contact provides a relatively high unit pressure for sealing. At the same time, it allows low total ring force against the cylinder. This results in low ring friction. Pressure in the combustion chamber acts on the top piston ring. The pressure forces the ring to flatten on the bottom side of the piston ring groove. This action seals the ring-to-piston joint. Pressure behind the ring will also force it against the cylinder wall to seal the ring-to-cylinder wall contact surface. This action produces a **dynamic sealing force** that makes an effective moving combustion chamber seal.

■ RING GAP

The piston **ring gap** will allow some leakage past the top compression ring. This leakage is useful in providing pressure on the second ring to develop a dynamic sealing force. The amount of piston ring gap is critical. Too much gap will allow excessive **blowby.** Blowby is the leakage of combustion gases past the rings. Blowby will blow oil from the cylinder wall. This oil loss is followed by piston ring scuffing. Too little gap, on the other hand, will allow the piston ring ends to butt when the engine is hot. Ring end butting increases the mechanical force against the cylinder wall, causing excessive wear and possible engine failure.

A butt-type piston ring gap is the most common type used in automotive engines. Some low-speed industrial engines and some diesel engines use a more expensive tapered or seal-cut ring gap. These gaps are necessary to reduce losses of the high-pressure combustion gases. At low speeds, the gases have more time to leak through the gap. Typical ring gaps are illustrated in Figure 17–40.

■ PISTON RING CROSS SECTIONS

As engine speeds have increased, inertia forces on the piston rings have also increased. As a result, engine manufacturers have found it desirable to reduce inertia forces on the rings by reducing their weight. This has been done by narrowing the piston ring from 1/4 inch (6 millimeters) to as little as 1/16 inch (1.6 millimeters).

Typical compression ring cross sections are illustrated in Figure 17–41. A discussion of piston ring cross sections must start with their original rectangular shape. This was first modified with a **taper face** that would contact the cylinder wall at the lower edge of the piston ring. When either a chamfer or counter bore relief is made on the *upper inside* corner of the piston ring, the ring cross section is unbalanced. This will cause the ring to twist in the groove in a positive direction. **Positive twist** will give the same wall contact as the taper-faced ring. It will also provide a line contact

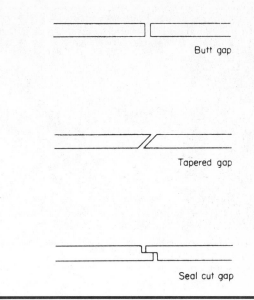

Figure 17–40 Typical ring gaps.

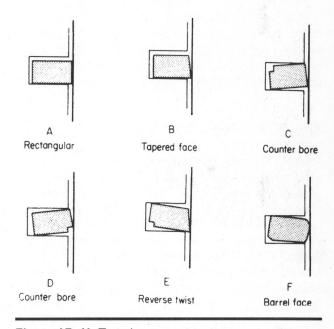

Figure 17–41 Typical compression ring cross sections.

seal on the bottom side of the groove. Sometimes, twist and a taper face are used on the same compression ring.

Some second rings are notched on the *outer lower* corner. This, too, provides a positive ring twist. The sharp lower outer corner becomes a scraper that helps in oil control, but this type of ring has less compression control than the preceding types.

By chamfering the ring's *lower inner* corner, a **reverse twist** is produced. This seals the lower outer section of the ring and piston ring groove, thus improving oil control. Reverse twist rings require a greater taper face or barrel face to maintain the desired ring face-to-cylinder wall contact.

Some rings replace the outer ring taper with a barrel face. The barrel is 0.0003 inch per 0.100 inch (0.0076

Figure 17–42 Cross-sectional view showing piston ring groove wear. *(Courtesy of Dana Corporation)*

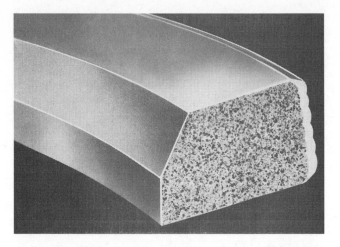

Figure 17–43 Chromium facing can be seen on the right side of the sectional view of the piston ring. *(Courtesy of Sealed Power Corporation)*

millimeter per 0.254 millimeter) of piston ring width. Barrel faces are found on rectangular and torsionally twisted rings. See Figure 17–42 for an example of how piston ring twist during engine operation can wear the ring groove of the piston, as well as the face of the ring.

■ CHROMIUM PISTON RINGS

A chromium facing on cast-iron rings greatly increases piston ring life, especially where abrasive materials are present in the air. During manufacture, the chromium-plated ring is slightly chamfered at the outer corners. About 0.0004 inch (0.010 millimeter) of chrome is then plated on the ring face. Chromium-faced rings are prelapped or honed before they are packaged and shipped to the customer. The finished chromium facing is shown in a sectional view in Figure 17–43.

■ MOLYBDENUM PISTON RINGS

Early in the 1960s, molybdenum piston ring faces were introduced. These rings proved to have good service life, especially under scuffing conditions. The plasma method is a spray method used to deposit molybdenum on cast iron to produce a long-wearing and low-friction piston ring. The plasma method involves an electric arc plasma (ionized gas) that generates an extremely high temperature to melt the molybdenum and spray-deposit a molten powder of it onto a piston ring. Therefore, plasma rings are molybdenum (moly) rings that have the moly coating applied by the plasma method. Most molybdenum-faced piston rings have a groove that is 0.004 to 0.008 inch (0.1 to 0.2 millimeter) deep cut into the ring face. This groove is filled with molybdenum, using a metallic (or plasma) spray method, so that there is

Figure 17–44 Molybdenum facing can be seen on the right side of the sectional view of the piston ring. *(Courtesy of Sealed Power Corporation)*

a cast-iron edge above and below the molybdenum. This edge may be chamfered in some applications. A sectional view of a molybdenum-faced ring is shown in Figure 17–44.

Molybdenum-faced piston rings will survive under high-temperature and scuffing conditions better than chromium-faced rings. Under abrasive wear conditions, chromium-faced rings will have a better service life. There is little measurable difference between these two facing materials with respect to blowby, oil control, break-in, and horsepower. Piston rings with either of these two types of facings are far better than plain cast-iron rings with phosphorus coatings. A molybdenum-faced ring, when used, will be found in the top groove, and a plain cast-iron or chromium-faced ring will be found in the second groove.

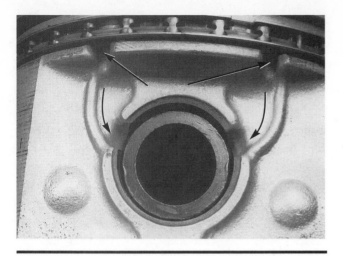

Figure 17–45 The oil scraped from the cylinder walls by the oil control ring is directed to lubricate the piston pin in this design.

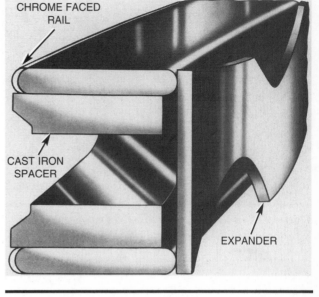

Figure 17–46 Oil ring with a cast-iron spacer, two chrome-faced rails, and an expander. *(Courtesy of Dana Corporation)*

■ MOLY-CHROME-CARBIDE RINGS

Rings with moly-chrome-carbide coating are also used in some original equipment (OE) and replacement applications. The coating has properties that include the hardness of the chrome and carbide combined with the heat resistance of molybdenum. Ceramic-coated rings are also being used where additional heat resistance is needed, such as in some heavy-duty, turbocharged, or supercharged engines.

■ OIL CONTROL RINGS

The scraping action of the oil control ring allowed oil to return through the ring and openings in the piston. Figure 17–45 shows how the scraping action of the oil control ring can be used to lubricate the piston pin. Steel spring expanders were placed in the ring groove behind the ring to improve static radial tension. They forced the ring to conform to the cylinder wall. Many expander designs are used. One type of expander (Figure 17–46) acts as a spring between the ring groove base and the ring. The action of another type of expander (Figure 17–47) results from radial force when the two ends of the expander butt together. This creates static tension as the ring is forced into the piston ring groove by the cylinder.

Steel **rails** with chromium or other types of facings are used on most oil control rings. The rails are backed with **expanders** and separated with a **spacer** as seen in Figure 17–48.

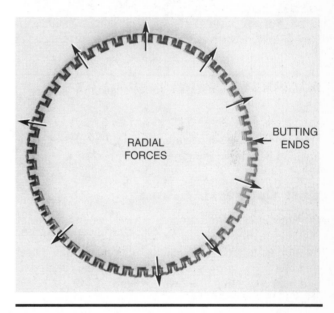

Figure 17–47 Oil ring expander type that provides radial force as it is compressed with the ends butting together.

■ CONNECTING RODS

The connecting rod transfers the force and reciprocating motion of the piston to the crankshaft. The small end of the connecting rod reciprocates with the piston. The large end rotates with the crankpin. These dynamic motions make it desirable to keep the connecting rod as light as possible while still having a rigid beam section. Use of lightweight rods also reduces the total connecting rod material cost.

Figure 17–48 On the left is an oil ring having an expander-spacer and two chrome-faced rails. On the right is an oil ring having one chrome-faced rail and a combination expander-spacer rail.

Figure 17–49 Rough casting for a connecting rod.

Connecting rods are manufactured by casting, forging, and powdered (sintered) metal processes.

Cast Connecting Rods

Casting materials and processes have been improved so that they are used in most vehicle engines with high production standards. Cast connecting rods can be identified by their *narrow parting line*. A typical rough connecting rod casting is shown in Figure 17–49.

Forged Connecting Rods

Forged connecting rods have been used for years. They are always used in high performance engines. They are generally used in heavy-duty, high performance engines. Generally, the forging method produces lighter weight and stronger but more expensive connecting rods. Forged connecting rods can be identified by their *wide parting line* as seen in Figure 17–50. Also see Figure 17–51.

Powdered Metal Connecting Rods

Some production engines, such as the General Motors Northstar, switched from forged to powdered metal (PM) rods, which proved to be stronger. Each of the rods is blended into a tapered I-beam section.

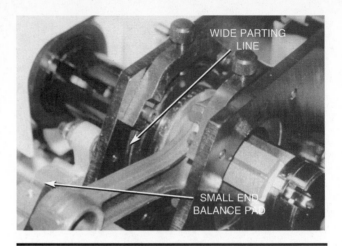

Figure 17–50 A forged connecting rod being reconditioned. Note the wide parting line and the extra metal at the small end used to balance the rod. Grinding some metal from this pad (called balancing pads or balancing boss) reduces the weight of the small end of the rod.

NOTE: Most powdered (sintered) metal connecting rods are broken at the parting end of the big end of the connecting rod. This rough broken surface helps ensure a perfect match when the pieces are bolted together. See Figure 17–52.

■ CONNECTING ROD DESIGN

The big end of the connecting rod must be a perfect circle. Therefore, the rod caps must not be interchanged. Assembly bolt holes are closely reamed in both the cap and connecting rod to ensure alignment. The connecting rod bolts have **piloting surfaces** that closely fit these reamed holes. The fit of the connecting rod bolts is so tight that a press must be used to remove the bolts when they are to be replaced as shown in Figure 17–53 on page 420.

In some engines, offset connecting rods provide the most economical distribution of main bearing space and crankshaft cheek clearance. Some V-6 engines have the connecting rods offset by approximately 0.100 inch (2.54 millimeters). An example is shown in Figure 17–54 on page 420.

Connecting rods are made with **balancing bosses (pads)** so that their weight can be adjusted to specifications. Some have balancing bosses only on the rod cap. Others also have a balancing boss above the piston. Some manufacturers put balancing bosses on the side of the rod, near the center of gravity of the connecting rod. Typical balancing bosses can be seen in Figure 17–55 on page 420. Balancing is done on automatic balancing machines as the final machining operation before the rod is installed in an engine.

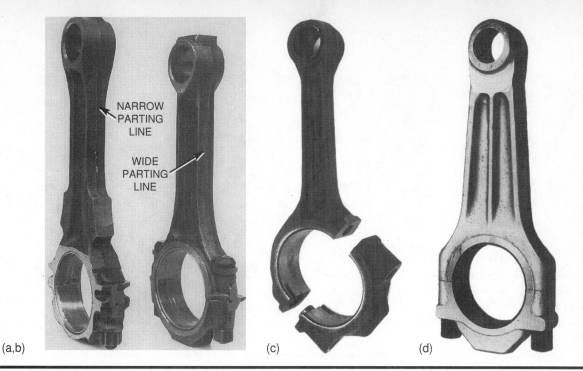

NARROW PARTING LINE

WIDE PARTING LINE

(a,b)　　　　　　　　(c)　　　　　　　(d)

Figure 17–51 Connecting rod types. (a) Cast iron; note the thin parting line. (b) Forged steel; note the wide parting line. (c) Cap separated at an angle on a forged rod. (d) Forged aluminum racing rod.

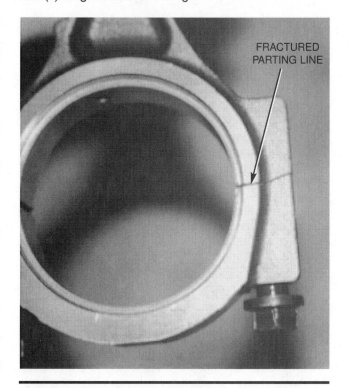

FRACTURED PARTING LINE

Figure 17–52 Powdered metal connecting rod with a fractured parting line at the big end of the rod.

Most connecting rods have a **spit hole** that bleeds some of the oil from the connecting rod journal. On inline engines, oil is thrown up from the spit hole into the cylinder in which the rod is located. On V-type engines, it is thrown into a cylinder in the opposite bank. The oil that is spit from the rod is aimed so that it will splash into the interior of the piston. This helps to lubricate the piston

pin. A hole similar to the spit holes may be used. It is called a **bleed hole.** Its only purpose is to control the oil flow through the bearing. See Figure 17–56 on page 421.

■ ROD TWIST

During connecting rod reconditioning, the rod should be checked for twist. In other words, the hole at the small end and the hole at the big end of the connecting rod should be parallel. No more than 0.002 inch (0.05 millimeter) twist is acceptable. See Figure 17–57 on page 421 for the fixture used to check connecting rods for twist. If measured rod twist is excessive, some specialty shops can remove the twist by bending the rod cold. Both cast and forged rods can be straightened. However, many engine builders replace the connecting rod if it is twisted. See Figure 17–58 on page 421.

TECH TIP

Successful Engine Building Is in the Details

A technician checked every new fastener that was purchased and discovered one connecting rod nut that was manufactured crooked. See Figure 17–59 on page 421. If the technician had not checked, this nut could have been installed on a connecting rod to the torque specifications, yet not provide enough clamping force on the rod bearing. This simple flaw in one nut could have caused catastrophic engine damage.

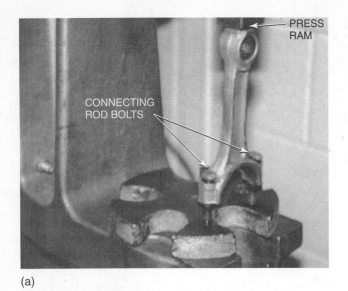

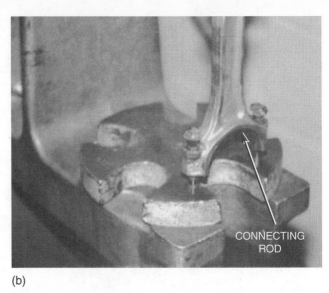

(a)

(b)

Figure 17–53 (a) Using a hand-operated press to remove connecting rod bolts. (b) Pressing out the old bolts and pressing in the new bolts should be done as evenly as possible to avoid creating stress in the connecting rods. After bolt replacement, the rods should be reconditioned.

Figure 17–54 On the left side is a piston and connecting rod from a V-6 engine. Note the full skirt piston and offset connecting rod. On the right is a piston and connecting rod from another V-6 that does not require an offset rod because the cylinder bores line up with the crankshaft throws directly. Note also the use of a lighter-weight piston.

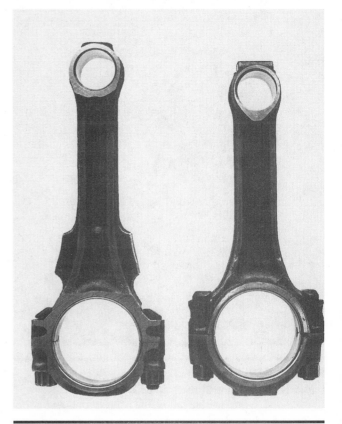

Figure 17–55 Typical locations of balancing bosses on connecting rods.

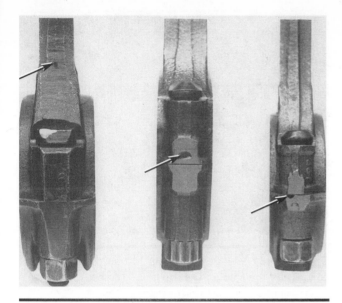

Figure 17–56 Connecting rod spit and bleed holes.

Figure 17–57 Fixture used to check a connecting rod for twist.

ANGLE WEAR ON THE PISTON SKIRT

EDGE WEAR ON THE BEARING

Figure 17–58 Signs of connecting rod misalignment.

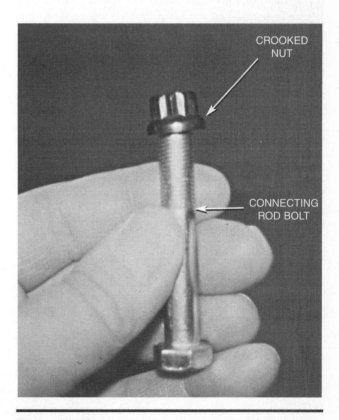

CROOKED NUT

CONNECTING ROD BOLT

Figure 17–59 A new connecting rod bolt and nut. Notice how the nut does not fit correctly on the bolt. Thankfully, the technician discovered this problem before the part was used in the engine.

■ CONNECTING ROD SERVICE

As an engine operates, the forces go through the large end of the connecting rod. This causes the crankshaft end opening of the rod (eye) to gradually deform. The large eye of the connecting rod is resized during precision engine service.

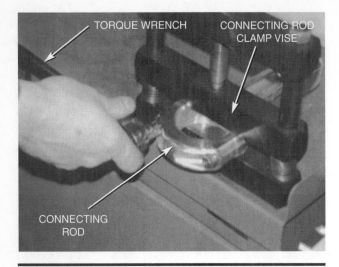

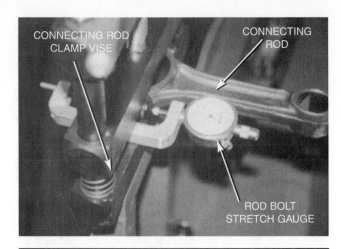

Figure 17–60 Always use a connecting rod clamp vise when assembling or disassembling the cap from big end of the rod.

Figure 17–61 Using a connecting rod bolt stretch gauge to measure the amount the rod bolt stretches to tighten the fastener to its ultimate strength.

Step 1 The parting surfaces of the rod and cap are smoothed to remove all high spots before resizing. A couple of thousandths of an inch of metal is removed from the rod cap parting surface. This is done using the same grinder that is used to remove a slight amount of metal from the parting surface of main bearing caps. The amount removed from the rod and rod cap only reduces the bore size 0.003 to 0.006 inch (0.08 to 0.15 millimeter).

Step 2 The cap is installed on the rod, and the nuts or cap screws are properly torqued as shown in Figures 17–60 and 17–61. The hole is then bored or honed to be perfectly round and of the size and finish required to give the correct connecting rod

NOTE: Powdered metal connecting rods cannot be reconditioned using this method. Most manufacturers recommend replacing worn powdered metal connecting rods.

bearing crush. Figure 17–62 shows the setup for resizing the rod on a typical hone used in engine reconditioning.

Even though material is being removed at the big end of the rod, the compression ratio is changed very little. The inside of the bore at the big end should have a 60- to 90-microinch finish for proper bearing contact and heat transfer.

Figure 17–62 Resizing the big end of the connecting rod with a hone. To help ensure a more accurate and straighter job, hone two connecting rods at a time.

(a)

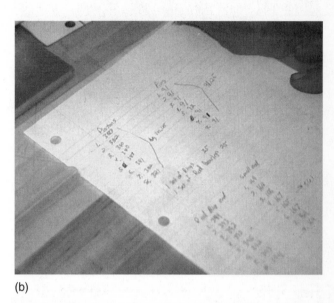

(b)

Figure 17–63 (a) Weighing the big end of the connecting rod. Both ends should be weighed. (b) Record the weight of both ends of all connecting rods and then grind material from the balancing pads to achieve the weight of the lightest rod.

■ PISTON AND ROD BALANCING

All pistons should be weighted and recorded as shown in Figure 17–63. Carefully grind weight off of all but the lightest piston to match their weights.

All connecting rods should be weighted separately at both ends. Grind material from the balance pad area of each end to achieve equal weight for all rods matching the weight of the lightest rod.

■ PISTON AND ROD ASSEMBLY

To assemble the piston and rod, the piston pin is put in one side of the piston. The small end of the connecting rod should be checked for proper size as shown in Figure 17–64. The small eye of the connecting rod is heated before the pin is installed. See Figure 17–65. This causes the rod eye to expand so that the pin can be pushed into place with little force. The pin must be rapidly pushed into the correct center position. There is only one chance to get it in the right place because the rod will quickly seize on the pin as the rod eye is cooled by the pin.

Full-floating piston pins operate in a bushing in the small eye of the connecting rod. The bushing can be replaced. The bushing and the piston are honed to the same diameter. This allows the piston pin to slide freely through both. The full-floating piston pin is held in place with a lock ring at each end of the piston pin. The lock ring expands into a small groove in the pin hole of the piston.

> **NOTE:** The lock rings should always be replaced with new rings.

Care must be taken to ensure that the pistons and rods are in the correct cylinder. They must face in the correct direction. There is usually a **notch** on the piston head indicating the *front.* Using this will correctly position the piston pin offset toward the right side of the engine. The connecting rod **identification marks** on pushrod inline engines are normally placed on the camshaft side.

> **NOTE:** The camshaft side of an inline OHV engine is also the oil filter side of most engines.

The notch and numbers on a piston and rod assembly can be seen in Figure 17–66 on page 425. On V-type engines, the connecting rod cylinder identification marks are on the side of the rods that can be seen from the bottom of the engine when the piston and rod assemblies are installed in the engine. The service manual should be checked for any special piston and rod assembly instructions.

Figure 17–64 Precision gauge used to check the small-end diameter of a connecting rod for taper and out-of-round.

■ PISTON RING SERVICE

Each piston ring, one at a time, should be placed backward in the groove in which it is to be run. Its **side clearance** in the groove should be checked with a feeler gauge, as shown in Figure 17–67. If a ring is tight at any spot, check for deposits or burrs in the ring groove. Each piston ring, one at a time, is then placed in the cylinder in which it is to operate.

> **NOTE:** See Chapter 16 for block preparation procedures that should be complete before the following operations are performed.

After the block and cylinder bores have been reconditioned, invert the piston and push each ring into the lower quarter of the cylinder (Figure 17–68); then measure the **ring gap** (Figure 17–69 on page 426). It should be approximately 0.004 inch for each inch of bore diameter (0.004 millimeter for each centimeter of bore diameter). If necessary, use a file or hand-operated piston ring grinder to achieve the necessary ring gap. See Figure 17–70 on page 426.

The oil rings are installed first. The expander-spacer of the oil ring is placed in the lower ring groove.

(a)

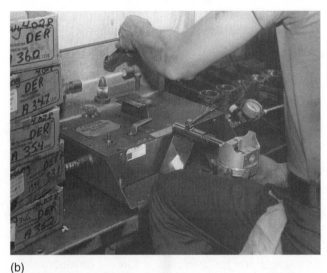

(b)

Figure 17–65 (a) Flame-type connecting rod heater, the type most often used by remanufacturers because of the rapid heating. The rod should not be heated to more than 700°F (370°C). (If the rod turns blue, it is too hot.) (b) An operator removing the heated connecting rod and preparing to install it on the piston. Note the fixture used to hold the piston pin, and the dial indicator (gauge) used to ensure proper positioning.

Figure 17–66 Position of the notch at the front of the piston, and the connecting rod numbers.

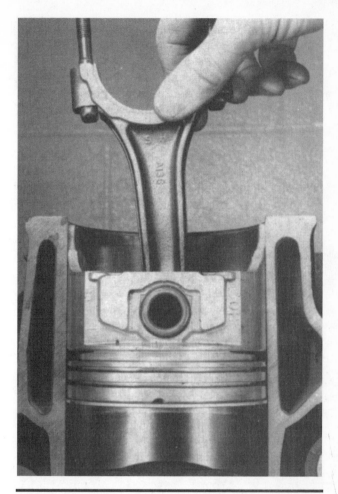

Figure 17–68 A piston is used to push the ring squarely into the cylinder.

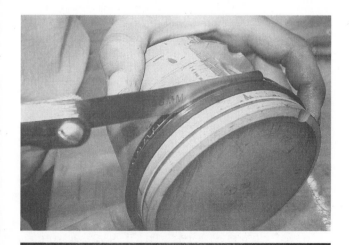

Figure 17–67 The side clearance of the piston ring is checked with a thickness (feeler) gauge.

One oil ring rail is carefully placed above the expander-spacer by winding it into the groove. The other rail is placed below the expander-spacer. The ring should be rotated in the groove to ensure that the expander-spacer ends have not overlapped. If they have, the ring must be removed and reassembled correctly.

Installing the compression rings requires the use of a **piston ring expander** tool that will only open the ring gap enough to slip the ring on the piston. Figure 17–71 shows one type of piston ring expander in use for engine repair. Be careful to install the ring with the correct side up. The top of the compression ring is marked with a dot, the letter *T,* or the word *top* (Figure 17–72). After the rings are installed, they should be rotated in the groove to ensure that they move freely, and checked to ensure that they will go fully into the groove so that the ring face is flush with the surface of the piston ring lands. Usually, the rings are placed on all pistons before any pistons are installed in the cylinders. See Chapter 19 for details on engine assembly.

Figure 17–69 The ring gap is measured with a feeler gauge.

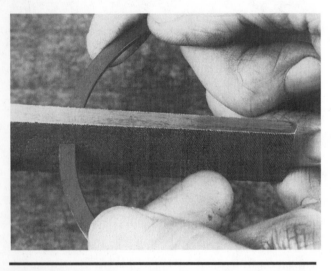

Figure 17–70 Method used to file the butt ends of a ring when the gap is too small.

Figure 17–71 One type of good-quality ring expander being used to install a piston ring.

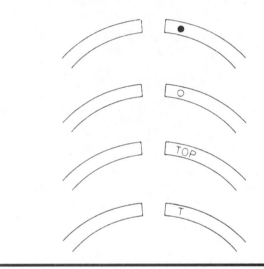

Figure 17–72 Identification marks used to indicate the side of the piston ring to be placed toward the head.

■ SUMMARY

1. The connecting rods should be marked before disassembly.

2. Pistons are cam ground so that when operating temperature is reached, the piston will have expanded enough across the piston pin area to become round.

3. Replacement pistons should weigh the same as the original pistons to maintain proper engine balance.

4. Some engines use an offset piston pin to help reduce piston slap when the engine is cold.

5. Piston rings usually include two compression rings at the top of the piston and an oil control ring below the compression rings.

6. If the ring end gap is excessive, blowby gases can travel past the rings and into the crankcase.

7. Many piston rings are made of coated cast iron to provide proper sealing.

8. If the connecting rod is twisted, diagonal wear will be noticed on the piston skirt.

9. Powdered metal connecting rods are usually broken at the big end parting line. Because of this rough junction, powdered metal connecting rods cannot be reconditioned—they must be replaced if damaged or worn.

10. The piston and the connecting rod must be correctly assembled according to identifying notches or marks.

PHOTO SEQUENCE   Piston Ring Fitting

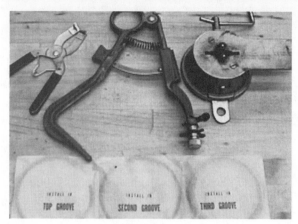

PS 28–1 New piston rings, piston ring expanders, piston groove cleaner, and a piston ring grinder are necessary items to fit piston rings to a particular cylinder.

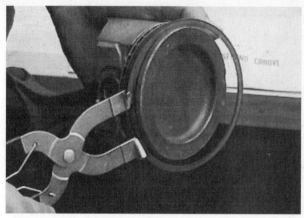

PS 28–2 Remove the old piston rings from the piston using a piston ring expander tool.

PS 28–3 Carefully clean the piston ring grooves using a piston ring groove cleaning tool.

PS 28–4 The oil drain holes behind the oil control rings should be cleaned.

PS 28–5 When fitting piston rings to pistons, always be certain to properly assemble the piston on the connecting rod. The rod should be marked with its cylinder position in the engine.

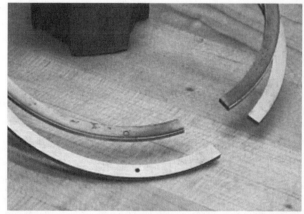

PS 28–6 Piston rings should be checked for proper size and application. Consult the instructions for the meaning of the marks (data) on the rings.

Piston Ring Fitting—continued

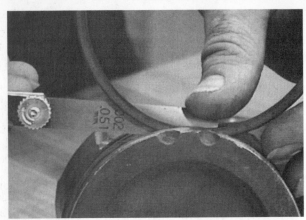

PS 28–7 Measure the side clearance between the piston ring and the piston ring groove using a feeler (thickness) gauge. Compare the readings with factory specifications (usually between 0.001 in. and 0.003 in.).

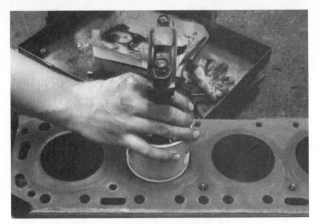

PS 28–8 Insert a piston ring into the proper cylinder and use a piston upside down to help position the ring squarely in the cylinder bore.

PS 28–9 Use a feeler gauge to measure the piston ring end gap and compare with factory specifications (usually 0.004 in. per inch of bore).

PS 28–10 If the piston ring end gap is too close, use a grinder to remove material from the ends of the piston rings until the proper end gap has been achieved.

PS 28–11 Carefully install the piston rings onto the piston using a piston ring expander.

PS 28–12 Be sure to position the gap of the rings according to factory recommendations before installing the piston in the cylinder.

PHOTO SEQUENCE   Rod Reconditioning

PS 29–1 This precision grinder is used to grind material from the connecting rod caps so that the big end can be resized back to its original inside diameter.

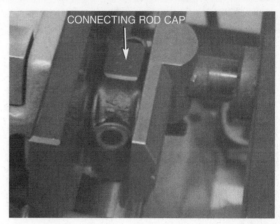

CONNECTING ROD CAP

PS 29–2 The cap from a connecting rod is installed in the vise of the grinder. A small amount of material is removed from the cap.

PS 29–3 For best results, the same amount of material should be removed from the mating surface of all connecting rod caps used in the engine.

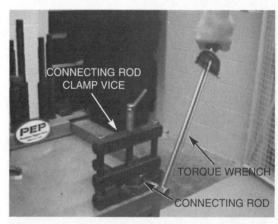

CONNECTING ROD CLAMP VICE

TORQUE WRENCH

CONNECTING ROD

PS 29–4 The connecting rod is then placed into a vise and the attaching nuts (or bolts) are torqued to factory specifications. (If new bolts are going to be used, they should be installed now before the reconditioning process is performed.)

PS 29–5 A typical connecting rod resizing machine.

PS 29–6 Measure the big end of all connecting rods using the precision hone gauge to ensure that the two rods being reconditioned together are the same size.

Rod Reconditioning—continued

PS 29–7 Install two connecting rods onto the arbor of the reconditioning machine. By using two rods, the resizing of the big end is more likely to be straight with a reduced chance of machining in a taper or barrel shape to the inside of the big end. The dial indicates the amount of force exerted on the grinding stones.

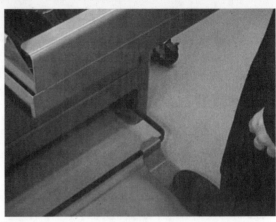

PS 29–8 The foot pedal releases the tension of the grinding stones and allows the operator to remove and reinstall the rods over the stones.

PS 29–9 Start the resizing operation by turning the machine on and, as the arbor containing the grinding stone rotates, move both rods away from you and toward you several times.

PS 29–10 Stop the grinding operating and remove the rods and place the front rod to the rear and the rear rod to the front.

Rod Reconditioning—continued

PS 29–11 Repeat the grinding operation with the two rods in the other position. This step helps ensure consistent big-end resizing without taper.

PS 29–12 Stop the grinding operation again and this time change the direction in which the rods are pointing.

PS 29–13 Repeat the resizing operation by again moving the rods toward you and then away from you several times as the arbor rotates the cutting stones inside the big end.

PS 29–14 Measure the big end for size and taper frequently. If too much has been removed, the cap will have to be reground and the process repeated. The final results should be within two-tenths of one thousandth of an inch (0.0002 in.) of the specified dimension.

PHOTO SEQUENCE Rod Weighing

PS 30–1 The equipment needed to weigh connecting rods includes the scale and the connecting rod big-end and small-end holding fixtures.

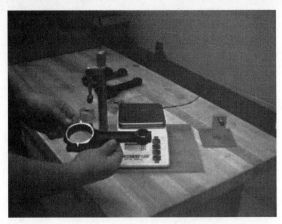

PS 30–2 Before starting, double-check that all rods have been reconditioned and that the bolts and nuts are replaced if necessary.

PS 30–3 Start the weighing process by weighing the fixture used to hold the small end of the rod and then set the scale to zero.

PS 30–4 Select the proper-size holding fixture for the big end of the rod.

PS 30–5 Insert the big end of the rod into the holding fixture and place the small end on the scale.

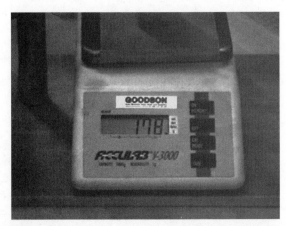

PS 30–6 Read and record the weight of the small end of the rod.

Rod Weighing—continued

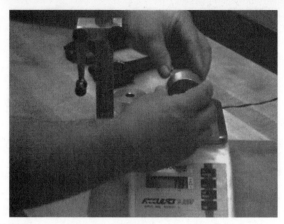

PS 30–7 Install the big-end fixture on the scale.

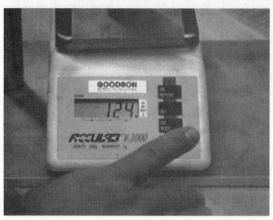

PS 30–8 Set the scale to zero which disregards the weight of the holding fixture. The weight of the holding fixture is called the tare weight.

PS 30–9 Weigh the big end of the rod.

PS 30–10 Record all weights from all connecting rods to be used in the engine. Compare the readings and determine where weight must be removed to make all rods weigh the same as the lightest rod in the set.

PS 30–11 Use a grinder to remove material from the small-end or big-end balancing pad to achieve the proper weight.

PS 30–12 Remeasure the weight of the rod after grinding.

PHOTO SEQUENCE Assembling Rod to Piston

PS 31–1 A typical connecting rod heater used to heat the small end of the rod.

PS 31–2 The first step is to position the piston into the holding fixture and adjust the piston pin stop.

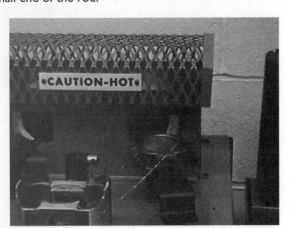

PS 31–3 Insert the small end of the rod into the heating element. It should be placed into the heater so that it can be installed on the piston in the correct direction. Always consult the factory service manual for the correct connecting rod installation direction.

PS 31–4 After double-checking that everything is ready to go, start the rod heating process by pushing the button on the heater. The light indicates that the heater is on.

PS 31–5 Next to the heater on light is a timer control that can be set to limit the time the rod is heated.

PS 31–6 The electric heating coils glow red as the small end of the rod is heated.

Assembling Rod to Piston—continued

PS 31–7 Before the rod reaches temperature, the technician is practicing inserting the piston pin into the piston using the pushrod.

PS 31–8 As soon as the light goes out, the technician has just several seconds to get the rod and insert the piston pin before the small end of the rod cools.

PS 31–9 The technician has grasped the rod by the big end and is starting to guide it into position in the piston.

PS 31–10 As soon as the rod is in position, the piston pin is inserted.

PS 31–11 After the rod has cooled for a minute or two, the piston/rod assembly is removed from the heater.

PS 31–12 The piston/rod assembly is checked for proper assembly.

■ REVIEW QUESTIONS

1. Describe the procedure for correctly removing the piston and rod assembly from the engine.

2. What methods are used to control piston heat expansion?

3. Why are some piston skirts tin plated?

4. Describe the effect of the piston pin offset as it controls piston slap.

5. Why is it important to keep the connecting rod cap with the rod on which it was originally used, and to install it in the correct way?

6. What causes the piston ring groove clearance to widen in service?

7. Describe how connecting rods are reconditioned.

8. How is the piston pin installed in the piston and rod assembly?

■ ASE CERTIFICATION-TYPE QUESTIONS

1. Connecting rod caps should be marked (if they were not marked at the factory) before the piston and connecting rod assembly is removed from the engine _____ .
   a. Because they are balanced together
   b. Because they are machined together
   c. To make certain that the heavier rod is matched to the heavier piston
   d. To make certain that the lighter rod is matched to the lighter piston

2. Many aluminum piston skirts are plated with _____ .
   a. Tin
   b. Lead
   c. Antimony
   d. Terneplate

3. A hypereutectic piston has _____ .
   a. A higher weight than a eutectic piston
   b. A higher silicon content
   c. A higher tin content
   d. A higher nickel content

4. The purpose of casting steel struts into an aluminum piston is to _____ .
   a. Provide increased strength
   b. Provide increased weight at the top part of the piston where it is needed for stability
   c. Provide increased heat transfer from the piston head to the piston pin
   d. Control thermal expansion

5. Full-floating piston pins are retained by _____ .
   a. Lock rings
   b. A drilled hole with roll pin
   c. An interference fit between rod and piston pin
   d. An interference fit between piston and piston pin

6. When balancing pistons, _____ .
   a. Choose the heaviest and add weight to the others
   b. Choose the heaviest and grind weight off until it matches the *average* of all the others
   c. Choose the lightest and grind material from the other pistons until all pistons are of equal weight
   d. Balance the piston only after it is assembled with the connecting rod

7. A misaligned connecting rod causes what type of engine wear?
   a. Cylinder taper
   b. Barrel-shaped cylinders
   c. Ridge wear
   d. Angle wear on the piston skirt

8. Side clearance is a measure taken between the _____ and the _____ .
   a. Piston (side skirt); cylinder wall
   b. Piston pin; piston pin retainer (clip)
   c. Piston ring; piston ring groove
   d. Compression ring; oil control ring

9. Piston ring gap should only be measured _____ .
   a. After all cylinder work has been performed
   b. After installing the piston in the cylinder
   c. After installing the rings on the piston
   d. Both a and c

10. Piston damage is most likely to be caused by _____ .
    a. Valves hitting the piston head
    b. Abnormal combustion
    c. Lugging the engine during operation
    d. High engine speeds that can break piston heads

Crankshafts and Bearings

Objectives: After studying Chapter 18, the reader should be able to:

1. Distinguish a cast crankshaft from a forged crankshaft.
2. Describe the purpose and function of a vibration damper.
3. Explain how crankshafts are reground and polished.
4. Discuss engine balance shafts and how they function.

All engine power is delivered through the crankshaft. The shaft must have the necessary shape and must be made from the proper materials to meet the power demands placed on it.

■ CRANKSHAFT PURPOSE AND FUNCTION

Power from expanding gases in the combustion chamber is delivered to the crankshaft through the piston, piston pin, and connecting rod. The connecting rods and their bearings are attached to a bearing journal on the crank throw. The crank throw is offset from the **crankshaft centerline.** The combustion force is applied to the crank throw after the crankshaft has moved past top center. This produces the turning effort or **torque,** which rotates the crankshaft. The crankshaft rotates on main bearings. These bearings are split in half so that they can be assembled around the crankshaft main bearing journals.

The bearing journal is the surface of the crankshaft that operates on a bearing. Parts of a typical crankshaft are illustrated in Figure 18–1. Crankshafts used in vehicles equipped with a manual transmission use a **pilot bearing** in the end of the crankshaft to support the input shaft of the transmission. See Figure 18–2. Some crankshafts are drilled through the center to help lighten the reciprocating weight of the crankshaft. See Figure 18–3.

■ FORGED CRANKSHAFTS

Crankshafts used in high-production automotive engines may be either forged or cast. Forged crankshafts are stronger than the cast crankshaft, but they are more

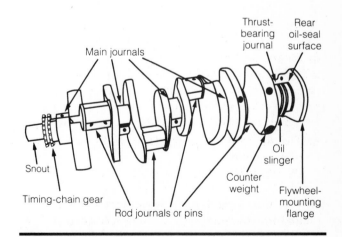

Figure 18–1 Typical crankshaft with main journals that support the crankshaft in the block. Rod journals are offset from the crankshaft centerline.

REAR FLANGE OF CRANKSHAFT

PILOT BEARING

Figure 18–2 A pilot bearing is placed in the end of the crankshaft to support the input shaft of the transmission if the vehicle is equipped with a manually shifted transmission.

HOLES THROUGH CENTER OF CRANKSHAFT

Figure 18–3 This crankshaft from a Chevrolet LS-1, V-8 shows holes drilled through the center of the crankshaft. Not only do these holes lighten the weight of the crankshaft, but they also help with equalizing airflow in the crankcase as the pistons move up and down in the cylinders.

Figure 18–4 Wide separation lines where the flashings have been removed from this forged crankshaft show that it has been twisted to index the crank throws.

expensive. Forged crankshafts have a wide separation line as seen in Figure 18–4.

Forged crankshafts are made from SAE 1045 or a similar type of steel. The crankshaft is formed from a hot steel billet through the use of a series of forging dies. Each die changes the shape of the billet slightly. The crankshaft blank is finally formed with the last die. The blanks are then machined to finish the crankshaft. Forging makes a very dense, tough crankshaft with the metal's grain structure running parallel to the principal direction of stress.

Two methods are used to forge crankshafts.

- One method is to forge the crankshaft *in place*. This is followed by straightening. The forging in place method is primarily used with forged four- and six-cylinder crankshafts.
- A second method is to forge the crankshaft in a *single plane*. It is then twisted in the main bearing journal to index the throws at the desired angles.

■ CAST CRANKSHAFTS

Casting materials and techniques have improved cast crankshaft quality so that cast crankshafts are used in most production automotive engines. Automotive crank-

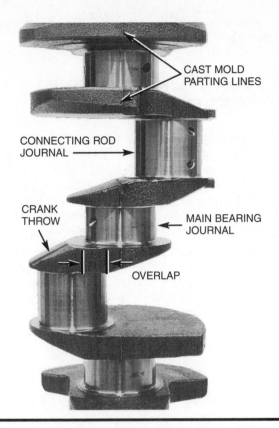

Figure 18-5 Cast crankshaft showing the bearing journal overlap and a straight, narrow cast mold parting line.

shafts may be cast in steel, nodular iron, or malleable iron. The major advantage of the casting process is that crankshaft material and machining costs are less than they are with forging. The reason is that the crankshaft can be made close to the required shape and size, including all complicated counterweights. The only machining required on a carefully designed cast crankshaft is the grinding of bearing journal surfaces and the finishing of front and rear drive ends. Metal grain structure in the cast crankshaft is uniform and random throughout; thus, the shaft is able to handle loads from all directions. Counterweights on cast crankshafts are slightly larger than counterweights on a forged crankshaft, because the cast shaft metal is less dense and therefore somewhat lighter. The narrow mold parting surface lines can be seen on the cast crankshaft pictured in Figure 18–5.

Frequently Asked Question   **???**

What Is the Difference Between the Throw of a Crankshaft and the Stroke of the Crankshaft?

Throws are the offset part of the crankshaft. The amount of throw offset determines the piston stroke. The throw is one-half the stroke.

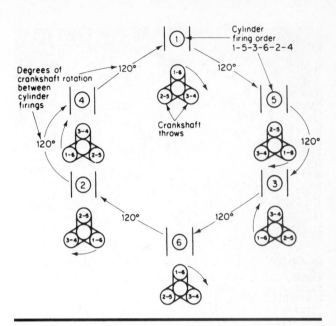

Figure 18–6 Crankshaft of an even-firing, inline, six-cylinder engine.

■ SIX-CYLINDER ENGINE CRANKSHAFTS

The inline six-cylinder engine has six crank throws in three matched pairs. The throw is ground to make a crankpin. The smooth surface of the crankpin is called the bearing journal. Each pair of throws on an inline six-cylinder engine is 120 degrees from the other pairs. This causes one pair of pistons to reach top center at each 120 degrees of crankshaft rotation. Pistons in cylinders #1 and #6, #2 and #5, and #3 and #4 move together as pairs. Each piston in a pair of pistons is 360 degrees out of phase with its mate in the 720-degree four-stroke cycle. This arrangement gives smooth, low-vibration operation. There are even-power strokes, one at each 120 degrees of crankshaft rotation, as illustrated in Figure 18–6. The crankshafts for these engines usually have one main bearing journal between each throw, making seven main bearings. Some have two throws between each main bearing, making four main bearings.

■ V-8 ENGINE CRANKSHAFTS

The V-8 engine has four inline cylinders in each of the two blocks that are placed at a 90-degree angle to each other. Each group of four inline cylinders is called a **bank.** The crankshaft for the V-8 engine has four throws. The connecting rods from two cylinders are connected to each throw, one from each bank. This can be seen in the cutaway V-type engine pictured in Figure 18–7. This arrangement results in a condition of being only minimally unbalanced. The V-8 engine

Figure 18–7 Cutaway of a V-type engine. Note the compact design.

crankshaft has two planes, so there is one throw every 90 degrees. A plane is a flat surface that cuts through the part. These planes could be seen if the crankshaft were cut lengthwise through the center of the main bearing and crankpin journals. Looking at the front of the crankshaft with the first throw at 360 degrees (up), the second throw is at 90 degrees (to the right), the third throw is at 270 degrees (to the left), and the fourth throw is at 180 degrees (down). There is one main bearing journal between each throw, so there are five main bearings in a V-8 engine. In operation with this arrangement, one piston reaches top center at each 90 degrees of crankshaft rotation so that the engine operates smoothly with even firing at each

90 degrees of crankshaft rotation. This can be seen in Figure 18–8.

■ FOUR-CYLINDER ENGINE CRANKSHAFTS

The crankshaft used on four-cylinder inline engines has four throws on a single plane. There is usually a main bearing journal between each throw, making it a five-main-bearing crankshaft (Figure 18–9). Pistons also move as pairs in this engine. Pistons in #1 and #4 cylinders move together, and pistons #2 and #3 move together. Each piston in a pair is 360 degrees out of phase with the other piston in the 720-degree four-stroke cycle. With this arrangement, the four-cylinder inline engine fires one cylinder at each 180 degrees of crankshaft rotation. This is illustrated in Figure 18–10. A four-cylinder opposed engine and a 90-degree V-4 engine have crankshafts that look like that of the four-cylinder inline engine.

■ FIVE-CYLINDER ENGINE CRANKSHAFTS

The inline five-cylinder engine has a five-throw crankshaft with one throw at each 72 degrees. Six main bearings are used on this crankshaft. The piston in one cylinder reaches top center at each 144 degrees of crankshaft rotation. The throws are arranged to give a firing order of 1-2-4-5-3. Dynamic balancing has been one of the major problems with this engine design, yet the vibration was satisfactorily dampened and isolated on both the Audi and Acura five-cylinder engines.

Figure 18–8 Crankshaft of an even-firing V-8 engine.

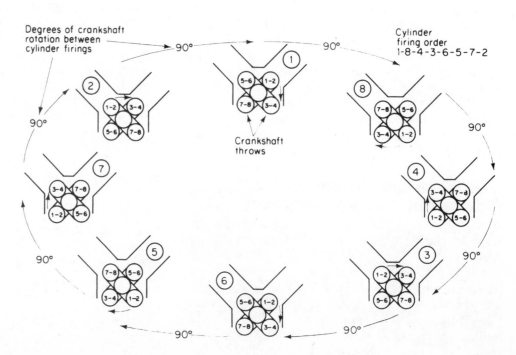

Figure 18–9 Five-main-bearing crankshaft for an inline four-cylinder engine.

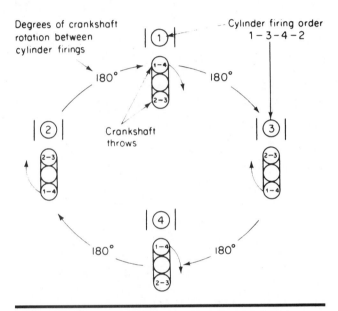

Figure 18–10 Crankshaft of an even-firing, inline, four-cylinder engine.

Diagnostic Story

The Mysterious Engine Vibration

A Buick-built, 3.8-liter V-6 engine vibrated the whole car after a new short block had been installed. The technician who had installed the replacement engine did all of the following:

1. Checked the spark plugs
2. Checked the spark plug wires
3. Checked the distributor cap and rotor
4. Disconnected the torque converter from the flex plate (drive plate) to eliminate the possibility of a torque converter or automatic transmission pump problem
5. Removed all accessory drive belts one at a time

Yet the vibration still existed.

Another technician checked the engine mounts and found that the left (driver's side) engine mount was out of location, ripped, and cocked. The transmission mount was also defective. After the technician replaced both mounts and made certain that all mounts were properly set, the vibration was eliminated. The design and location of the engine mounts are critical to the elimination of vibration, especially on 90-degree V-6 engines.

-90°-150°-90°, as illustrated in Figure 18–11. This firing pattern produces unequal pulses that have to be isolated with engine mounts that have been carefully designed.

■ THREE-CYLINDER ENGINE CRANKSHAFTS

A three-cylinder engine uses a 120-degree three-throw crankshaft with four main bearings. This engine requires a balancing shaft that turns at crankshaft speed, but in the opposite direction, to reduce the vibration to an acceptable level.

■ ODD-FIRING 90-DEGREE V-6 ENGINE CRANKSHAFTS

The 90-degree V-6 engine uses a three-throw crankshaft with four main bearings. The throws are 120 degrees apart. As in typical V-type engines, each crank throw has two connecting rods attached, one from each bank. This V-6 engine design does not have even firing impulses, because the pistons, connected to the 120-degree crankpins, do not reach top center at even intervals. The engine has a firing pattern of 150°-90°-150°

■ EVEN-FIRING 90-DEGREE V-6 ENGINE CRANKSHAFTS

The crank throws for an even-firing V-6 engine are split, making separate crankpins for each cylinder. The split throw can be seen in Figure 18–12. This angle between the crankpins on the crankshaft throws is called a **splay angle.** Figure 18–13 on page 443 illustrates how the 30-degree splay angle allows even firing. A flange was left between the split crankpin journals. This provides a continuous fillet or edge for machining and grinding operations. It also provides a normal flange for the rod and bearing. This flange between the splayed crankpin journals is sometimes called a **flying web.**

■ 60-DEGREE V-6 ENGINE CRANKSHAFTS

The 60-degree V-6 engine is similar to the even-firing 90-degree V-6 engine. The adjacent pairs of crankpins on the crankshaft used in the 60-degree V-6 engine

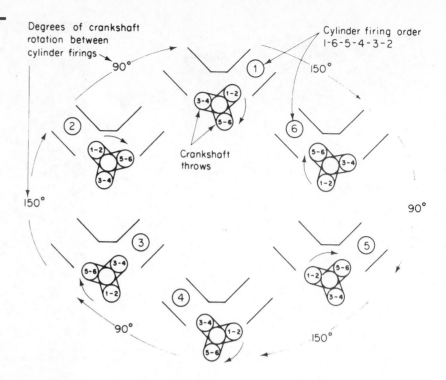

Figure 18–11 Odd-firing pattern produced by a crankshaft with the crank throws 120 degrees apart operating in a 90-degree V-6 block.

Figure 18–12 Split crankpin journals splayed at 30 degrees used in an even-firing 90-degree V-6 block.

have a splay angle of 60 degrees. This design allows even firing as shown in Figure 18–14. With this large 60-degree splay angle, the flange or flying web between the splayed crankpins is made heavier than on crankshafts with smaller splay angles. This is necessary to give strength to the crankshaft. The crankshaft of the 60-degree V-6 engine also uses four main bearings.

■ CRANKSHAFT OILING HOLES

The crankshaft is drilled, as shown in Figure 18–15 on page 444 to allow oil from the main bearing oil groove to be directed to the connecting rod bearings. The oil on the bearings forms a hydrodynamic oil film to support bearing loads. Some of the oil may be sprayed out through a spit or bleed hole in the connecting rod. The rest of the oil leaks from the edges of the bearing. It is thrown from the bearing against the inside surfaces of the engine. Some of the oil that is thrown from the crankshaft bearings will land on the camshaft to lubricate the lobes. A part of the throw-off oil splashes on the cylinder wall to lubricate the piston and rings.

Stress tends to concentrate at oil holes drilled through the crankshaft journals. These holes are usually located where the crankshaft loads and stresses are the lowest. The edges of the oil holes are carefully chamfered to relieve as much stress concentration as possible. Chamfered oil holes are shown in Figure 18–16 on page 444.

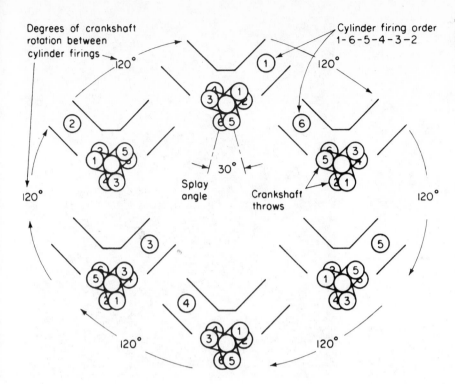

Figure 18–13 Even firing of a 90-degree V-6 engine using a crankshaft with 30-degree splayed crankpin journals.

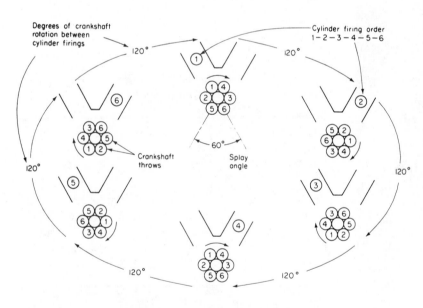

Figure 18–14 Even-firing pattern of a 60-degree V-6 engine using a crankshaft with 60-degree splayed crankpin journals.

■ CRANKSHAFT LIGHTENING HOLES

Lightening holes in the crankpins do not reduce crankpin strength if the hole size is less than half of the crankpin diameter. Lightening holes will often increase crankshaft strength by relieving some of the natural stress in the crankshaft. The hole in the center of the crank throw is used for balancing, through control of the hole depth (Figures 18–17 and 18–18 on pages 444–445).

■ CRANKSHAFT FORCES

Each time combustion occurs, the force deflects the crankshaft as it transfers torque to the output shaft. This deflection occurs in two ways, to bend the shaft sideways and to twist the shaft in torsion. The crankshaft must be rigid enough to keep the deflection forces to a minimum.

Crankshaft deflections are directly related to operating roughness of an engine. When back-and-forth

Figure 18–15 Crankshaft sawed in half, showing drilled oil passages between the main and rod bearing journals.

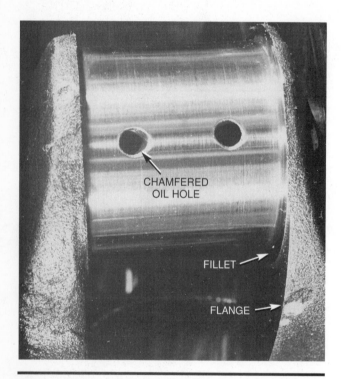

CHAMFERED
OIL HOLE

FILLET

FLANGE

Figure 18–16 Typical chamfered hole in a crankshaft bearing journal.

Figure 18–17 Balance hole drilled in a crankpin.

consists of a cast-iron **inertia ring** mounted to a cast-iron **hub** with an **elastomer** sleeve.

> **HINT:** Push on the rubber (elastomer sleeve) of the vibration damper with your fingers or a pencil. *If the rubber does not spring back, replace the damper.*

Two examples are shown in Figure 18–20. Elastomers are actually synthetic, rubberlike materials. The inertia ring size is selected to control the **amplitude** of the crankshaft vibrations for each specific engine model. See Figure 18–21 on page 446.

HIGH PERFORMANCE TIP

High Engine Speeds Require High Performance Parts

Do not go racing with stock parts. The harmonic balancer shown in Figure 18–22 on page 446 came apart and the resulting vibration broke the crankshaft when the owner attempted to race with his stock engine. The owner had made some engine modifications, but he did not change the stock harmonic balancer even though all other changes allowed the engine to rev to much higher speeds than stock parts normally would permit.

deflections occur at the same vibration **frequency** (number of vibrations per second) as that of another engine part, the parts will vibrate together. When this happens, the parts are said to **resonate.** These vibrations may become great enough to reach the audible level, producing a thumping sound. If this type of vibration continues, the part may fail. See Figure 18–19.

Harmful crankshaft twisting vibrations are dampened with a torsional vibration damper. It is also called a harmonic balancer. This damper or balancer usually

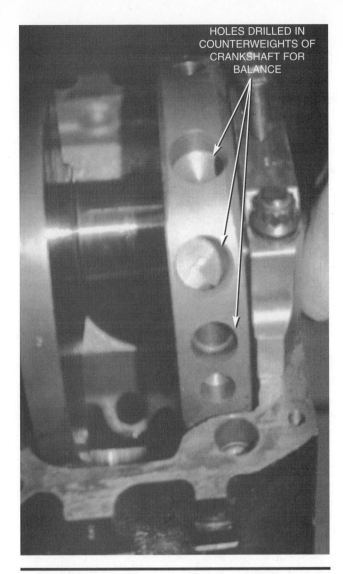

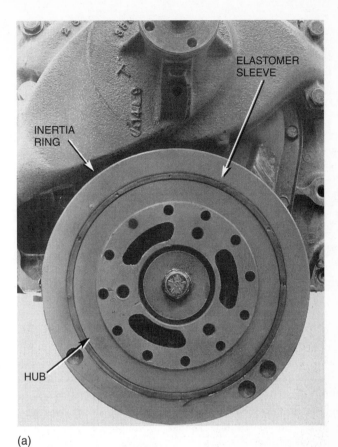

(a)

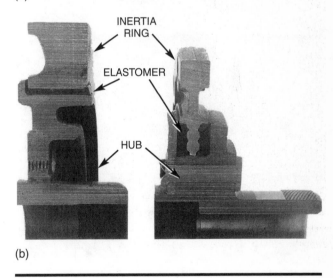

(b)

Figure 18–20 Crankshaft torsional dampers: (a) front view, and (b) sectional view of two different types of dampers.

Figure 18–18 Crankshaft balance is accomplished by drilling holes in the counterweights for balance. The deeper and larger in diameter the hole, the more weight is removed.

Figure 18–19 A crankshaft broken as a result of using the wrong torsional vibration damper.

■ CRANKSHAFT BALANCE

Most crankshaft balancing is done during manufacture. Holes are drilled in the counterweight to lighten it to improve balance. Sometimes these holes are drilled after the crankshaft is installed in the engine. Some manufacturers are able to control casting quality so closely

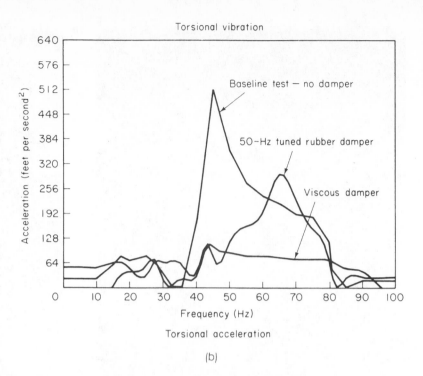

(a)

(b)

Figure 18–21 (a) Typical vibration damper showing where material has been drilled to balance the assembly. (b) Graphic showing forces involved without a damper and with two styles of vibration dampers. A viscous damper is commonly used on heavy-duty diesel engines.

Figure 18–22 Harmonic balancer that separated at high engine speed.

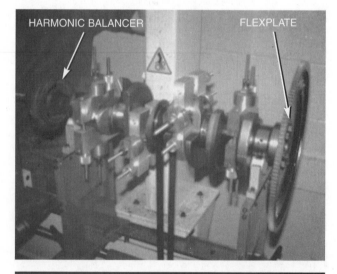

Figure 18–23 An externally balanced crankshaft being balanced. Notice that both the harmonic balancer and flexplate are installed on the crankshaft.

that counterweight machining for balancing is not necessary.

There are two ways engine manufacturers balance an engine:

- **Externally balanced**—weight is added to the harmonic balancer (vibration damper) and flywheel or the flexplate (see Figure 18–23).

- **Internally balanced**—All rotating parts of the engine are individually balanced including the harmonic balancer and flywheel (flexplate).

For example, the 350-cubic-inch Chevrolet V-8 is internally balanced, whereas the 400-cubic-inch Chevro-

Figure 18–24 Thrust bearing located on one of the crankshaft main bearings.

Figure 18–25 Scored connecting rod bearing journal.

let V-8 uses an externally balanced crankshaft. The harmonic balancer used on an externally balanced engine has additional weight.

■ THRUST SURFACE

Automatic transmission fluid pressure in the torque converter tends to push the crankshaft toward the front of the engine. Thrust bearings in the engine will support thrust loads and maintain the crankshaft position. Smooth thrust bearing journal surfaces are ground on a small boss located on the crankshaft cheek next to one of the main bearing journals (Figure 18–24). One main bearing has thrust bearing flanges that ride against these thrust bearings. Thrust bearings may be located on any one of the main bearing journals.

■ CRANKSHAFT INSPECTION

Shaft damage includes scored bearing journals, bends or warpage, and cracks. Damaged shafts must be reconditioned or replaced.

The crankshaft is one of the most highly stressed engine parts. *The stress on the crankshaft increases by four times every time the engine speed doubles.* Any sign of a crack is a cause to reject the crankshaft. Most cracks

can be seen during a close visual inspection. Crankshafts should also be checked with Magnaflux, which will highlight tiny cracks that would lead to failure.

Bearing journal scoring is a common crankshaft defect. Scoring appears as scratches around the bearing journal surface. Generally, there is more scoring near the center of the bearing journal, as shown in Figure 18–25.

Crankshaft journals should be inspected for nicks, pits, or corrosion. See Figures 18–26 and 18–27. Roughness and slight bends in journals can be corrected by grinding the journals.

> **HINT:** If your fingernail catches on a groove when rubbed across a bearing journal, the journal is too rough to reuse and must be reground. Another test is to rub a copper penny across the journal. If any copper remains on the crankshaft, it must be reground. See Figure 18–28.

■ CRANKSHAFT GRINDING

Crankshaft journals that have excessive scoring, out-of-round, or taper should be reground. See Figure 18–29. Crankshafts may require straightening before grinding.

Both crankshaft ends are placed in rotating heads on one style of crankshaft grinder. The main bearing journals are ground on the centerline of the crankshaft. The crankshaft is then offset in the two rotating heads just enough to make the crankshaft main bearing journal centerline rotate around the centerline of the

Figure 18–26 Nicked crankshaft journal that scratched the bearing.

Figure 18–27 The pitted part of the main bearing journal rides in the main bearing oil groove.

Figure 18–28 Damaged connecting rod journal.

Figure 18–29 Connecting rod journal badly worn from lack of lubrication.

crankpin. The crankshaft will then be rotating around the crankpin centerline. The journal on the crankpin is reground in this position. The crankshaft must be repositioned for each different crankpin center.

In another type of crankshaft grinder, the crankshaft always turns on the main bearing centerline. The grinding head is programmed to move in and out as the crankshaft turns to grind the crankpin bearing journals. The setup time is reduced when this type of grinder is used. Figure 18–30 shows a crankshaft being ground. Crankshafts are usually ground to the following undersize:

- 0.010 inch
- 0.020 inch
- 0.030 inch

The finished journal should be accurately ground to size with a smooth-surface finish. The radius of the fillet area on the sides of the journal should also be the

Figure 18–30 A crankshaft being ground.

Figure 18–31 All crankshafts should be polished after grinding. Both the crankshaft and the polishing cloth are being revolved.

Figure 18–32 After grinding and polishing, the crankshaft should be thoroughly cleaned. All oil passages should be cleaned with a brush. The operator shown here is using a solvent spray with a powered brush to clean the oil passages.

same as the original. The journal is polished after grinding using a 320-grit polishing cloth and oil to remove the fine metal "fuzz" remaining on the journal. See Figure 18–31. This fuzz feels smooth when the shaft turns in its direction. As the shaft turns in the opposite direction, the fuzz feels like a fine milling cutter. Polishing removes this fuzz. The crankshaft is rotated in its normal direction of rotation so that the polishing cloth can remove the fuzz. This leaves a smooth shaft with the proper surface finish. *Most crankshaft grinders grind in the direction opposite of rotation and then polish in the same direction as rotation.* The oil hole chamfer in the journal should be smoothed so that no sharp edge remains to cut the bearing. Finally, the crankshaft oil passages are thoroughly cleaned. See Figures 18–32 through 18–34. The reground journals are coated with oil to keep them from rusting until they are to be cleaned for assembly.

■ WELDING A CRANKSHAFT

Sometimes it is desirable to salvage a crankshaft by building up a bearing journal and then grinding it to the

original journal size. This is usually done by either electric arc welding or a metal spray. See Figure 18–35. Sometimes the journal is chrome plated. Chrome plating makes an excellent bearing surface when the chrome is well bonded. If the bonding loosens, it will cause an immediate bearing failure.

■ BALANCING A CRANKSHAFT

It is desirable to balance an engine that is to be operated at high RPM levels. Balancing will also improve the durability of a low-speed engine. It is reported that 0.4 ounce (10 grams) of unbalance on a standard automotive crankshaft can cause an unbalance effect of 60 pounds at 6000 RPM.

Figure 18–33 After the crankshaft is ground, the knurled part of the crankshaft that operates under a rope-type seal must be redone.

Reciprocating Weight

Reciprocating weight (also called **inertia weight**) refers to the weight of those engine parts that move up and down (reciprocate) during operation. The parts include:

- Pistons
- Piston rings
- Piston pins
- Connecting rods
- Connection rod bearings

All of these parts should weigh the same for each cylinder and piston; and rods must be taken apart for the weighing process.

Rotary Weight

Rotary or **rotating weight** is the weight of those engine components that rotate during normal engine operation. These parts include:

- Crankshaft
- Flywheel (flex plate)
- Harmonic balancer
- Timing gear

Bob Weight

A **bob weight** is the weight added to the crankshaft connecting rod journals to offset the weight of the counterweights. See Figure 18–36.

Figure 18–34 This photo was taken at a small remanufacturing company where every crankshaft is labeled using a rotary file. Most large remanufacturers use a color code system to identify the type of crankshaft and the undersize measurement.

Figure 18–35 A crankshaft that has had the journals welded in preparation for grinding. An extremely worn or damaged crankshaft can be returned to service using this repair procedure.

The bob weights are installed on the crank throws. Externally balanced crankshafts must also have the flywheel and damper installed. The balancer spins the crankshaft, usually at a low RPM level. The unbalance readout is similar to that of modern wheel balancers. Counterweights that are too heavy are drilled or ground to reduce their weight as seen in Figure 18–37. Heavy metal is added to light counterweights to add the weight required for balance if necessary.

Figure 18–36 Bob weights are installed on the connecting rod journals during the crankshaft balancing procedure.

Figure 18–37 Instead of drilling into the counterweight, a carbide cutter is being used to remove a little weight from the counterweight. The display on the balancer indicated where and how much weight needed to be removed.

■ STRESS RELIEVING THE CRANKSHAFT

The greatest area of stress on a crankshaft is the fillet area. Stress relief is achieved by blasting the fillet area of the journals with #320 steel shot. This strengthens the fillet area and helps to prevent the development of cracks in this area. Gray duct tape is commonly used to cover the journal to prevent damage to the rest of it. Stress relief procedures are usually performed after the grinding and polishing of the crankshaft.

■ AUXILIARY SHAFTS

Pushrod engines operate all accessories from either the crankshaft or the camshaft. External engine acces-

Figure 18–38 Typical auxiliary shaft.

sories are driven by belts from a crankshaft pulley on the front of the engine. Inside the engine, the oil pump, fuel pump, and distributor are usually driven by the camshaft at one-half the crankshaft speed.

It is not so easy to drive the internal engine accessories with the camshaft on engines using overhead camshafts. These engines often use a small auxiliary shaft. Sometimes this shaft is called a **jackshaft.** It is driven by the timing belt or timing chain and often drives (turns) the distributor and oil pump. Figure 18–38 shows a typical auxiliary shaft in the engine block.

■ BALANCE SHAFTS

Some engines use balance shafts to dampen normal engine vibrations. **Dampening** is reducing the vibration to an acceptable level. A balance shaft that is turning at crankshaft speed, but in the opposite direction, is used on a three-cylinder inline engine. Weights on the ends of the balance shaft move in a direction opposite to the direction of the end piston. When the piston goes up, the weight goes down, and when the piston goes down, the weight goes up. This reduces the end-to-end rocking action on the three-cylinder inline engine.

Another type of balance shaft system is designed to counterbalance vibrations on a four-stroke, four-cylinder engine. Two shafts are used, and they turn at *twice* the engine speed. One shaft turns in the same direction as the crankshaft, and the other turns in the opposite direction. The oil pump gears are used to drive the reverse-turning shaft. Counterweights on the balance shafts are positioned to oppose the natural rolling action of the engine, as well as the secondary vibrations caused by the piston and rod movements. This design is shown in Figure 18–39.

Balance shafts are commonly found on the larger-displacement (over 2.0 liter) four-cylinder automotive

Figure 18–39 Two counter-rotating balance shafts used to counterbalance the vibrations of a four-cylinder engine.

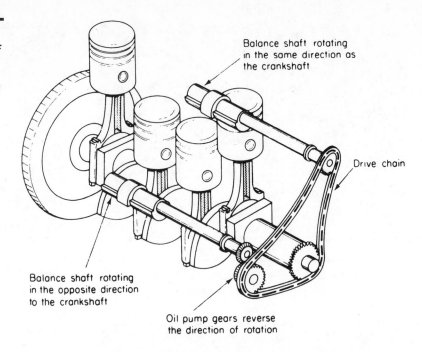

Balance shaft rotating in the same direction as the crankshaft

Drive chain

Balance shaft rotating in the opposite direction to the crankshaft

Oil pump gears reverse the direction of rotation

engines. Mitsubishi introduced counterbalance shafts on four-cylinder engines in 1974. In 1988, both Ford and General Motors added a balance shaft to some of their 3.8-L V-6 engines. The addition of balance shafts makes a big improvement in the smoothness of the engine. In V-6 engines, the improvement is most evident during idling and low-speed operation, whereas in the four-cylinder engines, balance shafts are especially helpful at higher engine speeds.

■ CAUSES OF UNBALANCE

Primary Unbalance

When the piston goes down in the cylinder, it tends to force the engine downward. When it goes up, it tends to force the engine upward. This causes a vertical shake in each direction on each crankshaft revolution. The piston moves farther and faster when the crankshaft is rotating in the upper half of the stroke than it does when the crankshaft is rotating in the lower half of the stroke, as shown in Figure 18–40. This greater imbalance when the crankshaft is in the upper half of the stroke is called **primary unbalance.** See Figure 18–41.

The counterweights could be sized large enough to balance the crankshaft, connecting rod, and piston. With this type of balance, the counterweight rotating upward would balance the piston going downward. The counterweight rotating downward would balance the piston going upward. As a result, there would be no vertical vibrating force or shake on the main bearings.

A counterweight this large would cause a side shake as great as the original up-and-down shaking caused by the primary unbalance, because there is no side-to-side weight to balance the crankshaft counterweight. See Figure 18–42. As a result, the crankshaft counterweight is made to be about half of the weight needed to balance the piston and connecting rod, so the counterweight does not balance all of the primary vertical shake. Some vertical and some horizontal primary shaking remains.

Secondary Unbalance

The piston is accelerated as it moves from bottom center until it reaches maximum speed, slightly over halfway up on the upward stroke. Acceleration increases and then drops to zero as the piston reaches its maximum speed at slightly more than halfway up the stroke. Negative acceleration slows the piston during the last half of the stroke. Negative acceleration drops to zero as the piston stops again at top center. The acceleration force changes twice on each stroke. The change in acceleration causes a **secondary vibration** at twice the engine speed, and the secondary vibration rotates in a direction opposite to the crankshaft rotation.

In four-cylinder inline engines, the pistons in the two middle cylinders move upward as the pistons in the two end cylinders move downward. See Figure 18–43. This tends to balance the primary vertical unbalance. Horizontal primary unbalance remains. This, combined with secondary unbalance, causes engine vibration.

Shaking Unbalance

Shaking forces from the secondary unbalance in inline engines can be countered with two balance shafts rotating in opposite directions at twice the engine speed.

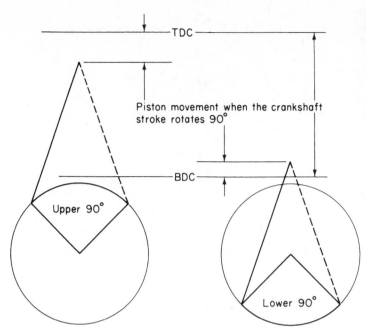

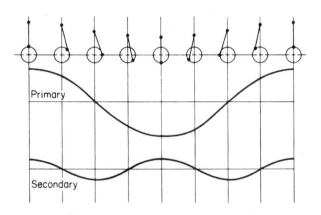

Figure 18–41 Primary and secondary vibrations in relation to piston pin position.

Figure 18–43 In an inline four-cylinder engine, the pistons in the two middle cylinders move together and in the direction opposite to that of the two pistons on the end.

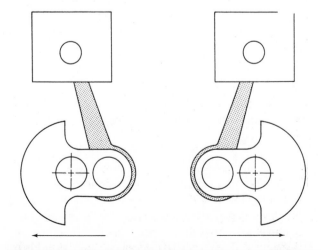

Figure 18–42 Counterweight unbalance in the horizontal direction.

Four-cylinder inline engines with balance shafts use two balance shafts in this way. An example is shown in Figure 18–44.

In 90-degree V-type engines, two connecting rods are fastened to the same crankpin on the crankshaft. The cylinders for the pistons on these connecting rods are at 90 degrees to each other. The crankshaft counterweight is large enough to fully balance one piston and connecting rod. Side shake caused by a fully balanced counterweight for one cylinder is offset by the piston and connecting rod in the second cylinder. What would have caused horizontal side shake on a

Figure 18–44 Typical balance shaft as installed in an inline four-cylinder engine.

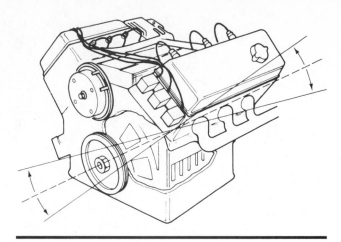

Figure 18–46 Direction of forces of a rolling couple.

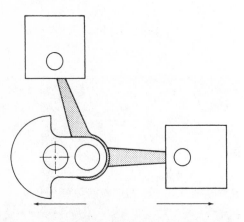
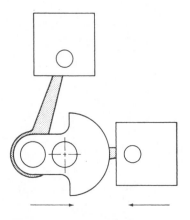

Figure 18–45 Balance of one crankpin on a V-type engine.

single-cylinder engine becomes the balance weight for the paired cylinder. See Figure 18–45.

Rolling Couple

The crank throws on a V-6 engine do not balance each other from end to end, as the throws on a four-cylinder inline engine do. This causes a rolling action as the throws on each end of the crankshaft rotate. This is called **rolling couple** and is illustrated in Figure 18–46. The engine can be balanced so that the unbalanced rolling couple will move the engine vertically, horizontally, or at any angle in between; but some roll will be present. A **balance shaft** with a heavy unbalanced section is placed in the block above the camshaft. See Figure 18–47. It is driven at crankshaft speed. The movement of unbalanced section is timed to oppose and minimize the unbalanced roll to make a smooth-running engine. Using soft engine mounts usually absorbs any remaining vibration.

■ ENGINE BEARINGS

Engine bearings are the main supports for the major moving parts of any engine. Engine bearings are important for the following reasons:

1. The clearance between the bearings and the crankshaft is a major factor in maintaining the proper oil pressure throughout the entire engine. Most engines are designed to provide the maximum protection and lubrication to the engine bearings above all else.
2. Engine durability relies on bearing life. Bearing failure usually results in immediate engine failure.
3. Engine bearings are designed to support the operating loads of the engine and, with the lubricant, provide minimum friction. This must be achieved at all designed engine speeds. The bearings must be able to operate for long periods of time, even when small foreign particles are in the lubricant.

(a)

(b)

(c)

Figure 18–47 (a) Balance shaft in a 90-degree V-6 engine. (b) The balance shaft is driven off of the camshaft gear at two times camshaft speed (this is the same as crankshaft speed). (c) A narrower than usual timing chain and sprocket are used to complete the installation.

Most engine bearings are of the **plain** or **sleeve bearing** type. Both need a constant flow of lubricating oil. In automotive engines, the lubricating system supplies oil to each bearing continuously when the engine runs. Bearings and journals *only* wear when the parts come in contact with each other or when foreign particles are present.

Oil enters the bearing through the oil holes and grooves. It spreads into a smooth wedge-shape oil film that supports the bearing load.

■ BEARING LOADS

It is important that the engine have large enough bearings that the bearing load is within the strength limits of the bearings. Bearing load capacity is calculated by dividing the bearing load in pounds by the projected area of the bearing. The projected area is the bearing length multiplied by the bearing diameter. The load on engine bearings is determined by developing a polar bearing load diagram that shows the amount and direction of the instantaneous bearing loads. Bearing load diagrams are shown in Figure 18–48.

The forces on the engine bearings vary with engine speed and load. On the intake stroke, the inertia force is opposed by the force of drawing in the air-fuel mixture. On the compression and power strokes, there is also an opposing force on the rod bearings. On the exhaust stroke, however, there is no opposing force to counteract the inertia force of the piston coming to a stop at TDC. The result is a higher force load on the *bottom* rod

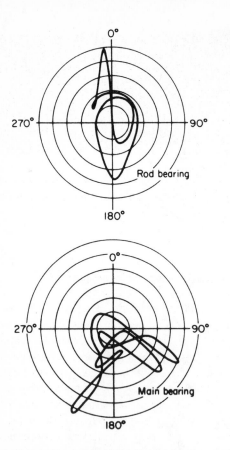

Figure 18–48 Typical rod and main bearing load diagrams. The circles on these polar diagrams indicate the amount of force on the bearing as it rotates. Notice that most of the forces on the connecting rod bearing are vertical (up and down) as you would expect; and most of the forces on the main bearing are downward again as expected.

bearing due to inertia at TDC of the exhaust stroke. These forces tend to stretch the big end of the rod in the direction of rod movement.

1. As engine speed (RPM) increases, rod bearing loads decrease because of the balancing of inertia and opposing loads.
2. As engine speed (RPM) increases, the main bearing loads increase.

> **NOTE:** This helps explain why engine blocks with four-bolt main bearing supports are really only needed for high-engine speed stability.

3. Because the loads on bearings vary and affect both rod and main bearings, it is generally recommended that *all* engine bearings be replaced at one time.

The Knock of a Flex Plate

The source of a knocking noise in an engine is often difficult to determine without disassembling the engine. Generally, a deep engine knocking noise means that serious damage has occurred to the rods or main bearings and related parts. A flex plate (drive plate) is used on automatic transmission–equipped engines to drive the torque converter and provide a ring gear for the starter motor to crank the engine. Two common flex plate–related noises and their causes are as follows:

- Torque converter attaching bolts or nuts can loosen (this is most common in four-cylinder engines, where vibration is more severe than in six- or eight-cylinder engines). The torque converter can then pound on the holes of the flex plate, causing a loud knocking sound. However, if there is a load on the engine, as when the transmission is in drive or while driving under load, the sound should stop. At idle in park or neutral, the noise will be loudest, because the torque converter can float and will hit the sides of the holes in the flex plate.
- If the flex plate is cracked, the resulting noise is very similar to a connecting rod or main bearing knock. The noise also seems to change at times, leading many technicians to believe that it involves a moving internal part that is lubricated, such as a rod or main bearing. The drive belts can also make a similar noise when they are loose, and belt-driven accessories can also produce similar noises.

Diagnosis should proceed as follows:

During the diagnostic procedure, the technician should disconnect one drive belt at a time (if there is more than one) and then start the engine in an attempt to isolate the noise. Noises can be transmitted throughout the entire length of the engine through the crankshaft, making the source of the noise more difficult to isolate. If the flex plate is cracked, the noise is most noticeable when there is a change in engine speed or load. To help diagnose a cracked flex plate, raise engine speed to a high idle (1500 to 2000 RPM), then turn the ignition switch off. Before the engine stops, turn the ignition back on. If a knocking noise is heard when the engine restarts, the flex plate is cracked.

■ BEARING FATIGUE

Bearings tend to flex or bend slightly under changing loads. This is especially noticeable in reciprocating engine bearings. Bearing metals, like other metals, tend to

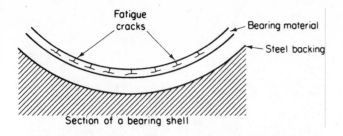

Figure 18–49 Shape of fatigue cracks in a bearing. If the bearing is subjected to continued high loads, the cracks expand and eventually cause the bearing material to flake off from the steel backing.

Figure 18–51 Bearing material missing from the bearing as a result of fatigue failure.

fatigue and break after being flexed or bent a number of times. Flexing starts fatigue, which shows up as fine cracks in the bearing surface because the bearing material became **work hardened.** These cracks gradually deepen almost to the bond between the bearing metal and the backing metal. The cracks then cross over and intersect with each other, as illustrated in Figure 18–49. In time, this will allow a piece of bearing material to fall out. The length of time before fatigue will cause failure is called the **fatigue life** of the bearing. Bearings must have a long fatigue life for normal engine service. The harder the bearing material, the longer is its fatigue life. Soft bearings have a short fatigue life and low bearing load strength. They are generally low in cost and can only be used where the bearing requirements are low. See Figures 18–50 and 18–51.

■ BEARING CONFORMABILITY

The ability of bearing materials to creep or flow slightly to match shaft variations is called **conformability.** The bearing conforms to the shaft during the engine break-in period. In modern automobile engines, there is little need for bearing conformability or break-in, because automatic processing has achieved machining tolerances that keep the shaft very close to the designed size. See Figure 18–52.

■ BEARING EMBEDABILITY

Engine manufacturers have designed engines to produce minimum crankcase deposits. This has been done by providing them with oil filters, air filters, and closed crankcase ventilation systems that minimize contaminants. Still, some foreign particles get into the bearings. The bearings must be capable of embedding these particles into the bearing surface so that they will not score the shaft. To fully embed the particle, the bearing material gradually works across the particle, completely covering it. The bearing property that allows it to do this is called **embedability.** Embedability is illustrated in Figures 18–53 and 18–54.

■ BEARING DAMAGE RESISTANCE

Under some operating conditions, the bearing will be temporarily overloaded. This will cause the oil film to break down and allow the shaft metal to come in contact with the bearing metal. As the rotating crankshaft contacts the bearing high spots, the spots become hot from friction. The friction causes localized

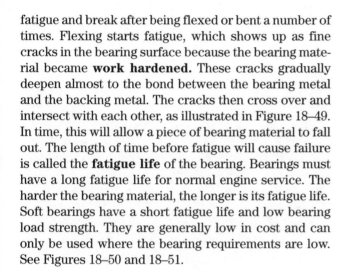

Figure 18–50 Bearing material missing from the shell as a result of fatigue.

Figure 18–52 Bearing wear caused by a misaligned journal. A bent connecting rod could also cause similar bearing wear.

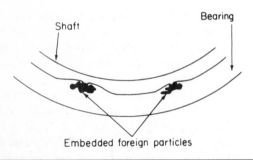

Figure 18–53 Bearing material covers foreign material as it embeds into the bearing.

Figure 18–54 Foreign particles such as dirt embedded in the bearing material.

hot spots in the bearing material that seize or weld to the crankshaft. The crankshaft then breaks off particles of the bearing material and pulls the particles around with it, scratching or scoring the bearing surface. See Figures 18–55 and 18–56. Bearings have a characteristic called **score resistance.** It prevents the bearing materials from seizing to the shaft during oil film breakdown.

By-products of combustion form acids in the oil. The bearings' ability to resist attack from these acids is called **corrosion resistance.** Corrosion can occur over the entire surface of the bearing. This will remove material and increase the oil clearance. It can also leach or eat into the bearing material, dissolving some of the bearing material alloys. Either type of corrosion will reduce bearing life.

Figure 18–55 Bearing material starting to leave the steel backing.

(a)

(b)

Figure 18–56 Typical results of oil pressure loss:
(a) extreme wear of the connecting rod journal,
(b) overheating finally leading to failure of the bearing.

■ BEARING MATERIALS

Three materials are used for automobile engine bearings: **babbitt, copper-lead alloy,** and **aluminum.** A layer of the bearing materials 0.010 to 0.020 inch (0.25 to 0.50 millimeter) thick is applied over a low carbon steel backing. An engine bearing is called a **bearing shell,** which is a steel backing with a surface coating of bearing material. The steel provides support needed for the shaft load. The bearing material meets the rest of the bearing operating requirements.

Babbitt

Babbitt is the oldest automotive bearing material. Isaac Babbitt (1799–1862) first formulated this material in 1839. An excellent bearing material, it was originally made from a combination of lead, tin, and antimony. Lead and tin are alloyed with small quantities of copper and antimony to give it the required strength. Babbitt is still used in applications in which material is required for soft shafts running under moderate loads and speeds. It will work with occasional borderline lubrication and oil starvation without failure.

Tri-Metal

Copper-lead alloy is a stronger and more expensive bearing material than babbitt. It is used for intermediate- and high-speed applications. Tin, in small quantities, is often alloyed with the copper-lead bearings. This bearing material is most easily damaged by corrosion from acid accumulation in the engine oil. Corrosion results in bearing journal wear as the bearing is eroded by the acids.

Many of the copper-lead bearings have an **overlay,** or third layer, of metal. This overlay is usually of babbitt. Babbitt-overlayed bearings have high fatigue strength, good conformity, good embedability, and good corrosion resistance. The overplated bearing is a premium bearing. It is also the most expensive because the overplating layer, from 0.0005 to 0.001 inch (0.0125 to 0.025 millimeter) thick, is put on the bearing with an **electroplating** process. The layers of bearing material on a bearing shell are illustrated in Figure 18–57.

Aluminum

Aluminum was the last of the three materials to be used for automotive bearings. Automotive bearing aluminum has small quantities of tin and silicon alloyed with it. This makes a stronger but more expensive bearing than either babbitt or copper-lead alloy.

Most of its bearing characteristics are equal to or better than those of babbitt and copper lead. Aluminum bearings are well suited to high-speed, high-load conditions and do not contain lead, which is a benefit to the environment both at the manufacturing plant and for the technician who may be exposed to the bearings.

■ BEARING MANUFACTURING

Modern automotive engines use **precision insert-type bearing shells** sometimes called **half-shell bearings.** The bearing is manufactured to very close tolerance so that it will fit correctly in each application. The bearing, therefore, must be made from precisely the correct materials under closely controlled manufacturing conditions.

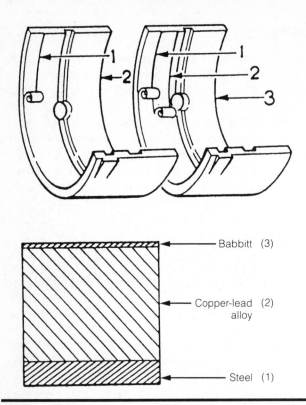

Babbitt (3)

Copper-lead (2)
alloy

Steel (1)

Figure 18–57 Typical two-layer and three-layer engine bearing insert showing the relative thickness of the various materials.

Figure 18–58 shows the typical bearing shell types found in modern engines.

■ BEARING SIZES

Bearings are usually available in standard (std) size, and in measurements 0.010, 0.020, and 0.030 inch *undersize*. Even though the bearing itself is thicker for use on a machined crankshaft, the bearing is referred to as undersize because the crankshaft journals are undersize. Factory bearings may be available in 0.0005 or 0.001 inch undersize for precision fitting of a production crankshaft.

Before purchasing bearings, be sure to use a micrometer to measure *all* main and connecting rod journals.

■ BEARING CLEARANCE

The bearing-to-journal clearance may be from 0.0005 to 0.0025 inch (0.025 to 0.060 millimeter), depending on the engine. Doubling the journal clearance will allow more than *four* times as much oil to flow from the edges of the bearing. The oil clearance must be large enough to allow an oil film to build up, but small enough to prevent excess oil leakage, which would cause loss of oil

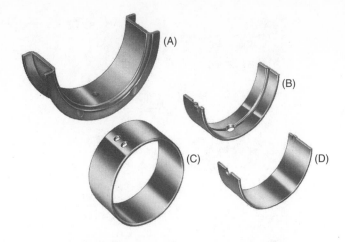

Figure 18–58 Typical bearing shell types found in modern engines: (a) half-shell thrust bearing, (b) upper main bearing insert, (c) lower main bearing insert, (d) full round-type camshaft bearing. *(Courtesy of Sealed Power Corporation)*

pressure. A large amount of oil leakage at one of the bearings would starve other bearings farther along in the oil system. This would result in the failure of the oil-starved bearings.

■ BEARING SPREAD AND CRUSH

The bearing design also includes bearing **spread** and **crush,** as illustrated in Figure 18–59. The bearing shell has a slightly larger arc than does the bearing housing. This difference is called bearing spread and it makes the shell 0.005 to 0.020 inch (0.125 to 0.500 millimeter) wider than the housing bore. A lip or **tang** locates the bearing endwise in the housing. The tang can be identified in Figure 18–60. Spread holds the bearing shell in the housing while the engine is being assembled. When the bearing is installed, each end of the bearing shell is slightly above the parting surface. When the bearing cap is tightened, the ends of the two bearing shells touch and are forced together. This force is called bearing crush. Crush holds the bearing in place and keeps the bearing from turning when the engine runs. Crush must exert a force of at least 12,000 psi (82,740 kPa) at 250°F (121°C) to hold the bearing securely in place. A stress of 40,000 psi (275,790 kPa) is considered maximum to avoid damaging the bearing or housing. Bearing shells that do not have enough crush may rotate with the shaft. The result is called a **spun bearing,** as pictured in Figure 18–61.

Replacement bearings should be of a quality as good as or better than that of the original bearings. The replacement bearings must also have the same oil holes and grooves.

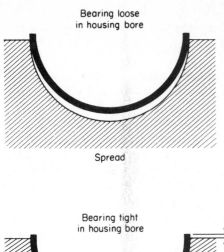

Bearing loose
in housing bore

Spread

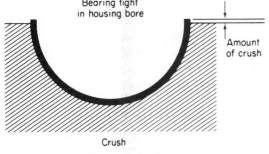

Bearing tight
in housing bore

Amount
of crush

Crush

Figure 18–59 Bearing spread and crush.

Figure 18–60 Tang on a bearing used to properly locate the bearing during assembly.

> *CAUTION:* Some bearings may have oil holes in the top shell only. If these are incorrectly installed, no oil will flow to the connecting rods or main rods, which will result in instant engine failure.

Modified engines have more demanding bearing requirements and therefore usually require a higher-quality bearing to provide satisfactory service.

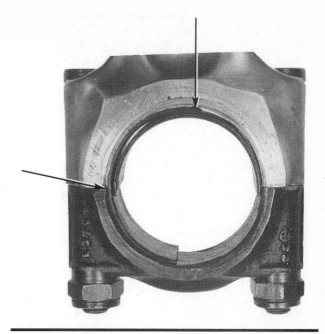

Figure 18–61 Spun bearing. The lower cap bearing has rotated under the upper rod bearing.

TECH TIP ✔

Count Your Blessings and Your Pan Bolts!

Replacing cam bearings can be relatively straightforward or can involve keeping count of the number of oil pan bolts! For example, Buick-built V-6 engines use different cam bearings depending on the number of bolts used to hold the oil pan to the block.

- Fourteen bolts in the oil pan: The front bearing is special, but the rest of the bearings are the same.
- Twenty bolts in the oil pan: Bearings #1 and #4 use two oil feed holes. Bearings #2 and #3 use single oil feed holes.

■ CAM BEARINGS

The camshaft in pushrod engines rotates in **sleeve bearings** that are pressed into bearing bores within the engine block. Overhead camshaft bearings may be either sleeve-type bushings called **full round bearings** or **split-type (half-shell) bearings,** depending on the design of the bearing supports. In pushrod engines, the cam bearings are installed in the block. The best rule of thumb to follow is to replace the cam bearings whenever the main bearings are replaced. The replacement cam bearings must have the correct outside diameter to fit snugly in the cam bearing bores of the block. They must have the correct oil holes and be positioned correctly. Cam bearings must also have the proper inside

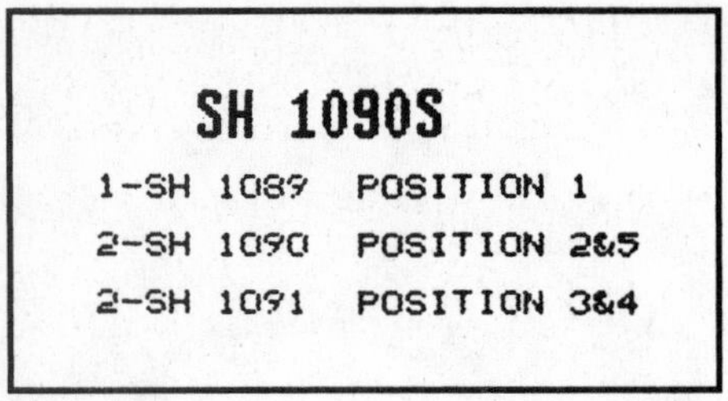

```
SH 1090S
1-SH 1089    POSITION 1
2-SH 1090    POSITION 2&5
2-SH 1091    POSITION 3&4
```

Figure 18–62 Typical cam bearing identification (instruction) sticker that accompanies replacement cam bearings. The cam bearing in position 1 is the front cam bearing. Proper cam bearing installation is critical to proper engine operation.

diameter to fit the camshaft bearing journals. See Figure 18–62. See Chapter 16 for block preparation procedures to be performed before installing camshaft bearings.

In many engines, each cam bearing is a different size—the largest is in the front and the smallest is in the rear. The cam bearing journal size must be checked and each bearing identified before assembly is begun. The location of each new cam bearing can be marked on the outside of the bearing with a felt-tip marker to help avoid mixing up bearings. Marking in this way will not affect the bearing size or damage the bearing in any way. Cam bearings should be installed "dry" (not oiled) to prevent the cam bearing from moving (spinning) after installation. If the cam bearing were oiled, the rotation of the camshaft could cause the cam bearing to rotate and block oil holes that lubricate the camshaft.

PHOTO SEQUENCE   Plastigage a Main Bearing

PS 32–1 The tools required to measure the main bearing oil clearance include a torque wrench, appropriate-size socket(s), and Plastigage material.

PS 32–2 Start the measuring process by thoroughly cleaning the main bearing journal.

PS 32–3 Place a strip of Plastigage onto the main bearing journal.

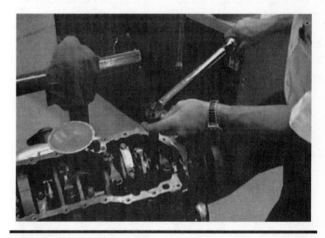

PS 32–4 Carefully install the main bearing cap and torque the retaining bolts to factory specifications.

PS 32–5 After torquing the main bearing cap to specifications, loosen the bolts and carefully remove the bearing cap.

PHOTO SEQUENCE   Plastigage a Main Bearing

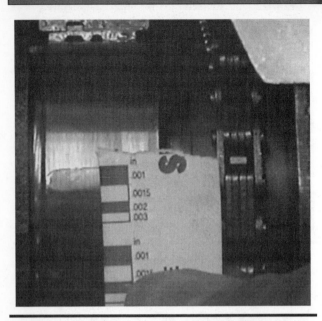

PS 32–6 Using the scale on the package of Plastigage, determine the main bearing oil clearance by comparing the width of the squeezed plastic gauging strip. In this case, the width is about equal to the green 0.001-in. strip. The wider the strip of Plastigage is, the narrower the bearing oil clearance.

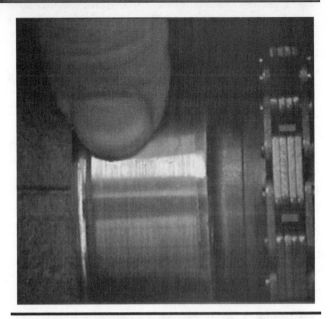

PS 32–7 After comparing the width of the Plastigage to the scale on the package, all of the squeezed Plastigage material must be removed from the crankshaft journal. Removal often requires using your fingernail to get all of the material removed.

PS 32–8 After measuring all main rod bearing oil clearances, the main bearing caps can be reinstalled this time using assembly lube on the crankshaft journal before installing the main bearing cap.

PS 32–9 After replacing the main bearing cap, torque the bolts to factory specifications.

PS 33–1 Before the crankshaft can be checked for balance, the crankshaft has to be installed onto the balancer and the sensor at the end adjusted to eliminate any runout.

PS 33–2 The bearings on which the crankshaft rides must be properly lubricated.

PS 33–3 All necessary dimensions and weights are entered into the balancer and the balancer itself does the necessary calculations.

PS 33–4 After the correct Bob weights have been attached to the rod bearing journals and all necessary preliminary steps have been completed, the balancer is turned on and the crankshaft is spun.

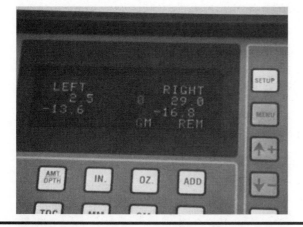

PS 33–5 After the crankshaft stops spinning, the balancer displays the amount of weight (in grams) that should be removed and its location.

PS 33–6 An air-powered die grinder is being used to remove a small amount of weight from the crankshaft in the location specified by the balancer.

Crankshaft Balancing—continued

PS 33–7 Before spinning the crankshaft to recheck the balance, the rubbing blocks are again lubricated.

PS 33–8 The crankshaft is spun again to check the balance after material has been removed.

PS 33–9 A small amount of additional material is being removed using a hand grinder.

PS 33–10 If more weight needs to be removed, the balancer is programmed to direct the technician as to how deep to drill into the counterweight and with which diameter drill bit.

PS 33–11 This counterweight has been drilled to reduce its weight. The bigger the diameter and the deeper the hole is drilled, the more weight is removed from the crankshaft counterweight.

PS 33–12 After weight has been drilled or ground from the crankshaft, the display will indicate that it is within acceptable balance tolerance.

■ SUMMARY

1. Forged crankshafts have a wide separation line.

2. Cast crankshafts have a narrow mold parting line.

3. Most crankshafts have counterweights that offset the weight and the forces of the piston and connecting rod assembly.

4. Even-fire 90-degree V-6 engines require that the crankshaft be splayed to allow for even firing.

5. Lubrication to the main bearings is fed through the main oil gallery in the block. Oil for the rod bearings comes from holes in the crankshaft drilled between the main journal and the rod journal.

6. A vibration damper, also known as a harmonic balancer, is used to dampen harmful twisting vibrations of the crankshaft.

7. Most engines are internally balanced. This means that the crankshafts and vibration damper are both balanced. Other engines use the vibration damper to balance the crankshaft and are called externally balanced engines.

8. Most crankshafts can be reground to be 0.010, 0.020, or 0.030 inch undersize.

9. Crankshafts are ground in the direction opposite of rotation and polished in the same direction as rotation.

10. Most engine bearings are constructed with a steel shell for strength and are covered with a copper-lead alloy. Many bearings also have a thin overlay of babbitt.

11. Bearings should have spread and crush to keep them from spinning when the crankshaft rotates.

■ REVIEW QUESTIONS

1. Describe the difference between a forged and a cast crankshaft.

2. How many degrees of crankshaft rotation are there between cylinder firings on an inline four-cylinder engine, an inline six-cylinder engine, and a V-8 engine?

3. Explain how and why crankshafts should be polished after grinding.

4. Explain the operation and use of auxiliary shafts.

5. Describe the use of balance shafts in an engine and explain how they help control engine vibration.

6. List four engine bearing properties.

7. Describe bearing crush and bearing spread.

■ ASE CERTIFICATION-TYPE QUESTIONS

1. A forged crankshaft _____ .
   a. Has a wide parting line
   b. Has a thin parting line
   c. Has a parting line in one plane
   d. Has both b and c

2. A typical V-8 engine crankshaft has _____ main bearings.
   a. Three
   b. Four
   c. Five
   d. Seven

3. A four-cylinder engine fires one cylinder at every _____ degrees of crankshaft rotation.
   a. 270
   b. 180
   c. 120
   d. 90

4. A splayed crankshaft is a crankshaft that _____ .
   a. Is externally balanced
   b. Is internally balanced
   c. Has offset main bearing journals
   d. Has offset rod journals

5. The thrust bearing surface is located on one of the main bearings to control thrust loads caused by _____ .
   a. Lugging the engine
   b. Torque converter or clutch release forces
   c. Rapid deceleration forces
   d. Both a and c

6. If any crankshaft is ground, it must also be _____ .
   a. Shot peened
   b. Chrome plated
   c. Polished
   d. Externally balanced

7. If bearing-to-journal clearance is doubled, how much oil will flow?
   a. One-half as much
   b. The same amount if the pressure is kept constant
   c. Double the amount
   d. Four times the amount

8. Typical journal-to-bearing clearance is _____ .
   a. 0.00015 to 0.00018 inch
   b. 0.0005 to 0.0025 inch
   c. 0.150 to 0.250 inch
   d. 0.020 to 0.035 inch

9. A bearing shell has a slightly larger arc than the bearing housing. This difference is called _____ .
   a. Bearing crush
   b. Bearing tang
   c. Bearing spread
   d. Bearing saddle

10. Bearing _____ occurs when a bearing shell is slightly above the parting surface of the bearing cap.
    a. Overlap
    b. Crush
    c. Cap lock
    d. Interference fit

Engine Assembly

All parts are attached to the engine block. The block, therefore, must be prepared before assembly can begin. The key to proper assembly of any engine is cleanliness. The work area and workbench space must be clean to prevent dirt or other engine-damaging particles from being picked up and causing possible serious engine damage.

■ BLOCK PREPARATION

All surfaces should also be checked for damage resulting from the machining processes. As mentioned in Chapter 16, items that should be done before assembly begins include the following:

1. The block including the oil gallery passages should be thoroughly cleaned.
2. All threaded bolt holes should be chamfered.
3. All threaded holes should be cleaned with a tap.

■ INSTALLING CUPS AND PLUGS

Oil gallery plugs should be installed using sealant on the threads. See Figure 19–1.

> **CAUTION:** Avoid using Teflon tape on the threads of oil gallery plugs. The tape is often cut by the threads, and thin strips of the tape are then free to flow through the oil galleries where the tape can cause a clog, thereby limiting lubricating engine oil to important parts of the engine.

Core holes left in the external block wall are machined and sealed with **soft core plugs** or **expansion plugs** (also called **freeze plugs** or **Welsh plugs**).

Soft plugs are of two designs:

- **Convex type**—the core hole is counter bored with a shoulder. The convex soft plug is placed in the

Figure 19–1 Oil passage (gallery) plug being installed with a T-handle wrench.

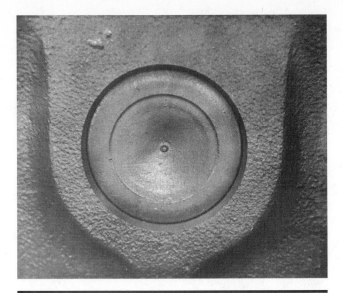

Figure 19–2 Installed convex-type soft plug.

Figure 19–3 Installed cup-type soft plug.

counter bore, convex side out. It is driven in and upset with a fitted seating tool. This causes the edge of the soft plug to enlarge to hold it in place. Figure 19–2 shows an installed convex soft plug. A convex plug should be driven in until it reaches the counter bore of the core plug hole.

- **Cup type**—the most common type, it fits into a smooth, straight hole. The outer edge of the cup is slightly bell mouthed. The bell mouth causes it to tighten when it is driven into the hole to the correct depth with a seating tool. An installed cup-type soft plug is shown in Figures 19–3 and 19–4. A cup plug is installed about 0.020 to 0.050 inch (0.5 to 1.3 millimeters) below the surface of the block, using sealant to prevent leaks.

■ CAM BEARINGS

A cam bearing installing tool is required to insert the new cam bearing without damage to the bearing. A number of tool manufacturers design and sell cam bearing installing tools. Their common feature is a shoulder on a bushing that fits inside the cam bearing, with a means of keeping the bearing aligned as it is installed. Figure 19–5 shows a camshaft bearing on the removing and installing tool. The bearing is placed on the bushing of the tool and rotated to properly align the oil hole. The bearing is then forced into the bearing bore of the block by either a pulling screw or a slide hammer. A pulling screw type of tool is illustrated in Figure 19–6. The installed bearing must be checked to make sure that it has the correct depth and that the oil hole is indexed with

Figure 19–4 Cup plugs (also called expansion plugs or core plugs) being installed in cylinder heads before final assembly. Note the use of sealer on the plugs.

the oil passage in the block. No additional service is required on cam bearings that have been properly installed. See Figures 19–7 and 19–8 on page 471. The opening at the back of the camshaft is closed with an expansion plug (Figure 19–9 on page 471).

Figure 19–5 Cam bearing tool being used to remove a used cam bearing.

■ CAUSES OF PREMATURE BEARING FAILURE

According to a major manufacturer of engine bearings, the major causes of premature (shortly after installation) bearing failure include the following:

Dirt (45%)

Misassembly (13%)

Misalignment (13%)

Lack of lubrication (11%)

Overloading or lugging (10%)

Corrosion (4%)

Other (4%)

Many cases of premature bearing failure may result from a combination of several of these items. Therefore, to help prevent bearing failure, *keep everything as clean as possible.*

■ MEASURING MAIN BEARING CLEARANCE

The engine is assembled from the inside out. Checks are made during assembly to ensure correct fits and proper assembly of the parts.

The main bearings are properly fit before the crankshaft is lubricated or turned. The oil clearance of both main and connecting rod bearings is set by selectively fitting the bearings. In this way, the oil clearance can be adjusted to within 0.0005 inch of the desired clearance.

> **CAUTION:** Avoid touching bearings with bare hands. The oils on your fingers can start corrosion of the bearing materials. Always wear protective cloth or rubber gloves to avoid the possibility of damage to the bearing surface.

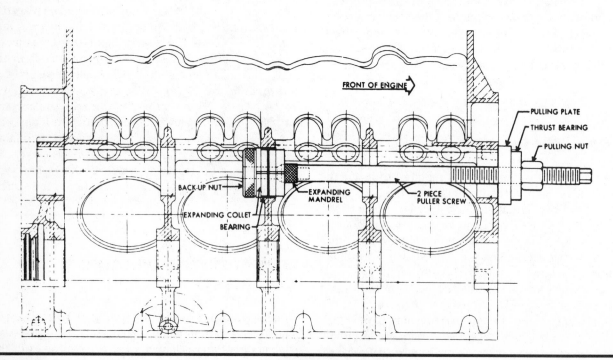

Figure 19–6 Screw-type puller being used to install a new cam bearing. Most cam bearings are **crush fit.** The full, round bearing is forced into the cam bearing bore. (*Courtesy of Buick Motor Division, GMC*)

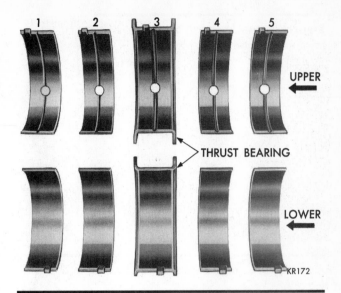

Figure 19–7 Cam bearing damaged by improper engine assembly.

Figure 19–8 Cam bearing that was driven in too far. The oil feed hole to the cam bearing was slightly covered.

Figure 19–9 The opening in the back of the camshaft is closed with a cup-type expansion plug. Screw-type plugs are installed in the oil passages.

Figure 19–10 Typical main bearing set. Note that the upper halves are grooved for better oil flow and the lower halves are plain for better load support. This bearing set uses the center main bearing for thrust control. (*Courtesy of Chrysler Corporation*)

Bearings are usually made in 0.010, 0.020, and 0.030 inch undersize for use on reground journals. See Figure 19–10 for a typical main bearing design.

The crankshaft bearing journals should be measured with a micrometer to select the required bearing size. Remember that each of the main bearing caps will only fit one location and the caps must be positioned correctly. The correct-size bearings should be placed in the block and cap, making sure that the bearing tang locks into its slot. The upper main bearing has an oil feed hole. Carefully rest the clean crankshaft in the block on the upper main bearings. Lower it squarely, as shown in Figure 19–11, so that it does not damage the thrust bearing. Place a strip of Plastigage (gauging plastic) on each main bearing journal. Install the main bearing caps and tighten the bolts to specifications. Remove each cap and check the width of the Plastigage with the markings on the gauge envelope, as shown in Figure 19–12. This will indicate the oil clearance. If the shaft is out-of-round, the oil clearance should be checked at the point that has the *least* oil clearance.

■ CORRECTING BEARING CLEARANCE

The oil clearance can be reduced by 0.001 inch by replacing both bearing shells with bearing shells that 0.001 inch undersize. The clearance can be reduced by 0.0005 inch by replacing only one of the bearing shells with a bearing shell that is 0.001 inch smaller. This smaller bearing shell should be placed in the engine-block side

Figure 19–11 Crankshaft being carefully lowered into place.

Figure 19–12 Checking the width of the plastic gauging strip to determine the oil clearance of the main bearing. An alternate method of determining oil clearance includes careful measurement of crankshaft journal and bearings after they are installed and the main housing bore caps are torqued to specifications.

TECH TIP

"One to Three"

When engine technicians are talking about clearances and specifications, the unit of measure most often used is thousandths of an inch (0.001 inch). Therefore, a clearance expressed as "one to three" would actually be a clearance of 0.001 to 0.003 inch. The same applies to parts of a thousandth of an inch. For example, a specification of 0.0005 to 0.0015 inch would be spoken of as simply being "one-half to one and one-half." The unit of a thousandth of an inch is assumed, and this method of speaking reduces errors and misunderstandings.

HINT: Most engine clearance specifications fall within one to three thousandths of an inch. The written specification could be a misprint; therefore, if the specification does not fall within this general range, double-check the clearance value using a different source.

of the bearing (the upper shell). Oil clearance can be adjusted accurately using this procedure. Never mismatch the bearing shells by more than a 0.001-inch difference in size. Oil clearances normally run from 0.0005 to 0.002 inch.

The crankshaft is removed once the correct oil clearance has been established. The rear oil seal is installed in the block and cap; then the crankshaft journals are lubricated with assembly lubricant.

■ LIP SEAL INSTALLATION

Seals are always used at the front and rear of the crankshaft. Overhead cam engines may also have a seal at the front end of the camshaft and at the front end of an auxiliary accessory shaft. Either a lip seal or a rope seal is used in these locations. See Figures 19–13 and 19–14. The rear crankshaft oil seal is installed after the main bearings have been properly fit.

The lip seal may be molded in a steel case or it may be molded around a steel stiffener. The counter bore or guide that supports the seal must be thoroughly clean. In most cases, the back of the lip seal is dry when it is installed. Occasionally, a manufacturer will recommend the use of sealants behind the seal. The engine service manual should be consulted for specific sealing in-

Figure 19–13 Lip-type rear main bearing seal in place. The crankshaft is removed.

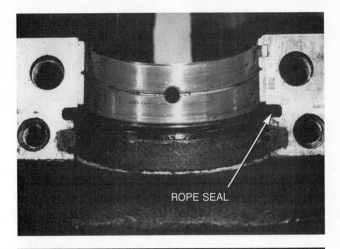

Figure 19–15 Rope-type rear main bearing seal in place, with the crankshaft removed.

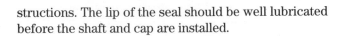

Figure 19–14 Lip seal with spring tension. This spring is called a garter spring.

Figure 19–16 Rolling a rope-type seal in a main bearing cap.

structions. The lip of the seal should be well lubricated before the shaft and cap are installed.

> **CAUTION:** Teflon® seals should not be lubricated. This type of seal should be installed dry. When the engine is first started, some of the Teflon® transfers to the crankshaft so a Teflon®-to-Teflon® surface is created. Even touching the seal with your hands could remove some of the outer coating on the seal and could cause a leak. Carefully read the installation instructions that should come with the seal.

■ ROPE SEAL INSTALLATION

Rope-type seals (**braided fabric seals**) are sometimes used as rear crankshaft oil seals. Some engines manufactured by Buick use rope-type seals at both the front and rear of the crankshaft. Rope-type oil seals must be compressed tightly into the groove so that no oil can leak behind them. With the crankshaft removed, the up-

per half of the rope seal is put in a clean groove and compressed by rolling a round object against it to force it tightly into the groove. A piece of pipe, a large socket, or even a hammer handle can be used for this, as shown in Figure 19–15. When the seal is fully seated in the groove, the ends that extend above the parting surface are cut to be flush with the surface using a sharp single-edge razor blade (Figure 19–16) or a sharp tool specially designed to cut the seal. The same procedures are used to install the lower half of the rope seal in the rear main bearing cap or seal retainer.

The front rope-type oil seal packing is held in place with a retainer called a **shredder.** The old seal and shredder are driven from the timing cover case. The shredder is staked in place. A staked shredder is pictured in Figure 19–17. Staking is done by upsetting the timing cover metal over the edge of the seal in several places around the seal. See Figure 19–18.

Figure 19–17 Trimming the rope-type seal to length.

Figure 19–19 Sealing strip being placed in the side groove of the main bearing cap.

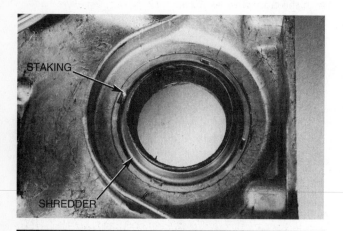

STAKING

SHREDDER

Figure 19–18 The shredder is staked in place to hold the rope-type seal in a timing cover.

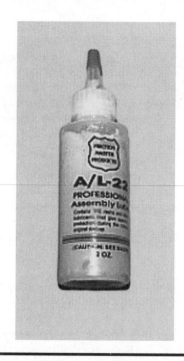

Figure 19–20 Engine assembly lubricant is best to use because it contains additives that provide protection to engine parts during the critical original start-up phase.

■ ADDITIONAL SEALING LOCATIONS

Engines that have the oil pan rail extended below the crankshaft centerline have an additional rear seal requirement. The small gap between the side main bearing cap or seal retainer and the block must be sealed.

Sealing Strips

Most of these spaces are sealed with a swelling-type seal strip. The sealing strip is put into a groove in the cap or retainer after the cap or retainer has been torqued in place. The sealing strip is first soaked for several minutes in petroleum solvent and then inserted in a groove, as shown in Figure 19–19. It may be necessary to use a blunt tool to firmly seat the sealing strip in the groove. The solvent and engine oil cause the sealing strip to swell in place to seal the gap.

■ INSTALLING THE CRANKSHAFT

The main bearing saddles, the caps, and the back of all the main bearing shells should be wiped clean; then the bearing shells can be put in place. It is important that each bearing tang line up with the slot in the bearing support. The bearing shells must have some spread to hold them in the bearing saddles and caps during assembly. The surface of the bearings is then given a thin coating of assembly lubricant to provide initial lubrication for engine start-up. See Figure 19–20.

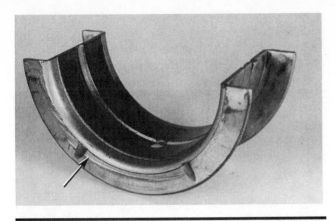

Figure 19–21 Damage to the thrust surfaces of the thrust bearing from careless assembly.

Figure 19–22 Checking crankshaft thrust bearing clearance with a feeler gauge. The technician in this photo has not yet installed the thrust bearing cap; this allows a better view of the actual movement and clearance as the crankshaft is pried back and forth.

The crankshaft with lubricant on the journals is carefully placed in the bearings to avoid damage to the thrust bearing surfaces. Figure 19–21 shows thrust surface damage resulting from careless assembly. The bearing caps are installed with their identification numbers correctly positioned. The caps were originally machined in place, so they can only fit correctly in their original position. The main bearing cap bolts are tightened finger tight, and the crankshaft is rotated. It should rotate freely.

■ THRUST BEARING CLEARANCE

Pry the crankshaft forward and rearward to align the cap half of the thrust bearing with the block saddle half. Most engine specifications for thrust bearing clearance (also called **crankshaft end play**) can range from 0.002 to 0.012 inch (0.02 to 0.3 millimeter). This clearance or play can be measured with a feeler gauge (Figure 19–22) or a dial indicator (Figure 19–23).

If the clearance is too great, oversize main thrust bearings may be available for the engine. Semifinished bearings may have to be purchased and machined to size to restore proper tolerance.

■ TIGHTENING PROCEDURE FOR THE MAIN BEARING

Tighten the main bearing caps to the specified assembly torque, and in the specified sequence. Many manufacturers require that the crankshaft be pried forward or rearward during the main bearing tightening process. The crankshaft should turn freely after all main bearing cap bolts are fully torqued. See Figure 19–24. It should never require over 5 pound-feet [6.75 Newton-meters (N-m)] of torque to rotate the crankshaft. An increase in

(a)

(b)

Figure 19–23 (a) Using a pry bar to move the crankshaft front to rear and rear to front as the thrust bearing clearance (crankshaft end play) is being measured on the dial indicator as shown in (b).

Figure 19–24 Measuring the crankshaft turning torque after each main bearing cap is properly tightened. An abnormal increase in torque indicates a problem that should be corrected before additional assembly.

Figure 19–25 Before camshaft gears are installed on the camshaft, some gears must be heated. These gears are being warmed in *cooking oil!* The cooking oil heats the gears evenly so that they can be readily installed on the camshaft.

the torque needed to rotate the crankshaft is often caused by a foreign particle that was not removed during cleanup. It may be on the bearing surface, on the crankshaft journal, or between the bearing and saddle.

■ INSTALLING TIMING CHAINS AND GEARS

On pushrod engines, the timing gears or chain and sprocket can be installed after the crankshaft. See Figures 19–25 and 19–26. The timing marks on the gears must align when the gears are installed, as shown in Figure 19–27. The same is true of the sprockets, as shown in Figure 19–28. When used, the replaceable fuel-pump

Figure 19–26 Installing a crankshaft gear.

Figure 19–27 Timing marks on both the cam gear (*top*) and the crankshaft gear (*bottom*) should align to time the camshaft to the crankshaft.

eccentric is installed as the cam sprocket is fastened to the cam. The crankshaft should be rotated several times to see that the camshaft and timing gears or chain rotate freely. The timing mark alignment should be rechecked at this time. If the engine is equipped with a slinger ring, it should also be installed on the crankshaft, in front of the crankshaft gear. The slinger ring is positioned so that the outer edge faces away from the gear or sprocket, as shown in Figure 19–29.

Figure 19–28 Timing marks on chain sprockets should be aligned to time the camshaft to the crankshaft.

It is assumed that the front oil seal is installed in the cover. The timing cover and gasket are placed over the timing gears and/or chain and sprockets. The attaching bolts are loosely installed to allow the damper hub to align with the cover as it fits in the seal. The damper is installed on the crankshaft. On some engines, it is a press-fit and on others it is held with a large center bolt. After the damper is secured, the attaching bolts on the timing cover can be tightened to the specified torque.

■ PISTON FITTING

After thorough block cleaning, the piston-to-cylinder clearance should be checked to ensure that the piston properly fits the cylinder in which it is to operate. The fit can be checked by determining the difference in the measured size of the piston and cylinder. A **strip feeler gauge** placed between the piston and the cylinder can be used to measure the piston-to-cylinder clearance. See Figure 19–30. The gauge thickness is the desired clearance measurement. Typical piston clearances range from about 0.0005 (1/2 thousandth) of an inch to

Figure 19–29 Typical slinger ring behind the front crankshaft oil seal.

.0025 (2 1/2 thousandths) of an inch (0.02 to 0.06 millimeter).

The cylinders and pistons, without rings, are wiped thoroughly clean to remove any excess protective lubricant and dust that may have accumulated on the surface. The strip thickness (feeler) gauge is placed in the cylinder along the thrust side. The piston is inserted in the cylinder upside down, with the piston thrust surface against the thickness (feeler) gauge. The piston is held in the cylinder with the connecting rod as the strip gauge is withdrawn. A moderate pull (from 5 to 10 pounds) on the gauge indicates that the clearance is the same as the gauge thickness. A light pull indicates that the clearance is greater than the gauge thickness, whereas a heavy pull indicates that the clearance is smaller than the gauge thickness.

All pistons should be tested in all cylinder bores. Even though all cylinders were honed to the exact same dimension and all pistons were machined to the same diameter, some variation in dimensions will occur. *Each piston should be selectively fitted to each cylinder.* This procedure helps to prevent mismatched assembled components and results in a better- performing and longer-lasting engine. By checking all cylinders, the technician is also assured that the machining of the block was done correctly. See Figure 19–31.

■ RING END GAP

The bottom of the combustion chamber is sealed by the piston rings. They have to fit correctly in order to seal properly. Piston rings are checked both for side clearance and for gap, as discussed in Chapter 17.

Figure 19–30 Measuring the clearance between the piston and the cylinder wall with a strip thickness (feeler) gauge. There are no rings on the piston when this measurement is made.

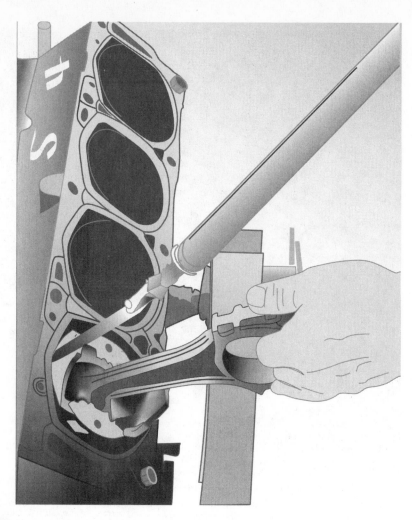

Figure 19–31 A V-8 block on an assembly line of an engine remanufacturer after it has been checked for piston-to-cylinder clearance. Note that the top two cylinders need some additional honing for proper clearance.

Typical ring gap clearances are about 0.004 inch per inch of cylinder bore or as follows:

Piston Diameter	Ring Gap Clearance
2 to 3 inches	0.007 to 0.018 inch
3 to 4 inches	0.010 to 0.020 inch
4 to 5 inches	0.013 to 0.023 inch

NOTE: If the gap is greater than recommended, some engine performance is lost. However, too small a gap will result in scuffing because of ring butting during operation, which forces the rings to scrape the cylinders.

If the ring gap is too large, the ring should be replaced with one having the next oversize diameter. If the ring gap is too small, the ring should be removed and filed to make the gap larger.

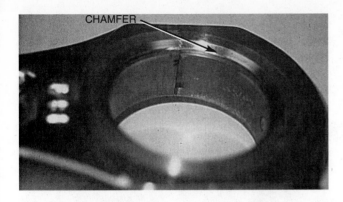

Figure 19–32 On V-type engines that use paired rod journals, the side of the rod with the large chamfer should face toward the crank throw (outward).

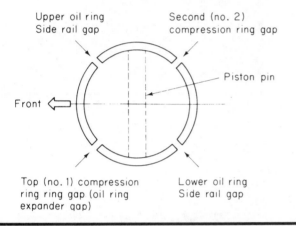

Figure 19–33 One method of piston ring installation showing the location of ring gaps. Always follow the manufacturer's recommended method for the location of ring gaps and for ring gap spacing.

Figure 19–34 Dipping the piston, with rings installed, into a container of engine oil is one method that can be used to ensure proper lubrication of pistons during installation in the engine cylinder. This method also ensures that the piston pin will be well lubricated.

■ INSTALLING PISTON AND ROD ASSEMBLIES

Be sure to note which piston/rod assembly goes into which cylinder. Double-check the following:

1. The piston notch "front" or arrow points toward the front of the engine.
2. Be sure that the valve reliefs end up closest to the lifter valley on a V-type OHV engine.
3. Be sure that the larger valve reliefs always match the intake valve.
4. Make sure the connecting rod has been installed on the piston correctly—the chamfer on the side of the big end should face outward (toward the crank throw). See Figure 19–32.
5. Be sure the piston ring gaps are set according to the manufacturer's recommendations. See Figure 19–33.

The cylinder is wiped with a lintless cleaning cloth. It is then given a liberal coating of clean engine oil. This oil is spread over the entire cylinder wall surface by hand.

The connecting rod bearings are prepared for assembly in the same way, as are the main bearings. The piston can be dipped in a bath of clean engine oil to lubricate the piston pin as well as the piston rings. See Figure 19–34.

> **NOTE:** Some overlapping (gapless) piston rings are installed dry, without oil. Some manufacturers recommend oiling only the oil control ring. Always check the piston ring instruction sheet for the exact procedure.

When the piston is lifted from the oil, it is held to drip for a few seconds. This allows the largest part of the oil to run out of the piston and ring grooves. The **piston ring compressor** is then put on the piston to hold the rings in their grooves. See Figures 19–35 through 19–37.

Figure 19–35 Before installing the piston-connecting rod assembly into the cylinder, be sure to cover the connecting rod bolts with protective covers such as these given away free at a trade show for automotive engine rebuilders.

Figure 19–37 Piston being installed in a cylinder on a production line of an engine remanufacturer. Crankshaft protectors have been installed on connecting rod bolts. Note the T handle on the crankshaft used to rotate the engine as pistons are installed.

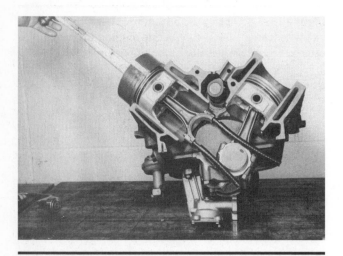

Figure 19–36 Installing a piston and rod assembly using a cast-iron ring compressor and placing short pieces of hose over the connecting rod bolts.

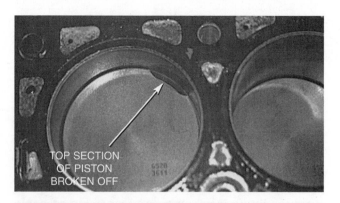

TOP SECTION OF PISTON BROKEN OFF

Figure 19–38 Here is what can happen if the ring compressor does not fully compress the top piston ring. Notice that a part of the piston has been broken when the top ring got caught on the deck surface of the block during piston installation.

The bearing cap is removed from the rod, and protectors are placed over the rod bolts. The crankshaft is rotated so that the crankpin is at the bottom center. The upper rod bearing should be in the rod, and the piston should be turned so that the notch on the piston head is facing the front of the engine.

The piston and rod assembly is placed in the cylinder through the block deck. The ring compressor must be kept tightly against the block deck as the piston is pushed into the cylinder. The ring compressor holds the rings in their grooves so that they will enter the cylinder. See Figures 19–38 and 19–39. The piston is pushed into the cylinder until the rod bearing is fully seated on the journal. See Figure 19–40.

Figure 19–39 Installing a piston in a cylinder using a band-type ring compressor. The ring compressor should cover the area near the rings only. The lower part of the piston is already in the cylinder. If everything is well lubricated and the ring compressor is tight, one good tap with the handle of a hammer should install the piston in the cylinder.

Figure 19–40 Two commercially available connecting rod bolt protectors of different lengths. After the piston is installed, the protectors can be removed and the rod cap installed.

Connecting Rod Bearing Clearance

The rod cap, with the bearing in place, is put on the rod. There are two methods that can be used to check for proper connecting rod clearance:

- Use Plastigage following the same procedure discussed for main bearing clearance.
- Measure the assembled connecting rod big-end devices with the bearing installed and the caps torqued to specification. Subtract the diameter of the rod journal to determine the bearing clearance.

NOTE: Be certain to check for piston-to-crankshaft counterweight clearance. Most manufacturers specify a minimum 0.060 inch (1.5 millimeters).

TECH TIP ✔

Tightening Tip for Rod Bearings

Even though the bearing clearances are checked, it is still a good idea to check and record the torque required to rotate the crankshaft with all piston rings dragging on the cylinder walls. Next, the retaining nuts on one bearing should be torqued; then the torque required to rotate the crankshaft should be rechecked and recorded. Follow the same procedure on all rod bearings. If tightening any one of the rod bearing caps causes a large increase in the torque required to rotate the crankshaft, immediately stop the tightening process. Determine the cause of the increased rotating torque using the same method as used on the main bearings. Rotate the crankshaft for several revolutions to make sure that the assembly is turning freely and that there are no tight spots.

The rotating torque of the crankshaft with all connecting rod cap bolts fully torqued should be as follows:

- Four-cylinder engine: 20 pound-feet maximum (88 Newton-meters)
- Six-cylinder engine: 25 pound-feet maximum (110 Newton-meters)
- Eight-cylinder engine: 30 pound-feet maximum (132 Newton-meters)

Figure 19–41 The connecting rod side clearance is measured with a feeler gauge.

Figure 19–42 Fixture being used to hold bucket-type cam followers down as the camshaft is being slid endways into the cam bearings on an overhead cam engine.

■ CONNECTING ROD SIDE CLEARANCE

The connecting rods should be checked to make sure that they still have the correct side clearance. This is measured by fitting the correct thickness of feeler gauge between the connecting rod and the crankshaft cheek of the bearing journal (Figure 19–41). A dial gauge can also be set up to measure the connecting rod side clearance.

- *If the side clearance is too great*, excessive amounts of oil may escape that can cause lower-than-normal oil pressure. To correct excessive clearance:

1. Weld and regrind or replace the crankshaft.
2. Carefully measure all connecting rods and replace those that are too thin or mismatched.

- *If the side clearance is too small*, there may not be enough room for heat expansion. To correct a side clearance that is too small:

1. Regrind the crankshaft.
2. Replace the rods.

■ INSTALLING THE CAMSHAFT FOR OVERHEAD CAM ENGINES

The camshaft is usually installed on overhead cam engines before the head is fastened to the block deck. Some engines have the camshaft located directly over the valves. The cam bearings on these engines can be ei-

ther one piece or split. A fixture is required on one type of engine that has a one-piece cam bearing to hold the valves open as the cam is slid endways into the cam bearings, as shown in Figure 19–42. The cam bearings and journals are lubricated before assembly. In other engine types, the camshaft bearings are split to allow the camshaft to be installed without the valves being depressed. The caps are tightened evenly to avoid bending the camshaft. The valve clearance or lash is checked with the overhead camshaft in place. Some engines use shims under a follower disc as shown in Figure 19–43. On these, the camshaft is turned so that the follower is on the base circle of the cam. The clearance of each bucket follower can then be checked with a feeler gauge. The amount of clearance is recorded and compared with the specified clearance. The cam is then removed, and shims of the required thickness are put in the top of the bucket followers. See Figure 19–44.

■ HEAD GASKETS

The head gasket is under the highest clamping loads. It must seal passages that carry coolant with antifreeze and often is required to seal a passage that carries hot engine oil. The most demanding job of the head gasket is to seal the combustion chamber. As a rule of thumb, about 75% of the head bolt clamping force is used to seal the combustion chamber. The remaining 25% seals the coolant and oil passages.

The gasket must seal when the temperature is as low as 40° below zero and as high as 400°F (204°C). The combustion pressures can get up to 1000 psi (6900 kPa) on gasoline engines.

Cylinder head bolts are tightened to a specified torque, which stretches the bolt. The combustion pressure tries to push the head upward and the piston downward on the power stroke. This puts additional stress

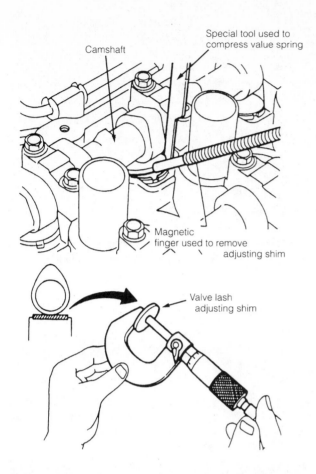

Some overhead camshaft engines use valve lash adjusting shims to adjust the valve lash. A special tool is usually required to compress the valve spring so that a magnet can remove the shim.

Figure 19–43 Some overhead camshaft engines use valve lash adjusting shims to adjust the valve lash. A special tool is usually required to compress the valve spring so that a magnet can remove the shim.

on the head bolts and it reduces the clamping load on the head gasket just when the greatest seal is needed. On a normally aspirated engine (without turbocharging), a partial vacuum on the intake stroke tries to pull the head more tightly against the gasket. As the crankshaft rotates, the force on the head changes from pressure on the combustion stroke to vacuum on the intake stroke, then back to pressure. Modern engines have lightweight thin-wall castings. The castings are quite flexible, so that they move as the pressure in the combustion chamber changes from high pressure to vacuum. The gasket must be able to compress and recover fast enough to maintain a seal as the pressure in the combustion chamber changes back and forth between pressure and vacuum. As a result, the modern head gasket is made of several different materials assembled in numerous ways depending on the model of engine.

> **NOTE:** Older gasket designs often contained asbestos and required that the head bolts be retorqued after the engine had been run to operating temperature. Head gaskets today are dense and do not compress like those older-style gaskets. Therefore, most gaskets are called **no-retorque**-type gaskets, meaning the cylinder head bolts do not have to be retorqued after the engine has run. New gaskets do not contain asbestos.

Embossed Gaskets

The first no-retorque gasket was the **embossed steel shim** gasket (see Figure 19–45), made from steel from 0.015 to 0.021 inch (0.4 to 0.5 millimeter) thick.

Figure 19–44 Split-type cam bearings on an overhead cam engine using bucket-type cam followers. One bucket follower is removed to show the valve tip, retainer, and locks (keepers).

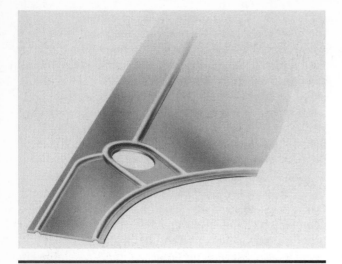

Figure 19–45 Embossed steel head gasket. (*Courtesy of Fel-Pro Incorporated*)

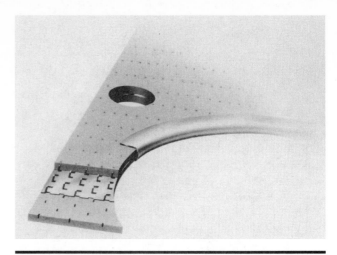

Figure 19–46 Perforated steel core head gasket. (*Courtesy of Fel-Pro Incorporated*)

TECH TIP ✔

Wow—I Can't Believe a Cylinder Can Deform That Much!

An automotive instructor uses a dial bore gauge in a four-cylinder, cast-iron engine block cylinder to show students how much a block can deform. Using just one hand, the instructor was able to grasp both sides of the block and squeeze—the dial bore gauge showed that the cylinder deflected about 0.0003 inch (3/10,000 of an inch) just by squeezing the block with one hand—and this is with a cast-iron block!

After this demonstration, the students were more careful during engine assembly and always used a torque wrench on each and every fastener that was installed in or on the engine block.

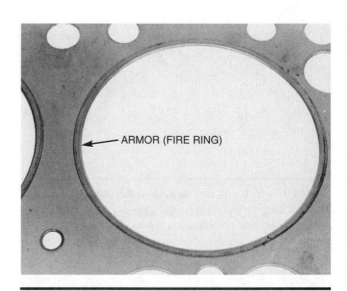

Figure 19–47 Head gasket with armor.

The embossed beads are from 0.06 to 0.1 inch (0.15 to 0.25 centimeter) wide and from 0.007 to 0.03 inch (0.17 to 0.7 millimeter) high. Shim gaskets may be coated with aluminum or with a plastic to aid in sealing. They have no resilient fiber so they do not relax. Shim gaskets require smooth sealing surfaces because there are no fibers to conform to sealing surface roughness. Shim gaskets also require a flat sealing surface, because the steel cannot compensate for slight warpage of the head and block deck. The steel shim gasket makes a good original equipment gasket when manufacturers use smooth, flat sealing surfaces. The shim gasket is not a good aftermarket gasket, because used engines will usually have some warpage and often have rough sealing surfaces. Even if the warpage is removed by machining, often the resurfacing does not give a finish as smooth as the original finish.

Improved Perforated Steel Core Gaskets

A variation of this gasket design uses a wire mesh core. Another design has rubber-fiber facings cemented to a solid steel core with an adhesive. See Figure 19–46. The thickness of the gasket is controlled by the thickness of the metal core. The facing is thick enough to compensate for minor warpage and surface defects.

The fiber facing is protected around the combustion chamber with a metal **armor** (also called **fire ring**). See Figure 19–47. The metal also increases the gasket thickness around the cylinder so that it uses up to 75% of the clamping force and forms a tight combustion seal.

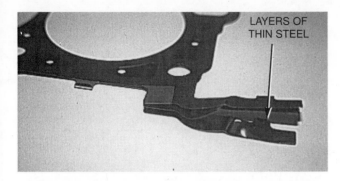

Figure 19–48 Multilayer steel (MLS) gaskets are used on many newer all-aluminum engines as well as engines that use a cast block with aluminum cylinder heads. This type of gasket allows the aluminum to expand without losing the sealing ability of the gasket.

Figure 19–49 As a final check before installing a cylinder head, draw a file sideways across the head surface. Any burrs or nicks will be indicated by a bright spot. Because the file is being drawn lightly across the surface, no material is being removed except for small high spots.

Figure 19–50 Typical head gasket markings.

TECH TIP ✔

Use a Credit Card to Scrape an Aluminum Head

Only a plastic or wooden scraper should be used to remove gasket material from an aluminum cylinder head or block deck. A commonly used trick is to use an old credit card or other plastic card such as discarded hotel room plastic entry card. The plastic card will do no harm, is easy to store, and inexpensive to replace if broken.

Multilayered Steel Gaskets

Multilayered steel (MLS) is being used from the factory on many newer engine designs such as the overhead camshaft Ford V-8s. The many layers of thin steel reduce bore and overhead camshaft distortion with less clamping force loss than previous designs. See Figure 19–48. The use of multilayered steel gaskets also reduces the torque requirement and, therefore, reduces the stresses on the fastener and engine block.

■ INSTALLING THE HEAD GASKET

The block deck and head surfaces should be rechecked for any handling nicks that could cause a gasket leak. All tapped holes should be cleaned with the correct-size bottoming tap to remove any dirt or burrs. See Figure 19–49. There are usually alignment pins or dowels at the front and rear of the block deck to position the gasket and head. Care should be taken to properly position any head gasket with markings (up, top, front, and so forth). See Figure 19–50. The gasket and head are placed on the block deck. All the head bolts are loosely installed. Very often, the head bolts have different lengths. Make sure that a bolt of the correct length is put into each location.

Put sealer on the threads of the assembly bolts that go into the cooling system. Put antiseize compound on bolts that hold the exhaust manifold. Lightly oil the threads of bolts that go into blind holes. See the Tech Tip, "Watch Out for Wet and Dry Holes."

> **NOTE:** Most manufacturers recommend putting oil on the threads of bolts (not in the block holes!) during reassembly. Lubricated threads will give as much as 50% more clamping force at the same bolt torque than threads that are tightened dry.

Often, the assembly bolts have different lengths. Make sure that the correct length of bolt is put into each hole.

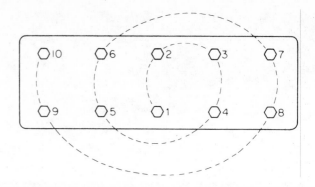

Figure 19–51 Typical cylinder head tightening sequence.

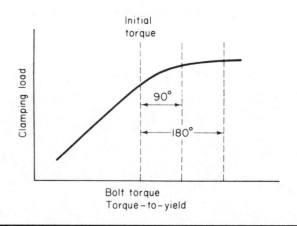

Figure 19–52 Due to variations in clamping force with turning force (torque) of head bolts, some engines are specifying the torque-to-yield procedure. The first step is to torque the bolts by an even amount called the initial torque. Final clamping load is achieved by turning the bolt a specified number of degrees. Bolt stretch provides the proper clamping force.

■ HEAD BOLT TORQUE SEQUENCE

The torque put on the bolts is used to control the clamping force. The clamping force is correct only when the threads are clean and properly lubricated. In general, the head bolts are tightened in a specified torque sequence in three steps. By tightening the head bolts in three steps, the head gasket has time to compress and conform to the block deck and cylinder head gasket surfaces. Follow that sequence and tighten the bolts to *one-third* the specified torque. Tighten them a second time following the torque sequence to *two-thirds* the specified torque. Follow the sequence with a final tightening to the specified torque. See Figure 19–51.

■ TORQUE-TO-YIELD BOLTS

Many engines use a tightening procedure called the **torque-to-yield,** or **torque-angle,** method. The purpose of the torque-to-yield procedure is to have a more constant clamping load from bolt to bolt. This aids in head gasket sealing performance and eliminates the need for retorquing. The torque-to-yield head bolts are made with a narrow section between the head and threads. As the bolts are tightened past their elastic limit, they yield and begin to stretch in this narrow section.

Torque-to-yield head bolts will not become any tighter once they reach this elastic limit, as you can see on the graph in Figure 19–52.

As a result, many engine manufacturers specify *new* head bolts each time the head is installed. If these bolts are reused, they are likely to break during assembly or fail prematurely as the engine runs. If there is any doubt about the head bolts, replace them.

Torque-to-yield bolts are tightened to a specific initial torque, from 18 to 50 pound-feet (25 to 68 Newton-meters). The bolts are then tightened a specified number of degrees, following the tightening sequence. In some cases they are turned a specified number of degrees two or three times. Some specifications limit the maximum torque that can be applied to the bolt while the degree turn is being made. Torque tables in a service manual will show how much initial torque should be applied to the bolt and how many degrees the bolt should be rotated after torquing.

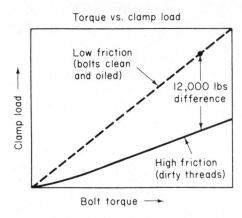

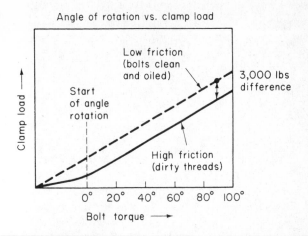

Figure 19–53 To ensure consistent clamp force (load), many manufacturers are recommending the torque-angle or torque-to-yield method of tightening head bolts. The torque-angle method specifies tightening fasteners to a low torque setting and then giving an additional angle of rotation. Notice that the difference in clamping force is much smaller than it would be if just a torque wrench with dirty threads were used.

NOTE: The torque-turn method does not necessarily mean torque-to-yield. Some engine specifications call for a beginning torque and then a specified angle, but the fastener is not designed to yield. These head bolts can often be reused. Always follow the manufacturer's recommended procedures.

Head bolts are tightened following a sequence specified in the service manual or torque tables. In general, the tightening sequence starts at the center of the head and moves outward, alternating front to rear and side to side. The bolts are usually tightened to approximately one-half the specified torque, following the tightening sequence. They are then retorqued to the specified torque following the same tightening sequence. See Figures 19–53 and 19–54.

■ TIMING DRIVES FOR OVERHEAD CAM ENGINES

After the head bolts have been torqued, the cam drive can be installed on overhead cam engines. This is done by aligning the timing marks of the crankshaft and camshaft drive sprockets with their respective timing marks. The location of these marks differs between engines, but the marks can be identified by looking carefully at the sprockets. See Figure 19–55. The tightening idler may be on either or both sides of the timing belt or chain. After the camshaft drive is engaged, rotate the crankshaft through two full revolutions. On the first full revolution, you should see the exhaust valve almost close and the intake valve just starting to open when the

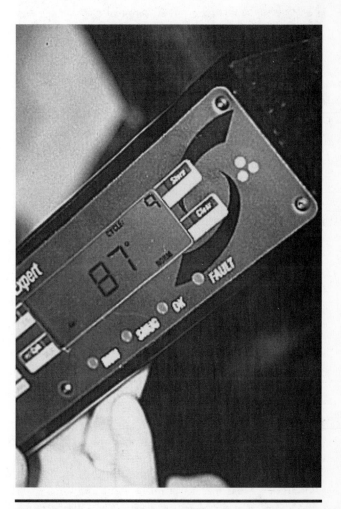

Figure 19–54 An electronic torque wrench showing the number of degrees of rotation. These very accurate and expensive torque wrenches can be programmed to display torque or number of degrees of rotation.

Figure 19–55 Timing belt that drives the cam and auxiliary shaft.

crankshaft timing mark aligns. At the end of the second revolution, both valves should be closed, and all the timing marks should align on most engines. This is the position the crankshaft should have when cylinder #1 is to fire.

> **NOTE:** Always check the manufacturer's recommended timing chain installation procedure. Engines that use primary and secondary timing chains often require an exact detailed procedure for proper installation.

TECH TIP ✔

Soak the Timing Chain

Many experts recommend that a new timing chain be soaked in engine oil prior to engine assembly to help ensure full lubrication at engine start-up. The timing chain is one of the last places in the engine to get lubrication when the engine first starts. This procedure may even extend the life of the chain.

■ LIFTER AND PUSHROD INSTALLATION

The outside of the lifters and the lifter bores in the block should be cleaned and coated with assembly lubricant. The lifters are installed in the lifter bores and the pushrods put in place. There are different-length pushrods on some engines. Make sure that the pushrods are installed in the proper location. The rocker arms are then put in place, aligning with the valves and pushrods. Rocker arm shafts should have their retaining bolts tightened a little at a time, alternating between the retaining bolts. This keeps the shaft from bending as the rocker arm pushes some of the valves open.

■ HYDRAULIC LIFTERS

The retaining nut on some rocker arms mounted on studs can be tightened to a specified torque. The rocker arm will be adjusted correctly at this torque when the valve tip has the correct height. Other types of rocker arms require tightening the nut to a position that will center the hydraulic lifter. The general procedure for adjusting the hydraulic lifter types is to tighten the retaining nut to the point that all of the free lash is gone. The lifter plunger starts to move down after the lash is gone. From this point, the retaining nut is tightened by a specified amount, such as three-fourths of a turn or one and one-half turns.

> **HINT:** This method usually results in about three threads showing above the adjusting nut on a *stock* small-block Chevrolet V-8 equipped with flat-bottom hydraulic lifters.

■ SOLID LIFTERS

The valve clearance or **lash** must be set on a solid lifter engine, so that the valves can positively seat. Some service manuals give an adjustment sequence to follow to set the lash. If this is not available, then the following procedure can be used on all engines requiring valve lash adjustment. The valve lash is adjusted with the valves completely closed. See Figure 19–56.

After the valve lash on cylinder #1 is set, the crankshaft is rotated in its normal direction of rotation to the next cylinder in the firing order. This is done by turning the crankshaft 90 degrees on eight-cylinder engines, 120 degrees on even-firing six-cylinder engines, and 180 degrees on four-cylinder engines. The valves on this next cylinder are adjusted in the same manner, as were those on cylinder #1. This procedure is repeated on each cylinder *following the engine firing order* until all the valves have been adjusted.

The same valve lash adjustment sequence is used on overhead cam engines. Those engines with rocker arms or with adjustable finger follower pivots are adjusted in the same way, as are pushrod engines with rocker arms.

■ ASSEMBLY SEALANTS

RTV Silicone

RTV silicone is used by most technicians in sealing engines. **RTV,** or **room temperature vulcanization,** means that the silicone rubber material will cure at room temperature. It is not really the temperature that causes RTV silicone to cure, but the moisture in the air. RTV silicone cures to a tack-free state in about 45 minutes. It takes 24 hours to fully cure.

CAUTION: Some RTV silicone sealers use **acetic acid,** and the fumes from this type can be drawn through the engine through the PCV system and cause damage to oxygen sensors. Always use an **amine-type** RTV silicone or one that states on the package that it is safe for oxygen sensors.

RTV silicone is available in several different colors. The color identifies the special blend within a manufacturer's product line. Equal grades of silicone made by different manufacturers may have different colors. RTV silicone can be used in two ways in engine sealing:

1. It can be used as a gasket substitute between a stamped cover and a cast surface.
2. It is used to fill gaps or potential gaps. A joint between gaskets or between a gasket and a seal is a potential gap.

Figure 19–57 Improperly sealed valve cover gasket. Note the use of RTV silicone sealant on a cork-rubber gasket. The cover bolts were also overtightened, which deformed the metal cover around the bolt holes.

NOTE: RTV silicone should *never* be used around fuel because the fuel will cut through it. Silicone should not be used as a sealer on gaskets. It will squeeze out to leave a bead inside and a bead outside the flange. The inside bead might fall into the engine, plugging passages and causing engine damage. The thin film still remaining on the gasket stays uncured, just as it would be in the original tube. The uncured silicone is likely to let the gasket or seal slip out of place. See Figure 19–57.

Anaerobic Sealers

Anaerobic sealers are sealers that cure in the absence of air. They are used as thread lockers (such as Loctite), and they are used to seal rigid machined joints between cast parts. Anaerobic sealers lose their sealing ability at temperatures above 300°F (149°C). On production lines, the curing process is speeded up by using ultraviolet light.

When the anaerobic sealer is used on threads, air does not get to it so it hardens to form a seal to prevent the fastener from loosening. Teflon is added to some anaerobic sealers to seal fluids better. Anaerobic sealers can be used to seal machined surfaces without a gasket. The surfaces *must* be thoroughly clean to get a good seal. Special primers are recommended for use on the sealing surface to get a better bond with anaerobic sealers.

■ INSTALLING MANIFOLDS

The intake manifold gasket for a V-type engine may be a one-piece gasket or it may have several pieces. V-type engines with open-type manifolds have a cover over the lifter valley. The cover may be a separate part or it may be part of a one-piece intake manifold gasket. Closed-type intake manifolds on V-type engines require gasket pieces at the front and rear of the intake manifold. Inline engines usually have a one-piece intake manifold gasket.

The intake manifold is put in place over the gaskets. Use a contact adhesive to hold the gasket and end seal if there is a chance they might slip out of place. Just before the manifold is installed, put a spot of RTV silicone on each of the four joints between the intake manifold gasket and end seals. Install the bolts and tighten to the specified torque following the correct tightening sequence.

Only some exhaust manifolds use gaskets. The gaskets and exhaust manifolds are installed. The exhaust manifold operates at very high temperatures, so there is usually some expansion and contraction movement in the manifold-to-head joint. It is very important to use attachment bolts, cap screws, and clamps of the correct type and length. They must be properly torqued to avoid both leakage and cracks.

> **NOTE:** When the exhaust manifold gasket has facing on one side, put the facing toward the head and let the manifold rest against the metal side of the gasket.

■ COVER GASKET MATERIALS

The gasket must be *impermeable* to the fluids it is designed to seal in or out. The gasket must *conform* to the shape of the surface, and it must be *resilient*, or elastic, to maintain the sealing force as it is compressed. Gaskets work best when they are compressed about 30%.

Cork Gaskets

Cork is the bark from a Mediterranean evergreen oak tree. It is made of very small, flexible, 14-sided, air-filled

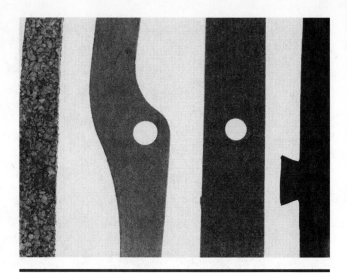

Figure 19–58 *Left to right:* cork-rubber, paper, composite, and synthetic rubber (elastomer) gaskets.

fiber cells, about 0.001 inch (0.025 millimeter) in size. The air-filled cells act like a pneumatic system. This gives resiliency to the cork gasket until the air leaks out. Because cork is mostly wood, it expands when it gets wet and shrinks when it dries. This causes cork gaskets to change in size when they are in storage and while they are installed in the engine. Oil gradually wicks through the organic binder of the cork, so a cork gasket often looks like it is leaking. Problems with cork gaskets led the gasket industry to develop cork cover gaskets using synthetic rubber as a binder for the cork. This type of gasket is called a **cork-rubber gasket.** These cork-rubber gaskets are easy to use, and they outlast the old cork gaskets. See Figure 19–58.

Fiber Gaskets

Some oil pans use fiber gaskets. Covers with higher clamping forces use gaskets with fibers that have greater density. For example, timing covers may have either fiber or paper gaskets.

Synthetic Rubber Gaskets

Molded, oil-resistant synthetic rubber is being used in more applications to seal covers. When it is compounded correctly, it forms a superior cover gasket. It operates at high temperatures for a longer period of time than does a cork-rubber cover gasket. See Figure 19–59.

Sealers

Sealers are nonhardening materials. Examples of sealer trade names include Form-A-Gasket 2, Pli-A-Seal, Tight Seal 2, Aviation Form-A-Gasket, Brush Tack, Copper Coat, Spray Tack, and High Tack. Sealers are always

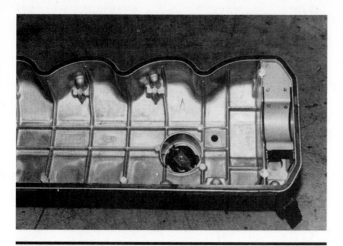

Figure 19–59 Typical cast-aluminum cam (valve) cover. Note the rubber gasket in the cast groove of the cover.

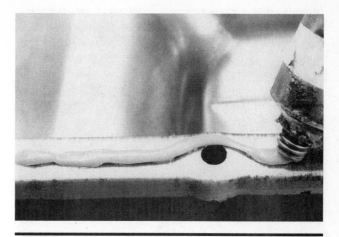

Figure 19–60 A 1/8- to 3/16-inch (3- to 5-millimeters) bead of RTV silicone on a parting surface with silicone going around the bolt hole.

used to seal the threads of bolts that break into coolant passages. Sealers for sealing threads may include Teflon. Sealer is often recommended for use on shim-type head gaskets and intake manifold gaskets. These gaskets have a metal surface that does not conform to any small amounts of surface roughness on the sealing surface. The sealer fills the surface variations between the gasket and the sealing surface.

Sealer may be used as a sealing aid on paper and fiber gaskets if the gasket needs help with sealing on a scratched, corroded, or rough surface finish. The sealer may be used on one side or on both sides of the gasket.

> **CAUTION:** Sealer should *never* be used on rubber or cork-rubber gaskets. Instead of holding the rubber gasket or seal, it will help the rubber to slip out of place because the sealer will never harden.

Antiseize Compounds

Antiseize compounds are used on fasteners in the engine that are subjected to high temperatures to prevent seizing caused by galvanic action between dissimilar metals. These compounds minimize corrosion from moisture. Exhaust manifold bolts and nuts, oxygen sensors, and spark plugs, especially those that go into aluminum heads, are kept from seizing. The antiseize compound minimizes the chance of threads being pulled or breaking as the oxygen sensor or spark plug is removed.

■ HINTS FOR GASKET USAGE

Never reuse an old gasket. A used gasket or seal has already been compressed, has lost some of its resilience, and has taken a set. If a used gasket does reseal, it will not seal as well as a new gasket or seal.

A gasket should be checked to make sure it is the correct gasket. Also check the list on the outside of the gasket set to make sure that the set has all the gaskets that may be needed *before* the package is opened.

An instruction sheet is included with most gaskets. It includes a review of the things the technician should do to prepare and install the gaskets to give the best chance of a good seal. The instruction sheet also includes special tips on how to seal spots that are difficult to seal or that require special care to seal on a particular engine.

■ INSTALLING TIMING COVERS

Most timing covers are installed with a gasket, but some use RTV sealer in place of the gasket. Cast covers use anaerobic compound as a gasket substitute. A bead of RTV silicone 1/8 to 3/16 inch in diameter is put on the clean sealing surface (see Figure 19–60). Encircle the bolt holes with the sealant. Install the cover before the silicone begins to cure so that the uncured silicone bonds to both surfaces. While installing the cover, do not touch the silicone bead; otherwise, the bead might be displaced, causing a leak. Carefully press the cover into place. Do not slide the cover after it is in place. Install the assembly bolts finger tight, and let the silicone cure for about 30 minutes; then torque the cover bolts.

■ INSTALLING THE VIBRATION DAMPER

Vibration dampers are seated in place by one of three methods.

- The damper hub of some engines is pulled into place using the hub-attaching bolt. See Figures 19–61 and 19–62.

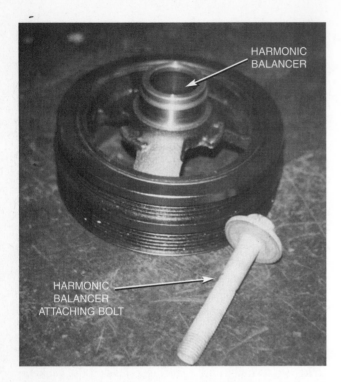

Figure 19–61 A typical harmonic balancer with the attaching bolt.

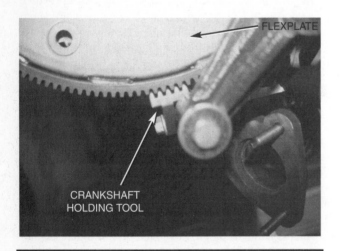

Figure 19–62 Whenever the harmonic balancer attaching bolt is torqued, the engine should be kept from rotating. This is usually achieved by installing a flywheel holding tool as shown.

- The second method uses a special installing tool that screws into the attaching bolt hole to pull the hub into place. The tool is removed and the attaching bolt installed and torqued.
- The last method is used on engines that have no attaching bolt. These hubs depend on a press-fit to hold the hub on the crankshaft. The hub is seated using a hammer and a special tube-type driver.

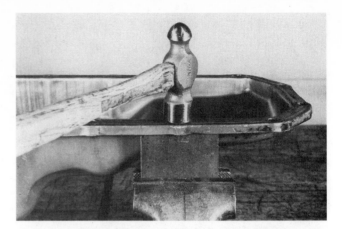

Figure 19–63 Using a hammer to straighten the gasket rail surface before installing a new gasket. When the retaining bolts are tightened, some distortion of sheet-metal covers occurs. If the area around the bolt holes is not straightened, leaks can occur with the new gasket.

■ INSTALLING THE OIL PUMP

When an engine is rebuilt, the oil pump should be replaced with a new pump. This ensures positive lubrication and long pump life. Oil pump gears should be coated with assembly lubricant before the cover is put on the pump. This provides initial lubrication, and it primes the pump so that it will draw the oil from the pan when the lubrication system is first operated.

■ THE OIL PAN

The oil pan should be checked and straightened as necessary. See Figure 19–63. With the oil pump in place, the oil pan gaskets are properly positioned. A spot of RTV silicone is placed at each gasket joint just before the pan is installed. The oil pan is carefully placed over the gaskets. All oil pan bolts should be started into their holes before any are tightened. The bolts should be alternately snugged up; then they should be properly torqued.

■ INSTALLING THE WATER PUMP

A reconditioned, rebuilt, or new water pump should be used. Gaskets are fitted in place. The pump is secured with assembly bolts tightened to the correct torque.

A new thermostat is usually installed at this time. It is put in place, with care being taken to place the correct side of the thermostat toward the engine. The thermostat gasket is put in place. Sealers are used on the gasket where they are required. The thermostat housing

Diagnostic Story

The New Oil Pump That Failed

A technician replaced the oil pump and screen on a V-8 with low oil pressure. After the repair, the oil pressure returned to normal for two weeks, but then the oil pressure light came on and the valve train started making noise. The vehicle owner returned to the service garage where the oil pump had been replaced. The technician removed the oil pan and pump. The screen was almost completely clogged with the RTV sealant that the technician had used to "seal" the oil pan gasket. The technician had failed to read the instructions that came with the oil pan gasket. Failure to follow directions and using too much of the wrong sealer cost the repair shop an expensive comeback repair.

TECH TIP ✔

Oil Pump Precautions

The oil pump is the heart of any engine, and any failure of the oil circulation system often results in severe and major engine damage. To help prevent possible serious oil pump–related failures, many engine builders recommend the following precautions:

1. Always be sure that the oil pump pickup tube (screen) is securely attached to the oil pump to prevent the pickup tube from vibrating out of the pump.
2. Use modeling clay to check pickup screen-to-oil pan clearance. For proper operation, there should be about 1/4 inch (6 millimeters) between the oil pump pickup screen and the bottom of the oil pan.

Figure 19–64 Partially assembled engine being spray painted at an engine remanufacturing plant.

All parts that should not be painted must be covered before spray painting. This can be done with old parts, such as old spark plugs and old gaskets. This can also be done by taping paper over the areas to be covered. If the intake manifold of an inline engine is to be painted, it can be painted separately. Engine assembly can continue after the paint has dried.

is installed, and the retaining bolts are tightened to the proper torque.

■ ENGINE PAINTING

Painting an engine helps prevent rust and corrosion and makes the engine look new. See Figure 19–64. Standard engine paints with original colors are usually available at automotive parts stores. Engine paints should be used rather than other types of paints. Engine paints are compounded to stay on the metal as the engine temperatures change. Normal engine fluids will not remove them. These paints are usually purchased in pressure cans so that they can be sprayed from the can directly onto the engine.

■ CHECKING FOR PROPER OIL PRESSURE

With oil in the engine and the distributor out of the engine, oil pressure should be established before the engine is started. This can be done on most engines by rotating the oil pump by hand. This ensures that oil is delivered to all parts of the engine before the engine is started. A socket speed handle makes an ideal crank for turning the oil pump. A flat-blade adapter that fits the speed handle will operate on General Motors engines. The V-type Chrysler engine requires the use of the same flat-blade adapter, but it also requires an oil pump drive. One can be made by removing the gear from an old oil pump hex driveshaft. A 1/4-inch drive socket can be used on Ford engines. Examples of these are pictured in Figure 19–65. Engines that do not drive the oil pump with the distributor will have to be cranked with the spark plugs removed to establish oil pressure. The load on the starter and battery is reduced with the spark plugs out so that the engine will have a higher cranking speed. A pressurized oil container or an aerosol can containing engine oil could also be used as shown in Figure 19–66.

See Figure 19–67 for an example of a tester used to spin the crankshaft of the engine to check for proper compression, oil leaks, or other problems.

Figure 19–65 Drivers used to rotate oil pumps to prelubricate all parts of the engine before installing the distributor and starting the engine.

Figure 19–66 The engine can be pressurized with engine oil from an aerosol can as shown or from a pressurized oil container designed for preoiling the engine.

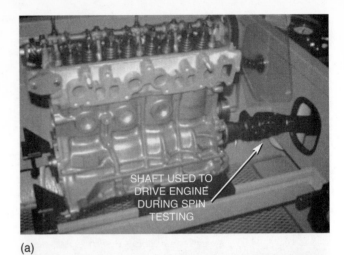

SHAFT USED TO DRIVE ENGINE DURING SPIN TESTING

(a)

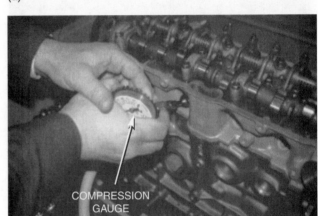

COMPRESSION GAUGE

(b)

OIL PRESSURE TEST LINE TO GAUGE

(c)

Figure 19–67 (a) A newly rebuilt engine is placed in the tester and the crankshaft is connected to an electric drive motor. (b) As the engine is being spun by the drive motor, a technician can check cylinder compression by using a compression gauge. (c) Oil pressure can be measured and recorded at various engine speeds.

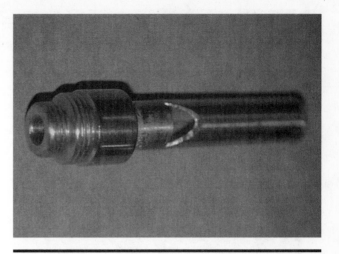

Figure 19–68 A whistle stop is used to help locate top dead center (TDC) of the compression stroke for #1 cylinder. With the whistle in the spark plug hole for #1 cylinder, rotate the engine. The whistle will sound as the piston is coming up on the compression stroke and will stop when the piston reaches TDC.

■ SETTING INITIAL IGNITION TIMING

After oil pressure is established, the distributor, if equipped, can be installed. Rotate the crankshaft in its normal direction of rotation until there is compression on cylinder #1. This can be done with the starter or by using a wrench on the damper bolt. The compression stroke can be determined by covering the opening of spark plug #1 with a finger as the crankshaft is rotated. Continue to rotate the crankshaft slowly as compression is felt, until the timing marks on the damper align with the timing indicator on the timing cover. See Figure 19–68.

The angle of the distributor gear drive will cause the distributor rotor to turn a few degrees when installed. Before the distributor is installed, the shaft must be positioned to compensate for the gear angle. After installation, the rotor should be pointing to the #1 tower of the distributor cap.

The distributor position should be close enough to the basic timing position to start the engine. If the distributor hold-down clamp is slightly loose, the distributor housing can be adjusted to make the engine run smoothly after the engine has been started.

PHOTO SEQUENCE Preoiling an Engine

PS 34–1 Whenever an engine has been disassembled and then reassembled, it is important to make sure that all internal parts are preoiled before starting the engine. Start by filling the crankcase with the specified amount of oil.

PS 34–2 Attach an oil pressure gauge to the engine. On this small-block Chevrolet V-8, the oil pressure tap is located near the distributor at the top of the block.

PS 34–3 To rotate the oil pump, an old distributor was cut down and the shaft installed in the chuck of an electric drill.

PS 34–4 Rotating the oil pump using an electric drill results in the oil pressure increasing to over 50 psi.

PS 34–5 The drill should continue being used to prime the engine with oil until oil is observed coming from the rocker arms, indicating that oil has reached the highest part of the engine.

PS 34–6 An overall view of the oil pump drive adapter made from an old distributor and the oil pressure gauge. After the engine has been primed, the distributor can be installed and the engine can be installed into the vehicle.

■ SUMMARY

1. All oil galleries must be thoroughly cleaned before engine assembly can begin.

2. All expansion cups and plugs should be installed with a sealer to prevent leaks. Avoid the use of Teflon tape on threaded plugs.

3. The cam bearings should be installed using a cam bearing installation tool.

4. Main bearings and rod bearings should be checked for proper oil clearance by precision measuring the crankshaft journals and inside diameter of bearings or by using plastic gauging material.

5. The piston and rod assembly should be installed in the cylinder after being carefully fitted for each bore.

6. Connecting rod side clearance should be checked with a feeler (thickness) gauge.

7. Double-check the flatness of the block deck and cylinder head before installing the cylinder head.

8. Torque the cylinder head bolts according to the proper sequence and procedures.

9. Many cylinder heads use the torque-to-yield method, wherein the head bolts are tightened to a specified torque and then rotated a specified number of degrees.

10. The oil pressure should be tested before installation of the engine in the vehicle.

■ REVIEW QUESTIONS

1. Describe the procedure for fitting pistons to a cylinder.

2. Explain how main bearings should be checked and fitted to the crankshaft.

3. How is plastic gauging material used to determine oil clearance?

4. What is the procedure for checking thrust bearing clearance?

5. How should the connecting rod side clearance be measured and corrected?

6. How is the piston and connecting rod assembly installed in the engine?

7. What procedures should be followed for installing and torquing the cylinder head?

8. Describe the torque-to-yield head bolt tightening procedure.

■ ASE CERTIFICATION-TYPE QUESTIONS

1. Typical piston-to-cylinder clearance is _____ .
   a. 0.001 to 0.003 inch
   b. 0.010 to 0.023 inch
   c. 0.100 to 0.150 inch
   d. 0.180 to 0.230 inch

2. If the gauging plastic strip is wide after the bearings are tightened, this indicates _____ .
   a. A large oil clearance
   b. An old, dried strip of plastic gauging material
   c. A small oil clearance
   d. A small side (thrust) clearance

3. The most common cause of premature bearing failure is _____ .
   a. Misassembly
   b. Dirt
   c. Lack of lubrication
   d. Overloading

4. Typical thrust bearing clearance is:
   a. 0.001 to 0.003 inch
   b. 0.002 to 0.012 inch
   c. 0.025 to 0.035 inch
   d. 0.050 to 0.100 inch

5. Piston ring gap clearance can be *increased* by _____ .
   a. Filing the ring to make the gap larger
   b. Installing oversize rings
   c. Sleeving the cylinder
   d. Knurling the piston

6. The cylinder should be tightened (torqued) in what general sequence?
   a. The four outside bolts first, then from the center out
   b. From the outside bolts to the inside bolts
   c. From the inside bolts to the outside bolts
   d. Starting at the front of the engine and torquing bolts from front to rear

7. The torque-angle method involves _____ .
   a. Turning all bolts the same number of turns
   b. Torquing to specifications and loosening by a specified number of degrees
   c. Torquing to one-half specifications, then to three-quarter torque, then to full torque
   d. Turning bolts a specified number of degrees after initial torque

8. Turning the oil pump before starting the engine should be done _____ .
   a. To lubricate engine bearings
   b. To lubricate valve train components
   c. To supply oil to the camshaft
   d. All of the above

9. Most bolt torque specifications are for _____ .
   a. Clean threads only
   b. Clean and lubricated threads
   c. Dirty threads
   d. Dirty threads, but 50% can be added for clean threads

10. Cam bearings should be installed _____ .
    a. Dry
    b. Oiled
    c. With at least 0.010 inch of crush
    d. Both b and c

Engine Installation and In-Vehicle Service

Objectives: After studying Chapter 20, the reader should be able to:

1. List the steps necessary to install and start up a rebuilt engine.
2. Discuss the importance of torquing all bolts or fasteners that connect accessories to the engine block.
3. Describe what precautions must be taken to prevent damage to the engine when it is first started.
4. Explain how to break in a newly rebuilt engine.

The engine installation will have to be thoroughly checked to make sure that the engine is in proper condition to give the customer dependable operation for a long time.

All operating accessories have to be reinstalled on the engine. They have to be adjusted so that the engine will operate correctly. Some of the accessories can be checked as they are assembled, whereas others will have to be checked after the engine is running. See Figure 20–1.

■ MANUAL TRANSMISSION INSTALLATION

If the engine was removed with the transmission attached, the transmission should be reinstalled on the engine before other accessories are added. The flywheel is installed on the back of the crankshaft. Often,

the attaching bolt holes are unevenly spaced so that the flywheel will fit in only one way to maintain engine balance. The pilot bearing or bushing in the rear of the crankshaft is usually replaced with a new one to minimize the possibility of premature failure of this part.

The clutch is installed next. Usually, a new clutch is used; at the least, a new clutch friction disk is installed. The clutch friction disk must be held in position using an alignment tool (sometimes called a dummy shaft) that is secured in the pilot bearing. This holds the disk in position while the pressure plate is being installed. Finally, the engine bell housing is put on the engine, if it

Figure 20–1 Remanufactured engine being run on a stand. Note the small carburetor that is used for this test. Coolant is fed through the engine from passages attached with quick-disconnect fittings. No fuel pump or rocker arm (valve) cover gaskets are used, but the splashed-out oil flows under the grates on the floor and is used again.

Figure 20–2 Bell housing alignment dowel pins are used to ensure proper alignment between the engine block and the transmission.

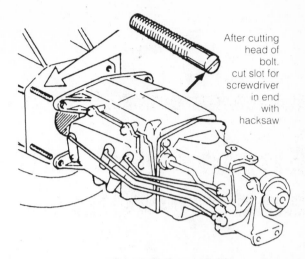

After cutting head of bolt, cut slot for screwdriver in end with hacksaw

Figure 20–3 Headless long bolts can be used to help install a transmission to the engine.

was not installed before. The alignment of this type of bell housing is then checked. See Figure 20–2.

> **CAUTION:** Perfectly round cylinders can be distorted whenever another part of the engine is bolted and torqued to the engine block. For example, it has been determined that after the cylinders are machined, the rear cylinder bore can be distorted to be as much as 0.006 inch (0.15 millimeter) out-of-round after the bell housing is bolted onto the block! To help prevent this distortion, always apply the specified torque to all fasteners going into the engine block and tighten in the recommended sequence.

The clutch release yoke should be checked for free movement. Usually, the clutch release bearing is replaced to ensure that the new bearing is securely attached to the clutch release yoke. The transmission can then be installed.

The transmission clutch shaft must be guided straight into the clutch disk and pilot bearing. See the Tech Tip, "The Headless Bolt Trick." The transmission clutch shaft is rotated, as required, to engage in the splines of the clutch disk. The assembly bolts are secured when the transmission fully mates with the bell housing.

> **CAUTION:** Always adjust the clutch free play *before* starting the engine to help prevent thrust bearing damage.

■ AUTOMATIC TRANSMISSION INSTALLATION

The drive plate is attached to the back of the crankshaft. Its assembly bolts are tightened to the specified torque.

TECH TIP ✔

The Headless Bolt Trick

Sometimes parts do not seem to line up correctly. Try this tip the next time. Cut the head off of extra-long bolts that are of the same diameter and thread as those being used to retain the part, such as a transmission. See Figure 20–3. Use a hacksaw to cut a slot in this end of the guide bolts for a screwdriver slot. Install the guide bolts; then install the transmission. Use a straight-blade screwdriver to remove the guide bolts after securing the transmission with the retaining bolts.

The bell housing is part of the transmission case on most automatic transmissions. Usually, the torque converter (Figure 20–4) will be installed on the transmission before the transmission is put on the engine. The torque converter should be rotated as it is pushed onto the transmission shafts until the splines of all shafts are engaged in the torque converter. The torque converter is held against the transmission as the transmission is fitted on the back of the engine. The transmission mounting bolts are attached finger tight. The torque converter should be rotated to make sure that there is no binding. The bell housing is secured to the block; then the torque converter is fastened to the drive plate. The engine should be rotated. Any binding should be corrected before any further assembly is done.

■ STARTER

It is generally easier to install the starter before the engine is put in the chassis. The starter should be checked

Figure 20–4 Typical automatic transmission torque converter.

to make sure that the starter drive pinion does not bind on the ring gear. Shims can be installed between the starter mounting pad and the starter to adjust the pinion-to-ring gear clearance on the GM-type mounting. The starter mounting bolts are then tightened to the specified torque.

■ ACCESSORIES

All belt-driven engine accessories are mounted on the front of the engine. Some engines drive all these accessories with one belt. Other engines use as many as four belts. The service manual or decal under the hood should be checked to determine the specific belt routing for the accessories used on the engine being built up. On some engines it is more convenient to install the front accessories before the engine is installed; on other engines, it is easier to put the engine in the chassis before installing the front accessories.

Install new spark plugs and spark plug wires. The service manual should be checked for the proper routing of the plug wires.

■ ENGINE INSTALLATION

A sling, either a chain or lift cable, is attached to the manifold or head bolts on the top of the engine. A hoist is attached to the sling and snugged up to take the weight and to make sure that the engine is supported and balanced properly.

> **NOTE:** Many engines for front-wheel-drive vehicles are installed from underneath the vehicle. Often the entire drivetrain package is placed back in the vehicle while it is attached to the cradle. Always check the recommended procedure for the vehicle being serviced.

The engine must be tipped as it was during removal to let the transmission go into the engine compartment first. The transmission is worked under the floor pan on rear-wheel-drive vehicles as the engine is lowered into the engine compartment. The front engine mounts are aligned; then the rear cross-member and rear engine mount are installed. The engine mount bolts are installed, and the nuts are torqued. Then the hoist is removed. Controls are connected to the transmission under the vehicle. This is also a good time to connect the electrical cables and wires to the starter. The exhaust system is then attached to the exhaust manifolds. If any of the steering linkage was previously disconnected, it can be reattached while work is being done under the vehicle. After the engine is in place, the front engine accessories can all be installed, if they were not installed before the engine was put in the chassis. The air-conditioning compressor is reattached to the engine, with care being taken to avoid damaging the air-conditioning hoses and lines.

■ COOLING SYSTEM

The radiator is installed and secured in place, followed by the cooling fan and shroud. The fan and new drive belts are then installed and adjusted. New radiator hoses, including new heater hoses, should be installed. Coolant, a 50/50 mixture of antifreeze and water, is put in the cooling system after making sure that the radiator petcock is closed and the block drain plugs are in place. See Chapter 7 for proper procedures to follow to bleed trapped air from the cooling system. See Figure 20–5 for additional precautions.

■ FUEL AND EMISSION CONTROLS

The carburetor (if the vehicle is so equipped) should be installed with a new gasket. The fuel and vacuum hoses

(a)

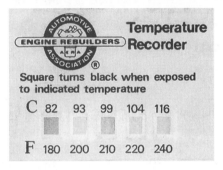

(b)

Figure 20–5 Most engine rebuilders install a temperature-sensitive device on the engine. These sensors are used by the rebuilders for warranty purposes to record any occurrence of engine overheating. (a) This small disk is glued to the engine block and will pop out if the engine overheats. (b) A sticker style. (*Courtesy of the Automotive Engine Rebuilders Association*)

should be inspected carefully and replaced as required. The fuel-injection system (if the vehicle is so equipped) should be carefully inspected for damage while it is off the engine and then reinstalled, being certain to follow recommended procedures and torque settings. The fuel and air filters should be replaced. If the vacuum hoses and/or electrical wiring were not marked, refer to the engine emission decal and service manual for the proper location and routing.

> **NOTE:** The oxygen sensor should be replaced, especially if the engine had a blown head gasket or other problem that could have caused coolant to get on the sensor.

■ ELECTRICAL SYSTEM

Connect all wiring to the starter and generator (alternator) as required. Connect the instrument wires to the

electrical sending units on the engine. Double-check the condition and routing of all wiring, being certain that wires have not been pinched or broken, before installing a fully charged battery. Attach the positive cable first and then the ground cable. Check to make sure that the starter will crank the engine. Install and time the distributor; then connect the ignition cables to the spark plugs, again being sure that they are routed according to the manufacturer's recommendations.

■ BREAK-IN ENGINE OIL

Many years ago, vehicle manufacturers used straight weight nondetergent engine oil as break-in oil. Today, the engine oil recommended for break-in (running in) is the same type of oil that is recommended for use in the engine. No special break-in oil is recommended or used by the factory in new vehicles. SAE 5W-30 or SAE 10W-30 engine oil is usually the specified viscosity recommended by most vehicle manufacturers.

■ ENGINE BREAK-IN

The engine installation should be given one last inspection to ensure that everything has been put together correctly before the engine is started. If the engine overhaul and installation are done properly, the engine should crank and start on its own fully charged battery without the use of a fast charger or jumper battery. As soon as the engine starts and shows oil pressure, it should be brought up to a fast idle speed and *kept there* to ensure that the engine gets proper lubrication. The fast-running oil pump develops full pressure, and the fast-turning crankshaft throws plenty of oil on the cam and cylinder walls.

> **NOTE:** In camshaft-in-block engines, the only lubrication sent to the contact point between the camshaft lobes and the lifters (tappets) is from the splash off the crankshaft and connecting rods. At idle, engine oil does not splash enough for proper break-in lubrication of the camshaft.

As soon as you can tell that no serious leaks exist, and the engine is running reasonably well, the vehicle should be driven to a road having minimum traffic. Here, the vehicle should be accelerated, full throttle, from 30 to 50 miles per hour (48 to 80 kilometers per hour). Then the throttle is fully closed while the vehicle is allowed to return to 30 miles per hour (48 kilometers per hour). This sequence is repeated 10 to 12 times. The acceleration sequence puts a high load on the piston rings to properly seat them against the cylinder walls. The piston rings are the only part of the modern engine that needs to be broken in. Good ring seating is indicated by a dry coating inside the tailpipe at the completion of the ring seating drive.

The vehicle is returned to the service area, where the basic ignition timing is set and the idle speed is properly adjusted if possible. The engine is again checked for visible fluid leaks. If the engine is dry, it is ready to be turned over to the customer.

The customer should be instructed to drive the vehicle in a normal fashion, neither babying it at slow speeds nor beating it at high speeds for the first 100 miles (160 kilometers). The oil and filter should be changed at 500 miles (800 kilometers) to remove any dirt that may have been trapped in the engine during assembly and to remove the material that has worn from the surfaces during the break-in period.

A well-designed engine that has been correctly reconditioned and assembled using the techniques described should give reliable service for many miles.

■ NORMAL OPERATING TEMPERATURE

Normal operating temperature is the temperature at which the upper radiator hose is hot and pressurized. Another standard method used to determine when normal operating temperature is reached is to observe the operation of the electric cooling fan, when the vehicle is so equipped. Many manufacturers define **normal operating temperature** as being reached when the cooling fan has cycled on and off at least once after the engine has been started. Some vehicle manufacturers specify that the cooling fan should cycle twice. This method also helps assure the technician that the engine is not being overheated.

■ HOW TO WARM UP A COLD ENGINE

The greatest amount of engine wear occurs during start-up. The oil in a cold engine is thick, and it requires several seconds to reach all the moving parts of an engine. After the engine starts, the engine should *not* be raced, but rather allowed to idle at the normal fast idle speed as provided for by the choke fast idle cam (on carburetor-equipped engines) or by the computer-controlled speed on fuel-injected engines. After the engine starts, allow the engine to idle until the oil pressure peaks. This will take from 15 seconds to about 1 full minute, depending on the outside temperature. *Do not allow the engine to idle for longer than 5 minutes.* Because an engine warms up faster under load, drive the vehicle in a normal manner until the engine is fully warm. Avoid full-throttle acceleration until the engine is completely up to normal operating temperature. This method of engine warm-up also warms the rest of the power train, including transmission and final drive component lubricants.

■ BREAK-IN PRECAUTIONS

Any engine overhaul represents many hours of work and a large financial investment. Precautions should be taken to protect the investment, including the following:

1. Never add cold water to the cooling system while the engine is running.
2. Never lug any engine. **Lugging** is increasing the throttle opening without increasing engine speed (RPM). Applying loads to an engine for *short periods* of time creates higher piston ring pressure against the cylinder walls and helps in the breaking-in process by helping to seat the rings.
3. Change oil and filter at 500 miles (800 kilometers) or after 20 hours of operation.
4. Remember that the proper air-fuel ratio is important to the proper operation and long life of any engine. Any air leak (vacuum leak) could cause engine damaging detonation.
5. Be certain to use spark plugs for the proper heat range.

PHOTO SEQUENCE   Oil Change

PS 35–1 Begin the oil change process by safely hoisting the vehicle.

PS 35–2 Locate and remove the oil drain plug. On this 5.0L, V-8 Ford Mustang, two oil drain plugs are used. This is the front drain plug.

PS 35–3 Loosen and remove the rear oil drain plug.

PS 35–4 Allow the oil to drain into a suitable container. For best results, the oil drain should be close to the oil pan to help prevent the possibility of the oil splashing onto the floor or onto the service technician.

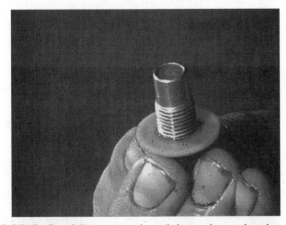

PS 35–5 Carefully inspect the oil drain plug and gasket. Replace the gasket as needed or specified by the vehicle manufacturer (for example, Honda specifies that the aluminum seal on the drain plug be replaced at every oil change).

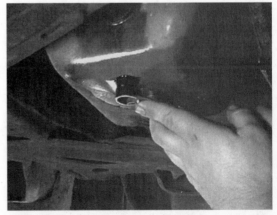

PS 35–6 After all of the oil has been allowed to drain from the oil pan, reinstall the plug in the rear portion of the oil pan.

Oil Change—continued

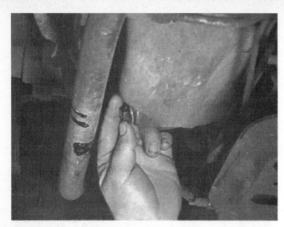

PS 35–7 Also replace the oil drain plug in the front portion of the oil pan.

PS 35–8 Using an oil filter wrench, remove the oil filter. Remember, "righty, tighty and lefty, loosy." Also be sure the oil drain pan is placed under the oil filter because oil will often drain from the filter and engine passages as the oil filter is removed.

PS 35–9 Check the area where the oil filter gasket seats to be sure that no part of the gasket remains that could cause an oil leak if not fully removed.

PS 35–10 Also check the old oil filter to make sure the gasket has been removed with the oil filter. Also compare the replacement filter with the oil filter to double-check that the correct filter will be installed.

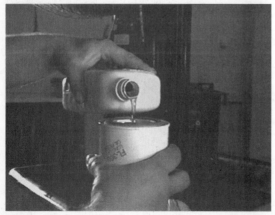

PS 35–11 The wise service technician adds oil to the oil filter whenever possible. This provides faster filling of the filter during start-up and a reduced amount of time that the engine does not have oil pressure.

PS 35–12 Apply a thin layer of clean engine oil to the gasket of the new filter. This oil film will allow the rubber gasket to slide and compress as the oil filter is being rotated on the oil filter thread.

Oil Change—continued

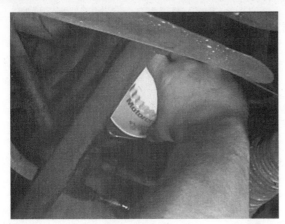

PS 35–13 Install the new oil filter and tighten the recommended amount—usually 3/4 of a turn after the gasket contacts the engine.

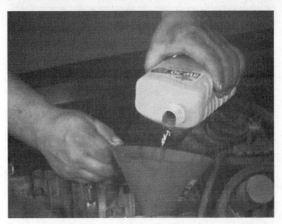

PS 35–14 Use a funnel to help avoid spills and add the specified amount of oil to the engine at the oil-filling opening. Oil capacity for passenger vehicles can vary from 3 quarts (liters) to over 7 quarts (liters).

PS 35–15 Inspect and clean the oil-fill cap and reinstall before starting the engine.

PS 35–16 Start the engine and allow it to idle while watching the oil pressure gauge and/or oil pressure warning lamp.

PS 35–17 The oil pressure gauge should register and the oil pressure warning lamp should go out within 15 seconds of starting the engine. If not, stop the engine and determine the cause before starting the engine again.

PS 35–18 Look underneath the vehicle to check for any oil leaks at the oil drain plug(s) or oil filter. Pull out the oil-level dipstick and wipe it clean with a shop cloth.

Oil Change—continued

PS 35–19 Reinstall the oil-level dipstick to check the oil level.

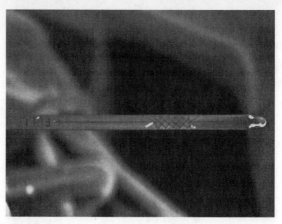

PS 35–20 Remove the dipstick a second time and read the oil level. The oil level should be at the full mark as shown. If overfilled, hoist the vehicle and drain some oil out. An engine that has been overfilled with oil can be damaged because the oil can be aerated (filled with air like a milkshake) reducing the lubricating properties of the engine oil. Be sure to thoroughly wash your hands with soap and water after touching used engine oil or wear protective rubber gloves.

PHOTO SEQUENCE   Water Pump and Timing Belt Replacement

PS 36–1 A view of the 3.0L, V-6 Dodge minivan that needs a new water pump because it is leaking from the weep hole.

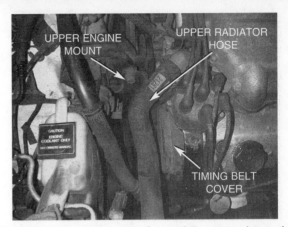

PS 36–2 Because the entire front of the engine has to be disassembled including the removal of the upper engine mount on the passenger side, the timing belt will also be replaced.

PS 36–3 After draining the cooling system, the upper radiator hose and the accessory drive belt are removed.

PS 36–4 The vehicle is hoisted and the right front wheel/tire assembly is removed to gain access to the front of the engine.

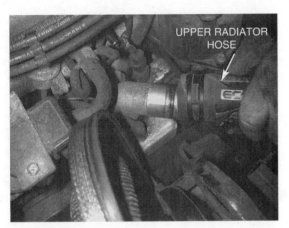

PS 36–5 The splash shield has to be removed to gain access to the front accessory drive pulley.

PS 36–6 The retaining bolts are removed holding the accessory drive belt pulley to the harmonic balancer.

Water Pump and Timing Belt Replacement—continued

PS 36–7 A puller is used to remove the harmonic balancer.

PS 36–8 While under the vehicle, the air-conditioning compressor bracket is removed.

PS 36–9 Before removing the upper engine mount, the engine is being supported by a floor jack. Notice that a block of wood is placed between the oil pan and the jack.

PS 36–10 With the engine supported from underneath, the upper engine mount is removed.

PS 36–11 The accessory support plate is removed.

PS 36–12 The timing belt cover(s) can now be removed.

Water Pump and Timing Belt Replacement—continued

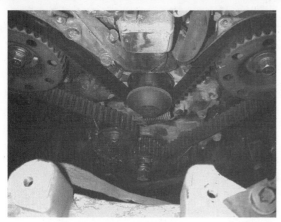

PS 36–13 A view of the front of the engine with the timing belt covers removed.

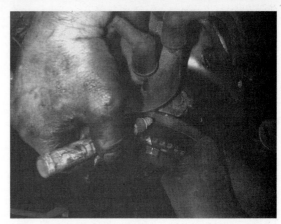

PS 36–14 Before removing the timing belt, the wise service technician marks the location of the belt and pulley as a precaution to be sure that the new replacement belt will be placed back into proper time.

PS 36–15 The spring tensioner is moved and the belt removed.

PS 36–16 To save time, this service technician is cutting off the head of one bolt that holds a support bracket. This bolt cannot be removed without removing the entire intake manifold.

PS 36–17 With the bolt head removed, the bracket is lifted up slightly, allowing room to remove the water pump. The bracket is still retained by another bolt.

PS 36–18 After the water pump retaining bolts have been removed, a screwdriver or pry bar is needed to remove the water pump.

Water Pump and Timing Belt Replacement—continued

PS 36–19 Removing the water pump from the front of the engine.

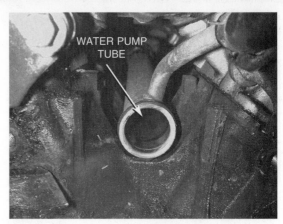

PS 36–20 After the water pump is removed, the tube used to transfer coolant the length of the block is visible. The water pump slides over the seal on the end of the tube. This tube and seal are the reason why a pry bar was needed to remove the water pump.

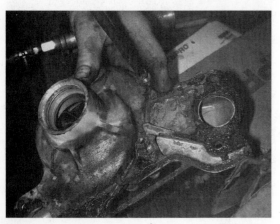

PS 36–21 The replaceable part of the water pump has to be removed from the housing. There is a hidden Phillips screw on the backside that has to be removed.

PS 36–22 After removing the Phillips screw on the backside, turn the water pump over and remove the rest of the retaining bolts.

PS 36–23 After all retaining bolts have been removed, separate the water pump from the housing.

PS 36–24 A fiber disc on an air grinder is being used to remove the old gasket material.

Water Pump and Timing Belt Replacement—continued

PS 36–25 Gasket adhesive is being applied to the gasket surface of the replacement water pump.

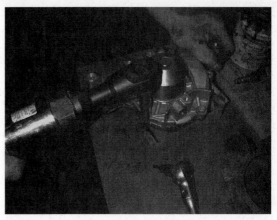

PS 36–26 Assembling the new water pump onto the original water pump housing.

PS 36–27 Attaching new gaskets to the outlet flanges of the water pump.

PS 36–28 Before installing the water pump, the block has to be cleaned of the old gaskets.

PS 36–29 A view of the front of the engine with the replacement water pump installed.

PS 36–30 After the water pump is installed, the new timing belt can be installed.

Water Pump and Timing Belt Replacement—continued

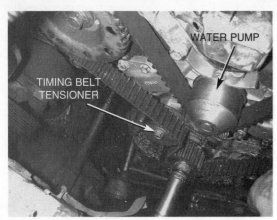

PS 36–31 Notice that the timing belt drives the water pump. This is the reason why both the timing belt and the water pump are being replaced. The spring-loaded tensioner applies tension to the timing belt.

PS 36–32 Before reinstalling everything, the cooling system is connected and partially filled and then pressure tested to check to make sure there are no leaks. This step is very important on this engine because of the design of the water pump fitting over the transfer tube.

PS 36–33 After making sure that everything is okay with the installation of the water pump and there are no leaks, the timing belt cover and upper engine mount can be reinstalled.

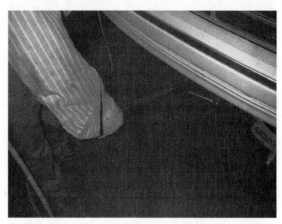

PS 36–34 After the engine mount has been replaced, the floor jack being used to support the engine is removed.

PS 36–35 All the other brackets and hoses can now be reinstalled.

PS 36–36 The vehicle is hoisted and the harmonic balancer and air-conditioning bracket is reinstalled.

Water Pump and Timing Belt Replacement—continued

PS 36–37 The accessory drive pulley is then installed on the harmonic balancer and the bolts torqued to factory specifications.

PS 36–38 After the drive pulley has been installed, the accessory drive belt is installed.

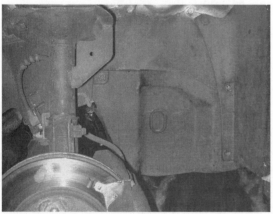

PS 36–39 After double-checking that everything is properly reinstalled and torqued, the splash shield can be installed.

PS 36–40 Install the wheel/tire assembly and wheel cover.

PS 36–41 The vehicle is now lowered and the cooling system filled with new coolant.

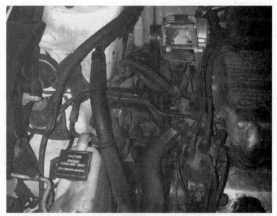

PS 36–42 The repair is completed four hours after starting. The vehicle should be test driven and all connections double-checked before returning the vehicle to the customer.

■ SUMMARY

1. Carefully install all accessories.
2. When installing the transmission and other components on the engine block, be sure to use a torque wrench and tighten all fasteners to factory specifications.
3. Always adjust the clutch free play before starting the engine.
4. Temperature recording sensors should be installed on cylinder heads. This lets the rebuild technician know if the engine has been overheated.
5. A new oxygen sensor(s) should be installed to ensure that the engine operation is within acceptable limits. If the oxygen sensor is defective, the engine may operate too lean. A lean-operating engine runs hotter than normal.
6. Change the engine oil after 500 miles (800 kilometers) or sooner, and use SAE 5W-30 or SAE 10W-30 engine oil.

■ REVIEW QUESTIONS

1. How are the clutch and bell housing installed?
2. What should be done to help prevent rear cylinder distortion when the bell housing is being installed on the engine?
3. Describe the engine break-in procedure.

■ ASE CERTIFICATION-TYPE QUESTIONS

1. Every automotive engine should be filled with at least _____ quarts of engine oil before the engine is prelubricated or started.
   a. 2
   b. 3
   c. 4
   d. 5
2. If the bell housing is not properly torqued to the engine block, _____ .
   a. The bell housing will distort
   b. The engine block will crack
   c. The rear cylinder can be distorted (become out of round)
   d. The crankshaft will crack
3. Break-in engine oil is _____ .
   a. Of the same viscosity and grade as that specified for normal engine operation
   b. SAE 40
   c. SAE 30
   d. SAE 20W-50

4. Normal operating temperature is reached when _____ .
   a. The radiator cap releases coolant into the overflow
   b. The upper radiator hose is hot and pressurized
   c. The electric cooling fan has cycled at least once (if the vehicle is so equipped)
   d. Both b and c occur
5. Lugging an engine means _____ .
   a. Wide-open throttle in low gear above 25 miles per hour
   b. That engine speed does not increase when the throttle is opened wider
   c. Starting a cold engine and allowing it to idle for longer than 5 minutes
   d. Both b and c
6. Which computer sensor should be replaced if the engine had been found to have a defective head gasket or cracked head?
   a. Throttle position sensor
   b. Oxygen sensor
   c. Manifold absolute pressure sensor
   d. Engine coolant temperature sensor
7. For best results, the oil should be drained when the engine is _____ .
   a. At normal operating temperature
   b. At room temperature
   c. Cold—not yet started
8. A water pump failed shortly after it was replaced. Technician A says the accessory drive belt could have been adjusted too tight. Technician B says that the engine-driven cooling fan could be out of balance. Which technician is correct?
   a. Technician A only
   b. Technician B only
   c. Both Technician A and B
   d. Neither Technician A nor B
9. The valves could be bent if the timing belt breaks on a _____ .
   a. Freewheeling engine design
   b. Interference engine design
10. Two technicians are discussing the installation of a rebuilt engine into a vehicle. Technician A says that the radiator should be flow tested to help ensure that the engine will not overheat. Technician B says that a new thermostat should be installed. Which technician is correct?
    a. Technician A only
    b. Technician B only
    c. Both Technician A and B
    d. Neither Technician A nor B

Engine Repair Sample ASE Certification Test

1. Two technicians are discussing the markings on the heads of bolts (cap screws). Technician A says the higher the number of lines, the higher the strength of the bolt. Technician B says the higher the number on metric bolts, the higher the grade. Which technician is correct?
   a. Technician A only
   b. Technician B only
   c. Both Technician A and B
   d. Neither Technician A nor B

2. A metric bolt size of M8 means that _____ .
   a. The bolt is 8 millimeters long
   b. The bolt is 8 millimeters in diameter
   c. The pitch (the distance between the crest of the threads) is 8 millimeters
   d. The bolt is 8 centimeters long

3. On a metric bolt sized M8 × 1.5, the 1.5 means that _____ .
   a. The bolt is 1.5 millimeters in diameter
   b. The bolt is 1.5 centimeters long
   c. The bolt has 1.5 millimeters between the crest of the threads
   d. The bolt has a strength grade of 1.5

4. Prevailing torque (lock) nuts should be replaced rather than reused after removal.
   a. True
   b. False

5. If the bore of an engine is increased without any other changes except for the change to proper-size replacement pistons, the displacement will _____ and the compression rate will _____ .

   a. Increase; increase
   b. Increase; decrease
   c. Decrease; increase
   d. Decrease; decrease

6. A battery is being tested. Technician A says that the surface charge should be removed before the battery is load tested. Technician B says that the battery should be loaded to two times the CCA rating of the battery for 15 seconds. Which technician is correct?
   a. Technician A only
   b. Technician B only
   c. Both Technician A and B
   d. Neither Technician A nor B

7. A starter motor cranks the engine too slowly to start. Technician A says that the cause could be a weak or defective battery. Technician B says that the cause could be loose or corroded battery cable connections. Which technician is correct?
   a. Technician A only
   b. Technician B only
   c. Both Technician A and B
   d. Neither Technician A nor B

8. The charging system voltage is found to be lower than specified by the vehicle manufacturer. Technician A says that a loose or defective drive belt could be the cause. Technician B says that a defective generator (alternator) could be the cause. Which technician is correct?
   a. Technician A only
   b. Technician B only
   c. Both Technician A and B
   d. Neither Technician A nor B

9. An engine uses an excessive amount of oil. Technician A says that clogged oil drain-back holes in the cylinder head could be the cause. Technician B says that worn piston rings could be the cause. Which technician is correct?
   a. Technician A only
   b. Technician B only
   c. Both Technician A and B
   d. Neither Technician A nor B

10. Battery voltage during cranking is below specifications. Technician A says that a defect in the engine may be the cause. Technician B says that the starter motor may be defective. Which technician is correct?
    a. Technician A only
    b. Technician B only
    c. Both Technician A and B
    d. Neither Technician A nor B

11. Two technicians are discussing distributorless (EI) ignition. Technician A says that the crankshaft sensor triggers the module. Technician B says that the module controls the primary circuit of the ignition coil. Which technician is correct?
    a. Technician A only
    b. Technician B only
    c. Both Technician A and B
    d. Neither Technician A nor B

12. An engine cranks but will not start. No spark is available at the end of a spark plug wire with a spark tester connected and the engine cranked. Technician A says that a defective pickup coil could be the cause. Technician B says that a defective ignition module could be the cause. Which technician is correct?
    a. Technician A only
    b. Technician B only
    c. Both Technician A and B
    d. Neither Technician A nor B

13. An engine miss is being diagnosed. One spark plug wire measured OL on a digital ohmmeter set to the K ohm scale. Technician A says that the spark plug should be replaced. Technician B says that the spark plug wire is okay. Which technician is correct?
    a. Technician A only
    b. Technician B only
    c. Both Technician A and B
    d. Neither Technician A nor B

14. Two technicians are discussing torquing cylinder head bolts. Technician A says that many engine manufacturers recommend replacing the head bolts after use. Technician B says that many manufacturers recommend tightening the head bolts to a specific torque, then turning the bolts an additional number of degrees. Which technician is correct?
    a. Technician A only
    b. Technician B only

    c. Both Technician A and B
    d. Neither Technician A nor B

15. Engine ping (spark knock or detonation) can be caused by _____ .
    a. Advanced ignition timing
    b. Retarded ignition timing

16. Two technicians are discussing the diagnosis of a lack-of-power problem. Technician A says that a worn (stretched) timing chain could be the cause. Technician B says that retarded ignition timing could be the cause. Which technician is correct?
    a. Technician A only
    b. Technician B only
    c. Both Technician A and B
    d. Neither Technician A nor B

17. Technician A says that low fuel pressure can cause the engine to produce low power. Technician B says that all fuel pumps should be able to pump at least 2 pints (1 liter) per minute. Which technician is correct?
    a. Technician A only
    b. Technician B only
    c. Both Technician A and B
    d. Neither Technician A nor B

18. An engine equipped with a turbocharger is burning oil (blue exhaust smoke all the time). Technician A says that a defective wastegate could be the cause. Technician B says that a plugged PCV system could be the cause. Which technician is correct?
    a. Technician A only
    b. Technician B only
    c. Both Technician A and B
    d. Neither Technician A nor B

19. An engine idles roughly and stalls occasionally. Technician A says that using fuel with too high an RVP level could be the cause. Technician B says that using winter-blend gasoline during warm weather could be the cause. Which technician is correct?
    a. Technician A only
    b. Technician B only
    c. Both Technician A and B
    d. Neither Technician A nor B

20. A customer was concerned about using unleaded fuel in a vehicle designed for leaded gasoline. Technician A says that valve recession is likely to occur if unleaded fuel is used even if the vehicle is driven only a few miles. Technician B says that an additive must be used to prevent serious and rapid engine damage from occurring. Which technician is correct?
    a. Technician A only
    b. Technician B only
    c. Both Technician A and B
    d. Neither Technician A nor B

21. Technician A says that coolant flows through the engine passages and does not flow through the radiator until the thermostat opens. Technician B says that the temperature rating of the thermostat indicates the temperature of the coolant when the thermostat is opened fully. Which technician is correct?
   a. Technician A only
   b. Technician B only
   c. Both Technician A and B
   d. Neither Technician A nor B

22. Technician A says the higher the concentration of antifreeze, the better. Technician B says that a 50/50 mix of antifreeze and water is the ratio recommended by most vehicle manufacturers. Which technician is correct?
   a. Technician A only
   b. Technician B only
   c. Both Technician A and B
   d. Neither Technician A nor B

23. Technician A says that the radiator pressure cap is designed to raise the boiling point of the coolant. Technician B says that the radiator pressure cap helps prevent cavitation and, therefore, improves the efficiency of the water pump. Which technician is correct?
   a. Technician A only
   b. Technician B only
   c. Both Technician A and B
   d. Neither Technician A nor B

24. Technician A says that used antifreeze coolant is often considered to be hazardous waste. Technician B says that metals absorbed by the coolant when it is used in an engine are what makes antifreeze harmful. Which technician is correct?
   a. Technician A only
   b. Technician B only
   c. Both Technician A and B
   d. Neither Technician A nor B

25. A water pump has been replaced three times in three months. Technician A says that the drive belt(s) may be installed too tightly. Technician B says that a cooling fan may be bent or out of balance. Which technician is correct?
   a. Technician A only
   b. Technician B only
   c. Both Technician A and B
   d. Neither Technician A nor B

26. Two technicians discuss the "hot" light on the dash. Technician A says that the light comes on if the cooling system temperature is too high for safe operation of the engine. Technician B says that the light comes on whenever there is a decrease (drop) in cooling system pressure. Which technician is correct?
   a. Technician A only
   b. Technician B only
   c. Both Technician A and B
   d. Neither Technician A nor B

27. Two technicians diagnose an engine noise. Technician A says that a double knock is likely to be due to a worn rod bearing. Technician B says that a knock only when the engine is cold is usually due to a worn piston pin. Which technician is correct?
   a. Technician A only
   b. Technician B only
   c. Both Technician A and B
   d. Neither Technician A nor B

28. A compression test gave the following results: cylinder #1 = 155, cylinder #2 = 140, cylinder #3 = 110, cylinder #4 = 105

Technician A says that a defective (burned) valve is the most likely cause. Technician B says that a leaking head gasket could be the cause. Which technician is correct?
   a. Technician A only
   b. Technician B only
   c. Both Technician A and B
   d. Neither Technician A nor B

29. Two technicians are discussing a compression test. Technician A says that the engine should be turned over with the pressure gauge installed for "3 puffs." Technician B says that the maximum difference between the highest-reading cylinder and the lowest-reading cylinder should be 20%. Which technician is correct?
   a. Technician A only
   b. Technician B only
   c. Both Technician A and B
   d. Neither Technician A nor B

30. Technician A says that oil should be squirted into all cylinders before taking a compression test. Technician B says that if the compression greatly increases when some oil is squirted into the cylinders, it indicates defective or worn piston rings. Which technician is correct?
   a. Technician A only
   b. Technician B only
   c. Both Technician A and B
   d. Neither Technician A nor B

31. During a cylinder leakage (leak-down) test, air is noticed coming out of the oil-fill opening. Technician A says that the oil filter may be clogged. Technician B says that the piston rings may be worn or defective. Which technician is correct?
   a. Technician A only
   b. Technician B only
   c. Both Technician A and B
   d. Neither Technician A nor B

32. A cylinder leakage (leak-down) test indicates 30% leakage, and air is heard coming out of the air inlet. Technician A says that this is a normal reading for a slightly worn engine. Technician B says that one or more intake valves are defective. Which technician is correct?
    a. Technician A only
    b. Technician B only
    c. Both Technician A and B
    d. Neither Technician A nor B

33. Two technicians are discussing a cylinder power balance test. Technician A says the more the engine RPM drops, the weaker the cylinder. Technician B says that all cylinder RPM drops should be within 50 RPM of each other. Which technician is correct?
    a. Technician A only
    b. Technician B only
    c. Both Technician A and B
    d. Neither Technician A nor B

34. Technician A says that cranking vacuum should be the same as idle vacuum. Technician B says that a sticking valve is indicated by a floating valve gauge needle reading. Which technician is correct?
    a. Technician A only
    b. Technician B only
    c. Both Technician A and B
    d. Neither Technician A nor B

35. Technician A says that black exhaust smoke is an indication of a too rich air-fuel mixture. Technician B says that white smoke (steam) is an indication of coolant being burned in the engine. Which technician is correct?
    a. Technician A only
    b. Technician B only
    c. Both Technician A and B
    d. Neither Technician A nor B

36. Excessive exhaust system back pressure has been measured. Technician A says that the catalytic converter may be clogged. Technician B says that the muffler may be clogged. Which technician is correct?
    a. Technician A only
    b. Technician B only
    c. Both Technician A and B
    d. Neither Technician A nor B

37. Two technicians are a possible head gasket failure. Technician A says that an exhaust analyzer can be used to check for HC when the tester probe is held above the radiator coolant. Technician B says that a chemical-coated paper changes color in the presence of combustion gases. Which technician is correct?
    a. Technician A only
    b. Technician B only

    c. Both Technician A and B
    d. Neither Technician A nor B

38. Technician A says that pistons should be removed from the crankshaft side of the cylinder when disassembling an engine to prevent possible piston or cylinder damage. Technician B says that the rod assembly should be marked before disassembly. Which technician is correct?
    a. Technician A only
    b. Technician B only
    c. Both Technician A and B
    d. Neither Technician A nor B

39. Before the valve is removed from the cylinder head, _____ .
    a. The valve spring should be compressed and locks removed
    b. The valve tip edges should be filed
    c. The ridge should be removed
    d. Both a and b

40. A steel wire brush should be used to clean the gasket surface of an aluminum cylinder head.
    a. True
    b. False

41. The heat shield was removed from the bottom of a V-8 intake manifold. Technician A says that the engine will run cooler. Technician B says that the oil may coke (harden) without the shield. Which technician is correct?
    a. Technician A only
    b. Technician B only
    c. Both Technician A and B
    d. Neither Technician A nor B

42. Technician A says that most engines equipped with a carburetor or throttle-body injection unit use a heated intake manifold to help in vaporization. Technician B says that engines equipped with port fuel injection do not require that the manifold be heated. Which technician is correct?
    a. Technician A only
    b. Technician B only
    c. Both Technician A and B
    d. Neither Technician A nor B

43. Technician A says that the purpose of the exhaust gas recirculation system is to reburn the exhaust gases to reduce emissions. Technician B says that the exhaust in the EGR system helps prevent high combustion temperatures inside the combustion chamber. Which technician is correct?
    a. Technician A only
    b. Technician B only
    c. Both Technician A and B
    d. Neither Technician A nor B

44. Technician A says that all valve train parts that are to be reused should be kept together. Technician B says that before testing valve springs for tension,

the damper spring should be removed if used. Which technician is correct?
   a. Technician A only
   b. Technician B only
   c. Both Technician A and B
   d. Neither Technician A nor B

45. A cast-iron cylinder head is checked for warpage using a straightedge and a feeler (thickness) gauge. The amount of warpage on a V-8 cylinder head was 0.002 inch (0.05 millimeter). Technician A says that the cylinder head should be resurfaced. Technician B says that the cylinder head should be replaced. Which technician is correct?
   a. Technician A only
   b. Technician B only
   c. Both Technician A and B
   d. Neither Technician A nor B

46. The higher the microinch finish, the _____ the surface.
   a. Rougher
   b. Smoother

47. The valve guide should be reconditioned or replaced *before* the valve seats are reconditioned.
   a. True
   b. False

48. Technician A says that a dial indicator (gauge) is often used to measure valve guide wear by measuring the amount by which the valve head is able to move in the guide. Technician B says that a ball gauge can be used to measure the valve guide. Which technician is correct?
   a. Technician A only
   b. Technician B only
   c. Both Technician A and B
   d. Neither Technician A nor B

49. Technician A says that a worn valve guide can be reamed and a valve with an oversize stem can be used. Technician B says that a worn valve guide can be replaced with a bronze insert to restore the cylinder head to useful service. Which technician is correct?
   a. Technician A only
   b. Technician B only
   c. Both Technician A and B
   d. Neither Technician A nor B

50. Technician A says that worn integral guides can be repaired by knurling. Technician B says that worn integral guides can be replaced. Which technician is correct?
   a. Technician A only
   b. Technician B only
   c. Both Technician A and B
   d. Neither Technician A nor B

51. Typical valve-to-valve guide clearance should be _____ .
   a. 0.001 to 0.003 inch (0.025 to 0.076 millimeter)
   b. 0.010 to 0.030 inch (0.25 to 0.76 millimeter)
   c. 0.035 to 0.060 inch (0.89 to 1.52 millimeters)
   d. 0.100 to 0.350 inch (2.54 to 8.90 millimeters)

52. Before a valve spring is reused, it should be checked for _____ .
   a. Squareness
   b. Free height
   c. Tension
   d. All of the above

53. Many manufacturers recommend that valves be ground with an interference angle. This angle is the difference between the _____ .
   a. Valve margin and valve face angles
   b. Valve face and valve seat angles
   c. Valve guide and valve face angles
   d. Valve head and margin angles

54. To narrow and lower a 45-degree valve seat, the technician should use a _____ .
   a. 30-degree stone
   b. 45-degree stone
   c. 60-degree stone
   d. 75-degree stone

55. To widen a valve seat without lowering or raising its position, the technician should use a _____ .
   a. 30-degree stone
   b. 45-degree stone
   c. 60-degree stone
   d. 75-degree stone

56. Valve stem height and installed height mean the same thing.
   a. True
   b. False

57. Valve spring inserts are used _____ .
   a. Under the valve spring
   b. To restore proper installed height
   c. To restore proper spring tension after the valves and valve seats have been reconditioned
   d. For all of the above

58. Technician A says that valve stem seals of the O-ring type are installed on top of the valve locks (keepers). Technician B says that a vacuum pump can be used to determine if the valve stem seal is correctly seated. Which technician is correct?
   a. Technician A only
   b. Technician B only
   c. Both Technician A and B
   d. Neither Technician A nor B

59. Two technicians are diagnosing a problem with an OHV V-8. The valve covers have been removed and the engine is running. One pushrod is not rotating. Technician A says that the camshaft is worn and

must be replaced. Technician B says that the lifter is worn and must be replaced. Which technician is correct?
   a. Technician A only
   b. Technician B only
   c. Both Technician A and B
   d. Neither Technician A nor B

60. A noisy valve train is being diagnosed. Technician A says that the rocker arm may be adjusted too tightly. Technician B says that the rocker arm may be adjusted too loosely or may be worn. Which technician is correct?
   a. Technician A only
   b. Technician B only
   c. Both Technician A and B
   d. Neither Technician A nor B

61. A cylinder is 0.002 inch out-of-round. Technician A says that the block should be bored and oversize pistons installed. Technician B says that oversize piston rings should be used. Which technician is correct?
   a. Technician A only
   b. Technician B only
   c. Both Technician A and B
   d. Neither Technician A nor B

62. After the engine block has been machined, the block should be cleaned with _____ .
   a. A stiff brush and soap and water
   b. A clean rag and engine oil
   c. WD-40
   d. Spray solvent washer

63. Technician A says that piston rings should be installed with the dot or mark facing up (toward the cylinder head). Technician B says that the mark on the piston rings is used to identify the position (groove) in which the ring should be installed. Which technician is correct?
   a. Technician A only
   b. Technician B only
   c. Both Technician A and B
   d. Neither Technician A nor B

64. Two technicians are discussing ring gap. Technician A says that the ring should be checked in the same cylinder in which it is to be installed. Technician B says that the ends of the piston ring can be filed if the clearance is too small. Which technician is correct?
   a. Technician A only
   b. Technician B only
   c. Both Technician A and B
   d. Neither Technician A nor B

65. Technician A says that connecting rod caps should be marked when the connecting rod is disassem-

bled and then replaced in the exact same location and direction on the rod. Technician B says that each piston should be fitted to each individual cylinder for best results. Which technician is correct?
   a. Technician A only
   b. Technician B only
   c. Both Technician A and B
   d. Neither Technician A nor B

66. Two technicians are discussing bearing clearance measurement. Technician A says that the main and rod bearing clearance should be measured with plastic gauging material (Plastigage). Technician B says that the engine crankshaft should be rotated for two complete revolutions when Plastigage is used between the crankshaft and the main or rod bearings. Which technician is correct?
   a. Technician A only
   b. Technician B only
   c. Both Technician A and B
   d. Neither Technician A nor B

67. When pistons are installed in the block, the notch on the piston should be facing _____ .
   a. Toward the lifter side of the block
   b. Toward the front of the engine
   c. Toward the rear of the engine
   d. Away from the lifter side of the block

68. A bearing shell is being installed in a connecting rod. The end of the bearing is slightly above the parting line. Technician A says that this is normal. Technician B says that the bearing is too big. Which technician is correct?
   a. Technician A only
   b. Technician B only
   c. Both Technician A and B
   d. Neither Technician A nor B

69. Two technicians are discussing the cause of low oil pressure. Technician A says that a worn oil pump could be the cause. Technician B says that worn main or rod bearings could be the cause. Which technician is correct?
   a. Technician A only
   b. Technician B only
   c. Both Technician A and B
   d. Neither Technician A nor B

70. Oil is discovered inside the air cleaner assembly. Technician A says that the cause could be excessive blowby past the piston rings. Technician B says that the cause could be a clogged PCV valve, hose, or passage. Which technician is correct?
   a. Technician A only
   b. Technician B only
   c. Both Technician A and B
   d. Neither Technician A nor B

Cylinder Head Specialist Sample ASE Certification Test

1. An aluminum cylinder head is to be removed from an engine. Machinist A says that the head bolts should be loosened in a sequence starting at the center of the cylinder head and working toward the ends of the cylinder head. Machinist B says that the engine should be at room temperature before the cylinder head is removed. Which machinist is correct?
   a. Machinist A only
   b. Machinist B only
   c. Both Machinist A and B
   d. Neither Machinist A nor B

2. Machinist A says that all pushrods should be kept and arranged so that they can be replaced in their original locations when the engine is reassembled. Machinist B says that a rocker arm should be kept with the pushrod that it contacted. Which machinist is correct?
   a. Machinist A only
   b. Machinist B only
   c. Both Machinist A and B
   d. Neither Machinist A nor B

3. Machinist A says that a putty knife can be used to clean the gasket surface of cast-iron or aluminum cylinder heads. Machinist B says that a steel wire brush can be used to clean cast-iron and aluminum cylinder heads. Which machinist is correct?
   a. Machinist A only
   b. Machinist B only
   c. Both Machinist A and B
   d. Neither Machinist A nor B

4. Machinist A says that some chemicals can turn an aluminum cylinder head black. Machinist B says that an aqueous-based chemical cleaning method can be used to clean both cast-iron and aluminum cylinder heads. Which machinist is correct?
   a. Machinist A only
   b. Machinist B only
   c. Both Machinist A and B
   d. Neither Machinist A nor B

5. Machinist A says that thermal cleaning in a pyrolytic oven is best suited for cast-iron cylinder heads. Machinist B says that shot blasting or tumbling may also be necessary after a cylinder head is cleaned in an oven. Which machinist is correct?
   a. Machinist A only
   b. Machinist B only
   c. Both Machinist A and B
   d. Neither Machinist A nor B

6. Machinist A says that magnetic flux testing can be used to check for cracks in aluminum and cast-iron cylinder heads. Machinist B says that dye penetrant testing can be used to check for cracks in aluminum and cast-iron cylinder heads. Which machinist is correct?
   a. Machinist A only
   b. Machinist B only
   c. Both Machinist A and B
   d. Neither Machinist A nor B

7. Machinist A says that fluorescent penetrant testing can be used to check for cracks in aluminum and cast-iron cylinder heads. Machinist B says that

pressure testing can be used to check for cracks in aluminum and cast-iron cylinder heads. Which machinist is correct?

 a. Machinist A only
 b. Machinist B only
 c. Both Machinist A and B
 d. Neither Machinist A nor B

8. Cracks in cylinder heads can be repaired by

 _____ .

 a. Stop drilling
 b. Welding
 c. Plugging
 d. All of the above

9. Before a crack in cast iron is welded, the cylinder head must first be _____ .

 a. Pinned with cast-iron plugs
 b. Heated
 c. Brazed
 d. Machined

10. Machinist A says that aluminum cylinder heads can be welded to repair a crack. Machinist B says that the valve seat insert should be removed if the crack is near the combustion chamber. Which machinist is correct?

 a. Machinist A only
 b. Machinist B only
 c. Both Machinist A and B
 d. Neither Machinist A nor B

11. Machinist A says that tapered plugs can be used to repair a crack in a cast-iron cylinder head. Machinist B says that the tapered plugs should be coated in sealant and installed side by side with other plugs. Which machinist is correct?

 a. Machinist A only
 b. Machinist B only
 c. Both Machinist A and B
 d. Neither Machinist A nor B

12. A V-8 cylinder head has 0.001 inch (0.05 millimeter) of total warpage. Machinist A says that the cylinder head should be resurfaced. Machinist B says the cylinder head should also be checked for bend and twist. Which machinist is correct?

 a. Machinist A only
 b. Machinist B only
 c. Both Machinist A and B
 d. Neither Machinist A nor B

13. Cylinder head gasket surface finish is measured in what unit?

 a. Millimeters
 b. Centimeters
 c. Microinches
 d. Nanometers

14. Machinist A says that the finish of a cast-iron cylinder head gasket surface should be between 60 and 100 units. Machinist B says that the finish of an aluminum cylinder head gasket surface should be between 50 and 60 units. Which machinist is correct?

 a. Machinist A only
 b. Machinist B only
 c. Both Machinist A and B
 d. Neither Machinist A nor B

15. Machinist A says that the valve timing will be *retarded* if material is removed from the head-to-block surface of the cylinder head of an overhead camshaft engine. Machinist B says that the valve timing will be *advanced* if material is removed from the cylinder head on an overhead valve type of engine. Which machinist is correct?

 a. Machinist A only
 b. Machinist B only
 c. Both Machinist A and B
 d. Neither Machinist A nor B

16. A V-type engine has had the head gasket surface refinished. What other machining operation should be performed?

 a. Machining the deck at least 0.008 inch to ensure a proper seal
 b. Machining the intake manifold
 c. Machining the exhaust manifolds
 d. All of the above

17. Two machinists are discussing stress relieving a warped aluminum cylinder head. Machinist A says that the head should be machined before stress relieving. Machinist B says that the head should be bolted to a thick slab of steel and placed in an oven to soak for 5 hours. Which machinist is correct?

 a. Machinist A only
 b. Machinist B only
 c. Both Machinist A and B
 d. Neither Machinist A nor B

18. A four-cylinder overhead camshaft engine cylinder head with integral cam bearings is being machined. Machinist A says that the camshaft centerline should be realigned by boring the camshaft journals. Machinist B says that the cylinder head should be straightened *before* the machining operation. Which machinist is correct?

 a. Machinist A only
 b. Machinist B only
 c. Both Machinist A and B
 d. Neither Machinist A nor B

19. Machinist A says that a loose valve seat should be staked. Machinist B says that the valve seat should be replaced. Which machinist is correct?

 a. Machinist A only
 b. Machinist B only
 c. Both Machinist A and B
 d. Neither Machinist A nor B

20. Machinist A says that a ball gauge and a micrometer can be used to determine valve guide clearance. Machinist B says that holding a dial indicator against the side of the valve while the valve is held in the open position is specified by some manufacturers as a method for checking valve guide wear. Which machinist is correct?
    a. Machinist A only
    b. Machinist B only
    c. Both Machinist A and B
    d. Neither Machinist A nor B

21. Typical valve guide clearance is _____ .
    a. 0.0003 to 0.0008 inch (0.008 to 0.02 millimeter)
    b. 0.001 to 0.003 inch (0.025 to 0.076 millimeter)
    c. 0.005 to 0.008 inch (0.13 to 0.20 millimeter)
    d. 0.010 to 0.015 inch (0.25 to 0.38 millimeter)

22. Oversize stem valves are being installed in a cast-iron cylinder head with integral valve guides. Machinist A says that the old guide must be reamed. Machinist B says that the valve guide should be replaced. Which machinist is correct?
    a. Machinist A only
    b. Machinist B only
    c. Both Machinist A and B
    d. Neither Machinist A nor B

23. Two machinists are discussing knurling valve guides. Machinist A says that the valve guide should be reamed before the knurling operation. Machinist B says that the valve stem-to-valve guide clearance is usually one-half of the new guide clearance. Which machinist is correct?
    a. Machinist A only
    b. Machinist B only
    c. Both Machinist A and B
    d. Neither Machinist A nor B

24. Machinist A says that replacement guides are pressed into the cylinder head. Machinist B says that the replacement guide should be reamed or honed after installation. Which machinist is correct?
    a. Machinist A only
    b. Machinist B only
    c. Both Machinist A and B
    d. Neither Machinist A nor B

25. Machinist A says that a bronze thin-walled insert can be used to repair a worn valve guide. Machinist B says that a thin-walled insert is used with an oversize stem valve. Which machinist is correct?
    a. Machinist A only
    b. Machinist B only
    c. Both Machinist A and B
    d. Neither Machinist A nor B

26. Machinist A says that aluminized valves should not be machined. Machinist B says that the tip of the valve stem should be filed before the valve is removed from the cylinder head. Which machinist is correct?
    a. Machinist A only
    b. Machinist B only
    c. Both Machinist A and B
    d. Neither Machinist A nor B

27. Machinist A says that sodium-filled valves should not be ground. Machinist B says that sodium-filled valves require greater valve guide clearance than standard valves. Which machinist is correct?
    a. Machinist A only
    b. Machinist B only
    c. Both Machinist A and B
    d. Neither Machinist A nor B

28. Machinist A says that mushroomed valves should be replaced. Machinist B says that guttered valves should be replaced. Which machinist is correct?
    a. Machinist A only
    b. Machinist B only
    c. Both Machinist A and B
    d. Neither Machinist A nor B

29. Machinist A says that a dead-blow hammer should be used against the valve retainer before the valves are removed. Machinist B says that a valve spring should be compressed before the valve locks are removed. Which machinist is correct?
    a. Machinist A only
    b. Machinist B only
    c. Both Machinist A and B
    d. Neither Machinist A nor B

30. Valve springs should be tested for _____
    a. Free height
    b. Squareness
    c. Spring force
    d. All of the above

31. Machinist A says that damper springs should be removed before checking for spring force. Machinist B says that the spring force should be checked at the spring's free height dimension. Which machinist is correct?
    a. Machinist A only
    b. Machinist B only
    c. Both Machinist A and B
    d. Neither Machinist A nor B

32. Machinist A says that the valve stem should be squared and chamfered *before* the valve face is ground. Machinist B says that the stem height determines how much of the valve stem should be ground. Which machinist is correct?
    a. Machinist A only
    b. Machinist B only
    c. Both Machinist A and B
    d. Neither Machinist A nor B

33. Machinist A says that a 60-degree stone can be used to widen a 45-degree seat. Machinist B says that a 30-degree stone can be used to raise a 45-degree seat. Which machinist is correct?
    a. Machinist A only
    b. Machinist B only
    c. Both Machinist A and B
    d. Neither Machinist A nor B

34. A 45-degree seat has been ground and is too wide. Machinist A says to grind the seat using a 45-degree stone. Machinist B says to use both a 30-degree and a 60-degree stone to narrow the seat. Which machinist is correct?
    a. Machinist A only
    b. Machinist B only
    c. Both Machinist A and B
    d. Neither Machinist A nor B

35. A valve has been ground and has less than the specified margin. Machinist A says to grind a 1-degree interference angle on the valve face. Machinist B says to compensate by grinding the valve seat 1 degree less than specified by the manufacturer. Which machinist is correct?
    a. Machinist A only
    b. Machinist B only
    c. Both Machinist A and B
    d. Neither Machinist A nor B

36. Machinist A says that valves should be ground until the margin is at the minimum allowable thickness according to the manufacturer's specification. Machinist B says the thicker the margin left on a valve, the better. Which machinist is correct?
    a. Machinist A only
    b. Machinist B only
    c. Both Machinist A and B
    d. Neither Machinist A nor B

37. Machinist A says that a valve seat cutter should only be rotated clockwise. Machinist B says that a 60-degree cutter will raise and narrow a 45-degree valve seat. Which machinist is correct?
    a. Machinist A only
    b. Machinist B only
    c. Both Machinist A and B
    d. Neither Machinist A nor B

38. Machinist A says that a damaged or worn integral valve seat can be replaced with an insert valve seat. Machinist B says that a replacement valve seat insert should be welded in place. Which machinist is correct?
    a. Machinist A only
    b. Machinist B only
    c. Both Machinist A and B
    d. Neither Machinist A nor B

39. Machinist A says that valve stem height is the same as installed height. Machinist B says that installed height can be changed by grinding the tip of the valve stem. Which machinist is correct?
    a. Machinist A only
    b. Machinist B only
    c. Both Machinist A and B
    d. Neither Machinist A nor B

40. Machinist A says that the installation of valve stem seals of the O-ring type can be checked using a vacuum pump. Machinist B says that mineral spirits can be used in the combustion chamber to determine if the valve stem seals leak. Which machinist is correct?
    a. Machinist A only
    b. Machinist B only
    c. Both Machinist A and B
    d. Neither Machinist A nor B

Cylinder Block Specialist Sample ASE Certification Test

1. Machinist A says that all oil gallery plugs should be removed when the block is cleaned. Machinist B says that all core plugs should be removed before the block is cleaned. Which machinist is correct?
   a. Machinist A only
   b. Machinist B only
   c. Both Machinist A and B
   d. Neither Machinist A nor B

2. Machinist A says that aluminum blocks should only be cleaned using a blaster. Machinist B says that aluminum blocks can be cleaned in an oven. Which machinist is correct?
   a. Machinist A only
   b. Machinist B only
   c. Both Machinist A and B
   d. Neither Machinist A nor B

3. Before an engine block is machined, the machinist should first determine the minimum allowable

   _____ .
   a. Bore center
   b. Block deck height
   c. Pan rail length
   d. Saddle depth

4. Machinist A says that the main bearing caps should be installed and torqued to specification before the block is align honed. Machinist B says that the main bearing caps should be installed and torqued to specification before the block is bored. Which machinist is correct?
   a. Machinist A only
   b. Machinist B only

   c. Both Machinist A and B
   d. Neither Machinist A nor B

5. Machinist A says that the block deck should be machined before align boring is done. Machinist B says that the block deck should be machined before the cylinders are bored. Which machinist is correct?
   a. Machinist A only
   b. Machinist B only
   c. Both Machinist A and B
   d. Neither Machinist A nor B

6. When align honing, about how much material should be removed from the main bearing caps?
   a. 0.002 inch (0.05 millimeter)
   b. 0.004 inch (0.10 millimeter)
   c. 0.008 inch (0.20 millimeter)
   d. 0.010 inch (0.25 millimeter)

7. The surface finish of a cast-iron block deck should be _____ .
   a. 10 to 30 Ra
   b. 30 to 60 Ra
   c. 60 to 100 Ra
   d. 100 to 120 Ra

8. A cast-iron V-8 engine has two cylinders that are tapered 0.005 inch (0.13 millimeter). Machinist A says to hone all cylinders and use standard piston rings. Machinist B says to bore all cylinders to the same oversize measurement. Which machinist is correct?
   a. Machinist A only
   b. Machinist B only

  c. Both Machinist A and B
  d. Neither Machinist A nor B

9. A cast-iron V-8 block has one cylinder that is out of round 0.005 inch (0.13 millimeter). The other cylinders are worn just to the point of being 0.003 inch out of round. Machinist A says to sleeve the one cylinder. Machinist B says to bore the one cylinder. Which machinist is correct?
  a. Machinist A only
  b. Machinist B only
  c. Both Machinist A and B
  d. Neither Machinist A nor B

10. Machinist A says that an engine should be bored to the largest possible size. Machinist B says that 0.005 inch (0.13 millimeter) should be left for honing after the cylinder is bored. Which machinist is correct?
  a. Machinist A only
  b. Machinist B only
  c. Both Machinist A and B
  d. Neither Machinist A nor B

11. Machinist A says that torque plates should be attached to the block deck when cylinders are being bored. Machinist B says that torque plates should be used when honing cylinders. Which machinist is correct?
  a. Machinist A only
  b. Machinist B only
  c. Both Machinist A and B
  d. Neither Machinist A nor B

12. Machinist A says that a sizing hone can be used to straighten a wavy cylinder. Machinist B says that a flexible hone should be used after the cylinder has been bored. Which machinist is correct?
  a. Machinist A only
  b. Machinist B only
  c. Both Machinist A and B
  d. Neither Machinist A nor B

13. Machinist A says that a hone stone with a high grit number produces a rougher surface than does a hone with a lower grit number. Machinist B says that the stone grit recommended for use with moly piston rings is 150. Which machinist is correct?
  a. Machinist A only
  b. Machinist B only
  c. Both Machinist A and B
  d. Neither Machinist A nor B

14. A finished honed cylinder should have a maximum out-of-round and taper of _____ .
  a. 0.0005 inch (0.013 millimeter)
  b. 0.003 inch (0.096 millimeter)
  c. 0.005 inch (0.127 millimeter)
  d. 0.008 inch (0.20 millimeter)

15. After the block is machined, all bolt holes should be _____ .

  a. Enlarged to the next size with a tap
  b. Chamfered
  c. Beveled
  d. Plugged

16. Machinist A says that the piston ring grooves should be machined before installing replacement piston rings. Machinist B says that pistons can be knurled to be used in worn cylinders. Which machinist is correct?
  a. Machinist A only
  b. Machinist B only
  c. Both Machinist A and B
  d. Neither Machinist A nor B

17. A full-floating piston pin should have about how much clearance?
  a. No clearance—should be press fit
  b. No clearance—should be interference fit
  c. 0.0005 inch (0.013 millimeter)
  d. 0.002 inch (0.05 millimeter)

18. Machinist A says that all connecting rods should be checked for twist. Machinist B says that forged connecting rods cannot be straightened if bent. Which machinist is correct?
  a. Machinist A only
  b. Machinist B only
  c. Both Machinist A and B
  d. Neither Machinist A nor B

19. Machinist A says that powdered metal connecting rods can be reconditioned using the same method as that used for standard cast rods. Machinist B says that all connecting rods of the same engine can be interchanged. Which machinist is correct?
  a. Machinist A only
  b. Machinist B only
  c. Both Machinist A and B
  d. Neither Machinist A nor B

20. When the big end of a connecting rod is resized, _____ .
  a. The center-to-center dimension of the rod is lengthened slightly
  b. The center-to-center dimension of the rod is shortened slightly
  c. The diameter of the big end is reduced by about 0.003 inch (0.08 millimeter)
  d. The diameter of the big end is increased by about 0.003 inch (0.08 millimeter)

21. A connecting rod can be straightened by _____ .
  a. Bending the rod while it is cold
  b. Placing the rod in a hydraulic press
  c. Heating the rod and twisting it to be straight using a special tool
  d. Machining the cheeks of the small end and large end of the rod to be parallel to each other

22. Machinist A says that the connecting rods should be balanced to ensure a smoothly operating engine. Machinist B says that material should be removed from the heaviest connecting rod so that its weight matches that of the lightest rod in the engine. Which machinist is correct?
    a. Machinist A only
    b. Machinist B only
    c. Both Machinist A and B
    d. Neither Machinist A nor B

23. A forged crankshaft can be identified by _____ .
    a. Its heavy weight as compared with that of a cast crankshaft
    b. A thick parting line
    c. A thin parting line
    d. Its being harder than a cast crankshaft

24. Machinist A says that if your fingernail catches when rubbed across a bearing journal, the journal must be reground. Machinist B says that both the main and the rod bearing journal should be ground by the same amount to maintain proper crankshaft balance. Which machinist is correct?
    a. Machinist A only
    b. Machinist B only
    c. Both Machinist A and B
    d. Neither Machinist A nor B

25. Machinist A says that the crankshaft should be ground in the direction opposite that of normal rotation of the crankshaft. Machinist B says that the crankshaft should be polished after grinding, in the same direction as that of normal crankshaft rotation. Which machinist is correct?
    a. Machinist A only
    b. Machinist B only
    c. Both Machinist A and B
    d. Neither Machinist A nor B

26. Machinist A says that undersize crankshaft journals can be welded up, then ground to size. Machinist B says that the fillet area of the crankshaft can be shot blasted to increase the crankshaft strength. Which machinist is correct?
    a. Machinist A only
    b. Machinist B only
    c. Both Machinist A and B
    d. Neither Machinist A nor B

27. Crankshafts should be polished using what grit of polishing cloth?
    a. 150
    b. 180
    c. 220
    d. 320

28. What is attached to the crankshaft while it is being spin tested for balance?
    a. Bob weights
    b. External balance weights
    c. Internal balance weights
    d. Pistons with connecting rods

29. An externally balanced crankshaft can be changed to an internally balanced crankshaft by replacing the vibration damper.
    a. True
    b. False

30. Machinist A says that grinding the crankshaft relieves the stresses in the crankshaft. Machinist B says that blasting the fillet area of the journals with #320 steel shot relieves the stress. Which machinist is correct?
    a. Machinist A only
    b. Machinist B only
    c. Both Machinist A and B
    d. Neither Machinist A nor B

31. The recommended microinch surface finish for crankshaft journals is _____ .
    a. 10 to 14 Ra
    b. 18 to 32 Ra
    c. 45 to 72 Ra
    d. 60 to 100 Ra

32. The recommended microinch surface finish for the connecting rod big end is _____ .
    a. 10 to 14 Ra
    b. 18 to 32 Ra
    c. 45 to 72 Ra
    d. 60 to 100 Ra

33. The recommended microinch surface finish for a honed cylinder is _____ .
    a. 10 to 14 Ra
    b. 18 to 32 Ra
    c. 45 to 72 Ra
    d. 60 to 100 Ra

34. Machinist A says that the top of the cylinder bore should be chamfered after the cylinder is bored. Machinist B says that the bolt holes should be chamfered after the block has been decked. Which machinist is correct?
    a. Machinist A only
    b. Machinist B only
    c. Both Machinist A and B
    d. Neither Machinist A nor B

35. Machinist A says that the dowel pins should be removed from the block before the deck surface is machined. Machinist B says that plateau honing should be performed "dry" (without cooling lubricant). Which machinist is correct?
    a. Machinist A only
    b. Machinist B only
    c. Both Machinist A and B
    d. Neither Machinist A nor B

36. Machinist A says that all oil holes in the crankshaft should be cleaned with a brush and solvent after machining. Machinist B says that the rope seal

area of the crankshaft should be knurled after the crankshaft journals have been machined. Which machinist is correct?

    a. Machinist A only
    b. Machinist B only
    c. Both Machinist A and B
    d. Neither Machinist A nor B

37. Machinist A says that lifter bores should be cleaned and honed if necessary. Machinist B says that some lifter bores may be machined to be oversize at the factory. Which machinist is correct?

    a. Machinist A only
    b. Machinist B only
    c. Both Machinist A and B
    d. Neither Machinist A nor B

38. Connecting rods should not be heated to above
_____ .

    a. 250°F (120°C)
    b. 450°F (230°C)
    c. 650°F (340°C)
    d. 850°F (450°C)

39. Machinist A says that a cracked block may be repaired using a cylinder sleeve if the crack is located in the cylinder wall. Machinist B says that all cylinders should be bored to the same size in the same engine. Which machinist is correct?

    a. Machinist A only
    b. Machinist B only
    c. Both Machinist A and B
    d. Neither Machinist A nor B

40. Machinist A says that the cylinder hone should be stopped before it is removed from the finished cylinder. Machinist B says that the ridge at the top of the cylinder should be removed after the cylinder is honed. Which machinist is correct?

    a. Machinist A only
    b. Machinist B only
    c. Both Machinist A and B
    d. Neither Machinist A nor B

Engine Assembly Specialist Sample ASE Certification Test

1. After an engine block has been machined, it should be cleaned using _____ .
   a. WD-40 and a clean cloth
   b. A brush with soap and water
   c. Engine oil and a clean cloth
   d. Solvent spray and brake cleaner

2. Technician A says that oil gallery plugs have to be installed before core plugs are installed. Technician B says that the oil gallery passages should be cleaned after the block has been machined and before the gallery plugs are installed. Which technician is correct?
   a. Technician A only
   b. Technician B only
   c. Both Technician A and B
   d. Neither Technician A nor B

3. Technician A says that a bottoming tap should be used to clean all block threads before assembly of the engine begins. Technician B says that a taper tap should be used. Which technician is correct?
   a. Technician A only
   b. Technician B only
   c. Both Technician A and B
   d. Neither Technician A nor B

4. Technician A says that on a counter bore, convex plugs should be driven into the block until they stop. Technician B says that convex plugs should be installed with the convex side of the plug facing outward. Which technician is correct?
   a. Technician A only
   b. Technician B only

   c. Both Technician A and B
   d. Neither Technician A nor B

5. Technician A says that a cup-type plug should be installed flush with the block. Technician B says that a cup-type plug should be installed using sealant and pressed in to about 0.020 to 0.050 inch below the surface of the block. Which technician is correct?
   a. Technician A only
   b. Technician B only
   c. Both Technician A and B
   d. Neither Technician A nor B

6. Technician A says that dirt is the major cause of premature engine bearing failure. Technician B says that the main bearings should be installed and torqued to specification before the oil gallery plugs are installed. Which technician is correct?
   a. Technician A only
   b. Technician B only
   c. Both Technician A and B
   d. Neither Technician A nor B

7. A small-block Chevrolet V-8 engine is being assembled. Technician A says that the cam bearings should be installed before the crankshaft is installed. Technician B says that the oil gallery plugs must be installed before the cam bearings are installed. Which technician is correct?
   a. Technician A only
   b. Technician B only
   c. Both Technician A and B
   d. Neither Technician A nor B

8. Technician A says that cam bearing clearance must be determined and corrected, if necessary, before the camshaft is installed on an OHV-type engine. Technician B says that camshaft bearing clearance can be checked using plastic gauging material. Which technician is correct?
   a. Technician A only
   b. Technician B only
   c. Both Technician A and B
   d. Neither Technician A nor B

9. Technician A says that the crankshaft should be carefully inspected and measured after it is received back from the machine shop. Technician B says that the block should be carefully inspected and measured after it is received back from the machine shop. Which technician is correct?
   a. Technician A only
   b. Technician B only
   c. Both Technician A and B
   d. Neither Technician A nor B

10. Technician A says that both sides of the main bearing shells should be lubricated before installation. Technician B says that fingerprints can cause corrosion damage to bearings where they are touched by bare hands. Which technician is correct?
    a. Technician A only
    b. Technician B only
    c. Both Technician A and B
    d. Neither Technician A nor B

11. Technician A says that the crankshaft should be rotated for two complete revolutions after installing plastic gauging material when measuring main bearing oil clearance. Technician B says that crankshaft end play can be measured with a dial indicator (gauge). Which technician is correct?
    a. Technician A only
    b. Technician B only
    c. Both Technician A and B
    d. Neither Technician A nor B

12. Technician A says that plastic gauging material can be used to check crankshaft end play. Technician B says that plastic gauging material can be used to measure connecting rod bearing oil clearance. Which technician is correct?
    a. Technician A only
    b. Technician B only
    c. Both Technician A and B
    d. Neither Technician A nor B

13. Typical engine bearing oil clearance is
    _____ .
    a. 0.001 to 0.003 inch (0.025 to 0.076 millimeter)
    b. 0.010 to 0.030 inch (0.25 to 0.76 millimeter)
    c. 0.020 to 0.040 inch (0.51 to 1.02 millimeters)
    d. 0.060 to 0.080 inch (1.52 to 2.03 millimeters)

14. Technician A says that the rear main seal should be installed before checking for correct oil clearances. Technician B says that the main bearing caps must be torqued to specification when checking main bearing oil clearance using plastic gauging material. Which technician is correct?
    a. Technician A only
    b. Technician B only
    c. Both Technician A and B
    d. Neither Technician A nor B

15. Technician A says that the tang on the bearing shell should align with the slot in the bearing support. Technician B says that the tang is installed opposite to the slot in some engines. Which technician is correct?
    a. Technician A only
    b. Technician B only
    c. Both Technician A and B
    d. Neither Technician A nor B

16. Technician A says that a feeler (thickness) gauge can be used to measure thrust bearing clearance. Technician B says that oversize main thrust bearings may be available for engines on which the thrust bearing clearance is too great. Which technician is correct?
    a. Technician A only
    b. Technician B only
    c. Both Technician A and B
    d. Neither Technician A nor B

17. Technician A says that the vibration damper should be driven onto the nose of the crankshaft. Technician B says that some vibration dampers simply slip on the crankshaft. Which technician is correct?
    a. Technician A only
    b. Technician B only
    c. Both Technician A and B
    d. Neither Technician A nor B

18. Technician A says that each piston should be selectively fitted to each cylinder. Technician B says that a strip feeler (thickness) gauge should be used to determine proper piston-to-cylinder clearance. Which technician is correct?
    a. Technician A only
    b. Technician B only
    c. Both Technician A and B
    d. Neither Technician A nor B

19. The clearance between the piston and the cylinder is too great. Technician A says that the piston could be knurled. Technician B says that the cylinder could be honed to provide the proper clearance. Which technician is correct?
    a. Technician A only
    b. Technician B only
    c. Both Technician A and B
    d. Neither Technician A nor B

20. Two technicians are discussing piston ring end gap. Technician A says that if the gap is too great, excessive blowby can occur. Technician B says that if the gap is too small, the ring could break. Which technician is correct?
    a. Technician A only
    b. Technician B only
    c. Both Technician A and B
    d. Neither Technician A nor B

21. Typical piston ring end gap is _____ .
    a. 0.001 to 0.003 inch
    b. 0.100 to 0.300 inch
    c. 0.004 inch per inch of bore diameter
    d. 0.010 inch per inch of stroke length

22. Two technicians are discussing piston installation. Technician A says that the cylinder should be wiped with a lintless cloth and coated with a film of oil. Technician B says that the connecting rod bearing should be installed on the connecting rod before the piston is installed in the cylinder. Which technician is correct?
    a. Technician A only
    b. Technician B only
    c. Both Technician A and B
    d. Neither Technician A nor B

23. Technician A says that pistons should be installed with the notch on the top of the piston head facing the front of the engine. Technician B says that the valve reliefs should be closest to the lifter valley on V-type OHC engines. Which technician is correct?
    a. Technician A only
    b. Technician B only
    c. Both Technician A and B
    d. Neither Technician A nor B

24. Technician A says that the connecting rod can be installed on the piston pin facing in either direction. Technician B says that the piston pin should be lubricated before the piston-rod assembly is installed. Which technician is correct?
    a. Technician A only
    b. Technician B only
    c. Both Technician A and B
    d. Neither Technician A nor B

25. When an engine is being assembled, proper clearance should be maintained between the piston skirt and the crankshaft counterweight. Most manufacturers recommend a minimum clearance of

    _____ .
    a. 0.010 inch (0.25 millimeter)
    b. 0.025 inch (0.64 millimeter)
    c. 0.040 inch (1.02 millimeters)
    d. 0.060 inch (1.52 millimeters)

26. Two technicians are discussing connecting rod side clearance. Technician A says that if the clearance is too great, the crankshaft may require replacement. Technician B says that excessive side clearance may decrease oil pressure when the engine is running. Which technician is correct?
    a. Technician A only
    b. Technician B only
    c. Both Technician A and B
    d. Neither Technician A nor B

27. Technician A says that connecting rod side clearance can be measured using plastic gauging material. Technician B says that connecting rod side clearance can be measured with a micrometer. Which technician is correct?
    a. Technician A only
    b. Technician B only
    c. Both Technician A and B
    d. Neither Technician A nor B

28. Technician A says that the crankshaft should be rotated after the pistons are installed. Technician B says that the turning torque should be measured after the pistons have been installed. Which technician is correct?
    a. Technician A only
    b. Technician B only
    c. Both Technician A and B
    d. Neither Technician A nor B

29. Two technicians are discussing assembling an engine that has had both the cylinder head and the block deck machined. Technician A says that a thicker head gasket or a shim gasket can be used to compensate for the machining. Technician B says that longer pushrods should be used. Which technician is correct?
    a. Technician A only
    b. Technician B only
    c. Both Technician A and B
    d. Neither Technician A nor B

30. Two technicians are discussing head gaskets. Technician A says that all head gaskets require that the head bolts be retorqued after the engine has been run. Technician B says that the torque specifications for head bolts are for dry (nonlubricated) threads. Which technician is correct?
    a. Technician A only
    b. Technician B only
    c. Both Technician A and B
    d. Neither Technician A nor B

31. Technician A says that sealer should be used on head bolts that go into the cooling system. Technician B says that oil should be squirted into "dry" bolt holes before head bolts are installed. Which technician is correct?
    a. Technician A only
    b. Technician B only
    c. Both Technician A and B
    d. Neither Technician A nor B

32. Two technicians are discussing the tightening pro-
    cedure for cylinder head bolts. Technician A says
    that the specified torque should be applied to each
    bolt in the specified sequence. Technician B says
    that the head bolt tightening sequence should be
    repeated three times, increasing the amount of
    torque on the bolts each time and reaching the
    specified torque on the final (third) repetition.
    Which technician is correct?
    a. Technician A only
    b. Technician B only
    c. Both Technician A and B
    d. Neither Technician A nor B

33. Two technicians are discussing the torque-to-yield
    type of head bolts. Technician A says that many
    manufacturers specify the use of new head bolts
    when the engine is assembled. Technician B says
    that the bolt should be rotated a specified number
    of degrees after the bolt has been tightened to a
    torque specification. Which technician is correct?
    a. Technician A only
    b. Technician B only
    c. Both Technician A and B
    d. Neither Technician A nor B

34. A gear-driven camshaft becomes locked up and
    will not rotate after the thrust plate has been
    torqued to specifications. Technician A says that a
    spacer may be missing. Technician B says that the
    camshaft has not been timed correctly with the
    crankshaft. Which technician is correct?
    a. Technician A only
    b. Technician B only
    c. Both Technician A and B
    d. Neither Technician A nor B

35. Technician A says that all hydraulic valve lifters
    should be "pumped up" in a container of engine oil
    before installation. Technician B says that the bot-
    tom of flat lifters should be covered with extreme
    pressure-type lubricant before being installed.
    Which technician is correct?
    a. Technician A only
    b. Technician B only
    c. Both Technician A and B
    d. Neither Technician A nor B

36. Technician A says that valve lash (clearance)
    should be adjusted after the engine is started.
    Technician B says that all hydraulic lifters are self-
    adjusting and do not require any adjustment.
    Which technician is correct?
    a. Technician A only
    b. Technician B only
    c. Both Technician A and B
    d. Neither Technician A nor B

37. A type of assembly sealant that is used to fill voids
    or potential openings and that cures in the pres-
    ence of moisture is called _____ .
    a. RTV silicone
    b. Anaerobic
    c. Antiseize
    d. Contact adhesive

38. A type of assembly sealant that is used between
    two machined surfaces and that cures in the ab-
    sence of air is called _____ .
    a. RTV silicone
    b. Anaerobic
    c. Antiseize
    d. Contact adhesive

39. Technician A says that the distance between the oil
    pickup screen and the bottom of the oil pan should
    be measured. Technician B says that the distance
    between the oil pickup screen and the bottom of
    the oil pan should be about 0.25 inch (6 millime-
    ters). Which technician is correct?
    a. Technician A only
    b. Technician B only
    c. Both Technician A and B
    d. Neither Technician A nor B

40. Technician A says that the oil pump should be ro-
    tated to force oil through the engine before the en-
    gine is started. Technician B says that the engine
    should be started and kept running at a fast idle to
    help break in a flat lifter type of camshaft. Which
    technician is correct?
    a. Technician A only
    b. Technician B only
    c. Both Technician A and B
    d. Neither Technician A nor B

Fraction/Decimal/ Millimeter Conversion Chart

(1 mm = 0.03937″) (0.001″ = 0.0254 mm)					
Fractions	**Decimals**	**Millimeters**	**Fractions**	**Decimals**	**Millimeters**
1/64	0.015625	0.397	23/64	0.359375	9.128
1/32	0.03125	0.794	3/8	0.3750	9.525
3/64	0.046875	1.191	25/64	0.390625	9.922
1/16	0.0625	1.588	13/32	0.40625	10.319
5/64	0.078125	1.984	27/64	0.421875	10.716
3/32	0.09375	2.381	7/16	0.4375	11.113
7/64	0.109375	2.7780	29/64	0.453125	11.509
1/8	0.1250	3.175	15/32	0.46875	11.906
9/64	0.140625	3.572	31/64	0.484375	12.303
5/32	0.15625	3.969	1/2	0.5000	12.700
11/64	0.171875	4.366	33/64	0.515625	13.097
3/16	0.1875	4.763	17/32	0.53125	13.494
13/64	0.203125	5.159	35/64	0.546875	13.891
7/32	0.21875	5.556	9/16	0.5625	14.288
15/64	0.234375	5.953	37/64	0.578125	14.684
1/4	0.2500	6.350	19/32	0.59375	15.081
17/64	0.265625	6.747	39/64	0.609375	15.478
9/32	0.28125	7.144	5/8	0.6250	15.875
19/64	0.296875	7.541	41/64	0.640625	16.272
5/16	0.3125	7.938	21/32	0.65625	16.669
21/64	0.328125	8.334	43/64	0.671875	17.066
11/32	0.34375	8.731	11/16	0.6875	17.463

Fractions	Decimals	Millimeters	Fractions	Decimals	Millimeters
45/64	0.703125	17.859	55/64	0.859375	21.828
23/32	0.71875	18.256	7/8	0.8750	22.225
47/64	0.734375	18.653	57/64	0.890625	22.622
3/4	0.7500	19.050	29/32	0.90625	23.019
49/64	0.765625	19.447	59/64	0.921875	23.416
25/32	0.78125	19.844	15/16	0.9375	23.813
51/64	0.796875	20.241	61/64	0.953125	24.209
13/16	0.8125	20.638	31/32	0.96875	24.606
53/64	0.828125	21.034	63/64	0.984375	25.003
27/32	0.84375	21.431	1	1.00	25.400

Decimal Millimeters to Decimal Inches Chart

Millimeters	Inches
0.1	0.0039
0.2	0.0079
0.3	0.0118
0.4	0.0157
0.5	0.0197
0.6	0.0236
0.7	0.0276
0.8	0.0315
0.9	0.0354
1	0.0394

Fraction/Decimal Equivalents

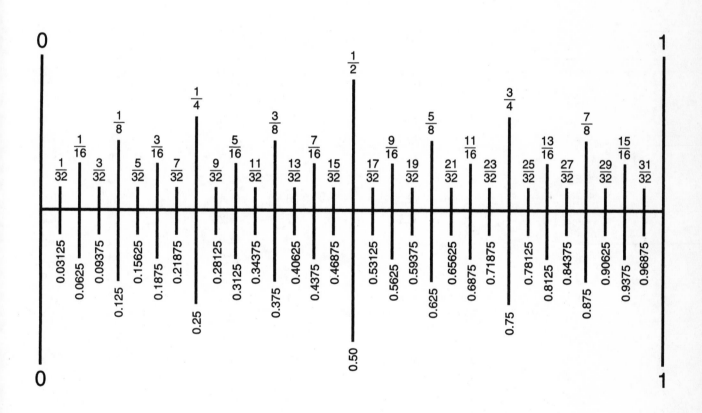

Newton-Meter to Pound-Feet Conversion Chart

(1 N-m = 0.074 lb-ft)							
N-m	Lb-ft	N-m	Lb-ft	N-m	Lb-ft	N-m	Lb-ft
1	0.74	26	19.2	51	37.7	76	56.2
2	1.5	27	20.0	52	38.5	77	57.0
3	2.2	28	20.7	53	39.2	78	57.7
4	3.0	29	21.5	54	40.0	79	58.5
5	3.7	30	22.2	55	40.7	80	59.2
6	4.4	31	22.9	56	41.4	81	59.9
7	5.2	32	23.7	57	42.2	82	60.7
8	5.9	33	24.4	58	42.9	83	61.4
9	6.7	34	25.2	59	43.7	84	62.2
10	7.4	35	25.9	60	44.4	85	62.9
11	8.1	36	26.6	61	45.1	86	63.6
12	8.9	37	27.4	62	45.9	87	64.4
13	9.6	38	28.1	63	46.6	88	65.1
14	10.4	39	28.9	64	47.4	89	65.9
15	11.1	40	29.6	65	48.1	90	66.6
16	11.8	41	30.3	66	48.8	91	67.3
17	12.6	42	31.1	67	49.6	92	68.1
18	13.3	43	31.8	68	50.3	93	68.8
19	14.1	44	32.6	69	51.0	94	69.6
20	14.8	45	33.3	70	51.8	95	70.3
21	15.5	46	34.0	71	52.5	96	71.0
22	16.3	47	34.8	72	53.3	97	71.8
23	17.0	48	35.5	73	54.0	98	72.5
24	17.8	49	36.3	74	54.8	99	73.3
25	18.5	50	37.0	75	55.5	100	74.0

Pound-Feet to Newton-Meter Conversion Chart

(1 lb-ft = 1.4 N-m)							
Lb-ft	**N-m**	**Lb-ft**	**N-m**	**Lb-ft**	**N-m**	**Lb-ft**	**N-m**
1	1.4	26	36.4	51	71.4	76	106.4
2	2.8	27	37.8	52	72.8	77	107.8
3	4.2	28	39.2	53	74.2	78	109.2
4	5.6	29	40.6	54	75.6	79	110.6
5	7.0	30	42.0	55	77.0	80	112.0
6	8.4	31	43.4	56	78.4	81	113.4
7	9.8	32	44.8	57	79.8	82	114.8
8	11.2	33	46.2	58	81.2	83	116.2
9	12.6	34	47.6	59	82.6	84	117.6
10	14.0	35	49.0	60	84.0	85	119.0
11	15.4	36	50.4	61	85.4	86	120.4
12	16.8	37	51.8	62	86.8	87	121.8
13	18.2	38	53.2	63	88.2	88	123.2
14	19.6	39	54.6	64	89.6	89	124.6
15	21.0	40	56.0	65	91.0	90	126.0
16	22.4	41	57.4	66	92.4	91	127.4
17	23.8	42	58.8	67	93.8	92	128.8
18	25.2	43	60.2	68	95.2	93	130.2
19	26.6	44	61.6	69	96.6	94	131.6
20	28.0	45	63.0	70	98.0	95	133.0
21	29.4	46	64.4	71	99.4	96	134.4
22	30.8	47	65.8	72	100.8	97	135.8
23	32.2	48	67.2	73	102.2	98	137.2
24	33.6	49	68.6	74	103.6	99	138.6
25	35.0	50	70.0	75	105.0	100	140.0

Celsius Degrees to Fahrenheit Degrees Conversion Chart

Celsius °	Fahrenheit °
−40°	−40°
−35°	−31°
−30°	−22°
−25°	−13°
−20°	−4°
−15°	5°
−10°	14°
15°	23°
0°	32°
5°	41°
10°	50°
15°	59°
20°	68°
25°	77°
30°	86°
35°	95°
40°	104°
50°	122°
60°	140°
70°	158°
80°	176°
90°	194°
100°	212°
110°	230°
120°	248°
130°	266°
140°	284°

Timing Belt Replacement Guide

(The number in parentheses represents a footnote at the end of the vehicle listing.)

Vehicle Manufacturer	Engine	Manufacturers' Recommended Replacement Intervals	Interference?	Engine Damage if Belt Breaks? (22)
ACURA	1.6L	(1)	Yes	Yes
	1.7L, 2.5L & 2.7L V-6	90,000 miles or 72 months	Yes	Yes
	2.2L	105,000 miles or 84 months	Yes	Yes
	1.8L, 2.5L 5-Cyl	(2)	Yes	Yes
	3.2L V-6 (Legend & 3.2TL)	(2)	Yes	Yes
	3.0L, 3.5L	(3)	Yes	Yes
	3.2L, 3.5L (SLX)	60,000 miles	Yes	Yes
ALFA ROMEO	3.0L	(1)	No	No
AMERICAN MOTORS	2.0L	(1)	No	No
AUDI	Gasoline Engines	(1)	No	No
	Diesel Engines	(1)	Yes	Yes
BMW	2.5L, 2.7L	60,000 miles (4)	Yes	Yes
CHRYSLER	1.4L, 1.5L, 1.6L SOHC and DOHC	60,000 miles	Yes	Yes
	1.8L, 3.0L SOHC	(5)	No	No
	3.0L DOHC	(5)	Yes	Yes
	1.7L	(1)	No	No
	2.0L, 2.4L SOHC	(6)	No	No
	2.0L DOHC	(6)	Yes	Yes
	2.2L SOHC, 2.5L	90,000 miles	No	No

Vehicle Manufacturer	Engine	Manufacturers' Recommended Replacement Intervals	Interference?	Engine Damage if Belt Breaks? (22)
	2.2L DOHC	90,000 miles	Yes	Yes
	2.3L Diesel	50,000 miles	Yes	Yes
	2.4L DOHC	(7)	Yes	Yes
	2.5L V-6	(8)	No	No
	3.5L	105,000 miles	No	No
Daewoo	1.6L, 2.0L	(1)	No	No
Daihatsu	1.0L	(9)	Yes	Yes
	1.3L	60,000 miles	Yes	Yes
Fiat	1.3L (Air Pump & Camshaft)	36,000 miles (10)	Yes	Yes
	1.5L, 2.0L	30,000 miles (10)	Yes	Yes
	1.6L	25,000 miles or 24 months (10)	Yes	Yes
	1.8L (1974–1977)	25,000 miles or 24 months (10)	Yes	Yes
	1.8L (1978)	25,000 miles (10)	Yes	Yes
Ford	1.3L, 1.6L SOHC (Ford)	60,000 miles	Yes	Yes
	1.6L SOHC (Mazda) & 1.6L DOHC, 1.8L	60,000 miles	No	No
	1.9L, 2.0L DOHC Gasoline (except Probe)	(1)	No	No
	2.0L SOHC Gasoline (except 1997 Escort/Tracer)	100,000 miles	No	No
	2.0L SOHC Gasoline (1997 Escort/Tracer)	(1)	No	No
	2.0L DOHC Gasoline (Probe), 2.5L V-6	60,000 miles	No	No
	2.2L	60,000 miles	Yes	Yes
	2.0L Diesel, 2.3L Diesel (Camshaft and Balance Shaft Belts)	(1)	Yes	Yes
	2.3L SOHC Gasoline	(1)	No	No
	3.0L & 3.2L SHO	100,000 miles	No	No
General Motors	1.0L, 1.4L, 1.6L, 1.8L Gasoline	(1)	No	No
	1.0L Diesel	(1)	Yes	Yes

Vehicle Manufacturer	Engine	Manufacturers' Recommended Replacement Intervals	Interference?	Engine Damage if Belt Breaks? (22)
	2.0L, 2.3L	(1)	No	No
	3.0L V-6	(1)	Yes	Yes
	1.5L, 2.2L Diesel	60,000 miles	Yes	Yes
	3.4L DOHC	60,000 miles	No	No
GEO	1.0L, 1.6L SOHC (Tracker)	(11)	No	No
	1.3L	100,000 miles	No	No
	1.5L	60,000 miles	Yes	Yes
	1.6L DOHC (Storm)	(1)	No	No
	1.6L SOHC & DOHC (Prizm), 1.8L DOHC, 1993 & Prior	60,000 miles	Yes	Yes
	1.6L SOHC & DOHC (Prizm)	(1)	No	No
	1.8L DOHC (Prizm) 1994 and Later	(1)	No	No
	1.8L DOHC (Storm) 1994 & Later	(1)	Yes	Yes
HONDA	1.2L, 1.3L, 1.8L	(1)	Yes	Yes
	1.5L, 1.6L, 2.0L DOHC	(12)	Yes	Yes
	2.0L SOHC	(12)	No	No
	2.1L, 2.3L	90,000 miles or 72 months	Yes	Yes
	2.2L SOHC & DOHC, 2.7L	(12)		
	2.6L	60,000 miles	Yes	Yes
	3.2L	60,000 miles	No	No
HYUNDAI	1.5L, 1.6L, 1.8L, 2.0L, 2.4L	60,000 miles	Yes	Yes
	3.0L (1995 & Prior)	60,000 miles	No	No
	1.5L, 1.6L, 1.8L, 2.0L, 2.4L	(1)	Yes	Yes
	3.0L (1996 & Later)	(1)	No	No
INFINITI	3.0L (1993 & Prior)	60,000 miles	Yes	Yes
	3.0L (1994 & Later)	105,000 miles	Yes	Yes
	3.3L	105,000 miles	Yes	Yes

Vehicle Manufacturer	Engine	Manufacturers' Recommended Replacement Intervals	Interference?	Engine Damage if Belt Breaks? (22)
ISUZU	1.5L, 1.6L DOHC, 1.8L DOHC Gasoline	60,000 miles	Yes	Yes
	1.6L SOHC	60,000 miles	No	No
	1.8L Diesel, 2.0L, 2.2L Diesel, 2.3L, 2.6L	60,000 miles	Yes	Yes
	3.2L, 3.5L	60,000 miles	Yes	Yes
JEEP	2.0L	(1)	No	No
KIA	1.6L DOHC, 1.8L DOHC, 2.0L DOHC	(13)	Yes	Yes
	1.6L SOHC, 2.0L SOHC	(13)	No	No
LANCIA	1.8L	25,000 miles	Yes	Yes
LEXUS	2.5L	60,000 miles	No	No
	3.0L Inline, 3.0L V-6, 4.0L V-8	(21)	No	No
MAZDA	1.6L SOHC & DOHC, 1.8L SOHC & DOHC 4-Cyl	60,000 miles	No	No
	1.8L V-6	105,000 miles	No	No
	2.0L SOHC	60,000 miles	No	No
	2.0L DOHC, 2.2L	60,000 miles	Yes	Yes
	2.0L Diesel (Camshaft & Injection Pump)	100,000 miles	Yes	Yes
	2.3L (B2300)	(1)	No	No
	2.3L V-6, 2.5L	60,000 miles	No	No
	3.0L SOHC & DOHC	60,000 miles	Yes	Yes
MITSUBISHI	1.5L, 1.6L SOHC & DOHC, 1.8L, 2.0L DOHC	(5)	Yes	Yes
	1.8L & 2.0L SOHC, 2.4L SOHC, 3.0L SOHC	(5)	No	No
	2.3L Diesel, 2.4L DOHC, & 3.0L DOHC, 3.5L	(5)	Yes	Yes
NISSAN	1.5L	(1)	Yes	Yes
	1.6L SOHC, 1.7L Diesel, 2.0L, 3.0L SOHC	(14)	Yes	Yes
	1.6L DOHC, 1.8L DOHC	60,000 miles	Yes	Yes

Vehicle Manufacturer	Engine	Manufacturers' Recommended Replacement Intervals	Interference?	Engine Damage if Belt Breaks? (22)
	3.0L DOHC	(15)	Yes	Yes
	3.3L	105,000 miles	Yes	Yes
PEUGEOT	1.9L	(1)	No	No
	2.2L	(1)	Yes	Yes
PORSCHE	2.0L, 2.5L, 2.7L, 3.0L	(16)	Yes	Yes
	4.5L, 4.7L, 5.0L, 5.4L	(17)	Yes	Yes
RENAULT	1.7L	(1)	Yes	Yes
	2.2L	(1)	No	No
SAAB	2.5L & 3.0L	(1)	Yes	Yes
STERLING	2.5L & 2.7L	(1)	Yes	Yes
SUBARU	1.2L, 2.2L, 2.7L, 3.3L, 1.8L (Impreza)	60,000 miles	No	No
	1.8L (except Impreza)	52,000 miles	No	No
SUZUKI	1.3L SOHC, 1.6L (8-Valve)	(18)	No	No
	1.3L DOHC, 1.6L (16-Valve)	(18)	Yes	Yes
TOYOTA	1.5L, 1.6L DOHC	(21)	Yes	Yes
	1.6L SOHC, 1.8L Gasoline	(21)	No	No
	1.8L Diesel, 2.2L Diesel	60,000 miles	Yes	Yes
	2.5L, 2.8L	60,000 miles	No	No
	2.0L, 2.2L Gasoline, 3.0L Inline, 3.0L V-6	(21)	No	No
	2.4L Diesel	100,000 miles	Yes	Yes
	3.4L	(1)	No	No
VOLKSWAGEN	Gasoline Engine	(1)	No	No
	Diesel Engine	(1)	Yes	Yes
VOLVO	2.1L, 2.3L (B23), 2.3L 4-Cyl (B230, B230F & B230FT)	(19)	Yes	Yes
	2.3L 4-Cyl (B234)	50,000 miles	Yes	Yes
	2.3L 5-Cyl, 2.4L 5-Cyl Gasoline	70,000 miles	Yes	Yes
	2.9L	70,000 miles	No	No
YUGO	1.1L & 1.3L	(20)	Yes	Yes

(1) Manufacturer does not recommend a specific maintenance interval.

(2) On 1996 and prior models, 90,000 miles or 72 months; on 1997 models, under normal conditions, 105,000 miles or 84 months (60,000 miles if the vehicle is operated at ambient temperatures under −20°F or above 110°F).

(3) Under normal conditions, 105,000 miles or 84 months (60,000 miles if the vehicle is operated at ambient temperatures under −20°F or above 110°F).

(4) When the tensioner roller has been released, regardless of belt age or condition. After replacement, a label indicating the mileage and date that service has been performed should be affixed to the cylinder head cover.

(5) On 1994 and prior models, 60,000 miles; on 1995 to 1997 California models, 60,000 miles is recommended but not required; on all 1995 to 1997 models, at 100,000 miles (if not previously replaced).

(6) 1994 and prior models, intervals of 60,000 miles; on 1995 to 1997 Breeze, Cirrus, Stratus, and Sebring Convertible models, 105,000-mile intervals is recommended but not required. On Avenger and Sebring (except convertible), Summit Wagon Talon California models, 60,000-mile intervals is recommended but not required. On all 1995 to 1997 Avenger, Sebring (except convertible), Summit Wagon, and Talon models, at 100,000 miles (if not previously replaced).

(7) On California models, 60,000-mile intervals is recommended but not required; on all models, replace at 100,000 miles (if not previously replaced).

(8) On Breeze, Cirrus, Stratus, and Sebring Convertible models, 105,000-mile intervals is recommended but not required; on Avenger and Sebring California models (except convertible), 60,000-mile intervals is recommended but not required; on Avenger and Sebring models (except convertible), at 100,000 miles (if not previously replaced).

(9) 60,000-mile intervals if vehicle operates under extensive idling, low-speed driving for long distances, on dusty, muddy, or rough roads.

(10) Timing belt must be replaced any time tension is relieved.

(11) On 1996 and prior models, inspect and adjust belt at 30,000 and 60,000 miles; replace timing belt at 60,000 miles. On 1996 and later models, inspect and adjust belt at 30,000- and 60,000-mile intervals; replace timing belt at 100,000 miles.

(12) On 1989 and prior models, manufacturer does not recommend a specific interval; on 1990 to 1996 models, 90,000-mile intervals or 72 months; on 1997 models, under normal conditions, at intervals of 105,000 miles or 84 months (60,000-mile intervals if operated at ambient temperatures under −20°F or above 110°F).

(13) On non-California models, 60,000-mile intervals; on California models, inspect at 60,000-mile intervals and replace at 90,000-mile intervals.

(14) On 1985 and prior models, manufacturer does not recommend a specific interval; on 1986 to 1993 models, 60,000-mile intervals; on 1994 to 1997 and later models, 105,000-mile intervals.

(15) On early 1993 and prior models, 60,000-mile intervals; on late 1993 and later models less turbo, 105,000-mile intervals; on late 1993 and later models with turbo, 60,000-mile intervals.

(16) Under normal operation, 45,000-mile intervals; check tension at 2000 miles, then every 15,000 miles.

(17) Under normal operation, 60,000-mile intervals; check tension at 2000 miles, then every 15,000 miles.

(18) On 1994 and prior models, manufacturer does not recommend a specific interval; on 1995 to 1997 California models, 60,000-mile intervals is recommended but not required; on all 1995 to 1997 models, at 100,000 miles (if not previously replaced).

(19) On 1985 and prior models, 40,000-mile intervals; 1986 to 1994 and later models, 50,000-mile intervals; 1995 and later models, 100,000-mile intervals.

(20) Inspect every 15,000 miles.

(21) On 1993 and prior models, replace at 60,000-mile intervals; on 1994 and later models, manufacturer does not recommend a specific maintenance interval.

(22) Always check for engine damage that can still occur in the event of a timing belt failure even if "no" is listed.

Answers to Even-Numbered ASE Certification-Type Questions

Glossary

4 × 2 The term used to describe a two-wheel-drive truck. The "4" indicates the number of wheels of the vehicle and the "2" indicates the number of wheels that are driven by the engine.

4 × 4 The term used to describe a four-wheel-drive vehicle. The first "4" indicates the number of wheels of the vehicle and the second "4" indicates the number of wheels that are driven by the engine.

AC generator Produces AC voltage but the output is rectified by diodes to produce DC voltage. Also called an *alternator*.

Additive A substance added in small amounts to something, such as gasoline.

AIR Air-injection reaction emission control system.

Alloy A metal that contains one or more other elements usually added to increase strength or give the base metal important properties.

Alternating current (AC) An electrical signal in which current and voltage vary in a repeating sequence.

Alternator An electric generator that produces alternating current but is rectified to DC current by diodes. Also called an *AC generator*.

Altitude Elevation as measured in relationship to the earth's surface at sea level.

Ambient air temperature The temperature of the air surrounding an object.

Ammeter An electrical test instrument used to measure amperes (unit of the amount of current flow).

Ampere The unit of the amount of current flow. Named for André Ampère (1775–1836).

Amplitude The difference between the highest and lowest level of a waveform.

Analog A type of dash instrument that indicates values by use of the movement of a needle or similar device. An analog signal is continuous and variable.

ANSI American National Standards Institute.

Antiknock index A measure of a fuel's ability to resist engine knock; stated as a number called the octane number.

Antimony A metal added to nonmaintenance-free or hybrid battery grids to add strength.

API American Petroleum Institute.

APRA Automotive Parts Rebuilders Association.

Aramid Generic name for aromatic polyamide fibers developed in 1972. Kevlar is the Dupont brand name for aramid.

Armature The rotating unit inside a DC generator or starter consisting of a series of coils of insulating wire wound around a laminated iron core.

ASE Abbreviation for the National Institute for Automotive Service Excellence, a nonprofit organization for the testing and certification of vehicle service technicians.

ASTM American Society for Testing Materials.

ATC After top center.

ATDC After top dead center.

Atmospheric pressure Pressure exerted by the atmosphere on all things based on the weight of the air.

Atom The smallest unit of matter that still retains its separate unique characteristic.

Atomize To reduce or separate into fine or minute particles.

AWG American wire gauge system.

Axial In line along with the axis or centerline of a part or component. Axial play in a ball joint means looseness in the same axis as the ball joint stud.

Back pressure The exhaust system's resistance to flow. Measured in pounds per square inch (psi).

Baffle A plate or shield used to direct the flow of a liquid or gas.

Bakelite A brand name of the Union Carbide Company for phenolformaldehyde resin plastic.

Balance shaft   A shaft in the engine that is designed so that, as it rotates, it reduces or cancels out any vibration.

Ballast resistor   A variable resistor used to control the primary ignition current through the coil.

Barometric pressure   The measure of atmospheric pressure, in inches of mercury (Hg), that reflects altitude and weather conditions.

Barrel shape   A brake drum having a frictional surface that is larger in the center than at the open end or the rear of the drum.

Battery   A chemical device that produces a voltage from two dissimilar metals submerged in an electrolyte.

Battery electrical drain test   A test to determine if a component or circuit is draining the battery with everything electrical turned off.

Bell housing   A bell-shape housing attached between the engine and the transmission.

Bendix drive   An inertia-type starter engagement mechanism not used on vehicles since the early 1960s.

Blowby gases   Combustion gases that leak past the piston rings into the crankcase during the compression and combustion strokes of the engine.

Boost   An increase in air pressure above atmospheric; measured in pounds per square inch (psi).

Bottom dead center (BDC)   The lowest position in the cylinder that a piston can travel without reversing its direction.

Brinelling   A type of mechanical failure used to describe a dent in metal such as what occurs when a shock load is applied to a bearing. Named after Johann A. Brinell, a Swedish engineer.

British thermal unit (Btu)   The amount of heat required to raise 1 pound of water 1°F at sea level.

Brushes   A copper or carbon conductor used to transfer electrical current from or to a revolving electrical part such as that used in an electrical motor or generator.

BTDC   Before top dead center.

Buffer   A component or circuit used to reduce the interaction between two electronic circuits.

CAFE   Corporate average fuel economy.

Calcium   A metallic chemical element added to the grids of a maintenance-free battery to increase strength.

Carbon dioxide (CO_2)   A colorless, odorless, nonflammable gas produced during the combustion process. The amount (%) in the exhaust can be used to evaluate the efficiency of an engine's combustion process.

Carbon monoxide (CO)   A colorless, odorless, and highly poisonous gas. It is formed by the incomplete combustion of gasoline.

Carbon pile   An electrical test instrument used to provide an electrical load for testing batteries and the charging circuit.

Catalytic converter   An emission control device located in the exhaust system that changes HC and CO into harmless H_2O and CO_2. In a three-way catalyst, NO_x is also divided into harmless nitrogen (N_2) and oxygen (O_2).

Cell   A group of negative and positive plates capable of producing 2.1 V.

CEMF   Counterelectromotive force.

Charging circuit   Electrical components and connections necessary to keep a battery fully charged.

Chassis   The frame, suspension, steering, and machinery of a motor vehicle.

Check engine light   A dashboard warning light that is controlled by the vehicle computer; also called the *malfunction indicator light* or *MIL*.

CO   Carbon monoxide.

Coefficient of friction   A measure of the amount of friction, usually in increments from 0 to 1. A low number (0.3) indicates low friction and a high number (0.9) indicates high friction.

Coil-on-plug ignition system   An ignition system without a distributor where each spark plug has its own ignition coil.

Cold cranking amperes (CCA)   The rating of a battery's ability to provide battery voltage during cold-weather operation.

Combustion   The rapid burning of the air-fuel mixture in the engine cylinders.

Combustion chamber   The space left within the cylinder when the piston is at the top of its combustion chamber.

Commutator   The name for the copper segments of the armature of a starter or DC generator.

Compression ratio   The ratio of the volume in the engine cylinder with the piston at bottom dead center (BDC) to the volume at top dead center (TDC).

Computer   Any device that can perform high-speed mathematical or logical calculations.

Concentric   Perfectly round; the relationship of two round parts on the same center.

Conductor   A material that conducts electricity and heat. A metal that contains fewer than four electrons in its atom's outer shell.

Continuity   Instrument setup to check wiring, circuits, connectors, or switches for breaks (open circuit) or short circuits (closed circuit).

Controller   A name commonly used to describe a computer or an electronic control module.

Conventional ignition system   Ignition system that uses a distributor, also called *distributor ignition (DI)*.

Conventional theory   The theory that electricity flows from positive (+) to negative (−).

Coolant   The liquid mixture of antifreeze and water in the engine cooling system.

Cranking circuit   Electrical components and connections required to crank the engine to start.

Cylinder hone   A tool that uses an abrasive to smooth out and bring to exact measurement such things as wheel cylinders.

DC   Direct current.

Deep cycling   The full discharge and then the full recharge of a battery.

Default setup   The setup that exists as long as there are no changes made to the settings.

Deflection   A bending or distorting motion; usually applied to a brake drum when it is forced out-of-round during brake application.

Delta wound   A type of stator winding where all three coils are connected in a triangle shape.

Detonation   A violent explosion in the combustion chamber created by uncontrolled burning of the air-fuel mixture; often causes a loud, audible knock.

Diagnostic trouble code (DTC)   An alphanumeric or numeric sequence indicating a fault in a vehicle operating system.

Direct current (DC)   A constant electric current that flows in one direction only.

DIS   Distributorless ignition system; also called *direct-fire ignition system.*

Distributor   Electromechanical unit used to help create and distribute the high voltage necessary for spark ignition.

Drive plate   See *flex plate.*

Driveability   The general evaluation of an engine's operating qualities, including idle smoothness, cold and hot starting, throttle response, and power delivery.

Dual-mass flywheel   A flywheel that consists of two parts separated by springs used to absorb vibration in the driveline.

Dual overhead camshaft (DOHC)   An engine design with two camshafts above each line of cylinders—one for the exhaust valves and one for the intake valves.

Duration   A rating system applied to engine camshafts that determines how long the valve will be open relative to crankshaft movement in degrees.

Duty cycle   On-time or off-time to period-time ratio expressed in a percentage.

Dwell   The amount of time, recorded on a dwell meter in degrees, that voltage passes through a closed switch.

Eccentric   The relationship of two round parts having different centers; a part that contains two round surfaces, not on the same center.

ECM   Electronic control module.

ECU   Electronic control unit.

EFI   Electronic fuel injection.

EGR   Exhaust gas recirculation. An emission control device to reduce NO_x (oxides of nitrogen).

Elastomer   Another term for *rubber.*

Electricity   The movement of free electrons from one atom to another.

Electrolyte   Any substance which, in solution, is separated into ions and is made capable of conducting an electric current; the acid solution of a lead-acid battery.

Electronic ignition   A general term used to describe any of various types of ignition systems that use electronic instead of mechanical components such as contact points.

Electronic spark control (ESC)   The computer system equipped with a knock sensor that can retard spark advance if necessary to eliminate spark knock.

Emissions   Gases and particles left over after the combustion event of an engine. The primary emissions of concern are hydrocarbons, carbon monoxide, and oxides of nitrogen.

Energy   Capacity for performing work.

Engine control module (ECM)   The on-board computer of the engine management system that controls fuel and emissions, as well as diagnostics, for the vehicle's engine management system.

Enleanment   The act of reducing fuel delivery to the air-fuel mix to create a leaner mixture.

Enrichment   The act of adding fuel to the air-fuel mix to create a richer mixture.

Environmental Protection Agency (EPA)   A federal government agency that oversees the enforcement of laws related to the environment. Included in these laws are regulations on the amount and content of automotive emissions.

EPA   Environmental Protection Agency.

Ethanol (grain alcohol)   An octane enhancer added, at a rate of up to 10 %, to gasoline that increases the octane rating of the fuel by 2.5 to 3.0 points. Ethanol is a fuel oxygenate because it contains oxygen.

Ethyl tertiary butyl ether (ETBE)   An octane enhancer for gasoline. It is also a fuel oxygenate that is manufactured by reacting isobutylene with ethanol; which results in high octane and low volatility. ETBE can be added to gasoline up to a level of approximately 13%.

Evaporative (EVAP) emissions   A control system used to prevent fuel vapors in the tank from entering the atmosphere as HC emissions.

Exhaust gas recirculation (EGR)   The process of passing a small, measured amount of exhaust gas back into the engine to reduce combustion temperatures and formation of NO_x (oxides of nitrogen).

Foot-pound   A measurement of torque; a 1-pound pull, 1 foot from the center of an object.

Fuel trim   A computer function that adjusts fuel delivery during closed-loop operation to bring the air-fuel mixture as close to 14.7:1 as possible.

FWD   Front-wheel drive.

Gassing   The release of hydrogen and oxygen gas from the plates of a battery during charging or discharging.

Gauge   Wire sizes as assigned by the American wire gauge system; the smaller the gauge number, the larger the wire.

Generator A device that converts mechanical energy into electrical energy.

Gram A metric unit of weight measurement equal to 1/1000 kilogram (1 oz × 28 = 1 gram). An American dollar bill or paper clip weighs about 1 gram.

Grid The lead-alloy framework (support) for the active materials of an automotive battery.

Ground The lowest possible voltage potential in a circuit; in electrical terms, the desirable return circuit path. Ground can also be undesirable and provide a shortcut path for a defective electrical circuit.

Hall effect switch The sensor operates by moving a magnetic field relative to a semiconductor creating a square-wave output; primarily used to determine position. Named for Edwin H. Hall, who discovered the Hall effect in 1879.

HC Hydrocarbon (unburned fuel) that when combined with NO_x and sunlight forms smog.

HD Heavy duty.

HEI General Motors name for its high-energy ignition.

Hertz A unit of measurement of frequency, abbreviated Hz. One Hertz is one cycle per second. Named for Heinrich R. Hertz, a nineteenth-century German physicist.

Hold-in winding One of two electromagnetic windings inside a solenoid; used to hold the movable core in the solenoid.

Horsepower A unit of power equivalent to 33,000 foot-pounds per minute. One horsepower equals 746 W.

Hydraulic lifter A valve lifter that, using simple valving and the engine's oil pressure, can adjust its length slightly, thereby maintaining zero clearance in the valve train. Hydraulic lifters reduce valve train noise and are maintenance free.

Hydrocarbon (HC) Any of a number of compounds of carbon and hydrogen used as fuel, such as gasoline. High levels of hydrocarbons in tailpipe emissions are a result of unburned fuel. When combined with NO_x and sunlight, they form smog.

Hydrometer An instrument used to measure the specific gravity of a liquid. A battery hydrometer is calibrated to read the expected specific gravity of battery electrolyte.

IAC Idle air control.

Ignition circuit Electrical components and connections that produce and distribute high-voltage electricity to ignite the air-fuel mixture inside the engine.

Ignition coil An electrical device consisting of two separate coils of wire—a primary and a secondary winding. The purpose of an ignition is to produce the high-voltage (20,000 to 40,000 V), low-amperage (about 80 mA) current necessary for spark ignition.

Ignition timing The exact point of ignition in relation to piston position.

Inductance The signal caused by the sudden change of a magnetic field. For example, the turning off of the current through a solenoid generates a voltage spike across the solenoid.

Inductive reactance An opposing current created in a conductor whenever there is a charging current flow in a conductor.

Insulator A material that does not readily conduct electricity and heat. A nonmetal material that contains more than four electrons in its atom's outer shell.

Intake air temperature (IAT) sensor A sensor that measures the air temperature of the air entering the engine.

Intermittent Irregular; a condition that happens with no apparent or predictable pattern.

Iron Refined metal from iron ore (ferrous oxide) in a furnace. Also see *steel*.

ISO International Standards Organization.

Kilo 1000; abbreviated k or K.

Knock sensor A sensor that can detect engine spark knock.

Lambda sensor Oxygen sensor or O_2 sensor. Lambda is the Greek letter that represents ratio, as in air-fuel ratio.

Lead peroxide The positive plate of an automotive-style battery, the chemical symbol is PbO_2.

Lead sulfate Both battery plates become lead sulfate when the battery is discharged. The chemical symbol for lead sulfate is $PbSO_4$.

LT Light truck.

Magnetic timing A method of measuring ignition that uses a magnetic pickup tool to sense the location of a magnet on the harmonic balancer.

Malfunction indicator lamp (MIL) This amber dashboard warning light may be labeled "check engine" or "service engine soon."

Manifold absolute pressure (MAP) A sensor used to measure the pressure inside the intake manifold compared with a perfect vacuum.

Manifold vacuum Low pressure (vacuum) measured at the intake manifold of a running engine (normally between 17 and 21 inches Hg at idle).

MAP Manifold absolute pressure.

Mass airflow (MAF) The volume of air passing into the engine; varies with temperature and humidity and used in calculating injector operation and spark timing.

Methanol (wood alcohol) Typically manufactured from natural gas. Methanol content, including cosolvents, in unleaded gasoline is limited by law to 5%.

Methyl tertiary butyl ether (MTBE) A fuel oxygenate that is permitted in unleaded gasoline up to a level of 15%.

MIL See *malfunction indicator lamp*.

Millisecond One thousandth of one second (1/1000).

Misfire A circumstance that occurs when complete combustion does not happen in one or more cylinders due to fuel, ignition, or cylinder compression.

MSDS   Material safety data sheets.

Mutual induction   The generation of an electric current due to a changing magnetic field of an adjacent coil.

NHTSA   National Highway Traffic Safety Administration.

Nitrile   A type of rubber that is okay for use with petroleum.

NLGI   National Lubricating Grease Institute. Usually associated with grease. The higher the NLGI number, the firmer the grease: #000 is very fluid whereas #5 is very firm. The consistency most recommended is NLGI #2 (soft).

NO$_x$ Oxides of nitrogen which, when combined with HC and sunlight, form smog.

O$_2$ sensor   Oxygen sensor; also called *O2S.*

Octane rating   The measurement of a gasoline's ability to resist engine knock. The higher the octane rating, the less prone the gasoline is to cause engine knock (detonation).

OE   Original equipment.

OEM   Original-equipment manufacturer.

Ohm   The unit of electrical resistance; named for Georg Simon Ohm (1787–1854).

Ohmmeter   An electrical test instrument used to measure ohms (unit of electrical resistance).

Ohm's law   An electrical law that requires 1 volt to push 1 ampere through 1 ohm of resistance.

Ω (Omega)   The last letter of the Greek alphabet; a symbol for ohm (Ω), the unit for electrical resistance.

Oscilloscope   A visual display of electrical waves on a fluorescent screen or cathode ray tube.

OSHA   Occupational Safety and Health Administration.

Oxidation catalysts   Platinum and palladium used in the catalytic converter to combine oxygen (O_2) with hydrocarbons (HC) and carbon monoxide (CO) to form nonharmful tailpipe emissions of water (H_2O) and carbon dioxide (CO_2).

Oxides of nitrogen (NO$_x$)   A primary emission produced in the combustion chamber under high temperatures when nitrogen combines with oxygen. Oxides of nitrogen contribute to the formation of smog [ground-level ozone (O_3)] when combined with HC and sunlight.

Oxygenate   An octane component containing hydrogen, carbon, and oxygen in its molecular structure. Types of oxygenates include ethers, such as MTBE, and alcohols, such as ethanol and methanol.

Oz-in.   Measurement of imbalance: 3 oz-in. means that an object is out-of-balance to the degree that it would require a 1-oz weight placed 3 inches from the center of the rotating object or a 3-oz weight 1 inch from the center or any other combination that when multiplied equals 3 oz-in.

Ozone   Oxygen-rich (O_3) gas created by sunlight reaction with unburned hydrocarbons (HCs) and oxides of nitrogen (NO$_x$); also called *smog.*

PAG   Polyalkaline glycol.

Partitions   Separations between the cells of a battery. Partitions are made of the same material as the outside case of the battery.

Pasting   The process of applying active battery materials onto the grid framework of each plate.

PCV   Positive crankcase ventilation.

Piezoelectric principle   The principle by which certain crystals become electrically charged when pressure is applied.

Ping   Secondary rapid burning of the last 3% to 5% of the air-fuel mixture in the combustion chamber causing a second flame front that collides with the first flame front producing a knock noise. Also called *detonation* or *spark knock.*

Plenum   A chamber located between the throttle body and the runners of the intake manifold used to distribute the intake charge more evenly and efficiently.

Polarity   The condition of being positive or negative in relation to a magnetic pole.

Porous lead   Lead with many small holes to make a porous surface for use in battery-negative plates; the chemical symbol for lead is Pb.

Ported vacuum   Low pressure (vacuum) measured above the throttle plates. As the throttle plates open, the vacuum increases and becomes of the same value as the manifold vacuum.

Positive crankcase ventilation (PCV)   A system used to prevent corrosive blowby gases (by products of combustion) in the crankcase from entering the atmosphere.

Positive temperature coefficient (PTC)   Primarily used in reference to a conductor or electronic circuit breaker. As the temperature increases, the electrical resistance also increases.

Potentiometer   A three-terminal variable resistor that varies the voltage drop in a circuit.

Power   In electrical terms, Amperes × Volts (Power = $I \times E$) expressed in watts.

Powertrain control module (PCM)   The on-board computer that controls both the engine management and transmission functions of the vehicle.

PPM   Parts per million.

Preignition   Ignition of the air-fuel mix before the timed ignition spark occurs.

Pressure regulator   A regulating device that maintains a specified pressure in a system.

Pull-in windings   One of two electromagnetic windings inside a solenoid used to move a movable core.

Pulse generators   An electromagnetic unit that generates a voltage signal used to trigger the ignition control module that controls (turns on and off) the primary ignition current of an electronic ignition system.

Pulse width   The amount of on-time of an electronic fuel injector or other electrical component.

Rebuilt   See *remanufactured.*

Reid vapor pressure (RVP)   A method of determining vapor pressure of gasoline and other petroleum products; widely used in the petroleum industry as an indicator of the volatility of gasoline.

Remanufactured   A term used to describe a component that is disassembled, cleaned, inspected, and reassembled using new or reconditioned parts. According to the Automotive Parts Rebuilders Association (APRA), this same component is also referred to as being *rebuilt.*

Renewal   A part built to be used as a replacement for the original-equipment (OE) part.

Reserve capacity   The number of minutes a battery can produce 25 A and still maintain a battery voltage of 1.75 V per cell (10.5 V for a 12-V battery).

Resistance   The opposition to current flow, measured in ohms.

Revolutions per minute (RPM)   A measure of how fast an object is rotating around an axis.

RFG   Reformulated gasoline.

Rise time   The time, measured in microseconds, for the output of a coil to rise from 10% to 90% of its maximum output.

RPM   Engine speed expressed in revolutions per minute of the crankshaft.

RTV   Room-temperature vulcanization.

SAE   Society of Automotive Engineers.

Schrader valve   A spring-loaded valve used in the service ports of the fuel rail and air-conditioning system. Invented in 1844 by August Schrader.

Secondary pickup   An accessory that can be clamped on the high-voltage coil wire used to measure secondary ignition patterns.

SEMA   Specialty Equipment Manufacturers Association.

Shelf life   The length of time that something can remain on a storage shelf and not be reduced in performance level from that of a newly manufactured product.

Smog   The term used to describe a combination of *smoke* and *fog.* Formed by NO_x and HC with sunlight.

Society of Automotive Engineers (SAE)   A professional organization made up of automotive engineers and designers that establishes standards and conducts testing for many automotive-related functions.

Spalling   A term used to describe a type of mechanical failure caused by metal fatigue. Metal cracks then break out into small chips, slabs, or scales of metal.

Spark knock   Secondary rapid burning of the last 3% to 5% of the air-fuel mixture in the combustion chamber causing a second flame front that collides with the first flame front and produces a knock noise.

Specific gravity   The ratio of the weight of a given volume of a liquid divided by the weight of an equal volume of water.

Spike   A (high) voltage pulse during a short period of time (sharp pulse).

Sponge lead   Lead made with many small holes to make its surface porous or spongelike for use in battery-negative plates; the chemical symbol for lead is Pb.

Starter drive   A term used to describe the starter motor drive pinion gear with overrunning clutch.

State of charge   The degree or the amount that a battery is charged. A fully charged battery would be 100% charged.

Stator   A name for three interconnected windings inside an alternator. A rotating rotor provides a moving magnetic field and induces a current in the windings of the stator.

Steel   Refined iron metal with most of the carbon removed.

Stoichiometric   Describes an air-fuel ratio of exactly 14.7:1. At this specific rate, all the gasoline is fully oxidized by all the available oxygen.

Stroboscopic   A very bright, pulsing light triggered from the firing of one spark plug used to check and adjust ignition timing.

Stud   A short rod with threads on both ends.

Tachometer (tach)   Instrument or gauge used to measure RPM (revolutions per minute).

TBI   Throttle-body injection.

TDC   Top dead center.

Tell-tale light   Dash warning light (sometimes called an *idiot light*).

Throttle body   A housing containing a valve to regulate the airflow through the intake manifold.

Throttle position (TP) sensor   A sensor that signals the computer as to the position of the throttle.

Top dead center (TDC)   The highest point in the cylinder that the piston can travel. The measurement from bottom dead center (BDC) to TDC determines the stroke length of the crankshaft.

Torque   A twisting force measured in pound-feet (lb-ft) or Newton-meters (N-m) that may or may not result in motion.

Torque converter   A special form of fluid coupling in which torque is increased.

Torque converter clutch   A clutch located inside the torque converter that locks the turbine and the impeller together to prevent any slippage. Also called a *lockup torque converter.*

Torque wrench   A wrench that registers the amount of applied torque.

Torx   A type of fastener that features a star-shape indentation for a tool. A registered trademark of the Camcar Division of Textron.

Turbocharger   An exhaust-powered supercharger.

Turbulence   The state of being violently disturbed, as in an engine; the rapid swirling motion of the air-fuel mixture entering the cylinder.

UNC Unified national coarse.

UNF Unified national fine.

VAC Vacuum sensor.

Vacuum Negative pressure (below atmospheric); measured in units of inches or centimeters of mercury (Hg).

Vacuum, manifold Vacuum in the intake manifold that develops as a result of the intake stroke of the cylinders.

Vacuum, ported A vacuum that develops on the intake side of the throttle plate as air moves past it.

Valve overlap The amount of time, in degrees of crank rotation; the intake and exhaust valves are both open.

Valve train The collection of parts that make the valves operate. The valve train includes the camshaft(s), related drive components, the various parts that convert the camshaft's rotary motion into reciprocating motion, and the valves and their associated parts.

Vapor lock Vaporized fuel, usually in the fuel line, that prevents or retards the necessary fuel delivery to the cylinders.

Vehicle control module (VCM) The on-board computer that controls the engine management, transmission, and other vehicle systems such as antilock brakes.

Vehicle identification number (VIN) Alphanumeric number identifying vehicle type, assembly plant, powertrain, etc.

Vibration An oscillation, shake, or movement that alternates in opposite directions.

VOC Volatile organic compounds.

Volatility A measurement of the tendency of a liquid to change to vapor.

Volt The unit of measurement for the amount of electrical pressure; named for Alessandro Volta (1745–1827).

Voltage drop Voltage loss across a wire, connector, or any other conductor. Voltage drop equals resistance in ohms times current in amperes (Ohm's law).

Voltage regulator An electronic or mechanical unit that controls the output voltage of an electrical generator or alternator by controlling the field current of the generator.

Voltmeter An electrical test instrument used to measure volts (unit of electrical pressure). A voltmeter is connected in parallel with the unit or circuit being tested.

Volumetric efficiency The ratio between the amount of air-fuel mixture that actually enters the cylinder and the amount that could enter under ideal conditions expressed as a percentage.

VSS Vehicle speed sensor.

Warning light A light on the instrument panel that alerts the driver when one-half of a split hydraulic system fails as determined by the pressure differential switch.

Watt An electrical unit of power; 1 watt equals current (amperes) $\times$ voltage (1/746 hp). Named after James Watt, a Scottish inventor.

WOT Wide-open throttle.

Zerk A name commonly used for a grease fitting. Named in 1922 for its developer, Oscar U. Zerk, an employee of the Alamite Corporation. A grease fitting is also called an *Alamite fitting*.

Index